THE COMPLETE BOOK OF
FOOTBALL

EDITED BY CHRIS HUNT

Dedicated to Cliff Hunt, a 'Gooner' until the end!

First published in Great Britain in 2003 by Hayden Publishing

Hayden Publishing Limited
32 Winifred Road
Apsley
Hemel Hempstead
HP3 9DX

Copyright © 2003 Hayden Publishing

ISBN 1 903635 16 0

A CIP catalogue record for this book can be obtained from the British Library.

This edition produced for The Book People Ltd,
Hall Wood Avenue, Haydock, St Helens WA11 9UL

A 'MILE AWAY CLUB' PRODUCTION
Designed by David Houghton
Colour Origination by PDQ Digital Media Solutions Ltd, Bungay
Printed and bound by Polygraf Print, Slovakia

CONTENTS

FOREWORD

Every football fan dreams of lifting the World Cup. And while very few of us ever manage to get our hands on that prized trophy, we grow up reading of the daring deeds of footballing legends like Pele and Moore, Maradona and Beckenbauer! We discover how matches can turn on a single instant of exquisite skill, how a football legend can be built in just one moment of instinctive brilliance, how dreams can be shattered by the consequences of a simple mistimed tackle. We learn that a football match takes just 90 minutes – but lasts forever.

And while each generation of football fan is brought up with its own heroes – today we have Beckham and Ronaldo, Zidane and Van Nistelrooy – it is often in books like this that we discover our heritage, the roots of the game, the legends who originally inspired our parents, and grandparents before them, to fall in love with the world's best and most popular sport.

This is a book for all of us who have dreamt of glorious victory. It is for those of us who have felt our heart quicken by the counter attack or the anguish of defeat. This book is a celebration of the beautiful game that conquered the world – football!

CHRIS HUNT Editor

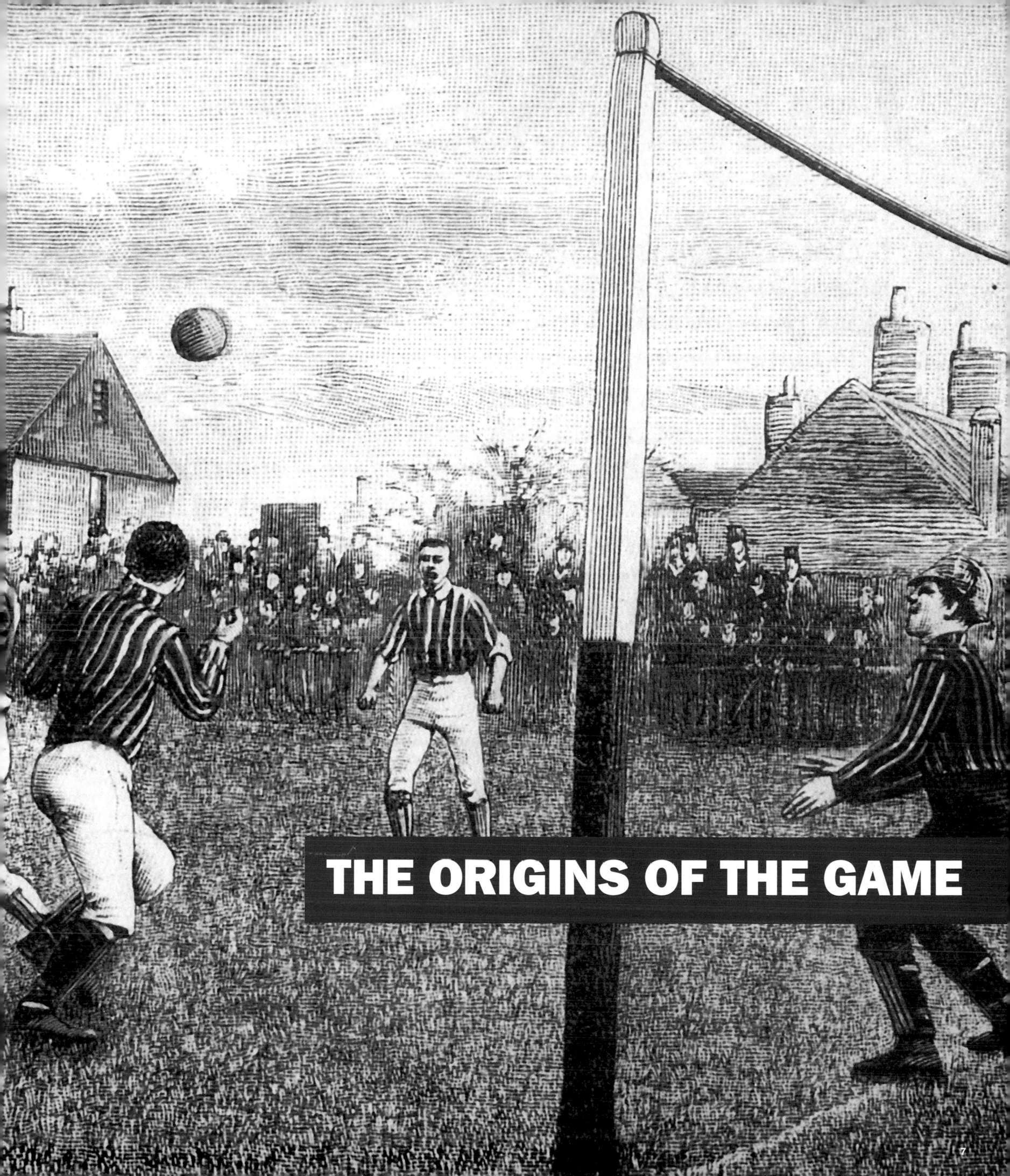

THE ORIGINS OF THE GAME

THE ORIGINS OF THE GAME

SPORT REALLY DOESN'T get any bigger than football in the 21st Century. Take the World Cup final in 2002: more than one billion people in 213 countries across the globe crowd around TV sets. For some it's the middle of the night, for others it's early morning, but even as 30 different wars rage in and between nations, from the shanty towns of Brazil to the ultra-sleek high-rise blocks of Tokyo, the world is united for one reason and for one reason only – to watch a game of football.

On a pristine playing surface, surrounded by advertising hoardings for some of the biggest brands on earth, men paid millions of pounds a year chase a scientifically designed, technologically advanced plastic sphere of air – kicking it, heading it, sometimes seeming to caress it with their feet. One of them, a buck-toothed Brazilian with an odd triangular patch of hair at the front of his head, twice kicks the ball between two white posts where it is caught by a fine white net. Each time the Brazilian wheels away, arms aloft and grinning, before being engulfed by a sea of yellow as his team-mates rush to hug and kiss him. Each time 69,000 spectators go wild. Each time a bald man, dressed all in black, blows a whistle while 11 players in white shirts look down at their feet disconsolately.

Then, 90 minutes after all the running, bustling, shouting and screaming began, the bald man lets out three long blasts on his whistle and the match is over. Up in the stands, delirious supporters jump up and down, singing songs and dancing. Down on the pitch, the tears begin to flow. The players in white are crying. So too are those in yellow. For everyone, the 69,000 inside the stadium and the one billion watching on TV, something important has happened. Brazil are the football champions of the world.

TO WATCH FOOTBALL at the beginning of the 21st Century is to watch a multi-million pound industry that creates global stars out of the most ordinary of people and stirs the emotions of billions of men, women and children around the world. In bars and cafés, homes and schools, from the Amazon to Zanzibar, the conversation is never far from 'the beautiful game'. Hours of TV coverage are devoted not just to showing matches, but to talking about them, endlessly arguing over rules and their interpretation, over tactics used by different coaches, and the relative merits of players. The world is obsessed with football.

But how did it get to this? How did a game so apparently simple become the *raison d'être* for millions, a worldwide religion?

The only thing that can be said with any real certainty about the early origins of football is that a variety of games were played in countries

around the world, which involved elements of today's football. Some featured little or no kicking, others lacked a competitive edge, but each embraced something recognisably part of the modern day game.

Recorded in a military manual dating back to the Han Dynasty (200-300 BC), it is usually said that the Chinese Tsu Chu is the earliest form of football known to man, though in truth it more closely resembles a fairground game than the football we know today. Two 30-feet high bamboo canes were used to suspend a large piece of silk cloth with a hole 30cm-40cm in diameter cut into it. Competitors would then attempt to kick a leather ball filled with hair and feathers through the hole, sometimes with the added difficulty of being pressured by opponents. Tsu Chu, it seems, was played to celebrate the Emperor's birthday. The penalty for losing was death.

Less sinister, and certainly less fatal, was Kemari, a non-competitive Japanese game dating from around the 5th Century AD. Best described as 'keepie-uppies', Kemari was contested among a group of eight players standing in a circle and passing the ball to each other without allowing it to touch the ground. Further south, in the Malay states, they played Sepak Raga, a similar game in which you were permitted to use any part of your body apart from your hands to keep the ball in the air. In South America, in 400 AD, the Mayans played Poktapok, a game between two teams using rubber balls. Much later, the Aztecs had a similar game called Ullamatzli, while in North Africa there was Koura, a Berber ball game probably linked to fertility rights.

It is unlikely that there was any common link among these different games, rather that each civilisation invented its own game with its own rules uninfluenced by people living thousands of miles away. It is difficult, therefore, to sustain the Chinese claim to have invented football, since the evidence that they took Tsu Chu to the world is at best threadbare. They may not even have invented the world's first ball game – there is actually evidence of ball games being played even earlier, in Greece, where the little-known Pheninda (or Episkyros) is mentioned in the writings of the Greek playwright Antiphanes, who lived in the 4th Century BC. Adding weight to his words is a bas relief at the foot of a marble column in Athens, believed to date from 600 BC, which shows a figure playing a game that looks very much like football. And Episkyros probably did influence later games, not least as the forerunner of Harpastum.

Used as a way of keeping the Roman army fit, Harpastum was played on a rectangular field with the aim of getting the ball over the opponents' boundary line. Kicking was limited and the game was probably more similar to rugby, but the growth of the Roman Empire took the game to new territories and it survived for 700 years. It may even have had some influence on the very early development of football in Britain – it is claimed that victory celebrations after a battle with the Romans in Derby in the 3rd Century involved something resembling a game of 'football'.

Yet despite the claims and counter-claims, none of these games was football as we know it. The game known around the world by that

Above: Part of a 14th Century misericord at Gloucester Cathedral depicts an early example of ball game players.

Opposite: A game of 'mob football' taking place in the streets of London in 1721.

Above: A depiction of a soccer game at the turn of the 18th Century.

Opposite: The original FA Challenge Cup, awarded to the victors of the world's first organised football tournament.

name did not really exist until the mid-19th Century and its home was certainly England.

THE ORIGINS OF the game in England are just as hazy as those elsewhere. Along with the story of the Romans in Derby, comes a tale from Chester of a game played with the severed head of a defeated Dane. Whether either is true is impossible to say, but what is clear is that from around the 12th Century, ball games were a common sight in the towns and villages of the British Isles. Often these games were for local pride, two teams in a village fighting it out for bragging rights, or neighbouring villages competing in an annual contest, usually staged on Shrove Tuesday (in northern France a similar game called La Soule was played on Shrove Tuesday, Sundays and Saints days, and it has been suggested that the Norman conquest of 1066 brought the tradition to England). But local pride came at a cost, often counted in broken limbs, sometimes in fatalities. The rules – if there were any – were vague. This was 'mob football', with no limit to the number of men on each side and virtually no method of play illegal. Nor was there necessarily much use of feet in contact with the ball. The general idea was to transport a ball (or pig's bladder) to one or other point within a village, but with so many players, games could last for days. (Annual games are still played today, albeit with less risk to life and limb, in places like Ashbourne in Derbyshire and Haxey in Lincolnshire, where they fight over a hood rather than a ball.)

By the 14th Century, these raucous street games were causing consternation among the authorities. So much so, in fact, that in 1314,

Right and opposite: Teams from Eton (nearest) and Harrow public schools in the 19th Century.

King Edward II tried to ban them with the threat of jail. A proclamation was issued: 'For as much as there is great noise in the city caused by hustling over large balls, from which many evils arise, which God forbid; we command and forbid on behalf of the King, on pain of imprisonment, such game be used in the city in future.'

Yet Edward II was just the first of several monarchs to try – and fail – to clamp down on

what was fast becoming 'the people's game'. When his son, Edward III, made his own attempt to ban football, he was not just concerned with public order issues but with the distraction football was causing at a time when England was at war with France. His subjects, he argued, should be focusing on more important business, like archery practice. But despite his attempts – and those of monarchs to come – mob football continued to flourish in England (and Scotland) mainly due to the people's desire to play.

Meanwhile in Italy in the 14th Century, the game of Il Calcio had begun to be played in the main square in Florence on the feast day of St John the Baptist, the city's patron saint. With its roots in the Roman game of Harpastum, Il Calcio was nevertheless closer to modern day football than its ancient predecessor – to begin with, its name came from *calciare*, Italian for 'to kick'.

The game, with its teams dressed in bright colours, was certainly more civilised than its English counterpart. In 1580, a set of rules was published for the first time by Giovanni Bardi, and the game may even have had an influence on the development of football in Britain after a match was played in front of the British Consul. But football in England remained firmly in the hands of the mobs (a character in Shakespeare's 1605 play *King Lear* refers to a 'base football player'). Rough, violent and a nuisance to the authorities, for several centuries no real progress was made in the development of the game.

The turning point came in the mid-19th Century. By then, football had long been played

in the major public schools of England, the virtues of team play, discipline and exercise were noted by teachers, and the rough and tumble excesses were a joy to the pupils. By their nature more organised, these games allowed for a gradual refinement of the 'rules' to the point where a more sophisticated game was starting to be played.

Still, however, there was no uniformity. Different schools played by their own evolved regulations, dependent on, for example, the area of ground they had at their disposal for games or the whims of the master in charge. Other rules were added piecemeal over the years by each school, so that when two schools faced each other they would adopt the rules of one of the two teams, the other adapting as best they could. But there were too many problems to make this satisfactory. There were irreconcilable differences, for example, in the degree to which handling was permitted. In some schools running with the ball in your hands was fine, in others only minimal use of the hands was allowed. More controversial was the use of hacking, a technique which essentially involved kicking away at an opponent's shins if he had the ball.

It was not until a group of footballers from various public schools found themselves together at Cambridge University that the first attempt to draw up a uniform set of rules was made. Published in 1848, the 'Cambridge Rules' were by no means universally adopted, but the group of students behind them were to play an important part in both raising awareness of the need for a standardised set of rules and in persuading various schools and

clubs to modify their own rules in order to develop unity.

Other rules were drawn up over the next 15 years (the best known being the 'Sheffield Rules' of 1857 and the 1862 'Rules for the Simplest Game' by Mr Thring, a teacher at Uppingham School), but the breakthrough came in October 1863 when representatives from 11 clubs – Barnes, Blackheath, Blackheath School, Crusaders, Crystal Palace, Forest (later Wanderers), Kensington School, No Names Kilburn, Perceval House, Surbiton and War Office – met to form the Football Association.

Two months later, the Football Association rules were published [see sidebar], and it was here that rugby and football went their separate ways and the football we know today really began to appear. Some clubs, Blackheath among them, opted to continue with their own game, based more on catching and passing the ball than kicking it, but those that stayed within the FA were determined that their 'football' should be played largely with the feet. For a while there was hope that the two groups – the rugby unionists and the association footballers as they became known – could be brought back under the same umbrella, but when, six years later, the FA banned all handling of the ball, the split became permanent and in 1871 the Rugby Football Union was formed.

The first FA laws were far from perfect – they did not, for example, stipulate the number of players on each side or the duration of the game and to begin with, many schools and clubs continued to follow their own rules. But gradually they began to be used all over the

country and when, in 1878, the 'Sheffield Rules' were absorbed into a new set of FA rules, uniformity was fast approaching. In 1886 responsibility for the laws of the game passed to the International Football Association Board comprising of one representative from each of the English, Scottish, Welsh and Irish FAs. (Since 1913 FIFA has also had a presence on the board, which now consists of four delegates making up 50 percent of any vote.)

As the FA grew bigger and stronger, there became apparent a desire among the top teams to test themselves in organised competition. So, at the start of the 1871-72 season, the world's oldest cup competition, the FA Challenge Cup was launched. Based on a knockout competition – Cock House – and

THE FOOTBALL ASSOCIATION RULES 1863

1. The maximum length of the ground shall be 200 yards, the maximum breadth shall be 100 yards, the length and breadth shall be marked off with flags; and the goal shall be defined by two upright posts, eight yards apart, without any tape or bar across them.

2. A toss for goals shall take place, and the game shall be commenced by a place kick from the centre of the ground by the side losing the toss for goals; the other side shall not approach within 10 yards of the ball until it is kicked off.

3. After a goal is won, the losing side shall be entitled to kick off, and the two sides shall change goals after each goal is won.

4. A goal shall be won when the ball passes between the goal-posts or over the space between the goal-posts (at whatever height), not being thrown, knocked on, or carried.

5. When the ball is in touch, the first player who touches it shall throw it from the point on the boundary line where it left the ground in a direction at right angles with the boundary line, and the ball shall not be in play until it has touched the ground.

6. When a player has kicked the ball, any one of the same side who is nearer to the opponent's goal line is out of play and may not touch the ball himself, nor in any way whatever prevent any other player from doing so, until he is in play; but no player is out of play when the ball is kicked off from behind the goal line.

7. In case the ball goes behind the goal line, if a player on the side to whom the goal belongs first touches the ball, one of his side shall be entitled to a free kick from the goal line at the point opposite the place where the ball shall be touched. If a player of the opposite side first touches the ball, one of his side shall be entitled to a free kick at the goal only from a point 15 yards outside the goal line, opposite the place where the ball is touched, the opposing side standing within their goal line until he has had his kick.

8. If a player makes a fair catch, he shall be entitled to a free kick, providing he claims it by making a mark with his heel at once; and in order to take such a kick he may go back as far as he pleases, and no player on the opposite side shall advance beyond his mark until he has kicked.

9. No player shall run with the ball.

10. Neither tripping nor hacking shall be allowed, and no player shall use his hands to hold or push his adversary.

11. A player shall not be allowed to throw the ball or pass it to another with his hands.

12. No player shall be allowed to take the ball from the ground with his hands under any pretext whatever while it is in play.

13. No player shall be allowed to wear projecting nails, iron plates, or gutta percha on the soles or heels of his boots.

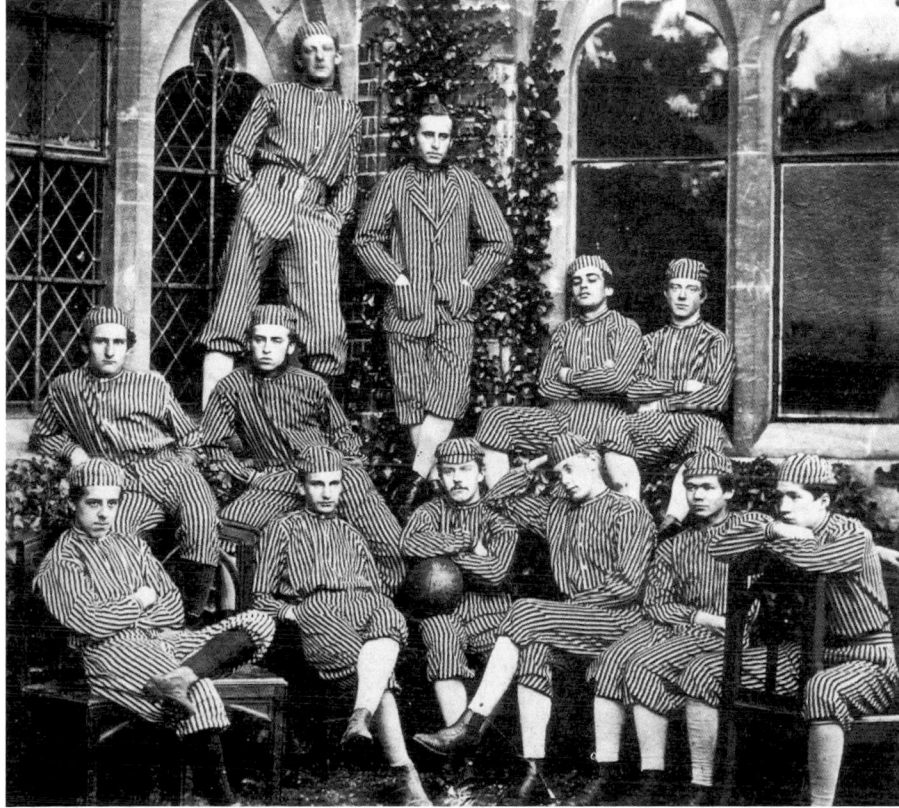

Above: An advert for equipment from the late 19th Century.

Right: The minutes recording the formation of the Football Association.

Opposite clockwise from top: An artist's impression of the 1891 FA Cup Final; Lord Kinnaird, who presided over the first ever international match; 1897 double-winners Aston Villa; Preston, the first double-winners in 1889.

Below: The 1897 FA Cup Final at Crystal Palace.

played at Harrow School, the inaugural FA Cup saw 15 entries; 13 from the London area, plus Donington School from Lincolnshire and Queen's Park from Glasgow, who were given a bye to the semi-finals because of the distance they had to travel. Sadly, having drawn their semi-final in London, the Scots decided they could not afford to return for the replay, so the first ever final, in 1872, pitted Royal Engineers against Wanderers, who won 1-0.

In October of the same year, England played Scotland in the first ever international match, a 0-0 draw in Glasgow. Just five months later, the Scottish FA was established at a meeting attended by Clydesdale, Dumbreck, Glasgow Eastern, Granville, Queen's Park, Rovers, Third Lanark and Vale Of Leven.

With football's popularity growing in England and attendances at matches rising, it was not long before the potential financial rewards of football were noted. Spectators, it became apparent, could be charged for admission. And since, unsurprisingly, the more successful teams attracted larger crowds, it was inevitable that ambitious clubs would look for ways to attract better players. There was little the FA could do to hold back the advent of professionalism. Having at first attempted to limit payments to players to 'wages lost' and expenses, in 1885 the FA gave in and permitted professional players.

Three years later, it was decided that the growing number of clubs warranted better organisation and the world's first Football League was established with 12 teams taking part – Accrington, Aston Villa, Blackburn Rovers, Bolton Wanderers, Burnley, Derby County, Everton, Notts County, Preston North End, Stoke, West Bromwich Albion and Wolverhampton Wanderers.

The FA was barely 25 years old yet English football had taken huge strides in the development of the game. It had a glamorous cup competition, a professional football league and a basic structure that would carry it well into the 20th Century. International football was under way too, with regular fixtures among the four home nations, England,

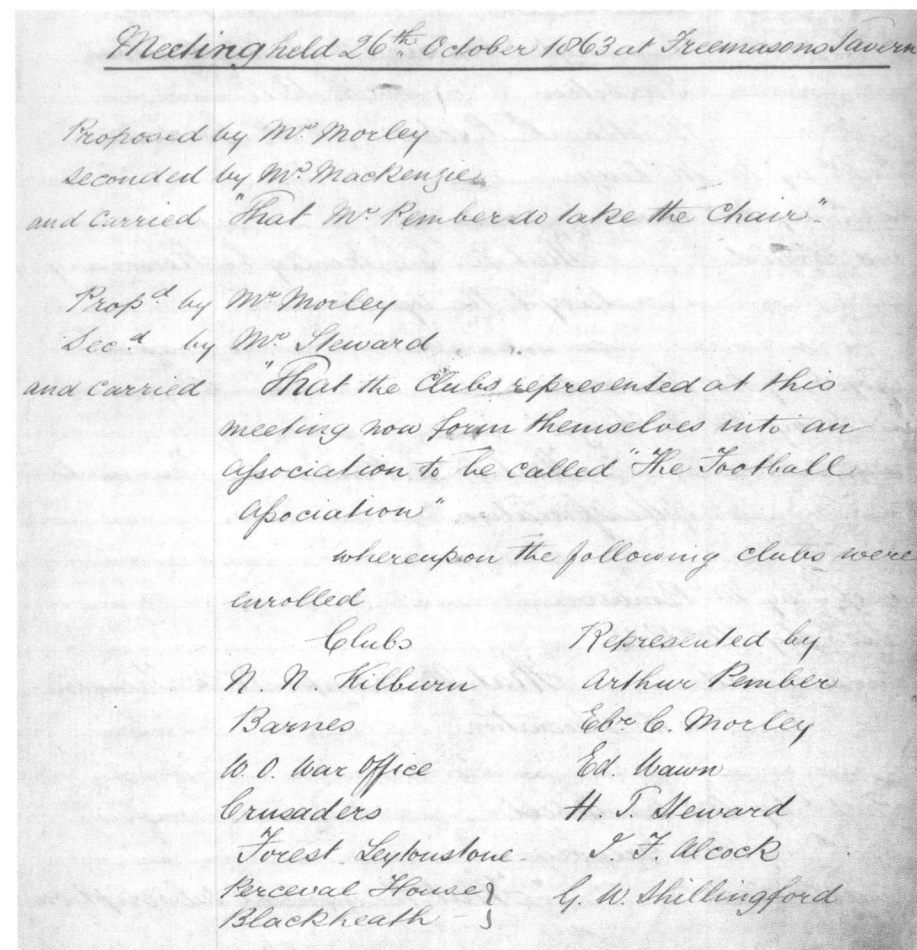

Scotland, Wales and Ireland. But already football was far more than just a British sport. It was still a long way from becoming the most popular pastime in the world, but by the turn of the century, travelling British workers and businessmen had taken football to all four corners of the globe.

IN 1930, URUGUAY hosted the first football World Cup, featuring 13 nations – France, Mexico, Chile, Argentina, Yugoslavia, Brazil, Bolivia, Romania, Peru, USA, Belgium, Paraguay and the hosts. Fifty years earlier, the competition could not have been played; would not, in fact, have even been dreamed of. But in the late-19th century, football had spread like wildfire, carried around the world by English sailors (to France), engineers (to Spain), schoolteachers (to Switzerland and Germany), textile workers (to Holland), businessmen (to Argentina), students (to Portugal and Uruguay) and Scottish shipyard workers (to Sweden).

As early as 1866, British students were playing football in Portugal. By 1869 it had been introduced to Swiss schools and in 1872, a group of British sailors formed the Le Havre club in France. At around the same time their colleagues were playing the first football games half a world away in Brazil.

British influence can still be seen in the names of clubs around the world – AC Milan (rather than Milano), Athletic (not Atlético)

Bilbao, Newell's Old Boys in Argentina, Young Boys of Berne, Corinthians of Brazil and Chile's Everton to name just a few.

But though they undoubtedly played the leading role, it wasn't just the British who helped the game to flourish worldwide. FC Barcelona, for example, who despite borrowing their club colours from the old school of one of several English players who turned out in their first game, were founded by a Swiss, Joan Gamper, who had learned and loved the game at school. Internazionale of Milan chose their name because of the cosmopolitan make-up of their team. Yes, the British took football to the world, but it wasn't long before the world adopted football as its own.

In Brazil, Charles Miller, son of an English father and a Brazilian mother, returned from studying in England with two footballs. Within the space of a year, the five teams Miller had organised for a São Paulo state championship had swelled to 70. In neighbouring Argentina, River Plate were founded by an Englishman and Boca Juniors by an Irishman, but it was the Italians who oversaw and pushed through the real growth of football there, as they did in Uruguay. Meanwhile, in Africa, colonialists – French, German and Portuguese, as well as English – introduced the game.

As football's popularity boomed around the world, so too did its organisation. In 1889, the Dutch and Danish Football Associations were established. By 1900, New Zealand, Argentina,

Above: France set-sail for the inaugural 1930 World Cup, they were one of only three European teams to compete.

Right: FIFA president Jules Rimet, the man who established the World Cup and lent his name to its original trophy.

Chile, Switzerland, Belgium, Italy, Germany and Uruguay were also up and running, and it was becoming increasingly apparent that, just as individual countries had football associations, so football would benefit from an organisation that could oversee the growth of the global game in the 20th Century.

So, in May of 1904, FIFA (Fédération Internationale de Football Association) arrived, founded by representatives from France, Belgium, Holland, Spain, Sweden and Switzerland. The English FA wrote to say they could see no need for the new federation. (It would not be the last time that arrogance meant the English were missing at the start – in later years, the World Cup, European Cup and European Championship would all begin without the presence of English teams.)

Initially FIFA struggled to make a mark. Within a year the idea of a world championship had been raised, but when the first competition was arranged for 1906 in Switzerland, no-one entered. Yet despite this setback, there was a growing clamour for nations to test themselves against each other. The first opportunity had come at the Olympic Games of 1896, but since the teams taking part came from Denmark, Athens and Izmir, it could hardly be seen as a real international tournament. The following two Olympics saw football played merely as a demonstration sport, but in 1908 in London the game was finally accepted, with England beating Denmark 2-0 in the final and repeating the trick four years later in Stockholm.

In those early years of the 20th Century, it was the European nations who led the way. By the mid-1920s, however, Europe was being forced to take note of the increasing strength of South American football. Uruguay won the 1924 Olympic title, thrashing Switzerland in the final, and in 1928 the final was a derby, Uruguay beating Argentina in a replay.

The South Americans had also organised their own international tournament, the Copa América. Initially beginning as an unofficial championship in 1910 featuring Argentina, Uruguay and Chile, the Copa América had developed into an annual opportunity for the major South American football-playing nations to test themselves against each other. The result was improving standards throughout and tough, competitive teams.

The FIFA president, a Frenchman by the name of Jules Rimet, watched with growing interest. A long-time advocate of a world championship, Rimet now sensed an opportunity to finally get his project off the ground, and when Uruguay offered to host and fund the inaugural World Cup, his dream became reality. Little did Rimet know as he set

out for South America with just four European countries agreeing to send teams, that his brainchild would become the biggest sporting event in the world.

FIFA HAD EXPERIENCED massive growth by the 1950s. Founded by the federations in Europe, in its first half-century football's world governing body had become truly global, its role much broader than initially envisaged, with the World Cup now established as the shining symbol of that development. With FIFA's attentions divided across Africa, Asia and the Americas, as well as Europe, the Europeans decided to create their own governing body to more carefully protect their interests and administer to their needs. In June 1954, at a meeting in Basle, Switzerland, UEFA was born.

Almost immediately, a plan was put in place for a national European Championship. The competition had actually been suggested nearly 30 years earlier by Henri Delaunay, a colleague of Jules Rimet at the French Federation, who considered the World Cup a bridge too far, arguing that the logical first step was to create a European Championship. The World Cup had captured FIFA's imagination, however, and the European Championship was duly forgotten – though never by Delaunay.

In fact, Europe was a late starter in having its own international competition. By the time of the first European Championship final in 1960, the Copa América was well established; the first African Nations Cup had kicked-off in 1957, with Egypt beating Ethiopia 4-0 in the final; the inaugural Asian Games had seen India victorious in 1951, with South Korea lifting the Asian Cup five years later; and the first CONCACAF Championship (for North and Central America) had been won by Costa Rica back in 1941.

If the Europeans were slow to organise their first international championship, however, they were the pioneers of international club competitions. The godfather of international club football was an Austrian, Hugo Meisl, who hit upon the idea of a competition between the very best teams from Hungary, Czechoslovakia, Yugoslavia and Austria. He called his creation the Mitropa Cup, from the German for central Europe – Mittel Europa. The format was simple, but ingenious: a two-legged (home and away) knockout with the winners progressing. The first competition, in 1927, was won by Sparta Prague, and in 1929 the Italians took part adding to the prestige. Sadly, World War II halted the competition in mid-flight and though it returned post-war, in 1955, the bigger European competitions were already on their way, signalling the beginning of the end. (Amazingly the competition continued until 1991, when Torino lifted the trophy.)

The Mitropa Cup was crucial to the development of international club football (as was the Latin Cup, a competition involving teams from Spain, Italy, Portugal and France which debuted in 1949). It was the forerunner – in both concept and format – to the competition that would go on to become the richest and most glittering club competition in the world; the European Champions Cup.

The European Cup was actually born out of arrogance – the arrogance, once again, of the English. Their over-the-top response to Wolverhampton Wanderers' victory over Hungary's Honvéd at a waterlogged Molineux prompted the editor of France's *L'Equipe* to propose what he called a 'proper European club cup', pitching the champions of each country against each other in a knockout format based on the Mitropa Cup. The English immediately banned champions Chelsea from taking part. But those more familiar with international club competitions, like Real Madrid, Milan and Sporting Lisbon, were enthusiastic, seeing the commercial and sporting benefits of playing against the top clubs from all over Europe. So, in 1955, the European Cup began, with immediate success.

In other circumstances Real Madrid's dominance – they won the first five trophies – could have caused the competition to stagnate, but the manner of their victories and the wonderful football they played merely raised the stakes and European football was soon climbing to new heights.

Before long, two other notable European competitions had kicked-off – the Cup Winners' Cup (a knockout between domestic cup winners) and the Inter-Cities Fairs Cup (later to become the UEFA Cup), a competition that owes its origins to an age when industrial trade fairs were held in Europe's major cities. UEFA's idea was to arrange a competition that could be played between city select XIs of the cities that hosted these fairs. To begin with the matches were only played when the fairs were taking place, with the result that the first competition kicked off in June 1955 but didn't finish until May 1958, when Barcelona defeated London in the first final.

By the early 1960s, however, all three competitions were annual events and had cemented their places in European football, broadening the football experience and horizons of all who took part. Their success saw replicas spring up around the world. CONCACAF launched their own Champions Cup in 1962, Mexico's Guadalajara taking the first honours, and the African Champions Cup arrived two years later, with Cameroon's Oryx Douala drawing first blood. The African Cup

Left: Henri Delaunay, the founder of the European Championship.

Winners' Cup followed in 1975 and the CAF Cup (essentially the African Federation's version of the UEFA Cup) in 1992. In Asia, a club championship launched in 1967 lasted just four years before falling apart (partly due to the huge geographical area covered), but the competition returned in 1985 with South Korea's Daewoo Royals triumphant, and it was joined by a Cup Winners' Cup in 1990.

Below: Léonidas and his Brazilian team-mates enjoy a kickabout while waiting for a train at the 1938 World Cup in France.

Above: Alfredo di Stéfano, whose move to the unofficial Colombian super league was an early example of 'player power'.

Above right: Celtic's Jimmy Johnstone takes on Racing Club of Argentina in the 1967 World Club Cup.

Opposite top: Manchester United players celebrate their 1999 Champions League win, while the accountants rub their hands.

Opposite bottom: Zinedine Zidane, the world's most expensive player at £47 million.

Right: The programme from the 1972 World Club Cup second-leg in Amsterdam, which pitted Ajax against Independiente. The Dutch won 4-1 on aggregate.

The Europeans were also responsible for South America's Copa Libertadores. In the mid-Fifties, just as the European Cup was taking off, Henri Delaunay suggested a match between the club champions of Europe and those of South America. The South Americans liked the idea – despite the absence of Africa, Asia and the rest of the Americas, football's powerhouses of Europe and South America considered this a world championship – but before it could take place they needed to establish who the South American champions were. For that, they needed a competition. They came up with the Copa Libertadores, won in its inaugural year, 1960, by Uruguay's Peñarol who gleefully headed off for a money-spinning tie with the European Champions, Real Madrid, in what was – and still is – known as the World Club Cup.

BY THE MID-1960s, the fundamental structure of world and domestic football was established. FIFA was at the head of the global game with UEFA (Europe), CONCACAF (Central and North America), CAF (Africa), CONMEBOL (South America), AFC (Asia) and OFC (Oceania) each taking control of their own geographical areas and running events such as the international club competitions and continental championships. The national football associations were then in charge of domestic football and their national teams.

In that sense, little has changed. But though the structure remains familiar, football at the beginning of the new millennium is hardly recognisable from the game of 40 years ago. In the Sixties, local heroes mixed with fans on the way to games, sharing buses, playing for the love of the game and earning a decent, but far from spectacular living. When their careers ended, they would seek other work and many struggled to make ends meet. The history books are full of tragic stories of great footballers (like Brazil's World Cup-winning Garrincha) whose lives ended in the gutter.

In contrast, today's football stars live a life of luxury, hidden away in palatial homes, treated like movie stars with flashy cars and bulging pay packets. When they retire in their 30s, many will never have to work again (some, like Raúl, Ronaldo and Michael Owen, were in that position by their early 20s).

The move towards big wages actually began in South America as long ago as the 1940s, when the best players in the world (like Alfredo Di Stéfano) were lured to earn their fortunes in Colombia's super league. In 1951, however, Colombia (who had been expelled) rejoined FIFA on condition that the foreign players left. Rubbing their hands with glee, Europe's top clubs were quick to capitalise – not least Real Madrid who, led by a Spanish lawyer called Santiago Bernabéu, were determined to become the world's best club. Bernabéu offered the likes of Di Stéfano and Hector Rial up to £10,000 a year. Not surprisingly they took him up on that offer, laying the foundations for Madrid's early dominance of the European Champions Cup.

Italian clubs followed suit, paying their top players huge salaries in search of glory, but elsewhere in Europe players earned far less. It was not until Jimmy Hill led a revolution in 1961 that the English Football League abandoned its maximum wage for players, while in Germany and Belgium, players were not professional until the mid-Sixties.

But even in the 1970s and 1980s, with wages theoretically limitless and hundreds of professional clubs watched by millions of fans, the idea of millionaire footballers was laughable. It was not until the 1990s that football, the world's most popular sport, finally became a big business.

Throughout the Seventies and Eighties, companies had increasingly used footballers to advertise their products or made use of sponsorship opportunities to publicise their brand on club shirts or pitchside hoardings, as the sport enjoyed a commercial awakening.

Transfer fees jumped to seven figures and top players lived well. But it was television that changed football forever.

In the late Eighties and early Nineties, new TV stations across Europe sought to challenge the state channels' monopolies and some of them – Rupert Murdoch's Sky in Britain, Silvio Berlusconi's Mediaset and the Kirch group in Germany – saw football, 'the people's game', as the best way to do that. Off the back of a hugely successful 1990 World Cup in Italy, and with hopes that hooliganism was finally coming under control, football was enjoying a boom in popularity and these new TV companies wanted in. The result was more and more TV coverage of the game with a resultant boost in exposure for any brands associated with clubs and players. What followed was an unseemly scramble as everyone from brewers to fast-food chains to mobile phone companies flocked to associate themselves with 'the beautiful game'.

The sudden commercial interest in the game did not go unnoticed in football's corridors of power. In England, the chairmen of the top clubs saw their opportunity to seize power from the FA and control the rapidly increasing TV revenues. In the 1992-93 season they launched the Premier League.

A year later UEFA followed with the Champions League, a reformatted European Cup guaranteeing more games (and therefore more TV coverage and money) for the top clubs. All of this meant more and more money flooding into the game. Merchandising sales rocketed, TV contracts were signed for billions of pounds and clubs paid huge transfer fees and unprecedented salaries. In 2001 the commercial boom hit its peak when Real Madrid paid a world record £47 million for one player, France's Zinedine Zidane.

That appears to have been the high water mark, however. A year later Madrid signed World Cup-winner Ronaldo for £22 million, and in 2003, the world's most marketable footballer, David Beckham, arrived at the Bernabéu for a fee that at most will be £25 million. However, many of Europe's top players still earn in excess of £5 million a year.

It's all a far cry from medieval rabbles or public schoolboys making up the rules as they went along. Who then could have predicted what football would become? Who now can guess what it will be like next century?

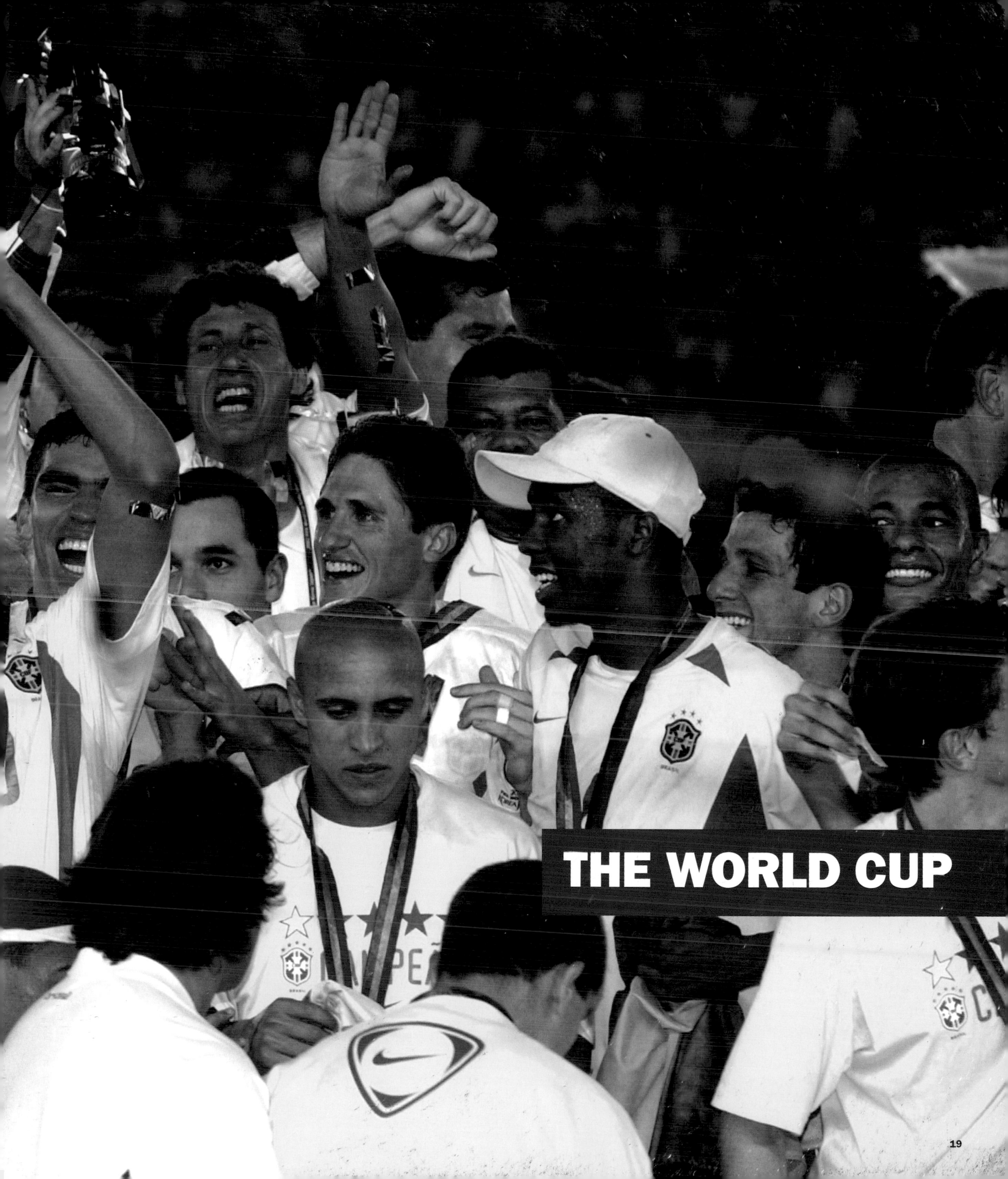

THE WORLD CUP

THE WORLD CUP

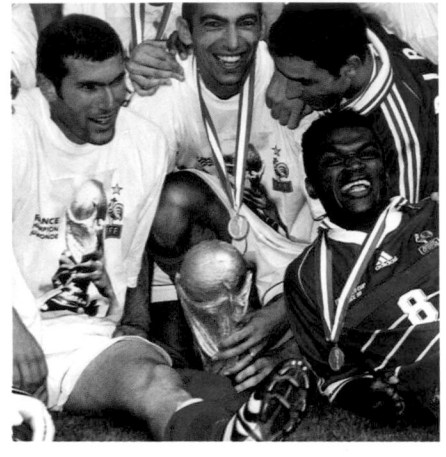
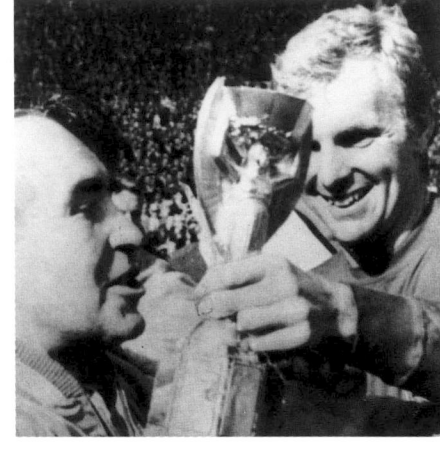

No other sporting event, with the possible exception of the Olympic Games, captures the imagination across the globe quite like the World Cup. Ever since the first competition in Uruguay in 1930, the tournament has grown in popularity and prestige – but that's not to say it hasn't been without its share of problems over the years. Indeed, the origins of the tournament were so wrapped up in politics that it took 26 years for the idea of a World Cup to become a reality.

During its inaugural meeting in 1904 FIFA agreed that it had the sole right to organise a tournament that brought together the world's strongest national football teams. However, it wasn't until the 1920s, nurtured by French administrator Jules Rimet, that the idea gained impetus. In the interim, the Olympic Games football tournament began to establish itself as the first truly international competition (England, representing Great Britain, ran out winners in both 1908 and 1912). In 1920, at FIFA's Antwerp congress, the World Cup was proposed and accepted in principle, and four

years later during the Paris Olympics it was talked about in finer, more realistic detail.

In 1928 Uruguay retained their Olympic title in Amsterdam, beating Argentina in the final. The tiny South American country were so eager to host the inaugural World Cup that not only did they say they would build a new stadium in Montevideo to stage the event, but they offered to pay the cost of all travel and accommodation for the visiting teams. Such unbridled willingness beat off competition from Italy, Holland, Spain and Sweden.

On July 13, 1930 the first game of the first World Cup kicked off in Pocitos Stadium, with France getting the better of Mexico 4-1. This marked the beginning of a long and wonderful World Cup history. But all was not sweetness and light, and not one of the other aspiring hosts made the journey to Uruguay – although it was, admittedly, a trip that took three weeks by sea. Indeed, at one stage it seemed that the competition would not feature any European sides, but ultimately four made the journey (France, Romania, Belgium and Yugoslavia).

It was the only World Cup not to involve the modern system of qualifying rounds.

Since that first competition, the 17 tournaments have seen only seven different winners. However, the FIFA World Cup has still been punctuated by some dramatic upsets that have helped create football history – the United States defeating England in 1950, North Korea's defeat of Italy in 1966, Cameroon's emergence in the 1980s and their opening match defeat of reigning champions Argentina in 1990.

The 1934 World Cup was held in Italy, and before a ball was kicked it was already heading for controversy. The holders Uruguay, still upset by the stay-away attitude of the European sides four years earlier, decided not to defend their own title and did not attend the competition. The tournament was the first to be run using the knockout format with 16 teams competing, and was also the first to host games in more than just one city. Sadly, not for the last time, the shadow of world politics threatened to eclipse the event as fascist

Above from left to right: The French team celebrate their victory as hosts in 1998; England manager Alf Ramsey and captain Bobby Moore admire the Jules Rimet Trophy in 1966; Brazil became the first team to win a World Cup final on penalties at USA 94.

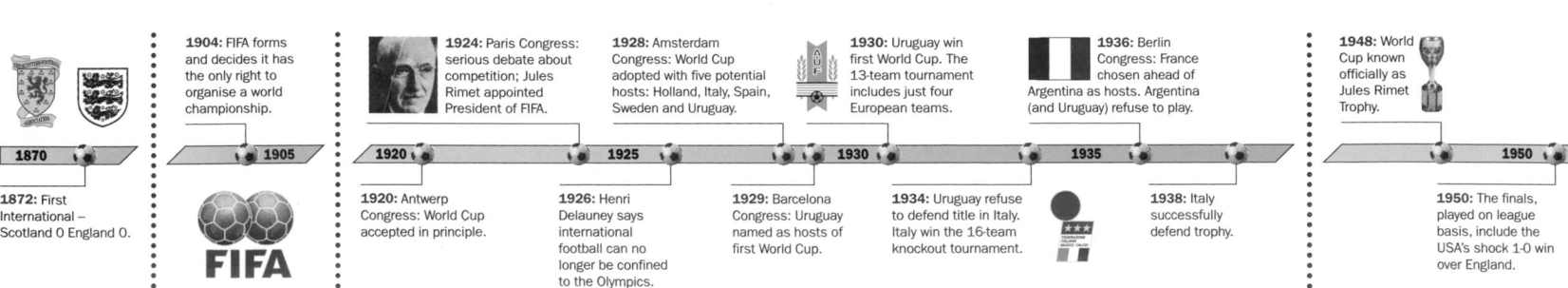

1904: FIFA forms and decides it has the only right to organise a world championship.

1924: Paris Congress: serious debate about competition; Jules Rimet appointed President of FIFA.

1928: Amsterdam Congress: World Cup adopted with five potential hosts: Holland, Italy, Spain, Sweden and Uruguay.

1930: Uruguay win first World Cup. The 13-team tournament includes just four European teams.

1936: Berlin Congress: France chosen ahead of Argentina as hosts. Argentina (and Uruguay) refuse to play.

1948: World Cup known officially as Jules Rimet Trophy.

1870   1905   1920   1925   1930   1935   1950

1872: First International – Scotland 0 England 0.

FIFA

1920: Antwerp Congress: World Cup accepted in principle.

1926: Henri Delauney says international football can no longer be confined to the Olympics.

1929: Barcelona Congress: Uruguay named as hosts of first World Cup.

1934: Uruguay refuse to defend title in Italy. Italy win the 16-team knockout tournament.

1938: Italy successfully defend trophy.

1950: The finals, played on league basis, include the USA's shock 1-0 win over England.

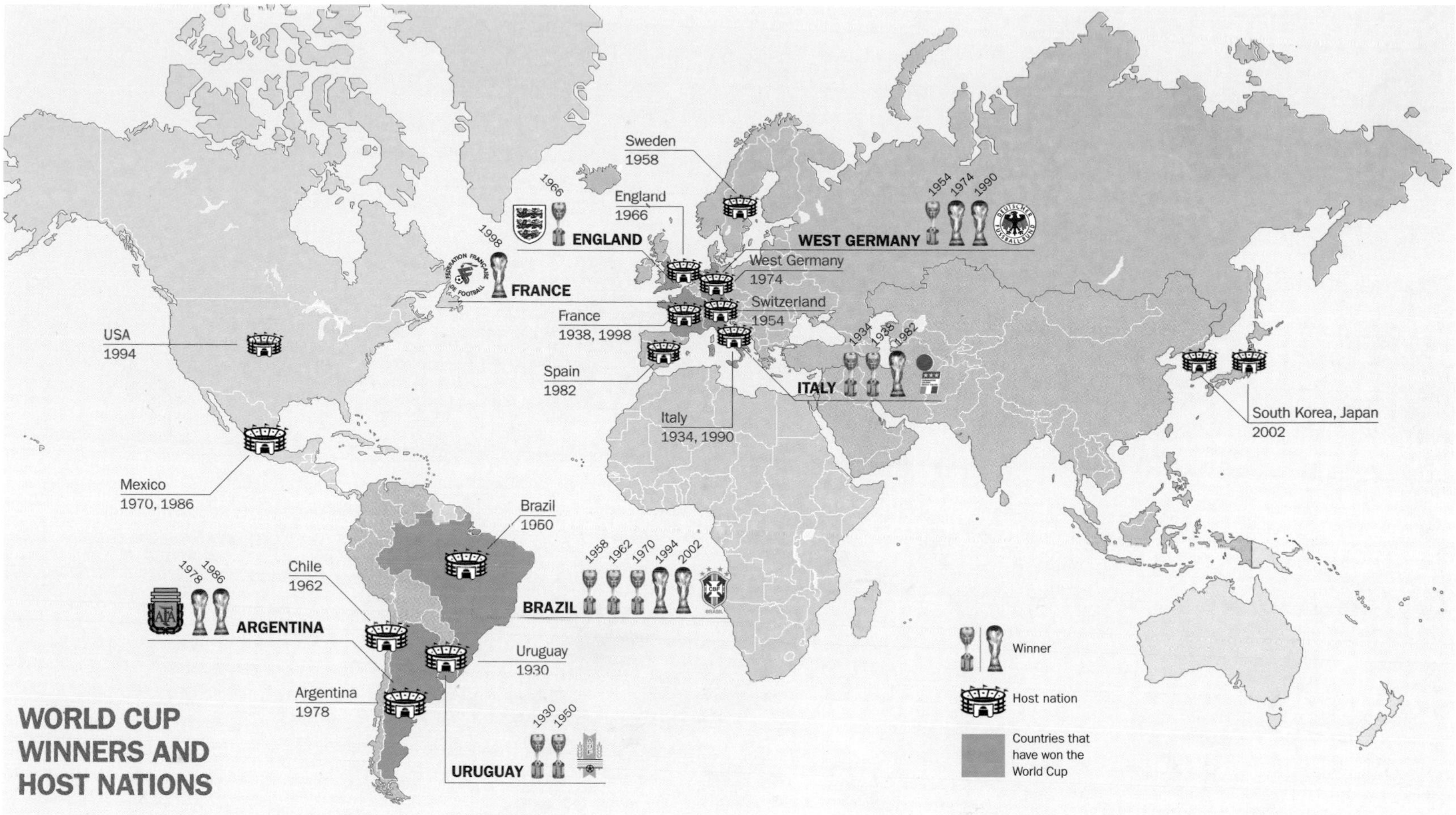

WORLD CUP WINNERS AND HOST NATIONS

Sweden
1958

England
1966

ENGLAND

West Germany
1974

1954 1974 1990

WEST GERMANY

FRANCE

France
1938, 1998

Switzerland
1954

ITALY

Italy
1934, 1990

USA
1994

Spain
1982

South Korea, Japan
2002

Mexico
1970, 1986

Brazil
1950

1958 1962 1970 1994 2002

BRAZIL

Chile
1962

1978 1986

ARGENTINA

Uruguay
1930

Argentina
1978

1930 1950

URUGUAY

Winner

Host nation

Countries that
have won the
World Cup

---

dictator Benito Mussolini attended many of the games. The 1938 tournament was plagued with similar problems. Spain was in the middle of a bloody civil war, while Austria had been annexed by Hitler's Germany – with many of their best players persuaded to change national allegiance.

The original trophy bore Jules Rimet's name and was contested twice more in the 1930s before the Second World War put a 12-year stop to the competition. In 1950, the World Cup was held in Brazil and the country built the Maracana, the largest stadium in the world, to host the event. It was the first time England competed. Again it was a tournament ravaged by no-shows, with several countries pulling out on the eve of the competition. This caused scheduling woes, but Brazil decided to stick to the original draw, so two groups consisted of four teams, while the other two consisted of three and two teams respectively – hardly the most equitable of systems.

The World Cup Committee rejigged the format again in the 1954 tournament, held in Switzerland. Each group of four in the first round possessed two seeded teams who were kept apart, and therefore only played the two unseeded teams in their group. This significantly increased the likelihood of teams ending up with the same number of points, and the need for play-offs meant that a massive 26 games had to be played in just 19 days – it was a system that was never used again.

Throughout the history of the tournament the number of countries registering with FIFA to qualify has increased. For instance, in 1954 it was 38, in 1958 it was 53, increasing to 56 in 1962. In 1974, the teams met in West Germany to compete for a new trophy – after the three-time winners Brazil had claimed the Jules Rimet Trophy.

The first major tournament change came in 1982, when FIFA president Joao Havelange expanded the field from 16 to 24 teams. Part

of the reasoning for the expansion was to open up the tournament to less established football nations. His expansionist philosophy was taken further when the World Cup was taken to the United States in 1994. As a fitting farewell to the man, France 98, Havelange's last tournament as FIFA president, saw the competition expanded to 32 teams. Still the tournament continues to evolve – as the 2002 competition in Japan and South Korea marked the first time the World Cup was held in Asia, and also the first occasion it had co-hosts.

Today, the FIFA World Cup holds the global public under its spell. It was estimated, for instance, that an audience of over 37 billion people watched the France 98 tournament, including 1.3 billion for the final alone, while over 2.7 million people flocked to watch the 64 matches. After all these years and so many changes and political strife, the focus of the World Cup still remains the same – to raise aloft the golden trophy.

PLAYER RATINGS

In our coverage of World Cup finals over the following pages, all available footage and match reports have been studied by an independent expert, with players awarded marks out of ten for their performance.

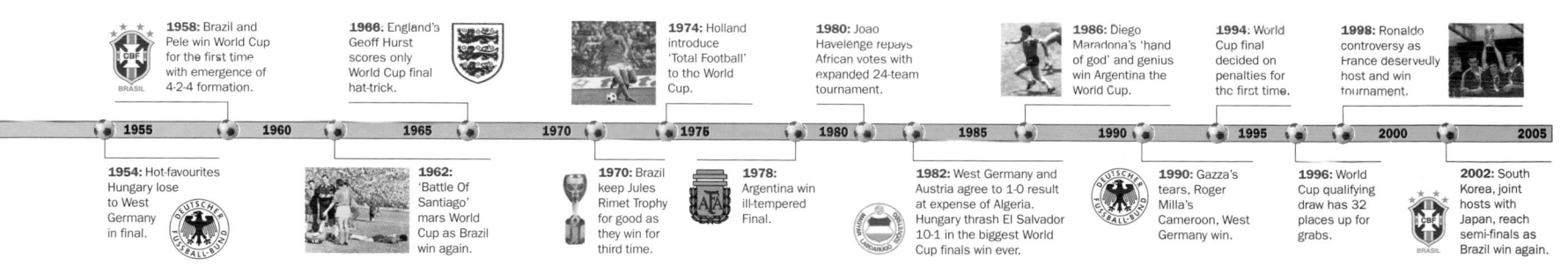

1958: Brazil and Pele win World Cup for the first time with emergence of 4-2-4 formation.

1966: England's Geoff Hurst scores only World Cup final hat-trick.

1974: Holland introduce 'Total Football' to the World Cup.

1980: Joao Havelenge repays African votes with expanded 24-team tournament.

1986: Diego Maradona's 'hand of god' and genius win Argentina the World Cup.

1994: World Cup final decided on penalties for the first time.

1998: Ronaldo controversy as France deservedly host and win tournament.

1955 1960 1965 1970 1975 1980 1985 1990 1995 2000 2005

1954: Hot-favourites Hungary lose to West Germany in final.

1962: 'Battle Of Santiago' mars World Cup as Brazil win again.

1970: Brazil keep Jules Rimet Trophy for good as they win for third time.

1978: Argentina win ill-tempered Final.

1982: West Germany and Austria agree to 1-0 result at expense of Algeria. Hungary thrash El Salvador 10-1 in the biggest World Cup finals win ever.

1990: Gazza's tears, Roger Milla's Cameroon, West Germany win.

1996: World Cup qualifying draw has 32 places up for grabs.

2002: South Korea, joint hosts with Japan, reach semi-finals as Brazil win again.

URUGUAY 1930

FIFA mandarins had been trying to get a world championship off the ground since shortly after the turn of the century, but it wasn't until visionary Frenchman Jules Rimet ascended to the presidency of FIFA after World War I that plans for such a tournament started to take shape, finally receiving a stamp of approval from FIFA's governing congress in 1928. The following year six countries bid to host the tournament – Holland, Hungary, Italy, Spain, Sweden and Uruguay – with the South Americans eventually getting the nod.

Thirteen countries (out of 41 that boasted FIFA membership) contested the inaugural tournament, with eight hailing from South America – Brazil, Bolivia, Mexico, Argentina, Chile, Peru, Paraguay and Uruguay. The other participants were made up of the United States and a disappointing turn-out from Europe – Yugoslavia, Belgium, France and Romania, who were coached by the country's reigning monarch, King Carol. Several European federations were undoubtedly deterred from

SEMI-FINALS
Argentina 6-1 USA
Uruguay 6-1 Yugoslavia

THIRD PLACE PLAY-OFF
Not held

TOP SCORERS
8 goals: Guillermo Stábile
(Argentina)
5 goals: Pedro Cea (Uruguay)
4 goals: Guillermo Suiabre (Chile)

FASTEST GOAL
1 minute: Adalbert Desu (Romania
v Peru)

TOTAL GOALS
70

AVERAGE GOALS
3,88 per game

Above: The opening ceremony of the 1930 World Cup at the Centenary Stadium in Montevideo. Opposite clockwise from top: Uruguay take on Argentina in the first World Cup final; the Argentina team take to the field; Uruguay celebrate winning the cup; despite having only one arm, Castro scored Uruguay's winning fourth goal in the final.

THE FINAL

URUGUAY (1) 4-2 (2) ARGENTINA

Date Wednesday July 30, 1930 **Attendance** 93,000
Venue Centenary Stadium, Montevideo

It was perhaps fitting that the tournament's first hosts should also end up as its first winners, in the country's centenary year. On top after 12 minutes through Pablo Dorado, Uruguay were nonetheless stunned when Carlos Peucelle brought the Argentinians level eight minutes later. Another setback for the hosts arrived in the 37th minute when Argentina took the lead through Stábile – the man who'd go on to be the tournament's highest scorer with eight goals.

Uruguay rallied after the break, Pedro Cea equalising in the 58th minute, and Santos Iriarte snatching a third ten minutes later. Argentina were unlucky when Pancho Varallo had a shot cleared off the line, and their ill fortune was compounded a minute before the end when Hector Castro snatched the winner.

HOW THE TEAMS LINED UP

URUGUAY:
COACH:
ALBERTO SUPPICCI

Ballesteros
Nasazzi   Mascheroni
Andrade   Fernandez   Gestido
Dorado Scarone Castro Cea Iriarte

ARGENTINA:
COACH:
AUGUSTO ROUQUETTE

Evaristo, M   Stábile   Peuccelle
Ferreira   Varallo
Suárez   Monti   Evaristo, J
Paternóster   Della Torre
Botasso

URUGUAY	
BALLESTEROS	6
NASAZZI	7
MASCHERONI	6
ANDRADE	7
GESTIDO	5
FERNÁNDEZ	5
SCARONE	
CEA	*8
Goal: 57 mins	
DORADO	7
Goal: 12 mins	
CASTRO	7
Goal: 89 mins	
IRIARTE	7
Goal: 68 mins	

ARGENTINA	
BOTASSO	6
DELLA TORRE	5
PATERNÓSTER	5
EVARISTO, J	6
MONTI	7
SUÁREZ	6
VARALLO	6
FERREIRA	5
PEUCCELLE	7
Goal: 20 mins	
STABILE	*8
Goal: 37 mins	
EVARISTO, M	6

Referee: Langenus (Belgium)

competing by the great distance to Uruguay (then only negotiable by boat), while others fulminated that Italy had been overlooked as hosts. None of the British sides were eligible to compete as they had withdrawn from FIFA a couple of years earlier following a pay row.

The rather unwieldy number of teams was split into four pools – four teams in one, three teams in the rest – and the draw itself didn't take place until all the sides had actually arrived in Uruguay. The very first match in a World Cup finals took place on July 13, 1930, and it saw France run out comfortable 4-1 winners over Mexico, their first goal scored by Lucien Laurent in the 19th minute. Disappointingly, the game took place not at the grand Centenario stadium in Montevideo as planned, because it wasn't yet finished, but in the much smaller Pocitos stadium in the same city.

France were probably the European side most likely to win the tournament – they'd even put four goals past the Mexicans despite being reduced to ten men when their goalkeeper went off injured in the first 20 minutes (there were no substitutes allowed in 1930). However, any such ambitions came grinding to a halt in their very next match, a controversial encounter with Argentina.

The South Americans were leading 1-0, but with the French slowly but surely getting on top it was an advantage that looked increasingly fragile. However, the Brazilian referee, Almeido Rego, blew the whistle for full-time with six minutes still left on the clock and France on the attack, provoking angry scenes and many accusations of foul play. Such was the furore that the referee called the players back out to complete the final six minutes. But by that stage the French had lost their rhythm and the game ended 1-0. Preferential treatment or not, Argentina went on to qualify for the semi-finals at a canter. They defeated Chile 3-1, but had been most impressive in their

previous game, a 6-3 win over Mexico, which had boasted five penalties and a hat-trick from young Argentine striker Guillermo Stábile.

Yugoslavia headed Pool 2 after wins over Brazil (2-1) and Bolivia (4-0). They were the only one of the European entrants to make the semi-finals, as Uruguay and the United States took the honours in Pools 3 and 4 respectively. Uruguay didn't concede a single goal as they despatched Peru and Romania, a feat matched by the Americans, who had little difficulty putting Belgium and Paraguay to the sword in two impressive 3-0 victories, the latter featuring two goals from Bertram Patenaude (although, to this day some sources list him as having scored a hat-trick, the first in World Cup history, while others attribute the disputed goal to either Thomas Florie or an own-goal).

Argentina and Uruguay ran up high scores against lesser opposition in the semi-finals, Argentina 6-1 winners against the USA. Uruguay, meanwhile, started their showdown with Yugoslavia slowly, even falling behind after four minutes when Brankil Sekulic struck for the visitors. The lead was short-lived, however, and the South Americans went in well ahead at half-time, Pedro Cea equalising after 18 minutes and Pelegrin Anselmo claiming a brace of goals before the interval to make it 3-1. Uruguayan domination continued after the interval. Iriarte made it 4-1 with half an hour still to play, and Cea completed an extraordinary hat-trick with goals in the 67th and 72nd minutes to cap a crushing victory.

Uruguay and Argentina had met in the Olympic final two years earlier in Amsterdam. Uruguay, also Olympic champions in 1924, ran out 2-1 winners in that encounter, and were too strong again in the first World Cup final. Argentina may have been the reigning South American champions, but they were unable to exact revenge on their great rivals, as Uruguay became the first world champions.

Above: The Brazilian entourage and their luggage arrive in Italy for the tournament. Opposite: Eventual winners Italy (top) edged past Spain 1-0 in the opening round thanks to a goal from Meazza (bottom left). In their semi-final they had to defeat Austria's much-vaunted 'Wunderteam', seen in action in the other pictures.

ITALY 1934

Italian dictator Benito Mussolini hoped to use the first World Cup on European soil to further the cause of his fascist regime, but while the tournament can claim to have been a success it was not without controversy. Following the widespread European boycott of the 1930 tournament, the South American nations retaliated with holders Uruguay not even sending a team, and both Brazil and Argentina fielding under-strength sides.

With 32 teams competing, qualification was required before 16 nations reached the preliminary round in Italy. Unlike the 1930 tournament in Uruguay which had been staged solely in Montevideo, eight venues across Italy played host to matches. On May 27, Genoa, Turin, Florence, Milan, Trieste, Rome, Naples and Bologna all witnessed preliminary round action, though naturally it was to be Rome that would eventually stage the showpiece final.

Brazil, Argentina, USA and Egypt were the only non-European countries in the final 16 and all were making the long journey home after just one game. Many of the Argentinians stars had moved to play in the European leagues and not one member of their 1930 team appeared against Sweden in Bologna. However, twice the Argentinians led before a late goal from Kroon sent the Swedes through 3-2. Brazil were barely in the game in Genoa before Spain took total control, leading 2-0 by the break. The South Americans pulled one back but their fate was sealed by Langara's second goal of the match.

France took a shock lead against the second-favourites Austria in Turin, and though Matthias Sindelar levelled, it wasn't until extra-time that Austria's superiority showed – it took a blatantly offside strike from Schall to unsettle the French before Josef Bican decided the match for the Austrians. A late penalty for the French was nothing more than a consolation.

Germany turned around a 2-1 half-time deficit to beat Belgium 5-2 in Florence, the victory owing much to a hat-trick in less than 15 minutes from Conen. The Dutch, meanwhile, crashed out of the competition 3-2 to Switzerland in Milan.

There were no such problems for favourites Italy against the USA. Angelo Schiavio netted a hat-trick in Rome as the hosts won 7-1. In Naples the first African challenge on the world stage succumbed in the second half as Egypt, who had put 11 goals past Palestine to qualify for the finals, went out of the competition with a 4-2 defeat to Hungary.

In Trieste, highly-fancied Czechoslovakia struggled past Romania. Dobai had given the Romanians the lead shortly before the break, but the Czechs possessed a formidable forward pairing of Antonin Puc and Oldrich Nejedly, who both scored to line-up a quarter-final meeting with the Swiss.

Once again the Czechs did not have it all their own way, falling behind to an early Kielholz goal before Svoboda levelled the tie. Sobotka put the Czechs ahead early in the second-half, but Switzerland hit back and once again it needed Nejedly to find the target seven minutes from time to decide the see-saw match and put Czechoslovakia through to the semi-finals.

Germany and Austria disposed of Sweden and Hungary respectively, but the most remarkable of the quarter-finals saw Italy triumph over Spain in Florence a full 24 hours after the game had kicked-off! The first encounter finished 1-1 and not even extra-time could separate the sides, so the first replay in World Cup history was arranged for the following day. The Spanish made seven

changes and the Italians five, but it was another close encounter, ultimately settled in favour of the hosts by prolific Inter Milan marksman Giuseppe Meazza.

There was little respite for Vittorio Pozzo's side and just 48 hours later, having now moved on to Milan's San Siro stadium, they took on Austria's 'Wunderteam' in the semi-finals. A first-half goal from Argentine-born winger Guarita was enough to take Italy through their fourth game in eight days.

The Czechs progressed through the other semi-final in Rome with a 3-1 victory over the Germans and Nejedly took centre stage once again, netting a hat-trick. But this encounter was witnessed by just 10,000 people, a full 50,000 less than at the Italy-Austria match.

Four days later Germany did at least salvage some pride by winning the inaugural third place play-off with a 3-2 victory over Hugo Meisl's Austria. But Mussolini and all of Italy had the dream they had longed for with the Azzuri in the final. For the second tournament running the hosts had gone all the way and now only Czechoslovakia stood before Pozzo's men and glory in Rome.

THE FINAL

ITALY (0) 2-1 (0) CZECHOSLOVAKIA
(aet; 1-1 at 90 mins)

Date Sunday June 10, 1934 **Attendance** 55,000

Venue Stadio del PNF, Rome

Czechoslovakia were less than ten minutes away from stunning the hosts and winning the World Cup in front of Mussolini. Antonin Puc, suffering with cramp, fired the Czechs ahead with little over 15 minutes remaining and an upset looked on the cards. Italy drew level though, through Raimondo Orsi in the 82nd minute, and five minutes into extra-time Pozzo's men grabbed a deserved winner through Angelo Schiavio's fourth goal of the competition.

The final saw Italy's Luis Monti set a unique record, appearing in his second straight final, but for different nations. Four years after finishing a runner-up with the country of his birth, Argentina, Monti was this time celebrating World Cup success with his adopted Italy.

HOW THE TEAMS LINED UP

ITALY
COACH: VITTORIO POZZO

CZECHOSLOVAKIA
COACH: CORNEL PETRU

ITALY	
COMBI	7
MONZEGLIO	5
ALLEMANDI	6
FERRARIS	6
MONTI	7
BERTOLINI	7
MEAZZA	6
FERRARI	7
GUAITA	7
SCHIAVIO	7
Goal: 95 mins	
ORSI	*9
Goal: 81 mins	

CZECHOSLOVAKIA	
PLÁNICKA	6
ZENISEK	5
CTYROKY	6
KOSTÁLEK	6
CAMBAL	*9
KRCIL	5
SVOBODA	7
NEJEDLY	6
JUNEK	6
SOBOTKA	6
PUC	8
Goal: 71 mins	

Referee: Eklind (Sweden)

SEMI-FINALS
Czechoslovakia 3-1 Germany
Italy 1-0 Austria

THIRD PLACE PLAY-OFF
Germany 3-2 Austria

TOP GOALSCORERS
5 goals: Oldrich Nejedly (Czechoslovakia)
4 goals: Angelo Schiavio (Italy), Edmund Conen (Germany)

FASTEST GOAL
30 seconds: Ernst Lehner (Germany v Austria)

TOTAL GOALS
70

AVERAGE GOALS
4.12 per game

FRANCE 1938

The 1938 World Cup brought us Italy, one of the greatest teams of all time, and Leónidas, the Brazilian striker who emerged as the outstanding individual of the tournament. While nobody could argue with Italy's eventual triumph, thanks largely to their outstanding mix of tactical astuteness and pragmatic defending, it was hard luck on Leónidas, known as 'the Black Diamond', that he ended without even a place in the final. As top scorer with seven goals, and with some magnificent performances, he was one of the earliest luminaries of the world game.

Yet Italy's all-round mix of resilience and flair was enough for a second consecutive triumph and confirmed Vittorio Pozzo as the foremost coach of his era. He had led the Italians to World Cup victory four years earlier and sandwiched the Olympic title in between. Who knows how great the Azzurri dynasty could have been but for World War II?

Impending conflict in Europe cast a shadow over the tournament from the outset. Adolf Hitler's Germany had annexed Austria and

SEMI-FINALS

Italy 2-1 Brazil
Hungary 5-1 Sweden

THIRD PLACE PLAY-OFF

Brazil 4-2 Sweden

TOP GOALSCORERS

8 goals: Leónidas (Brazil)
7 goals: Gyula Zsengeller (Hungary)
5 goals: Silvio Piola (Italy)

FASTEST GOAL

35 seconds: Arne Nyberg
(Sweden v Hungary)

TOTAL GOALS

84

AVERAGE GOALS

4.67 per match

Above: The Germans, complete with controversial Nazi salute, line up against Switzerland. Opposite clockwise from top: The captains of Brazil and Poland exchange pennants; Belgian goalkeeper Badjou punches away the ball against France; the teams run out in the same game; the German keeper Raftl makes a save against Swiss striker Abbeglen.

THE FINAL

ITALY (3) 4-2 (1) HUNGARY

Date Sunday June 19, 1938 **Attendance** 45,000
Venue Stade Olympique de Colombes, Paris

Italy won by a two-goal margin but it was no contest. Pozzo's side were much stronger than Hungary and far more decisive in attack. Colaussi opened the scoring when he collected a Piola cross in the sixth minute and prodded home past Szabó from close range. Titkos immediately equalised, but Hungarian hopes were dashed when Piola scored on 16 minutes, picking up a pass from Meazza to lash the ball high into the net. Colaussi added a third before half-time to put Italy in total control.

The reigning champions defended their lead in the second-half, even allowing for Sárosi's goal which reduced the lead, and Piola struck again with eight minutes remaining to seal victory. They were in a class of their own.

HOW THE TEAMS LINED UP

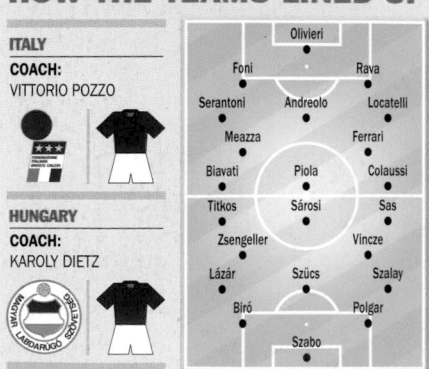

ITALY
COACH:
VITTORIO POZZO

HUNGARY
COACH:
KAROLY DIETZ

ITALY	
OLIVIERI	6
FONI	6
RAVA	7
SERANTONI	7
ANDREOLO	8
LOCATELLI	8
MEAZZA	*9
FERRARI	7
BIAVATI	6
PIOLA	7
Goal: 16 mins, 85 mins	
COLAUSSI	7
Goal: 6 mins, 35 mins	

HUNGARY	
SZABÓ	7
POLGAR	6
BIRÓ	7
SZALAY	6
SZÜCS	7
LÁZÁR	6
VINCZE	5
ZSENGELLER	6
SAS	6
SÁROSI	6
Goal: 70 mins	
TITKOS	6
Goal: 8 mins	

Referee: Capdeville (France)

Formation diagram:
Italy: Olivieri; Foni, Rava; Serantoni, Andreolo, Locatelli; Meazza, Ferrari; Biavati, Piola, Colaussi
Hungary: Titkos, Sárosi, Sas; Zsengeller, Vincze; Lázár, Szücs, Szalay; Biró, Polgar; Szabo

insisted the country's best players join the German side. Several did, but others refused, notably star striker Matthias Sindelar, who committed suicide a year later. Austria were forced to withdraw from the tournament, while Spain too pulled out, racked by civil war.

Champions eight years earlier, Uruguay also stayed at home, while Argentina pulled out over the decision to give the tournament to France. They had wanted to hold it themselves and felt FIFA should have alternated the venue between Europe and South America.

When the tournament finally kicked off, the three outstanding sides, Italy, Brazil and Hungary, were joined in the 16-team format by lesser nations such as Cuba and the Dutch East Indies. The competition was no less exciting for that. Italy needed a Silvio Piola goal in extra-time to win their opening match against Norway to reach the quarter-finals, while Cuba drew 3-3 with Romania and then stunned them by winning 2-1 in the replay. France beat Belgium 3-1, while Czechoslovakia knocked out Holland with a 3-0 win.

Switzerland, in a memorable clash, drew 1-1 with Germany and fell two goals behind in the replay but, despite playing much of the game with only ten fit men after an injury to Aebi, shocked the Germans with four second-half goals to send them home early.

The game of the first round, and arguably the best of any World Cup, saw Brazil facing Poland in Strasbourg on June 5. The 6-5 winning score-line was thanks mainly to Leónidas, who even wanted to continue to play the match barefoot when his boot fell apart in the mud, but was instructed by the referee to put his footwear back on. Three minutes into extra-time Leónidas became the first player to score four goals in the World Cup finals, and such was the brilliance of his performance in this astonishing match, it is often forgotten that Polish striker Ernest Wilimowski equalled the four goal haul just five minutes later.

Italy continued their fine form in the quarter-finals by putting out hosts France with a 3-1 win at Colombes; Piola adding two more goals to his tally and captain Giuseppe Meazza dominating in midfield. It meant the hosts would not win the World Cup for the first time, leaving 58,455 disappointed fans.

Following their attacking exploits in the previous round Brazil showed an ugly side to their game in the clash with Czechoslovakia. A brawl and the sending-off of three players blighted the first match, which ended 1-1, before Brazil won the replay through goals from Leónidas and Roberto. Hungary looked good, beating Switzerland 2-0, while Sweden crushed Cuba 8-0 to complete the final quartet.

In the semi-finals Brazil faced Italy, but Brazil coach Adhemar Pimenta left out Leónidas, a decision that proved their undoing. Some say Leónidas was rested arrogantly for the final, others that he was simply unable to play because of injuries collected in the warlike clash with Czechoslovakia. Whatever the reason, Italy gained the advantage immediately. Luigi Colaussi scored shortly after half-time and Meazza added a penalty on the hour. Brazil managed only a consolation goal three minutes from time through Romeu.

In the other semi-final Hungary ended Sweden's run with a 5-1 triumph despite conceding in the first minute. The Swedes' lead lasted 19 minutes before Hungary won through, thanks to Jakobsen's own goal, and strikes by Titkos, Sárosi and a brace from Zsengeller. The forward partnership between Gyula Zsengeller and Gyorgy Sárosi was perhaps the most thrilling in the tournament and revealed its power to devastating effect.

Ironically, Leónidas returned for the third place play-off and Brazil fell two goals behind to Sweden before fighting back to win 4-2. He scored twice to finish top-scorer with eight.

In the final the Italians confirmed their place as one of the greatest sides of all time.

BRAZIL 1950

The 1950 World Cup was, in many ways, the oddest of tournaments: withdrawals dominated the build-up, only 13 teams turned up in Brazil, and no final was scheduled by the organisers, the winners to be decided in a second league phase. Even the new Maracana stadium, built specifically for the tournament, wasn't ready when the first game kicked-off. But in the end the competition produced moments of pure drama and a game that will never be forgotten. The chaotic preparations eventually gave way to some excellent football and one of the greatest clashes the World Cup has ever seen.

The draw itself looked lop-sided, the opening round consisting of two groups of four, one of three and one of two. Argentina were among the many teams to pull-out before the qualifiers, while Scotland and Turkey withdrew after booking a place in the finals. India refused to turn up, according to some reports, because FIFA insisted they wore boots.

All eyes were on Group 1, where host nation Brazil and highly-fancied outsiders Yugoslavia immediately turned on the style. The host nation had a wonderfully entertaining line-up, boasting a trio of attackers – Ademir, Jair and Zizinho – who ranked among the finest in the world. They played skilful, inventive football and were the favourites to lift the trophy for the first time, making a superb start by thrashing Mexico 4-0 in their opener, with Ademir scoring twice. Yugoslavia kept pace with an impressive 3-0 win over Switzerland, maintaining their stunning form with a 4-1 win over Mexico in their second match.

Switzerland surprisingly held Brazil 2-2, but when the two group leaders met in the Maracana in front of 142,429 spectators, the hosts came out on top with a 2-0 win thanks to goals from Ademir and Zizinho, ensuring safe passage to the final pool. With only one team to go through, it was harsh on the talented Yugoslavs who went home early.

In Group B, England were the star attraction, taking part in their first World Cup. The team had lost star players Frank Swift and Tommy Lawton since the war but still boasted Billy Wright, Tom Finney and Stan Mortensen in their ranks. It was an impressive line-up and goals from Mortensen and Wilf Mannion secured a 2-0 win over Chile.

It looked as though they would cruise through but in their second game the United States inflicted on England one of the most embarrassing defeats in their history. The USA, who had lost their opening game 3-1 to Spain, recorded a 1-0 win in Belo Horizonte on June 29, with Joe Gaetjens scoring the 38th minute winner. It was a major shock for the English, who had assumed their side would reach the final pool at least.

Above: A packed Maracana hosts its only World Cup. Opposite clockwise from top: Schiaffino equalises for Uruguay in the 'final' against Brazil; Uruguay celebrate; England in action against Chile; Brazil open the scoring against Uruguay.

England's misery was doubled when Spain put the final nail in the coffin by beating them 1-0 to reach the final pool with a 100 per cent record. Walter Winterbottom's team returned home thoroughly humiliated.

In Group C, holders Italy, Sweden and Paraguay played each other, with Sweden earning an early advantage thanks to a 3-2 win over Italy. The Scandinavians' 2-2 draw with Paraguay in the next match was enough for them to clinch the top spot and Italy's 2-0 win over Paraguay was a mere consolation.

In the absurd two-team Group 4, Uruguay thrashed Bolivia 8-0 to make the final pool, with Juan Schiaffino catching the eye and Omar Miguez grabbing a hat-trick.

And so to the final pool – the World Cup trophy would go to whoever topped the mini-league table. It could have been an anti-climax if one team had wrapped it up early, but in the event it provided perhaps the most thrilling climax to any World Cup, with scorelines and scheduling throwing up an 'unofficial final' in front of the largest football crowd ever.

Certainly the hosts looked the best bet to win when the pool kicked-off, racking up a 7-1 win over Sweden, which included some of the finest attacking football ever seen. Ademir scored four goals in a truly blistering display as his understanding with Jair and Zizinho reached its peak. Next they thrashed Spain 6-1, all three strikers getting on the scoresheet, and Chico hit the target twice. The hosts began to look unstoppable.

Uruguay kept in touch by starting with a 2-2 draw against Spain in a tough physical encounter, and then a 3-2 win over Sweden was enough to retain a slim chance of causing an upset. It meant the final group match, between Brazil and Uruguay, would decide who would win the World Cup – although Uruguay needed to beat the favourites to triumph, while Brazil needed only a draw.

It looked a foregone conclusion, Brazil having played the better football and having the advantage of a home crowd in the Maracana. But the unimaginable happened. Uruguay came from behind and hit a winner with just 11 minutes remaining to leave the crowd shellshocked. It left a bitter feeling among the hosts that remains to this day.

THE FINAL POOL MATCH

URUGUAY (0) 2-1 (0) BRAZIL

Date Sunday July 16, 1950 **Attendance** 199,854
Venue Estadio Maracana, Rio de Janeiro

Thirty shots at goal, the will of a nation, and 200,000 fans in the stadium – but Uruguay refused to read the script and achieved a remarkable triumph. During a goalless first-half they weathered the storm, their defence doing everything to match the efforts of Brazil's famed attack, before they shocked in the second-half. Friaça scored two minutes after the break, making victory look inevitable, but on 66 minutes Juan Schiaffino swept in an equaliser. Uruguay stood firm and, on the break, Alcides Ghiggia attacked Barbosa's goal and scored from close range to seal a famous victory.

Uruguay had achieved the impossible and the supporters could hardly believe what they had seen. In the most dramatic circumstances, Brazil had yet again failed to lift the World Cup.

HOW THE TEAMS LINED UP

URUGUAY
COACH: JUAN LOPEZ

BRAZIL
COACH: FLAVIO COSTA

URUGUAY	
MÁSPOLI	*9
GONZÁLES M	7
ANDRADE	8
TEJERA	7
VARELA	8
GAMBETTA	7
PERÉZ	6
SCHIAFFINO ⚽	7
Goal: 66 mins	
GHIGGIA ⚽	8
Goal: 79 mins	
MIGUEZ	6
MORÁN	6

BRAZIL	
BARBOSA	6
AUGUSTO	6
JUVENAL	7
BAUER	5
DANILO ALVIM	7
BIGODE	6
ZIZINHO	6
JAIR	6
FRIAÇA ⚽	7
Goal: 47 mins	
ADEMIR MENEZES	7
CHICO	5

Referee: Reader (England)

FINAL POOL					
	P	W	D	L	Pts
Uruguay	3	2	1	0	5
Brazil	3	2	0	1	4
Sweden	3	1	0	2	2
Spain	3	0	1	2	1

TOP GOALSCORERS

9 goals: Ademir Menezes (Brazil)
5 goals: Juan Schiaffino (Uruguay), Estanislao Basora (Spain)

FASTEST GOAL

2 minutes: Alfredo (Brazil v Switzerland)

TOTAL GOALS:
88

AVERAGE GOAL
4.00 per game

SWITZERLAND 1954

🏆 Although it came nearly ten years after the end of the Second World War and even was seen by a privileged few in flickering black and white television pictures for the first time, the 1954 World Cup remained a marginal event, far removed from the global marketing phenomenon it is now.

But for all that, the tournament produced some of the most colourful attacking football in its history, with a massive 140 goals shared between 16 teams at an average of over five goals a game. The quarter-final between Austria and their Swiss hosts finished 7-5, the highest aggregate ever for a game at the finals, and several other matches finished with scorelines that appear improbable today.

Switzerland was a logical choice to host the first post-war tournament to be held in Europe, and not simply because it had escaped the devastation sustained across the rest of the continent. FIFA's headquarters were situated in Zurich and 1954 represented the 50th anniversary of its formation.

The Swiss had been granted the tournament at FIFA's first post-war congress in 1946, and they spent eight years building new stadiums for it. However, the finished grounds had small capacities and were not really up to the requirements of such a tournament. Despite this, it was a financial success, the organisers displaying early signs of grasping the World Cup's marketing potential, by having special commemorative coins minted.

The qualifying rounds featured the highest number of nations yet, with 38 entries. Sweden and Spain failed to qualify, the latter being beaten by Turkey who automatically became seeds, a ruling that was to have particular significance as the competition unfolded. England and Scotland came through the Home Nations group, though the latter were to lose both their games and make a rapid return. Once again the Soviet Union and Argentina were notable absentees.

Almost inevitably FIFA tampered with the set-up, reverting to a complicated pool phase featuring 16 teams divided into four groups, with two seeded sides in each who would not play each other. At the end the four winners played each other in a knock-out phase, as did the four runners-up. But the system was open to exploitation and the Germans did just that.

It was no surprise to find that Hungary, coached by Gusztav Sebes, were favourites. This was the era of the 'Magical Magyars'. Two years previously they had been crowned Olympic champions and now their players were at their peak. The line-up was crammed with legends, including the 'Galloping Major' Ferenc Puskás, striker Sándor Kocsis (dubbed 'The Man With The Golden Head'), midfield dynamo Josef Bozsik and deep-lying centre-forward Nandor Hidegkuti.

This was the core of the side which destroyed English pretensions to superiority with the dramatic 6-3 Wembley win in November 1953, the first ever at the venue, before dishing out a 7-1 pasting in Budapest six months later. The Magyars hammered South Korea 9-0 in their opening game in Zurich and put eight past a deliberately weakened German side, eventually scoring a record 27 goals in the tournament. Sandor Kocsis raced to the Golden Boot with 11 goals, including two hat-tricks.

However, Hungary's game against Brazil went down in football history for all the wrong reasons. Instead of the classic it promised, the match degenerated into hand-to-hand combat, since dubbed the 'Battle Of Berne'.

The bout was refereed by Arthur Ellis, who sent-off three players, Hungary's Bozsik and Brazil's Tozzi and Santos, after trouble broke out over a disputed penalty. The game degenerated from this point into violence that continued in the changing rooms after the match, embroiling both managers and even the official delegations.

Above: Santos and Boscik troop off during the 'Battle of Berne'. Opposite top: Tom Finney gets a header in for an England against Uruguay. Opposite bottom: Sandor Kocsis, whose goal put Hungary 2-0 up in their ill-fated final.

England, under Walter Winterbottom, topped a group featuring hosts Switzerland, Belgium and Italy. The side, featuring Billy Wright, Nat Lofthouse, Stanley Matthews and Tom Finney, should have gone further but came unstuck against Uruguay, losing 4-2 with goalkeeper Gil Merrick at fault for three goals. In the end the feeling was that their shattering 7-1 defeat at the hands of Hungary just weeks earlier had destroyed the team's confidence.

West Germany were admitted after their banishment following World War II and rapidly made a mockery of their non-seeding, beating Turkey 4-1, while France, another seeded side, lost to Yugoslavia. German manager Sepp Herberger then exploited the play-off system by electing to send out a weak side against Hungary in the knowledge that the group winners would play Brazil in the knock-out phase, while the runners-up would face Korea or Turkey. His plan worked and Germany duly thrashed Turkey and squeezed past the Yugoslavs 2-0, scoring early on and holding out until a late goal sealed the victory. A 6-1 semi-final victory over Austria sent out an ominous warning for the complacent.

Hungary's semi-final against holders Uruguay was another memorable encounter that put paid to the South Americans' unbeaten record in the competition, Hungary winning 4-2 in extra-time.

The final looked on paper to be a forgone conclusion. West Germany, unseeded, faced the might of Hungary, who had not lost in 31 games and four years, but the form book was discarded in a fascinating see-saw encounter that saw the Germans come back from 2-0 down to win the trophy for the first time. Hungary were stunned and when the Soviet Union crushed the country's uprising two years later the squad broke up, effectively ending its dominance forever.

SEMI-FINALS

West Germany 6-1 Austria
Hungary 4-2 Uruguay
(aet: 2-2 at 90 mins)

THIRD PLACE PLAY-OFF

Austria 3-1 Uruguay

TOP GOALSCORERS

11 goals: Kocsis (Hungary)
6 goals: Maximilian Morlock (West Germany), Josef Hügi (Switzerland), Erich Probst (Austria)

FASTEST GOAL

2 minutes: Mamat Suat (Turkey v West Germany)

TOTAL GOALS

140

AVERAGE GOALS

5.38 per game

THE FINAL

WEST GERMANY (2) 3-2 (2) HUNGARY

Date Sunday July 4, 1954 **Attendance** 60,000
Venue Wankdorf Stadium, Berne

Though carrying an injury, Puskás put his side ahead after only six minutes when he followed up a Kocsis shot. Two minutes later Czibor latched on to a weak back-pass to put them two up, but Morlock reduced the arrears after 11 minutes and a mistake by the Hungarian goalkeeper Grosics in the 18th minute allowed Rahn to equalise.

In the second-half Hidegkuti hit the post, Kocsis the bar, Kohlmeyer cleared off the line and Turek made a succession of great saves. Six minutes from time, winger Rahn picked up a half-hearted clearance, raced to the edge of the box and struck a low shot past Grosics, who appeared to slip. There was more drama when Puskás had a goal disallowed for offside; the Hungarians still arguing after the final whistle.

WEST GERMANY	
TUREK	*9
POSIPAL	6
KOHLMEYER	7
ECKEL	6
LIEBRICH	6
MAI	7
MORLOCK ⚽	7
Goal: 11 mins	
WALTER F	8
RAHN ⚽⚽	8
Goal: 18 mins, 84 mins	
WALTER O	6
SCHAFER	7

HUNGARY	
GROSICS	5
BUZANSZKY	6
LANTOS	6
BOZSIK	6
LORANT	7
ZAKARIAS	6
KOCSIS	*8
PUSKÁS ⚽	6
Goal: 6 mins	
CZIBOR ⚽	7
Goal: 9 mins	
HIDEGKUTI	6
TOTH M	5

Referee: Ling (England)

HOW THE TEAMS LINED UP

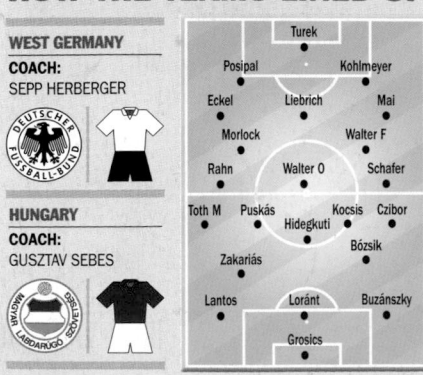

WEST GERMANY
COACH:
SEPP HERBERGER

Turek
Posipal   Kohlmeyer
Eckel   Liebrich   Mai
Morlock   Walter F
Rahn   Walter O   Schafer

HUNGARY
COACH:
GUSZTAV SEBES

Toth M   Puskás   Kocsis   Czibor
Hidegkuti
Bózsik
Zakariás
Lantos   Loránt   Buzánszky
Grosics

Above: One of Just Fontaine's record-breaking tally of 13 goals at the 1958 World Cup, this one part of his hat-trick against Paraguay. Opposite clockwise from top: Pele beats the Swedish goalkeeper – he was to score twice in the final; John Charles of Wales helps his side edge out Hungary; a 17-year-old Pele is overcome at the final whistle.

SWEDEN 1958

For fans of the beautiful game, the 1958 World Cup will always be remembered for the birth of a football nation, and in particular of its favourite son, Pele. Before Sweden '58, Brazil had never won the World Cup. Uruguay had forged a reputation as South America's finest side by twice lifting the trophy, but in 1958 the balance of power shifted. It has yet to shift again. Brazil, for the first of five times, became world champions.

They did so by pioneering a style of play that, in an era when defenders could – and did – get away with kicking the opposition's best players into the crowd, had football writers everywhere purring at its grace and beauty. The first strains of what was to become known as 'Samba football' were born in Sweden.

"Where skill alone counted Brazil stood alone," reported The Times of England. "The way each daffodil shirt of theirs pulled the ball down out of the sky, tamed it with a touch of the foot, caressed it and stroked it away into an open space was a joy."

Looking back, it is easy to over-romanticise about Brazil and to think that any team with so much skill, and with arguably the greatest ever player, was bound to succeed. But there was nothing inevitable about it. In the early decades of the World Cup, sides unfamiliar with foreign conditions did not travel well: until this tournament the winners had always been a team from the host continent. Brazil, third in 1938, spurned another great chance in 1950. This time, they meant business and even brought along a psychiatrist.

As for Pele, while everyone knew he was a bit special, at 17 no-one knew how special. His mere selection remained in doubt late, partly because of a niggling injury and partly because some believed he wasn't up to it.

The tournament, though, was something of a watershed. Although there were plenty of tasty tackles, Sweden marked the end of the more carefree, attack-minded post-war era of international football. In the 1960s, World Cup matches became increasingly cynical affairs characterised by defensive attitudes.

The party began without some familiar names as Uruguay and fellow two-time winners Italy both failed to qualify. For British football though, 1958 remains a high water mark with all four home nations qualifying for the only time. England, despite the Munich air disaster denying them such talents as Duncan Edwards, were among the favourites, particularly as they had never lost to any of the teams in their group. But it was to prove a hugely frustrating tournament for Walter Winterbottom's side. Creditable draws against the USSR and Brazil – incredibly the first goalless match in World Cup finals history – meant England only had to beat eliminated Austria to advance. But the draws continued and it came down to a play-off with the Soviets in the Ullevi Stadium, where England wilted.

Scotland set the tone for future World Cups by also going out in the first round, but Northern Ireland and Wales both advanced. The Irish, who had drawn 2-2 draw with West Germany in their group, beat Czechoslovakia in a play-off, a situation Wales were also catapulted into after drawing all three group matches. Inspired by John Charles, they came from behind to beat Hungary 2-1.

Charles was injured for the quarter-finals, where Wales met Brazil. For 70 minutes the Welsh dream lived on as the likes of Garrincha, Didi, Mazzola and Zagalo were continually thwarted. But when Pele scored the first of his 12 World Cup goals, it was all over.

The big guns were beginning to fire. In the quarter-finals, France ended Irish resistance with a 4-0 thumping. West Germany sneaked home 1-0 against Yugoslavia and Sweden put paid to the Soviet Union 2-0.

Although West Germany, the defending champions, were still in the competition, Sweden and Brazil had emerged as favourites. Sweden underlined their credentials in front of 53,000 fans in Gothenburg when they eliminated West Germany 3-1 in the semi-finals. The Germans hung on until the last ten minutes when the home team scored twice to trigger wild celebrations. It was one of West Germany's darkest World Cup moments. Erich Juskowiak was sent-off for kicking and they were reduced to nine men for a time when another player went off for treatment.

In the other semi-final in Stockholm, Brazil electrified the tournament with a 5-2 defeat of France, who had cruised through their quarter-final and were expected to pose a severe test. For half the match they did but they were blown away when Pele netted a hat-trick in 23 unforgettable second half minutes. French striker Just Fontaine had the consolation of scoring 13 goals in the tournament, a record that may never be broken.

The dream final had arrived and the era of Brazilian dominance was about to begin. That they have stayed ahead of their competition ever since, without forsaking their unique poetic style, is a sporting wonder.

THE FINAL

BRAZIL (2) 5-2 (1) SWEDEN

Date Sunday June 29, 1958 **Attendance** 49,737
Venue Rasunda Stadium, Solna, Stockholm

The Final was a summit meeting between football's new and old world orders. Heavy rain and a passionate home crowd suggested now wasn't the time or place for South American flair – especially when Liedholm fired the hosts ahead after five minutes. Four minutes later Vava equalised from Garrincha's cross, then Pele struck the post and Vava added a second. Suddenly Sweden were chasing shadows.

The second half was Pele's. His first goal in the 55th minute combined individual trickery with a rasping volley. Zagalo made it 4-1 before Simonsson restored hope for Sweden. But Pele had the final word, heading home for a 5-2 win. The Brazilians were overcome, weeping openly. They then sportingly carried the Swedish flag, bringing the stadium to its feet in acclaim.

HOW THE TEAMS LINED UP

BRAZIL
COACH:
VICENTE FEOLA

SWEDEN
COACH:
GEORGE RAYNOR

Gilmar

Santos D · Bellini · Orlando · Santos N

Didi · Zito

Garrincha · Vava · Pele · Zagalo

Skoglund · Simonsson · Hamrin

Liedholm · Gren

Parling · Gustavsson · Borjesson

Axbom · Bergmark

Svensson

Referee: Guigue (France)

BRAZIL	
GILMAR	6
SANTOS D	7
BELLINI	6
ORLANDO	7
SANTOS N	7
DIDI	8
ZITO	7
GARRINCHA	7
VAVA	8
Goal: 9 mins, 32 mins	
PELE	*9
Goal: 55 mins, 80 mins	
ZAGALO	7
Goal: 68 mins	

SWEDEN	
SVENSSON	5
BERGMARK	6
AXBOM	6
BORJESSON	5
GUSTAVSSON	6
PARLING	7
GREN	*8
LIEDHOLM	7
Goal: 4 mins	
HAMRIN	5
SIMONSSON	7
Goal: 80 mins	
SKOGLUND	5

SEMI-FINALS

Brazil 5-2 France
Sweden 3-1 West Germany

THIRD PLACE PLAY-OFF

France 6-3 West Germany

TOP GOALSCORERS

13 goals: Just Fontaine (France)
6 goals: Pele (Brazil), Helmut Rahn (West Germany)
5 goals: Vava (Brazil), Peter McParland (Northern Ireland)

FASTEST GOAL

90 seconds: Vava (Brazil v France)

TOTAL GOALS

126

AVERAGE GOALS

3.60 per game

CHILE 1962

SEMI-FINALS
Brazil 4-2 Chile
Czechoslovakia 3-1 Yugoslavia

THIRD PLACE PLAY-OFF
Chile 1-0 Yugoslavia

TOP GOALSCORERS
4 goals: Garrincha (Brazil),
Valentin Ivanov (Soviet Union),
Leonel Sánchez (Chile), Florian
Albert (Hungary), Drazan Jerkovic
(Yugoslavia), Vava (Brazil)
* Garrincha awarded Top Scorer
prize, drawn by lot

FASTEST GOAL
15 seconds: Vaclav Masek
(Czechoslovakia v Mexico)

TOTAL GOALS
89

AVERAGE GOALS
2.78 per game

🏆 "We have nothing, that is why we must have the World Cup," pleaded Carlos Dittborn, president of the Federación de Fútbol de Chile, after FIFA looked for an alternative host following the devastating earthquake that caused serious damage and loss of life in Chile in May 1960.

Chile kept the World Cup in the end and served up a tournament of extremes, ranging from the appalling 'Battle of Santiago' to the beautiful, crafted performances of the sublime Brazilians. Local interest in the games also wavered wildly, from disappointingly small attendances of under 6,000 at one extreme, to the crowds of over 60,000 who squeezed into the cauldron of Santiago. It was also a World Cup that witnessed the dawn of defensive football.

This largely dismal football showpiece reached its nadir with the infamous 'Battle of Santiago' between Italy and hosts Chile. Anti-Italian feeling had been whipped-up in Santiago as a result of the publication of derogatory articles about Chilean life by two Italian journalists. This was in addition to ill-feeling created by Italy's reputation for poaching South American players at both domestic and international level. Indeed, their line-up for the game included Argentinians Maschio and Sivori, and a veteran of Brazil's previous World Cup campaign, Jose Altafini.

The match, staged in front of a hostile over-capacity crowd in the Estadio Nacional, quickly descended into violence, which English referee Ken Aston failed to control. He did dismiss the Italian Ferrini for retaliation after just eight minutes, although the player refused to leave the field for a further ten minutes and was eventually removed by FIFA officials and the police. Aston also sent-off Ferrini's team-mate David in the second-half, however the referee did nothing when Sanchez, the son of a boxer, retaliated to Maschio's severe foul by breaking the Italian player's nose right in front of a linesman. The disgraceful violence on the field continued and Chile won the game 2-0.

The group stages were dominated by defensive play and excessive violence. After three match days the Chilean press reported there had been 34 serious injuries. Among the casualties was 21-year-old Pele, the result of a torn muscle from a groin injury sustained in a pre-tournament friendly – Pele had refused to declare it because of trainer Paulo Amaral's "don't train, don't play" policy.

Of course the opening stages did feature the odd decent match, the most amazing being the Group One clash between the Soviet Union and first time qualifiers Colombia in Arica. Three goals in three minutes gave the Soviets a 3-0 lead by the 11th minute, with two goals from Ivanov sandwiching a single strike from Chislenko. The game looked over, and an Aceros goal ten minutes later did nothing to change that opinion, with Ponedelnik adding to Colombian woe with a fourth for the Soviets early in the second-half. Colombia, however, staged a magnificent comeback to secure an amazing 4-4 draw, with Coll, Rada and Klinger all scoring. Indeed, Group One provided the most entertaining football of the early stages.

Outside of Santiago the games were poorly attended. The six Group Four matches in Rancagua, for example, attracted an average crowd of just 7,000, the worst attended being England's dull 0-0 draw against Bulgaria.

The quickest goal of the tournament was scored after just 15 seconds, Czechoslovakia's Vaclav Masek putting the ball past Mexican goalkeeper Carbajal, a veteran of three previous World Cups. Mexico won the game 3-1 but Czechoslovakia went on to the final along with group winners and holders Brazil.

Czechoslovakia had built a team around the successful Dukla Prague club with a strategy strongly built on defence. A cautious, counter-attacking team, they had held Brazil to a goalless draw and beaten a disharmonious

Above: Brazil's Garrincha goes past future World Cup winner Ray Wilson in their quarter-final with England. Opposite clockwise from top: Amarildo shows off his skills in the final; Chile's Rojas celebrates his country's last minute third place play-off win against Yugoslavia; Mauro lifts the Jules Rimet trophy after beating Chechoslovakia

Spain 1-0, reaching the quarter-finals on goal difference (being used for the first time at this World Cup) by virtue of conceding fewer goals than Mexico, thanks in no small part to Wilhelm Schrojf, the goalkeeper of the tournament. He was in magnificent form, particularly in the quarter-final and semi-final clashes with Hungary and Yugoslavia, a series of magnificent saves keeping his opponents at bay in both games.

Brazil suffered the loss of Pele after just two games but they remained unfazed by the loss of their star player, having unearthed Tavares Amarildo, who was quickly dubbed 'the white Pele'. It was Garrincha, though, who was Brazil's inspiration. The father of seven children, he was just as productive on the pitch when creating and scoring goals.

Brazil breezed through the quarter-finals, outclassing England who had finished runners-up in Group D. Garrincha, the smallest player on the field, opened the scoring with a header before later setting up Vava and finding the net again in a 3-1 win.

The semi-final pitched Brazil against hosts Chile in an open game that was streaked with spite. Garrincha gave Brazil a 2-0 lead through a volley and a header, although a Toro free-kick halved the deficit for the hosts before the break.

A Garrincha free-kick was headed home by Vava just after the interval, but Sanchez converted a penalty to keep Chile in touch. With 13 minutes remaining Zagalo dribbled through the Chilean defence and set up Vava with another header. Shortly afterwards Chile's Landa was sent-off and only minutes later Garrincha followed, finally retaliating to one on the many kicks he had suffered during the game. Nevertheless, now firm favourites Brazil progressed to the final, where they beat Czechoslovakia 3-1 to retain the trophy.

THE FINAL

BRAZIL (1) 3-1 (1) CZECHOSLOVAKIA

Date Thursday June 17, 1962 **Attendance** 68,679
Venue National Stadium, Santiago

Favourites Brazil named an unchanged side that included Garrincha, despite his semi-final sending-off. FIFA had imposed one-match bans on all of the other five players dismissed during the tournament. The experienced Brazil side included eight members of the team that had won in Sweden in 1958, but still they went 1-0 down to Masopust's opener for the Czechs.

Amarildo scored from an acute angle to equalise within two minutes and the match was closely-fought until the 69th minute when Amarildo's high pass was headed home by Zito.

The match was decided when Czech 'keeper Schrojf allowed a Djalma Santos high ball to fall through his hands, allowing Vava to stab home the loose ball for an unassailable 3-1 lead. It was the best match of the tournament.

BRAZIL	
GILMAR	7
SANTOS D	7
MAURO	7
ZOZIMO	6
SANTOS N	6
ZITO ⚽	7
Goal: 69 mins	
DIDI	7
GARRINCHA	6
VAVA ⚽	*8
Goal: 77 mins	
AMARILDO ⚽	7
Goal: 17 mins	
ZAGALO	6

CZECHOSLOVAKIA	
SCHROJF	5
TICHY	6
PLUSKAL	7
POPLUHAR	7
NOVAK	6
KVASNAK	6
MASOPUST ⚽	*8
Goal: 16 mins	
SCHERER	5
POSPICHAL	7
KADRABA	6
JELINEK	7

Referee: Latychev (USSR)

HOW THE TEAMS LINED UP

BRAZIL
COACH:
AYMORE MOREIRA

CZECHOSLOVAKIA
COACH:
RUDOLF VYTLACIL

Gilmar

Santos D — Mauro — Zózimo — Santos N

Zito — Didi — Zagalo

Garrincha — Vava — Amarildo

Jelinek — Kadraba — Scherer — Pospichal

Masopust — Kvasnak

Novak — Popluhar — Pluskal — Tichy

Schrojf

ENGLAND 1966

🏆 Most England fans remember the 1966 World Cup as their country's greatest sporting triumph, but the tournament itself was characterised by dour, often ugly defending, punctuated by occasional glimpses of brilliance and drama. The hosts England, boasted the likes of Bobby Moore, Bobby Charlton and Jimmy Greaves amongst their ranks and expectations were high, particularly after coach Alf Ramsey had promised the nation his team would prevail.

The draw pitted England against Uruguay, Mexico and France, but the opening game was an anticlimax with the negative Uruguayans blotting out England's sterile attack to leave the pitch with a 0-0 draw. England followed this up with a still less than convincing 2-0 win against Mexico, but qualification to the second stage was finally sealed with a 2-0 win against France.

In Group Two, meanwhile, West Germany got off to a flying start with a crushing 5-0 win over a Swiss side depleted by suspensions. The first surprise of the tournament came when a physical Argentina beat a Spain team built around the mighty Real Madrid side. While Spain recovered to beat the Swiss, West Germany faced Argentina and were subjected to the kind of brutal tactics which saw the South Americans pick up a FIFA warning. It did not prevent them progressing though, Argentina clinching qualification against Switzerland in front of a hostile crowd. West Germany, meanwhile, qualified top after an Uwe Seeler goal put Spain out.

Group Three favourites Brazil started well by beating Bulgaria 2-0 with two great strikes from Pele and Garrincha, though the game was marred by a series of ugly challenges. Hungary, meanwhile, faced Portugal without their first choice goalkeeper, which proved crucial as they lost 2-0.

Hungary against Brazil, minus the injured Pele, was to prove a classic match with the Hungarians showing a flair and skill rarely seen before or since in the finals. Bene gave them the lead after three minutes, then Brazil equalised against the run of play. The second half saw Hungary step up another gear, with the brilliant Albert at the heart of their 3-1 win. Portugal finished top of their group after beating Bulgaria and Brazil, and Hungary joined them in the quarter-finals.

Group Four opened at Ayresome Park with the Soviet Union overpowering outsiders North Korea 3-0 and Italy beating Chile 2-0. The English fans warmed to the energetic North Koreans and inspired them to a draw with Chile in their next game. The meeting of the group heavyweights saw a curiously unbalanced Italy run ragged by the Soviets, who were not flattered by their 1-0 win.

Italy faced Korea expecting to overcome their defeat to Russia and qualify in second place, but Italian coach Fabbri picked his slowest defenders and the quick Koreans revelled in the occasion, scoring the winning goal after 42 minutes. Italy were out.

England faced Argentina in the first quarter-final, with Geoff Hurst coming in for the country's best striker Jimmy Greaves, injured in the game with France. Argentina continued their ugly approach and just before half-time the referee lost patience and sent-off Rattin, sparking ten minutes of mayhem as he initially refused to leave the field and then started abusing the crowd. Ten-man

Above: Rattin is sent-off during Argentina's game with England. Opposite clockwise from top: England's one and only World Cup triumph; Portugal's Eusébio leaves three Hungarians behind on his way to the Golden Boot; Bonel and Gondet ponder France's elimination by England.

Argentina held out until 13 minutes from time when a header from Hurst put England into the semi-finals. On the final whistle England manager Alf Ramsey was so furious with the performance of the Argentinians – who he later described as 'animals' – that he took to the field, physically preventing his players from exchanging shirts with the opposition.

The second quarter-final was equally unpleasant. Uruguay had looked the better side in an open first-half, but the second-half descended into violence. The Germans reacted to the Uruguayan provocation – Emmerich kicked Troche, only for the Uruguayan to respond with a kick to the stomach. Troche was sent-off and he slapped Seeler in the face as he left the field. Minutes later Uruguay were down to nine men and Germany cruised home with four goals in the last 20 minutes.

The third quarter-final saw the Soviet Union press the Hungarians into making mistakes, as twice goalkeeper Gelei blundered and the Hungarians went down 2-1.

The most exciting game of the round brought the Koreans and Portugal together,

and unbelievably the Koreans were 3-0 up in just 20 minutes. Then, inspired by Eusébio (he would finish as the tournament's top scorer with nine goals), Portugal, began their comeback, with their star pulling two back before half-time. After the break Eusébio scored two more, before Augusto added a fifth.

The first semi-final saw West Germany face the USSR in another bruising encounter. Poor sportsmanship and violent conduct marred the game and the Soviet Union left the pitch with nine men, having lost 2-1.

England's match with Portugal was altogether different. Portugal struggled to breach England's resolute defence and Bobby Charlton was outstanding going forward, scoring in each half to put England two ahead. A penalty pulled one back for Portugal but it was too little too late and England, who had controversially retained Hurst in the line-up over Greaves, were in the final to face West Germany. Ramsey's team were about to fulfil the manager's prediction – and Geoff Hurst, not even a first choice selection at the start of the tournament, was about to write himself into the football history books.

THE FINAL

ENGLAND (1) 4-2 (1) WEST GERMANY
(aet: 2-2 at 90 mins)

Date Saturday July 30, 1966   **Attendance** 93,802
Venue Wembley Stadium

The match got off to the worst possible start for the hosts as Haller scored to give the Germans a 13th minute lead. It was short-lived though, as six minutes later a fine header from Geoff Hurst made it 1-1. Both sides continued to press forward in the second-half until with only 12 minutes left Peters latched on to a poor clearance to give England the lead. In the final minute, though, West Germany won a controversial free-kick and Weber equalised.

England went into extra-time on the attack and had already gone close twice when Hurst thumped a cross against the underside of the bar, the referee and his linesman giving the goal. In the final minute Hurst broke away to complete the only World Cup final hat-trick.

HOW THE TEAMS LINED UP

ENGLAND
COACH:
ALF RAMSEY

Banks
Cohen   Charlton J   Moore   Wilson
Ball   Stiles   Charlton R   Peters
Hunt   Hurst

WEST GERMANY
COACH:
HELMUT SCHÖN

Emmerich   Held   Seeler
Overath   Beckenbauer   Haller
Schnellinger   Weber   Schulz   Hottges
Tilkowski

ENGLAND

BANKS	7
COHEN	7
CHARLTON J	7
MOORE	8
WILSON	6
STILES	6
CHARLTON R	8
PETERS ⚽🟨	7

Goal: 78 mins. Booked.

BALL	8
HUNT	7
HURST ⚽⚽⚽	*9

Goal: 18 mins, 101 mins, 120 mins

WEST GERMANY

TILKOWSKI	5
HÖTTGES	6
SCHULZ	7
WEBER ⚽	7

Goal: 90 mins

SCHNELLINGER	5
HALLER ⚽	*8

Goal: 12 mins

BECKENBAUER	7
OVERATH	6
SEELER	7
HELD	6
EMMERICH	6

Referee: Dienst (Switzerland)

MEXICO 1970

Against all the odds Mexico 70 turned into a feast of football, and remains the most fondly remembered of all the World Cup competitions. Portents, however, didn't bode well. The problems of the extreme heat of the Mexican summer and the energy-sapping altitude threatened to stifle free-flowing, attacking football, especially in light of FIFA's decision to kick-off many games at midday to appease European broadcasters. Pre-tournament fears of ultra-defensive and violent play, a worrying trend in the game, also threatened to put a negative stranglehold on the competition. But thanks to the colourful flamboyance and daring excellence of the multi-skilled, Pele-inspired Brazilians, the beautiful game somehow managed to prosper like never before.

The first two qualifying groups saw the Soviet Union, Mexico, Italy and Uruguay come through without any surprises against lesser opposition. The ultra-cautious Italians qualified without conceding a goal, and scoring just two,

Above: Gerd Müller, who scored the winner, in action against England. Opposite clockwise from top left: Germany and Italy in semi-final action; Pele celebrates; Carlos Alberto lifts the Jules Rimet trophy; Pele and Bobby Moore swap shirts.

while the Soviet Union came out on top of their pile above Mexico on goals scored.

The outstanding match of the group stage was between twice-champions Brazil and the holders England. In a wonderful end-to-end game, famed for Gordon Banks' incredible save from a downward goal-bound Pele header, Brazil stole the honours with the only goal from the powerful Jairzinho, who was to score in all of Brazil's six matches. Both teams were to progress to the next stage. Meanwhile in Group 4, despite an early struggle against a spirited Morocco, the West Germans gained maximum points with 'Der Bomber', Gerd Müller, in typically prolific form, knocking in hat-tricks against Peru and Bulgaria.

In León, England were matched against West Germany in the first quarter-final. With goals from Alan Mullery and Martin Peters, England were 2-0 up and in control early in the second half. However, after a couple of rhythm-disturbing substitutions by Sir Alf Ramsey (Hunter and Bell for Bobby Charlton and Peters) the Germans clawed themselves back into the game, and goals from Franz Beckenbauer and Uwe Seeler took the tie to extra-time. A close-range volley from Müller past second-choice goalkeeper Peter Bonetti (Banks was ill with an upset stomach) finally eliminated the holders.

In the other quarter-finals, hosts Mexico lost out 4-1 to an untypically free-scoring Italy at Toluca, with the talented striker Gigi Riva scoring a brace. While in Guadalajara, Brazil continued their irrepressible form, getting the better of Peru in a six-goal thriller. In the lowest profile game of this stage, Uruguay narrowly defeated the Soviet Union with an extra-time goal by substitute Esparrago in the Azteca.

The match of the tournament came in Mexico City where the two European giants, Italy and West Germany, were pitted against each other in a thrilling semi-final. Italy took the lead through Roberto Boninsegna, and in

typical fashion withdrew to protect their lead. It was a tactic that very nearly worked, but an equaliser in the third minute of injury-time from Karl Heinz Schnellinger meant the game was not to be decided with the 90 minutes. Famously, Franz Beckenbauer remained on the field even with a dislocated shoulder, his arm in a sling strapped to his body. In extra-time the goals kept coming. Müller edged Germany into the lead, while Tarcisio Burgnich and Riva put Italy back in control at 3-2. Müller, the eventual Golden Boot winner, clawed it back to 3-3, before Rivera finally clinched one of the World Cup's most epic struggles for Italy.

The other semi-final pitted the old South American foes, Uruguay against Brazil, in Guadalajara. The Uruguayans took an early lead through Cubilla, and immediately tried to shut up shop. Not an easy task against Mario Zagalo's side, and Brazil were on equal terms late in the first-half when right-half Clodoaldo powered in the equaliser. Despite aggressive tackling from Uruguay, the Brazilians took hold of the game in the second 45 minutes, and goals from Jairzinho and the fabulous Rivelino sealed a 3-1 victory. Late on Pele almost hit the goal of the tournament, outrageously dummying Mazurkiewicz in the Uruguayan goal, before pulling his shot just wide.

Brazil were to play some of their most open and attacking football in the final, especially poignant as the team on the receiving end, the Italians, were the self-confessed masters of the defence-orientated game. Kicked out of the 1966 tournament, the competition was also a personal victory for Pele, his endeavours standing as a permanent testament to his football genius.

The 1970 World Cup was a triumph, and thanks, ironically, to television, a triumph on a global scale. How fitting it was that Mexico 1970 was to be first tournament to be shown in colour, and thanks to the fantasy football of the Brazilians it was glorious technicolour.

SEMI-FINALS
Italy 4-3 West Germany (aet)
Brazil 3-1 Uruguay

THIRD PLACE PLAY-OFF
West Germany 1-0 Uruguay

TOP GOALSCORERS
10 goals: Gerd Müller (West Germany)
7 goals: Jairzinho (Brazil)
5 goals: Teófilo Cubillas (Peru)

FASTEST GOAL
3 minutes: Ladislav Petras (Czechoslovakia v Romania)

TOTAL GOALS:
95

AVERAGE GOAL
2.97 per game

THE FINAL

BRAZIL (1) 4-1 (1) ITALY

Date Sunday June 21, 1970 **Attendance** 107,412
Venue Azteca Stadium, Mexico City

Pele opened the scoring after 18 minutes, athletically getting his head on the end of Rivelino's cross. Against the run of play, Boninsegna pounced on a careless mistake by Clodoaldo to level the score, but Italy were unable to push on. They were also unable to match the Brazilians in terms of possession, and the skill of the men in gold shirts left the Azzurri chasing shadows. In the 66th minute Gerson's left-footed cross-shot found the back of Albertosi's net, and it was followed by Jairzinho's customary goal. The *coup de grâce* was one of the most loved goals in football history. Jairzinho found Pele, he laid the ball off to his right into the stride of captain Carlos Alberto, who thundered it low into the corner. The Jules Rimet trophy was Brazil's to keep.

BRAZIL	
FÉLIX	6
CARLOS ALBERTO	7
Goal: 87 mins	
BRITO	6
PIAZZA	6
EVERALDO	7
JAIRZINHO	8
Goal: 71 mins	
CLODOALDO	7
GERSON	7
Goal: 66 mins	
TOSTAO	8
PELE	*9
Goal: 18 mins	
RIVELINO	7
Booked	

ITALY	
ALBERTOSI	6
BURGNICH	5
Booked	
CERA	6
BERTINI	6
Subbed: 75 mins (Juliano)	
FACCHETTI	6
ROSATO	5
DOMENGHINI	7
DE SISTI	6
MAZZOLA	*8
BONINSEGNA	7
Goal: 38 mins. Subbed: 84 mins (Rivera)	
RIVA	6
sub: JULIANO	6
sub: RIVERA	5

Referee: Glockner (East Germany)

HOW THE TEAMS LINED UP

BRAZIL
COACH:
MARIO ZAGALO

Felix
Carlos Alberto   Brito   Piazza   Everaldo
Clodoaldo   Gerson
Jairzinho   Tostao   Pele   Rivelino

ITALY
COACH:
FERRUCCIO VALCAREGGI

Riva   Boninsegna   Domenghini
De Sisti   Mazzola   Bertini
Facchetti   Rosato   Cera   Burgnich
Albertosi

WEST GERMANY 1974

The 1970 finals in Mexico had ended somewhat ignobly for the Europeans, with Italy on the receiving end of a 4-1 demolition from a seemingly unstoppable Brazil. This time, however, European countries found themselves most definitely in the ascendancy and, at the tournament's end, Poland, Holland and West Germany were installed as the world's three best teams. The latter pair contested the final itself, which, under a new system featuring 16 teams and two group stages, was the only proper 'knock-out' game of the tournament.

Although they'd struggled slightly during the qualifying stages, Holland, under manager Rinus Michels and boasting a plethora of stars from the all-conquering Ajax club side, cut a swathe through the group stages. Their unique brand of Total Football, in which players switched positions and roles with astonishing versatility, saw them score 14 goals in six games, conceding just one.

They began their first group stage campaign with a comfortable 2-0 win over the very first world champions, Uruguay, both goals coming from Ajax star Johnny Rep. Michels' men followed it up with a goalless draw against Sweden, but bounced back to record an impressive 4-1 rout of Bulgaria (including two penalties from another Ajax man, Johan Neeskens). This was enough for them to top the group and qualify for the last eight along with the Swedes.

A pre-tournament defeat of the West Germans had made Argentina seem a good 'dark horse' bet for glory at the finals, but after only just edging out Italy for a place in the last eight they were effectively dismantled by the rampant Dutch in their opening second group stage game. Goals from Rep, Cruyff (2) and Rudi Krol contributed to the 4-0 landslide. Holland's 2-0 win over East Germany, who'd beaten their West German neighbours earlier in the tournament, set up an all or nothing showdown with reigning world champions Brazil: the prize a place in the final.

Without Pele, who'd by now retired, the Brazilians were clearly not the force they had once been. They'd scraped through the first stage thanks to goalless draws with Yugoslavia and Scotland, and a 3-0 win over a hapless Zaïre side who had shipped nine against Yugoslavia. However, Brazil had started the second stage with something approaching their old swagger, beating East Germany 1-0, thanks to a second-half strike from Rivelino, and Argentina 2-1, with goals from Jairzinho and Rivelino again. Despite improving form, however, the Brazilians found it impossible to live with a Dutch side approaching the peak

Above: Joe Jordan in action for Scotland during their win over Zaïre. Opposite clockwise from top: Holland captain Johan Cruyff; German Gerd Müller fends off the Yugoslav Maric; Müller again, this time firing home against Poland; Beckenbauer lifts the World Cup in Munich.

of its powers. Two second-half goals, Cruyff's strike in the 65th minute following Neeskens' gorgeous lob in the 50th, saw Holland run out 2-0 winners and the self-destructing Brazilians finish with ten men after the dismissal of Luis Pereira. Holland, many assumed, were well on their way to a first and hugely deserved world championship.

In contrast, West Germany started the tournament slowly. After being held to a 0-0 draw by Chile and, in their final first stage game, losing 1-0 to neighbours East Germany, Helmut Schön's men had to rely on a 3-0 win over unfancied Australia (goals courtesy of Wolfgang Overath, Bernhard Cullman and Gerd Müller) to book their place in the last eight. Slowly but surely, however, the West German team started to gel.

Spurred on by inspirational skipper Franz Beckenbauer, they started the second group stage impressively – beating Yugoslavia 2-0 thanks to goals from Paul Breitner and the prolific Müller. Even better followed in the shape of a 4-2 victory over Sweden. Finely balanced at 2-2 with 14 minutes left, Jürgen Grabowski and Uli Hoeness put the tie beyond doubt, setting up a crucial final group game with Poland in the process – a match the Germans only needed to draw to advance to their third World Cup final appearance.

The Poles, who had surprisingly eliminated England during the qualifiers, were unbeaten thus far in the tournament and in Grzegorz Lato had a striker who would go on to become its highest scorer, with seven goals, including two in a 3-2 first stage victory over Argentina. He also scored a crucial second-half winner in the 2-1 victory over Yugoslavia that effectively brought Poland face-to-face with the West

THE FINAL

WEST GERMANY (2) 2-1 (1) HOLLAND

Date Sunday July 7, 1974 **Attendance** 77,822
Venue Olympic Stadium, Munich

Holland got off to the best possible start in this all-European final. After less than a minute had elapsed on the clock, Johan Cruyff was up-ended in the West German penalty area by Bayern Munich's Uli Hoeness. There had never been a penalty awarded in a World Cup final before, but Johan Neeskens calmly slotted the ball past goalkeeper Sepp Maier to put Rinus Michels' side a goal up.

The Dutch continued to dominate but surrendered their lead cheaply in the 25th minute when a surging Bernd Hölzenbein run was bought to an abrupt end by a trip in the Holland penalty area. Paul Breitner duly converted the spot-kick, and the Germans went on to snatch a decisive lead two minutes before half-time through Gerd Müller.

HOW THE TEAMS LINED UP

WEST GERMANY
COACH: HELMUT SCHÖN

HOLLAND
COACH: RINUS MICHELS

Maier

Vogts Schwarzenbeck Beckenbauer Breitner

Bonhof Hoeness Overath

Grabowski Müller Hälzenbein

Rensenbrink Cruyff Rep

Van Hanegem Neeskens Jansen

Krol Haan Rijsbergen Suurbier

Jongbloed

Germans for a place in the World Cup final.

It was an exciting but incredibly nervy game for both sides, especially after the kick-off was delayed due to a waterlogged pitch. Poland's best chances came in the first half, Robert Gadocha and the effervescent Lato forcing West Germany's goalkeeper Sepp Maier into a couple of excellent saves. In the second-half it was the turn of Maier's opposite number in the Polish goal, Jan Tomaszewski, to shine. He saved a penalty from Uli Hoeness, but it was to prove in vain. West Germany snatched the winner 14 minutes from time when Hoeness's shot deflected into the path of Müller, who clinically buried it into the back of the net in typical fashion.

A 1-0 third place play-off victory over Brazil (the goal coming courtesy of Lato) was scant consolation for the Poles, who'd surely been the tournament's biggest surprise package. The final, however, was now to be contested between hosts West Germany, who hadn't won the tournament since 1954, and Holland, who hadn't even managed to qualify since 1938. Efficiency, organisation and hard work against versatility, vision and precocious talent.

WEST GERMANY		
MAIER		6
VOGTS		7
Booked: 3 mins		
SCHWARZENBECK		7
BECKENBAUER		9
BREITNER		7
Goal: 25 mins (pen)		
BONHOF		6
HOENESS		6
OVERATH		7
GRABOWSKI		7
MÜLLER		8
Goal: 43 mins		
HÄLZENBEIN		6

HOLLAND		
JONGBLOED		6
SUURBIER		6
RIJSBERGEN		6
Subbed: 69 mins (De Jong)		
HAAN		7
KROL		7
JANSEN		6
NEESKENS		8
Goal: 2 mins (pen). Booked: 39 mins		
VAN HANEGEM		6
Booked: 22 mins		
REP		7
CRUYFF		*9
Booked: 45 mins		
RENSENBRINK		6
Subbed: 46 mins (R Van De Kerkhof)		
sub: R VAN DE KERKHOF		6
sub: DE JONG		6

Referee: Taylor (England)

SEMI-FINALS
Replaced by a second round group phase

THIRD PLACE PLAY-OFF
Poland 1-0 Brazil

TOP GOALSCORERS
7 goals: Gregorz Lato (Poland);
5 goals: Johan Neeskens (Holland), Anrdrzej Szarmach (Poland);
4 goals: Gerd Müller (Germany), Ralf Edström (Sweden), Johnny Rep (Holland)

FASTEST GOAL
80 seconds: Johan Neeskens (Holland v West Germany)

TOTAL GOALS:
97

AVERAGE GOAL
2.55 per game

ARGENTINA 1978

SEMI-FINALS

Replaced by a second round group phase

THIRD PLACE PLAY-OFF

Brazil 2-1 Italy

TOP GOALSCORERS

6 goals: Mario Kempes (Argentina)
5 goals: Teófilo Cubillas (Peru),
Rob Rensenbrink (Holland)
4 goals: Hans Krankl (Austria),
Leopoldo Luque (Argentina)

FASTEST GOAL

31 seconds: Bernard Lacombe
(France v Italy)

TOTAL GOALS:

102

AVERAGE GOAL

2.68 per game:

When Daniel Passarella hoisted the World Cup aloft in Buenos Aires, it was one of the most romantic and tragic moments in football history. For Argentina, named as hosts back in 1966, just to have staged the event was an achievement given the political turmoil that had prompted several participants to talk of a boycott. To then win the trophy sent the nation ecstatic.

Yet for Holland, whose players endured the victory night celebrations cooped up in their hotel, defeat in the final for the second consecutive time was cruel beyond measure. The country that had illuminated Seventies football, that probably did more to create the modern game than any other, were destined to end the decade without a major honour.

The tournament itself, in the wake of the great Brazil team's performance of 1970 and the Beckenbauer/Cruyff head-to-head of 1974, was not a vintage. Mario Kempes emerged as

Argentina's hero, but not to the extent that Diego Maradona would eight years later. But while Argentina 78 lacked a superstar or a great team, the extreme emotions it generated – not to mention the whiff of scandal – ensured its place in football folklore.

The threatened boycott in protest at the Videla regime never materialised and all 16 teams arrived, although Holland's enigmatic Cruyff stayed at home. Like 1974, there was no knockout stage. The top two teams in four groups would progress into a second group stage with the winners going into the final.

Most of the footballing superpowers had qualified, with the exception of Euro 76 winners Yugoslavia, the Soviet Union and, for the second consecutive finals, England. British interest centred on Scotland, who had assembled perhaps their greatest team, but their campaign degenerated into shambles and acrimony.

Poor results, coupled with their winger Willie Johnston failing a drugs test, ensured a shameful early exit for Scotland. Only then, when it was too late, did they show what they could do by beating Holland 3-2.

Peru had proven they weren't the expected pushover, while doubts persisted whether Holland without Cruyff could mount a serious challenge. West Germany qualified in equally unimpressive style as runners-up to Poland in perhaps the weakest group.

Brazil, under coach Claudio Coutinho, had gone from poetic to pragmatic. They too were far from convincing, managing only two goals in their first round group, but along with Austria they still squeezed through ahead of Spain and Sweden.

With so many big guns misfiring, the tournament appeared to be opening up. Italy, masters of the defensive approach that characterised football in this era, looked likely to prosper when they topped a group that also included Argentina, France and Hungary. Argentina's 2-1 defeat of France proved the decisive result for second place.

Despite their indifferent showings, all of the favourites had spluttered their way into a second round that fizzed with exciting match-ups. Group A featured European superpowers West Germany, Holland and Italy, plus a useful Austrian side gorging itself on the goals of Hans Krankl.

Group B included the less fancied Poles and Peru, plus arguably the fiercest rivals in world football – Argentina and Brazil. When the two met in Rosario, the weight of history and the fear of defeat were too much for either side to bear and the match fizzled out into an ill-tempered 0-0 draw.

With both sides having already recorded victories (Brazil had beaten Peru 3-0 and Argentina had defeated Poland 2-0), providing both could win their last matches the finalist would be decided on goal difference.

Above: Scotland's Archie Gemmill scores his wonder goal against eventual finalists Holland. Opposite clockwise from top left: Daniel Passarella lifts the trophy; the ticker tape welcome as Argentina took to the pitch; top scorer Mario Kempes; Rob Rensenbrink of Holland in action.

When Brazil overcame Poland 3-1 in Mendoza, the balance of power appeared to have swung their way. But owing to some blatantly unfair organisation, Argentina didn't kick-off their final game against Peru in Rosario until 45 minutes after Brazil v Poland had finished. Cesar Menotti's side had the massive advantage of knowing they had to win by four clear goals to reach the final.

Peru, who had looked so accomplished early in the tournament, at first looked up for the challenge, hitting the post. Then, in one of the most talked about matches in World Cup history, they rolled over and lost 6-0. Rumours, already fuelled by some controversial decisions in Argentina's favour against France in the first round, abounded that the matched was fixed. But when the dust settled, Argentina – 48 years after they had lost the first World Cup to Uruguay – had booked their ticket to the final of their own fiesta.

In the other group, Holland exploded into life with a 5-1 destruction of Austria to take an early stranglehold on the group, while Italy and West Germany drew 0-0. Holland strengthened their hand when, in a repeat of the 1974 final, goals from Haan and Rene van der Kerkhof earned them a useful 2-2 draw with West Germany.

With Italy beating Austria 1-0, the Dutch knew that unless the West Germans could manage a landslide against Austria, a draw with Italy would be sufficient. West Germany, a shadow of their 1974 side, were put out of their misery when they lost 3-2 to the already-eliminated Austrians. Holland did all that was required and more by beating Italy 2-1.

In the third-place play-off, Brazil overcame Enzo Bearzot's Italy 2-1 to maintain the only unbeaten record of the tournament. But in some ways the victory only upset Brazilians even more because, for the first time in the competition, they shed their inhibitions and played in the great Brazilian tradition. Why had they left it too late?

THE FINAL

ARGENTINA (1) **3-1** (1) **HOLLAND**
(AET; 1-1 at 90 mins)

Date Sunday June 25, 1978 **Attendance** 77,260
Venue River Plate Stadium, Buenos Aires

Argentina attempted to unnerve the Dutch by keeping them on the pitch for five minutes before their arrival to a sea of sky blue and white ticker tape. They then objected to a bandage on Rene van der Kerkhof's arm.

When play began, high skill mingled with barely restrained violence. Rep wasted a great chance for Holland before Kempes put Argentina ahead on 37 minutes. The Dutch were growing feverish with frustration when, in the 81st minute, substitute Nanninga headed the ball into the net. Then with a minute to go, Rensenbrink struck the foot of the post.

Kempes, the tournament's top scorer, scrambled the hosts back into the lead a minute before the first period of extra-time ended and, with four minutes to go, Bertoni made the game safe.

ARGENTINA	
FILLOL	7
OLGUIN	6
GALVAN	7
PASSARELLA	8
TARANTINI	6
ARDILES	7
Booked: 40 mins. Subbed: 66 mins (Larossa)	
GALLEGO	6
ORTIZ	6
Subbed: 75 mins (Houseman)	
BERTONI	7
Goal: 115 mins	
LUQUE	8
KEMPES	*9
Goal: 38, 105 mins	
sub: LAROSSA	6
Booked: 94 mins	
sub: HOUSEMAN	6

HOLLAND	
JONGBLOED	6
POORTVLIET	5
Booked: 96 mins	
KROL	*8
Booked: 15 mins	
BRANDTS	7
JANSEN	6
Subbed: 73 mins (Suurbier)	
NEESKENS	7
HAAN	6
VAN DE KERKHOF W	6
VAN DE KERKHOF R	6
REP	5
Subbed: 59 mins (Nanninga)	
RENSENBRINK	6
sub: NANNINGA	7
Goal: 82 mins	
sub: SUURBIER	
Booked: 94	6

Referee: Gonella (Italy)

HOW THE TEAMS LINED UP

ARGENTINA

COACH:
CESAR LUIS MENOTTI

Fillol

Olguin Galvan Passarella Tarantini

Ardiles Gallego Ortiz Bertoni

Luque Kempes

HOLLAND

COACH:
ERNST HAPPEL

Rensenbrink Rep

v d Kerkhof R v d Kerkhof W Haan Neeskens

Jansen Brandts Krol Poortvliet

Jongbloed

SPAIN 1982

Following the incident-free carnival played out in Argentina, there was a real sense of trepidation as the World Cup jamboree descended on Spain for the 1982 finals. Many doubted Spain's ability to host such a global spectacular and those fears were heightened as the draw, in January of that year, descended into chaos.

Peru and Chile were initially drawn with Brazil and Argentina, when it was decided that they should be kept apart from their illustrious neighbours. Scotland, meanwhile, found themselves in Argentina's group instead of Belgium's. The confusion led to a halt in proceedings, then to compound the situation, the cage containing the balls jammed and one split in half. Compelling TV, but the charade was met with worldwide condemnation.

The critics were given further ammunition with the tournament's expansion to 24 teams. There was a fear that games would descend into a procession as the likes of Kuwait, Honduras and El Salvador took to the stage, while conversely there was every indication that such teams would stifle the opposition and defend for their lives.

Thankfully, the inspirational opening ceremony and Belgium's subsequent 1-0 victory against champions Argentina allayed the fears and set the tone for a tournament that would promote the World Cup as a truly global affair.

Brazil were clear favourites. The flair and breathtaking skill – so absent four years earlier – had returned, while in Zico, Socrates, Falcao and Junior, they had a prowess that few could compete with. The 4-1 victory against Scotland – in which David Narey had the audacity to score first – and a 4-0 win over New Zealand indicated their intention.

Their rivals did not have it so easy. Italy made a less than auspicious start, drawing against Poland and Peru, and their progression was only confirmed in a winner-takes-all game against Cameroon. A Graziani header ensured another draw but, although he had secured a safe passage on goal difference, Italy were being ridiculed back home.

West Germany, another thoroughbred, lost their opener to Algeria, then contributed to one of the most distasteful ever World Cup moments. Having scored against neighbours Austria, and knowing a 1-0 score would ensure the progress of both sides, the second-half descended into farce at the expense of Algeria, whose complaint to FIFA fell on deaf ears.

Spain were also left sweating on their progression as a Gerry Armstrong goal for Northern Ireland stunned the home support, but the 1-0 defeat ensured both teams progressed, with Billy Bingham's side heading the group. The Irish also created history when

Above: England captain Bryan Robson celebrates scoring the tournament's quickest goal. Opposite clockwise from top left: Argentina captain Daniel Passarella; Norman Whiteside on the ball for Northern Ireland; the victorious Argentina squad with the World Cup; Poland's Lato shoots against France in the third place play-off.

their winger, Norman Whiteside, became the youngest player to appear in the finals, aged 17 years and 41 days.

Europe's other leading lights, France and England, were left to battle it out in Group Four. Aggrieved at England's seeding, the French were left to lick their wounds as Ron Greenwood's side put them to the sword in an emphatic 3-1 victory. Further wins against Czechoslovakia and Kuwait served to enhance England's reputation, while the French limped through, helped by a 4-1 defeat of Kuwait – a game remembered for coach Hidalgo's clash with police when a goal was disallowed.

With the second phase split into four groups of three, and with only the top side guaranteed a semi-final place, victory was imperative in the opening game, certainly in Group C which contained Brazil, Argentina and Italy. The latter's flaccid displays had them installed as elimination fodder, yet goals from Tardelli and Cabrini ensured a 2-1 win against Argentina. With Brazil also defeating their South American counterparts – a game that saw Maradona red-carded – the game between Brazil and Italy was billed as the clash of the tournament. The pendulum swung back and forth, yet it was the superlative finishing of Paolo Rossi that ensured Italy's 3-2 victory. His hat-trick, completed 15 minutes from time, created a hero and revitalised a nation.

England's progress, meanwhile, was halted by a lack of firepower. A sterile 0-0 draw against West Germany meant they had to beat Spain by two goals, but with the creativity of Kevin Keegan and Trevor Brooking still absent through injury, another 0-0 prevailed. Both players were desperately plunged into action with 27 minutes remaining, but a clearly unfit Keegan fluffed a simple header that could have provided the impetus so desperately needed.

France and Poland made up the quartet, but it was Italy who had the easiest route to the final against the Poles, who would sorely miss goalscorer Boniek. Rossi further enhanced his

credentials with a goal in either half, and although the 2-0 win raised few eyebrows, the other semi was a classic.

With Platini in sparkling form for France, the game against West Germany finished 1-1 after 90 minutes. But further goals from Giresse and Tresor had the French dreaming of the final. Yet, in typical fashion, the Germans refused to quit. Coach Derwall gambled by introducing half-fit captain Rummenigge and, having pulled a goal back in the 106th minute, Hrubesch then equalised with an overhead kick as the French tired.

The resulting penalty kicks went to sudden death and Hrubesch saw the Germans home. The hero was undoubtedly German goalkeeper Schumacher, yet he should not have been on the pitch following an appalling challenge on Battiston, which had left the Frenchman unconscious for three minutes.

The incident won the Germans few admirers, and with Italy on an upward spiral, there would be one winner and one hero...

THE FINAL

ITALY (0) 3-1 (0) WEST GERMANY

Date Sunday July 11, 1982 **Attendance** 77,260
Venue Santiago Bernabéu, Madrid

Italy were favourites to win their third World Cup but, with midfielder Antognoni injured, their anxieties were heightened further when Graziani left the field with an injured shoulder inside the first ten minutes. Things then got even worse when Cabrini became the first player to miss a penalty in the World Cup final. Yet despite the setbacks, Italy shaded a first-half dominated by fouls and the game finally came to life after 57 minutes when Rossi rose highest to connect with Gentile's pin-point cross.

Victory was secured 11 minutes later when Tardelli hit a superb left-foot shot from the edge of the area, and by the time Altobelli hammered home a Conti cross, the game had become a procession. Paul Breitner scored a late consolation but the Germans were left to pay the price of their epic semi-final. Italy claimed their third crown and toasted Rossi, who had become an overnight sensation.

HOW THE TEAMS LINED UP

ITALY
COACH:
ENZO BEARZOT

WEST GERMANY
COACH:
JUPP DERWALL

Zoff
Cabrini Scirea Gentile Collovati
Oriali Bergomi Tardelli
Conti Rossi Graziani
Fischer Rummenigge
Littbarski
Dremmler Briegel Breitner
Förster B Förster K-H Stieleke Kaltz
Schumacher

ITALY	
ZOFF	6
GENTILE	7
SCIREA	6
COLLOVATI	7
BERGOMI	7
CABRINI	6
Missed pen: 25 mins	
ORIALI	7
Booked: 73 mins	
TARDELLI	*8
Goal: 69 mins	
CONTI	7
Booked: 31 mins	
GRAZIANI	
Subbed: 8 mins (Altobelli)	
ROSSI	7
Goal: 57 mins	
sub: ALTOBELLI	7
Goal: 81 mins. Subbed: 88 mins (Causio)	
sub: CAUSIO	5

WEST GERMANY	
SCHUMACHER	6
KALTZ	5
STIELEKE	6
Booked: 73 mins	
FÖRSTER K-H	6
FÖRSTER B	6
LITTBARSKI	6
Booked: 88 mins	
DREMMLER	6
Booked: 61 mins. Subbed 63 mins (Hrubesch)	
BREITNER	7
Goal: 83 mins	
BRIEGEL	*7
FISCHER	6
RUMMENIGGE	5
Subbed: 70 mins (Muller H)	
sub: HRUBESCH	6
sub: MULLER H	6

Referee: Coelho (Mexico)

MEXICO 1986

SEMI-FINALS
Argentina 2-0 Belgium
West Germany 2-0 France

THIRD PLACE PLAY-OFF
France 4-2 Belgium
(aet: 2-2 at 90 mins)

TOP GOALSCORERS
6 goals: Gary Lineker (England)
5 goals: Emilio Butragueño
(Spain), Careca (Brazil), Diego
Maradona (Argentina)

FASTEST GOAL
63 seconds: Emilio Butragueño
(Spain v Northern Ireland)

TOTAL GOALS
132

AVERAGE GOAL
2.54 per game:

When Colombia decided they no longer had the financial muscle to host the 1986 World Cup, Mexico stepped into the breach to become FIFA's saviour in what proved to be another troubled episode for the game's governing body. Granted, the Mexicans hosted an exemplary tournament in 1970, but with their own financial crisis and unemployment at record levels, the decision looked dubious given the stability provided by the rival USA bid.

When it was revealed Mexican TV network Televisa would stage the tournament – whose president was a friend of FIFA president Joao Havelange – it drew outrage from the Americans. A strained relationship ensued – bombs were even found outside the US Embassy – and to compound the problems, some 25,000 people were killed in a huge earthquake prior to the tournament.

Mexico simply had to deliver, yet little did they realise that a pint-sized genius from Argentina would play the trump card. Diego Armando Maradona enlightened us all while exorcising the ghosts of Spain 82, when a lunge on Italian defender Gentile had ended his participation in the second round.

With a record transfer fee of £6.9million hanging above him, the Napoli midfielder was a marked man, and the succession of fouls inflicted by South Korea gave an indication of the fear he instilled. Yet he destroyed his opponents, setting up goals for Valdano and Ruggeri in a 3-1 Group A victory. A truer test came against champions Italy. No team knew the diminutive star better, yet he shone in a game of intrigue. In the 34th minute he eluded Napoli team-mate Bagni, his low centre of gravity enabling him to score from an acute angle. The goal was cancelled out by Altobelli's penalty but both teams progressed.

Yet if Maradona created headlines for his on-field exploits, the enthusiasm of the Mexico crowd proved unprecedented: 110,000 filled the Azteca for their opening win against Belgium and the 'Mexican Wave' phenomenon was born. Hero of the hour was Hugo Sanchez, whose feats were rivalling those of Maradona. Having scored in the 2-1 win, he was equally impressive against Paraguay and the consensus grew that the hosts could go far.

With the high altitude, European nations were given little chance. France were deemed a threat with Platini, Battison and Bossis providing experience and guile, but a 1-0 win against Canada was less than convincing, while a 1-1 draw with an impressive Soviet Union side left the European champions sweating on their progress. Their eventual qualification had more to do with the ineptitude of Canada and Hungary than their own creativity.

England also made heavy work of ensuring qualification as a 1-0 defeat against Portugal was followed by a sorry draw with Morocco. The 0-0 scoreline created a furore, and with captain Bryan Robson dislocating his shoulder and fellow midfielder Ray Wilkins being sent-off, victory against Poland was imperative. A Gary Lineker hat-trick spared a nation's blushes as a 3-0 win kept Bobby Robson in a job and England in the tournament.

Denmark appeared the European side best equipped to succeed in the tournament. An opening 1-0 win against Scotland was just an aperitif for the Michael Laudrup-inspired 6-1 demolition of Uruguay and a shock 2-0 victory over West Germany.

The second phase reverted to the knock-out format, with Brazil again looking dangerous. Having cruised through their group against Spain, Algeria and Northern Ireland, their 4-0 demolition of Poland saw a return to the flamboyance of four years earlier. Edinho's third goal, in particular, had the 45,000 Guadalajara crowd mesmerised.

Above: Gary Lineker after his hat-trick against Poland.
Opposite clockwise from top left: Argentina's Jorge Valdano fends off West Germany's Ditmar Jakobs; Diego Maradona celebrates victory against England; Bryan Robson about to dislocate his shoulder against Morocco; Uruguay's Jose Batista is sent-off against Scotland.

The expected nations progressed, with the exception of Denmark and Italy. The Danes had peaked and their emphatic 5-1 defeat at the hands of Spain is best remembered for Emilio Butragueño's four goals. The Italians, meanwhile, succumbed to a much-improved French team. Platini confirmed his class with a casual chip over Galli to set up a 2-0 win.

The French, playing as potential champions, would have to overcome Brazil in the quarter-finals if they had realistic ambitions, and with so much riding on the outcome, a game of cat and mouse ensued. With substitute Zico missing a crucial late penalty, the match was decided by a penalty shoot-out and France won 4-3, thanks to Fernandez's decider.

Shoot-outs decided three of the quarter-final ties, West Germany edging past Mexico and Belgium overcoming Spain. The process of elimination led to calls for sudden death football. Yet if this was knee-jerk anger on the part of the losers, their pain was nothing compared to that felt by England following their exit against Argentina.

With the scores level at 0-0, a harmless Hodge backpass was destined to reach Peter Shilton only for Diego Maradona to arrive and seemingly head home. At first glance, it appeared the altitude helped his elevation, but replays proved he had punched the ball. Blatant cheating, but the self-proclaimed 'Hand of God' goal only served to inspire Maradona, and his second, a fantastic solo effort six minutes later, put the game beyond doubt. A late flurry, which yielded Lineker's sixth goal of the tournament, gave England hope, but a bad taste had already been left in the mouth.

A virtuoso semi-final performance against Belgium, which included two breathtaking second-half goals, restored faith in Maradona and, although West Germany eased passed France 2-0 in a repeat of their 1982 semi-final, there was little stopping the Argentinian. His hands were already on the cup.

THE FINAL

ARGENTINA (1) 3-2 (0) WEST GERMANY

Date Sunday June 29, 1986 **Attendance** 116,026
Venue Azteca Stadium, Mexico City

Argentina proved they were no one-man team as their superior skill and creativity came to the fore against the Germans. With Burruchaga matching Maradona's performance, a 2-0 lead was established through Brown and Valdano. The Germans, who had so successfully stifled their opposition en route to the final, had no answer this time and the South American's were already dreaming of another ticker tape celebration back home.

Yet, as so often in the past, a wounded German animal is a dangerous beast and as the game limped to its conclusion, they finally showed the inventiveness that had been so absent. Two headers inside eight minutes, from Rummenigge and Völler, brought the tie level on 81 minutes. But cometh the hour, cometh the man. Maradona's inch-perfect pass found Burruchaga who beat the offside trap to power the ball past Schumacher.

ARGENTINA		
PUMPIDO		6
Booked: 85 mins		
BROWN		8
Goal: 23 mins		
CUCIUFFO		7
RUGGERI		6
OLARTICOECHEA		6
Booked: 77 mins		
GIUSTI		6
BATISTA		7
BURRUCHAGA		*9
Goal: 88 mins. Subbed: 89 mins. (Trobbiani)		
ENRIQUE		7
Booked: 81 mins		
MARADONA		8
Booked: 17 mins		
VALDANO		7
Goal: 56 mins		
sub: TROBBIANI		5

WEST GERMANY		
SCHUMACHER		5
JAKOBS		5
BERTHOLD		6
FÖRSTER K-H		6
BRIEGEL		*8
Booked: 62 mins		
MATTHÄUS		7
Booked: 21 mins		
BREHME		7
MAGATH		6
Subbed: 63 mins (Hoeness D)		
EDER		6
RUMMENIGGE		7
Goal: 74 mins		
ALLOFS		6
Subbed: 46 mins (Völler)		
sub: HOENESS D		6
sub: VÖLLER		7
Goal: 82 mins		

Referee: Arppi Filho (Brazil)

HOW THE TEAMS LINED UP

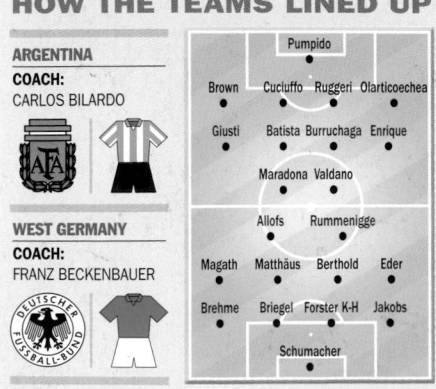

ARGENTINA
COACH:
CARLOS BILARDO

Pumpido
Brown Cuciuffo Ruggeri Olarticoechea
Giusti Batista Burruchaga Enrique
Maradona Valdano

WEST GERMANY
COACH:
FRANZ BECKENBAUER

Allofs Rummenigge
Magath Matthäus Berthold Eder
Brehme Briegel Forster K-H Jakobs
Schumacher

ITALY 1990

Italia 90 was the tournament where FIFA appeared to step up its campaign to have the World Cup recognised as a global marketing phenomenon, and no country was more suited to put on a mass footballing circus than Italy. As hosts for the second time, the Italians embarked on a major overhaul of ten stadiums and built two more in Turin and Bari in anticipation of the biggest tournament ever.

Sadly, the quality of play failed to live up to the vast hype and the carefully negotiated corporate endorsements, the competition being characterised by negativity, foul play and penalties. The statistics only underline its sorry reputation: a mere 115 goals were scored at a ratio of 2.21 per game, yet there were a record 16 dismissals and 164 bookings.

The format remained the same as four years previous, with 24 teams competing in six groups of four before progressing through to a knock-out second round, then quarter-finals, semi-finals and the final. Some strong teams were notably absent, including the 1986 semi-finalists France, coached by Michel Platini, and rising stars Denmark, but the Republic Of Ireland qualified for the first time.

Mexico and Chile were suspended for breaches of FIFA rules, the former for breaking regulations in a youth tournament, the latter after goalkeeper Rojas bizarrely attempted to fake an injury from a firecracker in a qualifier against Brazil.

Inevitably the hosts, under Azeglio Vicini, were hot favourites and their smooth progress only emphasised the feeling that their name was on the cup – they won all of their group games (against Austria, United States and Czechoslovakia) playing solid, attacking football without conceding a goal.

The nation also discovered a new Paolo Rossi in the shape of Palermo-born Salvatore 'Toto' Schillaci, a diminutive Juventus striker who rose from the substitute's bench to win the Golden Boot with six goals. Walter Zenga kept a clean sheet for a record 517 minutes, aided by a watertight defence superbly marshalled by Franco Baresi.

The Azzurri dream died against Argentina at the semi-final stage – not for the last time in a penalty shoot-out. Maradona had already attempted to divide the north and south of the country by appealing to Napoli fans to support his side. The hosts finished the tournament unbeaten, but still had to settle for third place while the nation mourned.

Of the other possible contenders, both Brazil and Holland went out tamely in the second round. European champions the Dutch, featuring Gullit, Rijkaard and Van Basten, were the biggest disappointments. Their encounter with old enemy West Germany is best remembered for Frank Rijkaard's rather too

Above: Roger Milla was one of the surprise stars of Italia 90. Opposite clockwise from top left: Jurgen Klinsmann and Guido Buchwald enjoy success against Holland; Paul Gascoigne in tears after England's semi-final exit; surprise top-scorer Toto Schillaci; Maradona prays for Argentina.

literal spat with Rudi Völler. Brazil topped a weak group featuring Sweden, Scotland and Costa Rica, but lacked the firepower to finish off Argentina when they had a chance.

For a while Cameroon looked like they might make history by winning the tournament. The 'Indomitable Lions' beat holders Argentina in a memorable opening encounter (despite being reduced to nine men) and became the first African nation to reach the quarter-finals when they beat Colombia after extra-time. Mixing some vibrant skills with a fairly strong physical presence, their unquenchable spirit was embodied by Roger Milla. A goal-scoring talisman who danced around the corner flag after each of his four strikes as a substitute, Milla was then 38 years old and playing for JS Saint-Pierroise, a local team from Reunion Island. Cameroon's recklessness in the tackle eventually proved their undoing, however, when they allowed England to pull level and win 3-2 in extra-time through two penalties in their quarter-final.

The English had travelled to the World Cup more in hope than expectation, having just scraped through qualification as second best of the second-placed teams in the European groups. Manager Bobby Robson's tenure as national coach had already involved the disastrous European Championship two years earlier and he was vilified by the British tabloid press for his team selections and tactics. However, in Gary Lineker the side had a proven goalscorer, there was real creativity in a midfield that featured Chris Waddle and Paul Gascoigne, Mark Wright was a defender who could switch to sweeper, and in the massively experienced Peter Shilton they had a 'keeper who had not conceded a goal in 540 minutes during qualification.

THE FINAL

WEST GERMANY (0) 1-0 (0) ARGENTINA

Date Sunday July 8, 1990 **Attendance** 73,603
Venue Olympic Stadium, Rome

Ranking as the worst final in World Cup history, the game was characterised by negativity and bad sportsmanship. Argentina arrived with a record of a foul every four minutes and were shorn of four players through suspension, but both teams were guilty of deeply cynical play.

West Germany held the upper hand for much of the game but the contest degenerated, Monzon becoming the first player to be sent-off in a World Cup final for a wild lunge at Jurgen Klinsmann. It was no surprise when the match was settled by a spot-kick following a foul by Sensini on Völler. Argentina lost control and two minutes later Dezotti was also sent-off.

Maradona conducted his side's protests and the enduring image is not Matthäus holding aloft the cup but the Argentinian's tear-stained face.

HOW THE TEAMS LINED UP

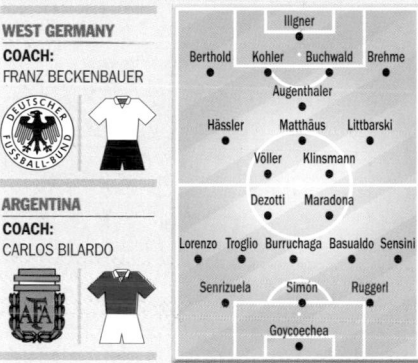

WEST GERMANY
COACH:
FRANZ BECKENBAUER

Illgner
Berthold Kohler Buchwald Brehme
Augenthaler
Hässler Matthäus Littbarski
Völler Klinsmann

ARGENTINA
COACH:
CARLOS BILARDO

Dezotti Maradona
Lorenzo Troglio Burruchaga Basualdo Sensini
Senrizuela Simon Ruggeri
Goycoechea

England made hard work of their group, progressing via two draws and a win, before stumbling past Belgium (thanks to David Platt's memorable last minute volley) and Cameroon. Their finest performance was in a pulsating encounter with West Germany that remains one of the great World Cup semi-finals, but their failure in the subsequent penalty shoot-out was to leave some deep psychological scars – and inspire at least one successful stage play.

Coached by Franz Beckenbauer, the Germans were strong in all departments, had Matthäus and Klinsmann both at their peak, and, typically, grew in stature as they progressed inexorably towards the final – their last as West Germany. However, for all their strengths, they did nothing to help Italia 90 finish on a high. Instead, the tournament got what it deserved in the final: stale, cynical football punctuated by fouls, histrionic diving and petulance. When a penalty with Argentina settled the final in West Germany's favour five minutes before time, the only sensation was relief that another 30 minutes would not have to be endured.

WEST GERMANY	
ILLGNER	6
AUGENTHALER	6
BERTHOLD	6
Subbed: 75 mins (Reuter)	
KOHLER	7
BUCHWALD	*8
BREHME	7
Goal: 85 mins (pen)	
HÄSSLER	7
MATTHÄUS	7
LITTBARSKI	6
KLINSMANN	6
VÖLLER	6
Booked: 52 mins	
sub: REUTER	6

ARGENTINA	
GOYCOECHEA	5
SIMÓN	6
SERRIZUELA	*7
RUGGERI	6
Subbed: 46 mins (Monzon)	
TROGLIO	5
Booked: 84 mins	
SENSINI	6
BURRUCHAGA	6
Subbed: 54 mins (Calderon)	
BASUALDO	5
LORENZO	5
DEZOTTI	6
Sent-off: 65 mins	
MARADONA	6
Booked: 87 mins	
sub: MONZON	5
Sent-off: 87 mins	
sub: CALDERON	6

Referee: Codesal (Mexico)

SEMI-FINALS
Argentina 1-1 Italy
(aet: Argentina won 4-3 on penalties)
West Germany 1-1 England
(aet: West Germany won 4-3 on penalties)

THIRD PLACE PLAY-OFF
Italy 2-1 England

TOP GOALSCORERS
6 goals: Salvatore Schillaci (Italy)
5 goals: Tomás Skuhravy (Czech)
4 goals: Míchel (Spain), Roger Milla (Cameroon), Gary Lineker (England), Lothar Matthäus (Germany)

FASTEST GOAL
4 minutes: Safet Susic (Yugoslavia v United Arab Emirates)

TOTAL GOALS
115

AVERAGE GOALS
2.21 per game

USA 1994

In light of their earlier snub in 1986, there was an air of inevitability when the United States were awarded the 1994 tournament. With rivals Morocco and Brazil unable to match the superior infrastructure, a lack of tradition was no barrier as FIFA used the competition to breach their final frontier.

There were, however, concerns that the competition would fail to capture the imagination – and the excruciating opening ceremony penalty miss by Diana Ross cemented the apprehension.

Yet the tournament would prove successful. Three points for victory ended those lifeless group games, while the introduction of motorised carts for 'injured' players saw feigning decrease. Stadiums were full and only the actions of one player blighted the festival. Diego Maradona came to America looking to play his third final and, on form, there was every chance the dream could become reality. However, a positive drug test ended his aspirations and his career.

SEMI-FINALS
Brazil 1-0 Sweden
Italy 2-1 Bulgaria

THIRD PLACE PLAY-OFF
Sweden 4-0 Bulgaria

TOP GOALSCORERS
6 goals: Oleg Salenko (Russia), Hristo Stoichkov (Bulgaria)
5 goals: Kennet Andersson (Sweden), Roberto Baggio (Italy), Jurgen Klinsmann (Germany), Romario (Brazil)

FASTEST GOAL
2 minutes: Gabriel Batistuta (Argentina v Greece)

TOTAL GOALS
141

AVERAGE GOAL
2.71 per game:

THE FINAL

BRAZIL (0) 0-0 (0) ITALY
(aet: Brazil won 3-2 on penalties)

Date Sunday July 17, 1994 **Attendance** 94,194
Venue Pasadena Rose Bowl, Los Angeles

Although much was expected, the game was a disappointment in which defences prevailed. Baresi, just three weeks after cartilage surgery, returned to shore up the Azzurri. Normal time saw just one clear opportunity, when Pagliuca pushed Silva's effort on to a post, while Bebeto and Baggio spurned chances in extra-time.

The game was destined for penalties and Baresi's opening miss set the trend for the drama to follow. Santos then missed for Brazil, but after Albertini and Evani for Italy and Romario and Branco for Brazil had all netted, the scores were level. Massaro saw his effort stopped by Taffarel, before Dunga converted for Brazil. This left Baggio needing to score but, cruelly, he shot over before sinking to his knees.

BRAZIL	
TAFFAREL	7
JORGINHO	6
Subbed: 22 mins (Cafu)	
ALDAIR	8
MARCIO SANTOS	*9
BRANCO	7
MAZINHO	6
Booked: 4 mins	
MAURO SILVA	7
DUNGA	7
ZINHO	6
Subbed: 106 mins (Viola)	
BEBETO	7
ROMARIO	8
sub: CAFU	6
Booked: 87 mins	
sub: VIOLA	6

ITALY	
PAGLIUCA	7
MUSSI	6
Subbed: 34 mins (Apolloni)	
BARESI	8
MALDINI	*9
BENARRIVO	7
BERTI	7
BAGGIO D	6
Subbed: 95 mins (Evani)	
ALBERTINI	7
Booked: 42 mins	
DONADONI	7
BAGGIO R	6
MASSARO	6
sub: APOLLONI	6
Booked: 41 mins	
sub: EVANI	6

Referee: Puhl (Hungary)

HOW THE TEAMS LINED UP

BRAZIL
COACH: CARLOS PARREIRA

Taffarel
Jorginho — Aldair — Marcio Santos — Branco
Mazinho — Mauro Silva — Dunga — Zinho
Bebeto — Romario

ITALY
COACH: ARRIGO SACCHI

Massaro — Baggio R
Donadoni — Albertini — Baggio D — Berti
Benarrivo — Maldini — Baresi — Mussi
Pagliuca

Above: Ray Houghton celebrates his strike against Italy. Opposite clockwise from top left: Brazil show off their spoils; Baggio and Taffarel experience differing emotions after the decisive penalty; Sweden salute their fans after semi-final defeat; Stoichkov's Bulgaria beat Germany.

The tournament began with Germany taking on Bolivia, and a solitary goal from Klinsmann spared the blushes although it was overshadowed by Bolivian star Etcheverry, red-carded four minutes after coming on as sub.

The dismissal of Spanish defender Nadal also proved costly in the group. Having taken a 2-0 lead against South Korea, the Spaniards conceded late goals and, with their match against Germany ending in stalemate, both superpowers teetered on the brink. Normality resumed as Caminero hit a brace against Bolivia, while Klinsmann took his tally to four in a 3-2 win against the Koreans.

Group A proved equally fascinating. Having defeated Brazil 5-0 in qualifying, Colombia were tipped to go far. Yet internal bickering and poor preparation caused their downfall, as a 3-1 defeat against Romania and subsequent defeat against the hosts sealed their fate. The USA result had tragic overtones as Andres Escobar – blamed for the defeat after scoring an own-goal – was murdered shortly after his return home.

Despite their tepid qualification, Brazil opened with a 2-0 victory against Russia, while Romario and Bebeto proved the catalysts of a 3-0 defeat of Cameroon. The Africans came with high expectations, following their exploits in 1990, yet returned early following a 6-1 mauling by Russia. Sweden also booked their place with Brolin and Dahlin's Euro 92 momentum carrying forward.

Prior to Maradona's cocaine exposé, Argentina had the look of champions. An emphatic 4-0 defeat of Greece was followed with victory over Nigeria, signalling Batistuta's arrival with three goals. The Africans hailed their own hero, Yekini, whose opener against Bulgaria was his country's first World Cup goal. With Stoichkov scoring twice for Bulgaria against Greece, and Nigeria also defeating the whipping boys, Argentina limped in third.

Italy, led by Roberto Baggio's guile, were regarded as certainties in Group E. Yet when they conceded Ray Houghton's solitary strike for Ireland it meant that victory against Norway was imperative. The sending-off of goalkeeper Pagliuca and injury to Baresi further troubled the Azzuri, yet Dino Baggio's goal ensured progress.

Bickering threatened Holland's Group F chances. A spat between Gullit and coach Advocaat led to the 32-year-old's omission, and a less than convincing 2-1 win against Saudi Arabia confirmed their troubles. The Saudis became the surprise package, beating Morocco 2-1 before Saeed Owairan, 'The Desert Pele', ran 60 yards through the Belgian rearguard to secure victory and qualification.

The Germans continued their ominous march as Rudi Völler inspired a 3-2 second round win over Belgium, while Spain's emphatic defeat of Switzerland was closer than the 3-0 scoreline suggests.

Two goals from Andersson enhanced his reputation as Sweden edged Saudi Arabia 3-1, while the tie of the round saw Argentina paired with Romania. Ortega did his best to fill Maradona's void, but it was the opposition playmaker, Hagi, who ran the midfield in a 3-2 victory. Argentina had ultimately been let down by their favourite son.

The heat of Orlando cost Ireland – errors by Phelan and Bonner sealed their fate against Holland, while USA's progress ended against Brazil, who had Leonardo sent-off for elbowing defender Ramos, who was later diagnosed with a fractured skull.

But what of Baggio? A last-minute equaliser against Nigeria and subsequent extra-time penalty signalled his arrival, made more significant by Zola's red card.

The final second round clash between Bulgaria and Mexico was delayed when a goalpost collapsed. It perhaps affected the Latin Americans as Aspe, Bernal and Rodrigues missed kicks when the game went to penalties.

Seven European sides from eight made the quarter-finals, with Italy in the ascendancy. Dino Baggio's two goals edged a thriller against Spain, while Brazil and Holland dished up a similarly scintillating show. Romario's drive and Bebeto's cool finish appeared to have won the game, but Bergkamp and Winter replied to set up a grandstand finish, which Brazil won thanks to Branco's free-kick.

Bulgaria provided the biggest shock, beating Germany 2-1 thanks to Stoichkov's free-kick and a text-book header by Letchkov, the tournament's star midfielder.

Sweden's tussle with Romania went to extra-time. Schwarz's sending-off at 1-2 made progression for Scandinavians unlikely, but Andersson's goal took the game to penalties where Ravelli saved from Belodedici to win.

Ravelli was inspired again against Brazil, but the South Americans would meet Italy in the final, who had two goals from Baggio to thank for their 2-1 defeat of Bulgaria.

FRANCE 1998

After the sterile final of 1994, and a tournament which failed to grip the imagination, France 98 came like a breath of fresh air, providing excitement, passion, drama and controversy. While it was the world's best footballer, Ronaldo, who would inflame the passions of the conspiracy theorists in the final, there was plenty of classic football action throughout the tournament.

The competition featured 32 teams, more than ever before, and that meant not only more games, but more sides from Africa, Asia and other emerging regions. Among those making a debut at the finals were Japan, Jamaica, South Africa and Croatia. There was also the introduction of the 'golden goal', meaning that if a game went into extra-time, the first goal scored would decide the match.

The hosts came into the tournament under pressure – they had failed to qualify for USA '94 and many claimed they had no strikers. But driven by Zinedine Zidane and his fabulous midfield, as well as the fanatical home support, goals didn't seem a problem in their group as they dispatched South Africa 3-0, Saudi Arabia 4-0, and Denmark 2-1.

Scotland kept up another tradition – giving the good teams a run for their money and flopping against the lesser lights. A narrow defeat to Brazil (2-1, with the winner coming from an own-goal by Tommy Boyd) was followed up by a 1-1 draw with Norway, and a 3-0 defeat against Morocco.

England went through the group stage with a 2-0 victory over Tunisia, defeat against Romania thanks to Dan Petrescu's last-minute winner, and a 2-0 win against Colombia. In the other groups the major football nations emerged relatively unscathed, with one major exception. Always a favourite 'outsider' for any title given the exceptional talent within their domestic league, Spain again promised much but delivered very little. They lost a thriller against Nigeria 3-2, drew 0-0 with Paraguay, and made a desperate effort in their last match, Bulgaria ending up on the wrong end of a 6-1 scoreline, but to no avail.

In the second phase, Brazil and Denmark were impressive, Italy and Croatia both crept through 1-0, Germany edged Mexico, the Dutch beat Yugoslavia in a thriller, and France's Laurent Blanc scored the tournament's first 'golden goal' to pip Paraguay.

The match of the round brought together two old foes: England and Argentina. The first-half was simply brilliant, Gabriel Batistuta giving the South Americans an early lead through a penalty before Alan Shearer converted a spot-kick for England. Then came one of those moments that build a reputation, as 17-year-old striker Michael Owen controlled a long pass, raced towards the Argentine goal

Above: The Romanian team celebrate progressing to the second round by dyeing their hair blond. Opposite clockwise from top left: Denmark's Brian Laudrup after scoring against Nigeria; France celebrate winning the World Cup on home soil; Michael Owen takes on Argentina's Jose Chamot; Holland's Edgar Davids in quarter-final action against Argentina.

leaving defenders floundering, and beat Carlos Roa with an unstoppable shot. England stayed ahead until just before the interval, when a clever free-kick routine saw Zanetti equalise.

The second-half saw drama of a different kind, and another of those defining moments. Within minutes of the re-start, Diego Simeone brought down David Beckham. While on the ground, the Englishman kicked Simeone on the leg – hardly vicious, but certainly foolish, and the Argentinian went down, perhaps a little too easily. Beckham was sent-off and England had to play the rest of the second-half, and 30 minutes of extra-time, with ten men.

England held their own, even having an effort from Sol Campbell disallowed and a penalty appeal refused. In the deciding penalty shoot out David Batty saw Roa save his spot-kick and England's dream was over, the fans blaming Beckham rather than Batty.

The World Cup carried on. Perhaps the best quarter-final was played out by Brazil and Denmark – the Europeans being pipped 3-2 thanks to Rivaldo's second-half winner. Holland and Argentina were both reduced to ten men in their game and an early goal apiece was all the scoring until near the end. Then Ariel Ortega was red-carded for head-butting goalkeeper Edwin Van Der Sar, and from the free-kick the ball was played to Dennis Bergkamp who finished with aplomb.

Croatia caused the upset of the round, two late goals from Davor Suker sealing a 3-0 win over Germany. Then the aristocracy of Europe played one of the dullest matches, Italy and France failing to register a goal. The game went to penalties, and when Luigi di Biagio's effort hit the bar, the hosts were through.

The first semi-final saw the debutants from Croatia come up against the hosts. Suker opened the scoring, then the team with no strikers once again relied on a defender to score, this time Lilian Thuram netting his first for his country, going on to score the winner. The other semi-final was also pure drama. Ronaldo's second-half goal looked enough, until a late Kluivert equaliser. Neither side

could grab the winner, and it went to penalties, the reigning champions winning 4-2.

The dream final was on – champions versus hosts, Ronaldo versus Zidane, style versus substance – what could go wrong?

THE FINAL

FRANCE (2) 3-0 (0) BRAZIL

Date Sunday July 12, 1998 **Attendance** 75,000
Venue Stade de France, Paris

The record will show the scoreline, the scorers and the fact that France's Marcel Desailly received his marching orders following a tackle on Cafu. What it won't show is the controversy which threatened to overshadow the final.

Brazil's World Player Of The Year, Ronaldo, wasn't named on coach Mario Zagalo's teamsheet when it was first handed in. An hour later his name was back on it again. It emerged that the previous day Ronaldo had suffered from convulsions and was taken to hospital. Zagalo named the team without him but the striker declared himself fit to play. The stadium was in uproar, Brazil – especially Ronaldo – looked lethargic, and Zinedine Zidane conducted the French orchestra to perfection, heading two goals, while Emmanuel Petit scored the breakaway third.

The country that had invented the World Cup had finally won it – on home soil!

HOW THE TEAMS LINED UP

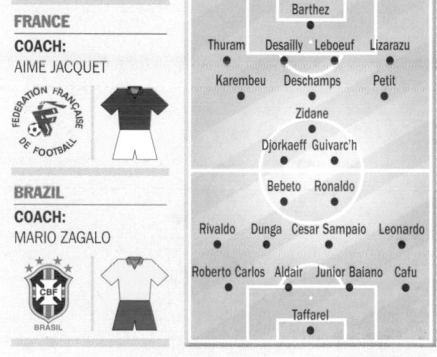

FRANCE
COACH: AIME JACQUET

BRAZIL
COACH: MARIO ZAGALO

SEMI-FINALS

Brazil 1-1 Holland
(aet. Brazil won 4-2 on penalties)
France 2-1 Croatia

THIRD PLACE PLAY-OFF

Croatia 2-1 Holland

TOP SCORERS

6 goals: Davor Suker (Croatia)
5 goals: Gabriel Batistuta (Argentina)

FASTEST GOAL

53 seconds: Celso Ayala (Paraguay v Nigeria)

TOTAL GOALS

171

AVERAGE GOALS

2.67 per game

FRANCE

BARTHEZ	7
THURAM	7
DESAILLY	6
Booked: 48 mins. Sent-off (second booking) 60 mins	
LEBOEUF	7
LIZARAZU	7
DESCHAMPS	7
Booked: 39 mins	
ZIDANE	*9
Goal: 27 mins, 45 mins	
PETIT	8
Goal: 90 mins	
KAREMBEU	7
Booked: 56 mins. Subbed: 56 mins (Boghossian)	
DJORKAEFF	8
Subbed: 74 mins (Vieira)	
GUIVARC'H	6
Subbed: 66 mins (Dugarry)	
sub: BOGHOSSIAN	6
sub: DUGARRY	7
sub: VIERA	6

BRAZIL

TAFFAREL	6
CAFU	6
JUNIOR BAIANO	5
Booked: 33 mins	
ALDAIR	6
ROBERTO CARLOS	*7
CESAR SAMPAIO	6
Subbed: 57 mins (Edmundo)	
LEONARDO	5
Subbed: 46 mins (Denilson)	
DUNGA	6
RIVALDO	6
RONALDO	5
BEBETO	5
sub: DENILSON	6
sub: EDMUNDO	5

Referee: S Belqola (Morocco)

KOREA/JAPAN 2002

The 17th World Cup finals in Japan and Korea were the first to be played in Asia, and as if to metaphorically signify a shift in the balance of global football dominance, from the very first game it was a competition full of shocks and surprise results. It was a tournament that saw plenty of countries with established reputations and big name players catch an early return flight home. However, Korea/Japan 2002 was also notable for the emergence of many unfancied countries, such as Senegal, Turkey and South Korea. Despite this, ironically enough the final was to be played out between the World Cup's two most established and successful sides.

It was World Cup debutantes Senegal who provided the biggest shock, in the opening game, with a 1-0 defeat of the holders and pre-tournament favourites France, with the goal scored by Pape Bouba Diop. In a physical game, the Africans over-powered a jaded looking French team, clearly missing the talismanic presence of an injured Zinedine

Above: South Korea watch the penalty shoot-out that will take them through to the semi-finals. Opposite clockwise from top left: Japan's Junichi Inamoto is mobbed by his team-mates after scoring against Russia; Roque Junior and Ronaldinho lift the World Cup; Senegal's goal celebrations after scoring against France; David Beckham gains revenge over Argentina.

SEMI-FINALS

Germany 1-0 South Korea
Brazil 1-0 Turkey

THIRD PLACE PLAY-OFF

Turkey 3-2 South Korea

TOP SCORERS

8 goals: Ronaldo (Brazil)
5 goals: Miroslav Klose (Germany); Rivaldo (Brazil)

FASTEST GOAL

10.8 seconds: Hakan Sükür (Turkey v South Korea)

TOTAL GOALS

161

AVERAGE GOALS

2.51 per game

THE FINAL

BRAZIL (0) 2-0 (0) GERMANY

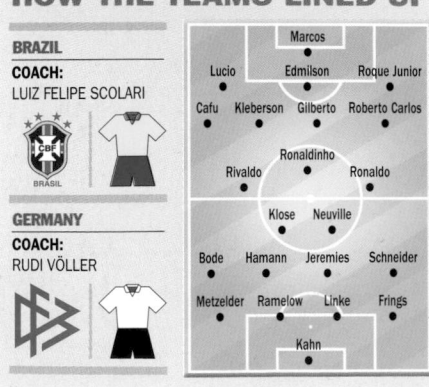

Date Sunday June 30, 2002 **Attendance** 69,029
Venue International Stadium, Yokohama

Despite sharing seven World Cup titles between them, Brazil and Germany had never met in the final stages of the tournament. Brazil started favouites – but they would have to beat Oliver Kahn, who had conceded just one goal in the tournament. A largely uneventful first half saw two bookings, while Kleberson hit the bar for Brazil and a couple of half-chances fell to Ronaldo. In the 67th minute, however, Kahn spilt Rivaldo's shot into the path of the grateful Ronaldo, who pounced on the ball to score.

He was on the scoresheet again 12 minutes later, curling the ball past Kahn to make it 2-0. Shortly after the final whistle, skipper Cafu, in his third World Cup final, was to lift the trophy to mark Brazil's record-breaking and wholly deserved fifth victory.

BRAZIL

MARCOS	7
LUCIO	8
EDMILSON	8
ROQUE JUNIOR	7
Booked: 6 mins	
CAFU	7
KLEBERSON	7
GILBERTO SILVA	6
ROBERTO CARLOS	6
RONALDINHO	7
Subbed: 85 mins (Juninho)	
RIVALDO	6
RONALDO	*9
Goal: 67 mins, 79 mins. Subbed: 90 mins (Denilson)	
sub: JUNINHO	5
sub: DENILSON	5

GERMANY

KAHN	7
LINKE	6
RAMELOW	7
METZELDER	6
FRINGS	7
JEREMIES	6
Subbed: 77 mins (Asamoah)	
HAMANN	7
SCHNEIDER	*8
BODE	6
Subbed: 84 mins (Ziege)	
NEUVILLE	7
KLOSE	6
Booked: 9 mins. Subbed: 74 mins (Bierhoff)	
sub: BIERHOFF	6
sub: ASAMOAH	6
sub: ZIEGE	5

Referee: Collina (Italy)

HOW THE TEAMS LINED UP

BRAZIL
COACH: LUIZ FELIPE SCOLARI

Marcos
Lucio — Edmilson — Roque Junior
Cafu — Kleberson — Gilberto — Roberto Carlos
Ronaldinho
Rivaldo — Ronaldo

GERMANY
COACH: RUDI VÖLLER

Klose — Neuville
Bode — Hamann — Jeremies — Schneider
Metzelder — Ramelow — Linke — Frings
Kahn

Zidane. Indeed, France failed to score a single goal in three qualifying games and were on a plane home much earlier than expected.

Joint favourites Argentina also suffered the ignominy of elimination at the group stage. After a narrow win in their opening game against Nigeria, courtesy of a Gabriel Batistuta header, two consecutive defeats against England and Sweden meant the hugely talented Argentinian squad were to play no further part in the tournament. The game against England was one of the most eagerly anticipated games of the competition, and saw David Beckham convert the match-winning penalty to gain revenge for his dismissal in the same fixture four years previous.

The much-fancied Portuguese side were the other high-profile casualties at this stage, losing out to both the USA and joint hosts South Korea, who topped their group after having never before won a match at the finals.

An impressive Brazil, looking more assured and confident with every game, and perennial under-achievers Spain were the only two countries to qualify from their respective groups with 100 per cent records, while Slovenia, China and Saudi Arabia went home without a point. Germany's 8-0 demolition of Saudi Arabia was, by quite a margin, the most one-sided of all the games of the tournament. The other group winners were Denmark, Germany, Sweden, Mexico and Japan – much to the delight of an enthusiastic co-host nation.

With Germany and England securing routine wins against Paraguay and Denmark in the opening games of the second round, it was left to South Korea to provide the major upset of this stage. Some controversial refereeing marred their 2-1 golden goal victory over the Italians, which saw golden boy Francesco Totti sent off for diving, and an apparently good goal ruled out.

Despite the loss of influential captain Roy Keane (who walked out on the squad before

they had even arrived at the World Cup), Ireland qualified for the knockout rounds, only to go out on penalties to Spain. The other games at this stage saw wins for USA over Mexico, Senegal over Sweden and Brazil over Belgium, while a headed goal from Turkey's Umit Davala ended the dreams of Japan.

The quarter-final stage consisted of four established football nations (Brazil, Germany, England, Spain), and four inexperienced at this level of competition (USA, South Korea, Turkey and Senegal). Brazil beat England 2-1, countering an opportunistic Michael Owen strike thanks to a freak long-range goal from Ronaldinho. Germany were fortunate to get past USA 1-0, especially after a blatant handball in their own penalty area had gone unnoticed. Turkey secured a golden goal victory over an unlucky Senegal, and South Korea were once again up to their giant-killing antics. This time Guus Hiddink's superbly conditioned and well-drilled team got the better of Spain, but again the victory was not without controversy, the Spanish side furious that two perfectly good goals had been disallowed.

The semi-finals finally saw the established powers assert some domination. Brazil eased past a spirited Turkey 1-0 with a memorable goal from a rejuvenated Ronaldo. Germany narrowly got the better of the co-hosts with a solitary goal from Michael Ballack, who got himself booked and missed the final.

Despite complaints over poor organisation in respect of ticket allocation, the first World Cup outside of Europe and the Americas was superbly staged by the host nations. The wide-eyed enthusiasm of the supporters from both of the host nations is sure to be considered one of the lasting memories of a successful tournament. No respecter of reputations, the 2002 Japan/Korea World Cup will also be remembered as one when the smaller football nations fought back, and very nearly succeeded in overthrowing the existing global power base.

WORLD CUP RESULTS

Above: Argentina score past Ballesteros in the 1930 final, but the goalkeeper's Uruguayan team would go on to triumph 4-2.

1930 URUGUAY

GROUP 1

France **4-1** Mexico
Argentina **1-0** France
Chile **3-0** Mexico
Chile **1-0** France
Argentina **6-3** Mexico
Argentina **3-1** Chile

	P	W	D	L	F	A	Pts
Argentina	3	3	0	0	10	4	6
Chile	3	2	0	1	5	3	4
France	3	1	0	2	4	3	2
Mexico	3	0	0	3	4	13	0

GROUP 2

Yugoslavia **2-1** Brazil
Yugoslavia **4-0** Bolivia
Brazil **4-0** Bolivia

	P	W	D	L	F	A	Pts
Yugoslavia	2	2	0	0	6	1	4
Brazil	2	1	0	1	5	2	2
Bolivia	2	0	0	2	0	8	0

GROUP 3

Romania **3-1** Peru
Uruguay **1-0** Peru
Uruguay **4-0** Romania

	P	W	D	L	F	A	Pts
Uruguay	2	2	0	0	5	0	4
Romania	2	1	0	1	3	5	2
Peru	2	0	0	2	1	4	0

GROUP 4

USA **3-0** Belgium
USA **3-0** Paraguay
Paraguay **1-0** Belgium

	P	W	D	L	F	A	Pts
USA	2	2	0	0	6	0	4
Paraguay	2	1	0	1	1	3	2
Belgium	2	0	0	2	0	4	0

SEMI-FINALS

Argentina **6-1** USA
Uruguay **6-1** Yugoslavia

THIRD PLACE PLAY-OFF

Not held

FINAL

Uruguay **4-2** Argentina

1934 ITALY

FIRST ROUND

Italy **7-1** USA
Czechoslovakia **2-1** Romania
Germany **5-2** Belgium
Austria **3-2** France
Spain **3-1** Brazil
Switzerland **3-2** Holland
Sweden **3-2** Argentina
Hungary **4-2** Egypt

SECOND ROUND

Germany **2-1** Sweden
Austria **2-1** Hungary
Italy **1-1** Spain
(aet)
Italy **1-0** Spain
(replay)
Czechoslovakia **3-2** Switzerland

SEMI-FINALS

Czechoslovakia **3-1** Germany
Italy **1-0** Austria

THIRD-PLACE PLAY-OFF

Germany **3-2** Austria

FINAL

Italy **2-1** Czechoslovakia
(aet)

1938 FRANCE

FIRST ROUND

Switzerland **1-1** Germany
(aet)
Switzerland **4-2** Germany
(replay)
Cuba **3-3** Romania
(aet)
Cuba **2-1** Romania
(replay)
Hungary **6-0** Dutch E. Indies
France **3-1** Belgium
Czechoslovakia **3-0** Holland
(aet)
Brazil **6-5** Poland
(aet)
Italy **2-1** Norway
(aet)
Sweden **w/o** Austria

QUARTER-FINALS

Sweden **8-0** Cuba
Hungary **2-0** Switzerland
Italy **3-1** France
Brazil **1-1** Czechoslovakia
(aet)
Brazil **2-1** Czechoslovakia
(replay)

SEMI-FINALS

Italy **2-1** Brazil
Hungary **5-1** Sweden

THIRD-PLACE PLAY-OFF

Brazil **4-2** Sweden

FINAL

Italy **4-2** Hungary

1950 BRAZIL

POOL 1

Brazil **4-0** Mexico
Yugoslavia **3-0** Switzerland
Yugoslavia **4-1** Mexico
Brazil **2-2** Switzerland
Brazil **2-0** Yugoslavia
Switzerland **2-1** Mexico

	P	W	D	L	F	A	Pts
Brazil	3	2	1	0	8	2	5
Yugoslavia	3	2	0	1	7	3	4
Switzerland	3	1	1	1	4	6	3
Mexico	3	0	0	3	2	10	0

POOL 2

Spain **3-1** USA
England **2-0** Chile
USA **1-0** England
Spain **2-0** Chile
Spain **1-0** England
Chile **5-2** USA

	P	W	D	L	F	A	Pts
Spain	3	3	0	0	6	1	6
England	3	1	0	2	2	2	2
Chile	3	1	0	2	5	6	2
USA	3	1	0	2	4	8	2

POOL 3

Sweden **3-2** Italy
Sweden **2-2** Paraguay
Italy **2-0** Paraguay

	P	W	D	L	F	A	Pts
Sweden	2	1	1	0	5	4	3
Italy	2	1	0	1	4	3	2
Paraguay	2	0	1	1	2	4	1

POOL 4

Uruguay **8-0** Bolivia

	P	W	D	L	F	A	Pts
Uruguay	1	1	0	0	8	0	2
Bolivia	1	0	0	1	0	8	0

FINAL POOL

Uruguay **2-2** Spain
Brazil **7-1** Sweden
Uruguay **3-2** Sweden
Brazil **6-1** Spain
Sweden **3-1** Spain
Uruguay **2-1** Brazil*

	P	W	D	L	F	A	Pts
Uruguay	3	2	1	0	7	5	5
Brazil	3	2	0	1	14	4	4
Sweden	3	1	0	2	6	11	2
Spain	3	0	1	2	4	11	1

THIRD PLACE

Sweden

FINAL (DECIDING MATCH)

Uruguay **2-1** Brazil*

the last game of the Final Pool decided the World Cup.

1954 SWITZERLAND

POOL 1

Yugoslavia **1-0** France
Brazil **5-0** Mexico
France **3-2** Mexico
Brazil **1-1** Yugoslavia
(aet)

	P	W	D	L	F	A	Pts
Brazil	2	1	1	0	6	1	3
Yugoslavia	2	1	1	0	2	1	3
France	2	1	0	1	3	3	2
Mexico	2	0	0	2	2	8	0

POOL 2

Hungary **9-0** South Korea
West Germany **4-1** Turkey
Hungary **8-3** West Germany
Turkey **7-0** South Korea

	P	W	D	L	F	A	Pts
Hungary	2	2	0	0	17	3	4
West Germany	2	1	0	1	7	9	2
Turkey	2	1	0	1	8	4	2
South Korea	2	0	0	2	0	16	0

PLAY OFF FOR 2ND GROUP PLACE

West Germany **7-2** Turkey

POOL 3

Austria **1-0** Scotland
Uruguay **2-0** Czechoslovakia
Austria **5-0** Czechoslovakia
Uruguay **7-0** Scotland

	P	W	D	L	F	A	Pts
Uruguay	2	2	0	0	9	0	4
Austria	2	2	0	0	6	0	4
Czechoslovakia	2	0	0	2	0	7	0
Scotland	2	0	0	2	0	8	0

POOL 4

England **4-4** Belgium
(aet)
England **2-0** Switzerland
Switzerland **2-1** Italy
Italy **4-1** Belgium

	P	W	D	L	F	A	Pts
England	2	1	1	0	6	4	3
Switzerland	2	1	0	1	2	3	2
Italy	2	1	0	1	5	3	2
Belgium	2	0	1	1	5	8	1

PLAY-OFF FOR 2ND GROUP PLACE

Switzerland **4-1** Italy

QUARTER-FINALS

West Germany **2-0** Yugoslavia
Hungary **4-2** Brazil
Austria **7-5** Switzerland
Uruguay **4-2** England

SEMI-FINALS

West Germany **6-1** Austria
Hungary **4-2** Uruguay
(aet)

THIRD-PLACE PLAY-OFF

Austria **3-1** Uruguay

FINAL

West Germany **3-2** Hungary

1958 SWEDEN

POOL 1

West Germany **3-1** Argentina
Northern Ireland **1-0** Czechoslovakia
West Germany **2-2** Czechoslovakia
Argentina **3-1** Northern Ireland
West Germany **2-2** Northern Ireland
Czechoslovakia **6-1** Argentina

Above: Dutch East Indies players line up in France in 1938 to face mighty Hungary.

Above: Jimmy Greaves in action for England at the 1962 World Cup in Chile.

	P	W	D	L	F	A	Pts
West Germany	3	1	2	0	7	5	4
Northern Ireland	3	1	1	1	4	5	3
Czechoslovakia	3	1	1	1	8	4	3
Argentina	3	1	0	2	5	10	2

PLAY-OFF FOR 2ND GROUP PLACE
Northern Ireland **2-1** Czechoslovakia
(act)

POOL 2
France **7-3** Paraguay
Yugoslavia **1-1** Scotland
Yugoslavia **3-2** France
Paraguay **3-2** Scotland
France **2-1** Scotland
Yugoslavia **3-3** Paraguay

	P	W	D	L	F	A	Pts
France	3	2	0	1	11	7	4
Yugoslavia	3	1	2	0	7	6	4
Paraguay	3	1	1	1	9	12	3
Scotland	3	0	1	2	4	6	1

POOL 3
Sweden **3-0** Mexico
Hungary **1-1** Wales
Wales **1-1** Mexico
Sweden **2-1** Hungary
Sweden **0-0** Wales
Hungary **4-0** Mexico

	P	W	D	L	F	A	Pts
Sweden	3	2	1	0	5	1	5
Wales	3	0	3	0	2	2	3
Hungary	3	1	1	1	6	3	3
Mexico	3	0	1	2	1	8	1

PLAY-OFF FOR 2ND GROUP PLACE
Wales **2-1** Hungary

POOL 4
England **2-2** Soviet Union
Brazil **3-0** Austria
England **0-0** Brazil
Soviet Union **2-0** Austria
Brazil **2-0** Soviet Union
England **2-2** Austria

	P	W	D	L	F	A	Pts
Brazil	3	2	1	0	5	0	5
Soviet Union	3	1	1	1	4	4	3
England	3	0	3	0	4	4	3
Austria	3	0	1	2	2	7	1

PLAY-OFF FOR 2ND GROUP PLACE
Soviet Union **1-0** England

QUARTER-FINALS
France **4-0** Northern Ireland
West Germany **1-0** Yugoslavia
Sweden **2-0** Soviet Union
Brazil **1-0** Wales

SEMI-FINALS
Brazil **5-2** France
Sweden **3-1** West Germany

THIRD-PLACE PLAY-OFF
France **6-3** West Germany

FINAL
Brazil **5-2** Sweden

1962 CHILE

GROUP 1
Uruguay **2-1** Colombia
Soviet Union **2-0** Yugoslavia
Yugoslavia **3-1** Uruguay
Soviet Union **4-4** Colombia
Soviet Union **2-1** Uruguay
Yugoslavia **5-0** Colombia

	P	W	D	L	F	A	Pts
Soviet Union	3	2	1	0	8	5	5
Yugoslavia	3	2	0	1	8	3	4
Uruguay	3	1	0	2	4	6	2
Colombia	3	0	1	2	5	11	1

GROUP 2
Chile **3-1** Switzerland
West Germany **0-0** Italy
Chile **2-0** Italy
West Germany **2-1** Switzerland
West Germany **2-0** Chile
Italy **3-0** Switzerland

	P	W	D	L	F	A	Pts
West Germany	3	2	1	0	4	1	5
Chile	3	2	0	1	5	3	4
Italy	3	1	1	1	3	2	3
Switzerland	3	0	0	3	2	8	0

GROUP 3
Brazil **2-0** Mexico
Czechoslovakia **1-0** Spain
Brazil **0-0** Czechoslovakia
Spain **1-0** Mexico
Brazil **2-1** Spain
Mexico **3-1** Czechoslovakia

	P	W	D	L	F	A	Pts
Brazil	3	2	1	0	4	1	5
Czechoslovakia	3	1	1	1	2	3	3
Mexico	3	1	0	2	3	4	2
Spain	3	1	0	2	2	3	2

GROUP 4
Argentina **1-0** Bulgaria
Hungary **2-1** England
England **3-1** Argentina
Hungary **6-1** Bulgaria
Argentina **0-0** Hungary
England **0-0** Bulgaria

	P	W	D	L	F	A	Pts
Hungary	3	2	1	0	8	2	5
England	3	1	1	1	4	3	3
Argentina	3	1	1	1	2	3	3
Bulgaria	3	0	1	2	1	7	1

QUARTER-FINALS
Yugoslavia **1-0** West Germany
Brazil **3-1** England
Chile **2-1** Soviet Union
Czechoslovakia **1-0** Hungary

SEMI-FINALS
Brazil **4-2** Chile
Czechoslovakia **3-1** Yugoslavia

THIRD-PLACE PLAY-OFF
Chile **1-0** Yugoslavia

FINAL
Brazil **3-1** Czechoslovakia

1966 ENGLAND

GROUP 1
England **0-0** Uruguay
France **1-1** Mexico
Uruguay **2-1** France
England **2-0** Mexico
Uruguay **0-0** Mexico
England **2-0** France

	P	W	D	L	F	A	Pts
England	3	2	1	0	4	0	5
Uruguay	3	1	2	0	2	1	4
Mexico	3	0	2	1	1	3	2
France	3	0	1	2	2	5	1

GROUP 2
West Germany **5-0** Switzerland
Argentina **2-1** Spain
Spain **2-1** Switzerland
Argentina **0-0** West Germany
Argentina **2-0** Switzerland
West Germany **2-1** Spain

	P	W	D	L	F	A	Pts
West Germany	3	2	1	0	7	1	5
Argentina	3	2	1	0	4	1	5
Spain	3	1	0	2	4	5	2
Switzerland	3	0	0	3	1	9	0

GROUP 3
Brazil **2-0** Bulgaria
Portugal **3-1** Hungary
Hungary **3-1** Brazil
Portugal **3-0** Bulgaria
Portugal **3-1** Brazil
Hungary **3-1** Bulgaria

	P	W	D	L	F	A	Pts
Portugal	3	3	0	0	9	2	6
Hungary	3	2	0	1	7	5	4
Brazil	3	1	0	2	4	6	2
Bulgaria	3	0	0	3	1	8	0

GROUP 4
Soviet Union **3-0** North Korea
Italy **2-0** Chile
Chile **1-1** North Korea
Soviet Union **1-0** Italy
North Korea **1-0** Italy
Soviet Union **2-1** Chile

	P	W	D	L	F	A	Pts
Soviet Union	3	3	0	0	6	1	6
North Korea	3	1	1	1	2	4	3
Italy	3	1	0	2	2	2	2
Chile	3	0	1	2	2	5	1

QUARTER-FINALS
England **1-0** Argentina
West Germany **4-0** Uruguay
Portugal **5-3** North Korea
Soviet Union **2-1** Hungary

SEMI-FINALS
West Germany **2-1** Soviet Union
England **2-1** Portugal

THIRD-PLACE PLAY-OFF
Portugal **2-1** Soviet Union

FINAL
England **4-2** West Germany
(aet)

1970 MEXICO

GROUP 1
Mexico **0-0** Soviet Union
Belgium **3-0** El Salvador
Soviet Union **4-1** Belgium
Mexico **4-0** El Salvador
Soviet Union **2-0** El Salvador
Mexico **1-0** Belgium

	P	W	D	L	F	A	Pts
Soviet Union	3	2	1	0	6	1	5
Mexico	3	2	1	0	5	0	5
Belgium	3	1	0	2	4	5	2
El Salvador	3	0	0	3	0	9	0

GROUP 2
Uruguay **2-0** Israel
Italy **1-0** Sweden
Uruguay **0-0** Italy
Sweden **1-1** Israel
Sweden **1-0** Uruguay
Italy **0-0** Israel

	P	W	D	L	F	A	Pts
Italy	3	1	2	0	1	0	4
Uruguay	3	1	1	1	2	1	3
Sweden	3	1	1	1	2	2	3
Israel	3	0	2	1	1	3	2

GROUP 3
England **1-0** Romania
Brazil **4-1** Czechoslovakia
Romania **2-1** Czechoslovakia
Brazil **1-0** England
Brazil **3-2** Romania
England **1-0** Czechoslovakia

	P	W	D	L	F	A	Pts
Brazil	3	3	0	0	8	3	6
England	3	2	0	1	2	1	4
Romania	3	1	0	2	4	5	2
Czechoslovakia	3	0	0	3	2	7	0

Above: Captain Bobby Moore is carried off with the Jules Rimet trophy by his team-mates after England's 1966 success.

WORLD CUP RESULTS

Above: Joe Jordan heads for goal during Scotland's 0-0 draw with holders Brazil at the 1974 tournament in West Germany.

GROUP 4

Peru **3-2** Bulgaria
West Germany **2-1** Morocco
Peru **3-0** Morocco
West Germany **5-2** Bulgaria
West Germany **3-1** Peru
Morocco **1-1** Bulgaria

	P	W	D	L	F	A	Pts
West Germany	3	3	0	0	10	4	6
Peru	3	2	0	1	7	5	4
Bulgaria	3	0	1	2	5	9	1
Morocco	3	0	1	2	2	6	1

QUARTER-FINALS

West Germany **3-2** England
(aet)
Brazil **4-2** Peru
Italy **4-1** Mexico
Uruguay **1-0** Soviet Union
(aet)

SEMI-FINALS

Italy **4-3** West Germany
(aet)
Brazil **3-1** Uruguay

THIRD-PLACE

West Germany **1-0** Uruguay

FINAL

Brazil **4-1** Italy

1974 WEST GERMANY

GROUP 1

West Germany **1-0** Chile
East Germany **2-0** Australia
West Germany **3-0** Australia
East Germany **1-1** Chile
Australia **0-0** Chile
East Germany **1-0** West Germany

	P	W	D	L	F	A	Pts
East Germany	3	2	1	0	4	1	5
West Germany	3	2	0	1	4	1	4
Chile	3	0	2	1	1	2	2
Australia	3	0	1	2	0	5	1

GROUP 2

Brazil **0-0** Yugoslavia
Scotland **2-0** Zaïre
Brazil **0-0** Scotland
Yugoslavia **9-0** Zaïre
Yugoslavia **1-1** Scotland
Brazil **3-0** Zaïre

	P	W	D	L	F	A	Pts
Yugoslavia	3	1	2	0	10	1	4
Brazil	3	1	2	0	3	0	4
Scotland	3	1	2	0	3	1	4
Zaïre	3	0	0	3	0	14	0

GROUP 3

Holland **2-0** Uruguay
Bulgaria **0-0** Sweden
Holland **0-0** Sweden
Bulgaria **1-1** Uruguay
Holland **4-1** Bulgaria
Sweden **3-0** Uruguay

	P	W	D	L	F	A	Pts
Holland	3	2	1	0	6	1	5
Sweden	3	1	2	0	3	0	4
Bulgaria	3	0	2	1	2	5	2
Uruguay	3	0	1	2	1	6	1

GROUP 4

Italy **3-1** Haiti
Poland **3-2** Argentina
Argentina **1-1** Italy
Poland **7-0** Haiti
Argentina **4-1** Haiti
Poland **2-1** Italy

	P	W	D	L	F	A	Pts
Poland	3	3	0	0	12	3	6
Argentina	3	1	1	1	7	5	3
Italy	3	1	1	1	5	4	3
Haiti	3	0	0	3	2	14	0

SECOND ROUND GROUP A

Brazil **1-0** East Germany
Holland **4-0** Argentina
Holland **2-0** East Germany
Brazil **2-1** Argentina
East Germany **1-1** Argentina
Holland **2-0** Brazil

	P	W	D	L	F	A	Pts
Holland	3	3	0	0	8	0	6
Brazil	3	2	0	1	3	3	4
East Germany	3	0	1	2	1	4	1
Argentina	3	0	1	2	2	7	1

SECOND ROUND GROUP B

Poland **1-0** Sweden
West Germany **2-0** Yugoslavia
Poland **2-1** Yugoslavia
West Germany **4-2** Sweden
Sweden **2-1** Yugoslavia
West Germany **1-0** Poland

	P	W	D	L	F	A	Pts
West Germany	3	3	0	0	7	2	6
Poland	3	2	0	1	3	2	4
Sweden	3	1	0	2	4	6	2
Yugoslavia	3	0	0	3	2	6	0

THIRD-PLACE PLAY-OFF

Poland **1-0** Brazil

FINAL

West Germany **2-1** Holland

1978 ARGENTINA

GROUP 1

Argentina **2-1** Hungary
Italy **2-1** France
Argentina **2-1** France
Italy **3-1** Hungary
Italy **1-0** Argentina
France **3-1** Hungary

	P	W	D	L	F	A	Pts
Italy	3	3	0	0	6	2	6
Argentina	3	2	0	1	4	3	4
France	3	1	0	2	5	5	2
Hungary	3	0	0	3	3	8	0

GROUP 2

West Germany **0-0** Poland
Tunisia **3-1** Mexico
Poland **1-0** Tunisia
West Germany **6-0** Mexico
Poland **3-1** Mexico
West Germany **0-0** Tunisia

	P	W	D	L	F	A	Pts
Poland	3	2	1	0	4	1	5
West Germany	3	1	2	0	6	0	4
Tunisia	3	1	1	1	3	2	3
Mexico	3	0	0	3	2	12	0

GROUP 3

Austria **2-1** Spain
Sweden **1-1** Brazil
Austria **1-0** Sweden
Brazil **0-0** Spain
Spain **1-0** Sweden
Brazil **1-0** Austria

	P	W	D	L	F	A	Pts
Austria	3	2	0	1	3	2	4
Brazil	3	1	2	0	2	1	4
Spain	3	1	1	1	2	2	3
Sweden	3	0	1	2	1	3	1

GROUP 4

Peru **3-1** Scotland
Holland **3-0** Iran
Scotland **1-1** Iran
Holland **0-0** Peru
Peru **4-1** Iran
Scotland **3-2** Holland

	P	W	D	L	F	A	Pts
Peru	3	2	1	0	7	2	5
Holland	3	1	1	1	5	3	3
Scotland	3	1	1	1	5	6	3
Iran	3	0	1	2	2	8	1

SECOND ROUND GROUP A

Italy **0-0** West Germany
Holland **5-1** Austria
Italy **1-0** Austria
Holland **2-2** West Germany
Holland **2-1** Italy
Austria **3-2** West Germany

	P	W	D	L	F	A	Pts
Holland	3	2	1	0	9	4	5
Italy	3	1	1	1	2	2	3
West Germany	3	0	2	1	4	5	2
Austria	3	1	0	2	4	8	2

SECOND ROUND GROUP B

Argentina **2-0** Poland
Brazil **3-0** Peru
Argentina **0-0** Brazil
Poland **1-0** Peru
Brazil **3-1** Poland
Argentina **6-0** Peru

	P	W	D	L	F	A	Pts
Argentina	3	2	1	0	8	0	5
Brazil	3	2	1	0	6	1	5
Poland	3	1	0	2	2	5	2
Peru	3	0	0	3	0	10	0

THIRD-PLACE PLAY-OFF

Brazil **2-1** Italy

FINAL

Argentina **3-1** Holland
(aet)

1982 SPAIN

GROUP 1

Italy **0-0** Poland
Peru **0-0** Cameroon
Italy **1-1** Peru
Poland **0-0** Cameroon
Poland **5-1** Peru
Italy **1-1** Cameroon

	P	W	D	L	F	A	Pts
Poland	3	1	2	0	5	1	4
Italy	3	0	3	0	2	2	3
Cameroon	3	0	3	0	1	1	3
Peru	3	0	2	1	2	6	2

GROUP 2

Algeria **2-1** West Germany
Austria **1-0** Chile
West Germany **4-1** Chile
Austria **2-0** Algeria
Algeria **3-2** Chile
West Germany **1-0** Austria

Above: Gerry Armstrong's goal gives Northern Ireland a shock 1-0 win over hosts Spain at the 1982 World Cup.

Above: Tigana goes for the ball during France and Italy's 1986 second round clash.

	P	W	D	L	F	A	Pts
West Germany	3	2	0	1	6	3	4
Austria	3	2	0	1	3	1	4
Algeria	3	2	0	1	5	5	4
Chile	3	0	0	3	3	8	0

GROUP 3

Belgium **1-0** Argentina
Hungary **10-1** El Salvador
Argentina **4-1** Hungary
Belgium **1-0** El Salvador
Belgium **1-1** Hungary
Argentina **2-0** El Salvador

	P	W	D	L	F	A	Pts
Belgium	3	2	1	0	3	1	5
Argentina	3	2	0	1	6	2	4
Hungary	3	1	1	1	12	6	3
El Salvador	3	0	0	3	1	13	0

GROUP 4

England **3-1** France
Czechoslovakia **1-1** Kuwait
England **2-0** Czechoslovakia
France **4-1** Kuwait
France **1-1** Czechoslovakia
England **1-0** Kuwait

	P	W	D	L	F	A	Pts
England	3	3	0	0	6	1	6
France	3	1	1	1	6	5	3
Czechoslovakia	3	0	2	1	2	4	2
Kuwait	3	0	1	2	2	6	1

GROUP 5

Spain **1-1** Honduras
Northern Ireland **0-0** Yugoslavia
Spain **2-1** Yugoslavia
Northern Ireland **1-1** Honduras
Yugoslavia **1-0** Honduras
Northern Ireland **1-0** Spain

	P	W	D	L	F	A	Pts
Northern Ireland	3	1	2	0	2	1	4
Spain	3	1	1	1	3	3	3
Yugoslavia	3	1	1	1	2	2	3
Honduras	3	0	2	1	2	3	2

GROUP 6

Brazil **2-1** Soviet Union
Scotland **5-2** New Zealand
Brazil **4-1** Scotland
Soviet Union **3-0** New Zealand
Scotland **2-2** Soviet Union
Brazil **4-0** New Zealand

	P	W	D	L	F	A	Pts
Brazil	3	3	0	0	10	2	6
Soviet Union	3	1	1	1	6	4	3
Scotland	3	1	1	1	8	8	3
New Zealand	3	0	0	3	2	12	0

SECOND ROUND GROUP A

Poland **3-0** Belgium
Soviet Union **1-0** Belgium
Soviet Union **0-0** Poland

	P	W	D	L	F	A	Pts
Poland	2	1	1	0	3	0	3
Soviet Union	2	1	1	0	1	0	3
Belgium	2	0	0	2	0	4	0

SECOND ROUND GROUP B

West Germany **0-0** England
West Germany **2-1** Spain
England **0-0** Spain

	P	W	D	L	F	A	Pts
West Germany	2	1	1	0	2	1	3
England	2	0	2	0	0	0	2
Spain	2	0	1	1	1	2	1

SECOND ROUND GROUP C

Italy **2-1** Argentina
Brazil **3-1** Argentina
Italy **3-2** Brazil

	P	W	D	L	F	A	Pts
Italy	2	2	0	0	5	3	4
Brazil	2	1	0	1	5	4	2
Argentina	2	0	0	2	2	5	0

SECOND ROUND GROUP D

France **1-0** Austria
Northern Ireland **2-2** Austria
France **4-1** Northern Ireland

	P	W	D	L	F	A	Pts
France	2	2	0	0	5	1	4
Austria	2	0	1	1	2	3	1
Northern Ireland	2	0	1	1	3	6	1

SEMI-FINALS

Italy **2-0** Poland
West Germany **3-3** France
(aet)
West Germany won 5-4 on penalties

THIRD PLACE PLAY-OFF

Poland **3-2** France

FINAL

Italy **3-1** West Germany

1986 MEXICO

GROUP A

Bulgaria **1-1** Italy
Argentina **3-1** South Korea
Italy **1-1** Argentina
Bulgaria **1-1** South Korea
Argentina **2-0** Bulgaria
Italy **3-2** South Korea

	P	W	D	L	F	A	Pts
Argentina	3	2	1	0	6	2	5
Italy	3	1	2	0	5	4	4
Bulgaria	3	0	2	1	2	4	2
South Korea	3	0	1	2	4	7	1

GROUP B

Mexico **2-1** Belgium
Paraguay **1-0** Iraq
Mexico **1-1** Paraguay
Belgium **2-1** Iraq
Paraguay **2-2** Belgium
Mexico **1-0** Iraq

	P	W	D	L	F	A	Pts
Mexico	3	2	1	0	4	2	5
Paraguay	3	1	2	0	4	3	4
Belgium	3	1	1	1	5	5	3
Iraq	3	0	0	3	1	4	0

GROUP C

Soviet Union **6-0** Hungary
France **1-0** Canada
Soviet Union **1-1** France
Hungary **2-0** Canada
France **3-0** Hungary
Soviet Union **2-0** Canada

	P	W	D	L	F	A	Pts
Soviet Union	3	2	1	0	9	1	5
France	3	2	1	0	5	1	5
Hungary	3	1	0	2	2	9	2
Canada	3	0	0	3	0	5	0

GROUP D

Brazil **1-0** Spain
Northern Ireland **1-1** Algeria
Spain **2-1** Northern Ireland
Brazil **1-0** Algeria
Spain **3-0** Algeria
Brazil **3-0** Northern Ireland

	P	W	D	L	F	A	Pts
Brazil	3	3	0	0	5	0	6
Spain	3	2	0	1	5	2	4
Northern Ireland	3	0	1	2	2	6	1
Algeria	3	0	1	2	1	5	1

GROUP E

West Germany **1-1** Uruguay
Denmark **1-0** Scotland
Denmark **6-1** Uruguay
West Germany **2-1** Scotland
Scotland **0-0** Uruguay
Denmark **2-0** West Germany

	P	W	D	L	F	A	Pts
Denmark	3	3	0	0	9	1	6
West Germany	3	1	1	1	3	4	3
Uruguay	3	0	2	1	2	7	2
Scotland	3	0	1	2	1	3	1

GROUP F

Morocco **0-0** Poland
Portugal **1-0** England
England **0-0** Morocco
Poland **1-0** Portugal
England **3-0** Poland
Morocco **3-1** Portugal

	P	W	D	L	F	A	Pts
Morocco	3	1	2	0	3	1	4
England	3	1	1	1	3	1	3
Poland	3	1	1	1	1	3	3
Portugal	3	1	0	2	2	4	2

SECOND ROUND

Mexico **2-0** Bulgaria
Belgium **4-3** Soviet Union
(aet)
Brazil **4-0** Poland
Argentina **1-0** Uruguay
France **2-0** Italy
West Germany **1-0** Morocco
England **3-0** Paraguay
Spain **5-1** Denmark

QUARTER-FINALS

France **1-1** Brazil
(aet)
France won 4-3 on penalties
West Germany **0-0** Mexico
(aet)
West Germany won 4-1 on penalties
Argentina **2-1** England
Spain **1-1** Belgium
(aet)
Belgium won 5-4 on penalties

SEMI-FINALS

Argentina **2-0** Belgium
West Germany **2-0** France

THIRD PLACE PLAY-OFF

France **4-2** Belgium

FINAL

Argentina **3-2** West Germany

1990 ITALY

GROUP A

Italy **1-0** Austria
Czechoslovakia **5-1** USA
Italy **1-0** USA
Czechoslovakia **1-0** Austria
Italy **2-0** Czechoslovakia
Austria **2-1** USA

	P	W	D	L	F	A	Pts
Italy	3	3	0	0	4	0	6
Czechoslovakia	3	2	0	1	6	3	4
Austria	3	1	0	2	2	3	2
USA	3	0	0	3	2	8	0

GROUP B

Cameroon **1-0** Argentina
Romania **2-0** Soviet Union
Argentina **2-0** Soviet Union
Cameroon **2-1** Romania
Argentina **1-1** Romania
Soviet Union **4-0** Cameroon

	P	W	D	L	F	A	Pts
Cameroon	3	2	0	1	3	5	4
Romania	3	1	1	1	4	3	3
Argentina	3	1	1	1	3	2	3
Soviet Union	3	1	0	2	4	4	2

GROUP C

Brazil **2-1** Sweden
Costa Rica **1-0** Scotland
Brazil **1-0** Costa Rica
Scotland **2-1** Sweden
Brazil **1-0** Scotland
Costa Rica **2-1** Sweden

	P	W	D	L	F	A	Pts
Brazil	3	3	0	0	4	1	6
Costa Rica	3	2	0	1	3	2	4
Scotland	3	1	0	2	2	3	2
Sweden	3	0	0	3	3	6	0

GROUP D

Colombia **2-0** UAE
West Germany **4-1** Yugoslavia
Yugoslavia **1-0** Colombia
West Germany **5-1** UAE
West Germany **1-1** Colombia
Yugoslavia **4-1** UAE

	P	W	D	L	F	A	Pts
West Germany	3	2	1	0	10	3	5
Yugoslavia	3	2	0	1	6	5	4
Colombia	3	1	1	1	3	2	3
UAE	3	0	0	3	2	11	0

Above: David Platt's last gasp extra time volley sends England into the 1990 quarter-finals at Belgium's expense.

WORLD CUP RESULTS

Above: Letchkov celebrates the goal that gave Bulgaria a shock win over Germany and took them to the USA 94 semi-finals.

GROUP E

Belgium **2-0** South Korea
Uruguay **0-0** Spain
Belgium **3-1** Uruguay
Spain **3-1** South Korea
Spain **2-1** Belgium
Uruguay **1-0** South Korea

	P	W	D	L	F	A	Pts
Spain	3	2	1	0	5	2	5
Belgium	3	2	0	1	6	3	4
Uruguay	3	1	1	1	2	3	3
South Korea	3	0	0	3	1	6	0

GROUP F

England **1-1** Rep. Of Ireland
Holland **1-1** Egypt
England **0-0** Holland
Egypt **0-0** Rep. Of Ireland
England **1-0** Egypt
Holland **1-1** Rep. Of Ireland

	P	W	D	L	F	A	Pts
England	3	1	2	0	2	1	4
Rep. Of Ireland	3	0	3	0	2	2	3
Holland	3	0	3	0	2	2	3
Egypt	3	0	2	1	1	2	2

SECOND ROUND

Cameroon **2-1** Colombia
(aet)
Czechoslovakia **4-1** Costa Rica
Argentina **1-0** Brazil
West Germany **2-1** Holland
Rep. Of Ireland **0-0** Romania
(aet)
Rep. Of Ireland won 5-4 on penalties
Italy **2-0** Uruguay
Yugoslavia **2-1** Spain
(aet)
England **1-0** Belgium
(aet)

QUARTER-FINALS

Argentina **0-0** Yugoslavia
(aet)
Argentina won 3-2 on penalties

Italy **1-0** Rep. Of Ireland
West Germany **1-0** Czechoslovakia
England **3-2** Cameroon
(aet)

SEMI-FINALS

Argentina **1-1** Italy
(aet)
Argentina won 4-3 on penalties
West Germany **1-1** England
(aet)
West Germany won 4-3 on penalties

THIRD-PLACE PLAY-OFF

Italy **2-1** England

FINAL

West Germany **1-0** Argentina

1994 USA

GROUP A

USA **1-1** Switzerland
Colombia **1-3** Romania
USA **2-1** Colombia
Romania **1-4** Switzerland
USA **0-1** Romania
Switzerland **0-2** Colombia

	P	W	D	L	F	A	Pts
Romania	3	2	0	1	5	5	6
Switzerland	3	1	1	1	5	4	4
USA	3	1	1	1	3	3	4
Colombia	3	1	0	2	4	5	3

GROUP B

Cameroon **2-2** Sweden
Brazil **2-0** Russia
Brazil **3-0** Cameroon
Sweden **3-1** Russia
Russia **6-1** Cameroon
Brazil **1-1** Sweden

	P	W	D	L	F	A	Pts
Brazil	3	2	1	0	6	1	7
Sweden	3	1	2	0	6	4	5
Russia	3	1	0	2	7	6	3
Cameroon	3	0	1	2	3	11	1

GROUP C

Germany **1-0** Bolivia
Spain **2-2** South Korea
Germany **1-1** Spain
South Korea **0-0** Bolivia
Bolivia **1-3** Spain
Germany **3-2** South Korea

	P	W	D	L	F	A	Pts
Germany	3	2	1	0	5	3	7
Spain	3	1	2	0	6	4	5
South Korea	3	0	2	1	4	5	2
Bolivia	3	0	1	2	1	4	1

GROUP D

Argentina **4-0** Greece
Nigeria **3-0** Bulgaria
Argentina **2-1** Nigeria
Bulgaria **4-0** Greece
Greece **0-2** Nigeria
Argentina **0-2** Bulgaria

	P	W	D	L	F	A	Pts
Nigeria	3	2	0	1	6	2	6
Bulgaria	3	2	0	1	6	3	6
Argentina	3	2	0	1	6	3	6
Greece	3	0	0	3	0	10	0

GROUP E

Italy **0-1** Rep. Of Ireland
Norway **1-0** Mexico
Italy **1-0** Norway
Mexico **2-1** Rep. Of Ireland
Rep. Of Ireland **0-0** Norway
Italy **1-1** Mexico

	P	W	D	L	F	A	Pts
Mexico	3	1	1	1	3	3	4
Rep. Of Ireland	3	1	1	1	2	2	4
Italy	3	1	1	1	2	2	4
Norway	3	1	1	1	1	1	4

GROUP F

Belgium **1-0** Morocco
Holland **2-1** Saudi Arabia
Belgium **1-0** Holland
Saudi Arabia **2-1** Morocco

Morocco **1-2** Holland
Belgium **0-1** Saudi Arabia

	P	W	D	L	F	A	Pts
Holland	3	2	0	1	4	3	6
Saudi Arabia	3	2	0	1	4	3	6
Belgium	3	2	0	1	2	1	6
Morocco	3	0	0	3	2	5	0

SECOND ROUND

Germany **3-2** Belgium
Spain **3-0** Switzerland
Saudi Arabia **1-3** Sweden
Romania **3-2** Argentina
Holland **2-0** Rep. Of Ireland
Brazil **1-0** USA
Nigeria **1-2** Italy
(aet)
Mexico **1-1** Bulgaria
(aet)
Bulgaria won 3-1 on penalties

QUARTER-FINALS

Italy **2-1** Spain
Holland **2-3** Brazil
Germany **1-2** Bulgaria
Sweden **2-2** Romania
(aet)
Sweden won 5-4 on penalties

SEMI-FINALS

Brazil **1-0** Sweden
Italy **2-1** Bulgaria

THIRD PLACE PLAY-OFF

Sweden **4-0** Bulgaria

FINAL

Brazil **0-0** Italy
(aet)
Brazil won 3-2 on penalties

1998 FRANCE

GROUP A

Brazil **2-1** Scotland
Morocco **2-2** Norway
Brazil **3-0** Morocco
Scotland **1-1** Norway
Brazil **1-2** Norway
Scotland **0-3** Morocco

	P	W	D	L	F	A	Pts
Brazil	3	2	0	1	6	3	6
Norway	3	1	2	0	5	4	5
Morocco	3	1	1	1	5	5	4
Scotland	3	0	1	2	2	6	1

Above: Marc Overmars helps Holland see off South Korea in 1998.

GROUP B

Italy **2-2** Chile
Austria **1-1** Cameroon
Chile **1-1** Austria
Italy **3-0** Cameroon
Chile **1-1** Cameroon
Italy **2-1** Austria

	P	W	D	L	F	A	Pts
Italy	3	2	1	0	7	3	7
Chile	3	0	3	0	4	4	3
Austria	3	0	2	1	3	4	2
Cameroon	3	0	2	1	2	5	2

GROUP C

Saudi Arabia **0-1** Denmark
France **3-0** South Africa
France **4-0** Saudi Arabia
South Africa **1-1** Denmark
France **2-1** Denmark
South Africa **2-2** Saudi Arabia

	P	W	D	L	F	A	Pts
France	3	3	0	0	9	1	9
Denmark	3	1	1	1	3	3	4
South Africa	3	0	2	1	3	6	2
Saudi Arabia	3	0	1	2	2	7	1

GROUP D

Paraguay **0-0** Bulgaria
Spain **2-3** Nigeria
Nigeria **1-0** Bulgaria
Spain **0-0** Paraguay
Nigeria **1-3** Paraguay
Spain **6-1** Bulgaria

	P	W	D	L	F	A	Pts
Nigeria	3	2	0	1	5	5	6
Paraguay	3	1	2	0	3	1	5
Spain	3	1	1	1	8	4	4
Bulgaria	3	0	1	2	1	7	1

GROUP E

South Korea **1-3** Mexico
Holland **0-0** Belgium
Belgium **2-2** Mexico
Holland **5-0** South Korea
Belgium **1-1** South Korea
Holland **2-2** Mexico

	P	W	D	L	F	A	Pts
Holland	3	1	2	0	7	2	5
Mexico	3	1	2	0	7	5	5
Belgium	3	0	3	0	3	3	3
South Korea	3	0	1	2	2	9	1

GROUP F

Germany **2-0** USA
Yugoslavia **1-0** Iran
Germany **2-2** Yugoslavia
USA **1-2** Iran
Germany **2-0** Iran
USA **0-1** Yugoslavia

	P	W	D	L	F	A	Pts
Germany	3	2	1	0	6	2	7
Yugoslavia	3	2	1	0	4	2	7
Iran	3	1	0	2	2	4	3
USA	3	0	0	3	1	5	0

GROUP G

England **2-0** Tunisia
Romania **1-0** Colombia
Colombia **1-0** Tunisia
Romania **2-1** England
Romania **1-1** Tunisia
Colombia **0-2** England

	P	W	D	L	F	A	Pts
Romania	3	2	1	0	4	2	7
England	3	2	0	1	5	2	6
Colombia	3	1	0	2	1	3	3
Tunisia	3	0	1	2	1	4	1

GROUP H

Argentina **1-0** Japan
Jamaica **1-3** Croatia
Japan **0-1** Croatia
Argentina **5-0** Jamaica
Argentina **1-0** Croatia
Japan **1-2** Jamaica

	P	W	D	L	F	A	Pts
Argentina	3	3	0	0	7	0	9
Croatia	3	2	0	1	4	2	6
Jamaica	3	1	0	2	3	9	3
Japan	3	0	0	3	1	4	0

SECOND ROUND

Italy **1-0** Norway
Brazil **4-1** Chile
France **1-0** Paraguay
(aet)
France won with golden goal
Nigeria **1-4** Denmark
Germany **2-1** Mexico
Holland **2-1** Yugoslavia
Romania **0-1** Croatia
Argentina **2-2** England
(aet)
Argentina won 4-3 on penalties

Above: Francesco Totti's Italy crashed controversially out of the 2002 World Cup.

QUARTER-FINALS

Italy **0-0** France
(aet)
France won 4-3 on penalties
Brazil **3-2** Denmark
Holland **2-1** Argentina
Germany **0-3** Croatia

SEMI-FINALS

Brazil **1-1** Holland
(aet)
Brazil won 4-2 on penalties
France **2-1** Croatia

THIRD-PLACE PLAY-OFF

Holland **1-2** Croatia

FINAL

Brazil **0-3** France

2002 KOREA/JAPAN

GROUP A

France **0-1** Senegal
Uruguay **1-2** Denmark
Denmark **1-1** Senegal
France **0-0** Uruguay
Senegal **3-3** Uruguay
Denmark **2-0** France

	P	W	D	L	F	A	Pts
Denmark	3	2	1	0	5	2	7
Senegal	3	1	2	0	5	4	5
Uruguay	3	0	2	1	4	5	2
France	3	0	1	2	0	3	1

GROUP B

Paraguay **2-2** South Africa
Spain **3-1** Slovenia
Spain **3-1** Paraguay
South Africa **1-0** Slovenia
South Africa **2-3** Spain
Slovenia **1-3** Paraguay

	P	W	D	L	F	A	Pts
Spain	3	3	0	0	9	4	9
Paraguay	3	1	1	1	6	6	4
South Africa	3	1	1	1	5	5	4
Slovenia	3	0	0	3	2	7	0

GROUP C

Brazil **2-1** Turkey
China **0-2** Costa Rica
Brazil **4-0** China
Costa Rica **1-1** Turkey
Costa Rica **2-5** Brazil
Turkey **3-0** China

	P	W	D	L	F	A	Pts
Brazil	3	3	0	0	11	3	9
Turkey	3	1	1	1	5	3	4
Costa Rica	3	1	1	1	5	6	4
China	3	0	0	3	0	9	0

GROUP D

South Korea **2-0** Poland
USA **3-2** Portugal
South Korea **1-1** USA
Portugal **4-0** Poland
Portugal **0-1** South Korea
Poland **3-1** USA

	P	W	D	L	F	A	Pts
South Korea	3	2	1	0	4	1	7
USA	3	1	1	1	5	6	4
Portugal	3	1	0	2	6	4	3
Poland	3	1	0	2	3	7	3

GROUP E

Rep. Of Ireland **1-1** Cameroon
Germany **8-0** Saudi Arabia
Germany **1-1** Rep. Of Ireland
Cameroon **1-0** Saudi Arabia
Cameroon **0-2** Germany
Saudi Arabia **0-3** Rep. Of Ireland

	P	W	D	L	F	A	Pts
Germany	3	2	1	0	11	1	7
Rep. Of Ireland	3	1	2	0	5	2	5
Cameroon	3	1	1	1	2	3	4
Saudi Arabia	3	0	0	3	0	12	0

GROUP F

Argentina **1-0** Nigeria
England **1-1** Sweden
Sweden **2-1** Nigeria
Argentina **0-1** England
Sweden **1-1** Argentina
Nigeria **0-0** England

	P	W	D	L	F	A	Pts
Sweden	3	1	2	0	4	3	5
England	3	1	2	0	2	1	5
Argentina	3	1	1	1	2	2	4
Nigeria	3	0	1	2	1	3	1

GROUP G

Croatia **0-1** Mexico
Italy **2-0** Ecuador
Italy **1-2** Croatia
Mexico **2-1** Ecuador
Mexico **1-1** Italy
Ecuador **1-0** Croatia

	P	W	D	L	F	A	Pts
Mexico	3	2	1	0	4	2	7
Italy	3	1	1	1	4	3	4
Croatia	3	1	0	2	2	3	3
Ecuador	3	1	0	2	2	4	3

GROUP H

Japan **2-2** Belgium
Russia **2-0** Tunisia
Japan **1-0** Russia
Tunisia **1-1** Belgium
Tunisia **0-2** Japan
Belgium **3-2** Russia

	P	W	D	L	F	A	Pts
Japan	3	2	1	0	5	2	7
Belgium	3	1	2	0	6	5	5
Russia	3	1	0	2	4	4	3
Tunisia	3	0	1	2	1	5	1

2ND ROUND

Germany **1-0** Paraguay
Denmark **0-3** England
Sweden **1-2** Senegal
(aet)
Senegal won with golden goal
Spain **1-1** Rep. Of Ireland
(aet)
Spain won 3-2 on penalties
Mexico **0-2** USA
Brazil **2-0** Belgium
Japan **0-1** Turkey
South Korea **2-1** Italy
(aet)
South Korea won with golden goal

QUARTER-FINALS

England **1-2** Brazil
Germany **1-0** USA
Spain **0-0** South Korea
(aet)
South Korea won 5-3 on penalties
Senegal **0-1** Turkey
(aet)
Turkey won with golden goal

SEMI-FINALS

Germany **1-0** South Korea
Brazil **1-0** Turkey

THIRD PLACE MATCH

South Korea **2-3** Turkey

FINAL

Germany **0-2** Brazil

Above: Rivaldo celebrates after Brazil win the World Cup for the fifth time at Korea/Japan 2002, beating Germany 2-0 in the final.

THE EUROPEAN CHAMPIONSHIP

THE EUROPEAN CHAMPIONSHIP

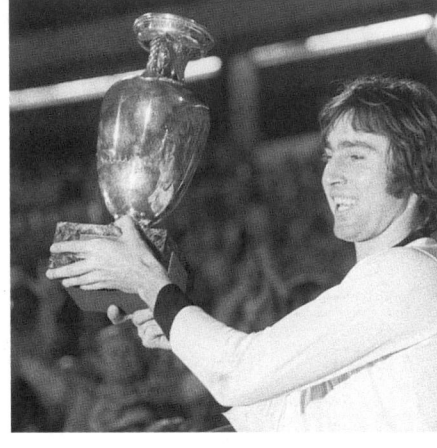

Above from left to right: Jurgen Klinsmann accepts the trophy from the Queen in 1996; Czechoslovakia enjoy their 1976 win after beating West Germany on penalties; Denmark proved unlikely winners in 1992, only qualifying as late replacements for suspended Yugoslavia.

The European Championship is the most prestigious European competition for national teams, and falls second in significance only to the World Cup in the football pecking order. It is contested every four years, and the finals are staged two years after (and hence two years before) the World Cup. The championship is open to all members of UEFA.

As early as 1927 Henri Delauney, head of the French FA, proposed the idea of a championship involving the top European countries – he was also a driving force behind the foundation of the World Cup. However, after the setting up of UEFA on June 15, 1954, the idea was raised once again, and two years later the planning got underway for the competition Delauney had dreamed of. Sadly, he passed away in 1955, but in his honour the trophy played for will forever hold his name.

In 1958, the first qualifying matches for the European Nations' Cup were played. The format for the early tournament remained in place for some time, and consisted of a series of two-legged qualifying rounds, played home and away, producing four finalists who would contest the semi-finals and final in a host country – with these games to be played over the space of a week.

Appropriately enough in the summer of 1960, the first finals of the European Nations' Cup were held in Delauney's native France. Just like the World Cup, the inaugural competition could not remain unspoilt by world politics. The quarter-finals drew the Soviet Union against Spain, whose fascist dictator Franco refused the Communist side entry to his country, and in so doing forfeited the tie. This worked in the USSR's favour, as they ran out eventual winners under the inspirational leadership of Lev Yashin, beating Yugoslavia 2-1 in the first ever final.

Hosts Spain and Italy ran out winners in 1964 and 1968 respectively, a sequence that was broken by West Germany in 1972 – but even then they were given a scare by hosts Belgium in a close fought semi-final. This tournament was also notable for the change of name from the unwieldy European Nations' Cup to the European Championship.

In 1976 the tournament was held in an Eastern Bloc country for the first time with Yugoslavia hosting. Quarter-finals were added to the existing format for the first time as well, and yet another first was created in the final when a spirited Czech side held the holders West Germany to a draw, and the game was decided on penalties. The Czechs held their nerve and ran out 5-3 winners, with Antonin Panenka famously dinking his penalty over a stranded Sepp Maier to claim the trophy.

The 1980 competition saw the final stage format change again with the quarter-final and semi-final stages dispensed with, and eight teams competing in two mini-leagues, with the winners of both groups advancing directly to the final. Once again the strength of West Germany saw them through – where they narrowly defeated Belgium with a late goal from match-winner Horst Hrubesch.

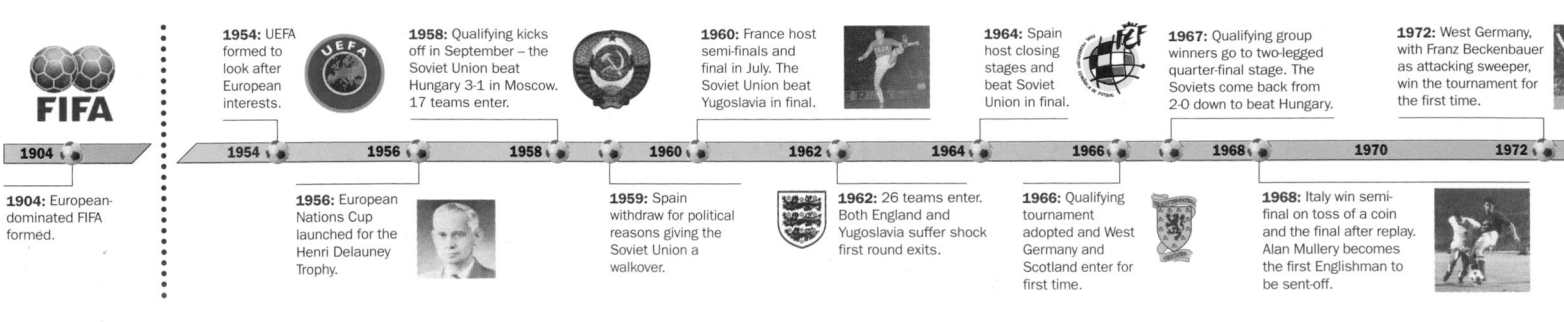

1954: UEFA formed to look after European interests.

1958: Qualifying kicks off in September – the Soviet Union beat Hungary 3-1 in Moscow. 17 teams enter.

1960: France host semi-finals and final in July. The Soviet Union beat Yugoslavia in final.

1964: Spain host closing stages and beat Soviet Union in final.

1967: Qualifying group winners go to two-legged quarter-final stage. The Soviets come back from 2-0 down to beat Hungary.

1972: West Germany, with Franz Beckenbauer as attacking sweeper, win the tournament for the first time.

1904: European-dominated FIFA formed.

1956: European Nations Cup launched for the Henri Delauney Trophy.

1959: Spain withdraw for political reasons giving the Soviet Union a walkover.

1962: 26 teams enter. Both England and Yugoslavia suffer shock first round exits.

1966: Qualifying tournament adopted and West Germany and Scotland enter for first time.

1968: Italy win semi-final on toss of a coin and the final after replay. Alan Mullery becomes the first Englishman to be sent-off.

EUROPEAN CHAMPIONSHIP WINNERS & HOST NATIONS

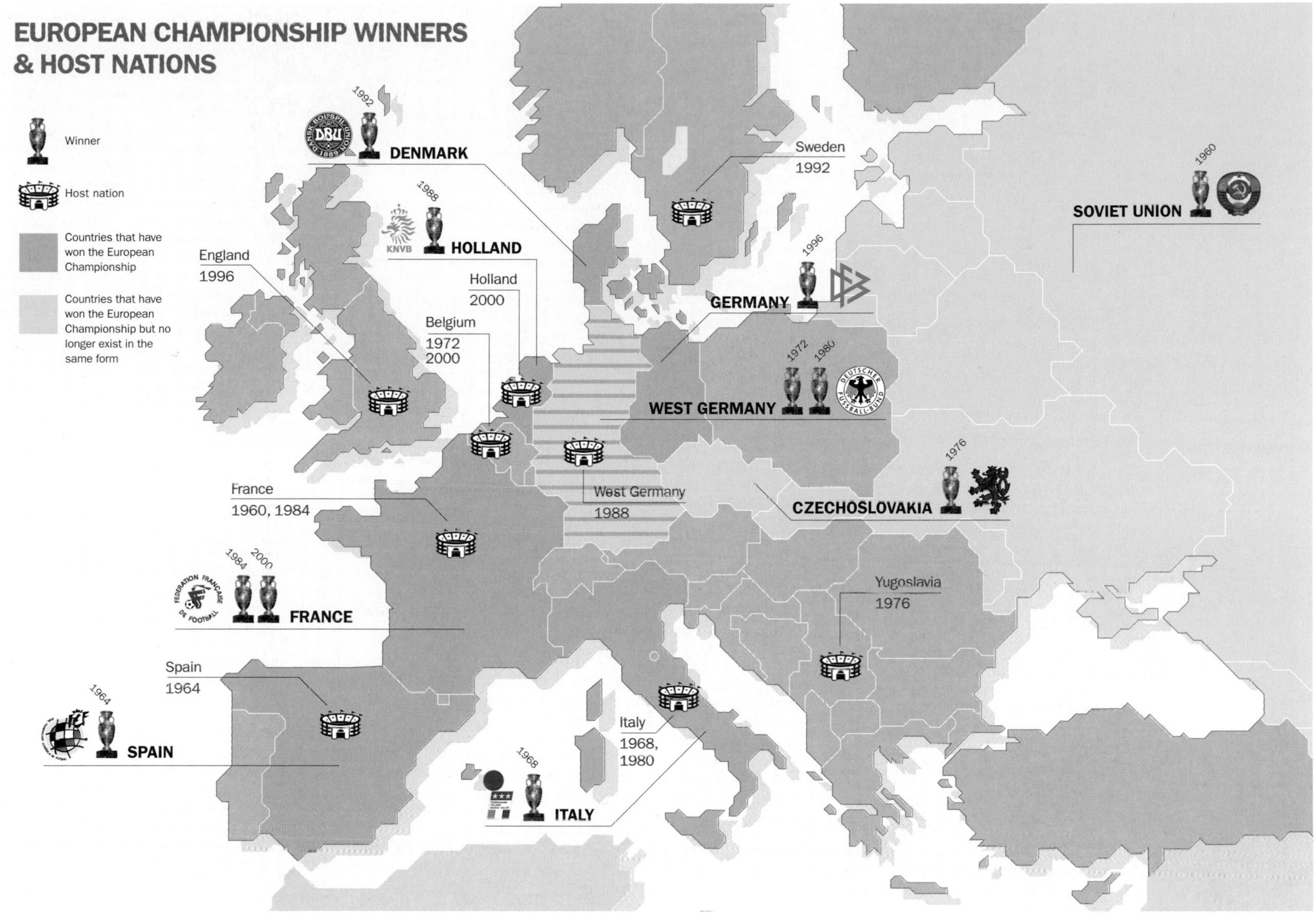

Winner

Host nation

Countries that have won the European Championship

Countries that have won the European Championship but no longer exist in the same form

DENMARK 1992

Sweden 1992

SOVIET UNION 1960

England 1996

HOLLAND 1988

Holland 2000

GERMANY 1996

Belgium 1972 2000

WEST GERMANY 1972 1980

France 1960, 1984

West Germany 1988

CZECHOSLOVAKIA 1976

Yugoslavia 1976

Spain 1964

Italy 1968, 1980

FRANCE 1984 2000

SPAIN 1964

Italy 1968

ITALY

Forever tinkering with the format, UEFA reintroduced semi-finals to the tournament in 1984, with the top two teams from each group playing for a place in the final. France, under the inspirational captaincy of Michel Platini swept all other teams aside, and for the third time in seven tournaments it was the hosts who claimed victory.

The format for the final stages of the 1988 and 1992 European Championships remained unaltered. The tournaments are best remembered for Dutch master Marco Van Basten's wonderstrike in the final against the Soviet Union in 1988, and Denmark almost literally coming from nowhere to defeat the Germans in 1992. Having failed to qualify, Denmark were only playing as last-minute replacements for the suspended Yugoslavia.

The success of the tournament saw further expansion in 1996 with 16 teams competing in four leagues to produce eight quarter-finalists. This was the tournament when football came home, as the success of Euro 96 went a long way to rehabilitating the reputation of English football both on and off the pitch. Despite this, it was still Germany who claimed the trophy. A close final against the Czech Republic was notable for Oliver Bierhoff's 94th minute goal – it was the first time a golden goal winner had decided the outcome of a major international competition. Four years later, and France's David Trezeguet would be repeating the trick against Italy to conclude another wonderful final.

The European Championship is to be held in Portugal in 2004. It is testament to a tournament that has grown in strength and prestige every time it has been played that all the football nations of Europe are now not only determined to qualify for the finals, but are also desperate to get their hands on the Henri Delauney Trophy.

PLAYER RATINGS

In our coverage of European Championship finals over the following pages, all available footage and match reports have been studied by an independent expert, with players awarded marks out of ten for their performance.

Red and yellow card information not available before 1984.

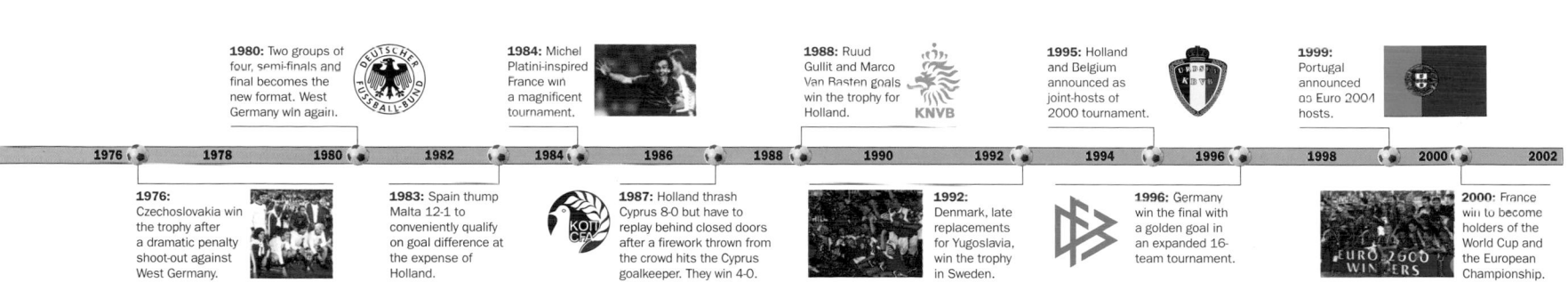

1980: Two groups of four, semi-finals and final becomes the new format. West Germany win again.

1984: Michel Platini-inspired France win a magnificent tournament.

1988: Ruud Gullit and Marco Van Basten goals win the trophy for Holland.

1995: Holland and Belgium announced as joint-hosts of 2000 tournament.

1999: Portugal announced as Euro 2004 hosts.

1976	1978	1980	1982	1984	1986	1988	1990	1992	1994	1996	1998	2000	2002

1976: Czechoslovakia win the trophy after a dramatic penalty shoot-out against West Germany.

1983: Spain thump Malta 12-1 to conveniently qualify on goal difference at the expense of Holland.

1987: Holland thrash Cyprus 8-0 but have to replay behind closed doors after a firework thrown from the crowd hits the Cyprus goalkeeper. They win 4-0.

1992: Denmark, late replacements for Yugoslavia, win the trophy in Sweden.

1996: Germany win the final with a golden goal in an expanded 16-team tournament.

2000: France win to become holders of the World Cup and the European Championship.

FRANCE 1960

France has provided the game with some of its greatest visionaries. So it is no real surprise to discover that it was a Frenchman, Henri Delaunay, head of the French Football Federation, who came up with the idea for a tournament between Europe's top nations.

The European Championship, or The European Nations Cup as it was originally called, was finally established at the third UEFA Congress in Stockholm on June 6, 1958, but Delaunay had actually conceived the idea as far back as 1927. At that time, however, getting the World Cup off the ground was the priority. It was Delaunay who chaired the original commission set up by Jules Rimet in 1926 to look into a world football tournament and this took precedence.

When UEFA was created in 1954 Delaunay became its general secretary and rapidly installed two competitions, one for club teams and one for national sides. His aim was to bring into a single competition the three regional tournaments that already existed: the British Home Championship, the Nordic Cup and the Central European Championship. Sadly, Delaunay died in 1955 before he could see his scheme fulfilled, but his son Pierre took over the reins and the trophy was named in his father's honour.

It was agreed to hold the tournament once every four years, in between the World Cups, but UEFA initially struggled to find enough countries who were willing to compete and much behind the scenes negotiating went on to ensure that there was a competitive first tournament. The cause was not helped by the predictable refusal of British teams, fearing the end of the Home Internationals, to participate. Other refuseniks included 1958 World Cup hosts and runners-up Sweden, along with West Germany and Italy.

In the end 17 out of 33 countries affiliated to UEFA agreed to take part, and after a two-legged eliminator between Ireland and Czechoslovakia had whittled the number of sides down to an even 16 for the qualifiers, the first match in the European Nations Cup was played between the Soviet Union and Hungary.

The remaining 14 nationals to enter the qualifying phase were Austria, Bulgaria, Czechoslovakia, Denmark, France, West Germany, Greece, Norway, Poland, Portugal, Romania, Spain, Turkey, and Yugoslavia. The entry fee was £50 and it was agreed gate receipts would be split 50-50 between FIFA and UEFA. The initial structure of the competition was very different from the European Championship as we know it today. Teams played home and away matches, the losing team being eliminated, and the winner proceeding to the next round.

There were further problems, too, when Spain were drawn against the Soviet Union. Under Helenio Herrera, and with stars like Di Stéfano, Suarez and Gento in their squad, the Spanish would have been strong contenders. However, Spain's fascist dictator at the time, General Franco, refused to allow his nation to play against the Communists, Spain losing by default and putting the Soviets through to the semi-finals. Thus four games, the semi-finals, the third place play-off and the final, constituted the tournament proper and were played over five days between July 6 and 10 in Paris and Marseilles.

The hosts had to qualify like the other sides and beat Austria convincingly to go through to a semi-final against Yugoslavia, a game which proved to be the most emotionally charged game of the tournament. The French, third in the 1958 World Cup, were without Raymond Kopa and Golden Boot winner Just Fontaine, but put on a good performance coming back from an early goal deficit and leading Yugoslavia 4-2 just 15 minutes before the final whistle. However, Tomislav Knez started the comeback and a brace by Drazen Jerkovic was enough to knock France out and stun the host nation.

The Soviet Union proved much too strong for Czechoslovakia in the other semi-final, with Victor Ponedelnik, a poacher in the Jimmy Greaves mould, scoring twice as the USSR eased to a 3-0 win that brought them face to face with Yugoslavia in the final.

The match was a repeat of the 1956 Olympic Games final in Melbourne, which had been won 1-0 by the USSR. Whether this gave them a psychological advantage as the teams lined-up in the early evening at the Parc Des Princes is unclear, but the Soviets were to prove too strong for their opponents once more. They became the first team to lift the Henri Delaunay trophy after coming through in extra-time to win 2-1 and claim their first and only major tournament victory.

SEMI-FINALS
Soviet Union 3-0 Czechoslovakia
Yugoslavia 5-4 France

THIRD PLACE PLAY-OFF
Czechoslovakia 2-0 France

TOP GOALSCORERS
2 goals: François Heutte (France), Valentin Ivanov (Soviet Union), Victor Ponedelnik (Soviet Union), Milan Galic (Yugoslavia), Drazen Jerkovic (Yugoslavia)

FASTEST GOAL
11 minutes: Milan Gallic (Yugoslavia v France)

TOTAL GOALS
17

AVERAGE GOALS
4.25 per game

Above: Hosts France took a 4-2 lead in their semi-final with Yugoslavia, only to be undone by three goals in the last 15 minutes. Opposite: The USSR and Yugoslavia battle out the first European Championship final under floodlights.

THE FINAL

SOVIET UNION (0) 2-1 (1) YUGOSLAVIA
(aet; 1-1 at 90 minutes)

Date Sunday July 10, 1960 **Attendance** 18,000

Venue Parc Des Princes, Paris

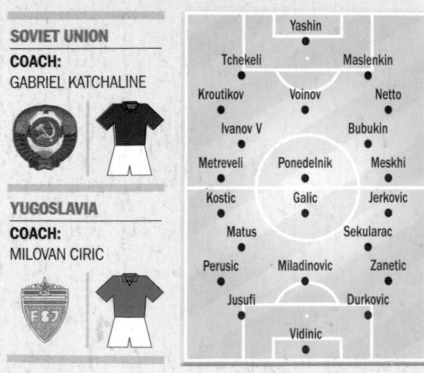

Played under floodlights in persistent drizzle on a heavy pitch, the inaugural European Nations Cup final was a credit to both sides. The conditions favoured the more technical skills of the Yugoslavs and they started strongly, eventually taking the lead in the 43rd minute as Galic nodded home after a cross by Erkovic.

The Yugoslavs should have capitalised on several more opportunities, but Lev Yashin made some spectacular saves. Four minutes into the second half the Soviets equalised through Metreveli and the match became increasingly tactical until the final whistle found both teams locked at 1-1. The Soviets proved stronger in extra-time and in the 113th minute, Ponedelnik headed home from Meskhi's cross.

SOVIET UNION	
YASHIN	*8
TCHEKELI	6
MASLENKIN	6
KROUTIKOV	7
VOINOV	7
NETTO	7
IVANOV V	7
BUBUKIN	6
METREVELI ⚽	7
Goal: 49 mins	
PONEDELNIK ⚽	7
Goal: 114 mins	
MESKHI	6

YUGOSLAVIA	
VIDINIC	*8
DURKOVIC	6
JUSUFI	7
ZANETIC	5
MILADINOVIC	6
PERUSIC	6
SEKULARAC	5
MATUS	6
JERKOVIC	7
GALIC ⚽	7
Goal: 41 mins	
KOSTIC	6

Referee: Ellis (England)

HOW THE TEAMS LINED UP

SOVIET UNION
COACH: GABRIEL KATCHALINE

Yashin
Tchekeli — Maslenkin
Kroutikov — Voinov — Netto
Ivanov V — Bubukin
Metreveli — Ponedelnik — Meskhi

YUGOSLAVIA
COACH: MILOVAN CIRIC

Kostic — Galic — Jerkovic
Matus — Sekularac
Perusic — Miladinovic — Zanetic
Jusufi — Durkovic
Vidinic

Above: Spain celebrate winning the Nations Cup on home soil. Opposite: Soviet Union goalkeeper Lev Yashin concedes the opening goal in the final.

SPAIN 1964

The European Championship was still in its infancy and struggling to make its mark in the international calendar. In 1963, however, one result in the qualifying stages captured the headlines and made Europe sit up and take notice. Luxembourg, with a population of just 300,000, produced a remarkable performance over two legs, beating Holland to achieve the greatest victory in their history and the first real upset of the fledgling competition.

Luxembourg's triumph fired the public imagination, but to make matters worse for the humiliated Dutch, both legs were played in their own country. The first, in Amsterdam in September 1963, ended in a 1-1 draw as Nuninga gave the Grand Duchy the lead after five minutes, with May equalising half an hour later. The second leg, played in Rotterdam, saw a host of changes in the Dutch line-up but Dimmer gave Luxembourg another shock lead. After Kruiver equalised the outsiders survived an onslaught before Dimmer grabbed an unexpected second 11 minutes from time to seal a famous victory.

Amazingly Luxembourg nearly repeated the feat against Denmark in the quarter-finals, drawing 3-3 and 2-2 before losing the play-off 1-0 – a game played, ironically, on neutral territory in Amsterdam.

They were out but had created the sensation of the competition and the biggest success in their history. Elsewhere, France crushed England over two legs, while Italy, making their first appearance, also lost out. Despite earlier shocks the latter stages had a familiar look, as Spain, Hungary, the Soviet Union and Denmark won through to the last four, with the finals to be played in Spain.

The finals took place over four days in June 1964. While the football was of a decent standard, it failed to grab the attention in the way of the World Cup. Luxembourg's giant-killing acts were entertaining at the time but the spread of matches over a lengthy period did little to concentrate the minds of fans across Europe, and with only four teams making the finals it had little mass appeal.

But there were still players to admire. Spain were favourites thanks to home advantage and the wing skills of Luis Suarez, while the USSR had the best goalkeeper in the world in Lev Yashin, and Hungary's centre-forward Florian Albert, later a European Footballer Of The Year, was a superbly balanced striker who gave hope to his ageing side.

In the semi-final Spain met Hungary in Madrid in front of 125,000 people and witnessed Jose Villalonga's side make it through in extra-time. Pereda gave them a first-half lead from Suarez's cross before Bene struck an equaliser six minutes before full-time. It took an Amancio goal in the 115th minute to decide the outcome.

In the other semi-final, the USSR saw off outsiders Denmark with a comfortable 3-0 victory in the Nou Camp to set up a final that would see if Spain could finally match the club achievements of Real Madrid with a national team triumph.

They did, and with it came Spain's first major trophy. It was a fitting tribute to the country that had dominated club football for half a decade, but the national team was not moulded in the same style. They lacked the flair, the grace and the sheer dazzling brilliance of the famous team in white. Despite occasional flashes of skill from Suarez and Amancio, both among the best players in the world at the time, Spain would not go down in history as one of the great sides.

SEMI-FINALS
Spain 2-1 Hungary
(aet: 1-1 at 90 mins)
Soviet Union 3-0 Denmark

THIRD PLACE PLAY-OFF
Hungary 3-1 Denmark
(aet: 1-1 at 90 mins)

TOP GOALSCORERS
2 goals: Jesus Maria Pereda (Spain), Ferenc Bene (Hungary), Dezso Novák (Hungary)

FASTEST GOAL
6 minutes: Jesus Maria Pereda (Spain v Soviet Union)

TOTAL GOALS
13 goals

AVERAGE GOALS
3.25

THE FINAL

SPAIN (1) 2-1 (1) SOVIET UNION

Date Sunday June 21, 1964 **Attendance** 125,000
Venue Santiago Bernabéu, Madrid

The largest crowd ever at a European Championship final turned up to see the home side lift the trophy. They did, but only just. It was a tense affair, although in front of fascist dictator Franco, the Spanish got off to a dream start with a sixth-minute goal from Pereda.

Khusainov struck back two minutes later and a defensive game ensued, with little excitement. All the pre-match build-up about Lev Yashin facing the deft skills of the Spanish attack came to little on the big day.

The match seemed destined for extra-time and more nervousness, but the supporters at the Bernabéu found salvation when Marcelino struck a winner with a diving header from a Pereda cross in the 84th minute. The Soviets, with so little time to come back, were beaten.

HOW THE TEAMS LINED UP

SPAIN
COACH:
JOSE VILLALONGA

SOVIET UNION
COACH:
CONSTANTINI BESKOV

Iribar
Rivilla   Olivella
Calleja   Zoco   Fuste
Pereda   Suarez
Amancio   Marcelino   Lapetra
Khusainov   Ponedelnik   Chislenko
Korneev   Ivanov V
Anichkin   Voronin   Mudrik
Shesternev   Chustikov
Yashin

SPAIN

IRIBAR	6
RIVILLA	7
OLIVELLA	7
CALLEJA	6
ZOCO	7
FUSTE	7
PEREDA	7
Goal: 6 mins	
SUAREZ	*9
AMANCIO	7
MARCELINO	8
Goal: 84 mins	
LAPETRA	6

SOVIET UNION

YASHIN	*8
CHUSTIKOV	6
SHESTERNEV	6
MUDRIK	7
VORONIN	6
ANICHKIN	7
IVANOV V	6
KORNEEV	7
CHISLENKO	6
PONEDELNIK	6
KHUSAINOV	6
Goal: 8 mins	

Referee: Holland (England)

ITALY 1968

The competition to win the Henri Delaunay Trophy underwent a change of name and format in 1968, as the European Nations Cup became the European Football Championship. The original two-legged knockout tournament was dropped and for the first time replaced with eight qualifying groups totalling a record 31 teams, including newcomers Scotland and West Germany. The eight group winners qualified for the quarter-finals which were played over two legs.

The big tie of the quarter-finals pitched World Cup-winners England against the defending European Champions Spain. Bobby Charlton scored the only goal of the first leg at Wembley, and in the return England won 2-1 in Madrid with goals from Martin Peters and Norman Hunter.

Italy were named as hosts of the latter stages of the tournament after a magnificent 4-3 aggregate win over Bulgaria's best-ever side, featuring the likes of Hristo Bonev and Petar Jekov. It was Jekov who had clinched the winner in a five-goal thriller in Sofia, but in Naples a fortnight later Italy became the first team to qualify for the semi-finals, winning 2-0 with goals from Prati and Domenghini.

Yugoslavia's young and energetic team easily overcame France, after a 1-1 draw in Marseille they thrashed the French 5-1 in Belgrade with two goals each from Petkovic and Musemic, and a single strike from Dzajic.

The best performance in the quarter-finals was by the Soviet Union, who overturned

Above: The Soviets before their play-off with England. Opposite clockwise from top left: Italy dominated the final replay; Facchetti celebrates winning the decisive toss after the USSR semi; England's Bobby Charlton; Italy before the final replay.

a 2-0 defeat by Hungary in Budapest with a magnificent home performance in Moscow, running out 3-2 aggregate winners. It was a tremendous comeback against a team who, later the same year, would be crowned as Olympic Champions.

The Soviet Union's reward was a semi-final clash with hosts Italy in Naples. A hard enough challenge in itself, team selection was made even harder by circumstances when winger Igor Chislenko and half-back Murtaz Khurtzilava sustained injuries in an Olympic qualifier against Czechoslovakia just days before. It all meant that team manager Mikhail Yakushin arrived in Italy with an injury-decimated squad.

The 75,000 crowd in the San Paulo Stadium were forced to witness a dreadful game, played in appalling weather conditions, between a makeshift Soviet side and an Italian team with a mortal fear of losing. The Soviets did dominate the first-half, but they squandered the few good chances they created. After the break Rivera returned to the pitch following an enforced first-half absence caused by a collision with the Soviet full-back, Afonin, and an impatient Italian crowd saw Italy improve and have the better of the second-half. This time, however, it was the turn of the Soviet defence to hold firm. The closing minutes saw Italy produce attack after attack, during which Domenghini hit the post, but even extra-time brought no goals. So a place in the 1968 European Championship Final was decided in the dressing room with the spin of a 1916 French ten-franc coin. The hosts won the toss and it was Italy who progressed to the final.

The other semi-final in Florence between favourites England and the gifted young Yugoslav side was equally dismal. Played in a humid, thundery atmosphere, one reporter described the match as a technical dirge. It was a frustrating game involving uncompromising tackling from both sides. After just five minutes England's Norman Hunter had inflicted an ankle injury on Yugoslavian playmaker Ivica Osim, making him a virtual passenger for the rest of the game. It set the tone for the rest of the match in which there were a staggering 49 free-kicks awarded.

The decisive action took place in the 85th minute when the excellent Dragan Dzajic beat goalkeeper Gordon Banks with an exquisite volley for the winning goal. It got worse for England before the final whistle when Alan Mullery, after being ruthlessly brought down by Trivic, retaliated with a blatant kick on his assailant. He became the first England player ever to be sent-off, and that in 96 years of international football.

England, without the suspended Mullery, the injured Alan Ball, and hayfever sufferer Colin Bell, recovered to win an entertaining Third Place Play-Off clash with the Soviet Union. Goals from Bobby Charlton and Geoff Hurst gave an England a deserved 2-0 win.

SEMI-FINALS

Italy 0-0 Soviet Union
(aet: Italy won on toss of coin)
Yugoslavia 1-0 England

THIRD PLACE PLAY-OFF

England 2-0 Soviet Union

TOP GOALSCORER

2 goals: Dragan Dzajic
(Yugoslavia)

FASTEST GOAL

11 mins: Gigi Riva
(Italy v Yugoslavia replay)

TOTAL GOALS

7

AVERAGE GOALS

1.4 per game

FINAL GAME

ITALY

ZOFF	7
BURGNICH	6
FACCHETTI	*8
FERRINI	7
GUARNERI	6
CASTANO	5
DOMENGHINI ⚽	7
Goal: 80 mins	
JULIANO	5
LODETTI	7
ANASTASI	7
PRATI	6

YUGOSLAVIA

PANTELIC	*9
FAZLAGIC	8
DAMJANOVIC	7
PAVLOVIC	6
PAUNOVIC	7
HOLCER	8
TRIVIC	7
ACIMOVIC	7
PETKOVIC	6
MUSEMIC	6
DZAJIC ⚽	7
Goal: 39 mins	

Referee: Dienst (Switzerland)

THE FINAL

ITALY (0) 1-1 (1) YUGOSLAVIA (AET)

Date Saturday June 8, 1968 **Attendance** 69,000
Venue Olympic Stadium, Rome

Italy were favourites but Yugoslavia dominated. Goalkeeper Dino Zoff kept Italy in the game, but was unable to stop Dzajic scoring in the 39th minute. The inability to beat Zoff again proved Yugoslavia's undoing. With ten minutes to go Domenghini's 25-yard free-kick crashed in. Extra-time saw no goals.

REPLAY

ITALY (2) 2-0 (0) YUGOSLAVIA

Date Monday June 10, 1968 **Attendance** 50,000
Venue Olympic Stadium, Rome

Italy made five changes and in came Rosato, Salvadore, Mazzola, De Sisti and Riva. The transformed team dominated the replay and Yugoslavia never recovered after Italy's magnificent start. After 11 minutes Riva scored with a great left-foot shot. After 32 Anastasi fired on the turn to make it 2-0.

HOW THE TEAMS LINED UP

ITALY

Zoff
Burgnich · Facchetti · Ferrini · Guarneri
Castano · Domenghini · Juliano · Lodetti
Anastasi · Prati
Dzajic · Musemic · Petkovic · Acimovic
Trivic · Holcer
Paunovic · Pavlovic · Damjanovic · Fazlagic
Pantelic

ITALY COACH: FERRUCCIO VALCAREGGI

YUGOSLAVIA COACH: RAJKO MITIC

Zoff
Burgnich · Facchetti · Salvadore · Guarneri
Rosato · Domenghini · Mazzola · De Sisti
Anastasi · Riva
Dzajic · Musemic · Hosic · Acimovic
Trivic · Holcer
Paunovic · Pavlovic · Damjanovic · Fazlagic
Pantelic

REPLAY

ITALY

ZOFF	7
BURGNICH	6
FACCHETTI	6
SALVADORE	7
GUARNERI	7
ROSATO	6
DOMENGHINI	6
MAZZOLA	*9
DE SISTI	7
ANASTASI ⚽	8
Goal: 32 mins	
RIVA ⚽	7
Goal: 11 mins	

YUGOSLAVIA

PANTELIC	*8
FAZLAGIC	7
DAMJANOVIC	6
PAVLOVIC	6
PAUNOVIC	6
HOLCER	5
TRIVIC	5
ACIMOVIC	6
HOSIC	5
MUSEMIC	6
DZAJIC	7

Referee: Ortiz de Mendibil (Spain)

Above: The Soviet Union line up before the final. Below right: Belgium's Van Himst wins a challenge. Opposite clockwise from top: Gerd Müller lifts the trophy after West Germany's 3-0 victory; West Germany charge forward; Müller nets one of his two goals; the Germans inspect the trophy.

BELGIUM 1972

It may not be remembered as one of the great international football tournaments of all time, but the 1972 European Championship was significant for one reason: it saw West Germany pick up their first major international trophy since the 1954 World Cup, beginning a golden era of almost 25 years that would see the Germans become arguably the most powerful nation in world football.

To be fair to the Germans, the success had been coming. Finishing a creditable third behind the greatest Brazilian team of all time at the 1970 World Cup had indicated there was something special to come, but 1972 saw the new young team built by coach Helmut Schön truly come of age.

Qualifying for the tournament had begun in 1970, with 32 European nations involved. Italy and Germany were among the favourites, as both had come into the tournament off the back of promising World Cup campaigns, finishing as runners-up and third respectively. England, meanwhile, were also still considered to be a major football power, despite failing to live up to expectations in Mexico.

In the first qualifying phase, these three each finished top of their groups and remained unbeaten, while the Soviet Union also came through impressively without losing a single game, making them serious contenders for a place in the final.

The quarter-finals saw Hungary eliminate Romania 2-1 in a play-off, the original two-legged encounter finishing 3-3, while the Soviet side cruised through 3-0 against Yugoslavia, their vanquished opponents in the first ever European Championship final. A physical Belgian outfit muscled past Italy, winning 2-1 on aggregate, but the big tie of the round was undoubtedly West Germany against England.

West Germany travelled to Wembley in April 1972 and completed an impressive 3-1 away win in the first leg, the first ever win by Germany on English soil. This result was enough to see them through as the return match ended in a scoreless draw.

Belgium was voted host nation for the final stages and they were drawn against the West Germans, who had now emerged as clear favourites. Home advantage counted for little for the Belgians, as so many German fans made the relatively short trip to Antwerp to cheer on their team. Belgium started well enough, containing the German threat, but a great header from Müller gave the favourites the lead going in at half-time. The Belgians, to their credit, threw men forward in the second period and brought some great saves out of the young German goalkeeper Sepp Maier, but the game turned decisively in West Germany's favour in the 71st minute when Müller put his side two up. Belgium pulled a goal back late on but it was to no avail.

While a crowd of nearly 60,000 had watched the first semi-final, only 3,500 fans were at the Parc Astrid in Brussels to witness a disappointing display between two of Eastern Europe's top footballing nations. The skilful Hungarians faced the Soviet Union, a nation with an impressive record in the tournament. But with neither side threatening in the first-half, the game only came to life when Konkov blasted the Soviets in front after the break. Hungary rallied but failed to equalise, even missing a late penalty.

Before the final came the third place play-off. Another disappointing crowd of only 10,000 saw the Belgians live up to their physical reputation, grinding out a 2-1 win over the Hungarians.

Three days later at the Heysel Stadium in Brussels, West Germany, playing in front of a largely German crowd, faced the Soviet

Union as clear favourites. Beckenbauer and his team-mates did not disappoint lifting the trophy with a comprehensive 3-0 victory.

The tournament's best team had won and it wouldn't be the last time a German side would return from a major international competition brandishing silverware. Despite it only being the very beginning of a long and successful spell, many critics now believe that this was the best of all the great German sides, even better than the team who went on to lift the World Cup two years later.

THE FINAL

WEST GERMANY (1) 3-0 (0) SOVIET UNION

Date Sunday June 18, 1972 **Attendance** 43,437
Venue Heysel Stadium, Brussels

The Germans were on the offensive from the start, mounting wave after wave of attack. Netzer ran the midfield, impressively supported by sweeper Beckenbauer, while Gerd Müller ran the Soviet defence ragged.

Heroics early on from the Soviet 'keeper Rudakov kept the Germans at bay until late in the first half when Müller met a cross with his chest, brought the ball down and slotted home. The Germans raised their game yet another level after the break. Wimmer, having a fine game, played a one-two with Heynckes, before crashing the ball home to put daylight between the two sides. Five minutes later, Müller put the West Germans three ahead, wrong footing the goalkeeper to score. The goal made him the tournament's top scorer.

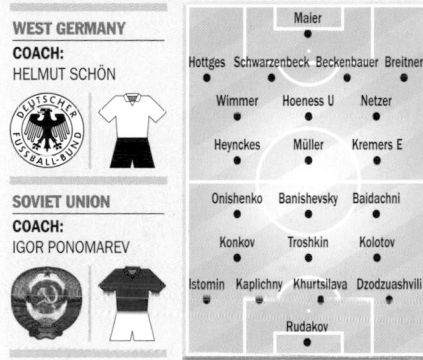

HOW THE TEAMS LINED UP

WEST GERMANY
COACH:
HELMUT SCHÖN

SOVIET UNION
COACH:
IGOR PONOMAREV

Maier

Hottges Schwarzenbeck Beckenbauer Breitner

Wimmer Hoeness U Netzer

Heynckes Müller Kremers E

Onishenko Banishevsky Baidachni

Konkov Troshkin Kolotov

Istomin Kaplichny Khurtsilava Dzodzuashvili

Rudakov

WEST GERMANY

MAIER	7
HÖTTGES	6
BECKENBAUER	8
SCHWARZENBECK	7
BREITNER	7
HOENESS U	7
WIMMER ⚽	8
Goal: 52 mins	
NETZER	*9
HEYNCKES	6
MÜLLER G ⚽⚽	8
Goal: 27 mins, 58 mins	
KREMERS E	6

SOVIET UNION

RUDAKOV	*8
DZODZUASHVILI	7
ISTOMIN	6
KHURTSILAVA	7
KAPLICHNY	6
KOLOTOV	6
TROSHKIN	6
BAIDACHNI	7
BANISHEVSKY	5
Subbed: 66 mins (Kozinkevich)	
KONKOV	5
Subbed: 46 mins (Dolmatov)	
ONISHENKO	7
sub: KOZINKEVICH	6
sub: DOLMATOV	6

Referee: Marschall (Austria)

SEMI-FINALS
West Germany 2-1 Belgium
Soviet Union 1-0 Hungary

THIRD PLACE PLAY-OFF
Belgium 2-1 Hungary

TOP GOALSCORERS
4 goals: Gerd Müller (West Germany)

FASTEST GOAL
24 mins: Raoul Lambert (Belgium v Hungary); Gerd Müller (West Germany v Belgium)

TOTAL GOALS
10

AVERAGE GOALS
2.5 per game

YUGOSLAVIA 1976

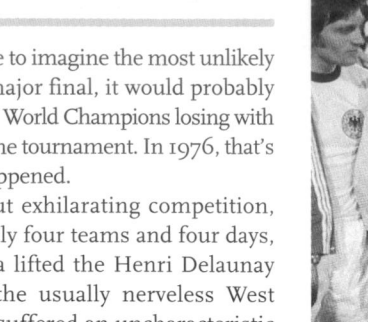

If you were to imagine the most unlikely end to a major final, it would probably involve the World Champions losing with the last kick of the tournament. In 1976, that's exactly what happened.

In a brief but exhilarating competition, restricted to only four teams and four days, Czechoslovakia lifted the Henri Delaunay trophy when the usually nerveless West German team suffered an uncharacteristic outbreak of penalty shoot-out nerves. However, the 1976 championship was about so much more than Uli Hoeness's hoof over the bar. At the peak of a golden era of European football, brilliant, attacking play dominated throughout and the underdog prevailed.

Yugoslavia 76 was the closest major tournament ever staged. Every match, both semi-finals, the final and third-place play-off went into extra-time. The quality of play throughout was both exhilarating and, for those not at the party, a chilling reminder of how far the game had moved on, led by Dutch Total Football and the powerful athleticism of West Germany.

SEMI-FINALS

Czechoslovakia 3-1 Holland
(aet: 1-1 at 90 mins)

West Germany 4-2 Yugoslavia
(aet: 2-2 at 90 mins)

THIRD PLACE PLAY-OFF

Holland 3-2 Yugoslavia
(aet: 2-2 at 90 mins)

TOP GOALSCORERS

4 goals: Dieter Müller (West Germany)

FASTEST GOAL

8 mins: Jan Svehlík
(Czechoslovakia v West Germany)

TOTAL GOALS

17

AVERAGE GOALS

4.25 per game

THE FINAL

CZECHOSLOVAKIA (2) 2-2 (1) WEST GERMANY
(aet: Czechoslovakia won 5-3 on penalties)

Date Sunday June 20, 1976 **Attendance** 45,000
Venue Red Star Stadium, Belgrade

The highly-fancied Germans were stunned by Czechoslovakia's attacking start, and after 25 minutes they were 2-0 down after goals from Svehlík and Dobiás. Müller grabbed one back straight away, but the Czechs looked to be holding on. Wave after wave of West German attacks finally paid off with a dramatic equaliser in the final minute. Now nothing, it appeared, would deny Beckenbauer another trophy in his 100th international appearance. But the Czechs were kept alive in extra-time by 'keeper Viktor and it went to penalties. When Hoeness blasted over and Panenka slotted home, the trophy was on its way to Prague.

CZECHOSLOVAKIA	
VIKTOR	7
PIVARNÍK	6
ONDRUS	7
CAPKOVIC	7
GÖGH	7
DOBIÁS ⚽	8
Goal: 25 mins. Subbed: 94 mins (Vesely)	
MÓDER	8
PANENKA	7
MASNY	*9
SVEHLÍK ⚽	7
Goal: 8 mins. Subbed: 79 mins (Jurkemik)	
NEHODA	7
sub: JURKEMIK	7
sub: VESELY	7

WEST GERMANY	
MAIER	7
VÖGTS	• 7
SCHWARZENBECK	6
BECKENBAUER	*8
DIETZ	6
WIMMER	6
Subbed: 46 mins (Flohe)	
BONHOF	7
BEER	5
Subbed: 80 mins (Bongartz)	
HOENESS U	5
MÜLLER D ⚽	7
Goal: 28 mins	
HÖLZENBEIN ⚽	7
Goal: 89 mins	
sub: FLOHE	5
sub: BONGARTZ	6

Referee: Gonella (Italy)

HOW THE TEAMS LINED UP

CZECHOSLOVAKIA
COACH:
VACLAV JEZEK

Viktor

Pivarnik Ondrus Capkovic Gögh

Dobiás Móder Panenka

Masny Svehlík Nehoda

WEST GERMANY
COACH:
HELMUT SCHÖN

Hölzenbein Müller D Hoeness U

Bonhof Beer Wimmer

Dietz Beckenbauer Schwarzenbeck Vögts

Maier

Above: The victorious Czech team. Opposite clockwise from top left: The final was a close affair between the Czechs and West Germany; the Czechs lift the cup after a penalty shoot-out; an exhausted Franz Beckenbauer; Ivo Viktor celebrates.

For some traditional footballing powers, Yugoslavia 76 rudely showed how far the game had changed and how they were being left behind. Italy, World Cup finalists just six years earlier, only finished third in their group during qualification.

England, world champions ten years earlier, also failed to progress beyond the group stages – although typically false promise came before the fall. In the opening match of their qualification group, Don Revie's men trounced the eventual winners of the tournament 3-0 at Wembley. Defeat in the return fixture, coupled with an inability to beat Portugal home or away, spelled elimination as group runners-up one point behind the Czechs.

Qualification for the quarter-finals was a straightforward battle for supremacy across eight groups. Of the British nations, only Wales made it this far after overcoming a group containing Hungary, Austria and Luxembourg. Quarter-finals over two legs then determined which four teams would receive their exclusive invites to the midsummer festival of football. Yugoslavia made sure they wouldn't miss their own party by beating Wales 2-0 at home, then drawing 1-1 in Cardiff. The other bright spot for the British teams was Don Givens, whose eight goals for Northern Ireland in the qualification phase wasn't bettered during the entire tournament.

Joining the hosts in the last four were West Germany, the outrageously talented Dutch and the neat but lightly fancied Czechs. Such a brief tournament needed to catch fire immediately, and in a sensational opening game three players were sent-off as Holland crashed out. For Johan Cruyff and his team-mates, this tournament, sandwiched between their two World Cup final appearances, should

have been payback time for their 1974 World Cup final defeat by West Germany. But instead they paid the price for overconfidence, ending their game against the Czechs with nine men. Their opponents scored two goals in extra-time to run out 3-1 winners.

Holland's exit appeared to pave the way for West Germany. They duly earned their place in the final courtesy of a 4-2 defeat of the hosts, although it was much closer than the score suggests. In one of the competition's classic encounters, watched by 70,000 fans in Belgrade, Yugoslavia raced into a two-goal lead with little more than 30 minutes played. They were still a goal to the good with ten minutes remaining when West Germany brought on Dieter Müller. Within two minutes he had equalised to send the match into extra-time, where he netted twice more to complete his hat-trick and Yugoslavia's misery.

Utterly deflated, the Yugoslavs did well to force the third-place play-off against Holland into extra-time, where the Dutch scored the winning goal to edge the game 3-2 and gain scant consolation in front of just 7,000 people.

All eyes now focused on Belgrade: could the Czechs, a talented but hardly feared football power, possibly match the might of the confident, powerful world champions? Franz Beckenbauer was at the height of his powers and his side contained incredible talent, even by the high standards of the mid-Seventies.

Müller's three goals in the semi-final were enough to retain his place in the German starting line-up, but in Viktor, crowd favourites the Czechs boasted the goalkeeper of the tournament. He was kept busy in a final match that proved worthy of this wonderful tournament, and one that eventually resulted in a surprise win for the Czechs.

ITALY 1980

With the 1976 Championship in Yugoslavia hailed an unmitigated success of skill, technique and drama, the tournament played out some four years later was nothing short of disastrous.

Negative football, poor refereeing and hooliganism were the abiding memories of Euro 80, while the depressing statistic of just 1.93 goals per game no doubt contributed to attendances that dropped as low as 9,000 for the Czechoslovakia v Greece game. Even the opening fixture between West Germany and the Czechs attracted just 11,000 fans in Rome. In hindsight, staying away was a wise choice considering the fear-riddled game that was settled by a Rummenigge header.

With the competition split into two groups of four teams, and the winners of each group contesting the final, the formula was a disaster waiting to happen. Teams that lost their opening fixture invariably had a mountain to climb and therefore played out meaningless ties, while those in contention for the top spot approached games in a chess-like fashion rather than expressing their true capabilities.

Indeed, it explained why Greece, in their first major tournament, were regarded the most expressive team in Group One, despite losing their opening games against Holland and the Czechs. A creditable stalemate with West Germany secured their fate, but the fact that a team who ended up with one point were the most talked about of the competition spoke volumes for the entertainment on show.

England, again, flattered to deceive and their opening fixture against Belgium in Turin was shrouded in controversy and disgrace. With 15 minutes to play and the game poised at 1-1, German referee Aldinger disallowed a perfectly valid goal by Woodcock for offside and prompted clashes between fans and riot police on the terraces. The game had already been halted for three minutes in the first-half, following Ceulemans' equaliser, which left England goalkeeper Clemence needing treatment for the effects of tear gas. With Italy drawing their opening fixture 0-0 against Spain, and all four teams in Group B with a point a-piece, the hosts' clash with England was billed as a war of attrition both on and off the terraces. Yet while the visiting fans remained calm, the players received a battering by an Italian team determined to stay in the competition at all costs. In a game of cat and mouse football played out in front of 59,000 supporters, a rare slip by Liverpool full-back Phil Neal proved costly as Tardelli headed home with just 11 minutes remaining.

Although England went on to beat Spain 2-1 in Naples, it was left to Belgium and Italy to fight out a place in the final. Having beaten Spain 2-1, Guy Thys' side knew that a draw

against the Italians would see them progress on goal difference, thus causing one of the all-time tournament shocks. With a vociferous 60,000 crowd behind them in Rome the Italians failed spectacularly in a game riddled with bookings and defensive football. The 0-0 stalemate was enough to see Belgium through. Italy were undone by their defensive instincts, scoring just one goal in three games.

With Holland and West Germany winning their opening games in Group One, it was assumed that both would fight it out for a place in the final, yet with the Cruyff-inspired Total Football conspicuous by its absence, the Dutch were put to the sword in their pivotal second game against the Germans. The 3-2 scoreline flattered the Dutch and only in their final group game against the Czechs, did the real Holland emerge. But by then the 1-1 draw was too little too late and they even lost out on a third play play-off appearance.

West Germany's final points tally of five indicated their dominance in a group that rarely saw them break sweat. Without the likes of Beckenbauer, Bonhof and Müller, they still reached the final by playing only 60 minutes of top-quality football, against Holland where they established a 3-0 lead before taking their foot off the pedal. Safe in the knowledge that a place in the final was assured, West Germany played out a 0-0 draw in their final game against the Greeks.

The hope was that the final would be the tournament's saving grace, and the omens were good as the third place play-off preamble proved an exciting affair in Naples. With extra-time banished in the hope of more attacking football, Czechoslovakia took the lead against the hosts when Jurkemik scored in the 53rd minute from a Panenka corner. The strike prompted the Italians to emerge from their tournament slumber and they were finally rewarded when a Causio free-kick was headed home by Graziani with 17 minutes remaining.

The Czechs should have wrapped the game up when Nehoda's shot was brilliantly saved by Zoff late in the game, but Barmos silenced the home side with the winner in a 9-8 penalty shoot-out spectacular.

Above: The Italians went out in the semi-finals. Opposite clockwise from top left: Horst Hrubesch scored both goals in West Germany's final win; Karl Heinz Rummenigge clears; Schuster takes on the Belgian defence; West Germany celebrate.

SEMI-FINALS
Group winners progressed to the final

THIRD PLACE PLAY-OFF
Czechoslovakia 1-1 Italy
(no extra time: Czechoslovakia won 9-8 on penalties)

TOP GOALSCORERS
3 goals: Klaus Allofs (West Germany)

FASTEST GOAL
6 mins: Antonin Panenka (Czechoslovakia v Greece)

TOTAL GOALS
27

AVERAGE GOALS
1.93 per game

THE FINAL

WEST GERMANY (1) 2-1 (0) BELGIUM

Date Sunday June 22, 1980 **Attendance** 47,864
Venue Olympic Stadium, Rome

Belgium's refusal to play the bridesmaid ensured a lacklustre ten days of football were brought to an exciting climax. The pattern was set as early as the 10th minute, when an inch-perfect pass from Schuster was met by 20-year-old Hamburg striker Horst Hrubesch, who rounded Millecamps before sliding his shot into the corner of the net.

The goal brought Belgium out of their shell, but the Germans should have doubled their lead when Schuster and Allots brought fine saves out of goalkeeper Pfaff before the break.

The Belgians drew level with Vandereycken's penalty, awarded for a challenge from Stielike on Van der Elst which was clearly outside the box, but with a minute remaining, Hrubesch met Rummenigge's corner to win it for the Germans.

WEST GERMANY
SCHUMACHER	6
KALTZ	7
FÖRSTER K-H	7
STIELIKE	8
DIETZ	6
BRIEGEL	7
Subbed: 55 mins (Cullmann)	
SCHUSTER	*9
MÜLLER H	6
ALLOFS K	7
RUMMENIGGE K-H	7
HRUBESCH ⚽⚽	8
Goal: 10 mins, 88 mins	
sub: CULLMANN	6

BELGIUM
PFAFF	7
GERETS	7
MILLECAMPS L	6
MEEUWS	*8
RENQUIN	5
COOLS	6
VANDEREYCKEN ⚽	7
Goal: 72 mins (pens)	
VAN MOER	6
MOMMENS	7
VAN DER ELST	7
CEULEMANS	5

Referee: Rainea (Romania)

HOW THE TEAMS LINED UP

WEST GERMANY
COACH:
JUPP DERWALL

Schumacher
Kaltz Förster K-H Stielike Dietz
Briegel Schuster Müller H
Rummenigge K-H Hrubesch Allofs K

BELGIUM
COACH:
GUY THYS

Ceulemans Van der Elst
Mommens Van Moer Vandereycken Cools
Renquin Meeuws Millecamps L Gerets
Pfaff

FRANCE 1984

For the French, the 1984 European Championship represented nothing less than a date with destiny. The country was in danger of becoming famous for instigating major football tournaments without ever actually winning them.

Two years earlier, at the World Cup, they had exuded quality before being physically battered by West Germany in Seville and losing their nerve in a semi-final they should have won. Now they were desperate to make amends and fulfil their promise. As hosts for the second time, they knew they might never have a better opportunity.

Against this background the 1984 European Championship produced some of the finest football the tournament has ever seen. The final competition was restricted to just eight sides, making qualification a tight business, and by June 1984 there were some notable absentees, including World Cup winners Italy, who made a dreadful qualifying bid coming second from bottom of their group. Also

Above: Michel Platini opens the final scoring from this free kick. Opposite clockwise from top left: Platini on the attack again; Platini gets his hands on the Henri Delaunay trophy, France's first major honour; the French team greets the final whistle with joy; mixed emotions as Spanish 'keeper Luis Arconada allows Platini's free-kick to slip through his grasp.

absent were Holland, Sweden and the Soviet Union, while the failure of England, Scotland, Northern Ireland and Wales to get through to the finals made it a disastrous clean sweep for the British Isles.

England were largely in transition under new manager Bobby Robson. They came second in their group behind Denmark after a 1-0 defeat at home. As the cream of Europe assembled in France that June they went off to play a friendly tournament in South America, ironically throwing up one of the enduring images of English football when John Barnes scored his wonderful solo effort in the Maracana.

There was no great shame in losing to Denmark, as it turned out, because they were an emerging football nation with world class talents like Preben Elkjaer and Michael Laudrup in their ranks. The Danes would go as far as the semi-finals when they got to France, though it was clear that the home nation and World Cup runners-up, West Germany, were the favourites.

Under Michel Hidalgo Les Bleus were, if anything, an even stronger outfit than they had been two years previous – particularly with the addition of Joel Bats in goal, probably the country's finest ever goalkeeper, and Luis Fernandez in midfield. They also boasted a tight defence that was still being carefully orchestrated by the dependable Maxime Bossis. That, in turn, sat behind possibly the best midfield in the world, even if they were nearly all in their thirties. The only question mark hung over the team's lack of true strike power, which is where Platini's presence was to prove crucial.

Once the tournament got under way France eased through Group A, winning all of their games, including a 5-0 thumping of neighbours Belgium. Platini was already hitting form, scoring two perfect hat-tricks

(left foot, right foot, header) in succession. Denmark qualified for the semi-finals behind them in second.

The real shock came in Group B, with holders West Germany failing to make the semi-finals. Even though they were held to a draw by Portugal, the Germans were still tipped to progress to the later stages,. However, a last-minute header by Antonio Maceda in their final group showdown with Spain sent them home stunned. Spain, who also missed a penalty in that match, took their place in the last four, with Portugal completing the semi-final line-up.

The first semi-final, on June 23, paired France with Portugal in the Stade Vélodrome in a match now regarded as a classic. After a slow start to the game France scored first through a Domergue free-kick, before being pegged back to 1-1 by a Jordao header with 16 minutes remaining. The home side then conceded a second goal in extra-time before Domergue, on his 27th birthday, scored again. With the prospect looming of a penalty shoot-out, one that France would surely have lost if recent form was anything to go by, Platini lashed home a Jean Tigana cross to put them through to the final with just 64 seconds remaining on the clock.

The other semi-final between Denmark and Spain was just as tight, if a little less open, and with the two sides locked at 1-1 it was Danish nerves that failed to hold in the penalty shoot-out. Nothing now was going to deny Les Bleus from seizing their moment. As David Miller wrote in *The Times* on the eve of the final, their name was morally already engraved on the European Championship trophy. Despite the weight of expectation, Platini's nerve held and he led his team to victory with his ninth goal in five games. It was one of his quieter matches, in truth, but he was rightly named the player of the tournament.

SEMI-FINALS

France 3-2 Portugal
(aet: 1-1 at 90 mins)

Spain 1-1 Denmark
(aet: Spain won 5-4 on penalties)

THIRD PLACE PLAY-OFF

Did not take place

TOP GOALSCORER

9 goals: Michel Platini (France)

FASTEST GOAL

3 mins: Michel Platini
(France v Belgium)

TOTAL GOALS

41

AVERAGE GOALS

2.73 per game

THE FINAL

FRANCE (0) 2-0 (0) SPAIN

Date Wednesday June 27, 1984 **Attendance** 47,368

Venue Parc Des Princes, Paris

The 1984 final started with some robust play from the Spaniards, designed no doubt to unsettle the hosts, which had the home crowd whistling. The Czech referee, Christov, quickly clamped down and play began to flow from end to end. Giresse had a shot as early as the first minute, but nevertheless there was no score at half-time. When the second-half restarted the French began to look edgy as they attempted to break the Spanish down, and it took a bad mistake from goalkeeper Arconada to settle Gallic nerves when he let a Platini free-kick squeeze past him. Spain held on and searched for an equaliser, but as they committed more men forward in the closing moments, Bellone was able to break clear and chip over the goalkeeper to seal the game.

FRANCE	
BATS	7
BATTISTON	6
Subbed: 72 mins (Amoros)	
LE ROUX	7
Sent-off: 85 mins	
BOSSIS	7
DOMERGUE	6
TIGANA	8
FERNANDEZ	7
PLATINI	*9
Goal: 57 mins	
GIRESSE	8
LACOMBE	6
Subbed: 80 mins (Genghini)	
BELLONE	7
Goal: 90 mins	
sub: AMOROS	6
sub: GENGHINI	5

SPAIN	
ARCONADA	5
URQUIAGA	6
SALVA	7
Subbed: 85 mins (Roberto)	
GALLEGO	*8
Booked.	
SENOR	6
FRANCISCO	6
VICTOR	5
CAMACHO	7
JULIO ALBERTO	6
Subbed: 77 mins (Sarabia)	
SANTILLANA	6
CARRASCO	7
Booked.	
sub: ROBERTO	5
sub: SARABIA	5

Referee: Christov (Czechoslovakia)

HOW THE TEAMS LINED UP

FRANCE
COACH:
MICHEL HIDALGO

SPAIN
COACH:
MIGUEL MUNOZ

FRANCE
Bats
Battiston Le Roux Bossis Domergue
Tigana Fernandez Platini Giresse
Lacombe Bellone

SPAIN
Carrasco Santillana
Julio Alberto Camacho Victor Francisco
Senor Gallego Salva Urquiaga
Arconada

Above: Holland enjoy collecting the trophy. Opposite clockwise from top left: Goalscorers Gullit and Van Basten celebrate during the final; Lineker of England; Brehme leaps with joy after Germany's semi win; Roberto Mancini takes on Denmark.

WEST GERMANY 1988

A decade after consecutive World Cup finals ended in bitterness and defeat, Holland achieved redemption in one of the most exciting tournaments of the 1980s. Dutch football had been plagued by a sense of unfulfilled potential since the twin losses of 1974 and 1978. In banishing old demons, they closed that chapter and ushered in a new golden era, centred around superstars such as Van Basten, Gullit and Rijkaard.

Holland were undoubtedly the best team of Euro 88, a tournament that produced possibly the finest football in these championships since 1976. Only eight teams qualified again and this time, with all the leading countries except defending champions France booking their places, fireworks were guaranteed.

Group 1, featuring hosts West Germany, Italy, Spain and Denmark, appeared to be the stronger of the two, and few thought that both eventual finalists would emerge from Group 2, made up of Holland, the USSR, Republic Of Ireland and England. But this group crackled with tension until the final moments when a late goal ended Ireland's adventure and sparked Holland's tournament into life.

By that point the competition had long gone sour for England. Strongly fancied after their World Cup quarter-final appearance in Mexico two years earlier, they suffered a shock 1-0 loss in the opening match against the Irish. The defeat, to a team coached by Englishman Jack Charlton, was a blow Bobby Robson's side never recovered from. They capitulated 3-1 to Holland, in a match remembered for Marco Van Basten's stunning hat-trick, and by the same score to the fast-improving Soviets.

For the Irish, beating England was the catalyst for an unlikely crusade into unknown territory, battering and bettering supposedly superior sides. Denied by a late equaliser in their next match against the Soviet Union, they headed into their final game against Holland knowing a draw would be enough for a place in the semi-finals. The Soviets, meanwhile, had beaten Holland in their opening match, and having scraped a draw against the Irish they required only a point against a dispirited England in their last game to qualify.

Despite their impressive showing against England, the Dutch were in danger of paying for their opening defeat: they had to beat the Irish. While the improving Soviets cruised past England, Holland struggled to make any impact on the solid, organised Irish, who came closest to scoring when McGrath headed against the post. With Charlton's men eight minutes away from the semi-finals, luck came to Holland's rescue when Koeman miss-hit a shot which Kieft was on hand to guide in.

In Group 1, a draw between West Germany and Italy enabled Spain to steal a march on their rivals by beating Denmark 3-2. However, the old superpowers went on to reassert their dominance; the Germans brushing aside the Danes 2-0 and Italy squeezing past Spain with a single goal. Italy completed their advance with a routine 2-0 defeat of the already-eliminated Danes, while West Germany clinically disposed of Spain by the same scoreline. The group was going according to expectations, with many experts believing the opening encounter between the hosts, World Cup finalists two years earlier, and the Italians, who were building a talented side for Italia 90, had been a dress rehearsal for the final.

The semi-finals threw up arguably the fiercest rivalry in European football as West Germany met Holland. The match inevitably provoked memories of 1974, when West Germany wore down the Cruyff-inspired Dutch. Holland's manager then was Rinus Michels, the man credited with creating Total Football. In a delicious twist of fate, he was back in charge of his national side.

In a match worthy of the final, Holland took the early initiative in Hamburg only for Matthäus to fire West Germany ahead from the penalty spot in the 53rd minute. The Dutch fell apart, their play growing ragged and the spectre of indiscipline returning to haunt them – until the 73rd minute when the referee levelled the score by awarding them a disputed penalty. Koeman equalised, then in the last minute of normal time Van Basten, out of favour early in the tournament, scored his fourth goal of the competition to derail the hosts and send Holland into the final.

In the other semi-final, the Soviets added a rugged approach to their fast, neat game to beat Italy 2-0 in Stuttgart. Quietly and effectively the Soviet Union had earned the right to contest the final for a fourth time.

Valery Lobanovsky, their manager, was as much a pioneer of the modern game as Dutch coach Michels, the man he would be pitting his wits against in the final. Lobanovsky had led Dynamo Kiev to seven championships before taking over the national side. Would he be the man to end his country's 28-year wait for a second major trophy, or would Michels, 14 years after the disappointment of losing the World Cup final, lead Holland to glory?

THE FINAL

HOLLAND (1) 2-0 (0) SOVIET UNION

Date Saturday June 25, 1988 **Attendance** 72,308
Venue Olympic Stadium, Munich

The final will always be remembered for Marco Van Basten's wonder goal ten minutes into the second half, but until that point the destiny of the trophy was far from certain. The Soviet Union started brightly and had the better of the opening 20 minutes, but gradually the Dutch began to draw their sting. Gullit took control of midfield, the 37-year-old Mühren started hitting probing passes, and Holland, who had the longer period to recover from their semi-final, suddenly looked to be in the ascendancy.

Twelve minutes before half-time Gullit headed Holland in front and Van Basten's vicious volley, which made him the tournament's top scorer with five, doubled the lead in the 54th minute. Van Breukelen saved a late penalty and Holland at last had the silverware they deserved.

HOW THE TEAMS LINED UP

HOLLAND
COACH: RINUS MICHELS

SOVIET UNION
COACH: VALERY LOBANOVSKY

Van Breukelen

Van Aerle Koeman R Rijkaard Van Tiggelen

Vanenburg Wouters Koeman E Mühren A

Gullit Van Basten

Belanov Protasov

Gotsmanov Mikhailichenko Zavarov Litovchenko

Rats Aleinikov Demianenko Khidiatulin

Dasaev

HOLLAND	
VAN BREUKELEN	6
VAN AERLE	7
Booked: 49 mins	
KOEMAN R	7
RIJKAARD	8
VAN TIGGELEN	6
VANENBURG	7
WOUTERS	7
KOEMAN E	6
MÜHREN A	7
GULLIT	8
Goal: 33 mins	
VAN BASTEN	*9
Goal: 54 mins	

SOVIET UNION	
DASAEV	6
KHIDIATULIN	6
Booked: 42 mins	
DEMIANENKO	7
Booked: 31 mins	
ALEINIKOV	5
RATS	7
LITOVCHENKO	5
Booked: 34 mins	
ZAVAROV	7
MIKHAILICHENKO	*8
GOTSMANOV	6
Subbed: 69 mins (Baltacha)	
PROTASOV	6
Subbed: 72 mins (Pasulko)	
BELANOV	5
sub: BALTACHA	5
sub: PASULKO	5

Referee: Vautrot (France)

SEMI-FINALS
West Germany 1-2 Holland
Soviet Union 2-0 Italy

THIRD PLACE PLAY-OFF
Did not take place

TOP GOALSCORER
5 goals: Marco Van Basten (Holland)

FASTEST GOAL
3 mins: Sergei Aleinikov (England v Soviet Union)

TOTAL GOALS
34

AVERAGE GOALS
2.26 per game

SWEEN 1992

This was an extraordinary tournament for a host of reasons. The redrawing of Europe's political map, following the fall of communism, had had a big effect on international football with the former USSR competing in Sweden as the Commonwealth Of Independent States (CIS), and East and West Germany present as a single unified country. Further political intrigue had seen Yugoslavia disqualified from the tournament in line with UN sanctions against Serbia. That meant a last minute call-up for Denmark, the team who had finished runners-up in Yugoslavia's qualifying group by a single point.

No-one gave Richard Moller Nielsen's men much chance of making an impact as the squad had barely a fortnight to prepare for the competition and many players had been recalled from their summer holidays. In true fairytale style, the Danes went on to prove their doubters spectacularly wrong.

Eight countries, split into two groups of four, contested the finals. Sweden, Denmark, France

Above: John Jensen opens the scoring in the final for Denmark. Below: Hässler and German team-mates enjoy a semi-final goal. Opposite clockwise from top left: Eventual winners Denmark opened with a 0-0 draw against England; Brian Laudrup kisses the trophy; Hosts Sweden equalise against England, they would go on to win; Scotland fell at the first stage.

and England were in Group A, producing only nine goals between them in six games. Sweden finished top of the group, thanks to wins against Denmark (1-0) and England (2-1, with the prolific Tomas Brolin hitting a terrific winner six minutes from time). The Danes followed them into the semi-final shake-up despite winning only one of their games, 2-1 over France, then managed by the legendary Michel Platini. Injury-ravaged England had once again disappointed on the big stage, returning home with only a single David Platt goal to their name just two years after a penalty shoot-out defeat against West Germany had denied them a place in the World Cup final.

Group B proved a little livelier, although predictably it was Germany and Holland who qualified for the semi-finals at the expense of Scotland and the hodgepodge of nations that made up the CIS. Indeed, the Dutch became red-hot favourites to retain the Henri Delaunay trophy after squashing Germany 3-1, thanks to goals from Frank Rijkaard, Rob Witschge and Ajax's Dennis Bergkamp, making his first major international tournament appearance. Bergkamp also grabbed Holland's early winner against Scotland in a 1-0 victory. Meanwhile, the Germans lived dangerously, and had Thomas Hässler not struck a last minute equaliser against the CIS in their opening game, it is doubtful they would have made it through to the last four at all.

The tournament really sprang into life at the semi-final stage with two memorable matches. World Champions Germany lived up to their prodigious reputation in a tough game with injury-depleted Sweden, Hässler giving Berti Vogts' side an early lead, before Karlheinz Riedle added a second with just over half an hour to go. But the hosts pulled one back when the irrepressible Brolin converted a penalty five minutes later, and even when Riedle added a third two minutes from time after a fine through ball from Thomas Helmer, it failed to kill them off. The Swedes reduced

the deficit immediately, setting up a nail-biting finale, which saw the Germans eventually hold on for the 3-2 win.

The semi-final between Denmark and Holland was even more dramatic, with the still unfancied Danes a goal up through Henrik Larsen after just five minutes following some good work down the right from Brian Laudrup. Bergkamp's equaliser for the Dutch, midway through the first half, provided short-lived relief as Larsen netted a second just past the half-hour mark. Rinus Michels' side threw everything they had at the Danes in the second-half, and their pressure finally told five minutes from the final whistle when Rijkaard grabbed a second equaliser from a corner. Somehow the shattered Danes pulled themselves together and kept Holland at bay during extra-time, meaning the tie had to be decided on penalties. It was Marco Van Basten, without a single goal in the tournament, who missed the vital spot-kick as Denmark pulled off the biggest surprise of the tournament, triumphing 5-4 in the shoot-out lottery.

The Danes had ridden their luck and eagerly grasped every opportunity that had come their way, but surely they couldn't now win a tournament for which they hadn't even truly qualified. Could they?

SEMI-FINALS

Sweden 2-3 Germany
Holland 2-2 Denmark
(aet: Denmark won 5-4 on penalties)

THIRD PLACE PLAY-OFF

Did not take place

TOP GOALSCORERS

3 goals: Dennis Bergkamp (Holland), Tomas Brolin (Sweden), Henrik Larsen (Denmark), Karlheinz Riedle (Germany)

FASTEST GOAL

2 mins: Frank Rijkaard (Holland v Germany)

TOTAL GOALS

32

AVERAGE GOALS

2.13 per game

THE FINAL

DENMARK (1) 2-0 (0) GERMANY

Date Friday June 26, 1992 **Attendance** 37,800
Venue Nya Ullevi Stadium, Gothenburg

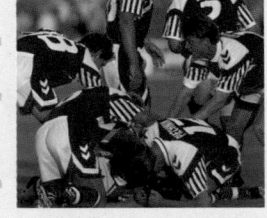

Germany started well as Denmark struggled to come to terms with the absence of suspended influential midfielder Henrik Andersen. However, having successfully soaked up the early pressure the Danes went ahead in the 18th minute, when John Jensen rifled the ball home past German keeper Bodo Illgner.

Germany tried to reassert themselves but were twice denied by Peter Schmeichel before the interval. The same pattern continued after the break with Vogts' men having the better of the chances. But Germany soon became frustrated at their inability to score and lost their discipline. With 12 minutes left Denmark sealed a famous win when Kim Vilfort made it 2-0, although Germans arguing that he controlled the ball with his hand had a point.

HOW THE TEAMS LINED UP

DENMARK
COACH:
R MOLLER NIELSEN

Schmeichel
Sivebaek Nielsen K Olsen L Christofte
Jensen Povlsen Laudrup B Piechnik
Larsen Vilfort

GERMANY
COACH:
BERTI VOGTS

Klinsmann Effenberg
Sammer Helmer Riedle Hässler
Buchwald Köhler Brehme Reuter
Illgner

DENMARK	
SCHMEICHEL	8
SIVEBAEK	6
Subbed: 65 mins (Christensen)	
NIELSEN K	6
OLSEN L	7
CHRISTOFTE	7
JENSEN	7
Goal: 18 mins	
POVLSEN	*9
LAUDRUP B	8
PIECHNIK	7
Booked 32 mins	
LARSEN	6
VILFORT	7
Goal: 78 mins	
sub: CHRISTENSEN	7

GERMANY	
ILLGNER	6
REUTER	6
Booked: 55 mins	
BREHME	*8
KÖHLER	7
BUCHWALD	6
HÄSSLER	6
Booked: 38 mins	
RIEDLE	6
HELMER	5
SAMMER	6
Subbed: 46 mins (Doll)	
EFFENBERG	5
Booked: 35 mins. Subbed: 78 mins (Thom)	
KLINSMANN	6
Booked 88 mins	
sub: DOLL	6
Booked 83 mins	
sub: THOM	5

Referee: Galler (Switzerland)

ENGLAND 1996

The golden goal rule was to decide the outcome of a successful European Championship, as Germany claimed the trophy from the Czech Republic in a repeat of the 1976 final. But the tournament will be remembered for much more than Oliver Bierhoff's late strike, as a great English summer saw three weeks of fantastic goals, enthusiastic support and penalty shoot-outs.

Held in England, it was important for the hosts not only to play well, but also to reconstruct their hooligan-tarnished image in front of the eyes of the football world. Under the shrewd management of Terry Venables England opened the tournament against Switzerland, but after a promising start they ran out of ideas and were held 1-1. Group A's other participants were Scotland and Holland, who played out a 0-0 draw.

The so-called Battle of Britain was one of the most eagerly awaited confrontations of the group stages, and the dramatic end-to-end action of the game did not disappoint. England took the lead with Alan Shearer's second goal of the tournament, and then came the passage of play that was to settle the contest. Scotland were awarded a second-half penalty, which David Seaman was fortunate to keep out from Gary McAllister via his elbow and the crossbar. From the resulting corner, England broke down the pitch and, latching on to a through ball, Paul Gascoigne deftly flicked the ball over Colin Hendry's head before volleying home one of the best goals of the tournament... and creating a much-loved moment English football history.

The team's confidence was high, and in a wonderful display of attacking football they defeated a complacent Dutch side 4-1. The consolation goal was to prove valuable, Patrick Kluivert's strike ensuring qualification for his country ahead of Scotland on goal difference.

Group B saw France finish top and go forward to the quarter-finals along with Spain, at the expense of the Eastern European representatives Bulgaria and Romania. In a low-scoring series of contests, no game was decided by more than one goal. The old war horses of Hristo Stoichkov and Gheorghe Hagi both failed to inspire their teams to get the better of a couple of sides blessed with a new generation of world-class talent.

Every world tournament produces one group packed with a seeming imbalance of strong sides, the so-called Group of Death, and Euro 96 was no exception. Italy, Russia, the Czech Republic and Germany were matched against each other, and something had to give. That something turned out to be Italian participation in the competition, and despite possessing arguably the most talented squad, in many ways they managed to engineer their own departure. A confident victory over Russia in the first game saw the Italians make changes to the starting 11 against the under-rated Czechs, who snatched a 2-1 victory. In the final game, Italy needed to defeat the already-qualified Germany to go through, but a 0-0 draw and the Czech Republic's point against Russia conspired against them.

Group D saw Portugal and world-stage newcomers Croatia grab the honours, with Denmark and Turkey exiting the tournament. The game of this group was played out by Croatia against holders Denmark, and will be remembered for Davor Suker's exquisite chipped finish against Peter Schmeichel.

After the open play of the group stages, the quarter-finals turned out to be tense affairs. England got the better of Spain via a penalty shoot-out, and France eliminated Holland in the same manner. England's shoot-out was notable for the redemption of left-back Stuart Pearce, who laid the ghost of his 1990 World Cup miss to rest after emphatically burying his spot-kick past Zubizarreta in the Spanish goal. The clash between Germany and Croatia turned out to be the most spiteful of the whole tournament, and despite possessing a trio of world-class talent in Davor Suker, Zvonimir Boban and Robert Prosinecki, Croatia temporarily put the football on hold and attempted to kick lumps out of their German opposition. Jurgen Klinsmann and his side limped out 2-1 winners. Thanks to mop-top Karel Poborsky's wonderful, improvised lob over Portugal's Vitor Baia, the Czechs continued their impressive run.

A 0-0 draw after extra-time between the Czech Republic and France at Old Trafford resulted in yet another semi-final shoot-out failure for the French. The other semi-final between hosts England and their old foe Germany also went to penalties, but not before an epic struggle in the game of the tournament. England made the start they wanted, with the eventual Golden Boot winner Alan Shearer heading them in front in the third minute. But England were unable to press home the advantage and Germany, through Stefan Kuntz, levelled the score. In extra-time England came agonisingly close to claiming a spot in the final through Darren Anderton and Gascoigne, while Kuntz had a headed goal disallowed. In a repeat of the events of 1990, once again England failed to see off the Germans. It fell to Gareth Southgate to miss the vital penalty and leave the hosts as nothing more than spectators for the final.

Above left: England's Stuart Pearce after his penalty shoot-out spot-kick in the quarter-final with Spain. Above right: Oliver Bierhoff enjoys scoring in the final. Opposite clockwise from top left: The Czech team celebrate semi-final victory; German goal machine Jurgen Klinsmann; England congratulate Paul Gascoigne for his goal versus Scotland; Italy's Pierluigi Casiraghi.

SEMI-FINALS

France 0-0 Czech Republic
(aet: Czechs won 6-5 on penalties)

England 1-1 Germany
(aet: Germany won 6-5 on penalties)

THIRD PLACE PLAY-OFF

Did not take place

TOP GOALSCORERS

5 goals: Alan Shearer (England)
3 goals: Jurgen Klinsmann (Germany); Brian Laudrup (Denmark), Hristo Stoichkov (Bulgaria)

FASTEST GOAL

3 mins: Alan Shearer (England v Germany); Hristo Stoichkov (Bulgaria v Romania)

TOTAL GOALS

64 goals

AVERAGE GOALS

2.06 per game

THE FINAL

GERMANY (0) **2-1** (1) **CZECH REPUBLIC**
(aet: 1-1 at 90 mins)

Date Sunday June 30, 1996 **Attendance** 73,611
Venue Wembley Stadium, London

Despite the exit of the hosts, the enthusiastic spirit of Euro 96 continued into the final in front of a full house at Wembley. Germany went into the game as favourites, and coach Berti Vogts' side were determined not to lose back-to-back European Championship finals. The underdog tag didn't deter the fast-improving Czech Republic side, who took the lead in the 59th minute with star player Patrik Berger converting a penalty past goalkeeper Kopke.

Substitute Oliver Bierhoff brought Germany back into the game only four minutes after coming on, and it was the tall striker who made football history by scoring the first ever golden goal in a major tournament final with just four minutes of extra-time on the clock.

WEST GERMANY		
KOPKE		7
BABBEL		7
SAMMER		7
Booked: 69 mins		
HELMER		6
Booked: 62 mins		
STRUNZ		6
HÄSSLER		6
EILTS		5
Subbed: 46 mins (Bode)		
SCHOLL		5
Subbed: 69 mins (Bierhoff)		
ZIEGE		7
Booked: 91 mins		
KLINSMANN		7
KUNTZ		6
sub: BODE		6
sub: BIERHOFF		*8
Goal: 73 mins, 95 mins		

CZECH REPUBLIC		
KOUBA		6
SUCHOPAREK		6
KADLEC		7
HORNAK		7
Booked: 47 mins		
RADA		5
POBORSKY		*8
Subbed: 88 mins (Smicer)		
NEDVED		7
NEMEC		6
BERGER		7
Goal: 59 mins (pen)		
BEJBL		5
KUKA		7
sub: SMICER		6

Referee: Pairetto (Italy)

HOW THE TEAMS LINED UP

GERMANY
COACH:
BERTI VOGTS

CZECH REPUBLIC
COACH:
DUSAN UHRIN

Kopke
Babbel Sammer Helmer Strunz
Hässler Eilts Scholl Ziege
Klinsmann Kuntz

Kuka Bejbl
Berger Nemec Nedved Poborsky
Rada Hornak Kadlec Suchoparek
Kouba

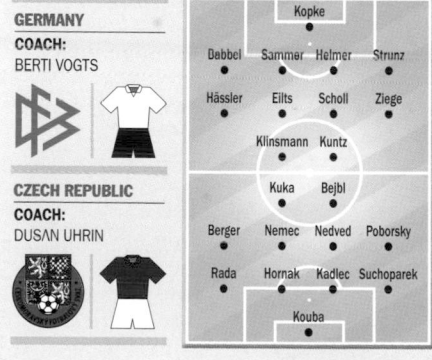

BELGIUM/HOLLAND 2000

SEMI-FINALS

Portugal 1-2 France
(aet: 1-1 at 90 mins)

Italy 0-0 Netherlands
(aet: Italy won 3-1 on penalties)

THIRD PLACE PLAY-OFF

Did not take place

TOP GOALSCORERS

5 goals: Patrick Kluivert (Holland)
Savo Milosevic (Yugoslavia)
4 goals: Nuno Gomes (Portugal)

FASTEST GOAL

3 mins: Paul Scholes
(England v Portugal)

TOTAL GOALS

85 goals

AVERAGE GOALS

2.74 per game

Above: Italy clinch a place in the final after a penalty victory over Holland. Opposite clockwise from top left: Alan Shearer wheels away after scoring the winner against Germany; Didier Deschamps holds the cup with the winning French squad; Luis Figo and Nuno Gomez led a talented Portuguese team to the semi-finals; Holland's Patrick Kluivert celebrates.

It was a tournament for purists, full of attacking flair, defensive ingenuity and high drama, most notably in the games played by the Dutch. But Euro 2000, held in Belgium and Holland, will be remembered for the extension of world champions France's footballing dominance, and the grace and guile of Zinedine Zidane. The midfielder, along with Portugal's Luis Figo, was undoubtedly the star of the tournament, entertaining fans with an armoury of tricks, flicks and defence-splitting passes. And while Figo and Portugal were the surprise package of the tournament, it was Zidane's France who extended their superiority following their World Cup win in 1998.

The opening game was indicative of how the tournament was to continue, mixing controversy with exciting football. But that drama would come at a cost, especially for Belgian goalkeeper Filip De Wilde, in the Group B clash between Belgium and Sweden.

THE FINAL

FRANCE (0) **2-1** (0) **ITALY**
(aet: 1-1 at 90 mins)

Date Sunday July 2, 2000 **Attendance** 50,000

Venue De Kuip Stadium, Rotterdam

Many would have preferred to see the attacking play of Holland against France, rather than the defensive Italians, but nevertheless the climax to Euro 2000 was a fascinating affair.

Having gone a goal down in the 54th minute to Marco Delvecchio, France threw on Sylvain Wiltord and David Trezeguet after 75 minutes. With full-time approaching, fortune favoured the French as Wiltord broke through in injury time to fire the ball beneath the body of goalkeeper Toldo and send the game into extra-time.

The first period was a typically cagey affair until Robert Pires hit a low cross into the Italian penalty area and David Trezeguet fired the ball into the roof of the net for the golden goal that would end the game and hand France victory.

HOW THE TEAMS LINED UP

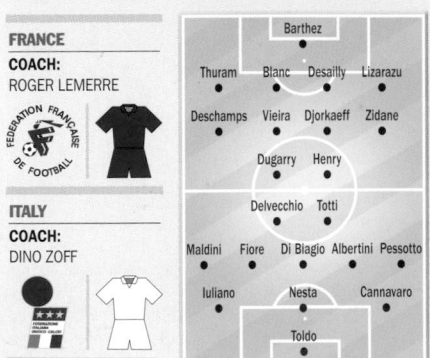

FRANCE

COACH:
ROGER LEMERRE

ITALY

COACH:
DINO ZOFF

FRANCE	
BARTHEZ	6
THURAM	6
Booked: 58 mins	
BLANC	*8
DESAILLY	7
LIZARAZU	6
Subbed: 86 mins (Pires)	
DESCHAMPS	6
VIEIRA	6
DJORKAEFF	6
Subbed: 76 mins (Trezeguet)	
ZIDANE	7
DUGARRY	6
Subbed: 57 mins (Wiltord)	
HENRY	7
sub: WILTORD	7
Goal: 90 mins	
sub: TREZEGUET	7
Goal: 103 mins	

ITALY	
TOLDO	7
CANNAVARO	*8
Booked: 41 mins	
NESTA	7
IULIANO	6
PESSOTTO	7
ALBERTINI	6
DI BIAGIO	6
Booked: 30 mins, Subbed: 66 mins (Ambrosini)	
FIORE	5
Subbed: 53 mins (Del Piero)	
MALDINI	7
TOTTI	6
Booked: 90 mins	
DELVECCHIO	7
Goal: 54 mins, Subbed: 86 mins (Montella)	
sub: AMBROSINI	6
sub: DEL PIERO	5
sub: MONTELLA	5

Referee: Frisk (Sweden)

He trod on the ball to allow Swedish striker Johan Mjallby to stroll past him and sweep the tournament's first goal into the net.

England's campaign started with equally catastrophic defensive incidents in Group A. After taking a two-goal lead against Portugal, Kevin Keegan's men were torn apart by Figo and conceded three goals. England went on to defeat arch-rivals Germany 1-0, but a defensive blunder from Phil Neville against Romania led to the penalty which knocked them, along with defending champions Germany, out of the tournament.

Almost immediately Keegan's credentials were criticised by the English press, as well as by a number of his own senior players, including first-team defender Martin Keown. The Arsenal centre-half accused the team of being inept tactically and claimed individual and collective errors had prevented England from beating teams they should have swept aside easily. The writing was already on the wall and Keegan's reign as England manager was to be short-lived. Meanwhile, Germany's failure to make it past the first round, almost unthinkable a few years earlier, was seen as indicative of a waning of their power.

Hosts Holland struggled to get out of first gear in their opening Group D game, defeating the Czech Republic by a single penalty, before demolishing Denmark 3-0 to cruise into the quarter-finals. It was here that Patrick Kluivert and his team-mates quickly upped the anté, firing six goals past a bemused Yugoslavian team in a performance that was pure perfection. But in their semi-final clash with Italy, who had defeated a strong Romanian side 2-0 in the quarter-finals, drama struck. Having been reduced to ten men after Gianluca Zambrotta was sent-off for a second bookable offence, Italy sat back and defended, with goalkeeper Francesco Toldo commanding his area admirably. Even with two penalty kicks in their favour, Holland, having been unable to convert either, failed to defeat the Italians. Worse was to come and after the golden goal period failed to produce a result, Holland missed the first three penalties of the shoot-out to gift the Italians victory. 'I think they could have played for the whole day shooting at our goal and they would never have scored', said Italian 'keeper Toldo. Dutch striker Dennis Bergkamp was more damning. 'We only have ourselves to blame,' he said, 'I don't know why Holland can't win a penalty shoot-out.'

Italy, who had infuriated fans and opponents alike with their ultra-defensive football in Group B, had ground their way to the final. Their qualifying group rivals Turkey were later knocked out of the quarter-finals by the Portuguese 2-0.

The French were ruthless in Group D, easing their way into the quarter-finals without ever looking stretched (a 3-2 defeat at the hands of the Dutch was played at half pace), dispensing with Spain 2-1 to progress into the semi-finals with goals from Zidane and Djorkaeff. Spain responded with a converted spot-kick from Mendieta, but minutes before the final whistle Raúl missed the game's second penalty, and with it the chance to take the game into extra-time. That the Spanish were unable to make it past the quarter-final stage in yet another international competition was proof that the tag of being perennial underachievers was hanging heavy.

Still, they had provided the game of the tournament when, in their final Group C clash against Yugoslavia, they came back from 3-2 down to score two goals in stoppage time and win the tie 4-3. At this stage in the competition many felt that the Spanish, with Raúl of Real Madrid and Valencia's Gaizka Mendieta hitting top form in attack, were likely contenders for the championships.

The French clearly had other ideas and, after sweeping aside Spain, they defeated the Portuguese in the semi-finals with an extra-time golden goal – Juventus striker David Trezeguet scoring with a thunderbolt of a shot from 12 yards. The battle between the tournament's two stars, Zidane and Figo, had gone in favour of the Frenchman. The final was set-up as a mouth watering battle between the attacking force of France and Italy's defence. But much more drama was to come.

EUROPEAN CHAMPIONSHIP RESULTS

Above: The England team managed third place in the 1968 European Championship, just two years after their World Cup win.

1960 FRANCE

SEMI-FINALS
Soviet Union **3-0** Czechoslovakia
Yugoslavia **5-4** France

THIRD PLACE PLAY-OFF
Czechoslovakia **2-0** France

FINAL
Soviet Union **2-1** Yugoslavia
(aet)

1964 SPAIN

SEMI-FINALS
Spain **2-1** Hungary
(aet)
Soviet Union **3-0** Denmark

THIRD PLACE PLAY-OFF
Hungary **3-1** Denmark
(aet)

FINAL
Spain **2-1** Soviet Union

1968 ITALY

SEMI-FINALS
Italy **0-0** Soviet Union
(aet)
Italy won on toss of a coin
Yugoslavia **1-0** England

THIRD PLACE PLAY-OFF
England **2-0** Soviet Union

FINAL
Italy **1-1** Yugoslavia
(aet)

REPLAY
Italy **2-0** Yugoslavia

1972 BELGIUM

SEMI-FINALS
West Germany **2-1** Belgium
Soviet Union **1-0** Hungary

THIRD PLACE PLAY-OFF
Belgium **2-1** Hungary

FINAL
West Germany **3-0** Soviet Union

1976 YUGOSLAVIA

SEMI-FINALS
Czechoslovakia **3-1** Holland
(aet)
West Germany **4-2** Yugoslavia
(aet)

THIRD PLACE PLAY-OFF
Holland **3-2** Yugoslavia
(aet)

FINAL
Czechoslovakia **2-2** West Germany
(aet)
Czechoslovakia won 5-4 on penalties

1980 ITALY

GROUP 1
West Germany **1-0** Czechoslovakia
Holland **1-0** Greece
West Germany **3-2** Holland
Czechoslovakia **3-1** Greece
Czechoslovakia **1-1** Holland
West Germany **0-0** Greece

	P	W	D	L	F	A	Pts
West Germany	3	2	1	0	4	2	5
Czechoslovakia	3	1	1	1	4	3	3
Holland	3	1	1	1	4	4	3
Greece	3	0	1	2	1	4	1

GROUP 2
Belgium **1-1** England
Spain **0-0** Italy
Spain **1-2** Belgium
Italy **1-0** England
Spain **1-2** England
Italy **0-0** Belgium

	P	W	D	L	F	A	Pts
Belgium	3	1	2	0	3	2	4
Italy	3	1	2	0	1	0	4
England	3	1	1	1	3	3	3
Spain	3	0	1	2	2	4	1

THIRD PLACE PLAY-OFF
Czechoslovakia **1-1** Italy
(no extra time)
Czechoslovakia won 9-8 on penalties

FINAL
West Germany **2-1** Belgium

1984 FRANCE

GROUP 1
France **1-0** Denmark
Belgium **2-0** Yugoslavia
France **5-0** Belgium
Denmark **5-0** Yugoslavia
France **3-2** Yugoslavia
Denmark **3-2** Belgium

	P	W	D	L	F	A	Pts
France	3	3	0	0	9	2	6
Denmark	3	2	0	1	8	3	4
Belgium	3	1	0	2	4	8	2
Yugoslavia	3	0	0	3	2	10	0

GROUP 2
West Germany **0-0** Portugal
Spain **1-1** Romania
West Germany **2-1** Romania
Portugal **1-1** Spain
West Germany **0-1** Spain
Portugal **1-0** Romania

	P	W	D	L	F	A	Pts
Spain	3	1	2	0	3	2	4
Portugal	3	1	2	0	2	1	4
West Germany	3	1	1	1	2	2	3
Romania	3	0	1	2	2	4	1

SEMI-FINALS
France **3-2** Portugal
(aet)
Spain **1-1** Denmark
(aet)
Spain won 5-4 on penalties

THIRD PLACE PLAY-OFF
Not held

FINAL
France **2-0** Spain

1988 WEST GERMANY

GROUP 1
West Germany **1-1** Italy
Denmark **2-3** Spain
West Germany **2-0** Denmark
Italy **1-0** Spain
West Germany **2-0** Spain
Italy **2-0** Denmark

	P	W	D	L	F	A	Pts
West Germany	3	2	1	0	5	1	5
Italy	3	2	1	0	4	1	5
Spain	3	1	0	2	3	5	2
Denmark	3	0	0	3	2	7	0

GROUP 2
England **0-1** Rep. Of Ireland
Holland **0-1** Soviet Union
England **1-3** Holland
Rep. Of Ireland **1-1** Soviet Union
England **1-3** Soviet Union
Rep. Of Ireland **0-1** Holland

	P	W	D	L	F	A	Pts
Soviet Union	3	2	1	0	5	2	5
Holland	3	2	0	1	4	2	4
Rep. Of Ireland	3	1	1	1	2	2	3
England	3	0	0	3	2	7	0

SEMI-FINALS
West Germany **1-2** Holland
Soviet Union **2-0** Italy

THIRD PLACE PLAY-OFF
Not held

FINAL
Holland **2-0** Soviet Union

1992 SWEDEN

GROUP A
Sweden **1-1** France
Denmark **0-0** England
France **0-0** England
Sweden **1-0** Denmark
Sweden **2-1** England
France **1-2** Denmark

	P	W	D	L	F	A	Pts
Sweden	3	2	1	0	4	2	5
Denmark	3	1	1	1	2	2	3
France	3	0	2	1	2	3	2
England	3	0	2	1	1	2	2

GROUP B
Holland **1-0** Scotland
Germany **1-1** CIS

Above: Franz Beckenbauer after West Germany's 1972 victory.

Above: Denmark's John Jensen in 1992.

	Germany	2-0	Scotland
Holland	0-0	CIS
Scotland	3-0	CIS
Holland	3-1	Germany

	P	W	D	L	F	A	Pts
Holland	3	2	1	0	4	1	5
Germany	3	1	1	1	4	4	3
Scotland	3	1	0	2	3	3	2
CIS	3	0	2	1	1	4	2

SEMI-FINALS

| Sweden | 2-3 | Germany |
| Holland | 2-2 | Denmark |

(aet)

Denmark won 5-4 on penalties

THIRD PLACE PLAY-OFF

Not held

FINAL

Denmark **2-0** Germany

1996 ENGLAND

GROUP A

England	1-1	Switzerland
Holland	0-0	Scotland
Switzerland	0-2	Holland
Scotland	0-2	England
Scotland	1-0	Switzerland
Holland	1-4	England

	P	W	D	L	F	A	Pts
England	3	2	1	0	7	2	7
Holland	3	1	1	1	3	4	4
Scotland	3	1	1	1	1	2	4
Switzerland	3	0	1	2	1	4	1

GROUP B

Spain	1-1	Bulgaria
Romania	0-1	France
Bulgaria	1-0	Romania
France	1-1	Spain
France	3-1	Bulgaria
Romania	1-2	Spain

	P	W	D	L	F	A	Pts
France	3	2	1	0	5	2	7
Spain	3	1	2	0	4	3	5
Bulgaria	3	1	1	1	3	4	4
Romania	3	0	0	3	1	4	0

GROUP C

Germany	2-0	Czech Republic
Italy	2-1	Russia
Czech Republic	2-1	Italy
Russia	0-3	Germany
Russia	3-3	Czech Republic
Italy	0-0	Germany

	P	W	D	L	F	A	Pts
Germany	3	2	1	0	5	0	7
Czech Republic	3	1	1	1	5	6	4
Italy	3	1	1	1	3	3	4
Russia	3	0	1	2	4	8	1

GROUP D

Denmark	1-1	Portugal
Turkey	0-1	Croatia
Portugal	1-0	Turkey
Denmark	0-3	Croatia
Croatia	0-3	Portugal
Denmark	3-0	Turkey

	P	W	D	L	F	A	Pts
Portugal	3	2	1	0	5	1	7
Croatia	3	2	0	1	4	3	6
Denmark	3	1	1	1	4	4	4
Turkey	3	0	0	3	0	5	0

QUARTER-FINALS

England **0-0** Spain
(aet)
England won 4-2 on penalties

France **0-0** Holland
(aet)
France won 5-4 on penalties

Germany **2-1** Croatia

Portugal **0-1** Czech Republic

SEMI-FINALS

France **0-0** Czech Republic
(aet)
Czech Republic won 6-5 on penalties

England **1-1** Germany
(aet)
Germany won 6-5 on penalties

THIRD PLACE PLAY-OFF

Not held

FINAL

Germany **2-1** Czech Republic
(aet)
Germany won with golden goal

2000 BELGIUM/HOLLAND

GROUP A

Germany	1-1	Romania
Portugal	3-2	England
Romania	0-1	Portugal
England	1-0	Germany
England	2-3	Romania
Portugal	3-0	Germany

	P	W	D	L	F	A	Pts
Portugal	3	3	0	0	7	2	9
Romania	3	1	1	1	4	4	4
England	3	1	0	2	5	6	3
Germany	3	0	1	2	1	5	1

GROUP B

Belgium	2-1	Sweden
Turkey	1-2	Italy
Italy	2-0	Belgium
Sweden	0-0	Turkey
Turkey	2-0	Belgium
Italy	2-1	Sweden

	P	W	D	L	F	A	Pts
Italy	3	3	0	0	6	2	9
Turkey	3	1	1	1	3	2	4
Belgium	3	1	0	2	2	5	3
Sweden	3	0	1	2	2	4	1

GROUP C

Spain	0-1	Norway
Yugoslavia	3-3	Slovenia
Slovenia	1-2	Spain
Norway	0-1	Yugoslavia
Yugoslavia	3-4	Spain
Slovenia	0-0	Norway

	P	W	D	L	F	A	Pts
Spain	3	2	0	1	6	5	6
Yugoslavia	3	1	1	1	7	7	4
Norway	3	1	1	1	1	1	4
Slovenia	3	0	2	1	4	5	2

GROUP D

France	3-0	Denmark
Holland	1-0	Czech Republic
Czech Republic	1-2	France
Denmark	0-3	Holland
France	2-3	Holland
Denmark	0-2	Czech Republic

	P	W	D	L	F	A	Pts
Holland	3	3	0	0	7	2	9
France	3	2	0	1	7	4	6
Czech Republic	3	1	0	2	3	3	3
Denmark	3	0	0	3	0	8	0

QUARTER-FINALS

Portugal	2-0	Turkey
Italy	2-0	Romania
Holland	6-1	Yugoslavia
France	2-1	Spain

SEMI-FINALS

Portugal **1-2** France
(aet)
France won with golden goal

Italy **0-0** Holland
(aet)
Italy won 3-1 on penalties

THIRD PLACE PLAY-OFF

Not held

FINAL

France **2-1** Italy
(aet)
France won with golden goal

Above: Oliver Bierhoff's golden goal wins the 1996 title for Germany.

Above: Winners in 1976, Czechoslovakia. Above top: France lift the trophy in 2000.

INTERNATIONAL COMPETITIONS

OLYMPIC GAMES

Football at the Olympics has gone through three distinct phases, evolving from a sport that hadn't convinced the International Olympic Committee of its popularity, before eventually becoming an essential ingredient to making any Olympic Games a success. The Olympic football tournament is now watched by more spectators than any other sporting discipline, including athletics. This has led to an uneasy partnership between the IOC and FIFA over the status of the Olympic football tournament.

There were unofficial tournaments at the first three Olympics, although a gold medal was awarded retrospectively at the 1904 games. The first official tournament was at the 1908 London Games. Six purely amateur teams competed, including French 'A' and 'B' teams. The two French sides were knocked-out by Denmark, who thrashed the 'B' team 9-0 and, in a game that included a ten-goal haul for Sophus Nielsen, the 'A' team 17-1. After such prolific success, the Danes ultimately lost the final to England 2-0.

The IOC were uncertain as to the popularity of football and actually questioned whether the sport warranted a place in the games in 1912, a competition which was again won by England. From 1920 to 1928, however, the Olympic football tournament was regarded as a world championship.

Belgium hosted and won the 1920 event held in Antwerp, beating Czechoslovakia 2-0 in the final – but the record books don't always mention the fact that after Larnoe had netted Belgium's second goal in the 78th minute, the Czech team walked off the pitch incensed at what they perceived as refereeing bias.

South American football dominated the

Olympics of 1924 and 1928 through the thrilling play of Uruguay, who won both tournaments. The World Cup was finally born two years later and from that point the two events would then rival one another until 1950, when the World Cup clearly established itself as football's premier event.

The post-war years brought the second phase of the Olympic football tournament. The Olympics still held firm to its amateur ethos, which was perfectly circumvented by the rising Eastern European Communist bloc countries. Under communist regimes, football was a leisure activity and the players were paid by, and deemed to work for, whatever national

institution or industry their club was affiliated to. Between 1952 and 1980 every Olympic football final was won by an East European team: Hungary (1952, 1964, 1968), USSR (1956), Yugoslavia (1960), Poland (1972), East Germany (1976) and Czechoslovakia (1980). Each final in this period, except for 1960, featured just East European teams.

The sequence was ended when France beat Brazil 2-0 in the 1984 final – but it was only because there had been a Communist bloc boycott of the Los Angeles Olympic Games in retaliation to the Western-led boycott of the Moscow Olympics four years earlier. For that tournament FIFA had already sought to address the problem and had ruled that any European or South American player who had played in a World Cup game became ineligible for the Olympics.

Ironically, it was the the Soviet Union that carefully planned their Olympic ambitions in conjunction with their European and World Cup hopes. The USSR had a hot property in 19-year-old Igor Dobrovolski who had five full caps, all in friendlies. Potentially he could have played at the European Championship in 1988, but he was redirected to the Olympics. It was well worth the gamble as Dobrovolski was excellent, helping the USSR to a gold medal, beating Brazil 2-1 in the final. Brazil were the only non-European side to make it as far as the semi-finals, but in Romario they produced the tournament's star player.

The competition also saw one of the greatest shocks in the history of the Olympics. Italy had been so determined to win the gold medal that they had gone as far as delaying the start of their domestic season to accommodate the

Olympic football tournament, but they were comprehensively beaten 4-0 by Zambia, with Kalusha Bwalya scoring a hat-trick.

Professional sport was now an integral part of the Olympics and the IOC wanted the football tournament to reflect that, with big names and big teams. FIFA, on the other hand, did not want a rival to the World Cup. In the third phase of Olympic football, and to the consternation of the IOC, FIFA decreed the tournament could only be an Under-23 event, with teams allowed to include just three over-age players.

Spain hosted and won the event in 1992, beating Poland 3-2 in a thrilling and dramatic final that attracted 95,000 spectators. In 1996 the final was played in Athens, Georgia, some 110 kilometres north west of the Olympic host city of Atlanta where no football matches were staged at all. Nevertheless, a staggering 1.36 million paying spectators witnessed the competition, culminating in Nigeria's 3-2 defeat of Argentina in the final.

Cameroon followed up that African success with victory in Australia in 2000, winning the gold medal in a penalty shoot-out with Spain. It was Cameroon's first Olympic gold medal in any sport, proving that the Olympics needs football, whatever its status.

COPA AMERICA
(SOUTH AMERICAN CHAMPIONSHIP)

The South American Championship is the oldest continental title in the world, having been staged 41 different times, including eight that are deemed unofficial. It has been played under various names and in varying formats, but since 1975 it has been known as the Copa América. There have been seven different winners of the championship over the years, but for the most part the competition has been dominated by the national sides of Argentina and Uruguay.

Argentina gave birth to the event in 1910, hosting and winning a triangular tournament that also involved Uruguay and Chile. Six years later, as part of the centenary celebrations to mark the country's independence from Spain, a second tournament was organised with the addition of Brazil, but this time the cup was won by Uruguay. Both events were actually unofficial, as the Confederación Sudamericana de Futbol (CONEMBOL) was only founded during the 1916 tournament.

The first official tournament took place in Uruguay just over a year later and was contested by the same four teams with the same outcome, Uruguay winners again. The championships were played on a league basis with all the games staged in one host city (except 1949) until 1975. During the 1920s the South American Championship was an annual event, but the rise of professionalism led to a hiatus of six years, when an unofficial professional championship was staged in Peru in 1935. The success of this tournament led to a revival in interest and a plethora of sanctioned and unsanctioned tournaments were staged during the Forties and Fifties. These competitions were invariably won by Argentina or Uruguay, except in 1939, 1949 and 1953, when Peru, Brazil and Paraguay triumphed respectively.

By the 1960s the championship began to suffer from the increased popularity of the international club game, and in particular the Copa Libertadores. Played just twice in the decade, in 1963 and 1967, the South American Championship disappeared for eight years from the football calendar after 30 rounds. When it did return in 1975, all ten members of CONEMBOL entered for the first time. The format was revamped and played on a home and away basis. The winners from three groups of three teams joined holders Uruguay in two-legged semi-finals. The final was

Right: Brazil lift the Copa
América trophy in 1989.

Below right: After victory
over Honduras, the USA's
Peter Vermes lifts the first
ever Gold Cup trophy in 1991.

COPA AMÉRICA
WINNERS

1910: Argentina*
1916: Uruguay*
1917: Uruguay
1919: Brazil
1920: Uruguay
1921: Argentina
1922: Brazil
1923: Uruguay
1924: Uruguay
1925: Argentina
1926: Uruguay
1927: Argentina
1929: Argentina
1935: Uruguay*
1937: Argentina
1939: Peru
1941: Argentina*
1942: Uruguay
1945: Argentina*
1946: Argentina*
1947: Argentina
1949: Brazil
1953: Paraguay
1955: Argentina
1956: Uruguay*
1957: Argentina
1959: Argentina
1959: Uruguay*
1963: Bolivia
1967: Uruguay
1975: Peru
1979: Paraguay
1983: Uruguay
1987: Uruguay
1989: Brazil
1991: Argentina
1993: Argentina
1995: Uruguay
1997: Brazil
1999: Brazil
2001: Columbia

* Unofficial Tournaments

contested by Peru and Colombia, with each team winning a match before Peru clinched a play-off victory 1-0 in Caracas.

In 1987 the Copa América reverted to being staged by a single host country. This was the ideal logistical solution. However, fans of the various host nations were notoriously fickle. For example, in Argentina that year only 500 fans bothered to turn up to watch Colombia play Bolivia. And in 1995, less than 100 fans watched Paraguay's clash with Venezuela in Uruguay, which at least did have the mitigating circumstances of being played in a torrential downpour.

It also has to be said that most tournaments have not produced good football. The 1987 event was dire and witnessed 14 players sent-off in 13 games. The final between Uruguay and Chile was a foul-riddled affair that saw four players dismissed. Uruguay, as holders, had been given a bye to the semi-finals and, therefore, had successfully defended the title by playing just two games.

The next tournament saw Brazil win their first major honour since the 1970 World Cup victory some 19 years earlier. The competition featured two groups of five teams, leading to a final round of four teams – that meant a schedule of 26 games in 12 days, with teams playing every other day to bring in the much needed TV revenues and gate receipts. CONEMBOL justified this as preparation for the 1990 World Cup, but as one player – Uruguay's Pablo Bengochea – failed a drugs

test which revealed more than the permitted amount of caffeine in his urine, it was a schedule too gruelling for some.

The other problem facing teams was that many of the European-based players were absent from the competition, while the best of the talent on display would invariably end up Europe-bound after catching-the-eye during the tournament. It was to become a problem that was further aggravated by CONEMBOL's decision to create a fixture-heavy World Cup qualifying programme. To earn the TV money, teams played up to 18 qualifying matches. The Copa América became a secondary concern to many teams, who fielded under-strength sides.

A desire to revitalise the event, plus a need for increased TV revenues, led CONEMBOL to invite other teams from around the world to take part. So far Mexico (finalists in 1993 and 2001), USA, Costa Rica, Japan and Honduras have all participated. Canada was invited in 2001 but when the event in Colombia looked set to be postponed they withdrew, along with Argentina.

Argentina won their 15th title in 1993, beating Mexico 2-1 in the final, while Uruguay's 14th trophy was won in 1995 following a penalty shoot-out win over Brazil. In 1997 Bolivia's Juan Baldivieso scored the Copa América's 2,000th goal, but it was Brazil who lifted the trophy that year, as they did again in 1999. Colombia became the seventh nation to win the Copa América when they hosted the 41st competition in 2001.

CONCACAF CHAMPIONSHIP
(GOLD CUP)

When Jack Warner was elected as President of CONCACAF in April 1990 he insisted on setting up an equivalent to the Nations Cup competitions that existed in Africa, Asia, Europe and South America.

Previous incarnations such as the CCCF Championship, run by the Confederación Centroamericana y del Caribe de Fútbol between 1941 and 1961, and the CONCACAF Championship, which ran from 1963 to 1989 had been limited successes. Mexico did not enter until 1963 and initially did not take the competition that seriously. The USA was another notable absentee as well.

In 1991 the CONCACAF Gold Cup was born. Twenty-eight teams entered chasing six qualifying places. The inaugural tournament was hosted by the USA, as have been all subsequent tournaments, although in 1993 they co-hosted the event with Mexico.

Under coach Bora Milutinovic, the USA won the first Gold Cup. Recording a 2-0 win over the Mexicans in the semi-final, it was their first victory over their near neighbours in 11 years, which led the Mexico coach Manuel Lapuente to resign on the spot. The final was played at the Coliseum in Los Angeles and after a goalless game the destination of the trophy was decided by penalty shoot-out. Sixteen penalties were taken in all, during which the USA's goalkeeper Tony Meola, who was voted the tournament's Most Valuable Player, saved three kicks. Spot kick number 15 saw Honduras's Espinoza fire the ball over the

bar, allowing Clavijo to convert for a 4-3 victory.

Two years later a rampant Mexico got their revenge. Despite being co-hosts, Mexico had originally submitted a 'B' team, but it was roundly rejected by CONCACAF Secretary Chuck Blazer. A full strength Mexico blew away most of the opposition, thrashing Martinique 9-0 (including seven goals for Zaguinho), Canada 8-0, and Jamaica 6-1 in a game that saw goalkeeper Jorge Campos switch to centre-forward when the reserve goalkeeper came on as a substitute in the second-half. In front of 120,000 screaming fans in Mexico City, the Mexicans, under coach Miguel Mejia Baron, comprehensively beat the Americans 4-0 in the final.

A switch of dates from July in odd years to January in even years began with the third tournament in 1996. There was a further change with the addition of an invited team – Brazil, who sent their Olympic Under-23 side for the nine-team tournament but still managed to reach the final where they faced Mexico, who were now under ex-USA boss Bora Milutinovic. Backed by the majority of the 88,155 crowd in the Los Angeles Coliseum, and playing in appalling conditions directly after the third place play-off match contested at the same venue, Mexico were cynically determined to win. They committed 38 fouls on the way to a 2-0 victory.

Brazil were invited again and allowed to play their games in Miami, despite California being firmly established as the home of the Gold Cup. This was connected to the revenue from television, as Los Angeles was some six hours ahead of Brazil, while Miami offered just a three-hour time difference. In a rain-affected tournament, one tie between Jamaica and El Salvador was postponed because of the weather. There was a low turn-out of 11,234 for the tournament's opening fixture between hosts USA and Cuba (the first meeting between the two countries since 1949), but USA went on to record their first ever win over Brazil at full international level thanks to a goal from Preki in the semi-finals. The real hero of the game was goalkeeper Kasey Keller who was magnificent under relentless Brazilian pressure. But it was Mexico, back under Manuel Lapuente, who were to complete a hat-trick of wins, beating the USA by a single Luis Hernandez goal in the final.

There were 12 teams battling for the £100,000 prize money in 2000, including guest teams Peru, South Korea and Colombia. It was also the tournament that revealed just how financially dependent the competition was on Mexican success. Mexico were knocked-out at the quarter-final stage by a 'golden goal' from Canada's Richard Hastings, and with hosts USA going out on penalties to Colombia at the same stage, attendance figures subsequently plummeted. The tournament's final between Canada and Colombia attracted just 6,197 spectators inside the Los Angeles Coliseum. Canada, who had earlier progressed through the group stage on the toss of a coin at the expense of South Korea, won 2-0 with a headed goal from Jason De Vos and a Carlo Corazzin penalty.

The 2002 event reverted to nine finalists, including guests Ecuador, who were knocked-out at the group stage by a draw of lots which allowed Canada and Haiti through. Mexico sent a 'B' team, under enormous pressure from the clubs back home not to select their best players, but they still managed to increase the disappointing crowds to an average of 18,500 for the event, which climaxed with the USA's 2-0 defeat of Costa Rica with goals from Josh Wolff and Jeff Agoos.

Mexico clinched a record fourth Gold Cup in 2003. A golden goal from Daniel Osorno in the 97th minute defeated favourites Brazil in the final.

ASIAN CUP

The second oldest continental competition in the world, the Asian Cup is played once every four years and has run uninterrupted since 1956, involving a qualifying competition from the outset. The first three Asian Cups were contested in a four-team league and won by South Korea in both 1956 and 1960, and Israel who had been runners up at the first two tournaments – in 1964. The 1964 competition was notable for its lack of skilled football and for its poor sportsmanship.

Iran made their debut in 1968, both hosting and winning the tournament. Iran's success was significant because it boosted the game of football in Arabic countries, where it had previously been banned due to religious reasons. The five-team finals marked the last appearance of Israel, while North Korea, the Asian heroes of the 1966 World Cup, bizarrely did not even enter.

THE CONCACAF CHAMPIONSHIP (GOLD CUP)

WINNERS

1941: Costa Rica
1943: El Salvador
1946: Costa Rica
1948: Costa Rica
1951: Panama
1953: Costa Rica
1955: Costa Rica
1957: Haiti
1960: Costa Rica
1961: Costa Rica
1963: Costa Rica
1965: Mexico
1967: Guatemala
1969: Costa Rica
1971: Mexico
1973: Haiti
1977: Mexico
1981: Honduras
1985: Canada
1989: Costa Rica
1991: USA
1993: Mexico
1996: Mexico
1998: Mexico
2000: Canada
2002: USA
2003: Mexico

Above left to right: Karim Bagheri of Iraq at the Asian Games in 1998; Japan lift the Asian Cup in Beirut in 2000.

THE ASIAN CUP
WINNERS

1956: South Korea

1960: South Korea

1964: Israel

1968: Iran

1972: Iran

1976: Iran

1980: Kuwait

1984: Saudi Arabia

1988: Saudi Arabia

1992: Japan

1996: Saudi Arabia

2000: Japan

THE ASIAN GAMES
WINNERS

1951: India

1954: Taiwan

1958: Taiwan

1962: India

1966: Burma

1970: Burma & South Korea *(title shared)*

1974: Iran

1978: South Korea & North Korea *(title shared)*

1982: Iraq

1986: South Korea

1990: Iran

1994: Uzbekistan

1998: Iran

2002: Iran

Semi-finals and a final were added to the six-team league stage in 1972, Iran dominating the revamped competition and winning the final with a 2-1 victory over South Korea after extra-time, Khalany scoring the 107th minute winner in Bangkok. The Iranians completed a hat-trick of triumphs in 1976 when, as hosts, they beat Kuwait 1-0. Iran went 17 successive Asian Cup games without defeat, with their magnificent run ultimately ended by Kuwait in the semi-finals of the 1980 competition. Kuwait went on to win the trophy in one of the most entertaining tournaments in the history of the Asian Cup – 76 goals were scored in the 24 games.

The number of entrants generally increased as the competition progressed, but in the politically volatile region there were inevitable withdrawals for various reasons – however, the Asian Cup increased in prestige, helped by the gradual rise of professionalism. Saudi Arabia beat China in the 1984 final and successfully defended the title four years later in a Middle East dominated competition, with seven out of the ten finalists from that region.

Japan were victorious at the 1992 Asian Cup, a tournament that was hit by political problems, with only 23 out of the 37 members entering. The finals were marred by violent play on the pitch, with eight players sent-off and 49 booked. Iran were the worst culprits, with three players facing one-year bans and another two receiving match bans.

At the 40th anniversary tournament in 1996 Iran were to win the Fair Play Award, as well as boasting both the highest goalscorer in Ali Daei and the Player Of The Tournament in Khodadad Azizi. The host nation lost a final for the very first time, when Saudi Arabia beat the United Arab Emirates in a penalty shoot-out to win the 12-team tournament. This was a particularly impressive display since three Saudi players had been suspended for breaking Islamic Sharia Law.

Japan beat Saudi Arabia 1-0 in Beirut to win the 2000 tournament, with a goal from Shigeyoshi Mochizuki, only playing in the final because Junichi Inamoto had been suspended. Earlier in the competition Japan had set a goalscoring record when they thrashed Uzbekistan 8-1. The tournament continues to go from strength to strength, and China will host the first 16-team event in 2004.

ASIAN GAMES

Football has always been part of the multi-sport Asian Games since the inaugural event was held in India in 1951. Six teams entered the first tournament, playing matches of 80 minutes in duration, but the standard was not particularly high with the hosts beating Iran 1-0 in the final.

From such humble beginnings the football tournament has increased in size, with Taiwan, mainly represented by players from Hong Kong, winning the finals in 1954 and 1958, beating South Korea on both occasions. The latter competition was marred by accusations of biased and incompetent refereeing.

In political terms the participation of both Taiwan and Israel were a problem in 1962 and hosts Indonesia ultimately rescinded their invitation to both teams. In 1974 both North and South Korea refused to play Israel, so after a 3-0 win over Burma, the Israelis found themselves in the final, where they lost to Iran by an own-goal.

On two occasions the gold medal has been shared. In both 1970 and 1978 South Korea were held to 0-0 draws, firstly by Burma and then by North Korea. South Korea finally won the gold medal outright in 1986, a competition noted for a quarter-final round decided entirely by penalty shoot-outs.

Iran has dominated the Asian Games since 1990, winning three out of four tournaments. Goalkeeper Ahadreze Abedzadeh was the hero in Beijing in 1990, saving two penalties in a 4-1 shoot-out victory over North Korea. That tournament was played in the shadow of the Iraqi invasion of Kuwait – the Kuwaiti team went on to reach the quarter-finals, while Iraq was banned from the competition and both India and Indonesia withdrew.

Iran won the gold medal again in 1998, beating Kuwait 2-0 in the first final between West Asian sides. Despite having Mehdi Mahdavikia sent-off late in the game, Iran outplayed a depleted Kuwait, with first-half goals from Ahmed Karimi and Karim Bagheri. By this point, the tournament had become a 24-team event (although Saudi Arabia withdrew) and was played over three weeks.

By the 2002 Asian Games, the football tournament had been revamped and turned into an Under-23 competition, with each team allowed to field up to three over-age players. The idea was to prepare Asian teams for the Olympics. However, this revamp seemed to have a detrimental effect on attendances.

Held in South Korea after the World Cup, the cream of Asian youth seemed a massive turn-off to Korean fans now accustomed to the big names of world football, and many of the games were played in half-empty stadiums. When South Korea were knocked out by Iran in the semi-finals, fans attempted to get refunds for their final tickets. Iran became the first team to retain the title outright, beating Japan 2-1 with goals from Kazemeyan and Bayatiniya. The tournament marked the return of Afghanistan after an 18-year absence, but they lost all three games, conceding 32 goals.

AFRICAN NATIONS CUP

The first African Nations Cup was held in Sudan in 1957 between Egypt, Ethiopia, South Africa and Sudan – the founder members of the Confédération Africaine de Football (CAF). However, South Africa were forced to withdraw when they refused to send a multi-racial team. They offered only an all-white or an all-black team, neither of which was acceptable to the other CAF members. South Africa did not return until they hosted and won the 1996 tournament.

In the Khartoum Stadium on February 16, 1957, the first African Nations Cup was decided when Egypt easily defeated Ethiopia 4-0, with all four goals scored by El Diba. It was appropriate that Egypt should be the first winners, since the trophy itself had been donated by Abdel Aziz Salem, the first president of CAF and an Egyptian. Since then the African Nations Cup has developed from a small three-team tournament to a 16-team event that is televised all over the world.

The 1960s saw the rise of Ghana, winners of the tournament in 1963 and 1965, runners-up in 1968 and 1970. Ghana had drawn on the experience of a number of European coaches and even embarked on a European tour in 1962, proving themselves to be far and away the best team in Africa at the time. Although successive Nations Cup triumphs were just 23 months apart, only one player, Odametey, played in both finals. Ghana finally won the Abdel Aziz Abdulla Salem Cup – as the original African Nations Cup trophy was officially known – outright in 1978.

For the 1968 tournament there was a qualifying round for the first time – and that year's final, when Zaire beat favourites Ghana 1-0 with a goal from Kalala, was the first

African Nations Cup match to be televised. In 1970 Sudan beat Ghana in the final, but it was Ivory Coast who broke the record for the biggest win in the finals with a 6-1 thrashing of Ethiopia, Pokou scoring a record haul of five goals in that game.

The African Nations Cup finally came of age in the Eighties. Nigeria, buoyant through oil money, staged a magnificent tournament in 1980, with state-of-the-art facilities and enormous spectator support. A total of 735,000 fans attended the 16 games, including an 80,000 capacity in the Surulere in Lagos for a final that saw Nigeria beat Algeria 3-0.

A new dimension was brought to the African Nations Cup in 1982 when all the games, staged in Libya, were played on artificial pitches. Technically it was a good tournament but goals were at a premium. The final itself was resolved by a penalty shoot-out, with Ghana overcoming the hosts 7-6 on penalties after a 1-1 draw.

Ivory Coast was consumed by football fever when they staged the tournament in 1984, but national pride – and local interest in the competition – was severely dented when the hosts went out in the first round. The crowds stayed away from the latter stages and the organisers were forced to give tickets away to get a capacity crowd for the final, in which Cameroon came from a goal down to beat Nigeria 3-1. This tournament was the first to seriously arouse the interest of European scouts following the impressive performance of the African nations at the 1982 World Cup. This proved the start of the plundering of African talent by the leading clubs of Europe,

a problem for the tournament in later years.

The refusal of European clubs to release players in 1990 contributed to a poor tournament. In 1992 CAF responded by switching the event to January and increasing the number of finalists to 12. Of the 263 players on call, some 83 were professionals from the European leagues. It was west Africa that dominated the tournament, which for the first time had comprehensive television coverage. Sadly it was not a great tournament, although the final produced a dramatic climax – after a goalless draw, the match was settled with a 20-minute penalty shoot-out involving 24 spot-kicks. Ivory Coast ultimately won the shoot-out 11-10 when Ghana's Tony Baffoe saw his kick saved after Kouame Akaa had converted with his second penalty of the shoot-out.

The 1994 final was one of the best in the history of the African Nations Cup. Zambia faced Nigeria, just a year after the air crash that had wiped out the Zambian national team. Litana put Zambia ahead after just three minutes, but Emmanuel Amunike equalised two minutes later and then scored the winner in the 47th minute. Amazingly it had been his first appearance in the tournament, making him the 19th squad player used by Nigeria in the finals.

In the following tournament, Mahmoud Al-Gohari became the first man to win the African Nations Cup as both a player (1959) and a coach (1998) when he guided Egypt to glory in Burkina Faso in 1998. In the most recent competitions, Cameroon became the first team in 37 years to retain the title when they lifted the trophy in 2000 and 2002.

Above: Cameroon celebrate victory in the African Nations Cup in Lagos in 2000.

Below left: After 39 years out of the competition, hosts South Africa lift the African Nations Cup at the first attempt in 1996.

AFRICAN NATIONS CUP
WINNERS

1957:	Egypt
1959:	Egypt
1962:	Ethiopia
1963:	Ghana
1965:	Ghana
1968:	Congo-Kinshasa
1970:	Sudan
1972:	Congo
1974:	Zaïre
1976:	Morocco
1978:	Ghana
1980:	Nigeria
1982:	Ghana
1984:	Cameroon
1986:	Egypt
1988:	Cameroon
1990:	Algeria
1992:	Ivory Coast
1994:	Nigeria
1996:	South Africa
1998:	Egypt
2000:	Cameroon
2002:	Cameroon

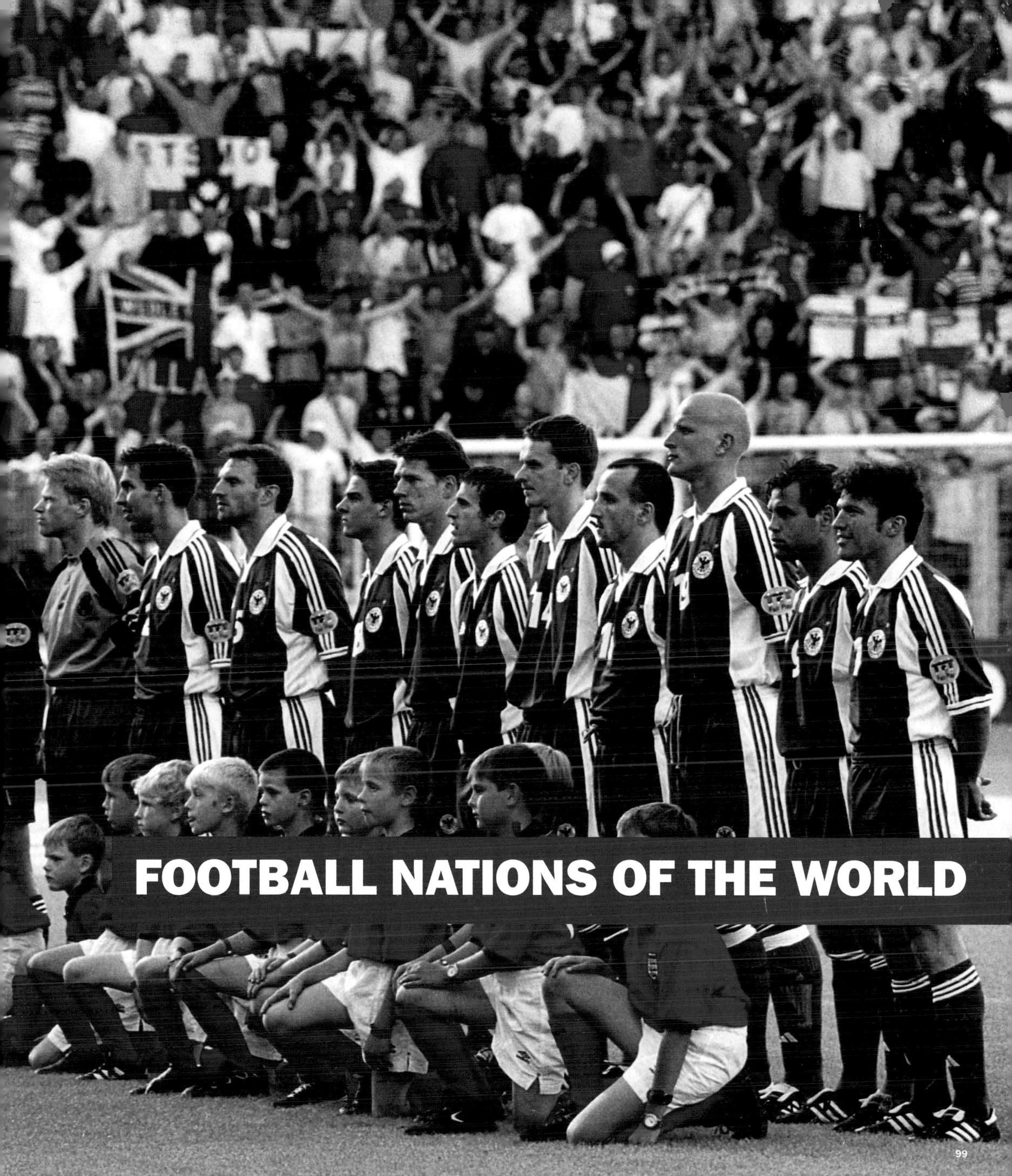

FOOTBALL NATIONS OF THE WORLD

THE COUNTRIES AND CONFEDERATIONS OF WORLD FOOTBALL

FIFA FÉDÉRATION INTERNATIONALE DE FOOTBALL ASSOCIATION

Founded: 1904 **Headquarters:** Zurich, Switzerland **Members:** 204

Competitions: World Cup, Women's World Cup, Under-17 World Championship, World Youth Championship, World Club Championship, Confederations Cup

The FIFA World rankings listed for each country in this chapter are as they stood in June 2003.

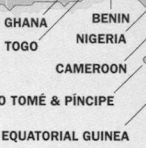

CONCACAF

CONFEDERATION OF NORTH, CENTRAL AMERICAN AND CARIBBEAN ASSOCIATION FOOTBALL

Founded: 1961

Headquarters: New York, USA

Members: 35

Competitions: Gold Cup, Women's Gold Cup, Champions Cup, Copa Pan-Americana

Seats On FIFA Executive

UEFA	👤👤👤👤👤👤👤👤
AFC	👤👤👤
CAF	👤👤👤👤
CONMEBOL	👤👤👤
CONCACAF	👤👤👤
FIFA	👤👤
OFC	👤

CONMEBOL

CONFEDERACIÓN SUDAMERICANA DE FÚTBOL

Founded: 1916

Headquarters: Asunción, Paraguay

Members: 10

Competitions: Copa América, Copa Libertadores, Copa Pan-Americana

Right: Albania's Fatmir Vata clears from England's Nick Barmby during a World Cup qualifier at St James' Park.

AFGHANISTAN

Federation: Afghanistan Football Federation
Founded: 1922
Joined FIFA: 1948
Confederation: AFC
FIFA world ranking: 199th

ALBANIA

Federation: Federata Shqiptare e Futbollit
Founded: 1930
Joined FIFA: 1932
Confederation: UEFA
FIFA world ranking: 88

Football arrived in Albania at the turn of the century but the ruling Turks actively prevented the locals playing the game. Independence in 1912 saw the game flourish and in 1930 the Football Association of Albania (FSF) was formed, along with the Albanian league championship. However, between 1938 and 1944 football activities ceased, with the country first under the control of Mussolini's fascists and then the Soviet-backed Communists.

Football returned after World War II and Albania claimed their only title as Balkan Cup winners in 1946. A period of self-imposed isolation followed and between 1954 and 1963 Albania played just one international. In the 1960s Albania began to compete at both club and national level for the first time. They remain one of Europe's football minnows, with a poor record. During the 1980s, for example, the national team won just two matches. On the domestic scene in Albania, the game is dominated by the Tirana clubs.

ALGERIA

Federation: Fédération Algérienne de Football
Founded: 1962
Joined FIFA: 1963
Confederation: CAF
FIFA world ranking: 68
Honours: African Nations Cup 1990

Right: Ali Benhalima, one of a handful of Algerian players to make an impact on the world stage.

Arguably the greatest moment in Algerian football history was the shock 2-1 defeat of the mighty West Germany at the 1982 World Cup. Algeria, under coach Mahieddine Khalef, gave

a resolute defensive performance against the attacking Germans, with goals from Rabah Madjer and Lakhdar Belloumi earning the landmark victory. However, Algeria were cheated out of a second round place by 'The Great Gijón Swindle' when a convenient 1-0 win for West Germany over Austria sent both those nations through at Algeria's expense. In 1990 Algeria finally experienced success when they hosted and won the African Nations Cup for the first time, an Oudjani goal beating Nigeria 1-0 in the final.

It was the French who introduced the game to Algeria at the turn of the century. By the 1920s the Muslim Algerians embraced the game and football quickly became the focus of a rising nationalist sentiment that was to lead to the country's independence from France in 1962. The first Algerian national league culminated in 1963 with USM Algeria winning the first title. JS Kabylie (aka JE Tizi-Ouzou), the Berber region team, have been the most successful Algerian side both at home and in the modern African game, having recently won a hat-trick of CAF Cups in 2000, 2001 and 2002.

AMERICAN SAMOA

Federation: American Samoa Football Association
Founded: 1984
Joined FIFA: 1998
Confederation: OFC
FIFA world ranking: 202

ANDORRA

Federation: Federacio Andorrana de Futbol
Founded: 1994
Joined FIFA: 1996
Confederation: UEFA
FIFA world ranking: 142 (joint)

The Principality of Andorra boasts an open eight-club top division vying for a fan-base from its 71,000 inhabitants. In November 2000 double winners Constellacio were relegated for alleged vote buying and financial irregularities. The national team has yet to win a competitive game and has chalked up just two friendly victories.

ANGOLA

Federation: Federação Angolana de Futebol
Founded: 1977
Joined FIFA: 1980
Confederation: CAF
FIFA world ranking: 81

ANGUILLA

Federation: Anguilla Football Association
Founded: 1990
Joined FIFA: 1996
Confederation: CONCACAF
FIFA world ranking: 197

ANTIGUA AND BARBUDA

Federation: Antigua/Barbuda Football Association
Founded: 1928
Joined FIFA: 1970
Confederation: CONCACAF
FIFA world ranking: 159

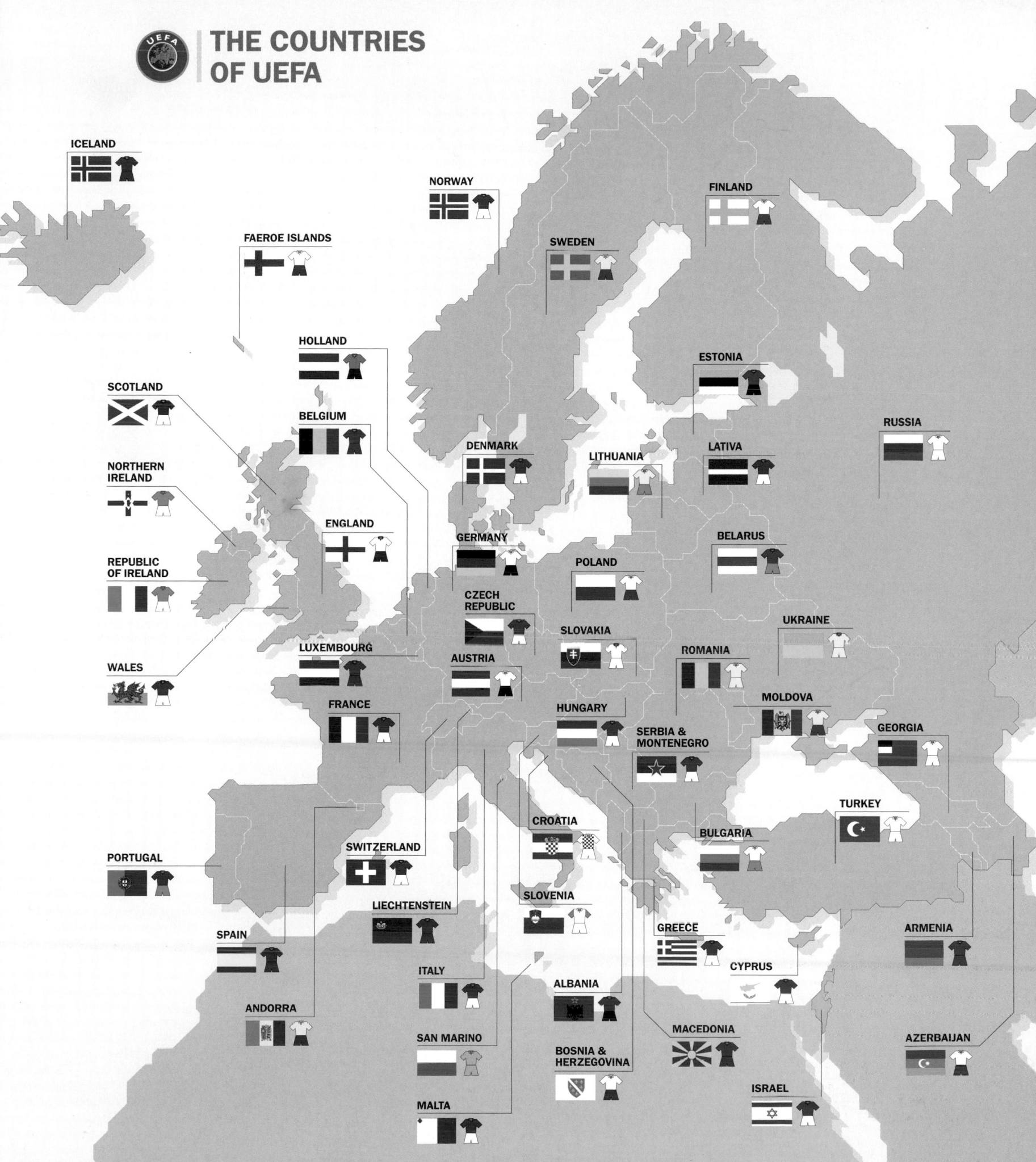

THE COUNTRIES OF UEFA

ICELAND

NORWAY

FINLAND

FAEROE ISLANDS

SWEDEN

HOLLAND

ESTONIA

RUSSIA

SCOTLAND

BELGIUM

DENMARK

LITHUANIA

LATIVA

NORTHERN
IRELAND

ENGLAND

GERMANY

POLAND

BELARUS

REPUBLIC
OF IRELAND

CZECH
REPUBLIC

SLOVAKIA

UKRAINE

WALES

LUXEMBOURG

AUSTRIA

ROMANIA

MOLDOVA

FRANCE

HUNGARY

SERBIA &
MONTENEGRO

GEORGIA

CROATIA

BULGARIA

TURKEY

PORTUGAL

SWITZERLAND

SLOVENIA

GREECE

ARMENIA

SPAIN

LIECHTENSTEIN

CYPRUS

ITALY

ALBANIA

ANDORRA

SAN MARINO

MACEDONIA

AZERBAIJAN

BOSNIA &
HERZEGOVINA

ISRAEL

MALTA

ARGENTINA

Federation: Asociación del Fútbol Argentina
Founded: 1893
Joined FIFA: 1912
Confederation: CONMEBOL
FIFA world ranking: 4
Honours: World Cup 1978, 1986; Copa América 1910, 1921, 1925, 1927, 1929, 1937, 1941, 1945, 1946, 1947, 1955, 1957, 1959, 1991, 1993

Argentina's football history can be traced back to 1867, when immigrant English and Italian rail workers and sailors introduced the game to the South American country. The English High School put together a club that captured ten of the 12 league titles following the formation of the Argentinian league in 1891 and although they were the most successful team, Buenos Aires FC claim to be the first formed in the country and the first outside of the British Isles and the USA.

The first international played outside of England also involved Argentina, who beat Uruguay 3-1 in 1901. The first South American championship was also hosted and won by the country some nine years later, although the tournament consisted of just two other teams, Uruguay and Chile.

The early years of the 20th Century saw the league's reputation grow in stature with the formation of the Buenos Aires 'Big Five': River Plate (founded by the English), Racing Club (the French and European descendants born in Argentina), Boca Juniors, Independiente and San Lorenzo, clubs that dominate the championship to this day.

The years either side of World War I saw the number of clubs rise to 20 and in the 1920s the league was at its most expansive, with 36 clubs. On the world stage Argentina had a good showing in the inaugural World Cup, losing to hosts and old foes Uruguay 4-2 in the final. This success led to the beginning of the professional era in 1932, with Boca Juniors setting the pace following three championship victories in the first four seasons. River Plate and Independiente would also enjoy extended spells of dominance, with the former enjoying a purple patch of five championships in six years during the 1950s.

It was within the first three decades of the formation of its professional league that Argentina established itself as a super power in world football. Attendances grew, stadiums improved and the international team won eight of its record 15 Copa América titles.

The ultimate prize of winning the World Cup had eluded the nation thus far. However, a league-restructuring programme in 1967

Above: The Argentina players celebrate winning the Copa América after their victory over Mexico in Ecuador in 1993.
Opposite: Diego Maradona capped a series of fine performances in the tournament by lifting the World Cup in 1986.

had a positive effect. The formation of two regional competitions, the Metropolitano and the Nacional, cut down on travelling times and expenses, leaving clubs to flourish and this was reflected with Racing Club, Estudiantes, Independiente and Boca Juniors all winning the World Club Cup within the next ten years.

Boca's victory against West German side Borussia Mönchengladbach in 1977 also proved to be the catalyst to World Cup success the following year. As hosts, Cesar Luis Menotti saw his team sweep all before them, including pre-tournament favourites Holland 3-1 in the final. Played out to a ticker tape welcome in the Monumental Stadium, Buenos Aires, Mario Kempes' two goals made him more popular than the country's president and as soon as the tournament ended, a statue was erected in the capital in the striker's honour.

Yet while Kempes had secured a place in Argentinian football history, his star would soon be cast into the shadows by the emerging talent of Diego Armando Maradona. Having started his career with Argentinos Juniors, where he scored 116 goals in 166 games, a move to Boca Juniors proved equally fruitful and the 20-year-old's performances secured his team the 1981 Metropolitano title.

Maradona's undoubted talents were thrust onto the world stage at the 1982 World Cup Finals in Spain and although he made an impression with his silky skills, unrivalled ball control and wonderful dribbles, his suspect temperament was also on show as a rash kick at Brazil substitute Batista brought an end to his participation with a red card.

Bowing out in round two proved to be a temporary blip for Argentinian football and having reverted to a single national league in

1985, Independiente's World Club Cup victory against Liverpool in 1984 and River Plate's success against Steaua Bucharest two years later only emphasised the buoyancy which carried itself through to the 1986 World Cup Finals, where Maradona reigned supreme.

Fans of Pelé might argue otherwise, but never in a World Cup finals had one player made such an impact. Although Real Madrid striker Jorge Valdano's contribution cannot be underestimated, Maradona literally took teams apart single-handedly, as both Belgium and England – the 'Hand of God' goal apart – would confirm. His second goal against Bobby Robson's side is regarded as one of the all-time great strikes, and although the skipper did not reach his usual dizzy heights in the 3-2 final win against West Germany, few would argue that he deserved to lift the trophy at the very peak of his career.

Argentina again reached the final in 1990 – when the Germans gained revenge – but their unsightly mix of roughhouse tactics and safety-first approach won them few friends and signalled a country in decline. Maradona's positive test for cocaine in 1994 was seen as the final nail in the coffin and, as Brazil began to re-establish themselves as South America's top nation, Argentina's decline continued.

The conveyor belt of Argentinian talent has not stopped, with the likes of Juan Sebastian Veron, Gabriel Batistuta and Hernan Crespo widely respected on the world stage, but while the best players ply their trade abroad, the domestic championship has fallen into decline. So too has the national side, whose first round exit at the 2002 World Cup finals in Korea and Japan was greeted with great derision from a restless nation.

1860

1870

1890

1900

1910

1920

1930

1965

1970

1975

1980

1985

1990

1995

2000

2005

1867: The first football matches in Argentina are played between immigrant English and Italian rail workers and Argentinians.

1870s: English High School build a team that captures ten of 12 titles in the early stages of Argentine football.

1893: The Argentine Association Football League is founded.

1901: Argentina and Uruguay contest the first international game outside England, while club side River Plate are formed.

1905: Boca Juniors are founded.

1910: The first South American Championship is hosted and won by Argentina.

1929 to **1959:** Argentina win 12 of their 14 Copa América titles during this period.

1930: Argentina reach the final of the first World Cup, losing 4-2 to hosts Uruguay.

1966: Antonio Rattin is sent off in an aggressive World Cup quarter-final with England, whose manager Alf Ramsey calls the Argentines 'animals'.

1970: Argentina fail to qualify for the Mexico World Cup.

1978: As hosts, Argentina reach their second World Cup final, beating Holland 3-1. Mario Kempes is the star of the side.

1986: Inspired by Diego Maradona, Argentina win their second World Cup, beating West Germany in the final in Mexico.

1990: Argentina lose the World Cup final to West Germany. Monzon becomes the first player to be sent-off in a World Cup final, followed by Dezotti.

1998: Argentina are knocked out of the World Cup in the quarter-finals by Holland.

2002: After defeat by England and a draw with Sweden, Argentina exit the World Cup in the first phase.

THE COUNTRIES OF CONCACAF

CANADA

UNITED STATES OF AMERICA

BERMUDA

US VIRGIN ISLANDS

BRITISH VIRGIN ISLANDS

PUERTO RICO

ANGUILLA

HAITI

DOMINICAN REPUBLIC

ST KITTS AND NEVIS

CUBA

ANTIGUA AND BARBUDA

TURKS AND CAICOS ISLANDS

MONTSERRAT

CAYMAN ISLANDS

BAHAMAS

DOMINICA

ST LUCIA

MEXICO

ST VINCENT AND THE GRENADINES

JAMAICA

BARBADOS

BELIZE

ARUBA

GRENADA

GUATEMALA

COLOMBIA

TRINIDAD AND TOBAGO

EL SALVADOR

NETHERLANDS ANTILLES

PANAMA

HONDURAS

VENEZUELA

NICARAGUA

SURINAM

ECUADOR

GUYANA

COSTA RICA

BRAZIL

PERU

PARAGUAY

BOLIVIA

URUGUAY

CHILE

ARGENTINA

THE COUNTRIES OF CONMEBOL

ARMENIA

Federation: Football Federation of Armenia
Founded: 1991
Joined FIFA: 1992
Confederation: UEFA
FIFA world ranking: 112

Ararat Yerevan are Armenia's leading side, forming the nucleus of the national team. In 1973 they won the Soviet league and cup double. The Armenian league rarely goes through a season without at least one team failing to complete the programme of fixtures.

ARUBA

Federation: Arubaanse Voetbal Bond
Founded: 1932
Joined FIFA: 1988
Confederation: CONCACAF
FIFA world ranking: 194

AUSTRALIA

Federation: Soccer Australia
Founded: 1961
Joined FIFA: 1963
Confederation: OFC
FIFA world ranking: 50
Honours: Oceania Nations Cup 1980, 1996, 2000

Football in Australia has minority sport status. Where the game does thrive is among ethnic communities and the club names reflect their origins, such as Adelaide City Juventus and Sydney Olympic. In 1977 a national league and cup competition were formed, galvanised by the 'Socceroos' qualifying for the 1974 World Cup Finals. In recent years Australian players such as Harry Kewell and Mark Viduka have made an impact in European club football.

Australia has no serious football opposition in the region and has suffered in World Cup qualification because the winner of the Oceania group have had to play-off against South American and European nations. Oceania had been granted an automatic place for the 2006 World Cup Finals, but when plans to enlarge the tournament to 36 teams were shelved, Oceania's guaranteed place disappeared.

AUSTRIA

Federation: Österreichischer Fussball-Bund
Founded: 1904
Joined FIFA: 1905
Confederation: UEFA
FIFA world ranking: 55 (joint)

On October 12, 1902, the first international football match between European nations outside of Britain was staged when Austria defeated Hungary 2-0 in Vienna, a city that became the centre of football excellence in central Europe. In Vienna, the emphasis was placed on the kind of skill, short passing and innovative tactics that had the rest of Europe astounded. In 1911 the Austrian league (albeit exclusively Vienna-based clubs) was formed, followed eight years later by the Austrian Cup, with both competitions dominated by FK Austria Vienna and SK Rapid Vienna.

The 1930s saw the arrival of Austria's 'Wunderteam', including the celebrated player Matthias Sindelar who scored 27 international goals in his career. Between February 1931 and June 1934 Austria were defeated just twice in a 30-game run that saw them score 101 goals. They were also World Cup semi-finalists in 1934, losing to Italy 1-0, and Olympic Games runners-up in 1936. Austria looked set to dominate the European game, but when the country was absorbed by Hitler's Germany, Austrian football ceased to exist.

In the Fifties the Austrian game experienced a brief renaissance under Walter Nausch that saw them reach the semi-finals of the 1954 World Cup. The side included Ernst Ocwirk and Gerhard Hanappi and will be remembered for the incredible 7-5 quarter-final victory over hosts Switzerland.

Austrian football influence then began to fade and the national team did not qualify for the World Cup again until 1978. At both club and international level the game had become quite ordinary, and despite unearthing such individual talents as Hans Krankl and Herbert Prohaska, the nadir was reached with a 1-0 defeat by the Faeroe Islands in 1990.

AZERBAIJAN

Federation: Azerbaycan Futbol Federasiyalari Assosiasiyasi
Founded: 1992
Joined FIFA: 1994
Confederation: UEFA
FIFA world ranking: 104 (joint)

Four clubs dominate Azerbaijani football: Neftchi Baku, Karabakh Agdam, Turan Taz and Kepez Ganca. In 1994-95 Turan became the first club from Azerbaijan to play in Europe, and the national side, enforced to play all their home games in Turkey, entered the European Championship. Since then home games have been played in Baku.

Left: Anton Pfeffer, one of the few modern heroes in the Austrian game.

Below: Mark Viduka, one of a new breed of Australians making an impact in the European leagues.

BAHAMAS

Federation: Bahamas Football Association
Founded: 1967
Joined FIFA: 1968
Confederation: CONCACAF
FIFA world ranking: 190

BANGLADESH

Federation: Bangladesh Football Federation
Founded: 1972
Joined FIFA: 1974
Confederation: AFC
FIFA world ranking: 145

BELARUS

Federation: Football Federation of the Republic of Belarus
Founded: 1992
Joined FIFA: 1992
Confederation: UEFA
FIFA world ranking: 82

BAHRAIN

Federation: Bahrain Football Association
Founded: 1951
Joined FIFA: 1966
Confederation: AFC
FIFA world ranking: 104 (joint)

BARBADOS

Federation: Barbados Football Association
Founded: 1910
Joined FIFA: 1968
Confederation: CONCACAF
FIFA world ranking: 94

Dinamo Minsk, the leading Belorussian side in the old Soviet Supreme League, dominated the early years of the Belarus championship and national team. Since then sides such as Slavia Mozyr, BATE Borisov and Belshina have all made their mark, while the national team have had highs (beating Holland) and lows (losing to Andorra). Among the nation's successful exports in recent years is Alexander Gleb, who plies his trade with German side Stuttgart, and was voted Belarus Player Of The Year in 2002.

Below right: Eric Gerets was a star of the Belgium team that reached the final of the 1980 European Championship.

Below: Enzo Scifo, Belgium's talismanic player of the 1990s, playing in the 1998 World Cup against Mexico.

BELGIUM

Federation: Union Royale des Societies de Football Association
Formed: 1895
Joined FIFA: 1904
Confederation: UEFA
FIFA world ranking: 17
Honours: Olympics 1920

Belgians loved football from the beginning and their contribution and promotion of the game is too often overlooked. The Royal Antwerp club was formed in 1880, the Belgian league began in 1896, and the national team played their first game against France in 1904.

Belgium were founder members of FIFA and heavily promoted the World Cup to the extent they were one of only four European sides to travel to Uruguay in 1930 for the first tournament. Indeed the first World Cup final referee was a Belgian, Jean Langenus. This unfettered enthusiasm saw the amateur game flourish. Semi-professionalism was reluctantly accepted later but it was not until 1972 that club football turned professional.

Anderlecht, after another round of the club mergers that have littered Belgian football history, took the domestic game up a level in 1973. Belgium's most successful club went on to lift the Cup Winners' Cup in both 1976 and 1978, and the UEFA Cup in 1983.

The national team have qualified for every World Cup since 1982, reaching the semi-final

BELIZE

Federation: Belize National Football Association
Founded: 1980
Joined FIFA: 1986
Confederation: CONCACAF
FIFA world ranking: 167

BENIN

Federation: Fédération Béninoise de Football
Founded: 1968
Joined FIFA: 1969
Confederation: CAF
FIFA world ranking: 127 (joint)

in 1986 and losing to a Maradona-inspired Argentina. In the European Championship they were runners-up in 1980 and have twice hosted the tournament (in 1972 and as co-hosts in 2000).

The most profound influence on the modern game was caused by a Belgian, when the Bosman Ruling shook football to its roots. Jean-Marc Bosman brought a court case that ultimately led to freedom of movement of foreign players within Europe and gained legal rights for players, allowing them to leave a club once their contract expires without the need for a transfer fee.

BERMUDA

Federation: Bermuda Football Association
Founded: 1928
Joined FIFA: 1962
Confederation: CONCACAF
FIFA world ranking: 179 (joint)

BHUTAN

Federation: Bhutan Football Federation
Founded: 1983
Joined FIFA: 2000
Confederation: AFC
FIFA world ranking: 193

BOLIVIA

Federation: Federación Boliviana Fútbol
Founded: 1925
Joined FIFA: 1926
Confederation: CONMEBOL
FIFA world ranking: 108 (joint)
Honours: Copa América 1963

Bolivia is a modest football nation, but on the international stage they have enormous home advantage due to the altitude at La Paz, which is 12,000 feet above sea level. Away from home they have not been so reliable. Their only Copa

América success was in 1963 when they hosted the tournament. Bolivia have reached the World Cup finals just three times: in 1930 (invited), 1950 (walk-over) and 1994. Down the years the domestic game in all its incarnations – La Paz League (1914), National Championship (1926) and the National League (1977) – has been dominated by three clubs: The Strongest, Jorge Wilsterman and Bolivar.

Above left: Bolivia's midfield playmaker, Marco Etcheverry.

Above: Kenan Hasagic, Bosnia Herzogovina's goalkeeper.

BOSNIA-HERZEGOVINA

Federation: Football Federation of Bosnia and Herzegovina
Founded: 1992
Joined FIFA: 1996
Confederation: UEFA
FIFA world ranking: 75

Bosnia's independence didn't provide a unified football scene. Initially there were three separate leagues for the Muslim, Croat and Serbian entities, but in 2002-03 Bosnia's national division was extended to 20 teams from all areas of the country. Similarly, non-Muslim players have only been selected for the national team since 1999.

BOTSWANA

Federation: Botswana Football Association
Founded: 1970
Joined FIFA: 1976
Confederation: CAF
FIFA world ranking: 127 (joint)

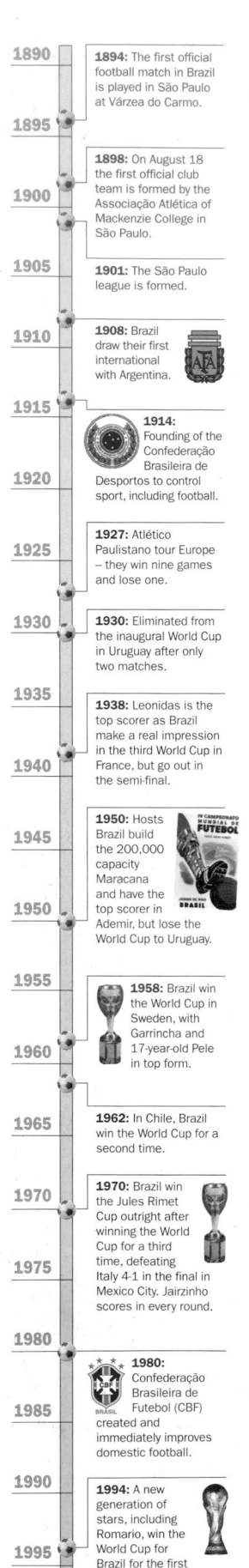

BRAZIL

Federation: Confederação Brasileira de Futebol

Founded: 1914

Joined FIFA: 1923

Confederation: CONMEBOL

FIFA world ranking: 1

Honours: World Cup 1958, 1962, 1970, 1994, 2002; Copa América 1919, 1922, 1949, 1989, 1997, 1999

Some quarters believe that football was brought to Brazil by British and Dutch sailors in the second half of the 19th Century. Yet the accepted consensus is that Charles Miller, who was born in Brazil but educated in Southampton, returned to his birthplace in 1894 with two footballs, a rule book and a set of playing kit to teach the locals of São Paulo the laws of the beautiful game.

The first recorded football match in Brazil took place took place that year between the employees of the local gas company and the São Paulo railway, which the latter side won 4-2. The game created fervent interest and within four years the first club side – Mackenzie Athletic Association – had been formed, creating a snowball effect throughout São Paulo and beyond.

In 1901 the São Paulo League was formally established, Rio de Janeiro followed suit and within seven years the Brazilian national team was born, drawing their first match 2-2 against neighbours Argentina.

The Brazilian Confederation of Sport was formed in 1914 and football became far more organised, yet competitions were still only organised within individual states and the game did not begin to resemble a professional sport until 1933. With many teams touring Europe, there was a real danger of a player exodus. Certainly Leonidas da Silva had achieved international fame by inventing the bicycle kick, while Friedenreich, a prolific striker, was said to have scored more than a thousand goals. It was imperative that suitable financial incentives were put in place to keep such players in Brazil, but this originally met with stiff resistance from clubs who wished to remain amateur. As a result it was an under-strength Brazil that participated in the first two World Cups of 1930 and 1934.

The internal bickering among the regions continued and it wasn't until 1960 and the birth of the Copa Libertadores (a South American competition for the best team in each country) that Brazil were prompted into forming the nationwide Taca do Brazil cup competition, while the national league (the Brasileiro) was created as late as 1971.

Above: Romario holds the World Cup aloft after Brazil's 3-2 penalty shoot-out victory over Italy in the final of USA 94

Opposite clockwise from top left: the stars of Brazil – Ronaldo, Zico, Pele, Jairzinho, Rivaldo and Ronaldinho, and Socrates. Opposite centre: Romario.

Both competitions were formed during a purple period in the history of Brazilian international football. Having hosted the 1950 World Cup Finals and built the famous Maracana Stadium, defeat in the final by Uruguay was an indication that the country was fast emerging as a major force in world football. Within eight years Brazil were hailed world champions in a tournament that saw the arrival of 17-year-old Pelé in a team that also included such esteemed names as Garrincha, Zagalo and Gilmar. In 1962, with the nucleus of the same team, Brazil lifted the World Cup again, as Czechoslovakia were defeated 3-1 in the final.

Dominance at international level was also reflected on the domestic front, as Pelé's team, Santos, won the World Club Cup in 1962 and 1963, defeating Benfica and AC Milan respectively. It would be another 18 years, however, until a Brazilian team, the Zico-inspired Flamengo, would again emerge victorious in the competition.

However you look at the history of Brazilian football, thoughts inevitably turn to the World Cup winning side of 1970, regarded by many as the greatest team in the history of the sport. With Pele at his peak, his team-mates Rivelino, Tostão, Gérson, Jairzinho and Carlos Alberto also became household names as the team swept all before them. The finals, held in Mexico, were also the first to be televised in colour, bringing another dimension to the samba flair on offer. Certainly Jairzinho's emphatic strike in the 4-1 final win against Italy remains an enduring image.

Pelé's retirement from the international fold led to an extended lull, and although the country continued to be a source of great talent, yielding the likes of Paulo Cesar, Zico, Falcao, Socrates and Cerezo, the country remained dormant on the world stage for 24 years.

So highly regarded had Brazilian players become that a player drain to Europe was inevitable. What remained was a weak national division that saw teams with ever-changing sides, and the first 20 seasons saw no fewer than 13 different champions – to this day the national league remains a fragile organisation and attendances reflect the entertainment on offer. Flamengo, arguably Brazil's most famous side, had an average attendance of fewer than 14,000 in 2002.

Yet there were signs of a renaissance with the national team; silver medals at the 1984 and 1988 Olympics provided the foundation for the 1994 World Cup winning team. Goalkeeper Taffarel, captain Dunga and star striker Romario formed the backbone of the Olympic sides and their potential finally came to fruition with World Cup victory against Italy, in a game settled on penalties.

A new belief had been restored to the national team and with the emerging young players Ronaldo, Denilson and Rivaldo added to the side, they made their intentions known with an appearance in the 1998 final, this time against hosts France. A mysterious illness to star player Ronaldo on the morning of the game put paid to any chances of victory, but four years on in Korea and Japan the Inter Milan forward was determined not to let lightning strike twice. Brazil swept all before them, their brand of free-flowing, attacking football and an inspired Ronaldo, who scored eight goals in the competition, made them worthy champions and restored their standing as the world's leading football nation.

BRITISH VIRGIN ISLANDS

Federation: British Virgin Islands Football Association
Founded: 1974
Joined FIFA: 1996
Confederation: CONCACAF
FIFA world ranking: 166

BRUNEI DARUSSALAM

Federation: Football Association of Brunei Darussalam
Founded: 1959
Joined FIFA: 1969
Confederation: AFC
FIFA world ranking: 192

BULGARIA

Federation: Bulgarski Futbolen Soius
Founded: 1923
Joined FIFA: 1924
Confederation: UEFA
FIFA world ranking: 38

Communism was good for football in Bulgaria. Prior to 1944, although football was played, it was not being played or organised very well – there was an aborted attempt at a national league and the national team failed to win a game in its first six years. The arrival of Soviet troops brought wholesale changes to Bulgarian life, and football was completely overhauled. A new national league with a pyramid feeder system was put in place, with promotion and relegation throughout. Clubs became affiliated to an official organisation: CSKA (Army), Levski (Interior Ministry) and Lokomotiv Sofia (railways). Players were professionals in all but name, while working for a power company or a government department, these workers embarked on a full-time regime of football training known and used throughout the Communist bloc as 'The System'.

The quality of Bulgarian football improved immeasurably, none more so than CSKA (then known as CDNA). Inspired by the goals of Ivan Kolev, between 1951 and 1962 CDNA were champions 11 times, a trend that ultimately made club football predictable. The army side provided much of the national team and Bulgaria were regarded as one of Europe's top teams, becoming World Cup regulars from 1962 (although they failed to win a single game at the finals). CSKA were unpopular despite their success, mainly because the army club could pick players by simply drafting them.

The fall of communism forced clubs to become financially independent, which led to the selling of players. Ironically, this has helped the national team, as their top stars have gained experience abroad. In 1994 Bulgaria reached the World Cup semi-finals, with Barcelona's Hristo Stoichkov the tournament's joint top scorer. Together with Levski, CSKA remain one of Bulgaria's strongest sides.

BURKINA FASO

Federation: Fédération Burkinabé de Football
Founded: 1960
Joined FIFA: 1964
Confederation: CAF
FIFA world ranking: 72

BURUNDI

Federation: Fédération de Football du Burundi
Founded: 1948
Joined FIFA: 1972
Confederation: CAF
FIFA world ranking: 138

CAMBODIA

Federation: Cambodian Football Federation
Founded: 1933
Joined FIFA: 1953
Confederation: AFC
FIFA world ranking: 170 (joint)

Below: Hristo Stoichkov, who finished as joint top scorer in the 1994 World Cup, where Bulgaria reached the semi-finals.

CAMEROON

Federation: Fedération Camérounaise de Football
Founded: 1960
Joined FIFA: 1962
Confederation: CAF
FIFA world ranking: 16
Honours: African Nations Cup 1984, 1988, 2000, 2002; Olympics 2000

Cameroon are known as the 'Indomitable Lions' and their roar was first heard on the world stage in 1982, when they boosted black African soccer with an unbeaten appearance at the World Cup, drawing their three group games against Peru, Poland and Italy. But it was eight years later in Italy that Cameroon took African soccer to the next level. A Roger Milla-inspired Cameroon defeated world champions Argentina 1-0 in their opening match and then went on a run that took them to within ten minutes of a semi-final place before they were defeated 3-2 by England.

Although Cameroon's subsequent World Cup appearances have not reached the same giddy heights there has been success in the African Nations Cup where they became the first side in 37 years to win successive cups in 2000 and 2002. They also won at the 2000 Olympics, beating Spain in the final. All three wins came after penalty shoot-outs.

Football had been played in both British and French protectorate regions of the pre-independence country, but did not really thrive until business began running the clubs in the 1940s. Independence from Britain and France saw the latter protectorate become Cameroon and the formation of a national league and cup soon followed in 1960. These competitions have been dominated by the two Yaoundé clubs, Canon and Tonnerre, with Union Douala providing the third force. In recent years they have been joined by Cotonsport, who have also made an impact.

Oryx Doula were the first African Cup winners in 1964, an achievement later matched by Canon Yaoundé and Union Doula. A number of Cameroonian players have been voted African Player Of The Year: Roger Milla (1976 and 1990), Thomas N'Kono (1979 and 1982), Jean Manga Onguene (1980) and Theophile Abega (1984). Many of their stars now play in Europe, with France the favoured destination.

Above: Roger Milla on the ball against England in the quarter-final of the 1990 World Cup. At 38 years of age, he was one of the stars of the Italia 90.

Above left: Cameroon's Patrick Suffo shares his Olympic gold medal with the crowd at Sydney in 2000.

CANADA

Federation: The Canadian Soccer Association
Founded: 1912
Joined FIFA: 1913
Confederation: CONCACAF
FIFA world ranking: 78
Honours: Olympics 1904; CONCACAF Championship 2000

In a land where ice hockey is king, football has struggled to make an impact, despite Olympic Games glory in 1904 courtesy of Galt FC. Although a national association was formed as early as 1912 there was no national league until 1987. From 1967 until 1984 the leading teams such as Vancouver Whitecaps and Toronto Blizzard joined the North American Soccer League (NASL), and in 1976 Toronto Blizzard (renamed Metros) won the Soccer Bowl. The demise of the NASL, combined with Canada's only appearance at the World Cup in 1986, led to the formation of a national league.

CAPE VERDE ISLANDS

Federation: Federação Cabo-Verdiana de Futebol
Founded: 1982
Joined FIFA: 1986
Confederation: CAF
FIFA world ranking: 144

CAYMAN ISLANDS

Federation: Cayman Islands Football Association
Founded: 1966
Joined FIFA: 1992
Confederation: CONCACAF
FIFA world ranking: 173

CENTRAL AFRICAN REP.

Federation: Fédération Centrafricaine de Football
Founded: 1937
Joined FIFA: 1963
Confederation: CAF
FIFA world ranking: 175 (joint)

Centre: Paul Peschisolido, a Canadian who has found some success in the English leagues.

CHAD

Federation: Fédération Tchadienne de Football
Founded: 1962
Joined FIFA: 1988
Confederation: CAF
FIFA world ranking: 165

CHILE

Federation: Federación de Fútbol de Chile
Founded: 1895
Joined FIFA: 1912
Confederation: CONMEBOL
FIFA world ranking: 70 (joint)

Valaparaiso FC became Chile's first club in 1889 and others, mainly British in origin, followed. In 1895 the second oldest football federation in South America was founded. The Chilean national team played its first international in 1910, but although it did not win a game until 1926, Chilean football took a turn for the better in 1925 when David Arellano founded the country's most successful and popular club, Colo Colo. Arellano and Colo Colo became the driving force behind the new professional national league in 1933. Through the years the league has been an open competition but from the 1970s it was Colo Colo who dominated.

On the international stage Chilean football has made little impact, although in 1991 Colo Colo did win the country's first international honour when they lifted the Copa Libertadores. Chile have occasionally appeared in the World Cup but without success, save for the 1962 competition, when as hosts they reached the semi-finals. The performance was marred by the appalling spectacle against Italy known as 'the Battle of Santiago'.

Chile were handed a ban in 1989 when goalkeeper Roberto Rojas faked an injury in a World Cup qualifier against Brazil.

CHINA

Federation: Football Association of the People's Republic of China
Founded: 1924
Joined FIFA: 1931-58, 1979
Confederation: AFC
FIFA world ranking: 70 (joint)

China played in the first international match in Asia at the Far Eastern Games in Manila in February 1913, losing out 2-1 to hosts the Philippines. The Chinese went on to win the remaining nine tournaments contested between China, Japan and the Philippines from 1915 to 1934. They even took part in the Munich and London Olympics of 1936 and 1948, and they joined FIFA in 1931 (but they did not enter the World Cup).

In 1958 China withdrew from FIFA in protest at the membership of Taiwan. This self-imposed exile did little for the domestic game,

even though the national league ran from 1953 to 1966. It was not until 1979 that China rejoined FIFA after cultural and sporting ties had begun to open up again. The national league was resurrected in 1976.

The quality of football was still very poor, although there were occasional highlights, such as Lioaning (the side of the Shenyang Army Unit) winning the Asian Champions Cup in 1989, and China finishing runners-up in the Asian Cup in 1984 and the Asian Games in 1994.

Professionalism was introduced and, in a relatively more open society, foreign players were allowed in the Chinese league. The most significant foreign import was a coach, Yugoslav Bora Milutinovic, who took over the national side and guided China to their first World Cup in 2002. Although they lost all three games and failed to score, their presence was a boost for the game and China are tipped to host the 2014 World Cup, providing the Beijing Olympics in 2008 go smoothly.

COLOMBIA

Federation: Federación Colombiana de Fútbol
Founded: 1924
Joined FIFA: 1936-50, 1954
Confederation: CONMEBOL
FIFA world ranking: 22
Honours: Copa América 2001

Colombia has had a dark and controversial football history, but illuminating the darkness are flamboyant players who have produced breathtaking moments, ranging from the spectacular goals of Carlos Valderrama to the astonishing 'scorpion' save of goalkeeper Rene Higuita in a friendly against England.

In 1948 a wealthy independent professional league (the DiMayor) was born in Colombia, and among the 18 wealthy clubs was Deportivo Municipal, who became known as 'Los Millonarios', because they were bankrolled by two extremely rich Bogotá businessmen.

In its four-year existence, this new league became known as the 'El Dorado' period – as it existed outside of FIFA jurisdiction, Colombian clubs refused to pay transfer fees and were able to lure star players from all over South America and Europe with offers of lucrative wages and signing-on fees. They attracted players of the calibre of Alfred Di Stéfano and Nestor Rossi, but by the time Colombia was readmitted to FIFA in 1954, the huge fees had smashed the Colombian game.

In the mid-Sixties a rival organisation challenged the incumbent football association and this political infighting led to FIFA taking on the running of Colombian soccer until the

Opposite page: Marcelo Salas was Chile's biggest star at the 1998 World Cup Finals, scoring four goals.

Left: Rene Higuita stunned world football with his amazing 'scorpion kick' save against England at Wembley.

Above: Croatia weren't unhappy with their third place play-off victory over Holland at the 1998 World Cup.

current FCF was formed. Colombia was due to host the 1986 World Cup but was forced to withdraw after being unable to provide sufficient facilities and communications for a 24-team tournament.

In the Eighties and Nineties Colombian league football was an exciting spectator sport, but off the pitch it had become unpleasant, with allegations of money-laundering by drug cartels and of high stake bets and bribes. Players, officials and investigators have all been brutally murdered during this period. In one of the more notorious incidents, international defender Andres Escobar was shot dead after returning from the 1994 World Cup because he had inadvertently scored an own-goal against the USA during the tournament.

The state of Colombian football has been so bad that there have been times when the league has been suspended and the national side has refused to play at home, but in 2001 Colombian football had a chance to celebrate once more when the national team won the Copa América for the first time, beating Mexico in the final.

CONGO

Federation: Fédération Congolaise de Football
Founded: 1962
Joined FIFA: 1962
Confederation: CAF
FIFA world ranking: 100
Honours: African Nations Cup 1972

Centre: Costa Rica's Paulo Wanchope, a familiar sight in the English leagues.

CONGO DR

Federation: Fédération Congolaise de Football Association
Founded: 1919
Joined FIFA: 1962
Confederation: CAF
FIFA world ranking: 58
Honours: African Nations Cup 1968, 1974

In 1974, when known as Zaire, the Democratic Republic of Congo became the first sub-Saharan – and black African – team to qualify for the World Cup. Heavily influenced by Europe – and Belgium in particular who had introduced the game to the country – Zaire were a major force in African football from the mid-Sixties to the mid-Seventies, winning the African Nations Cup twice.

COOK ISLANDS

Federation: Cook Islands Football Association
Founded: 1971
Joined FIFA: 1994
Confederation: OFC
FIFA world ranking: 188

COSTA RICA

Federation: Fedeacion Costarricense de Futbol
Founded: 1921
Joined FIFA: 1921
Confederation: CONCACAF
FIFA world ranking: 18 (joint)
Honours: CONCACAF Championship 1941, 1946, 1948, 1953, 1955, 1960, 1961, 1963, 1969, 1989

The formal birth of Costa Rican football was in 1921, the year the Federation was founded and the inaugural league championship kicked-off. CS Herediano were the dominant club before the war, while Deportivo Saprissa were the runaway team of the Sixties and Seventies, a period when the Costa Rican national team were the strongest in the region, winning seven of ten CCCF Championships and three of the subsequent CONCACAF titles before the tournament was again revamped in 1991. Despite such an impressive record Costa Rica shunned the World Cup until 1958. They have since qualified twice, in 1990, where they beat Scotland, and 2002.

CROATIA

Federation: Croatian Football Federation
Founded: 1912, 1991
Joined FIFA: 1992
Confederation: UEFA
FIFA world ranking: 26

During the Second World War Croatia, under German occupation, did have its own league and national team until Tito's Communists took over the Balkan region. Croatian players and clubs were among the powerhouses of Yugoslav football prior to real independence in 1991 and official FIFA recognition in 1992. Clubs such as Dinamo Zagreb and Hajduk Split were regular challengers to the Belgrade-based clubs, while in 1967 Dinamo Zagreb became the first Croatian (and Yugoslav) club to lift a European trophy when they won the Fairs Cup, defeating Leeds.

Great players such as Zvonimir Boban, Robert Jarni and Robert Prosinecki (half-Croat) were part of the Yugoslav national team that qualified for the European Championship in 1992, but by then Croatia had declared independence, their clubs had withdrawn from the Yugoslav league and Croatian players were forbidden from playing for Yugoslavia. The team were forced to withdraw from Euro 92.

In the shadow of civil war and grave economic problems, the Croatian league kicked-off in the 1992-93 season without the country's biggest stars, many having chosen to play their club football abroad. However, the Croatian game has gained in popularity because of the exploits of the national side, who made a startling impact at the 1996 European Championship by reaching the quarter-finals, and later going on to finish third at the 1998 World Cup.

CUBA

Federation: Asociación de Fútbol de Cuba
Founded: 1924
Joined FIFA: 1932
Confederation: CONCACAF
FIFA world ranking: 63

CYPRUS

Federation: Cyprus Football Association
Founded: 1934
Joined FIFA: 1948
Confederation: UEFA
FIFA world ranking: 83

Football was introduced to Cyprus by British servicemen in the late 1870s, although it wasn't until 1934 that an association was formed. A league and cup campaign was launched a year later, with Trast AC winning both titles. With a population of mainly Greek Cypriots, the most successful teams were of Greek origin and only one Turkish Cypriot side, Cetinkaya TSK, has ever taken the national title. Following the division of the island in 1974, teams from both communities found themselves displaced and although the so-called Turkish Republic of Northern Cyprus has a league, it is not recognised by FIFA. Throughout the 1990s, the Cypriot league

grew stronger, with Anorthosis Famagusta becoming the most prominent side. The national team took its biggest scalp in 1998, beating Spain 3-2 in a Euro 2000 qualifier.

CZECH REPUBLIC

Federation: Ceskomoravsky Fotbalovy Svaz
Founded: 1901
Joined FIFA: 1907
Confederation: UEFA
FIFA world ranking: 10
Honours: European Championship 1976; Olympics 1980 (both as Czechoslovakia)

From the 1993-94 season, Czechoslovakia split into two: the Czech Republic and Slovakia. It is fair to say that in footballing terms the Czech Republic was the stronger of the two. This was proved almost instantly when the Czech Republic not only qualified for 1996 European Championship (Slovakia didn't), but reached the final at Wembley, losing to Germany through a golden goal. The country's biggest names, like Patrik Berger and Pavel Nedved, have performed at the highest level, following in the tradition of former Czech greats like Masopust, Novak and Planicka.

Football had been played in the region since the 1890s. In Bohemia, a province of the Austro-Hungarian empire, both Slavia and Sparta clubs were formed in 1893. A Bohemian league and a football association were founded, and a national team existed until Czechoslovakia declared independence in 1918. Seven years later the regions of Bohemia, Monravia and Slovakia formed a new professional Czech league.

Czechoslovakia became a strong football nation. They reached the 1920 Olympic final but stormed off during the second-half of the game, complaining that the referee was biased against them. They were also the 1934 World Cup runners-up, losing to Italy in the final.

On the domestic front it was Slavia and Sparta who dominated both league and cup. In 1945 Communist rule led to clubs becoming affiliated to state organisations. Slavia and Sparta lost their stranglehold of the Czech game and were eclipsed by the army team, Dukla Prague. Dukla, in turn, became the core of the national side in the Sixties, when Czechoslovakia often came close without ever winning the final prize – they finished third in the 1960 European Championship, and were runners-up in the 1962 World Cup (to Brazil) and 1964 Olympics (to Hungary).

The late Seventies saw another resurgence with Czechoslovakia winning the 1976 European Championship in Yugoslavia, beating West Germany in a dramatic 5-3 penalty shoot-out. Four years later they were Olympic champions. At home Dukla's star began to fade even before independence and Sparta and Slavia re-emerged as dominant teams again in a free market economy.

Below: Pavel Nedved celebrates as the Czech Republic reach the final of Euro 96.

Above: Last-minute entrants, Denmark surprised everyone by taking the 1992 European Championship in Sweden.

DENMARK

Federation: Dansk Boldspil-Union
Founded: 1889
Joined FIFA: 1904
Confederation: UEFA
FIFA world ranking: 13
Honours: European Championship 1992

Denmark caused the biggest football shock of the Nineties. They had failed to qualify for the 1992 European Championship and just a week before the tournament many of their players were already sunning themselves on the beach when the call came that offered them the chance to become last-minute replacements for Yugoslavia. With no preparation the squad

went on to win the trophy, beating Germany 2-0 in the final with goals from John Jensen and Kim Vilfort. This was undoubtedly the finest hour in Denmark's football history.

The triumph followed a period in the 1980s when the Danish game had gained recognition and plaudits for its thrilling style, with the development of a talented crop of players, most notably the Laudrup brothers, Brian and Michael, Jesper Olsen, Jan Molby, John Sivebaek and Soren Lerby. These players took Denmark to their first World Cup in 1986, where they reached the second round only to meet an in-form Spain, who beat them 5-1. For the European Championship triumph, the squad also boasted Peter Schmeichel, Henrik Larsen and Flemming Povlsen.

The first truly great Danish player was Allan Simonsen, who was voted European Player Of The Year in 1977. He played for two great European sides, Barcelona and Borussia

Mönchengladbach, and his success as a professional led the DBU to allow professional players to be selected for the national team in 1976. The introduction of professionalism into the Danish game came in 1978.

Before 1978 Danish football had been strictly an amateur game ever since the first club KB Copenhagen was formed in 1876. Among the great amateur players of the early years was Niels Bohr, who later won the Nobel Prize for Physics. The first professional club was Brondby, who led the way in turning Danish football from a pastime into a national success story. The other significant move came in 1991 when the Superliga switched from a summer season to a winter season in line with the major leagues of Europe.

Though they missed out in 1994, Denmark recaptured some form in the 1998 World Cup, reaching the quarter-final, where they lost narrowly to Brazil.

DJIBOUTI

Federation: Fédération Djiboutienne de Football
Founded: 1977
Joined FIFA: 1994
Confederation: CAF
FIFA world ranking: 196

DOMINICA

Federation: Dominica Football Association
Founded: 1970
Joined FIFA: 1994
Confederation: CONCACAF
FIFA world ranking: 181

DOMINICAN REPUBLIC

Federation: Federación Dominicana de Fútbol
Founded: 1953
Joined FIFA: 1958
Confederation: CONCACAF
FIFA world ranking: 157

ECUADOR

Federation: Federación Ecuatoriana De Fútbol
Founded: 1925
Joined FIFA: 1926
Confederation: CONMEBOL
FIFA world ranking: 36

Ecuador qualified for the World Cup for the first time in 11 attempts in 2002, finishing runners-up to Argentina in the ten-strong CONMEBOL group. Notably, this magnificent achievement also included their first-ever win over Brazil. Ecuador did not get beyond the group stage in Japan, winning just one game. It was still impressive for a national side that had won just eight times between 1938 and 1975. The Ecuadorian league began in 1957 and has been dominated by five clubs: Barcelona (the only Ecuadorian side to reach a Libertadores final), Emelec, Deportivo, Nacional and Liga Deportivo Universitara.

EGYPT

Federation: Egyptian Football Association
Founded: 1921
Joined FIFA: 1923
Confederation: CAF
FIFA world ranking: 39
Honours: African Nations Cup 1957, 1959, 1986, 1998

Egypt were the initial trail-blazers for African football. They were the first African team to play in the Olympics in 1928 and the World Cup finals in 1934. A founder member of the Confédération Africaine de Football (CAF) in 1957, Egypt provided the organisation's first president in Abdel Aziz Abdullah Salem. Another leading Egyptian, General Abdelaziz Mustapha, donated the original African Nations Cup trophy in the same year, while the national team won the first two African Nations Cup tournaments.

Ever since football had arrived in the country at the turn of the century it had been a popular pastime. In 1907 native Egyptians got behind the newly-formed Al Ahly, an exclusive all-Egyptian sporting club and a beacon for nationalist pride. It is no surprise, then, that Al Ahly developed into Egypt's most popular and successful club. They dominated the Farouk Cup (1922-48) and, from 1949, the league championship and Cup of Egypt.

The presence of allied forces during World War Two had encouraged the domestic game and inspired the championship and cup competitions – Egyptian football, already well organised, was given a boost and this was reflected in the success that clubs such as Al Ahly, Ismaili and Zamalek have had in the African Cup down the years.

Above: Egypt's Ahmed Salah in action against Tunisia.

EL SALVADOR

Federation: Federacion Salvadorena de Futbol
Founded: 1935
Joined FIFA: 1938
Confederation: CONCACAF
FIFA world ranking: 85
Honours: CONCACAF Championship 1943

El Salvador have qualified for the World Cup just twice, causing a war and suffering the worst defeat in World Cup finals history. In 1969 the team were involved in a controversial three-game second round qualifying clash with neighbouring Honduras. Border infractions and rioting followed the first two games, and when El Salvador finally defeated Honduras 3-2 in neutral Mexico, the result inflamed an already tense border situation, causing the El Salvadorian Army to invade Honduras to protect its citizens (the migrant workers) from persecution. The action sparked all out war between the countries.

Back on the football field, in 1982 El Salvador were thrashed 10-1 by Hungary – the biggest ever defeat in a World Cup finals – and crashed out without a point.

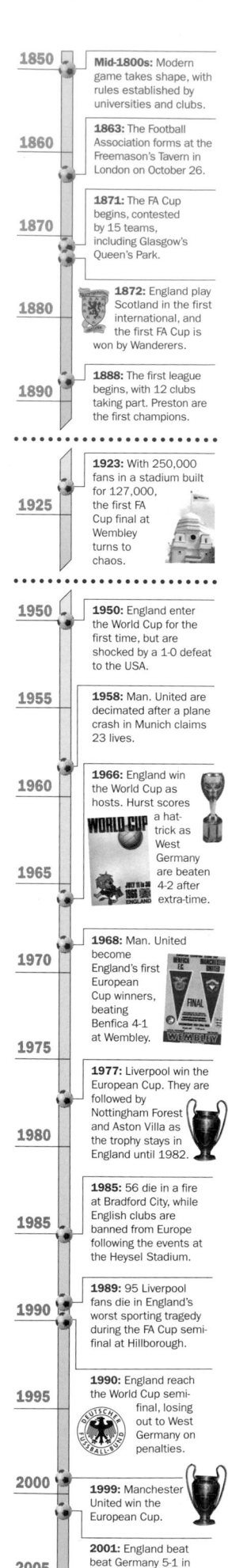

1850

Mid-1800s: Modern game takes shape, with rules established by universities and clubs.

1860

1863: The Football Association forms at the Freemason's Tavern in London on October 26.

1870

1871: The FA Cup begins, contested by 15 teams, including Glasgow's Queen's Park.

1880

1872: England play Scotland in the first international, and the first FA Cup is won by Wanderers.

1890

1888: The first league begins, with 12 clubs taking part. Preston are the first champions.

1925

1923: With 250,000 fans in a stadium built for 127,000, the first FA Cup final at Wembley turns to chaos.

1950

1950: England enter the World Cup for the first time, but are shocked by a 1-0 defeat to the USA.

1955

1958: Man. United are decimated after a plane crash in Munich claims 23 lives.

1960

1966: England win the World Cup as hosts. Hurst scores a hat-trick as West Germany are beaten 4-2 after extra-time.

1965

1970

1968: Man. United become England's first European Cup winners, beating Benfica 4-1 at Wembley.

1975

1977: Liverpool win the European Cup. They are followed by Nottingham Forest and Aston Villa as the trophy stays in England until 1982.

1980

1985: 56 die in a fire at Bradford City, while English clubs are banned from Europe following the events at the Heysel Stadium.

1985

1989: 95 Liverpool fans die in England's worst sporting tragedy during the FA Cup semi-final at Hillsborough.

1990

1990: England reach the World Cup semi-final, losing out to West Germany on penalties.

1995

2000

1999: Manchester United win the European Cup.

2005

2001: England beat beat Germany 5-1 in Munich.

ENGLAND

Federation: Football Association
Founded: 1863
Joined FIFA: 1905-28, 1946
Confederation: UEFA
FIFA world ranking: 8
Honours: World Cup winners 1966

England enjoys a lofty status as the home of football. The modern game was fashioned here in the mid 19th Century and rapidly exported all over the world. Its clubs are enshrined in the local community, have powerful historical roots and provide a focus for millions of people each week.

The basic structure of English football was pretty much in place by 1888 when the 12-member Football League was installed. The first FA Cup final had been won by Wanderers 16 years before and a football association had been founded back in 1863.

Developing the game inevitably gave England a head start. Its teams played the classic WM formation, essentially 2-3-5, that was to last for some 70 years, and, until the 1930s at least, England regularly drubbed foreign opposition – whenever they deigned to play them, that is.

However, this classically insular island approach, together with an overbearing sense of superiority, meant that the English Football Association repeatedly stood apart from the game's most significant developments. When FIFA pioneered a world tournament in the 1920s the FA declined to take part. It then resigned from the federation in 1928 and did not either rejoin until 1946 or enter a World Cup until 1950. As its insularity deepened, the English game remained oblivious to any thought of modernisation.

The myth of English superiority was rocked in 1953 when Hungary took the national side apart, winning 6-3 at Wembley. Yet when UEFA launched the European Nations Cup (later the European Championship) England initially refused to take part on the basis that it would undermine the all-important Home Internationals. For this reason a talented generation of players, including Billy Wright, Stanley Matthews and Tom Finney, were held back from the kind of competition that would have elevated their game further.

Still, justification for the FA's stance finally arrived in 1966 when England, led by one of its great ambassadors, Bobby Moore, hosted the World Cup finals and won in front of a passionate Wembley crowd, beating West Germany 4-2 with Geoff Hurst's hat-trick.

Yet English football failed to capitalise on the resultant euphoria. Four years later, with

Above: Gary Lineker, who retired at the age of 32 with a goal tally of 48, one short of Bobby Charlton's England record. Opposite clockwise from top left: the stars of England – the 1966 World Cup winning team; Paul Gascoigne sheds a tear at Italia 90; David Beckham proves a point against Argentina in 2002; and 'Captain Marvel' Bryan Robson.

arguably a better squad, they lost narrowly to eventual champions Brazil in a group game seen as a potential warm-up for the final. They then crashed out in a disastrous quarter-final confrontation with West Germany that signified a period of upheaval from which it took years to recover. The national team failed to qualify for two successive World Cups in the Seventies and were then hamstrung by technical shortcomings in the following decade. A semi-final appearance at Italia 90 with a side that included Paul Gascoigne, arguably the country's greatest talent ever, hardly heralded a new era given the failure to qualify for the World Cup again in 1994, or progress beyond the quarter-final stages since.

The nation's uneven international history is belied by the achievements of its clubs in Europe. Typically of the period, the FA advised league champions Chelsea not to take part in the inaugural European Cup competition created in 1955. However, Manchester United forged ahead a year later and would surely have won a trophy long before their eventual breakthrough in 1968 but for the tragedy of the 1958 Munich air disaster.

The late Seventies and early Eighties represented a golden era for English clubs in Europe, with four Champions Cup wins for Liverpool, one for Aston Villa and a brace of back-to-back trophies for Nottingham Forest. UEFA Cups and Cup Winners' Cups also arrived with regularity. But the dominance was ended abruptly in the wake of the 1985 Heysel tragedy, in which a pitched battle between Liverpool fans and Juventus supporters resulted in 39 deaths and a six-year ban from European competition for English clubs.

Domestically, English football has thrived and continues to support four professional divisions. In the modern era three clubs have largely held sway. Liverpool remain the all-time

most successful club in the country with 18 league championships and six FA Cups, having regularly built upon the revival overseen by Bill Shankly in the Sixties. Manchester United are the country's richest and most successful club of recent times, winning eight Premiership titles between 1993 and 2003, including three league and cup doubles. They also won a European Cup, with homegrown talents like David Beckham and Paul Scholes at the core of a team built by Sir Alex Ferguson. The sole London club to maintain a consistent challenge are Arsenal, who have won a total of 12 trophies, including two league and cup doubles under Frenchman Arsene Wenger in the past decade.

Hooliganism has been an unpleasant feature of English football and took a heavy toll in the Eighties. Gate receipts declined and further disasters – the 1985 Bradford fire and the 1989 Hillsborough tragedy – only served to underline the fact that the game's structure needed radical overhauling.

The 1990 Taylor Report and the consequent move to all-seater stadia helped usher in a new era for English football in the Nineties. Money flooded in via television and corporate sponsorship, and the advent of the Premier League in 1992 further revamped the game's image – in living rooms and on the terraces.

However, to conclude on a cautious note, English football has had to tighten its belt in the new millennium with several major clubs reporting huge losses. The deserved reputation that the Premiership maintains for exciting, fast-paced, attacking football is built on the talents of many top quality foreign imports, not on homegrown players. Until significant grassroots adjustments are made, England will always be seen as a nation forced to elevate work-rate over technique and suffer the consequences internationally.

EQUATORIAL GUINEA

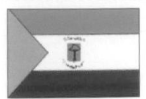 

Federation: Fédération Ecuatoguineana de Fútbol
Founded: 1976
Joined FIFA: 1986
Confederation: CAF
FIFA world ranking: 182

ERITREA

Federation: Eritrean National Football Federation
Founded: 1996
Joined FIFA: 1998
Confederation: CAF
FIFA world ranking: 155

ESTONIA

Federation: Eesti Jalgpalli Liit
Founded: 1921, 1992
Joined FIFA: 1923, 1992
Confederation: UEFA
FIFA world ranking: 62

Estonia was the first Baltic side to play a full international, when they were thrashed 6-0 by Finland in 1920. The game marked the first of a largely undistinguished 121-match record (including a failed qualification attempt for the 1938 World Cup) that ran until Estonia became a part of the Soviet Union. The return to independence in the early Nineties saw the revival of both the national team and league competition. Estonia's strongest team is Flora Tallinn, who also form the backbone to the national side. Some players have had careers abroad, most notably goalkeeper Mart Poom.

Above: Estonian export Mart Poom has played in England for Portsmouth, Derby and Sunderland.

Right: Finland's best known footballer Jari Litmanen takes a shot on goal against Albania.

ETHIOPIA

Federation: Ethiopian Football Federation
Founded: 1943
Joined FIFA: 1953
Confederation: CAF
FIFA world ranking: 132
Honours: African Nations Cup 1962

FAEROE ISLANDS

Federation: Fotboltssamband Føroya
Founded: 1979
Joined FIFA: 1988
Confederation: UEFA
FIFA world ranking: 115

The Faeroe Islands had a sensational debut on the international football stage. In their first competitive match in September 1990, the part-time players of the Faeroe Islands beat Austria 1-0 in Sweden, thanks to goalscorer Allan Morkore and bobble-hatted goalkeeper Martin Knudsen. Football has been played on the islands for more than a century with a league (1942) and cup competition (1967), and unofficial international matches against Iceland, Greenland and the Shetlands.

Local weather conditions and a lack of pitches had hindered their ability to host matches, but a grass pitch was laid in Tórshavn to allow the Faeroes to play their internationals at home. The leading sides are the Tórshavn clubs – HB, B36 and Fram, as well as KI Klaksvik and GÍ Gotu.

FIJI

Federation: Fiji Football Association
Founded: 1938
Joined FIFA: 1963
Confederation: OFC
FIFA world ranking: 149

FINLAND

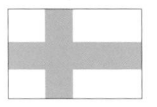 

Federation: Suomen Palloliito Finlands Bollförbund
Founded: 1907
Joined FIFA: 1908
Confederation: UEFA
FIFA world ranking: 45

Finland's most famous footballer is Jari Litmanen. A prolific goalscorer who has played for Europe's top clubs, including Barcelona, Ajax and Liverpool, he has won a host of trophies, including the European Cup in 1995. Litmanen's predecessors and team-mates have not made a similar impression. A Finnish league has been in existence since 1908 with HJK Helsinki and HPS Helsinki the most successful sides.

On the international stage Finland have made little impact, having failed to qualify for any major competitions, though they did achieve a fourth-place finish at the 1912 Olympics. Finnish clubs provide early round fodder in the European competitions, but Kuusysi Lahti did reach the Champions Cup quarter-finals in 1986.

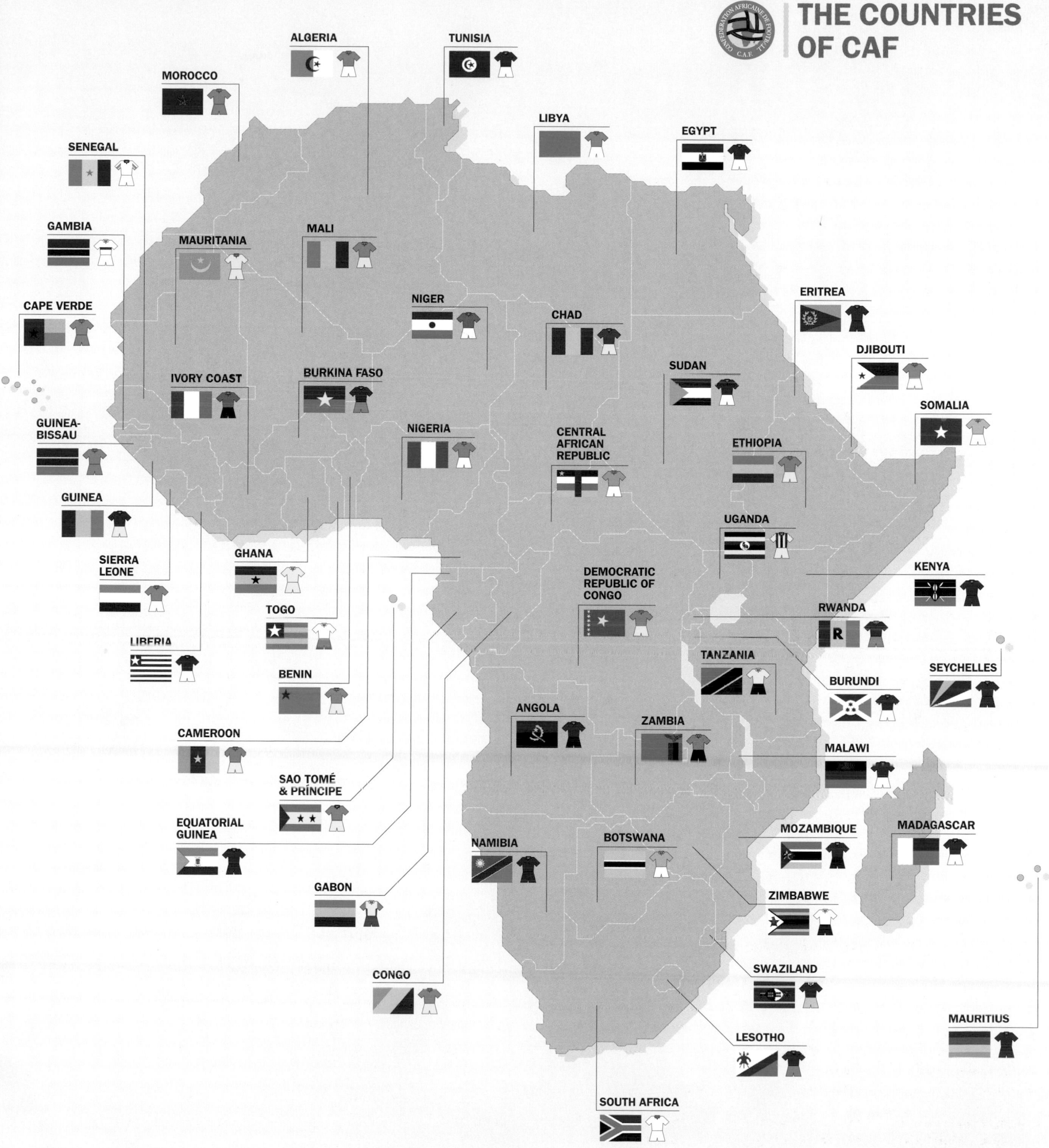

THE COUNTRIES OF CAF

MOROCCO

ALGERIA

TUNISIA

LIBYA

EGYPT

SENEGAL

GAMBIA

MAURITANIA

MALI

NIGER

CHAD

SUDAN

ERITREA

DJIBOUTI

CAPE VERDE

SOMALIA

IVORY COAST

BURKINA FASO

NIGERIA

CENTRAL AFRICAN REPUBLIC

ETHIOPIA

GUINEA-BISSAU

GUINEA

UGANDA

SIERRA LEONE

GHANA

DEMOCRATIC REPUBLIC OF CONGO

KENYA

TOGO

RWANDA

LIBERIA

TANZANIA

BURUNDI

SEYCHELLES

BENIN

ANGOLA

ZAMBIA

MALAWI

CAMEROON

SAO TOMÉ & PRÍNCIPE

MOZAMBIQUE

MADAGASCAR

EQUATORIAL GUINEA

NAMIBIA

BOTSWANA

GABON

ZIMBABWE

SWAZILAND

CONGO

MAURITIUS

LESOTHO

SOUTH AFRICA

FRANCE

Federation: Fédération Française de Football
Founded: 1919
Joined FIFA: 1904
Confederation: UEFA
FIFA world ranking: 2
Honours: World Cup 1998; European Championship 1984, 2000; Olympics 1984

France have played a key role in football development: inventing major competitions, pioneering youth training policies, and belatedly enjoying the success on the pitch their input off it deserved.

FIFA president Jules Rimet launched the World Cup in 1930; Gabriel Hanot, a former international and editor of sports paper *L'Equipe*, was the driving force behind the European Cup; and the name of the European Championship trophy is that of its founder, Henri Delaunay. Yet in the early days France was seen as an outsider, struggling to break through despite its involvement in the game. Poor domestic attendances in comparison to the English, Spanish and Italian leagues undermined attempts to make an impact.

Lille won the first professional league title in 1932, although Sochaux, backed by Peugeot, were the most prominent team of the era. France hosted the World Cup in 1938 and the tournament was considered a success, despite the home team going down 3-1 in a quarter-final defeat to eventual winners Italy.

After World War II the introduction of international club competitions gave France an opportunity to flourish. They did so thanks to Reims, who became the first of three dominant French club sides. Reims reached the final of the first Champions Cup, losing 4-3 to Real Madrid in Paris in 1956. The sides met three years later, with the same outcome, by which time Reims had become France's greatest team of the era.

Raymond Kopa was the French star of the time, playing for Reims before switching to Real Madrid to play alongside the likes of Ferenc Puskás and Alfredo Di Stéfano. An outside-right or centre-forward, he had a leading role at the 1958 World Cup Finals.

France reached the semi-finals as Kopa formed a brilliant partnership with Just Fontaine, who scored 13 goals, a tournament tally unlikely ever to be beaten. But the 1960s saw a decline and to improve standards the FFF introduced a national youth training programme with the aim of producing better-skilled professional players.

It would later bear fruit remarkably. In the meantime St Etienne filled the void. In the 1970s they became France's premier side and

Above: Michel Platini at the World Cup in 1986. His time in the national team coincided with a golden period for France.
Opposite clockwise from top: the stars of France – the 1998 World Cup winning team; Zinedine Zidane celebrates scoring the golden goal in the Euro 2000 semi-final; and Thierry Henry lifts the Henri Delaunay trophy in Rotterdam in 2000.

challenged for major honours but lost 1-0 in the Champions Cup final to Bayern Munich in Glasgow in 1976.

Their success barely hinted at even more exciting times to come. In the 1980s a French generation of such talent and flair emerged they were dubbed the 'Blue Brazil' and finally won France's first major international trophy. Michel Platini was the leading player as France reached the semi-finals of the 1982 World Cup, beaten on penalties by West Germany after a thrilling 3-3 draw made infamous by German goalkeeper Harald Schumacher's brutal foul on French defender Patrick Battiston.

The side was skilful and devastating to watch. Two years later, under manager Michel Hidalgo, France finally got their reward by becoming European champions on home soil. Platini scored nine goals in five matches and, aided by the likes of Jean Tigana and Alain Giresse, he led Hidalgo's champions as they beat Spain 2-0 in the final to earn their place among the tournament greats.

Platini's retirement in 1987 led to a slump for the national side but Marseille came along as the new heroes. Run by businessman Bernard Tapie, they were a dazzling side that left the rest trailing in France and became a genuine European superpower.

Marseille won four league titles from 1989 to 1992 and played a superb style of open, attacking football with a side boasting Chris Waddle, Abedi Pele and Jean-Pierre Papin. After near misses in 1990 and 1991 they became the first French side to lift the Champions Cup with a 1-0 win over AC Milan

in Munich in 1993. Triumph, however, turned to scandal when it emerged Marseille had fixed a league match against Valenciennes before the final. It tainted their European triumph and plunged French football into misery.

In the 1990s French players moved abroad in greater numbers because of the Bosman ruling and the national team improved dramatically as key players gained confidence from other leagues. Coach Aimé Jacquet built a superb side for the 1998 World Cup around the sublime skills of playmaker Zinedine Zidane. The side looked likely winners from the outset and went from strength to strength to reach the final, deservedly beating Brazil 3-0 at the Stade de France in Paris to achieve their greatest-ever success. Zidane scored twice on the big day and the nation celebrated with more than one million supporters pouring on to the Champs-Elysées.

France had found a winning formula and triumphed at the European Championship two years later with an even higher standard of play. Thierry Henry led a more potent attack, and Zidane once again produced some majestic midfield displays.

Domestically, French club football is weaker now as the best players continue to move abroad, but the future looks promising. Despite their disastrous showing at the 2002 World Cup in Korea and Japan, where three straight defeats and no goals led to an early exit, the seemingly endless supply of young players from their academies means France should continue to be a force to be reckoned with for several decades to come.

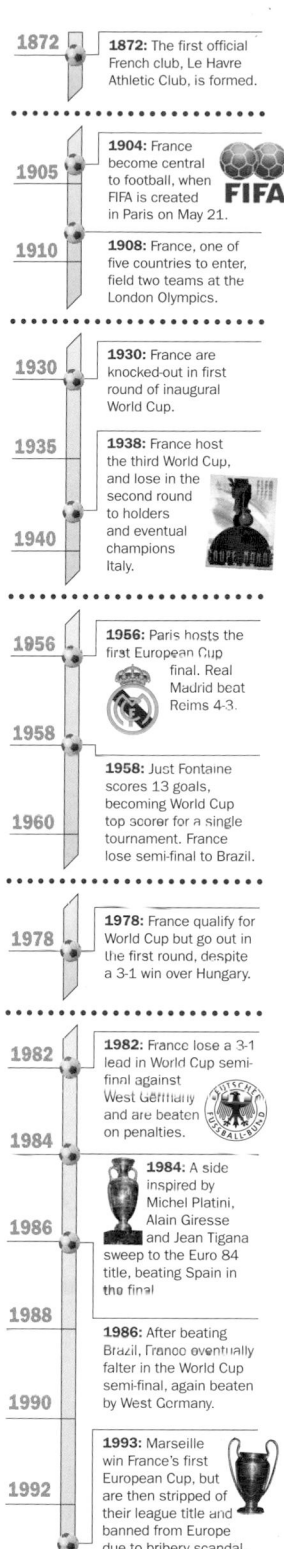

1872: The first official French club, Le Havre Athletic Club, is formed.

1904: France become central to football, when FIFA is created in Paris on May 21.

1908: France, one of five countries to enter, field two teams at the London Olympics.

1930: France are knocked-out in first round of inaugural World Cup.

1938: France host the third World Cup, and lose in the second round to holders and eventual champions Italy.

1956: Paris hosts the first European Cup final. Real Madrid beat Reims 4-3.

1958: Just Fontaine scores 13 goals, becoming World Cup top scorer for a single tournament. France lose semi-final to Brazil.

1978: France qualify for World Cup but go out in the first round, despite a 3-1 win over Hungary.

1982: France lose a 3-1 lead in World Cup semi-final against West Germany and are beaten on penalties.

1984: A side inspired by Michel Platini, Alain Giresse and Jean Tigana sweep to the Euro 84 title, beating Spain in the final

1986: After beating Brazil, France eventually falter in the World Cup semi-final, again beaten by West Germany.

1993: Marseille win France's first European Cup, but are then stripped of their league title and banned from Europe due to bribery scandal.

1998: At last, France win the World Cup, and on home soil. Zinedine Zidane inspires Les Bleus to a 3-0 win over Brazil.

2000: France prove their class in Euro 2000, held in Belgium and Holland. They beat Italy in a tense final.

2002: Shock, as highly-fancied France go out in the first round in Japan and Korea World Cup.

GABON

Federation: Fédération Gabonaise de Football
Founded: 1962
Joined FIFA: 1963
Confederation: CAF
FIFA world ranking: 122 (joint)

GAMBIA

Federation: Gambia Football Association
Founded: 1952
Joined FIFA: 1966
Confederation: CAF
FIFA world ranking: 137

GEORGIA

Federation: Georgian Football Federation
Founded: 1990
Joined FIFA: 1992
Confederation: UEFA
FIFA world ranking: 86 (joint)

Dinamo Tblisi were Georgia's leading force in the former Soviet Supreme League, winning the championship in 1964 and 1978, and lifting the Cup Winners' Cup in 1981. Since the Georgian league kicked-off in 1990 Tblisi have continued to dominate, winning every championship since. Such domination has had a detrimental effect on crowds.

Below: Georgi Kinkladze in action for the Georgian national team.

GERMANY

Federation: Deutscher Fussball-Bund
Founded: 1900
Joined FIFA: 1904
Confederation: UEFA
FIFA world ranking: 6
Honours: World Cup 1954, 1974, 1990;
European Championship 1972, 1980, 1996
[*all except 1996 won as West Germany]

Germany's outstanding tournament record is all the more remarkable given their late start in the game. They enjoyed barely any success before the Second World War, and until 1950 had virtually no international relations. It was, indeed, a modest beginning for one of football's superpowers. Yet since those difficult early days Germany has become a standard-bearer, winning trophies at every level and earning a reputation as one of the authentic masters of the modern era.

The nation has produced an array of great players over the past five decades, including arguably the world's greatest defender, Franz Beckenbauer, and deadliest goalscorer, Gerd Müller. Three times World Cup winners, finalists on three other occasions, and three times European champions, the nation's record is unequalled in Europe.

While success at national team level runs deep, their domestic clubs have also made a lasting impact. Bayern Munich have lifted the European Cup four times, their most recent success coming in 2001, and they have reached nine major continental finals. They are one of the richest and most successful clubs in the world. Other German sides, such as Borussia Mönchengladbach and Borussia Dortmund, have also triumphed on the European stage, and the quality of league

sides has been consistently high during the growth of club competitions.

German teams have developed a well-documented ability to rise to the occasion, no matter what the circumstances. They are noted – and envied – for making the most of their talents, and on occasion becoming greater than the sum of their parts. The German mix of skill, tactical nous and unshakeable self-belief goes beyond levels other nations attain. They have found a winning formula, yet their humble origins mean success is never taken for granted.

The start of the Bundesliga in 1963 saw standards improve following more than half a century of regionalised leagues. West Germany had emerged from the post-war doldrums to score their first major triumph when they won the 1954 World Cup, despite Hungary being the outstanding side of the era. They beat Ferenc Puskás's side 3-2 in the final and during the Sixties became a force to be reckoned with, losing 4-2 in extra-time to hosts England in the 1966 World Cup Final.

The tone for success was set. In 1972 they became European champions for the first time, beating the Soviet Union in the final, and two years later, on home soil, ran out World Cup winners for a second time when Müller, in typical fashion, scored the winner in a 2-1 victory over Holland in the newly-built Olympiastadion in Munich.

Beckenbauer was the star of his era, thanks to his revolutionary style of play. Originally a midfielder at the 1966 World Cup Finals, he became a free-moving defender who operated behind the markers and attacked from deep positions. The man nicknamed 'Der Kaiser' wooed crowds with his elegance on the ball and counter-attacking instincts.

Müller, the ultimate poacher, was equally important, creating little outside the box but scoring an astonishing total of 68 goals in 62 internationals. His stocky build and deceptive pace made him a nightmare for defenders to

handle and, alongside Beckenbauer, he also inspired Bayern Munich to a hat-trick of Champions Cup victories from 1974 to 1976, as both players deservedly picked up European Footballer Of The Year awards.

German football was built around the sweeper system, with the 3-5-2 formation using wing-backs and central strikers favoured by both club and country. In 1980, Bernd Schuster helped Germany become European champions, with Karl-Heinz Rummenigge as a centre-forward of pace and power.

West Germany's last triumph prior to re-unification came in 1990, when they won a third World Cup. Lothar Matthäus was the driving force behind their success in midfield, with Jürgen Klinsmann forming a potent attacking duo with Rudi Völler. They beat Argentina 1-0 in the final with an Andreas Brehme penalty gaining revenge for defeat to the same opponents in the 1986 final.

Their next success came thanks to a former East Germany star, Matthias Sammer, who was player of the tournament when a united Germany won Euro 96. He was the best example of a sweeper since Beckenbauer and inspired Borussia Dortmund to an unlikely Champions Cup triumph 12 months later, before retiring prematurely because of injury.

Yet German football struggled by its own standards in the 1990s, failing to meet expectations at a series of tournaments. Bayern Munich won a fourth European Cup in 2001, on penalties over Valencia, yet the 5-1 defeat to England in a World Cup qualifier in Munich in 2001 marked arguably the lowest point in the history of the national team. However, they bounced back in typical fashion at the 2002 World Cup and reached the final, thanks to the extraordinary goalkeeping of Oliver Kahn. They lost to Brazil 2-0, but Kahn was voted Player of the Tournament and Völler's side defied the critics. After 50 years of success, there are no signs of falling away. Germany, as every fan knows, can never be written off.

The stars of Germany: clockwise from top left – Oliver Kahn, voted the tournament's best player at Japan/Korea 2002; Michael Ballack and Torsten Frings celebrate in the 2002 semi-final; West Germany's Karl Heinz Rummenigge in full flight in Spain during the 1982 World Cup Final against Italy; 'Der Kaiser', Franz Beckenbauer, in commannding form during the 1974 World Cup Final; West Germany's Gerd Müller evades a Polish tackle during the 1974 World Cup.

1900
1900: The Deutscher Fussball Bund is founded in 1900.

1905
1904: The DFB becomes an official member of FIFA.

1935
1934: Germany make their World Cup finals debut, finishing in third place.

1940
1938: Germany lose a first round World Cup replay to Switzerland.

1955
1954: West Germany shock the world by defeating the invincible Hungarians to win the World Cup.

1960
1960: Eintracht Frankfurt lose 7-3 to Real Madrid in the greatest ever European Cup final.

1965
1966: West Germany reach the World Cup final, but lose to hosts England after a disputed goal.

1970
1972: One of the greatest West German sides wins the European Championship.

1975 
1974: After defeat in the first round to the East Germans, West Germany win the World Cup as hosts, beating Holland in the final.

1980
1980: Inspired by Bernd Schuster, West Germany collect another European Championship.

1985

1990
1990: West Germany win the World Cup in a poor final with Argentina.

1995
1996: Now known as Germany, the newly-unified national team win Euro 96, Bierhoff's goal beating the Czechs.

2000
1997: Borussia Dortmund win the Champions League.

2001: Bayern beat Valencia to win the Champions League.

2005
2002: Germany reach the final of the World Cup, losing to Brazil.

GHANA

Federation: Ghana Football Association
Founded: 1957
Joined FIFA: 1958
Confederation: CAF
FIFA world ranking: 69
Honours: African Nations Cup 1963, 1965, 1978, 1982, 1992

The 'Black Stars' of Ghana were the first team win the African Nations Cup four times. By the mid-Eighties they looked like the African team destined to make an impact on the world football stage, but the elusive World Cup qualification never came. There have been a number of great Ghanaian players, such as Ibrahim Sunday, Robert Mensah, Abdul Razak, Emmanuel Quarshie, Abedi Pelé, Nii Lamptey and Tony Yeboah, while clubs such as Asante Kotoko and Accra Hearts Of Oak have made their mark on the African game. Football was introduced to Ghana by the British and influenced to the extent that the great Stanley Matthews guested for Hearts Of Oak in 1957.

GREECE

Federation: Elliniki Podosferiki Omospondia
Founded: 1926
Joined FIFA: 1927
Confederation: UEFA
FIFA world ranking: 33 (joint)

Greek sport, including football, was for a long time dominated by the amateur ethos. Despite the massive popularity of the game, full-time professionalism did not arrive until 1979, making Panathinaikos's 1971 Champions Cup final appearance against Ajax at Wembley an even greater achievement – the game remains the only occasion that a Greek club has reached a major European final.

A national league kicked-off in 1960 and has since been dominated by three teams:

Right: Greece's Leonidas Vokolos fends off David Beckham in a World Cup qualifier.

Olympiakos Piraeus, Panathinaikos and AEK Athens. The previous so-called Greek league, founded in 1928, was restricted to clubs from just Athens and Salonica and it was one of the same big three clubs who topped the league in all but two seasons.

Aside from the all-embracing amateur ethos, in the first half of the 20th Century Greek football development also stalled in the face of greater adversity: civil war, the Balkan conflict, political instability and the Second World War. After professionalism was introduced in 1979, hooliganism blighted Greek football in the 1980s, but the game survived and the hooligan problem has lessened over the years.

Football has remained popular, despite the immense disappointment of the national side. Greece have qualified for just one European Championship in 1980, where they lost to Holland and Czechoslovakia and drew with West Germany, and the 1994 World Cup in the USA, where they failed to score and lost all of their group games.

GRENADA

Federation: Grenada Football Association
Founded: 1924
Joined FIFA: 1976
Confederation: CONCACAF
FIFA world ranking: 141

GUAM

Federation: Guam Football Association
Founded: 1976
Joined FIFA: 1996
Confederation: AFC
FIFA world ranking: 201

GUATEMALA

Federation: Federación Nacional de Fútbol de Guatemala
Founded: 1933
Joined FIFA: 1946
Confederation: CONCACAF
FIFA world ranking: 65 (joint)
Honours: CONCACAF Championship 1967

GUINEA

Federation: Fédération Guinéenne de Football
Founded: 1959
Joined FIFA: 1961
Confederation: CAF
FIFA world ranking: 118

GUINEA-BISSAU

Federation: Federação de Futebol da Guiné-Bissau
Founded: 1974
Joined FIFA: 1986
Confederation: CAF
FIFA world ranking: 189

GUYANA

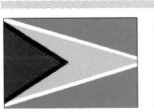

Federation: Guyana Football Federation
Founded: 1902
Joined FIFA: 1968
Confederation: CONCACAF
FIFA world ranking: 177

HAITI

Federation: Fédération Haïtienne de Football
Founded: 1904
Joined FIFA: 1933
Confederation: CONCACAF
FIFA world ranking: 84
Honours: CONCACAF Championship: 1957, 1973

Haiti were the first Caribbean side to play in the finals of the World Cup in 1974. Forward Sanon put Haiti ahead against Italy but they eventually lost 3-1. Disturbingly, Ernst Jean-Joseph failed a drug test, was beaten up by his own officials and sent back to Haiti. Heavy defeats by Poland (0-7) and Argentina (1-4) followed. Haiti have their own league, with clubs such as FICA, Violette Athlétique Club and Racing Club Haïtien picking up the title in recent years.

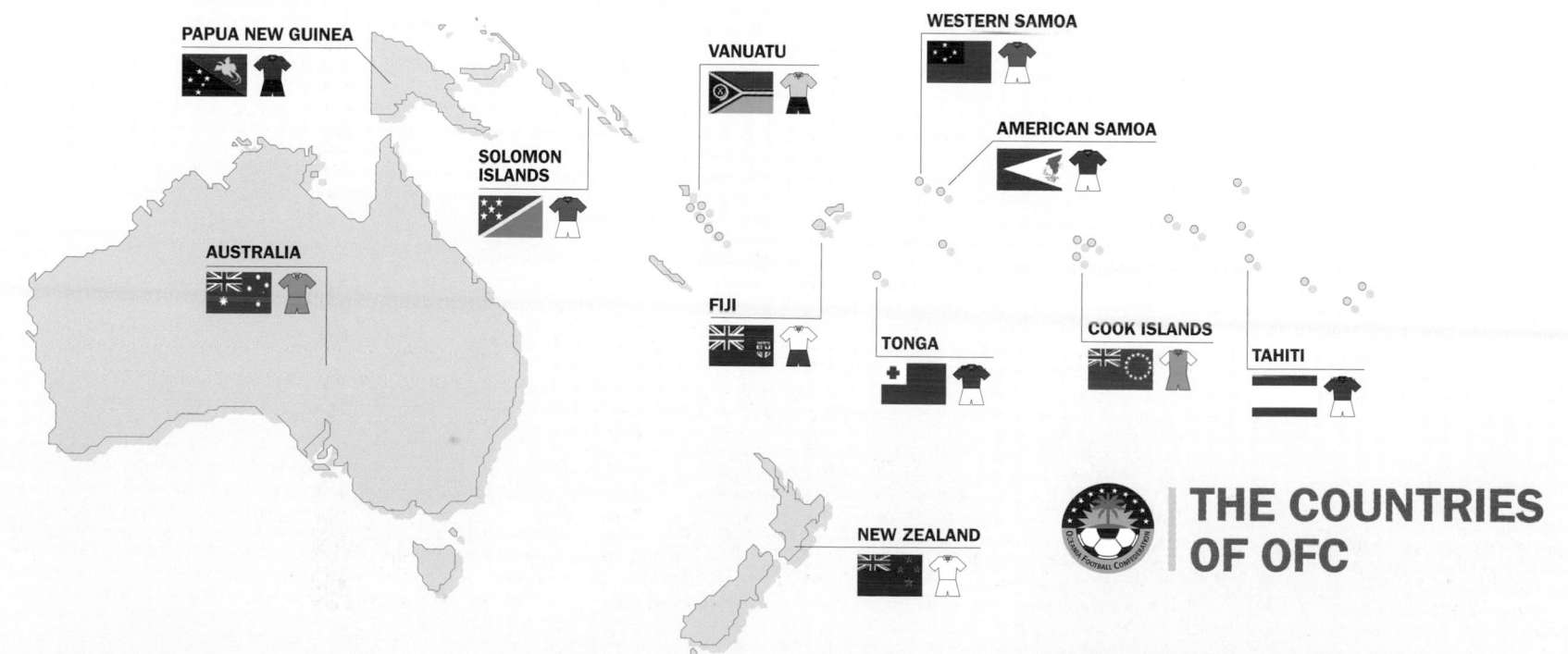

LEBANON

SYRIA

IRAN

IRAQ

KUWAIT

JORDAN

PALESTINE

SAUDI ARABIA

YEMEN

KAZAKHSTAN

TURKMENISTAN

UZBEKISTAN

AFGHANISTAN

BAHRAIN

QATAR

UEA

OMAN

KYRGYSTAN

TAJIKISTAN

NEPAL

PAKISTAN

INDIA

MALDIVES

MONGOLIA

BANGLADESH

BHUTAN

MYANMAR

SRI LANKA

THAILAND

SINGAPORE

MALAYSIA

NORTH KOREA

SOUTH KOREA

JAPAN

CHINA

LAOS

MACAO

TAIWAN

HONG KONG

GUAM

CAMBODIA

VIETNAM

BRUNEI

PHILIPPINES

INDONESIA

THE COUNTRIES OF AFC

Asian Football Confederation

PAPUA NEW GUINEA

SOLOMON ISLANDS

AUSTRALIA

VANUATU

FIJI

WESTERN SAMOA

AMERICAN SAMOA

TONGA

COOK ISLANDS

TAHITI

NEW ZEALAND

THE COUNTRIES OF OFC

HOLLAND

Federation: Koninklijke Nederlandse Voetbal Bond (KNVB)
Founded: 1889
Joined FIFA: 1904
Confederation: UEFA
FIFA world ranking: 5
Honours: European Championship 1988

Architects of 'Total Football' and birthplace of some of the game's finest talents, Holland remains one of the most innovative and exciting footballing cultures in the world – yet it was also one of its later developers.

Holland was one of the first countries outside of Britain to pick up on the appeal of football. The country's first club, Haarlemse FC, was founded in 1879 and its football association was set up ten years later. But while the Dutch football association's insistence on adhering to amateur, Calvinist principles yielded some return at the Olympics in the 1920s, it eventually proved to be a barrier to progress. In the post-war era it was evident that Holland lagged behind tactically and they regularly failed to make it through qualification for major championships.

Eventually the exodus of top players, like Ajax's Cor Van Der Hart and Xerxes' Faas Wilkes, to foreign clubs forced the KNVB to usher in professionalism in 1954. Ten years later the decision began to pay dividends as Dutch football accelerated into a new era, uncluttered by old traditions.

The breakthrough came in the mid-Sixties when the concept of Total Football took hold at Ajax with coach Rinus Michels and the young Johan Cruyff, Holland's most talented footballer ever. Their game plan relied on every player being comfortable on the ball, willing to play fluidly and move into space constantly. It has characterised the nation's football ever since – and influenced many other teams.

Ajax served notice that Dutch football had emerged from the dark ages with a memorable 5-1 thrashing of Bill Shankly's Liverpool in 1966. Three years later they made their first Champions Cup final appearance, losing to AC Milan, before winning the trophy on three successive occasions between 1971 and 1973.

At the 1974 World Cup Holland began to emerge as a real force on the international stage, but despite going 1-0 up in the first two minutes of the final against West Germany with a penalty from Neeskens, the team's over-confidence proved to be its downfall and they eventually lost to the hosts 2-1.

The psychological blow inflicted by that defeat then hung over Dutch football for a generation. Four years later in the final in

Above: Johan Neeskens lunges for the ball during the 1978 World Cup Final against Argentina. Opposite clockwise from top left: the stars of Holland – Frank Rijkaard; Johnny Rep in action at the 1978 World Cup; Ruud Gullit picks up the 1988 European Championship trophy; and Patrick Kluivert.

Argentina they were again undone by the hosts, on this occasion in extra-time.

The ghost was partially laid to rest in 1988 when the most talented Dutch team since the mid-Seventies, a side built around Ruud Gullit, Frank Rijkaard and Marco Van Basten, won the European Championship playing thrilling, attacking football – they also had the added satisfaction of gaining revenge over their German hosts in the semi-final.

Domestically the Dutch Eredivisie only came into existence in 1956 and has been totally dominated by three clubs ever since. Ajax (who won the inaugural title), PSV and Feyenoord annually turn the championship into a three-horse race. The lack of competition is another reason for the country's best (and most heavily-taxed) players regularly seeking more challenging climes. In 1973 Cruyff headed for Barcelona, while Rijkaard, Gullit and Van Basten became the bedrock for AC Milan's success in the early Nineties.

Ajax remain one of the most famous clubs in the world. Founded in 1900 the team began its early domination of Dutch football under Englishman Jack Reynolds, who enshrined its reputation for attacking play. Ajax have won the league on 28 occasions, most recently in 2002. In 1995 the club won the Champions Cup, thanks to a solitary goal from an 18-year-old Patrick Kluivert. A year later they moved to a state of the art stadium, the Amsterdam ArenA, which is also an international venue.

Amsterdam is effectively a one-club city and its bitterest rivals can be found in the port of Rotterdam at Feyenoord, the team that first

put Dutch football on the map when it lifted the Champions Cup in 1970. While Feyenoord fans still harbour an inferiority complex about the Amsterdamers, the club has had its fair share of success, not least in 14 championships and, in the Nineties, dominance in the cup competition, the KNVB Beker. Feyenoord's stadium, De Kuip, annually hosts the competition's final, and European glory also returned to De Kuip in May 2002 with a UEFA Cup win over Borussia Dortmund.

The third player in Holland's 'big three' is based in Eindhoven, home to industrial giant Philips, which also bankrolls PSV (Philips Sport Vereniging), the football club founded in 1913. Unsurprisingly PSV are the richest club in the Netherlands, though only the second most successful with 17 championship wins. The club's greatest era arrived with Ruud Gullit in the mid-Eighties, a period capped by a Champions Cup win in 1988.

On a general note, hooliganism became an unpleasant feature of Dutch football in the Nineties and a compulsory membership scheme was introduced in 1996.

Like many domestic leagues the Eredivisie began to feel the pinch at the start of the new millennium. In 2002 the KNVB announced the 36 professional clubs had suffered combined losses of £16million, necessitating squad cutbacks and wage cuts. This, and Holland's surprise failure to qualify for the 2002 World Cup Finals notwithstanding, the signs are there, especially with the revival of Ajax's famed youth policy, that the future is once again beginning to look orange.

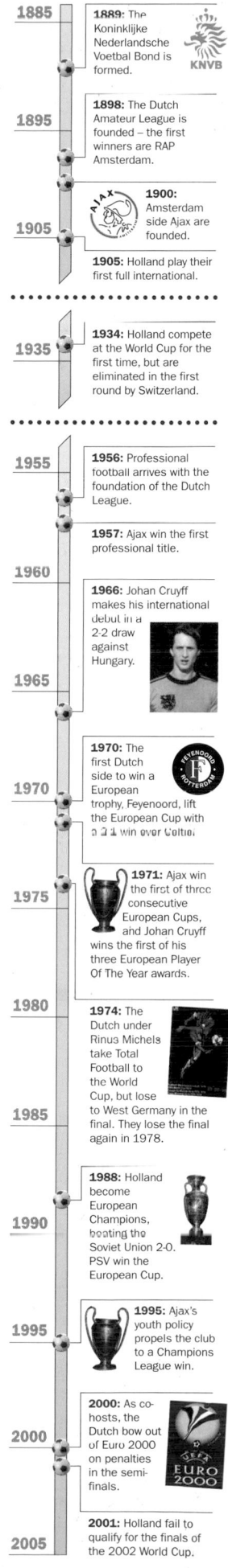

1885

1889: The Koninklijke Nederlandsche Voetbal Bond is formed.

1895

1898: The Dutch Amateur League is founded – the first winners are RAP Amsterdam.

1905

1900: Amsterdam side Ajax are founded.

1905: Holland play their first full international.

1935

1934: Holland compete at the World Cup for the first time, but are eliminated in the first round by Switzerland.

1955

1956: Professional football arrives with the foundation of the Dutch League.

1957: Ajax win the first professional title.

1960

1966: Johan Cruyff makes his international debut in a 2-2 draw against Hungary.

1965

1970: The first Dutch side to win a European trophy, Feyenoord, lift the European Cup with a 2-1 win over Celtic.

1970

1971: Ajax win the first of three consecutive European Cups, and Johan Cruyff wins the first of his three European Player Of The Year awards.

1975

1974: The Dutch under Rinus Michels take Total Football to the World Cup, but lose to West Germany in the final. They lose the final again in 1978.

1980

1988: Holland become European Champions, beating the Soviet Union 2-0. PSV win the European Cup.

1985

1990

1995: Ajax's youth policy propels the club to a Champions League win.

1995

2000: As co-hosts, the Dutch bow out of Euro 2000 on penalties in the semi-finals.

2000

2001: Holland fail to qualify for the finals of the 2002 World Cup.

2005

HONDURAS

Federation: Federación National Autónoma de Fútbol de Honduras
Founded: 1951
Joined FIFA: 1951
Confederation: CONCACAF
FIFA world ranking: 42 (joint)
Honours: CONCACAF Championship 1981

The early 1980s saw the heyday of football in Honduras – the nation won the CONCACAF Championship in 1981 and also qualified for the World Cup in Spain. Honduras, who drew with hosts Spain and Northern Ireland, could have qualified for the second stage but they lost to a Petrovic penalty against Yugoslavia.

HONG KONG

Federation: The Hong Kong Football Association
Founded: 1914
Joined FIFA: 1954
Confederation: AFC
FIFA world ranking: 136

The former British colony of Hong Kong was at the forefront of football development on the Asian continent. They were founder members of the Asian Football Confederation in 1954 and hosted the inaugural Asian Cup in 1956. The Hong Kong league was the first professional league on the continent, drawing players from abroad, especially British players. The league began in 1946 and was first won by the Royal Air Force team. Since then South China has become the biggest and most successful club, although in the late Seventies and early Eighties Seiko were unstoppable with seven successive titles.

Right: Iceland's Brynar Gunnarsson is challenged by Scotland's Don Hutchison in a European Championship qualifier.

HUNGARY

Federation: Magyar Labdarúgó Szövetség
Founded: 1901
Joined FIFA: 1906
Confederation: UEFA
FIFA world ranking: 49
Honours: Olympic winners 1952, 1964, 1968

Once numbered among the game's most innovative footballing cultures, Hungary is a shadow of its former self. Great promise failed to yield major trophies, talent drained away and socio-political decline has now left the country financially crippled.

The Hungarian football association was founded more than 100 years ago, but a professional league did not arise until the Twenties when Jewish-based club MTK (Magyar Testgyakorlók Köre) became so dominant under the coaching of Scotsman Jimmy Hogan that the need for organised competition necessitated one.

Pre-World War II Hungary began to display the ability and cohesion to challenge the hegemony of established footballing giants like England and Italy. The national side reached the 1938 World Cup Final before ushering in the era of the 'Magical Magyars', rewriting the way the game was played in the Fifties with a clutch of legends including Bozsik, Kocsis, Hidegkuti and Puskás. Their impact was vividly underlined in 1953 when they became the first team to beat England at Wembley with a resounding 6-3 victory.

In 50 games played between 1950 and 1955, Hungary lost just once – agonisingly it was the 1954 World Cup Final, where they threw away a 2-0 lead to end up losing 3-2 to West Germany. The team's promise ended abruptly with the Soviet invasion of their country in 1956. Many of the players were on tour with Honvéd and chose not to return. Kocsis and Czibor headed for Barcelona, while Puskás opted for Real Madrid.

Within six years, a talented new side had emerged, with the likes of striker Florian Albert taking Hungary to the quarter-finals of both the 1962 and 1966 World Cup finals. It was to be their last hurrah. Despite Olympic golds in 1964 and 1968, Hungary failed to qualify for the 1970 World Cup Finals and has not been represented since 1986, where they managed a first-round victory against Canada, but went out after heavy defeats to the Soviet Union and France. A fourth place in the 1972 European Championship remains their best showing in the modern era, where the team lost to a solitary goal in the semi-final against the Soviet Union.

At club level Hungarian football has rarely looked like capitalising on the brilliance of its national teams. Budapest-based Ferencváros dominated domestic football in the Nineties, but their only European success came as long ago as 1965 when they won the UEFA Cup, beating Juventus. They made one appearance in the Champions League in 1995-96. Local rivals Honvéd, once the army side which provided the core of the Golden Squad, Ujpesti TE, and 2002 winners Zalaegerszegi TE make up the running.

In 1999 the Hungarian Football Federation took drastic action to halt the alarming decline in quality footballers, revamping the entire grassroots structure of the game in an initiative known as the Bozsik Programme.

The financial strictures on clubs, however, continue to undermine the domestic game. In February 2003 First Division side Dunaferr SE parted company with almost their entire playing and coaching staff because of financial problems. The revival of the Magical Magyars remains a long way off.

ICELAND

Federation: Knattspyrnumsamband Island
Founded: 1947
Joined FIFA: 1947
Confederation: UEFA
FIFA world ranking: 59 (joint)

The Icelandic league, played between April and October, is dominated by the Reykjavik clubs – KR, Valur, Fram and Vikingur have been the big winners, but IA Akranes have also risen to prominence in recent years. Iceland is still regarded as a minor football nation but they rarely suffer heavy defeats and at home are very difficult to beat.

INDIA

Federation: All India Football Federation
Founded: 1937
Joined FIFA: 1948
Confederation: AFC
FIFA world ranking: 129

Like so many sports in India, football was introduced by the British. However, the Indian population has shown little interest in the game, instead preferring cricket and hockey. The early Calcutta league was strictly a British affair, but Indian teams such as Mohammedan Sporting, East Bengal and Mohon Bagan did spring up to challenge the British dominance.

re-emerged from a period of instability, qualifying for the 1998 World Cup and recording their first win at the finals, beating USA 2-1. Their best players, such as Ali Daei, also began making the grade in Europe.

IRAQ

Federation: Iraqi Football Association
Founded: 1948
Joined FIFA: 1950
Confederation: AFC
FIFA world ranking: 64

One of the top six sides on the Asian continent, more often than not it is Iraq that misses out on World Cup qualification and fails to make the final step in the Asian Cup. Iraq did qualify for the World Cup in 1986 under Brazilian coach Evaristo de Macedo, but they lost all three of their group games. The Iraqi FA, while under the control of Udey Hussein (son of Saddam), faced allegations of torturing its players when they have failed to perform on the international stage. The Iraqi league's most successful club has been Al Rasheed, with Al Talaba and Al Zewra consistent challengers.

ISRAEL

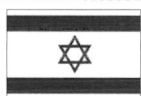 

Federation: Israel Football Association
Founded: 1928
Joined FIFA: 1929
Confederation: UEFA
FIFA world ranking: 44
Honours: Asian Cup 1964

Israel were a strong force in the Asian Football Confederation, runners-up twice in the first two Asian Cups of 1956 and 1960, before lifting the trophy in 1964. They also qualified for the World Cup finals in 1970, drawing with Italy and Sweden and losing to Uruguay.

However, Israel's national team were a political hot potato in Asian football. The AFC contrived that Israel avoided their Arab neighbours and grouped them with Far East opposition, such as Japan and South Korea. Arab disquiet was brought to a head and Israel were thrown out of the AFC in 1976, being shunted first into Europe and then Oceania, even facing South American opposition in World Cup play-offs. As a consequence Israel have had the distinction of having played World Cup qualifiers on every continent.

Israel was given a permanent football home in Europe when UEFA accepted them in 1991.

Mohon Bagan, to mark the club's centenary, were officially named 'The National Football Team of India'. Indian players have included Jumma Khan, the first Indian to play in boots, and Syed Abdus Sumad, 'the Indian Stanley Matthews', who played until he was 52.

INDONESIA

Federation: Persatuan Sepakbola Seluruh Indonesia
Founded: 1930
Joined FIFA: 1952
Confederation: AFC
FIFA world ranking: 89

IRAN

Federation: Football Federation of the Islamic Republic of Iran
Founded: 1920
Joined FIFA: 1945
Confederation: AFC
FIFA world ranking: 41
Honours: Asian Cup 1968, 1972, 1976

Iranian football rose to prominence in the Sixties and Seventies with the national team winning a hat-trick of Asian Cups and making the Olympic quarter-finals in 1976. The highlight was a deserved 1-1 draw with Scotland at the 1978 World Cup. In the Nineties Iran

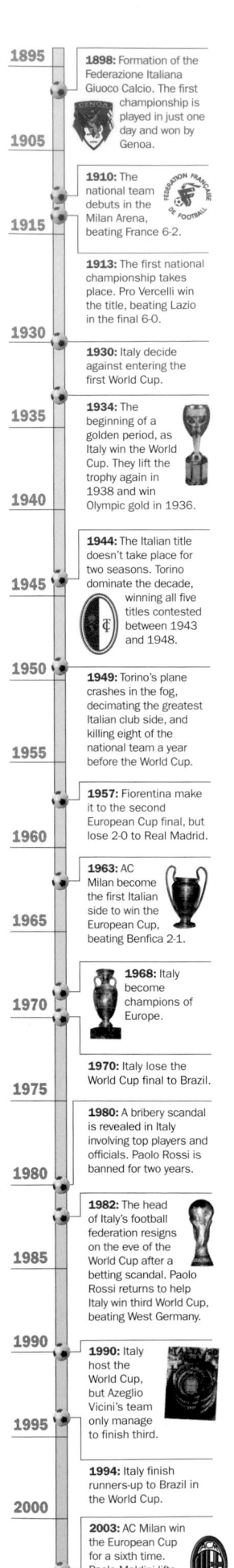

ITALY

Federation: Federazione Italiana Giuoco Calcio
Founded: 1898
Joined FIFA: 1905
Confederation: UEFA
FIFA world ranking: 11 (joint)
Honours: World Cup 1934, 1938, 1982; European Championship 1968; Olympics 1936

The Italian league, Serie A, wasn't founded until the 1929-30 season, but there had been a Football Association operating in the country since 1898. Italy's first four club sides – Juventus, AC Milan, Lazio and Internazionale – were established in a period stretching from 1897 to 1908, but they are all a dominant influence on European football to this day. In the 1980s and 1990s, Italian club football lavished money on expensive foreign players and consequently ruled European competition, AC Milan winning the Champions Cup in 1989, 1990 and 1994, and Juventus doing likewise in 1996. Furthermore, eight out of 11 UEFA Cup finals between 1989 and 1999 were won by Italian sides, with four of them being all-Italian affairs.

The country's national side enjoyed similar dominance in the 1930s, but hasn't hit the same heights since. Their appearance in the final of the European Championship in 2000 (where they were cruelly undone by a last-minute equaliser and golden goal by France) was their first in the tournament since winning it in 1968. Although Italy's recent record in the World Cup is slightly better, they haven't lifted the trophy since 1982. For most countries this catalogue of near misses would be acceptable, perhaps even laudable, but for Italy, the first European nation to not only stage the World Cup, but also to win it three times, it's underachievement on a grand scale and a thorn in the side of their passionate supporters.

Italy hadn't competed in the first finals in Uruguay in 1930, but were named hosts of the second, four years later. Their arrival on the world stage, under legendary manager Vittorio Pozzo, was marked with a crushing 7-1 win over the United States. Pozzo's side found Spain, their quarter-final opponents, a much tougher nut to crack, and had a controversial equaliser to thank for taking what had already been a bruising tie to a replay, which they duly won. Italy defeated Austria 1-0 in the semi-final and, cheered on by fascist dictator Benito Mussolini, came from behind to overcome Czechoslovakia with two late goals in the final.

To underline their superiority, Italy went on to win the gold medal at the Berlin Olympics in 1936 – they defeated Austria 2-1 in the final

Above: Marco Tardelli celebrates the first goal of Italy's 3-1 World Cup final win over West Germany in 1982. Opposite clockwise from top left: the stars of Italy – Sandro Mazzola in 1974; long-serving defender Paolo Maldini; Paolo Rossi, who despite being banned for match-fixing, returned to help Italy to World Cup triumph in 1982; and Roberto Baggio at USA 94.

and were no doubt glad to put to rest conspiracy theories about the nature of their World Cup victory two years earlier (some suggested Italy had unfairly benefited from their status as hosts).

The first European team to win the Jules Rimet trophy soon became the first nation to retain it, travelling to France in 1938 with a much remodelled side. Strangely enough it was Norway rather than hosts France or Brazil who caused the Italians most problems on their way to the final, but a fine display from goalkeeper Aldo Olivieri and an extra-time winner saw Pozzo's attack-minded side win 2-1 to progress to the quarter-finals. France were duly dispatched 3-1 and two second-half goals put paid to the Brazilians in the semi-finals (one, a penalty from Giuseppe Meazza, was scored as he struggled to hold up his shorts in which the elastic had snapped). Italy met Hungary in the final in Paris, running out 4-2 winners, with Silvio Piola and Luigi Colaussi bagging two each. It was a historic win not just for Italy, but with World War II just over a year away, for fascism also.

Post-war, Italy had to endure many years in the international wilderness. In 1949, the entire first team squad of reigning champions Torino were killed in a plane crash, effectively ripping the heart out of the national side a little over a year before they were expected to defend their world title in Brazil. Italy failed to make it past the first round in the finals and subsequently missed out on the finals altogether in 1958, having to endure the humiliation of losing to North Korea in 1966. Just two years later, however, Italian football got itself back on track when the country hosted – and won – the 1968 European Championship. Although they had to rely on the toss of a coin to defeat the Soviet Union in the semi-finals (the game had finished 0-0 after extra-time), and it had taken a replay to see off Yugoslavia in the final, coach Ferrucio

Valcareggi built on that success, taking his side all the way to the final of the 1970 World Cup, where it was heavily defeated by Brazil.

Under coach Enzo Bearzot, Italy finished fourth at the Argentina finals in 1978, but won the World Cup for a third time in 1982. They did it the hard way too, drawing all three of their first round games, before beating reigning champions Argentina and favourites Brazil in the second group phase. The latter match – a 3-2 win – was memorable thanks to an astonishing hat-trick from 25-year-old Paolo Rossi, who'd only recently returned to football following a two-year ban for match-fixing. Rossi hit two more in the semi-final against Poland and was the scorer of Italy's first goal in a 3-1 final triumph over West Germany.

Since then Italy have come close to claiming a fourth World Cup win. They finished third in 1990, losing to Argentina on penalties in the semi-final, and were beaten on penalties again in the final by Brazil in 1994. The team and nation will probably want to forget Italy's contribution to 2002's tournament though, where they were eliminated by hosts South Korea in the second round.

While Italian club sides remain some of the strongest in Europe, domestically the Italian league is still living in the wake of its spending spree in the 1990s. Many of the clubs who failed to deliver glory in exchange for unrealistic spending plans are now paying the price for over-ambition in a market that has seen attendances stagnating and uncertainties over TV revenues. But while Fiorentina, Napoli, Genoa and Sampdoria have struggled, Lazio opted to restructure their finances in 1998 with a partial flotation on the Italian stock exchange. The decision paid dividends two years later when they claimed their first title in 26 seasons. Neighbours Roma, and Turin giants Juventus, followed suit and both won the championship themselves in the subsequent campaigns.

Opposite: Junichi Inamoto, whose performances in the 2002 World Cup helped to put Japanese football on the map.

IVORY COAST

Federation: Fédération Ivoirienne de Football
Founded: 1960
Joined FIFA: 1960
Confederation: CAF
FIFA world ranking: 52
Honours: African Nations Cup 1992

It was the French that introduced football to the Ivory Coast. The West African nation has one of the best-organised and richest leagues on the continent, but this strength at home has not often been turned into success in the international arena. Stade Abidjan won the African Cup in 1966, while the national team, under coach Yeo Martial, won the African Nations Cup in 1992, beating Ghana in a dramatic 11-10 penalty shoot-out. Kouame Aka scored the decisive kick before goalkeeper Alain Gouamene saved. The victorious squad included two of the most famous Ivory Coast players, French league stars Youssef Fofana and Abdoulaye Traoré.

JAMAICA

Federation: Jamaica Football Federation
Founded: 1910
Joined FIFA: 1962
FIFA world ranking: 48
Confederation: CONCACAF

Below: Jamaica's Paul Hall escapes from Jose Chamot of Argentina during a World Cup match in 1998.

Jamaica has had a football federation, care of its former British colonial rulers, since 1910, although it does not have much history as an organised sport. The rise of the 'Reggae Boyz' in the late Nineties saw Jamaica qualify for their first World Cup under Brazilian coach Rene Simoes. For the first time Jamaica raided players from the English league and 'imported' players of Jamaican descent, such as Frank Sinclair, Fitzroy Simpson, Robbie Earle, Marcus Gayle, Paul Hall and Deon Burton, beating Japan 2-1 in their final group game following defeats by Croatia and Argentina. Jamaica were the inaugural winners of the Caribbean Cup in 1991.

JAPAN

Federation: The Football Association of Japan
Founded: 1921
Joined FIFA: 1929-45, 1950
Confederation: AFC
FIFA world ranking: 24 (joint)
Honours: Asian Cup 1992, 2000

Football has never been the biggest sport in Japan, but 2002 saw the country co-host (along with South Korea) the World Cup finals – and for a few short weeks at least, the land of the rising sun embraced the beautiful game.

Japan's only international successes have been in winning the Asian Cup, beating Saudi Arabia 1-0 in both 1992 and 2000. But having narrowly failed to qualify for the 1994 World Cup, hopes for the development of the Japanese game were placed with the future of the J.League. Set up in 1993 with $20million of investment and major TV and marketing support, Japan's first truly professional league tempted many veteran stars to conclude their careers in Japan, including England's Gary Lineker and Zico of Brazil.

In the J.League the corporate names of the old JSL were banned (Nissan Motors, for instance, becoming Yokohama Marinos), and at the league's insistence, clubs were strongly identified with their local communities. Initial success went to the strongest clubs of the former JSL, but after the initial boom years of the competition, the J.League has settled down. In recent years, some of the newer clubs like Kashima Antlers and Jubilo Iwata have enjoyed the most success.

Internationally Japan became a competitive side under the guidance of Frenchman Philip Troussier and the World Cup finals of 2002 saw them qualify for the second phase as the top team in their group. Having beaten Russia in progressing, they were eliminated by a strong Turkey side.

An increasing number of the Japanese national team are now playing abroad, players like Nakata and Inamoto have illuminated Italy's Serie A and the English Premiership respectively. Zico, having become a legend at Kashima Antlers as both player and general manager, has recently taken over the reins of the national team.

JORDAN

Federation: Jordan Football Association
Founded: 1949
Joined FIFA: 1958
FIFA world ranking: 77
Confederation: AFC

KAZAKHSTAN

Federation: Football Association of the Republic of Kazakhstan
Founded: 1914
Joined FIFA: 1994
FIFA world ranking: 124
Confederation: AFC

KENYA

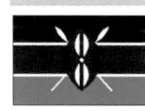 

Federation: Kenya Football Federation
Founded: 1960
Joined FIFA: 1960
FIFA world ranking: 76
Confederation: CAF

KUWAIT

Federation: Kuwait Football Association
Founded: 1952
Joined FIFA: 1962
Confederation: AFC
FIFA world ranking: 91 (joint)
Honours: Asian Cup 1980

Prince Fahid calling his team off the field after France had 'scored' a fourth goal at the 1982 World Cup is the abiding memory of Kuwaiti football. They did manage a draw with Czechoslovakia at the same tournament. Two years earlier Kuwait had hosted and won the Asian Cup, beating South Korea 3-0.

Above: Liechtenstein's Daniel Hasler in action at the tiny Rheinpark Stadium in Vaduz.

KYRGYZSTAN

Federation: Football Federation of Kyrgyz Republic
Founded: 1992
Joined FIFA: 1994
Confederation: AFC
FIFA world ranking: 170 (joint)

LAOS

Federation: Fédération Lao de Football
Founded: 1951
Joined FIFA: 1952
Confederation: AFC
FIFA world ranking: 163 (joint)

LATVIA

Federation: Latvijas Futbola Federacija
Founded: 1921
Joined FIFA: 1922, 1991
Confederation: UEFA
FIFA world ranking: 79

Between 1922 and 1949 Latvia were the strongest of the Baltic states but remained a minnow in football terms. They came within a whisker of qualifying for the 1938 World Cup but lost 2-1 to Austria in a play-off. Soviet occupation in 1940 eventually led to the demise of the Latvian national team, but after independence they competed in the qualifying stages for the 1994 World Cup and 1996 European Championship. Since their return

to international football, Latvia have yet to make any kind of impression on either competition. Latvia's leading club is Skonto Riga, who have dominated the first ten years of the revived Latvian championship.

LEBANON

Federation: Fédération Libanaise de Football Association
Founded: 1933
Joined FIFA: 1935
Confederation: AFC
FIFA world ranking: 121

LESOTHO

Federation: Lesotho Football Association
Founded: 1932
Joined FIFA: 1964
Confederation: CAF
FIFA world ranking: 125

LIBERIA

Federation: Liberia Football Association
Founded: 1936
Joined FIFA: 1962
Confederation: CAF
FIFA world ranking: 98

Liberian soccer has never been very strong but in striker George Weah, the country has produced one truly great player. Weah has been African, European and World Player Of The Year, plying his trade at a number of top Europan clubs and has provided enormous support to the game in his native nation.

LIBYA

Federation: Libyan Football Federation
Founded: 1962
Joined FIFA: 1963
Confederation: CAF
FIFA world ranking: 91 (joint)

LIECHTENSTEIN

Federation: Liechtensteiner Fussball-Verband
Founded: 1934
Joined FIFA: 1974
Confederation: UEFA
FIFA world ranking: 146

There is no national league in Liechtenstein, leaving the clubs to play their matches in the lower reaches of the Swiss League. The national team played occasional friendly matches before entering major UEFA and FIFA competitions from 1994. Regarded as one of the weakest team on the continent, they have yet to win a competitive match.

LITHUANIA

Federation: Lietuvos Futbolo Federacija
Founded: 1922
Joined FIFA: 1923, 1992
Confederation: UEFA
FIFA world ranking: 99

Despite the Soviet take-over of Lithuania, the football federation never actually cancelled its membership of FIFA and, following the country's independence, it was reactivated in 1992. Lithuania was the worst performing of the Baltic states, its clubs barely making an impact on the Soviet league until Zhalgiris

Right: George Weah is not only a former World Footballer Of The Year, but an ambassador for the Liberian game.

Vilnius won promotion to the Supreme Soviet League in 1982, finishing third in 1987. Sigitas Jakabauskas was the first Lithuanian to play for the USSR in 1985, while Viacheslav Sukristovas and Valdas Ivanauskas were Soviet Union Olympic gold medal winners in 1988. Zhalgiris have been the dominant teams in a Lithuanian league that lost many of its best players after independence.

LUXEMBOURG

Federation: Federation Luxembourgeoise de Football
Founded: 1908
Joined FIFA: 1910
Confederation: UEFA
FIFA world ranking: 153 (joint)

The part-time footballers of Luxembourg have one of the most dire records in Europe. Their clubs have suffered the worst aggregate defeats in European football, Dudelange losing 18-0 over two legs to Benfica, Jeunesse Hautcharage defeated 21-0 by Chelsea, and US Rumelange conceding 21 goals at the hands of Feyenoord. A European Championship quarter-final place in 1964 was the country's finest moment.

MACAO

Federation: Associacao de Futebol de Macau
Founded: 1939
Joined FIFA: 1976
Confederation: AFC
FIFA world ranking: 186

MACEDONIA FYR

Federation: Football Federation of Macedonia
Founded: 1909
Joined FIFA: 1994
Confederation: UEFA
FIFA world ranking: 90

In 2003, the country's leading clubs formed UPC – a union of premiership clubs – to take over the running of the Macedonian League from the federation. Leading club Vardar Skopje have gone down in history as the only Macedonian side to have won a national Yugoslav trophy, the Yugoslav Cup, in 1961.

MADAGASCAR

Federation: Fédération Malagasy de Football
Founded: 1961
Joined FIFA: 1962
Confederation: CAF
FIFA world ranking: 103

MALAWI

Federation: Football Association of Malawi
Founded: 1966
Joined FIFA: 1967
Confederation: CAF
FIFA world ranking: 101

MALAYSIA

Federation: Persatuan Bolasepak Malaysia
Founded: 1933
Joined FIFA: 1956
Confederation: AFC
FIFA world ranking: 116

MALDIVES

Federation: Football Association of Maldives
Founded: 1982
Joined FIFA: 1986
Confederation: AFC
FIFA world ranking: 152

MALI

Federation: Fédération Malienne de Football
Founded: 1960
Joined FIFA: 1962
Confederation: CAF
FIFA world ranking: 73

MALTA

Federation: Malta Football Association
Founded: 1900
Joined FIFA: 1959
Confederation: UEFA
FIFA world ranking: 130

Malta has a special place in footballing history as it was on the Mediterranean island that the first referee's whistle was heard, in a 1-1 draw between soldiers of the Shropshire Regiment and locals from Cospicua St Andrew's, in 1886. Malta did not join FIFA until 1959 and only then with the permission of the English FA, to whom they had been affiliated since 1900. They did not enter the World Cup until 1974 and have since had very limited success. One of Europe's smallest football nations, the Maltese league is dominated by Floriana and Sliema Wanderers, with Valletta a third force.

MAURITANIA

Federation: Fédération de Football de la République de Mauritanie
Founded: 1961
Joined FIFA: 1964
Confederation: CAF
FIFA world ranking: 179 (joint)

MAURITIUS

Federation: Mauritius Football Association
Founded: 1952
Joined FIFA: 1962
Confederation: CAF
FIFA world ranking: 133

Below left: Jeff Strasser in action for Luxembourg in 2000.

Above: The original Mexican wave. Mexico celebrate their goal against the Republic Of Ireland at USA 94.

MEXICO

Federation: Federación Mexicana De Fútbol Asociación
Founded: 1927
Joined FIFA: 1929
Confederation: CONCACAF
FIFA world ranking: 11 (joint)
Honours: CONCACAF Championship 1965, 1971, 1993, 1996, 1998

Mexico commands a special place in the hearts of international football fans worldwide for hosting the 1970 finals, which provided the canvas on which the great Brazilians of that era could let their artistry flow.

Mexico have regularly appeared at the World Cup finals, having taken part on ten occasions, their strongest showings coming in 1970 and 1986 where, as hosts, they progressed to the quarter-final stage. In 1986, it took a penalty shoot-out with eventual finalists West Germany to eliminate the team led by the great Hugo Sanchez, the most famous Mexican player of recent years. Sanchez, known for his extravagant and often over-the-top goal celebrations, was a familiar figure in Europe, having plied his trade very successfully for many years in Spain with Real Madrid.

Some argue that Mexican football has suffered internationally due to a lack of competition in the Central American region. Only in recent years, with the rise of the United States as a credible footballing force, have Mexico experienced a serious rival in a geographical neighbour. Many had argued that the nation, five times the CONCACAF championship winners, would benefit from joining the South American championship (the Copa América) and in 1993, together with the USA, they were invited to do so. Mexico reached the final at the first attempt, losing to Argentina 2-1 after a late Gabriel Batistuta strike, but since then they have continued to take part in the competition and have become one of the more dominant forces, finishing third in 1997 and 1999, and reaching the final again in 2001.

After the near miss of the 1986 World Cup, Mexico qualified for the 1990 tournament in Italy but did not attend because they were banned after fielding over-age players in an international youth tournament. In 1999 further controversy surrounded the Mexican side when, following the team's impressive third place in the Copa América, accusations were made of drug-taking among the players.

Of the 18 top flight clubs in the Mexican league all, apart from one, are subsidiaries of larger non-football companies. That one club is the unfashionable, and not very successful, Atlas of Guadalajara. Commercialism is rampant in Mexican football to the extent that allegations of corruption are constantly made because of all the vested interests from these outside businesses. The league itself has undergone enormous changes since it began, most recently in 1993 when it split the season into a winter and summer league.

The glamour club in Mexico is América from Mexico City. Bought by TV company Televisa and heavily promoted through the purchase of overseas stars and widespread TV exposure, the club quickly developed a nationwide following. América became a dominant force in Mexican football in the Eighties and since then, Televisas has also added Atlante and Necaxa to its stable. All three clubs play in the world famous Azteca national stadium in Mexico City, itself owned by the company. Since then, broadcasting rivals TV Azteca have followed suit, and bought into the Veracruz and Moriela clubs.

MOLDOVA

Federation: Federatia Moldoveneasca de Fotbal
Founded: 1990
Joined FIFA: 1994
Confederation: UEFA
FIFA world ranking: 106

When Nistru Kishinev (later renamed Zimbru Chisinau) finished sixth in the Soviet League in 1957, it was the best ever performance by a Moldovan club. Zimbru have subsequently proved the dominant team in a poor Moldovan league and, along with Serif and Tiligul Tiraspol, they provide most of the playing staff to a mediocre national side.

MONGOLIA

Federation: Mongolian Football Federation
Founded: 1959
Joined FIFA: 1998
Confederation: AFC
FIFA world ranking: 185

MONTSERRAT

Federation: Montserrat Football Association
Founded: 1973
Joined FIFA: 1996
Confederation: CONCACAF
FIFA world ranking: 204

MOROCCO

Federation: Fédération Royale Marocaine de Football
Founded: 1955
Joined FIFA: 1959
Confederation: CAF
FIFA world ranking: 37
Honours: African Nations Cup 1976

Morocco became the first African team to progress to the second round of the World Cup in 1986. After winning the group thanks to

o-o draws with England and Poland, and a 3-1 win over Portugal, they faced West Germany, but were beaten by a last minute goal. When Morocco made their very first World Cup appearance in 1970, the team was captained by Idriss Bamouss, who later became Moroccan FA President, and they shocked their German opponents by taking the lead before losing 2-1. They later drew 1-1 with Bulgaria. At the World Cup in 1994, Morocco lost all three group games by a single goal, while four years later, a 2-2 draw with Norway and an emphatic 3-0 win over Scotland was impressive enough but it still failed to take them through.

It was the French who introduced football to Morocco and several Moroccan-born players have featured for the French national team, including Larbi Ben Barek. Independence brought a remarkably robust and open league (which had been running since 1916) and two Moroccan sides – FAR Rabat in 1985 and Raja Casablanca in 1989 – have won the African Champions Cup, while Ahmed Faras (1975), Mohamed Timoumi (1985), Badou Zaki (1986) have been voted African Player Of The Year.

MOZAMBIQUE

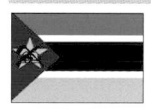  

Federation: Federação Mocambicana de Futebol
Founded: 1976
Joined FIFA: 1976
Confederation: CAF
FIFA world ranking: 131

MYANMAR

Federation: Myanmar Football Federation
Founded: 1947
Joined FIFA: 1957
Confederation: AFC
FIFA world ranking: 139 (joint)

NAMIBIA

Federation: Namibia Football Association
Founded: 1990
Joined FIFA: 1992
Confederation: CAF
FIFA world ranking: 134

Above: Morocco's Mustapha Hadji has been a hit in several European leagues.

NEPAL

Federation: All Nepal Football Federation
Founded: 1951
Joined FIFA: 1970
Confederation: AFC
FIFA world ranking: 163 (joint)

NETHERLANDS ANTILLES

Federation: Netherlands Antilliaanse Voetbal Unie
Founded: 1921
Joined FIFA: 1932
Confederation: CONCACAF
FIFA world ranking: 184

NEW ZEALAND

Federation: Soccer New Zealand
Founded: 1891
Joined FIFA: 1948
Confederation: OFC
FIFA world ranking: 53
Honours: Oceania Nations Cup 1973, 1998, 2002

New Zealand are known as the 'All Whites' to distinguish themselves from the dominant Rugby Union 'All Blacks'. With only Australia as serious rivals, New Zealand have made little impact, save for occasional Oceania Cup triumphs and a place at the 1982 World Cup. The national league did not begin until 1970.

Right: Norman Whiteside shoots at goal against France as Northern Ireland's good run at the 1982 World Cup comes to an end in the second phase.

NICARAGUA

Federation: Federación Nicaraguense de Fútbol
Founded: 1931
Joined FIFA: 1950
Confederation: CONCACAF
FIFA world ranking: 172

NIGER

Federation: Fédération Nigerienne de Football
Founded: 1967
Joined FIFA: 1967
Confederation: CAF
FIFA world ranking: 174

NIGERIA

Federation: Nigeria Football Association
Founded: 1945
Joined FIFA: 1959
Confederation: CAF
FIFA world ranking: 31 (joint)
Honours: African Nations Cup 1980, 1994; Olympics 1996

The formation of a football association and the launching of the Governor's Cup (later renamed the FA Challenge Cup in 1954) saw the formal birth of football in Nigeria after it had been introduced by the British. However, it was not until the 1970s that Nigerian football, despite its popularity, began to develop thanks to huge investment from petrol dollars.

A national league was quickly formed and the ever-popular FA Challenge Cup became strictly a club competition after previously accepting representative sides from outside the capital of Lagos. A combination of stability and investment began to reap rewards, most notably when Nigeria hosted and won the 1980 African Nations Cup, beating Algeria 3-0 in the final. More significant was the 1985 FIFA Under-16 World Cup victory which saw Nigeria beat West Germany 2-1, with goals from Sanni Adamu and Victor Igbinoba. It was the first world title won by an African nation. This was to provide the springboard that saw Nigeria's 'Super Eagles' qualify for three successive World Cups in 1994, 1998

and 2002, lift the African Nations Cup a second time in 1994, and win the Olympic football tournament in 1996. In addition, Rashidi Yekini (1993), Emmanuel Amunike (1994), Nwankwo Kanu (1996) and Victor Ikpeba (1997) have all been voted African Footballer Of The Year.

Nigerian players are in demand all over the world and these days a player from a Nigeria-based club is a rarity in the national squad. Players are often snapped up by European clubs at a young age and this experience of professionalism has helped the national team fulfil its potential.

NORTH KOREA

Federation: Football Association of the Democratic People's Republic of Korea
Founded: 1945
Joined FIFA: 1958
Confederation: AFC
FIFA world ranking: 117

Prior to the 1960s, North Korean football was strictly a domestic sport, with any contact at the international level limited to just the Communist countries. In 1966, however, North Korea entered the World Cup for the first time, qualifying for the finals after beating Australia in a play-off. The country astounded the world with their skill and sportsmanship, with Pak Doo Ik making history with a winning goal against the mighty Italy to take the Koreans into the quarter-finals against Portugal. Amazingly, Korea then stormed into

a 3-0 lead through Pak Seung Zin, Li Dong Woon and Yang Sung Kook but, equally astonishingly, ended up losing 5-3.

NORTHERN IRELAND

Federation: Irish Football Association
Founded: 1880
Joined FIFA: 1911
Confederation: UEFA
FIFA world ranking: 110 (joint)

The Irish FA is the fourth oldest football federation in the world and, until 1923, controlled football throughout Ireland. Their main opposition were England, Scotland and Wales in the annual Home International Championship, that ran from 1884 to 1984, although they were far from successful in the competition – winning it outright just three times (in 1914, 1980 and 1984).

Northern Ireland did not meet non-British opposition until 1951 – three years after they stopped picking players from southern Ireland. Successive World Cup qualification in 1982 and 1986 showcased the country's best team, featuring the likes of Martin O'Neill, Sammy McIlroy, Gerry Armstrong, Norman Whiteside and Pat Jennings. Northern Ireland's best World Cup performance, however, was in 1958 when a Danny Blanchflower-led team reached the quarter-finals in their first appearance.

George Best, the greatest Irish player, never got to play in a World Cup but won every other honour with his club Manchester United. There has been a league championship

Opposite: Nigeria's Jay Jay Okocha in action at the World Cup in France in 1998.

contested since 1891 but Northern Irish club football is semi-professional, with the best players often poached by the professional clubs of England and Scotland. There is also a sectarian element to Irish football with teams such as Linfield and Cliftonville regarded as Protestant and Catholic clubs respectively.

NORWAY

Federation: Norges Fotballforbund
Founded: 1902
Joined FIFA: 1908
Confederation: UEFA
FIFA world ranking: 23

It has taken Norway a long time to achieve the breakthrough on the international stage after years merely making up the numbers. After watching Scandinavian neighbours Denmark and Sweden make waves in world football, Norway finally broke through in the 1990s and qualification for three successive World Cups in 1994, 1998 and 2002 has given Norwegian football a great impetus. They even managed a 2-1 win over Brazil in the group stages of the 1998 World Cup in France, before losing to Italy in the second round.

The improvement has coincided with an increasing number of Norwegian players making their name abroad. This was largely because Norwegian players were proving cheaper to sign than other players across Europe in the Eighties and Nineties. Players such as Erik Thorstvedt, Stig Inge Bjornebye, Tore Andre Flo and Ole Gunnar Solksjaer have not only succeeded in the English Premiership, but have also won a host of honours.

Ironically, the domestic game in Norway has shifted from an open championship to being largely dominated by one club – Rosenborg. The Trondheim club won the Norwegian title on a record ten successive

Below: Ole Gunnar Solskjaer is one of many Norwegians to have starred in the major leagues of Europe.

occasions between 1993 and 2002 and have regularly featured in the Champions League.

Football has been played in Norway since the 1890s and the oldest club, Odds BK of Skein, was formed in 1894. A federation and cup competition were started in 1902, with the national team debuting in 1908 with an 11-3 defeat by Sweden. Norway did not win a game for ten years but they did win bronze at the 1936 Berlin Olympics, during which, in front of Hitler, they beat Germany 2-0.

OMAN

Federation: Oman Football Association
Founded: 1978
Joined FIFA: 1980
Confederation: AFC
FIFA world ranking: 113

PAKISTAN

Federation: Pakistan Football Federation
Founded: 1947
Joined FIFA: 1948
Confederation: AFC
FIFA world ranking: 160

PALESTINE

Federation: Palestine Football Federation
Founded: 1928
Joined FIFA: 1998
Confederation: AFC
FIFA world ranking: 148

PANAMA

Federation: Federación Nacional de Fútbol de Panamá
Founded: 1937
Joined FIFA: 1938
Confederation: CONCACAF
FIFA world ranking: 126
Honours: CONCACAF Championship 1951

PAPUA NEW GUINEA

Federation: Papua New Guinea Football Association
Founded: 1962
Joined FIFA: 1963
Confederation: OFC
FIFA world ranking: 169

PARAGUAY

Federation: Asociacion Paraguaya de Futbol
Founded: 1906
Joined FIFA: 1921
Confederation: CONMEBOL
FIFA world ranking: 20
Honours: Copa América 1953, 1979

Of the great footballing nations of South America, Paraguay remain one of the poorest and least glamorous. For a small country though, it can be proud of several of its international achievements. Twice winners of the South American Championships in 1953 and 1979, Paraguay have progressed past the group stages of the last two World Cups.

Having performed well in the South American qualifying group for the 1998 World Cup, they earned great respect on the continent after finishing a creditable second behind Argentina and ahead of Chile, Colombia, Uruguay and Peru. Their star player was undoubtedly goalkeeper Jose Luis Chilavert, the only Paraguayan player ever to be voted South American Footballer Of The Year. An immense presence marshalling the defence in front of him, Chilavert also took many of his side's free-kicks and penalties.

There was more to Paraguay than just the flamboyant Chilavert though, they were highly organised and qualified for the second phase after a 3-1 win against Nigeria. They put Spain out of the competition before finally succumbing to eventual champions France after a Laurent Blanc 'golden goal'.

Building on this success at the 2002 World Cup, Paraguay made it to the second phase before being knocked-out by Germany.

Olimpia are the most successful club side in Paraguay, having won the championship on 38 occasions since it began in 1906, including five titles in a row between 1956 and 1960, and six in a row between 1978 and 1983. They have also won the South American club Championship – the Copa Libertadores – on two occasions, in 1979 and 1990.

PERU

Federation: Federacion Peruana De Futbol
Founded: 1922
Joined FIFA: 1924
Confederation: CONMEBOL
FIFA world ranking: 80
Honours: Copa América 1939, 1975

Peru entered the international arena in the 1927 South American Championships – the Copa América – with a 4-0 defeat to Uruguay. It was to be a forgettable start for the Peruvians who went on to concede 26 goals in their first seven games. They did go on to win the tournament in 1939 though, and again in 1975.

On the world stage Peru have only really been a strong force in one era, qualifying for the World Cups of 1970, 1978 and 1982. Coached by former Brazilian star Didi, the team reached the quarter finals in 1970. The 1978 side included several memorable players,

POLAND

Federation: Polski Zwiazek Pilki Noznej
Founded: 1919
Joined FIFA: 1923
Confederation: UEFA
FIFA world ranking: 33 (joint)
Honours: Olympic 1972

Poland played its first international against Hungary in 1921 but had to wait 50 years for the game to come of age. In fact, Polish football effectively peaked in the 1970s, with a stylish brand of attacking play that produced a tournament victory at the 1972 Olympics and three excellent World Cup campaigns.

The Poles registered third place in West Germany in 1974 after famously eliminating England along the way to qualification. During this golden era, the team featured its finest talents ever, including Grzegorz Lato (who went on to win 95 caps and become an MP), Kazimierz Deyna, and the nation's top goalscorer, Wlodzimierz Lubanski.

The Poles were further strengthened by the addition of forward Zbigniew Boniek, who went on to play for Juventus and Roma and was later appointed national coach in August 2002. The side were unlucky not to progress further than the semi-finals in 1982, but by the mid-Eighties Polish football had slid into rapid decline, the game blighted by corruption, hooliganism and dwindling crowds.

such as the eccentric goalkeeper Ramon Quiroga, Hector Chumpitaz, and the real star of the side, Teofilo Cubillas. He inspired the team through to the second phase of the tournament, successfully negotiating a group which included Iran, a talented Scotland side, and eventual runners-up Holland. Cubillas

The national side subsequently failed to qualify for a single World Cup or European Championship in the Nineties and, after successfully qualifying for the 2002 World Cup, the team suffered total stage fright. Their results so enraged one fan that he attempted to sue Edyta Gorniak for singing the national anthem too slowly and making the team tired prior to the game against South Korea.

The Polish domestic game took off in the mining regions of Silesia in the early 20th Century. Three teams, Cracovia (famous for being Pope John Paul's side), Wisla Krakow and LKS Lodz formed in 1906, though the league has largely been dominated by the army side Legia Warsaw and Widzew Lodz. Both of those teams have reached the semi-finals of the European Cup but have never progressed further. Lodz, meanwhile, made just one solitary appearance in the 1996-97 Champions League stage of the competition.

Match-fixing and crowd trouble continue to plague the Polish game. Both Lodz and Legia had their stadiums closed in 1997, and in 1998 the government suspended the domestic league campaign in the face of a FIFA ban because of internal wrangling.

Further match-rigging scandals caused the league to be completely restructured for the 2001-02 season, but internal problems meant the format again had to be altered a year later. Hopes of a revival featuring the likes of Jerzy Dudek, who became the country's most expensive player when he moved to Liverpool from Feyenoord for £4.9million in 2001, and Emmanuel 'Oli' Olisadebe, a naturalised Nigerian striker, look misplaced.

was particularly impressive in his side's 3-1 defeat of the Scots, scoring a memorable goal.

The Peruvian capital Lima has always been the heart of the nation's club football. The Lima-based league was traditionally the strongest in the country until the national championship was set up in 1966. Club football today continues to be dominated by three teams, who are all from Lima: Alianza, Universitario and Sporting Crystal, though a Peruvian club side has still to achieve success beyond its national borders and pursue a successful Copa Libertadores campaign.

PHILIPPINES

Federation: Philippine Football Federation
Founded: 1907
Joined FIFA: 1928
Confederation: AFC
FIFA world ranking: 187

Left: One of Peru's leading goalscorers, Jorge Hirano, in action at the Copa América in 1989.

Below: Zbigniew Boniek on the ball for Poland in 1978. In 2002 he would become the manager.

PORTUGAL

Federation: Federação Portuguesa de Futebol
Founded: 1914
Joined FIFA: 1923
Confederation: UEFA
FIFA world ranking: 15

It is a close call as to which of the Iberian nations is the greatest underachiever. On reflection, given their ability to fall consistently short of expectation at both club and international level, Portugal must accept that unwanted accolade ahead of Spain.

In fact, for a nation with such a passionate footballing culture, a record of just three World Cup finals appearances is abysmal. A belated start in 1966 saw a side featuring Eusébio, 'the Black Pearl', unfortunate to be eliminated by hosts England. They finished third in the tournament but, rather than push on, it took Portugal 20 years to make another appearance, only to fail at the first round stage. A dispute between the federation and players at that tournament soured the late Eighties and resulted in Portugal attempting to qualify for the 1988 European Championship with their youth side.

At the same time, however, back-to-back World Youth Championship wins in 1989 and 1991 ushered in a group of young players including Luis Figo, Rui Costa and Paulo Sousa, who were rapidly hailed as 'the Golden Generation'. Figo would later become World Player Of The Year and the most expensive signing in the game's history.

Once again, though, performance failed to outstrip expectation, but at the European Championship in 2000 the team did progress to the semi-finals. However, a handball decision in sudden-death extra-time went against them and prompted acrimonious scenes. When the team finally qualified for another World Cup, in 2002, inconsistency saw elimination by hosts South Korea and further displays of bad sportsmanship.

The 2004 European Championship offers the Golden Generation one last chance at redemption, and recognising the opportunity, the FPF appointed Brazilian World Cup winner Luiz Felipe Scolari to the position of national team coach in 2002.

At club level, the Portuguese league is a tale of two cities: Lisbon and the northern port of Oporto. No club outside of these two centres has ever won the league. In the capital, it is Benfica who figure largest in the game's history. Founded in 1904, The Eagles have won the championship on more than 30 occasions. The club also won two European Champions Cups in succession in 1961 and 1962, inspired in the second final by Eusébio, the country's

greatest player and whose statue stands outside the club's Stadium Of Light.

While Sporting Lisbon won their first championship for 20 years in 2000, it was a minor blip since FC Porto have dominated domestically for the past decade, inspired by their European Cup winning success of 1987. Porto also won the final of the UEFA Cup in 2003 and, to underline the city's new found status, even smaller rivals Boavista managed a first ever championship win in 2001.

On a more downbeat note, Portuguese football is stalked by corruption. A match-fixing scandal broke in 1996 and then, in 2001, Benfica chairman Joao Vale e Azevedo was sentenced to five years for diverting club funds. A year later, the Vitoria Guimaraes chairman was also arrested for misuse of club finances.

PUERTO RICO

Federation: Federación Puertorriqueña de Fútbol
Founded: 1940
Joined FIFA: 1960
Confederation: CONCACAF
FIFA world ranking: 200

QATAR

Federation: Qatar Football Association
Founded: 1960
Joined FIFA: 1970
Confederation: AFC
FIFA world ranking: 74

REPUBLIC OF IRELAND

Federation: Football Association Of Ireland
Founded: 1921
Joined FIFA: 1923
Confederation: UEFA
FIFA world ranking: 14

The Football Association Of Ireland was founded in 1921, following the division of the country into two separate entities. The Republic played its first proper internationals at the 1924 Olympics in Paris, and in 1949 became the first foreign country to defeat England on home soil – a 2-0 win at Goodison

Above: Goalkeeper Pat Bonner celebrates the penalty shoot-out victory over Romania that took the Republic Of Ireland to the quarter-finals of Italia 90.

Opposite: One of the greatest players in the history of the game, Portugal's Eusébio takes on the Hungarian goalkeeper during the 1996 World Cup finals.

Park. Although Ireland had entered all but the inaugural World Cup competition, they had never qualified for the finals, despite going close on at least a couple of occasions. Their record in the European Championship was similarly anaemic, although they had made it to the quarter-finals in 1964.

Ireland's fortunes changed for the better with the appointment, in February 1986, of Jack Charlton as coach. Charlton had been a member of England's World Cup winning side, had enjoyed a long and distinguished career as a player at Leeds United, and had managed several English league clubs with varying degrees of success. Charlton scoured the English divisions looking for players who hadn't been picked for England, Scotland or Wales with a family link strong enough to qualify them to play for the Republic (at least one grandparent of Irish extraction). Soon he'd recruited the likes of John Aldridge, Kevin Sheedy and Ray Houghton, and had steered Ireland to the finals of 1988's European Championship in West Germany. Although they failed to reach the semi-final stage, Ireland did beat England 1-0, thanks to a goal after five minutes from Houghton and some inspired goalkeeping from Celtic's 'Packie' Bonner.

Ireland qualified for their first ever World Cup finals two years later and, having beaten Romania in a heart-stopping penalty shoot-out in the second round, made it to the quarter-finals. There it took a winner from the tournament's top scorer, Italy's Toto Schillaci,

to halt their ambitions. Despite remaining unbeaten during the qualifiers, Ireland didn't make it to the European Championship in 1992, but got their 1994 World Cup campaign off to an incredible start by beating eventual finalists Italy 1-0. Charlton's team were beaten 2-0 in the second round by Holland.

Charlton stepped down as manager in 1996 (the Republic had failed to qualify for that year's European Championship in England), to be replaced by former Ireland international Mick McCarthy. Having negotiated a difficult qualification group that included both Portugal and Holland, Ireland overcame Iran following a two-legged play-off, to book their place at the 2002 World Cup. Unfortunately, their tournament was completely overshadowed by the ill-tempered spat that erupted between McCarthy and his captain, Roy Keane, who then walked out on the team.

Following a heated row about the poor quality of the Irish team's preparation for the tournament, Keane returned home and subsequently announced his retirement from international football. Ireland went on to reach the tournament's second round, before being eliminated in a penalty shoot-out by Spain.

Following a disappointing start to Ireland's Euro 2004 qualification campaign, McCarthy quit his post and was replaced by Brian Kerr, who'd spent six years as coach of Ireland's highly successful youth teams. A surprise choice, but early results suggest he has a promising international career ahead.

Below: Making his final internaional appearance at Euro 2000, Romania's biggest star, Gheorghe Hagi.

ROMANIA

Federation: Federatia Romania de Fotbal
Founded: 1909
Joined FIFA: 1923
Confederation: UEFA
FIFA world ranking: 21

Romania played at the first three World Cups from 1930 onwards but subsequently missed out on qualifying for the world's premier competition until 1970. In the last three decades, however, Romanian football has become a potent force, notably through Steaua Bucharest, their leading club, and Gheorghe Hagi, their most outstanding player.

Steaua, the army team, were founded in 1948 as CCA Bucharest, and earned the right to be placed among the European greats in the 1980s when they produced a series of superb line-ups. They took the biggest prize of all in 1986 when they lifted the European Cup by beating Barcelona on penalties. The game, however, is widely regarded as a dour, goalless affair – not that Steaua cared.

RUSSIA

Federation: Russian Football Union
Founded: 1912
Joined FIFA: 1912
Confederation: UEFA
FIFA world ranking: 30
Honours: European Championship 1960; Olympics 1956, 1988

The Soviet Union, before its break-up, produced some of the finest football teams that Europe has ever seen. Often written off as too rigid in its tactical approach to the game, the USSR's real legacy is revealed by a glance at the history books. Soviet sides in their heyday played thrilling, effective football that was successful at the highest level. The USSR won the Olympic gold medal in 1956 and 1988, the inaugural European Championship in 1960, and produced teams in other decades ranked among the finest in the world. The 1980s generation under Valery Lobanovsky was the most exciting national side in recent memory.

Russia had great players too, such as Lev Yashin, considered by many to be the finest goalkeeper of all time. Oleg Blokhin was also an outstanding left-winger, while Igor Belanov deservedly won the European Footballer Of The Year award in 1986.

Steaua went on to reach the final again in 1989, with Hagi added to the team, but lost heavily (4-0) to an AC Milan team that cruised to victory following their opponents' poor show. A host of Romanian players moved abroad in the 1990s after the fall of dictator Nicolae Ceausescu, including Gheorghe Popescu, an elegant defender who starred for Barcelona among others, and striker Florin Raducioiu, who played in all five major European leagues. But the star was Hagi, a wonderfully gifted midfielder with a wicked left foot. He, more than anybody, was the driving force behind Romania's development.

The player never enjoyed a particularly glittering club career but stood out in national team colours. He played at the World Cup in 1990, and was one of the outstanding individuals in the United States four years later when Romania were unlucky not to progress further than the last eight, despite beating Argentina 3-2 in the second round.

Romanian club football has suffered from a continual exodus of its best players to Europe's bigger leagues, not to mention the whiff of corruption that surrounded its football in the 1980s, therefore the national team will always provide its best chances of success in the years to come.

Left: The Soviet Union's Oleg Blokhin takes on Belgium at the Nou Camp during the 1982 World Cup finals.

In the domestic league, Moscow dominated the game in the first half of the century and it was not until 1961 that a team from outside the capital won the title (Dynamo Kiev). But fittingly, Dynamo Moscow became the first Soviet side to reach a European final, losing 3-2 to Glasgow Rangers in the European Cup Winners' Cup in 1972.

The Soviet Union had really established a formidable reputation by that stage. Their 1960 European Championship triumph did not go unnoticed, even though the competition was low-key at the time. In the final, they beat Yugoslavia 2-1 after extra-time in Paris.

The USSR also reached the World Cup quarter-finals in 1962 and the semi-finals in England four years later. Yashin was the star of that side and was the first Soviet player to attract worldwide recognition.

In 1975 Blokhin, at his peak, inspired Dynamo Kiev to beat Ferencváros 3-0 in the European Cup Winners' Cup final to earn Soviet club football its first major trophy. He also collected the European Footballer Of The Year award, becoming the second winner after Yashin in 1963. He was an exciting talent who would have been a success abroad if allowed to leave his homeland.

Dinamo Tblisi also won the Cup Winners' Cup in 1981 and it was this generation that caught the eye in brilliant fashion at club and international level. Belanov starred for Dynamo Kiev and the USSR in 1986, helping his club win the Cup Winners' Cup with an emphatic 3-0 victory over Atletico Madrid and inspiring the Soviets to impressive displays at the World Cup finals – scoring a hat-trick in the 4-3 second round defeat to Belgium. Alexander Zavarov was his able midfield deputy who later played for Juventus, and Rinat Dassayev a worthy successor to Yashin in goal.

Lobanovsky, the godfather of Soviet football, was coach of their greatest triumphs in the Seventies and Eighties and continued to oversee the development of the most talented players and the structure of the national team until his death in 2002. However, since the break-up of the Soviet Union, Russia has struggled to make any kind of impact on the world stage, with Ukraine now seen as a bigger footballing power. Yet exports such as Victor Onopko and Valery Karpin have excelled in Spain, while Vladimir Beschastnykh boasts an impressive scoring record for the national side.

RWANDA

Federation: Fédération Rwandaise de Football Amateur
Founded: 1972
Joined FIFA: 1976
Confederation: CAF
FIFA world ranking: 119 (joint)

ST KITTS & NEVIS

Federation: St Kitts and Nevis Football Association
Founded: 1932
Joined FIFA: 1992
Confederation: CONCACAF
FIFA world ranking: 119 (joint)

ST LUCIA

Federation: St Lucia Football Association
Founded: 1979
Joined FIFA: 1988
Confederation: CONCACAF
FIFA world ranking: 110 (joint)

ST VINCENT AND THE GRENADINES

Federation: Saint Vincent and The Grenadines Football Federation
Founded: 1978
Joined FIFA: 1988
Confederation: CONCACAF
FIFA world ranking: 153 (joint)

SAN MARINO

Federation: Federazione Sammarinese Giouco Calcio
Founded: 1931
Joined FIFA: 1988
Confederation: UEFA
FIFA world ranking: 161

Davide Gualteri holds the record for the quickest goal in international football, scoring for San Marino after just 8.3 seconds against England in a World Cup qualifying defeat in November 1993. The Most Serene Republic of San Marino, located within Northern Italy, has run a national amateur league and cup competition since 1986, featuring teams such as Tre Fiori and Domagnano, yet it is Gualteri's goal against Graham Taylor's side which remains the nation's highlight to date.

SAO TOMÉ AND PRINCIPE

Federation: Federação Santomense de Futebol
Founded: 1975
Joined FIFA: 1986
Confederation: CAF
FIFA world ranking: 194 (joint)

Opposite: Kenny Dalglish in full flight as Scotland earn a draw from their clash with Brazil during the 1974 World Cup Finals in West Germany.

SAUDI ARABIA

Federation: Saudi Arabia Football Federation
Founded: 1959
Joined FIFA: 1959
Confederation: AFC
FIFA world ranking: 46
Honours: Asian Cup 1984, 1988, 1996

Saudi Arabia is the greatest exporter of oil in the world and it is from this influx of wealth that football got the kick-start it needed in the 1970s. Millions of dollars were invested in state-of-the-art facilities and clubs such as Al Hilal, Al Nasr and Al Ahli began to thrive.

Foreign coaches were lured to the country by the large salaries and in 1979 the Saudi Arabian league championship kicked-off. This investment and patience began to pay off as the Saudis won the Asian Cup in 1984 and 1988 – they beat China 2-0 in Singapore with goals from Shaye Nafisah and Majed Abdullah and retained the trophy four years later by beating South Korea 4-3 on penalties after a goalless draw in Qatar.

Below: El Hadji Diouf in action at the 2002 World Cup. Senegal were one of the big surprises of the tournament.

One year on and the World Under-17 Cup was won in Scotland. This Saudi Arabian side formed the basis of the country's future success, as three successive World Cup appearances followed. Their first appearance, in 1994, saw Saudi Arabia play Morocco in the first-ever all-Arab World Cup clash, while Saeed Owairan scored the goal of the tournament against Belgium. After the 2002 World Cup Finals, Asia's best goalkeeper Mohammed Al-Deayea retired after making a record 165th international appearance.

SCOTLAND

Federation: Scottish Football Association
Founded: 1873
Joined FIFA: 1910
Confederation: UEFA
FIFA world ranking: 59 (joint)

Scotland were involved in the first ever international football match. It was at home against England on November 30, 1872, and it began one of the world's great sporting rivalries. That first game ended in a goalless draw but, unlike England, the Scots never went on to taste glory at the highest level of international competition.

Despite being consistent qualifiers for the World Cup finals, Scotland have often under-performed against teams they really should have comfortably beaten, while performing heroically against far mightier opposition.

The Scots qualified for their first ever World Cup in 1950 but chose not to attend because they said they would only go as winners of the British Home Internationals tournament. Despite being eligible as runners-up to England, they chose not to go to Brazil.

Perhaps the Scotland team that should have had most impact on the greatest footballing stage was the one that went to the World Cup in Argentina under Ally MacLeod in 1978. A decent outside bet, this Scotland side were packed with talented players, many based in the English top flight, such as Dalglish, Souness, Gemmill, Jordan, Masson and Rioch.

Ally MacCleod recklessly promised the nation that Scotland would bring the World Cup home, a bold claim he would live to regret. Scotland disappointed, both on and off the field, losing to Peru and only scraping a draw with lowly Iran before, in typically Scottish fashion, beating well-fancied Holland and almost, but not quite, qualifying for stage two. The Dutch were the eventual tournament runners-up. Meanwhile, winger Willie Johnston was sent home in disgrace after failing a dope test.

Perhaps the most celebrated Scottish international win though, came not in a major

tournament but in 1967 against the 'Auld Enemy', England. The world champions, undefeated since lifting the trophy the previous year at Wembley, were beaten 3-2 by the skill, spirit and guile of Scottish legends Baxter, Bremner and Law.

Recent times have seen the rapid demise of Scottish football at international level, with too many foreign players preventing young local talent from getting top-flight club football often being cited as the main reason for the decline.

At club level, Scottish football has historically been dominated by the 'Old Firm' of Celtic and Rangers, possibly the fiercest rivalry in club football anywhere in the world. Celtic can claim 38 league titles and 31 Scottish Cups to Rangers' 50 titles and 31 Scottish Cups. Other clubs have had brief stays at the top, notably Edinburgh sides Hibernian and Hearts in the Fifties and Sixties, and for quite a while in the early Eighties it seemed that the 'new firm' of Aberdeen and Dundee United had broken the stranglehold, the former being quite dominant for a spell, winning three league titles, four Scottish Cups and a European Cup Winners' Cup in a six year period. Normal service was resumed by the middle of the decade though, and once again today it's Celtic or Rangers carving up the trophies between them.

In Europe both sides have struggled to really have an impact on the major competitions. Rangers' only European triumph came in the 1972 Cup Winners' Cup, but Celtic made history in 1967 when they became the first Scottish side to lift the European Cup, beating Inter Milan in the final, and they also reached the final of the UEFA Cup in 2003.

SENEGAL

Federation: Fédération Sénégalaise de Football
Founded: 1960
Joined FIFA: 1962
Confederation: CAF
FIFA world ranking: 28

Senegal, under French coach Bruno Metsu, caused a sensation with their first appearance at the World Cup finals in 2002 by reaching the quarter-finals, making a star of striker El Hadji Diouf along the way. They also beat defending world champions France 1-0, drew 1-1 with Denmark, led Uruguay 3-0 before being held to a draw, and then beat Sweden 2-1. The success owed much to Metsu's predecessor Peter Schnittiger – the German had been involved with Senegalese soccer since 1968, but in 1995 he had been appointed to structure a development programme for both the national team and the club game.

Above: Zvonimir Vukic on the ball for Serbia and Montenegro, the state formerly known as Yugoslavia.

SERBIA & MONTENEGRO

Federation: Football Association of Serbia and Montenegro
Founded: 1919
Joined FIFA: 1919
Confederation: UEFA
FIFA world ranking: 27
Honours: Olympics 1960 [*as Yugoslavia]

As from 2003, Yugoslavia were renamed Serbia and Montenegro – the last step of a disintegration that saw the former Yugoslavia break-up in 1991 after a bloody civil war. In football terms at least, the split was heartbreaking because Yugoslavia had one of the most exciting teams in Europe. They were serious contenders to win the European Championship in 1992, but by the time the finals were due to kick-off most of the non-Serbian players had refused to take part and UEFA took the decision to expel them from the competition. Their replacements Denmark went on to win the tournament.

Yugoslavia did not exist until after World War I, but several clubs in Serbia did. A Yugoslav championship began in 1923 but it was not until after the Second World War,

Right: Zlatko Zahovic celebrates during Slovenia's draw with Yugoslavia at Euro 2000.

under the rule of the Communist Tito, that the league began to take real shape. It was the Serbian clubs that dominated, such as Red Star Belgrade and Partizan Belgrade. In 1991, Red Star became the first and only Yugoslav side to win the European Cup when they beat Marseille 5-3 on penalties after a goalless draw.

Yugoslavia were one of only four European sides to play in the 1930 World Cup. They contested the football final at the Olympic Games on four successive occasions but were successful on only once, in 1960, when they beat Denmark 3-1.

In the World Cup, Yugoslavia boast two semi-final appearances (1930 and 1962) and have made it to the quarter-finals on three occasions (1954, 1958 and 1990). In 1968 they also reached the final of the European Championship, but lost to hosts Italy after a replay.

Yugoslavia have always produced some excellent individual footballers – Bobek, Dzajic, Prosinecki, Savicevic, Sekularec – but have never quiet combined for the final step to glory. Since 1992, Yugoslav football has been a shadow of its former self – despite now playing under another name, little has changed.

SEYCHELLES

Federation: Seychelles Football Federation
Founded: 1979
Joined FIFA: 1986
Confederation: CAF
FIFA world ranking: 178

SIERRA LEONE

Federation: Sierra Leone Football Association
Founded: 1967
Joined FIFA: 1967
Confederation: CAF
FIFA world ranking: 135

SINGAPORE

Federation: Football Association of Singapore
Founded: 1892
Joined FIFA: 1952
Confederation: AFC
FIFA world ranking: 95 (joint)

SLOVAKIA

Federation: Slovak Football Association
Founded: 1993
Joined FIFA: 1994
Confederation: UEFA
FIFA world ranking: 55 (joint)

Between 1939 and 1944 there was a Slovak league which was won four times by SK Slovan Bratislava. Slovan Bratislava and Spartak Trnava were also Slovakia's strongest clubs in the Czechoslovakian league until 1992. The resurrected, but much weaker, Slovak league has seen Kosice emerge as a leading club.

SLOVENIA

Federation: Football Association of Slovenia
Founded: 1920
Joined FIFA: 1992
Confederation: UEFA
FIFA world ranking: 29

Slovenian clubs made absolutely no impact on the former Yugoslav league championship. Since independence, the leading club side has been Maribor Branik, who qualified for the Champions League in 2000, the same year that the national team played in the finals of the European Championship, earning draws with Yugoslavia and Norway.

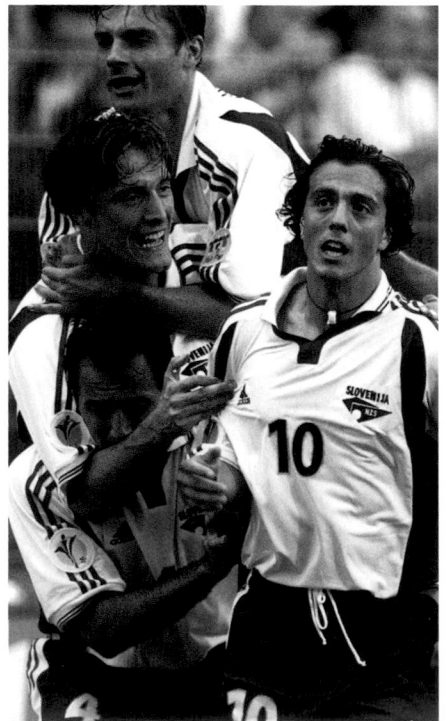

SOLOMON ISLANDS

Federation: Solomon Islands Football
Federation
Founded: 1979
Joined FIFA: 1988
Confederation: OFC
FIFA world ranking: 150

SOMALIA

Federation: Somalia Football Federation
Founded: 1951
Joined FIFA: 1960
Confederation: CAF
FIFA world ranking: 191

SOUTH AFRICA

Federation: South African Football Association
Founded: 1892, 1991
Joined FIFA: 1952-76, 1992
Confederation: CAF
FIFA world ranking: 33
Honours: African Nations Cup 1996

Football has been played in South Africa since the 1870s but the progress of the game was hindered for many years by the existence of apartheid. The all-white National Professional League initially kicked-off in 1959, while a rival, but highly successful and non-white National

Professional Soccer League was formed in 1972. The two leagues merged in 1978, but South Africa's apartheid policy had seen its FIFA membership suspended in 1952 and cancelled in 1976. In 1991, South Africa returned to international competition and they have subsequently won the African Nations Cup in 1996 and qualified for the 1998 and 2002 World Cup finals.

SOUTH KOREA

Federation: Korea Football Association
Founded: 1928
Joined FIFA: 1948
Confederation: AFC
FIFA world ranking: 24
Honours: Asian Cup 1956, 1960

South Korea gave Asian football a huge boost by reaching the semi-finals of the 2002 World Cup, a competition that they co-hosted with Japan. This was an amazing feat for a country who had failed to win a single match in their five previous World Cup tournaments.

Backed by stunning home support, and coached by Dutchman Guus Hiddink, the

Koreans overcame their inferiority complex and all of the pre-tournament predictions – they beat Poland 2-0, drew 1-1 with USA and defeated Portugal 1-0. The last group game was estimated to have been watched on television by 75 per cent of Korean households.

A sensational 2-1 second round win over Italy followed, while a tense 5-3 penalty shoot-out overcame Spain. It was Germany who put paid to the dream with a single goal victory.

South Korea have long been a consistent force in Asian football, although not always as winners. They produce many talented young players and have won the Asian Under-20 title on ten occasions. The creation of a professional league in 1983 (that later became the K-League) lifted Korean football and accounted for a development of the game that resulted in qualification for five successive World Cups from 1986 onwards.

Investment from big business has helped clubs and it is evident in club names such as Suwon Bluewings, Pusan Icons, Ulsan Hyundai and Pohang Steelers. This financial backing, however, does not necessarily translate into high wages for Korean players and several star names have moved abroad, with Japan a popular destination. South Korea's greatest player was Hong Myung-bo, who played in four successive World Cups and won a host of domestic honours.

Above. Ki Hyeon savours the moment as South Korea dump Italy out of the 2002 World Cup.

Left: Lucas Radebe congratulates his team-mates as South Africa pull themselves back from 2-0 down against Paraguay during the 2002 World Cup finals.

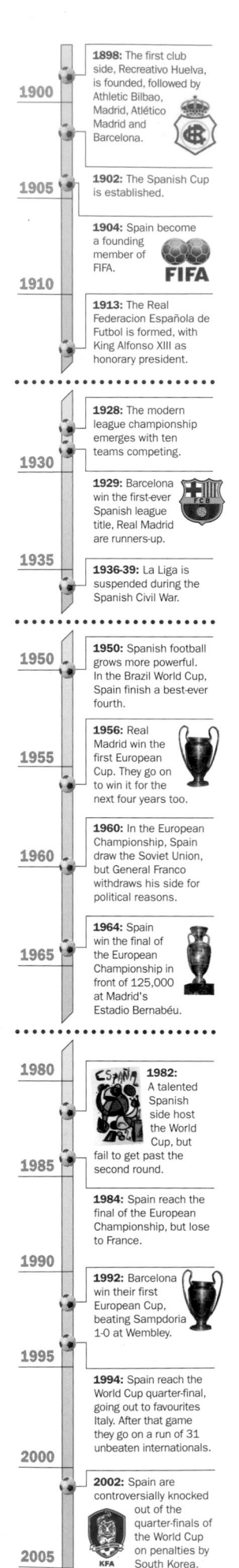

SPAIN

Federation: Real Federación Española De Fútbol

Founded: 1913

Joined FIFA: 1904

Confederation: UEFA

FIFA world ranking: 3

Honours: European Championship 1964; Olympics 1962

Football came to Spain in the latter part of the 19th Century, a result of British businessmen operating throughout the country's northern ports. A relative latecomer to a game that had already grown throughout Europe, Bilbao – the industrial port closest to England – became the first city associated with the game, and the city's flagship side, Athletic Bilbao, display their English roots to this day in the club's colours.

The game spread quickly among students in the port towns and, as had been seen in England, throughout the industrial cities. Irun, Gijon, Seville, La Coruna and Valencia all boasted teams, but Recreativo Huelva hold the honour of being the first club formed, in 1898.

The more revered football names of Real Madrid, Atlético Madrid and Barcelona soon followed, but with the exception of Real (then known simply as Madrid FC), the game never reached the highest level in the interior of the country. It was as late as 1913, under the honorary presidency of King Alfonso XII, that a number of regional unions consolidated to form the nationwide Real Federación Española de Fútbol.

Yet thanks to the representatives of Madrid FC, the dominant club side in the country, Spain had already become a founding member of FIFA, while the Spanish Cup, formed some 11 years earlier, was thriving and is now regarded as one of the oldest, if not most prestigious, cup competitions in Europe.

Indeed, it was predicted that the cup would have greater longevity than its league counterpart following a very inauspicious start. From its inception, the championship was a professional establishment but it took some time for it to become a truly countrywide competition, and it did not emerge in its modern form until the 1928-29 season, when just ten clubs competed for the main prize.

Madrid FC were given the name 'Real' as a gift by King Alfonso prior to the league's inception, and they continued their dominance, signing goalkeeper Zamora for £2,000 which, at the time, was a price tag more commonplace in the financially buoyant English league.

The Spanish Civil War between 1936 and 1939 saw its political overtones spread into the football arena and highlighted the bitter rivalry

Above: Real Madrid striker Rául is the golden boy of Spanish football. Opposite clockwise from top left: Midfielder Luis Enrique shows his poise at the 1994 World Cup Finals; one of Spain's greatest strikers, Emilio Butragueño; inspirational captain Fernando Hierro; and Michel, a star of the late Eighties.

that had grown between Barcelona and Real Madrid. As the flagship side of Catalonia, a region seeking independence from Spain, Barça associated their rivals with fascist dictator Franco and once the league campaign resumed, matches between the two sides proved to be bruising affairs. To further fuel the antipathy, teams from the Basque provinces also had their own agenda, and to this day Athletic Bilbao will only employ players who were born in the region.

The distain between clubs only served to establish 'La Liga Española' as one of the most competitive in Europe, and by the 1950s, Barça and Real were leading the way with seven titles in the decade between them, while both regularly boasting crowds approaching the 100,000 mark. Their dominance was unrivalled and the next logical step for both sides was to test themselves against the continent's finest clubs.

Following the inception of the European Champions Cup in 1956, Real Madrid won five finals in succession, the first being an exciting 4-3 victory against French side Stade de Reims. Leading the line for Real was Alfredo Di Stéfano, who scored the team's opening goal and who proceeded to score in each of the next four finals. His feats are now legendary, likewise the Real team who took their fifth Champions Cup success with an emphatic 7-3 victory against Eintracht Frankfurt. Di Stéfano netted a hat-trick while Hungarian wing wonder, Ferenc Puskás, scored four.

It took Barcelona some 36 years to win their solitary Champions Cup, when a Ronald Koeman free-kick defeated Italian side Sampdoria 1-0 at Wembley. Indeed, they have lived in the shadow of their fierce rivals for longer than their fans care to remember, despite winning 16 Spanish championships and ten European trophies by 2003. Although lagging behind Real both on the continent and in terms of domestic title wins, they do have the edge in Spanish Cups (24 to 17). Their wonderful Nou Camp stadium has also been the home to such legendary players as Johan Cruyff, Diego Maradona, Hristo Stoichkov, Romario and Ronaldo down the years.

Today, the Spanish League is widely regarded as the best in Europe, not only reflected by the exciting football displayed but also in terms of the contributions made to the Champions Cup by its teams. Real Madrid won three of the five finals between 1998 and 2002, while the emerging and widely underrated force of Valencia finished runners-up in both the 2000 and 2001 finals.

Yet despite a flourishing domestic league, a bugbear of all Spanish football fans is their underachieving national team. Some point to the intense regionalism as the root cause of Spain's underachievement but, whatever the reason, their 2-1 1964 European Championship victory against the Soviet Union, in front of 125,000 fans in Madrid's Bernabéu Stadium, remains their most significant success on the international stage.

SRI LANKA

Federation: The Football Federation of Sri Lanka
Founded: 1939
Joined FIFA: 1950
Confederation: AFC
FIFA world ranking: 139 (joint)

SUDAN

Federation: Sudan Football Association
Founded: 1936
Joined FIFA: 1948
Confederation: CAF
FIFA world ranking: 107

SURINAM

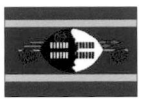  

Federation: Surinaamse Voetbal Bond
Founded: 1920
Joined FIFA: 1929
Confederation: CONCACAF
FIFA world ranking: 147

SWAZILAND

Federation: National Football Association of Swaziland
Founded: 1968
Joined FIFA: 1976
Confederation: CAF
FIFA world ranking: 114

SWEDEN

Federation: Svenska Fotbollförbundet
Founded: 1904
Joined FIFA: 1904
Confederation: UEFA
FIFA world ranking: 18 (joint)
Honours: Olympics 1948

There's no doubt that in football terms, Sweden – with a population in 2003 of around nine million and a domestic game that isn't even fully professional – have always punched above their weight on the international stage. The Swedish FA was founded in 1904 and its national team qualified for their first World Cup tournament in 1934. The Scandinavians shocked the mighty Argentina 3-2 during a run that took them all the way to the quarter-finals, where they were edged out 2-1 by Germany. They went one better in 1938, reaching the semi-finals (where they were defeated 5-1 by Hungary) before going down 4-2 to Brazil in the third-place play-off.

In 1948, an Englishman, George Raynor, was appointed national team coach, and he led them to a gold medal at the 1948 Olympic Games in London. However, Sweden's success at the Olympics had its downside as AC Milan, hugely impressed by the form of several of the country's top players, wasted no time in signing them up to professional contracts in Italy's lucrative Serie A.

With strict rules barring players from the national team if they made their living abroad, Raynor had access to only two of his Olympic gold medal-winning side for the 1950 World Cup Finals in Brazil. Despite such limitations, the remodelled Swedish team pulled off a major surprise in the tournament's first round by beating Italy's professional stars 3-2. Despite a crushing 7-1 defeat by Brazil, they went on to pip Spain to third place.

A bronze medal at the 1952 Olympics in Helsinki was achieved despite major injury problems, and in time for the 1958 World Cup finals, held on home turf, the Swedish FA finally rescinded its rule that only home-based players could appear for the national side.

As a result, Sweden fielded what many claim was its best ever team, with previously barred veterans such as Gunnar Gren and Nils Liedholm returning to international action. Buoyed by home advantage, Sweden made it all the way to the final, defeating the likes of West Germany and Hungary, before being cut down to size 5-2 by Brazil.

Since then Sweden's World Cup adventures have been less successful although, under highly-regarded coach Tommy Svensson, they did shock many observers by finishing third

Below: Until Lothar Matthäus broke his record, Sweden's Thomas Ravelli was Europe's most capped player, having made 143 appearances for his country.

Left: Stephane Chapuisat
was among the goalscorers as
Switzerland beat Romania 4-1
at the 1994 World Cup Finals.

TAHITI

Federation: Fédération Tahitienne de Football
Founded: 1989
Joined FIFA: 1990
Confederation: OFC
FIFA world ranking: 122 (joint)

TAIWAN

Federation: Chinese Taipei Football Association
Founded: 1936
Joined FIFA: 1954
Confederation: AFC
FIFA world ranking: 156

TAJIKISTAN

Federation: Tajikistan National Football
Federation
Founded: 1936
Joined FIFA: 1994
Confederation: AFC
FIFA world ranking: 175 (joint)

TANZANIA

Federation: Football Association of Tanzania
Founded: 1930
Joined FIFA: 1964
Confederation: CAF
FIFA world ranking: 158

THAILAND

Federation: Football Association of Thailand
Founded: 1916
Joined FIFA: 1925
Confederation: AFC
FIFA world ranking: 65 (joint)

in 1994, losing out to eventual winners Brazil in the semi-finals by a single goal.

Sweden haven't fared nearly as well in the European Championship, qualifying only twice in the competition's 45-year history, and on one of those occasions – 1992, when they progressed all the way the semi-finals – they did so as the tournament hosts.

SWITZERLAND

Federation: Schweizerischer Fussballverband
Founded: 1895
Joined FIFA: 1904
Confederation: UEFA
FIFA world ranking: 40

Switzerland is the home to both the European and world governing bodies of football, UEFA and FIFA, and was instrumental in each organisation's formation. They had plenty of experience, having been introduced to football by the English in the 1860s. British influence was enormous and is reflected in the club names, such as Grasshoppers, the country's most successful side, and Young Boys. The first club to be formed was St Gallen in 1879.

A Swiss championship was contested as early as 1898, although a national league did not kick-off until 1934. Switzerland played internationals from 1903, and in the first half of the century they had a strong team, winning an Olympic silver medal in 1924 and reaching the World Cup quarter-finals in 1934 and 1938.

Karl Rappan, Switzerland's Austrian coach, revolutionised tactics when he devised the 'Swiss Bolt' in the 1930s, a forerunner of the sweeper system. Switzerland's star began to fade after the war and the club game never elevated itself. The national side was not helped by the rivalry between the French, German and Italian communities of the country, who down the years have accused various coaches of bias towards one another.

SYRIA

Federation: Association Arabe Syrienne de
Football
Founded: 1936
Joined FIFA: 1937
Confederation: AFC
FIFA world ranking: 93

Right: Hakan Sükür, pictured at the 2002 World Cup, is the greatest player in Turkish history.

TOGO

Federation: Fédération Togolaise de Football
Founded: 1960
Joined FIFA: 1962
Confederation: CAF
FIFA world ranking: 86 (joint)

TONGA

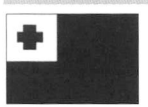 

Federation: Tonga Football Association
Founded: 1965
Joined FIFA: 1994
Confederation: OFC
FIFA world ranking: 183

TRINIDAD AND TOBAGO

Federation: Trinidad and Tobago Football Federation
Founded: 1908
Joined FIFA: 1963
Confederation: CONCACAF
FIFA world ranking: 54

TUNISIA

Federation: Fédération Tunisienne de Football
Founded: 1956
Joined FIFA: 1960
Confederation: CAF
FIFA world ranking: 42 (joint)

Tunisia was the first African team to win a match at the finals of the World Cup when they beat Mexico 3-1 in 1978, but it was in the mid-Nineties that Tunisian soccer really began to take off with successive World Cup qualifications. Club Africain became the first Tunisian club to win the African Champions Cup in 1991, and in 1998 Tunisian clubs achieved success in various competitions – Etoile Sahel winning the African Cup Winners' Cup, Esperence succeeding in the CAF Cup, and the successful Club Africain lifting the Arab Champions Cup.

TURKEY

Federation: Turkiye Futbol Federasyonu
Founded: 1923
Joined FIFA: 1923
Confederation: UEFA
FIFA world ranking: 7

Football had a hard time in establishing itself in Turkey. The rulers of the Ottoman Empire disliked the game that had been introduced by the British. Furthermore, football was not seen as a priority at a time when there were the Balkan Wars, World War I, Civil War and war with Greece. However, once Turkey was declared a republic in 1923, a football federation was formed, regional competition got under way, and the national team made its first forays into the international arena.

A professional league was launched in 1959 and the national team began to get some serious attention, however it was not until the 1990s that Turkey began to make an impact. The nation qualified for their first European Championship in 1996 and also, for the first time in 48 years, the World Cup in 2002. In 2000, Galatasaray, Turkey's leading club alongside Besiktas and Fenerbahce, won the UEFA Cup, beating Arsenal on spot kicks.

The Turkish league has been boosted by importing players and coaches from around the world, while the fans are among the most passionate in the game, creating one of the noisiest and most intimidating atmospheres in international football. Leading Turkish players such as Hakan Sükür, Alpay Özalan, Emre Belozoglu and Tayfun Korkut have also proved sought-after among Europe's top clubs.

TURKS & CAICOS ISLANDS

Federation: Turks and Caicos Islands Football Association
Founded: 1996
Joined FIFA: 1998
Confederation: CONCACAF
FIFA world ranking: 203

TURKMENISTAN

Federation: Football Federation of Turkmenistan
Founded: 1992
Joined FIFA: 1994
Confederation: AFC
FIFA world ranking: 142 (joint)

UGANDA

Federation: Uganda Football Association
Founded: 1924
Joined FIFA: 1959
Confederation: CAF
FIFA world ranking: 102

UKRAINE

Federation: Football Federation of Ukraine
Founded: 1991
Joined FIFA: 1992
Confederation: UEFA
FIFA world ranking: 47

Dynamo Kiev are, without doubt, Ukraine's most successful club, having won 16 Soviet league titles, the European Cup Winners' Cup in 1975 and 1986 – and dominated the Ukrainian league since its inception in 1992. Former Soviet (but Ukraine-born) greats include Oleg Blokhin and Igor Belanov, who were voted European Footballers Of The Year in 1975 and 1986 respectively.

UNITED ARAB EMIRATES

Federation: United Arab Emirates Football Association
Founded: 1971
Joined FIFA: 1972
Confederation: AFC
FIFA world ranking: 95 (joint)

Football, disliked by the region's religious leaders, took time to gain popularity. When the UAE was formed in 1971, football began to be taken seriously. Leading coaches were enticed to the country, including England boss Don Revie and Brazil's Carlos Alberto Parreira. It was the Brazilian ethos that was adopted and UAE qualified for the World Cup in 1990.

UNITED STATES

Federation: United States Soccer Federation
Founded: 1913
Joined FIFA: 1913
Confederation: CONCACAF
FIFA world ranking: 9
Honours: CONCACAF Championship 1991, 2002

'Soccer', as it is affectionately known in America, was introduced to the USA in Boston as early as 1862. In its formative years it resembled rugby, but in 1884 the American Football Association was formed, in affiliation with the FA in England, to bring the game in line with that played across the Atlantic. European immigrants filled most teams, mainly on the Eastern seaboard, and leagues appeared and disappeared with regularity.

The formation of the American Amateur Football Association (later to become the US Soccer Federation) in 1913 saw affiliation to FIFA and the beginnings of an American Soccer League. This professional attitude led, in 1930, to the national team reaching the semi-finals of the inaugural World Cup finals.

Soccer, however, failed to capture the imagination of a country brought up on 'American football' and baseball and few eyebrows were raised when the ASL folded in 1933. Regional leagues continued, but three silent decades followed and even the famous 1-0 victory against England in the 1950 World Cup failed to stir the passions.

The formation of the North American Soccer League in 1968 brought the game to the mainstream, attracting such football giants as Pele, who played for the New York Cosmos, Johan Cruyff and Franz Beckenbauer. Attendances boomed, yet when these great names hung up their boots, crowds tailed-off and the league was disbanded in 1984.

The NASL did, however, succeed in making football one of the most popular youth sports in the country and the fruits were realised when USA qualified for the 1990 World Cup, then went on to win the Gold Cup against Honduras the following year.

The decision to take the 1994 World Cup to America made the formation of the Major Soccer League a prerequisite for hosting the tournament. The country's progress to the second phase (elimination came at the hands of eventual winners Brazil) and the undoubted success of the tournament set the ball rolling and the MSL initially boomed.

Columbus Crew, DC United and San Jose Earthquakes drew crowds of over 30,000 and the national team continued their upward spiral, reaching the semi-finals of the 1995 Copa América. The MSL remains in operation but, with the better players seeking their fortune elsewhere, the standard has dropped.

Yet the national team continues to thrive, beating Costa Rica 2-0 to win the Gold Cup in 2002, before going on to reach the quarter-finals of the World Cup that year.

Below: Brad Friedel saves a penalty against South Korea at the 2002 World Cup.

URUGUAY

Federation: Asociación Uruguaya de Fútbol
Founded: 1900
Joined FIFA: 1923
Confederation: CONMEBOL
FIFA world ranking: 31 (joint)
Honours: World Cup 1930, 1950; Copa América 1916, 1917, 1920, 1923, 1924, 1926, 1935, 1942, 1956, 1959, 1967, 1983, 1987, 1995; Olympics 1924, 1928

The tiny South American nation was arguably the biggest force in world football in the first half of the 20th Century, winning Olympic gold medals in 1924 and 1928, and being crowned world champion in 1930 and 1950. Not only were they very successful, the Uruguayans were also stylish, playing imaginative pass-and-move football which stood in stark contrast to the physicality then prevalent elsewhere in the world game.

Uruguay were the first South American country to enter the Olympic football tournament and made an immediate impact in 1924 in Paris. Europeans had rarely encountered skills such as those displayed by team captain Jose Nasazzi and strikers such as Hector Castro, Pedro Cea and Hector Sarone. The South Americans cantered along to the final, where goals from Pedro Petrone, Cea and Angel Romano gave them an easy 3-0 victory over Switzerland.

Four years later Uruguay returned to the Olympics – this time held in Amsterdam – to defend their title. They beat fellow South Americans, Argentina, 2-1 to win gold after a replay. Uruguay's success in the Olympics led to the country being offered the chance to host the first World Cup in 1930. Because of the distance, many European countries stayed away from the tournament and as a result the Uruguayan hosts had to make do with only 13 entrants, including themselves. However, the low turnout didn't seem to distract the South Americans from the matter at hand: they repeated their excellent Olympic form and won the competition. Again it was neighbours and rivals Argentina who Uruguay put to the sword in the final, this time 4-2, with one of their goals coming from the one-armed Hector Castro.

Apparently upset at Europe's seeming lack of interest in the tournament, Uruguay turned down the chance to defend their world title in 1934. They didn't compete in the finals again until 1950, when the first post-World War II tournament was held in Brazil. As it turned out, the wait proved more than worth it for Uruguay. They thumped Bolivia 8-0, with Omar Miguez scoring a hat-trick, before joining Brazil, Spain and Sweden in a 'mini league' to decide the champions. It ended up in an all-or-nothing showdown with the hotly fancied hosts in front of more than 205,000 fans packed into the Maracana stadium. Despite falling behind in the second-half, Uruguay clinched their second World Cup victory in 20 years with goals from Juan Schiaffino and Alcide Ghiggia.

They made the semi-finals in 1954 and the quarter-finals in 1966, but there was no doubting Uruguay's World Cup star was seriously on the wane. After beating Australia in a two-legged play-off, they qualified for the 2002 World Cup Finals, something they hadn't managed since 1990. Unfortunately, coach Victor Pua's side failed to win any of their three group games and were soon heading home to South America.

Additionally, Uruguay have an excellent record in the South American Championship (the Copa América) – they even contested the tournament's very first match, in 1910, chalking up a 3-0 win over Chile in Buenos Aires. They went on to win eight of the first 18 tournaments up to 1942, an astonishing run. Their last appearance in a Copa América final came in 1999, when they were humbled 3-0 by Brazil. They finished fourth in 2001's tournament after losing a third-place play-off to Honduras on penalties.

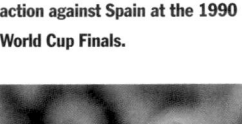
Below: Uruguay's Ruben Sosa in action against Spain at the 1990 World Cup Finals.

US VIRGIN ISLANDS

Federation: US Virgin Islands Soccer Federation
Founded: 1998
Joined FIFA: 1998
Confederation: CONCACAF
FIFA world ranking: 198

UZBEKISTAN

Federation: Uzbekistan Football Federation
Founded: 1946
Joined FIFA: 1994
Confederation: AFC
FIFA world ranking: 108 (joint)

VANUATU

Federation: Vanuatu Football Federation
Founded: 1934
Joined FIFA: 1988
Confederation: OFC
FIFA world ranking: 162

VENEZUELA

Federation: Federación Venezolana de Fútbol
Founded: 1926
Joined FIFA: 1952
Confederation: CONMEBOL
FIFA world ranking: 55 (joint)

VIETNAM

Federation: Vietnam Football Federation
Founded: 1962
Joined FIFA: 1964
Confederation: AFC
FIFA world ranking: 95 (joint)

WALES

Federation: Football Association of Wales
Founded: 1876
Joined FIFA: 1910-20, 1924-28, 1946
Confederation: UEFA
FIFA world ranking: 51

Football in Wales has always been a poor second to Rugby Union, despite the existence of a national team since March 1876 and a national FAW Cup competition since 1878.

What Wales lacked was a national league, which did not arrive until 1993, although its semi-professional status did not attract the country's strongest sides – Cardiff City, Swansea City and Wrexham – who have been playing in the English league since the 1920s.

Cardiff actually won the English FA Cup in 1927, while other clubs such as Colwyn Bay and Merthyr Tydfil also ply their trade in England. This situation, along with English clubs plundering the best of Welsh talent, leaves domestic Welsh football a poor product. Nevertheless, the national side qualified for the 1958 World Cup, reached the 1976 European Championship quarter-finals – at the time only the semis and finals were played as one tournament – and lifted the British Championship outright on seven occasions.

Wales have produced a host of great players, including Ivor Allchurch, John Charles, Ryan Giggs, Ian Rush and Mark Hughes. Hughes, as coach, has also guided Wales through their best unbeaten sequence in the team's history.

WESTERN SAMOA

Federation: Samoa Football (Soccer) Federation
Founded: 1968
Joined FIFA: 1986
Confederation: OFC
FIFA world ranking: 168

YEMEN

Federation: Yemen Football Association
Founded: 1962
Joined FIFA: 1980
Confederation: AFC
FIFA world ranking: 151

ZAMBIA

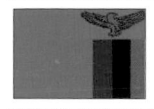  

Federation: Football Association of Zambia
Founded: 1929
Joined FIFA: 1964
Confederation: CAF
FIFA world ranking: 67

On April 28, 1993 tragedy struck Zambian football when a plane carrying the national team crashed into the Atlantic, killing 18 players and five officials. The loss was devastating at a time when Zambia looked set to qualify for the 1994 World Cup. The team had finished third at the 1990 African Nations Cup and were quarter-finalists in 1992. In 1988 they had reached the quarter-finals of the Olympic tournament after thrashing Italy 4-0, a game which saw African Player Of The Year Kalusha Bwalya (not on the plane) score a hat-trick. Power Dynamos had won the African Cup Winners' Cup in 1991 – the first Zambian club team to win an international trophy – but since the disaster, the country has failed to hit such heady heights.

ZIMBABWE

Federation: Zimbabwe Football Association
Founded: 1965
Joined FIFA: 1965
Confederation: CAF
FIFA world ranking: 61

Apartheid policies of the former Rhodesia kept the country out of the international arena until the 1970 World Cup. However, CAF did not accept the renamed Zimbabwe until 1980 after the instigation of black majority rule. Despite producing players of the calibre of Bruce Grobbelaar and Peter Ndlovu, Zimbabwe have yet to impact on the international stage, although they came within one game of reaching the 1994 World Cup finals.

Left: Welsh goal machine Ian Rush celebrates scoring against Germany in 1991.

CLUB COMPETITIONS OF THE WORLD

EUROPEAN CUP & CHAMPIONS LEAGUE

The origins of the European Cup – or the European Champions Clubs Cup to give its more precise name – came into being following a boast by the English press that the First Division champions Wolverhampton Wanderers were the best club side in world football. The outlandish claim was the result of a 3-2 friendly victory in 1954 against Hungarian side Honvéd under the new Molineux floodlights. It was also a knee-jerk reaction from Fleet Street journalists, who had witnessed the England national team comprehensively beaten the previous year by Hungary's 'Magical Magyars' – 6-3 at Wembley and then 7-1 in Budapest six months later.

With the Hungarians inspired by the continental skill and tactical awareness of Puskás, Czibor and Kocsis, both results finally buried the myth that England remained the best exponents of the beautiful game. The pride of a nation had been dented, yet the result at Molineux – and the subsequent 4-0 victory by Wolves against Spartak Moscow – saw some pride restored to a bruised ego.

The boast, however, fell on deaf ears on the continent; Gabriel Hanot, editor of French sports newspaper *L'Equipe* and a former French international, was particularly aggrieved by the claims from England. In response to the *Daily Mail*'s comment that Wolves were 'the best team in the world', Hanot suggested that a new European tournament – devised for teams from nominated countries played on a home-and-away basis – should be implemented to determine the best team on the continent.

His observations received a somewhat lukewarm reaction from a number of the associations, with the English Football Association particularly concerned at the impact that a new league would have on their own domestic campaign. Yet, following a meeting in Paris on April 2, attended by 15 of Europe's leading clubs, it was decided that Hanot's format should be presented to FIFA for it to receive international recognition.

Within four weeks, the world's governing body gave the competition its seal of approval and handed responsibility for its smooth running to UEFA, its European subsidiary, which was certainly a relief to Hanot. The new European Champions Clubs Cup saw its first match kick-off between Sporting Lisbon and Partizan Belgrade on September 4, 1955. In total, 16 countries had teams represented in the inaugural competition, but English champions Chelsea were conspicuous by their absence, their place going to Polish side Gwardia Warsaw.

Although these were humble beginnings, 38,000 fans attended the first final between Real Madrid and Reims, and so was born a tournament that has thrilled and excited the world of football for almost 50 years. The amazing final of 1960, which saw Real Madrid run out 7-3 victors against Eintracht Frankfurt, is now widely regarded as the greatest spectacle of club football ever seen.

Other highlights include Celtic's shock win against Inter Milan in 1967, the dominance of the Johan Cruyff-inspired Ajax sides of the early

1970s, likewise the stranglehold that English clubs seemed to have on the competition towards the end of that decade and into the early Eighties.

If England had little to do with the competition upon its inception, the nation has been intrinsically linked with the European Cup ever since – and not always for the happiest of reasons. For Manchester United, February 6, 1958 marks the darkest day in the club's long and illustrious history after eight of the fabled 'Busby Babes' were tragically killed on a Munich runway on the way back from their 5-4 aggregate quarter-final win against Red Star Belgrade.

Having stopped to refuel, the snowy conditions caused two aborted take-offs and on the third attempt the plane failed to gain altitude, hit a house and burst into flames. Roger Byrne, Geoff Bent, Mark Jones, David Pegg, Liam Whelan, Eddie Colman and Tommy Taylor died instantly, while the game's rising star – Duncan Edwards – passed away two weeks later. Manager Sir Matt Busby survived, but it took him another ten years to rebuild his team into European champions.

Yet the darkest moment in the competition's history came on May 29, 1985, when drunken Liverpool 'fans' went on the rampage inside the Heysel Stadium, Brussels, prior to the club's final appearance against Juventus. As the Italian supporters, who came under a hail of missiles and were faced with a spontaneous charge behind the goal, cowered in the corner of Terrace Z, a wall gave way under the

EUROPEAN CUP & CHAMPIONS LEAGUE WINNERS

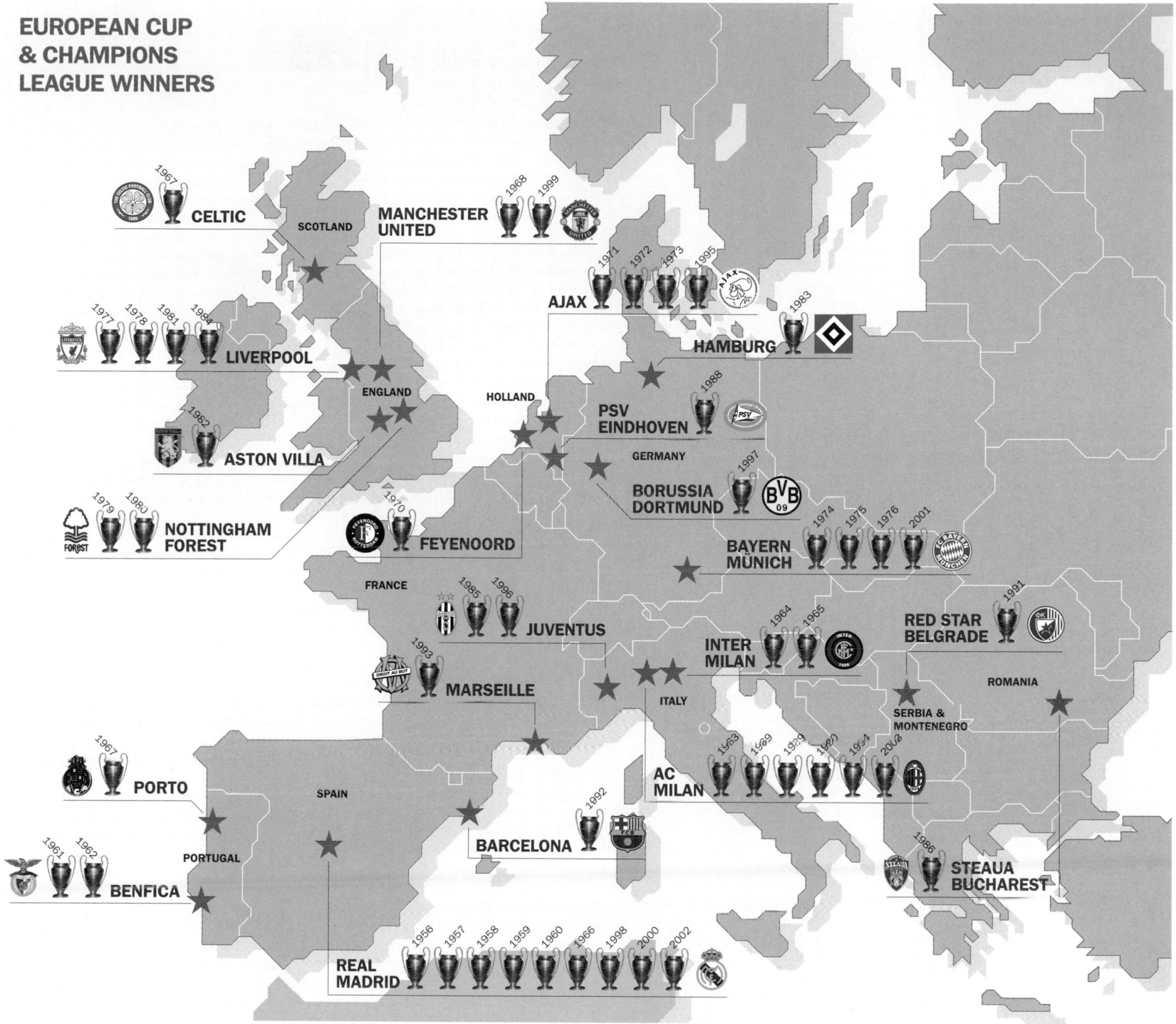

CELTIC 1967

MANCHESTER UNITED 1968 1999

AJAX 1971 1972 1973 1995

HAMBURG 1983

LIVERPOOL 1977 1978 1981 1984

PSV EINDHOVEN 1988

ASTON VILLA 1962

BORUSSIA DORTMUND 1997

NOTTINGHAM FOREST 1979 1980

FEYENOORD 1970

BAYERN MUNICH 1974 1975 1976 2001

JUVENTUS 1985 1996

INTER MILAN 1964 1965

RED STAR BELGRADE 1991

MARSEILLE 1993

PORTO 1967

AC MILAN 1963 1969 1989 1990 1994 2003

BENFICA 1961 1962

BARCELONA 1992

STEAUA BUCHAREST 1986

REAL MADRID 1956 1957 1958 1959 1960 1966 1998 2000 2002

SCOTLAND · ENGLAND · HOLLAND · GERMANY · FRANCE · SPAIN · PORTUGAL · ITALY · SERBIA & MONTENEGRO · ROMANIA

pressure and 39 people were crushed to death while hundreds were injured.

This wanton act of barbarism brought shame on English football and, more importantly, prompted UEFA to ban all English clubs 'indefinitely' from all European club competition. It would be another six years before the country would be represented in the European Cup.

On their return English teams would find for themselves a very different competition. With commercialism beginning to exert a much stronger influence on the sport, the bigger clubs were looking for more financial revenue from the competition, while the breakdown of the Eastern Bloc meant more

quality teams and therefore a more exploitable overall package had been created.

In 1992 the format of the competition changed. The first and second rounds continued as normal, but the third round consisted of two mini leagues of four teams, with the winners of each meeting in the final. The league format met with widespread approval and guaranteed a cash windfall for those teams participating in the latter stages.

Realising there was even more money to be generated, UEFA revamped the competition again for the 1994-95 season with the formation of the Champions League. The holders and seven top seeded teams would progress to four league groups, each

containing four clubs – the other clubs coming from a round of preliminary ties. AC Milan were the first winners of the new-look competition, beating Barcelona 4-0. As the seasons have passed and further changes have been implemented so that the highest-placed finishers in certain domestic league are now guaranteed a place in the competition, and such is the windfall that many teams now bank on qualification to ensure financial stability.

The model is now in place for a European Super League to evolve, consisting of only the most elite of European clubs. And the likelihood is that Wolves, or Honvéd for that matter, will never again claim to be the continent's dominant club.

Right: AC Milan won Italy's first
European Cup, beating Benfica at
Wembley in 1963.

1956: REAL MADRID

PARC DES PRINCES, PARIS June 13

Real Madrid **4-3** Stade de Reims
(Spain)   (France)

With a vociferous crowd behind them, Reims
took a 2-0 lead through Leblond and Templin,
but favourites Real Madrid soon found their
composure and stamped their mark on the
game. Alfredo Di Stéfano scored from the edge
of the box and Rial's headed equaliser set up
a storming second-half. A goal from Real
winger Joseito was disallowed shortly after the
break and Reims took advantage when Hidalgo
headed in Kopa's free-kick to edge them back
in front. Madrid's 67th minute equaliser came
when a Marquitos shot was defected home,
and with ten minutes remaining Rial scored
his second to win the game.

1957: REAL MADRID

BERNABÉU STADIUM, MADRID May 30

Real Madrid **2-0** Fiorentina
(Spain)   (Italy)

Real's second final was played in front of
a partisan 124,000 crowd, and although the
Italians possessed skilful Brazilian Julinho and
Argentine striker Miguel Montuori, they were
no match for the Spaniards. The game was
a stale affair until the 70th minute when Real
winger Enrique Mateos was fouled and Alfredo
Di Stéfano converted the kick. Six minutes
later Gento found himself with the goalkeeper
to beat and he held his nerve to secure victory.

Below: Real Madrid's 1960 win
over Eintracht Frankfurt was
perhaps the greatest game ever.

1958: REAL MADRID

HEYSEL STADIUM, BRUSSELS May 28

Real Madrid **3-2** AC Milan (aet)
(Spain)   (Italy)
2-2 at 90 minutes

With Milan marshalled by Maldini, the
Italians kept Di Stéfano and Kopa at bay and
the match proved to be an edgy affair until the
59th minute when Schiaffino put Milan
into the lead. Di Stéfano equalised in the
74th minute, only for Grillo to put Milan
back into the lead a few minutes later.
Within 60 seconds, Rial levelled to take the
game into extra-time and Madrid made it
three successive wins when Gento scored at
the second attempt.

1959: REAL MADRID

NECKARSTADION, STUTTGART June 3

Real Madrid **2-0** Stade de Reims
(Spain)   (France)

In a dour affair, the French were criticised for
a lack of adventure as Real won at a canter. The
pattern was set as early as the second minute
when Mateos shot past Colonna and, shortly
after the re-start, Di Stéfano scored the second
to continue his record of scoring in every final.
After the game, Real's Frenchman Kopa moved
back to Reims. French football would not see
another team in the final until 1976.

1960: REAL MADRID

HAMPDEN PARK, GLASGOW May 18

Read Madrid **7-3** Eintracht Frankfurt
(Spain)   (West Germany)

Quite possibly the greatest attacking game of
football ever staged, Frankfurt were blown
away by the flair and imagination of Real.

A near post volley from Kress put the Germans
into the lead, but Di Stéfano netted twice
before Puskás crashed in a left-foot shot to
make it 3-1 at half-time. Ten minutes after the
break Puskás scored a penalty, then followed
up with a header from Gento's cross. He
scored his fourth with a shot on the turn,
before a Stein goal 15 minutes from time gave
the Germans some respectability. Yet almost
immediately, a Puskás pass set up Di Stéfano
for his hat-trick before Stein scored again
following a Madrid defensive blunder.

1961: BENFICA

WANKDORF STADIUM, BERNE May 31

Benfica **3-2** Barcelona
(Portugal)   (Spain)

Barcelona's attack of Kubala, Kocsis and Czibor
was rightly feared, but opponents Benfica, with
the likes of Augusto, Coluna and Germano,
were fast becoming the best team on the
continent. The Spaniards took the lead through
a Kocsis header on 19 minutes but found
themselves on the back foot as Benfica scored
twice in two minutes through Aguas and
a Ramellets own-goal. In the 55th minute
Benfica scored their third with a Coluna volley
before a Barça onslaught saw Czibor get one
back and he, Kocsis and Kubala all hit the post.

1962: BENFICA

OLYMPIC STADIUM, AMSTERDAM May 2

Benfica **5-3** Real Madrid
(Portugal)   (Spain)

Another classic encounter saw Puskás score
three times inside 38 minutes for Madrid,
becoming the only player to have scored hat-
tricks in two European Cup finals. Benfica cut
back the deficit by half-time through Aguas

and Cavem, but with Di Stéfano pulling the strings changes were made. He was man-marked by Cavem in the second-half and the game swung in Benfica's favour. Coluna pounced on a slip by Puskás to level and the stage was set for 19-year-old Eusébio to weave his magic. Having won a penalty, he slammed the kick past Araquistain in the 65th minute, and three minutes later connected with a pass from Coluna to secure victory.

1963: AC MILAN

WEMBLEY STADIUM, LONDON May 22

AC Milan **2-1** Benfica
(Italy) (Portugal)

A half-full Wembley witnessed a no-nonsense display by Milan. The plan was to stifle Coluna, but the strategy played into Eusébio's hands as he left Trapattoni in his wake to score after 18 minutes. Milan's determination shone through in the second-half and when Rivera found Altafini, the Brazilian fired home. With Coluna a passenger following Pivatelli's crude challenge, there would be only one winner and that came via Altafini who, having picked up the ball on the halfway line, ran half the length of the pitch before firing past Costa Pereira at the second attempt.

1964: INTER MILAN

PRATER STADIUM, VIENNA May 27

Inter Milan **3-1** Real Madrid
(Italy) (Spain)

Having conceded just four goals in the tournament, Inter were favourites to win in Vienna, and when Mazzola scored from 25 yards in the 43rd minute, he had dealt a fatal blow. A 61st minute mistake by 'keeper Vicente let in Milani to put the Italians 2-0 ahead, and although Puskás hit a post, the writing was on the wall for Real. Felo cut the deficit with a 70th minute header but normality was resumed just six minutes later when Mazzola pounced on a bad clearance to secure victory.

1965: INTER MILAN

SAN SIRO, MILAN May 28

Inter Milan **1-0** Benfica
(Italy) (Portugal)

Prior to the game Benfica complained to UEFA that hosting the game at Inter's ground gave the Italians unfair advantage and threatened to field their youth team. They finally backed down when made fully aware of the financial benefits, but in hindsight their youngsters might have made a better job of it. Played in pouring rain, the players struggled with their footing and the match was settled when Jair's shot slithered through the hands of Costa Pereira in the 42nd minute.

1966: REAL MADRID

HEYSEL STADIUM, BRUSSELS May 11

Real Madrid **2-1** Partizan Belgrade
(Spain) (Yugoslavia)

Although the club was in its eighth final, it was an inexperienced Real side that faced the Yugoslavs and victory looked to be slipping away when Vasovic headed in Pirmajer's cross in the 56th minute. Real's response was to launch an all-out attack and in the 70th minute Amancio met a through pass from Grosso to shoot past Soskic. With their tails up, and Partizan's star striker Galic struggling with injury, Serena curled home from 25 yards to wrap the game up some six minutes later.

1967: CELTIC

ESTÁDIO NACIONAL, LISBON May 25

Celtic **2-1** Inter Milan
(Scotland) (Italy)

Celtic turned the Portuguese stadium into a sea of green and white – a sight that spurred Jock Stein's side into action against their much-

fancied and defensively-organised opponents. A good start was a necessity but when Craig felled Cappellini after six minutes, referee Tschenscher pointed to the spot and Mazzola sent Simpson the wrong way.

Lesser teams could have crumbled, but Celtic went for broke and when Auld and Gemmell hit the bar, it gave an indication of the Scots' dominance. They were finally rewarded in the 62nd minute when left-back Gemmell hit a 20-yard rocket into the corner of Sarti's net. The Inter defence was rattled and in the 83rd minute a Murdoch shot appeared to be going wide before Chalmers intercepted to guide the ball home.

1968: MANCHESTER UNITED

WEMBLEY STADIUM, LONDON May 29

Manchester United **4-1** Benfica (aet)
(England) (Portugal)
1-1 at 90 minutes

The first-half was a scrappy affair with chances at a premium, playmaker George Best being tightly marked by Cruz and Humberto. Sadler came closest to breaking the deadlock with two half-chances but it wasn't until the second-half, when Ashton began to cause problems down the left flank, that United looked dangerous. They were finally rewarded when Charlton headed home a Dunne cross in the 52nd minute, but 1-0 never looked a scoreline that would be enough to secure victory and, when Graca equalised with nine minutes to go, Benfica proved that the match was anything but over. Eusébio had a great chance to win the game in the dying seconds and it proved to be the defining moment as Best waltzed round two defenders to put United back in the lead early in extra-time. The goal demoralised Benfica and further strikes from Kidd and Charlton finally laid to rest the ghost of 1958.

Above: Benfica come unstuck in the 1965 final, losing to Inter Milan in the Italians' own San Siro home.

Left: Billy McNeill makes off with the European Cup after Celtic's 1967 success.

Above: Arie Haan seals Ajax's 1971 win over Panathinaikos at Wembley.

1969: AC MILAN

BERNABÉU STADIUM, MADRID May 28

AC Milan **4-1** Ajax
(Italy)   (Holland)

In a move rarely associated with Italian sides, Milan attacked from the start against an inexperienced Ajax. They opened the scoring as early as the sixth minute when Prati's looping header sailed over Bals' goal, and despite Ajax's best intentions, the lead was doubled when Prati's shot flew in from the edge of the box. The Dutch team were missing the injured Cruyff and although a dubious Vasovic penalty gave them hope on the hour, Sormani put away Milan's third just five minutes later and Prati completed his hat-trick after 74 minutes.

1970: FEYENOORD

SAN SIRO, MILAN May 6

Feyenoord **2-1** Celtic (aet)
(Holland)   (Scotland)
1-1 at 90 minutes

With Feyenoord underdogs, Celtic reverted to a 4-2-4 formation, believing an offensive action would win them game. That assumption appeared to be correct when, in the 29th minute, Gemmell swept home from 25 yards. But within three minutes the Dutch equalised when Hasil's free-kick was lofted over a static Celtic defence for captain Israel to head home. Feyenoord completely dominated the second-half but somehow Celtic made it to extra-time

and goalkeeper Williams kept them in the game with fine saves from Kindvall and Wery. He could do nothing when Kindvall took advantage of McNeill's slip to steer home the winner with four minutes remaining though.

1971: AJAX

WEMBLEY STADIUM, LONDON June 2

Ajax **2-0** Panathinaikos
(Holland)   (Greece)

Puskás's love affair with the European Cup continued as he guided the Greeks to their solitary final appearance as manager. They started as big underdogs against the Total Football of Ajax, who took a grip on the game as early as the fifth minute when Keizer whipped in a left-wing cross for Van Dijk to head clinically past Economopoulos. The Greek 'keeper then pulled off a number of fine saves, most notably from the impressive Cruyff, and although the Dutch seemed content to sit on their one goal advantage, Panathinaikos failed to seize the initiative. The game was won in the 87th minute when Haan finished off Cruyff's mazy run.

1972: AJAX

DE KUIP STADIUM, ROTTERDAM May 31

Ajax **2-0** Inter Milan
(Holland)   (Italy)

The Italians adopted their 'catenaccio' tactics in an attempt to overcome the Dutch masters, however it was clear from kick-off that they

were fighting a losing battle as Ajax played with the flair and imagination that had won them a domestic double back in Holland.

The loss of centre-half Giubertoni after 12 minutes did not help Inter's cause, but the deadlock wasn't breached until the 47th minute when Cruyff pounced on a mix-up between Bordon and Burgnich to stroke home. The goal forced the Italians to attack and Mazzola had a good chance to equalise before European Footballer Of The Year Cruyff made the game safe in the 77th minute.

1973: AJAX

RED STAR STADIUM, BELGRADE May 30

Ajax **1-0** Juventus
(Holland)   (Italy)

In a mirror image of the previous year's final, Dutch artistry overcame Italian stubbornness as Ajax became only the second team in history to win the cup three years in succession. On a humid night in Yugoslavia, Ajax went for an early kill and were rewarded when a deep Blankenburg cross was met by wonder-kid Johnny Rep, who rose above Marchetti to head home. Again, Cruyff teased the opposition and, although his team-mates couldn't take advantage, the result was never in doubt as the masters nonchalantly played possession football as the game drew to a close.

1974: BAYERN MUNICH

HEYSEL STADIUM, BRUSSELS May 15

Bayern Munich **1-1** Atlético Madrid (aet)
(West Germany)   (Spain)
0-0 at 90 minutes

In a closely-fought encounter Atlético had the better of the early exchanges, their flair and passing catching the Germans offguard. Bayern upped the tempo in the second-half but although Müller and Hoeness looked dangerous, the game went to extra-time. The deadlock was broken when a delightful Aragones free-kick beat Maier, and with seven minutes remaining the cup appeared to be heading to Spain. Yet, in typical fashion, the Germans rose from the ashes and with just seconds remaining, Schwarzenbeck unleashed a shot from 35 yards that flew past Reina. The title would be decided by a replay.

REPLAY

HEYSEL STADIUM, BRUSSELS May 17

Bayern Munich **4-0** Atlético Madrid

With playmaker Irureta suspended and centre-half skipper Adelardo later substituted through injury, Madrid were on the back foot and the match proved to be a one-sided affair. Although the score was 1-0 at half-time, thanks to Hoeness's 28th minute strike, the Germans turned the screw after the break and doubled their lead when Müller volleyed home

Kapellmann's cross. A delicate lob from Müller made it three and with eight minutes remaining, Hoeness scored his second by rounding the goalkeeper.

1975: BAYERN MUNICH

PARC DES PRINCES, PARIS May 28;

Bayern Munich **2-0** Leeds United
(West Germany)   (England)

With their physical, no-nonsense approach, United bossed the game in the opening half and had two legitimate appeals for a penalty turned down when Beckenbauer appeared to intercept a pass to Lorimer with his hand and later tripped Clarke inside the box. It simply wasn't going to be United's night, which was confirmed when Lorimer volleyed into the roof of the net after 67 minutes, only for the goal to be disallowed for offside. This decision caused rioting by a section of the Leeds following and they were further riled when Roth scored in the 72nd minute following good work from Müller. Although Leeds continued to throw men forward, the Germans wrapped the game up with eight minutes remaining as Müller ghosted past Madeley and beat Stewart at his near post.

1976: BAYERN MUNICH

HAMPDEN PARK, GLASGOW May 12

Bayern Munich **1-0** St Etienne
(West Germany)   (France)

Although the scoreline suggests a tight game, it was anything but as St Etienne's imagination was matched with Bayern's counter-attacking football. However, the Germans were denied a goal in the second minute when Müller was deemed offside as he slotted the ball past Curkovic. TV replays proved he'd been onside and the decision galvanised the French, who saw Bathenay and Santini hit the woodwork. Within 12 minutes of the restart Bayern landed the killer blow when a Beckenbauer free-kick that was lashed home by Roth.

1977: LIVERPOOL

OLYMPIC STADIUM, ROME May 25

Liverpool **3-1** Borussia
Mönchengladbach
(England)   (West Germany)

Liverpool's creativity was rewarded in the 27th minute when Heighway's cross was met by McDermott and his shot flew past Borussia goalkeeper Kneib. Yet within six minutes of the restart, Simonsen intercepted a poor Case back-pass and his left-foot shot beat Clemence emphatically. The goal lifted the Germans and the England goalkeeper was called into action on a number of occasions after that.

Having ridden the storm, Liverpool imposed themselves again and another Heighway cross was met by Smith, who rose quickest to make

it 2-0. With Keegan – in his last game for the club – running rings round the Germans, defender Vögts scythed him down and Neal converted the resulting spot kick.

1978: LIVERPOOL

WEMBLEY STADIUM, LONDON May 10

Liverpool **1-0** Club Brugge
(England)   (Belgium)

In total contrast to the previous year's final, Liverpool retained their crown in a totally uninspiring game. With the influential Lambert and Courant both absent through injury, Brugge's defence-first policy stifled Liverpool, themselves below par after another intense domestic season. A Case free-kick was the closest either side came to scoring in the first-half, but The Reds finally broke the deadlock in the 66th minute when Dalglish latched on to a through ball from Souness to delightfully chip over advancing goalkeeper Jensen. Liverpool became the first English team to win the European Cup twice, ample consolation for losing the championship and League Cup to Nottingham Forest.

1979: NOTTINGHAM FOREST

OLYMPIC STADIUM, MUNICH May 30

Nottingham Forest **1-0** Malmö
(England)   (Sweden)

Another poor final; Malmö were missing their influential defenders Larsson, Andersson and skipper Tapper, while Forest were without Gemmill and O'Neill. They did, however, have £1million man Trevor Francis in their ranks, and he scored the only goal of the game on the stroke of half-time when he met Robertson's cross with a far post header. Robertson also hit the post himself after the break, and Birtles

missed a sitter with just goalkeeper Möller to beat. A Ljungberg free-kick proved to be Malmö's only clear attempt at goal.

1980: NOTTINGHAM FOREST

BERNABÉU STADIUM, MADRID May 28

Nottingham Forest **1-0** Hamburg
(England)   (West Germany)

With Francis absent with an Achilles injury and goalkeeper Shilton struggling with a calf problem, Hamburg took the game to Forest with full-backs Kaltz and midfielder Memering keen to feed Kevin Keegan whenever possible. Yet as they pushed forward, Forest broke on the counter-attack – a move which worked to perfection in the 19th minute when Robertson played a neat one-two with Birtles before striking home from the edge of the box. Reimann had a goal disallowed for offside on the half-hour mark and although Keegan and Nogly went close, Forest held on.

1981: LIVERPOOL

PARC DES PRINCES, PARIS May 27

Liverpool **1-0** Real Madrid
(England)   (Spain)

With Camacho and Cortes shadowing Souness and Dalglish, and Real playmaker Stielike hustled off his game by Lee, an extremely tense first-half saw chances at a premium. Yet as the second-half got underway, Real skipper Camacho was clean through only to see his shot sail over the bar. It would act as a wake-up call to Liverpool, who then took a hold of the game, and a Ray Kennedy throw-in was chested down by Alan Kennedy who skipped past a tackle from Cortes before driving home from an acute angle. Liverpool held on and Bob Paisley became the first coach to win the European Cup three times.

Left: John Robertson and Peter Shilton enjoy Nottingham Forest's second successive European Cup win in 1980.

Below: David Johnson helps Liverpool to their third European Cup success, this time against Real Madrid in Paris.

Above: Graeme Souness lifts the fourth and last of Liverpool's European Cups in Rome.

1982: ASTON VILLA

DE KUIP, ROTTERDAM May 26

Aston Villa 1-0 Bayern Munich
(England)   (West Germany)

With a strong team that included German internationals Rummenigge and Hoeness, Bayern were clear favourites to lift the trophy in 1982, but it was Villa who started brightest and went close through both Withe and Evans. The early promise threatened to be undone, however, when goalkeeper Rimmer was taken off with an injured neck and replaced by 23-year-old Nigel Spink after just nine minutes. Any nerves that the youngster might have been experiencing were settled with two fantastic saves from Durnberger and Rummenigge,

however, inspiring his team-mates to fight back. Then, in the 67th minute, Morley's bobbling cross was met by Withe who spooned the ball home past Müller.

1983: HAMBURG

OLYMPIC STADIUM, ATHENS May 25

Hamburg 1-0 Juventus
(West Germany)   (Italy)

With six of Italy's World Cup-winning team in their ranks, and Platini and Rossi also added after the tournament, a Juve victory was seen as a formality. Yet it was German industry that actually reigned supreme, and within eight minutes Hamburg were ahead, as captain Magath's looping shot fooled 41-year-old Zoff. Platini and Rossi were poor throughout and the only Juventus player to emerge with any credit was Boniek, whose runs were a constant torment. But there was no denying Hamburg their victory, while Juve were left to rue the hype that had surrounded the team in the build-up to the game.

1984: LIVERPOOL

OLYMPIC STADIUM, ROME May 30

Liverpool 1-1 Roma (aet)
(England)   (Italy)
1-1 at 90 minutes; Liverpool won 4-2 on penalties

The Italians may have been spurred on by a vociferous home crowd, but Liverpool managed to silence them after just 15 minutes when Tancredi lost the ball under pressure and Neal gratefully stroked home. Within seconds Souness scored but was ruled offside, and The Reds were left to rue the decision as Pruzzo headed home Conti's cross on 38 minutes. Liverpool goalkeeper Grobbelaar made key saves from Falcao and Tancredi, and after extra-time stalemate the game went to penalties. In front of the Roma fans, Nicol missed the opening kick while Di Bartolomei scored. Neal then scored while Conti, distracted by the leg-wobbling antics of Grobbelaar, missed. Souness, Righetti and Rush all scored before Graziani hit the crossbar. It was left to Alan Kennedy to wrap the game up and he converted with consummate ease.

1985: JUVENTUS

HEYSEL STADIUM, BRUSSELS May 29

Juventus 1-0 Liverpool
(Italy)   (England)

The on-field events at Heysel were completely overshadowed by rioting on the terraces, which resulted in the deaths of 39 Juventus fans. Prior to kick-off, a group of Liverpool supporters charged at their Italian rivals behind the goal and, as the Juve fans fled the barrage of missiles being aimed in their direction, a wall collapsed under the immense pressure. The enormity of the disaster became apparent

as kick-off approached, with many fans being pulled out unconscious or dead. There is little doubt the crumbling stadium and lack of organisation was partly to blame, but it was the ugly face of English hooliganism that UEFA vented their fury at and, as a result, English teams were banned from European competition for six years. Juventus won the game thanks to Platini's penalty.

1986: STEAUA BUCHAREST

SÁNCHEZ PIZJUÁN STADIUM, SEVILLE May 7

Steaua Bucharest 0-0 Barcelona (aet)
(Romania)   (Spain)
Steaua won 2-0 on penalties

After a manic start that saw referee Vautrot hand out cards like confetti, the game settled down and Steaua took control through their playmakers Balint and Balan. Yet it was Schuster who went closest to breaking the deadlock with a header on the half-hour, though 0-0 at half-time was a fair reflection. The Romanian rearguard action shone in the second-half and Barça's closest effort came from Archibald, who headed over the crossbar. Extra-time failed to separate the sides and as the game went to penalties, the first four were saved. But as Lacatus and Balint converted, Barcelona's next two were saved, handing Steaua success.

1987: PORTO

PRATER STADIUM, VIENNA May 27

Porto 2-1 Bayern Munich
(Portugal)   (West Germany)

The Germans took a controversial lead when Porto's Magalhaes was illegally ordered back from a Bayern throw-in. As he retreated the ball was deflected off his head to Kögl, who headed home himself. The injustice unsettled Porto as Rummenigge and Matthäus also went close, but the second-half was a contrasting affair as Sousa began pulling the strings in midfield. The equaliser came in the 77th minute when Madjer cheekily backheeled the ball past Pfaff, and two minutes later Juary connected with Madjer's cross to seal victory.

1988: PSV EINDHOVEN

NECKAR STADIUM, STUTTGART May 25

PSV Eindhoven 0-0 Benfica (aet)
(Holland)   (Portugal)
PSV won 6-5 on penalties

With PSV boasting four players from the Dutch side that would win the European Championship that summer, they were clear favourites. Their chances were further boosted when Benfica skipper Diamantino was ruled out with injury. But as the Portuguese side launched a damage limitation exercise, the game petered out to a boring spectacle. Vanenburg and Gillhaus went close for PSV

after the break, while Nielsen missed an open goal, but extra-time proved equally dreary and only penalties lifted the gloom that had descended around the stadium. All penalties were expertly taken until Van Breukelen pushed out Veloso's weak effort.

1989: AC MILAN

NOU CAMP, BARCELONA May 24

AC Milan **4-0** Steaua Bucharest
(Italy)   (Romania)

With the likes of Gullit, Van Basten, Rijkaard and Maldini in their ranks, Milan confirmed their status as Europe's top side with a total demolition of Steaua. The passing and movement was a joy to behold and, although Lacatus and Hagi were early threats, the Romanians were soon under pressure. Milan took the lead after 18 minutes when Bumbescu fluffed a clearance and Gullit was on hand to tuck the ball home. Eight minutes later Van Basten rose to head home Tassotti's cross and, as the half drew to a close, Gullit received a pass from Donadoni and in one movement swivelled to volley past Lung. It could have been easy to shut up shop but within 60 seconds of the re-start Van Basten received Rijkaard's through ball to score the fourth.

1990: AC MILAN

PRATER STADIUM, VIENNA May 23

AC Milan **1-0** Benfica
(Italy)   (Portugal)

Milan adopted a more defensive approach than the previous year, due in part to Benfica's very lively forward line of Valdo and Magnusson. Indeed, the Portuguese made most of the running in the first-half, but it was Milan who came closest to breaking the deadlock when Van Basten's shot was well-saved by Silvino. The match was settled by the best move of the game involving Costacurta, Filippo Galli and Van Basten, whose through ball was coolly tucked home by Rijkaard. Gullit had a chance to make the final 15 minutes more comfortable, but despite a scare from Carlos, Milan held on.

1991: RED STAR BELGRADE

SAN NICOLA STADIUM, BARI May 29

Red Star Belgrade **0-0** Marseille (aet)
(Yugoslavia)   (France)
Red Star won 5-3 on penalties

With both sides renowned for their attacking instincts, it was somehow inevitable that the game would become a tedious affair. Red Star played with a lone striker in Pancev, a defensive midfield and an uncompromising defence, which meant the flair of Marseille's Papin and Waddle were given little space or time to shine. The first-half was entirely forgettable, but at least the French side took the game to their opponents after the break and Waddle went close in the 75th minute with a header that flashed wide. Papin also went close but it was Prosinecki who almost won the game for Red Star as his late free-kick shaved a post. In the penalty shoot-out Amoros missed, handing Red Star victory.

1992: BARCELONA

WEMBLEY STADIUM, LONDON May 20

Barcelona **1-0** Sampdoria (aet)
(Spain)   (Italy)
0-0 at 90 minutes

Barça took to the field in an unfamiliar orange kit and, although they showed more attacking instincts than their edgy opponents, Cruyff's side were nearly caught on the break when Lombardo's shot was well held by Zubizarreta.

The pace picked up in the second-half, with Vialli missing two guilt-edged chances, while Barça striker Stoichkov saw his shot rebound off a post. As the clock ticked away, anxiety set in and a melee followed Bakero's poor tackle on Cerezo.

Mancini had a chance to win the game with the ensuing free-kick but the game went to extra-time and, in the 110th minute, Barcelona controversially took the lead. Referee Schmidhuber wrongly judged that Invernezzi had fouled Eusebio on the edge of the box and from the resulting kick, Koeman's ferocious strike beat Pagliuca to secure victory.

1993: MARSEILLE

OLYMPIC STADIUM, MUNICH May 26

Marseille **1-0** AC Milan
(France)   (Italy)

It was all change for Milan, who left Gullit on the bench while Papin was sacrificed for Van Basten, making only his third appearance following ankle surgery. Marseille, on the other hand, had their own problems with rumours of match-fixing threatening to overshadow their very existence.

Milan dominated the opening half hour and could have been 2-0 up if Massaro had shown more composure, but the French gradually clawed their way back into the game. Völler went close with a shot that rebounded off goalkeeper Rossi's legs, while Boksic also saw an effort shave the bar. But the breakthrough finally came on the stroke of half-time when Boli rose to powerfully head home Pele's corner for the Frenchmen.

The second-half was one-way traffic as Milan pushed for an equaliser but, although Papin and Massaro both went close, they were left to rue Van Basten's shocking miss from just eight yards out in the 48th minute. Following the game, Marseille were found guilty of match fixing, banned from European football and relegated to the French Second Division.

Left: Ruud Gullit and AC Milan celebrate their 1989 demolition of Steaua Bucharest.

Below: Red Star Belgrade enjoy their 1991 success.

1994: AC MILAN

OLYMPIC STADIUM, ATHENS May 18

AC Milan **4-0** Barcelona
(Italy) (Spain)

With Barça displaying the attacking prowess of Stoichkov, Romario and Sergi, it was anticipated that the Italians would implement 'catenaccio' to the highest degree, yet the game was turned on its head as Milan displayed their own brand of breathtaking, offensive football. They showed their intentions from the start when Panucci's header was disallowed in the ninth minute, and although Romario forced a good save from Rossi, Massaro broke the deadlock from Savicevic's cross in the 22nd minute. He added a second on the stroke of half-time following good work from Donadoni, and the game was all but sealed in the 47th minute when Savicevic chipped the ball over Zubizarretta from 20 yards. Desailly, playing in midfield, scored a fourth and Savicevic had time to hit the post twice before the final whistle put Barça out of their misery.

1995: AJAX

ERNST HAPPEL STADIUM, VIENNA May 24

Ajax **1-0** AC Milan
(Holland) (Italy)

Although Van Gaal's young side had beaten Milan twice earlier in the competition, Milan had not conceded a goal for five European matches and started as clear favourites. As the first-half progressed, Milan took a hold of the game and, although they hadn't created much, they were bossing the midfield. Desailly, Baresi and Maldini, meanwhile, were comfortably dealing with the threat of Ajax forwards Litmanen, George and Overmars.

The first real chance of the game came via a Desailly shot on 41 minutes, while Van der Sar saved from Simone on the stroke of half-time. Ajax were happy to return to the dressing room on level terms and Van Gaal then played a master stroke by bringing on young strikers Kanu and Kluivert, who helped turn the game around with their pace and trickery. The winner came in the 85th minute when Rijkaard's through ball found Kluivert and, at 18 years and 327 days, he became the youngest ever European Cup final goalscorer.

1996: JUVENTUS

OLYMPIC STADIUM, ROME May 22

Juventus **1-1** Ajax (aet)
(Italy) (Holland)
1-1 at 90 minutes; Juventus win 4-2 on penalties

Although missing the injured Overmars, Ajax were everybody's tip to retain the trophy. But a defensive mix up between Frank De Boer and goalkeeper Van der Sar on 12 minutes let in Juve striker Fabrizio Ravanelli to score from the acutest of angles. Both sides had chances as the half progressed – most notably from Musampa and Del Piero – and in the 41st minute a foul by Vierchowod on Kanu resulted in a De Boer free-kick being turned home by Litmanen. Vialli and Del Piero had chances to win the game for Juve in the second-half but extra-time was required and Del Piero had a great chance at the death, but shot straight at Van der Sar. There was a feeling that it wasn't to be for the Italians, but they held their nerve in the shoot-out with Peruzzi saving from Davids and Silooy.

1997: BORUSSIA DORTMUND

OLYMPIC STADIUM, MUNICH May 28

Borussia Dortmund **3-1** Juventus
(Germany) (Italy)

With the Germans containing four ex-Juve players – Kohler, Möller, Paulo Sousa and Reuter – Dortmund had an added incentive to do well, but what followed was one of the biggest upsets in European Cup history.

For the first-half-hour Juve attacked with purpose through Boksic and Vieri, but it was the Germans who struck first when Lambert's chip was met by Riedle, who rifled the ball home. Within five minutes, Riedle had doubled Dortmund's lead, heading home Möller's cross. But the game was far from over for Juve, who saw Zidane hit the post and Vieri have a goal disallowed before half-time.

Throwing caution to the wind, Lippi replaced defender Porrini with Del Piero and it was a move that appeared to pay off when the substitute scored after 64 minutes. Yet, far from perturbed, Borussia scored a third when Ricken spotted Peruzzi off his line and lobbed the goalkeeper from 35 yards.

1998: REAL MADRID

AMSTERDAM ARENA, AMSTERDAM May 20

Real Madrid **1-0** Juventus
(Spain) (Italy)

With 21 internationals on the pitch and a further six on the bench, this game was billed as a clash of the giants. But although both started brightly, neither side could make their pressure pay. Davids and Carlos were both booked as frustrations grew and Mijatovic, causing constant problems down the left, was a target of some uncompromising Juventus defending.

Raúl missed a golden opportunity to open the scoring on the stroke of half-time, while Inzaghi repeated the feat for Juve soon after the restart, following good work from Davids. But just as the fans were beginning to look towards extra-time, Real took the lead with 20 minutes remaining. Seedorf crossed from the right and although Carlos's shot was saved, Mijatovic was on hand to slot the ball home from a tight angle.

1999: MANCHESTER UNITED

NOU CAMP, BARCELONA May 26

Manchester United **2-1** Bayern Munich
(England) (Germany)

With Keane and Scholes suspended, the odds were against United lifting the trophy for the first time in 31 years and their chances looked even more remote after a shaky start. As early

Below: 1999 winners Manchester United celebrate their last gasp heroics against Bayern Munich.

as the sixth minute, Johnsen fouled Jancker and from the resulting free-kick, Basler fired the ball over Schmeichel and into the net. United's creative force of Giggs and Blomqvist were contained, Effenberg and Jeremies had control of the midfield, while Cole and Yorke were given little opportunity to show their obvious talent. Indeed, as the game wore on and United became more desperate, they left themselves open and Effenberg went close while Scholl hit the bar.

As the game entered its 90th minute with the Bayern fans already celebrating their team's success, United 'keeper Schmeichel went up for a last-gasp Beckham corner. He failed to connect but the ball fell to Giggs, whose shot was intercepted by substitute Sheringham and the ball nestled in the back of the net. The Bayern players were clearly distraught and before they'd managed to rediscover their composure, Beckham sent in another corner, which was flicked on by Sheringham and diverted home by substitute Solskjaer.

2000: REAL MADRID

STADE DE FRANCE, PARIS May 24

Real Madrid 3-0 Valencia
(Spain)   (Spain)

In the first final between two teams from the same country, Real completely dominated with their brand of attacking football and breathtaking skill. With McManaman pulling the strings in midfield, wing-backs Carlos and Salgado marauding forward at every opportunity and Raúl a constant threat in attack, there was only ever going to be one winner. The only surprise was that it took 39 minutes for Real to open the scoring. A Carlos free-kick was deflected into the path of Anelka, whose ball found Morientes unmarked at the far post. In the 63rd minute McManaman was rewarded as he crashed home through a pack of players to put the game beyond Valencia's reach, but the best was saved until last as Raúl ran 70 yards before rounding Canizares and tucking the ball home.

2001: BAYERN MUNICH

SAN SIRO, MILAN May 23

Bayern Munich 1-1 Valencia (aet)
(Germany)   (Spain)
1-1 at 90 minutes; Bayern win 5-4 on penalties

In a game of penalties, Valencia opened the scoring as early as the second minute when Mendieta's shot was adjudged to have hit Andersson on the arm and the Spanish playmaker stepped up to convert the penalty kick himself. Incredibly, referee Jol awarded another spot-kick just five minutes later when Angloma scythed Effenberg down, but Scholl's kick was saved by the legs of Canizares.

The early edge, both psychological and in terms of goals, would not last for the Spaniards as Bayern enjoyed plenty of possession with Lizarazu and Salihamidzic causing problems down the left. Scholl went close with a free-kick and Carew could have made it 2-0 to Valencia with a header that flashed wide, but it was the introduction of Jancker that proved crucial. Within five minutes of coming on, the big striker's challenge on Carboni forced the Italian defender to handle the ball and Effenberg stepped up to send Canizares the wrong way. In extra-time, Canizares blocked a close range shot from Elber, Scholl fired a free-kick tamely wide, and the Valencia goalkeeper kept out an angled drive by Salihamidzic, but the Germans held their nerve to win a tense penalty shoot-out.

2002: REAL MADRID

HAMPDEN PARK, GLASGOW May 15

Real Madrid 2-1 Bayer Leverkusen
(Spain)   (Germany)

Zidane's breathtaking volley in the final minute of the first-half is the enduring image of a game that saw Real's class overcome Leverkusen's stubbornness. The French star, who had contributed little in the previous 44 minutes, met a left wing cross from Carlos and let fly from the edge of the area with a waist-high volley that flew past goalkeeper Butt.

Earlier, Raúl had struck in the ninth minute from a move that came from a long throw by Carlos, and Brazilian defender Lucio had headed the leveller in the 14th minute from a Schneider free-kick. But Zidane apart, the star of the show was young Real goalkeeper Casillas, who replaced the injured Sanchez in the 67th minute before making fine saves from a Basturk header and Berbatov's injury-time strike. The result meant that Madrid, beaten in the league and Spanish Cup final after being on course for the treble, finally won the biggest prize of all in their centenary year.

2003: AC MILAN

OLD TRAFFORD, MANCHESTER May 28

AC Milan 0-0 Juventus (aet)
(Italy)   (Italy)
Milan win 4-2 on penalties

In the first all-Italian final in the 48-year history of the competition, Juve faced Milan without suspended Czech midfielder Nedved. And the team lacked midfield urgency as Milan had three good scoring chances in the first 45 minutes. Shevchenko had the ball in the Juventus net in the eighth minute, but Rui Costa was adjudged offside, while Inzaghi went close with a diving header that was spectacularly saved by Buffon.

Six minutes before the break another chance fell to Rui Costa when Pirlo found him in front of goal, but the Portuguese midfielder pulled his shot wide of Buffon's right-hand post. An effort from Trezeguet and a Del Piero shot on the stroke of half-time were Juve's best of the half and, indeed, the game.

The second-half degenerated into a game of defensive mastery – and extra-time and penalties were inevitable. The kicks even proved very disappointing, and it was left to Shevchenko to score the winner and make up for his early disappointment.

Left: Real Madrid enjoy their win in 2000, one of three European titles won by the club in five seasons.

Below: Paolo Maldini (front centre) follows in his father's footsteps, lifting the European Cup for AC Milan in 2003.

INTER-CITIES FAIRS CUP & UEFA CUP

Above from left to right: Leeds legend Billy Bremner shows off the Fairs Cup after the Yorkshire side's 1968 success; Mick Mills drinks from the UEFA Cup after Ipswich's 1981 triumph; Napoli become the first Italian winners in 12 years in 1989.

Opposite clockwise from top left: Liverpool reclaim the cup in 2001; Porto enjoy their 2003 triumph; Lothar Matthäus lifts the cup in 1996; Feyenoord win on home turf in 2002.

Europe's second most prestigious international cup competition began life as something of an anomaly. Known originally as the Inter City Fairs Cup, it was thought up shortly after the inception of the European Cup in 1955 by the future president of FIFA, Sir Stanley Rous, and two future FIFA vice-presidents, Switzerland's Ernst Thommen and Italy's Ottorino Barrasi. Their idea was to hold a tournament for European cities which regularly organised trade fairs. Entry was unrelated to final league placings, which threw up some rather insignificant teams early on like DOS of Utrecht, as well as some peculiar representative sides featuring players from several clubs, like the London Select XI that starred in the first campaign.

The first Fairs Cup involved teams from Barcelona, Basle, Birmingham, Copenhagen, Frankfurt, Lausanne, Leipzig, London, Milan and Zagreb. Originally conceived as a two-year tournament, it actually lasted for three, during which time 23 games were played in a clumsy group system complicated by withdrawals (Cologne and Vienna).

The final was contested over two legs by Barcelona, using players exclusively from FC Barcelona, and the London representative XI which included Arsenal goalkeeper Jack Kelsey, Tottenham's Danny Blanchflower, Fulham's Johnny Haynes, and Jimmy Greaves, then with Chelsea. The Londoners, who had played several games under floodlights at Wembley, held Barça 2-2 in front of 45,000 fans at Stamford Bridge on March 5, 1958, but were

routed 6-0 in the return two months later.

Two years on the format was altered, limiting participation to 16 professional club sides from cities that held trade fairs. Barcelona held on to the trophy, beating Birmingham City who went on to lose two finals in a row, defeated the following year by AS Roma, the only Italian club to lift the 'Coppa Delle Fiere'.

Following this brief Italian interlude, Spanish clubs returned to their position of predominance in the competition. Between 1962 and 1964 the final was an all Spanish affair, with Valencia winning twice in succession before losing out in the third consecutive year to rivals Real Zaragoza in a one-legged confrontation at Barcelona's Nou Camp stadium. The Mediterranean hegemony was finally broken by Hungarians Ferencváros in 1965, before Barcelona reclaimed the title again a year later.

There were more changes in 1967 when the competition was renamed the European Fairs Cup and increased to 48 entrants, the first of a succession of expansions that saw 64 sides competing by the 1969-70 season, by which time it was unofficially known as the 'Runners-Up Cup'. Never was a title more merited than in 1968 when the winners proved to be Leeds United. Don Revie's Leeds United had earned the status of 'nearly men' in English domestic football and were the beaten Fairs Cup finalists the previous season, losing to Dinamo Zagreb. However, Leeds shook off their 'bridesmaid' image, progressing smoothly past Partizan Belgrade, Hibernian, Rangers and Dundee,

before holding on to a narrow 1-0 first leg lead against Ferencváros.

Leeds United's first victory opened the door for English clubs to dominate the competition for six years, with Newcastle picking up the trophy the following season. The Magpies had finished tenth in the First Division the previous season but qualified on a one-city, one-team rule. They demonstrated their worth by seeing off the likes of Sporting Lisbon, Real Zaragoza and Glasgow Rangers before a 6-2 victory over an Újpest Dozsa side that featured six Hungarian internationals.

In 1970 Arsenal strode to their first European trophy despite finishing 12th in the league, the lowest position ever for the competition's winners. That victory broke a barren run stretching back 17 years and they beat a powerful Ajax on the way to the final with Anderlecht. Facing a 3-1 deficit from the away leg, The Gunners looked set to notch up an unenviable record of three final defeats in succession (they had lost two consecutive League Cups previously) but romped to a 3-0 win at Highbury.

Leeds then returned to prominence in 1971, taking what proved to be the last ever Fairs Cup by beating Juventus on away goals, a rule used for the first time in the competition's history, after the original match was abandoned due to an unplayable pitch.

With the competition being turned over to UEFA the following season, Leeds and Barcelona, as the two sides with the best overall playing record in the competition, contested

a specially organised play-off on September 22, 1971. Barcelona won 2-1 and the trophy now resides permanently at the Nou Camp.

The first winners of the new 1972 trophy – a handless silver cup on a yellow marble plinth designed and crafted by the Bertoni workshops in Milan – were Tottenham Hotspur, who came out on top in an all English affair with Wolverhampton Wanderers.

Liverpool's first UEFA Cup win the following year was the culmination of eight consecutive seasons of continental action, including a Fairs Cup semi-final – a record no other English club could boast. Their two-legged final with Borussia Mönchengladbach was an epic that included a first leg abandoned at Anfield due to a waterlogged pitch. Bill Shankly used those 27 minutes of wasted play to rejig his side, replacing Brian Hall with John Toshack the following evening – a move that saw them post a 3-0 win that Borussia could not quite pull back in the return. Liverpool went on to win again in 1976 and 2001, the latter game a 5-4 thriller against Spanish side Alaves, decided by a golden own-goal.

The 1974 competition was notable for the outbreak of crowd trouble at the final after Spurs fans went on the rampage following a 2-0 defeat in Rotterdam to Feyenoord, a display which led to the club being banned from the competition for two years. However, ten years later a fan died in rioting and 200 arrests were made after the Londoners beat Anderlecht in the competition's first penalty shoot-out, goalkeeper Tony Parks writing his name in club history.

After Liverpool's 1976 victory over the Belgians Club Brugge, it would be four years before another English side lifted the UEFA Cup, with Juventus, PSV Eindhoven, Borussia Mönchengladbach and Eintracht Frankfurt passing the trophy around.

Bobby Robson's Ipswich Town restored English pride in 1981, with Frans Thijssen and Arnold Muhren squaring up to fellow Dutchmen AZ 67 Alkmaar and emerging 5-4 aggregate winners. One year on the cup went to a Scandinavian side for the first time with IFK Gothenberg overcoming Germans Hamburg. The Swedes would lift the trophy again in 1987.

Tottenham's 1984 triumph effectively saw the end of English dominance as the Heysel disaster in the European Cup final a year later led to the banning of English clubs for six years. No English side would compete in the competition again until Aston Villa were allowed to enter in September 1990, beating the Czechs Banik Ostrava. It was 11 years before an English team actually lifted the cup again, when Liverpool beat Spanish side Alaves in a 5-4 thriller decided by an own golden goal, though Arsenal did reach the final against Galatasaray in Copenhagen in 2000, an occasion that resulted in further violence and the first ever UEFA win for a Turkish team.

The late Eighties saw Italian football belatedly make its mark on the competition. Maradona's Napoli broke the drought, beating Stuttgart in 1989, opening the door for Serie A clubs to dominate the UEFA Cup for a six-year run broken only by Ajax in 1992. Juventus and Inter were the main beneficiaries with three of the finals all-Italian affairs.

After two wins for German clubs the 1998 final again featured two Italian clubs in the competition's first straight, one-legged, head-to-head final; Milan beating Lazio 3-0 at the Parc Des Princes in Paris. By then the expansion of the Champions League had resulted in a further raft of changes to the competition (whose organisation was already based on a complicated system of country co-efficients), with those clubs failing to qualify for the major competition's group stages getting a bye into the next round of the UEFA.

In the 1999-2000 season the trophy was effectively merged with the European Cup Winners' Cup and further qualification routes were opened up to the three 'winners' of the Intertoto Cup and, ludicrously, three clubs from the countries with the best disciplinary record – Manchester City, final league place ninth, being one prime English benefactor in the 2003-2004 season.

The continual aggrandisement of the Champions League only serves to diminish the status of UEFA Cup further, to the point that the original 'Runners-Up Cup' is now facing another overhaul with the introduction of a Champions League-style group system to placate those clubs who cannot cut it in the bigger competition.

Whatever happens, from now on any major club lifting the trophy with no handles will only ever view it as a consolation prize.

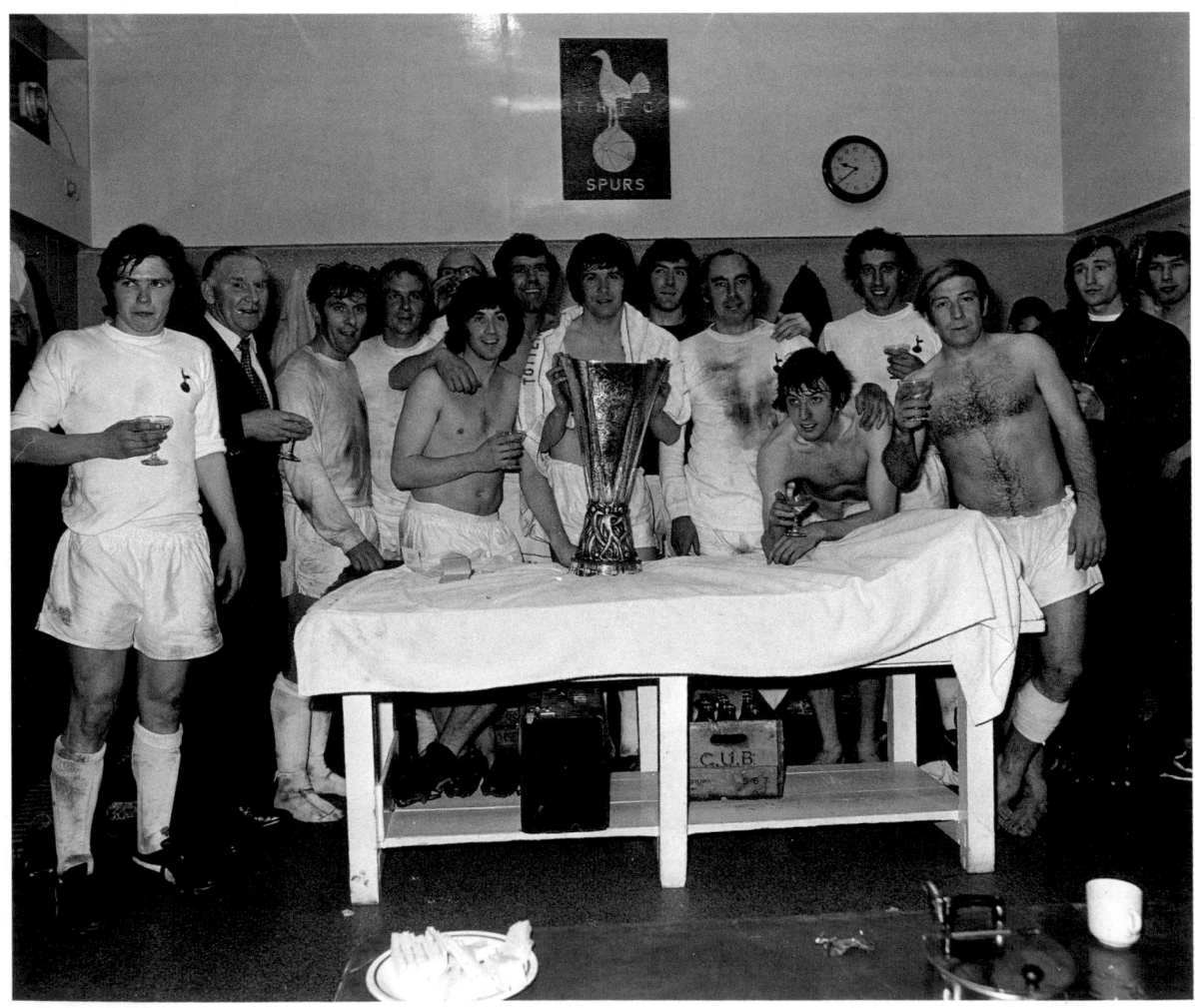

THE WINNERS OF THE FAIRS CUP/UEFA CUP

1958: BARCELONA
1ST LEG March 5
London Select XI **2-2** Barcelona
(England) (Spain)
2ND LEG May 1
Barcelona **6-0** London Select XI
Barcelona won 8-2 on aggregate

1960: BARCELONA
1ST LEG March 29
Birmingham City **0-0** Barcelona
(England) (Spain)
2ND LEG May 4
Barcelona **4-1** Birmingham City
Barcelona won 4-1 on aggregate

1961: AS ROMA
1ST LEG September 27
Birmingham City **2-2** Roma
(England) (Italy)
2ND LEG October 11
Roma **2-0** Birmingham City
Roma won 4-2 on aggregate

1962: VALENCIA
1ST LEG August 9
Valencia **6-2** Barcelona
(Spain) (Spain)
2ND LEG September 9
Barcelona **1-1** Valencia
Valencia won 7-3 on aggregate

1963: VALENCIA
1ST LEG June 12
Dynamo Zagreb **1-2** Valencia
(Yugoslavia) (Spain)
2ND LEG June 26
Valencia **2-0** Dynamo Zagreb
Valencia won 4-1 on aggregate

1964: REAL ZARAGOZA
NOU CAMP, BARCELONA June 25
Real Zaragoza **2-1** Valencia
(Spain) (Spain)

1965: FERENCVÁROS
COMUNALE, TURIN June 23
Ferencváros **1-0** Juventus
(Hungary) (Italy)

1966: BARCELONA
1ST LEG September 14
Barcelona **0-1** Real Zaragoza
(Spain) (Spain)
2ND LEG September 21
Real Zaragoza **2-4** Barcelona (aet)
Barcelona won 4-3 on aggregate

1967: DYNAMO ZAGREB
1ST LEG August 30
Dynamo Zagreb **2-0** Leeds United
(Yugoslavia) (England)
2ND LEG September 6
Leeds United **0-0** Dynamo Zagreb
Dynamo Zagreb won 2-0 on aggregate

1968: LEEDS UNITED
1ST LEG September 7
Leeds United **1-0** Ferencváros
(England) (Hungary)
2ND LEG September 11
Ferencváros **0-0** Leeds United
Leeds United won 1-0 on aggregate

1969: NEWCASTLE UNITED
1ST LEG May 29
Newcastle United **3-0** Újpest Dozsa
(England) (Hungary)
2ND LEG June 11
Újpest Dozsa **2-3** Newcastle United
Newcastle United won 6-2 on aggregate

1970: ARSENAL
1ST LEG April 22
Anderlecht **3-1** Arsenal
(Belgium) (England)
2ND LEG April 28
Arsenal **3-0** Anderlecht
Arsenal won 4-3 on aggregate

1971: LEEDS UNITED
1ST LEG May 26
Juventus **0-0** Leeds United
(Italy) (England)
Match abandoned after 51 mins waterlogged pitch
1ST LEG REPLAY May 28
Juventus **2-2** Leeds United
2ND LEG June 3
Leeds United **1-1** Juventus
Leeds United won on away goals rule

The Fairs Cup was replaced by The UEFA Cup in the 1971-72 season

1972: TOTTENHAM HOTSPUR
1ST LEG May 3
Wolverhampton **1-2** Tottenham
Wanderers Hotspur
(England) (England)
2ND LEG May 17
Tottenham **1-1** Wolverhampton
Hotspur Wanderers
Tottenham Hotspur won 3-2 on aggregate

1973: LIVERPOOL
1ST LEG May 9
Liverpool **0-0** Borussia
Mönchengladbach
(England) (West Germany)
Match abandoned after 27 mins waterlogged pitch
1ST LEG REPLAY May 10
Liverpool **3-0** Borussia
Mönchengladbach
2ND LEG May 23
Borussia **2-0** Liverpool
Mönchengladbach
Liverpool won 3-2 on aggregate

1974: FEYENOORD
1ST LEG May 21
Tottenham **2-2** Feyenoord
Hotspur
(England) (Holland)
2ND LEG May 29
Feyenoord **2-0** Tottenham
Hotspur
Feyenoord won 4-2 on aggregate

1975: B. MÖNCHENGLADBACH
1ST LEG May 7
Borussia **0-0** FC Twente
Mönchengladbach
(West Germany) (Holland)
2ND LEG September 11
FC Twente **1-5** Borussia
Mönchengladbach
Borussia Mönchengladbach won 5-1 on aggregate

1976: LIVERPOOL
1ST LEG April 28
Liverpool **3-2** Club Brugge
(England) (Belgium)
2ND LEG May 19
Club Brugge **1-1** Liverpool
Liverpool won 4-3 on aggregate

1977: JUVENTUS
1ST LEG May 4
Juventus **1-0** Athletic Bilbao
(Italy) (Spain)
2ND LEG May 18
Athletic Bilbao **2-1** Juventus
Juventus won on away goal rule

1978: PSV EINDHOVEN
1ST LEG April 26
SC Bastia **0-0** PSV Eindhoven
(France) (Holland)
2ND LEG May 9
PSV Eindhoven **3-0** SC Bastia
PSV Eindhoven won 3-0 on aggregate

1979: B. MÖNCHENGLADBACH
1ST LEG May 9
Red Star Belgrade **1-1** Borussia
Mönchengladbach
(Yugoslavia) (West Germany)
2ND LEG May 23
Borussia **1-0** Red Star Belgrade
Mönchengladbach
Borussia Mönchengladbach won 2-1 on aggregate

1980: EINTRACHT FRANKFURT
1ST LEG May 7
Borussia **3-2** Eintracht
Mönchengladbach Frankfurt
(West Germany) (West Germany)
2ND LEG May 21
Eintracht **1-0** Borussia
Frankfurt Mönchengladbach
Eintracht Frankfurt won on away goal rule

1981: IPSWICH TOWN
1ST LEG May 6
Ipswich Town **3-0** AZ 67 Alkmaar
(England) (Holland)
2ND LEG May 20
AZ 67 Alkmaar **4-2** Ipswich Town
Ipswich Town won 5-4 on aggregate

1982: IFK GOTHENBURG
1ST LEG May 5
IFK Gothenburg **1-0** Hamburg
(Sweden) (West Germany)
2ND LEG May 19
Hamburg **0-3** IFK Gothenburg
IFK Gothenburg won 4-0 on aggregate

1983: RSC ANDERLECHT
1ST LEG May 4
Anderlecht **1-0** Benfica
(Belgium) (Portugal)
2ND LEG May 18
Benfica **1-1** Anderlecht
RSC Anderlecht won 2-1 on aggregate

1984: TOTTENHAM HOTSPUR
1ST LEG May 9
Anderlecht **1-1** Tottenham
Hotspur
(Belgium) (England)
2ND LEG May 23
Tottenham **1-1** Anderlecht (aet)
Hotspur
Tottenham Hotspur won 4-3 on penalties

1985: REAL MADRID
1ST LEG May 8
Videoton **0-3** Real Madrid
(Hungary) (Spain)
2ND LEG May 22
Real Madrid **0-1** Videoton
Real Madrid won 3-1 on aggregate

1986: REAL MADRID
1ST LEG April 30
Real Madrid **5-1** Köln
(Spain) (West Germany)
2ND LEG May 6
Köln **2-0** Real Madrid
Real Madrid won 5-3 on aggregate

1987: IFK GOTHENBURG
1ST LEG May 6
IFK Gothenburg **1-0** Dundee United
(Sweden) (Scotland)
2ND LEG May 20
Dundee United **1-1** IFK Gothenburg
IFK Gothenburg won 2-1 on aggregate

1988: BEYER LEVERKUSEN
1ST LEG May 4
Espanyol **3-0** Bayer Leverkusen
(Spain) (West Germany)
2ND LEG May 18
Bayer Leverkusen **3-0** Espanyol (aet)
Bayer Leverkusen won 3-2 on penalties

1989: NAPOLI
1ST LEG May 3
Napoli **2-1** Vfb Stuttgart
(Italy) (West Germany)
2ND LEG May 17
Vfb Stuttgart **3-3** Napoli
Napoli won 5-4 on aggregate

1990: JUVENTUS
1ST LEG May 2
Juventus **3-1** Fiorentina
(Italy) (Italy)
2ND LEG May 16
Fiorentina **0-0** Juventus
Juventus won 3-1 on aggregate

1991: INTER MILAN
1ST LEG May 8
Inter Milan **2-0** AS Roma
(Italy) (Italy)
2ND LEG May 22
AS Roma **1-0** Inter Milan
Inter Milan won 2-1 on aggregate

1992: AJAX
1ST LEG April 29
Torino **2-2** Ajax
(Italy) (Holland)
2ND LEG May 13
Ajax **0-0** Torino
Ajax won on away goals rule

1993: JUVENTUS
1ST LEG May 5
Borussia **1-3** Juventus
Dortmund
(Germany) (Italy)
2ND LEG May 19
Juventus **3-0** Borussia
Dortmund
Juventus won 6-1 on aggregate

1994: INTER MILAN
1ST LEG April 26
Austria Salzburg **0-1** Inter Milan
(Austria) (Italy)
2ND LEG May 11
Inter Milan **1-0** Austria Salzburg
Inter Milan won 2-0 on aggregate

1995: PARMA
1ST LEG May 3
Parma **1-0** Juventus
(Italy) (Italy)
2ND LEG May 17
Juventus **1-1** Parma
Parma won 2-1 on aggregate

1996: BAYERN MUNICH
1ST LEG May 1
Bayern Munich **2-0** Bordeaux
(Germany) (France)
2ND LEG May 15
Bordeaux **1-3** Bayern Munich
Bayern Munich won 5-1 on aggregate

1997: FC SCHALKE 04
1ST LEG May 7
FC Schalke 04 **1-0** Inter Milan
(Germany) (Italy)
2ND LEG May 21
Inter Milan **1-0** FC Schalke 04
(aet)
FC Schalke 04 won 4-1 on penalties

1998: INTER MILAN
PARC DES PRINCES, PARIS May 6
Lazio **0-3** Inter Milan
(Italy) (Italy)

1999: PARMA
LUZHNIKI, MOSCOW May 12
Parma **3-0** Marseille
(Italy) (France)

2000: GALATASARAY
PARKEN, COPENHAGEN May 17
Galatasaray **0-0** Arsenal (aet)
(Turkey) (England)
Galatasaray won 4-1 on penalties

2001: LIVERPOOL
WESTFALENSTADION, DORTMUND May 16
Liverpool **5-4** Alavés (aet)
(England) (Spain)

2002: FEYENOORD
DEKUIP, ROTTERDAM May 8
Feyenoord **3-2** Borussia
Dortmund
(Holland) (Germany)

2003: FC PORTO
OLIMPICO, SEVILLE May 21
FC Porto **3-2** Celtic
(Portugal) (Scotland)

EUROPEAN CUP WINNERS' CUP

Above from left to right: Real Zaragoza, Aberdeen and Werder Bremen were among the smaller clubs who tasted success in the Cup Winners' Cup.

Opposite clockwise from top left: Dennis Wise and Gianluca Vialli after Chelsea became the last British club to win the cup in 1998; goalscorer Bruno N'Gotty lifts the cup after Paris Saint-Germain's 1996 win; Lazio celebrate winning the last ever Cup Winners' Cup in 1999; Tomas Brolin enjoys Parma's 1993 win at Wembley.

When Lazio's Pavel Nedved struck home the winning goal against Mallorca in the 81st minute of the 1999 European Cup Winners' Cup Final at Villa Park, he was not only ensuring the win for the Rome side, he was also entering the history books as the last ever player to score in the tournament. After 39 years the competition was discontinued, and swallowed up by the expanded UEFA Cup. This was due in the most part to the increased importance of the Champions League, and pressure on UEFA to streamline its European club fixtures. The final nail in the competition's coffin could be said to be Barcelona's decision to play in the Champions League rather than defend their title in 1998.

The European Cup Winners' Cup was launched in 1960, and organised to run in parallel with the UEFA Cup. Based on the same format as the European Cup, with home and away knock-out ties up to the final, the participants in the competition were generally the winners of their domestic cup, as well as the previous season's holders. However, if the cup winners were identical to the winners of the national championship (who would therefore be competing in the European Cup), the runners-up in the cup competition would-take part. At the time the tournament was established many European countries didn't possess a domestic cup competition, but the promise of qualification and extra revenue meant they soon acquired one.

The first Cup Winners' Cup tournament attracted teams from ten countries. Inspired

by legendary Swedish winger Kurt Hamrin, the trophy was won by Fiorentina – the first piece of European silverware to be won by an Italian side. They overcame Rangers 4-1 on aggregate in a final played over two legs (the format changed to a one-off game the following year). Rangers themselves reached the final after disposing of Wolverhampton Wanderers in a keenly contested all-British semi-final. With the competition deemed a success, the following year saw a far larger pool of entrants, with some 23 countries now taking part. The final again saw Fiorentina involved, but this time they were deprived of the distinction of retaining their title by Atlético Madrid, who lifted the cup after a 3-0 replay win. Curiously, the replay was played nearly four months after the original game.

In 1963 the holders once again had the opportunity to retain their trophy by making it to the final, but this time Atlético fell at the last hurdle. Their conquerors were Bill Nicholson's double-winning Tottenham side, and the result was an emphatic 5-1 win with the prolific Jimmy Greaves and Terry Dyson both getting on the scoresheet twice. The victory made Tottenham the first English club to get their hands on a European trophy. Over the course of its 39 years the Cup Winners' Cup saw many British clubs making it to the final. In 1965, in front of a 100,000 capacity Wembley crowd, West Ham United brought the trophy back to London with their 2-0 defeat of TSV 1860 Munich. Neighbours Chelsea made it a hat-trick for sides from the English

capital in 1971 with their stunning Peter Osgood-inspired replay victory over the mighty Real Madrid. The year before, northern pride had been restored with Manchester City's victory over Górnik Zabrze of Poland. The silverware heading to Maine Road thanks to goals by Neil Young and Francis Lee.

Rangers were also in on the act, and over the course of the 1972 final they narrowly got the better of Dynamo Moscow, coming out of the game 3-2 winners after leading 3-0 for much of the game. This was third time lucky for the Glasgow side, who were on the wrong end of two final defeats in 1960 and 1967. It wasn't always plain sailing for the English clubs that made the final either. In the 1966 final Liverpool were unlucky to lose out to Borussia Dortmund after extra-time, and a similar fate befell Leeds United (1973), West Ham (1976) and Arsenal (1980 and 1995) in subsequent finals. That 1980 defeat was against Valencia, and after a 0-0 draw it was the first European final to be decided on penalties. It was former England midfielder Graham Rix's failure from the spot that gave the Spaniards the trophy.

After an 11 year gap without any British success it was left to Alex Ferguson's Aberdeen to heroically recapture the Cup Winners' Cup in 1983, and they achieved it at the expense of Real Madrid. Played in atrocious weather conditions, the match was settled by substitute John Hewitt's diving header in extra-time and was a famous victory for the Scottish side. Since Aberdeen's triumph there have been four other British successes. In 1985 Howard

Kendall's Everton disposed of Rapid Vienna with a clinical 3-1 win with goals from Andy Gray, Trevor Steven and Kevin Sheedy. It was to be the last time English clubs participated in European competition until 1991, following their ban in the wake of the Heysel tragedy. This was the year that year saw Manchester United take the honours from Barcelona with Mark Hughes starring in a 2-1 win.

In 1994 Arsenal finally got their name on the trophy with a 1-0 victory, courtesy of an Alan Smith goal against the much-fancied Parma. The following year they were to suffer heartache as former Tottenham midfielder Nayim, now playing for Real Zaragoza, famously chipped David Seaman from the vicinity of the half-way line. The last English side to win the trophy were Chelsea, who secured the title for a second time with a narrow win against Stuttgart in Stockholm, thanks to an opportunistic Gianfranco Zola strike. The Italian had only come on a minute earlier as a substitute and found the roof of the net with his first touch.

Other teams to win the Cup Winners' Cup on more than one occasion were AC Milan (1968 and 1973), Anderlecht (1976 and 1978), and Dynamo Kiev (1975 and 1986). However, if there was one team who could lay claim to being the team of the tournament over its entire history, then it would have to be Barcelona. The Catalan side have lifted the trophy four times – ironic then, that their refusal to play in the tournament in 1998 would (indirectly) lead to the discontinuance of the competition.

Their first success was in the 1979 final when they edged out Fortuna Düsseldorf 4-3 in extra-time in one of the great finals. The 1982 final saw them storm to victory over Standard Liege in front of 100,000 fans in their own stadium, while a 2-0 victory over

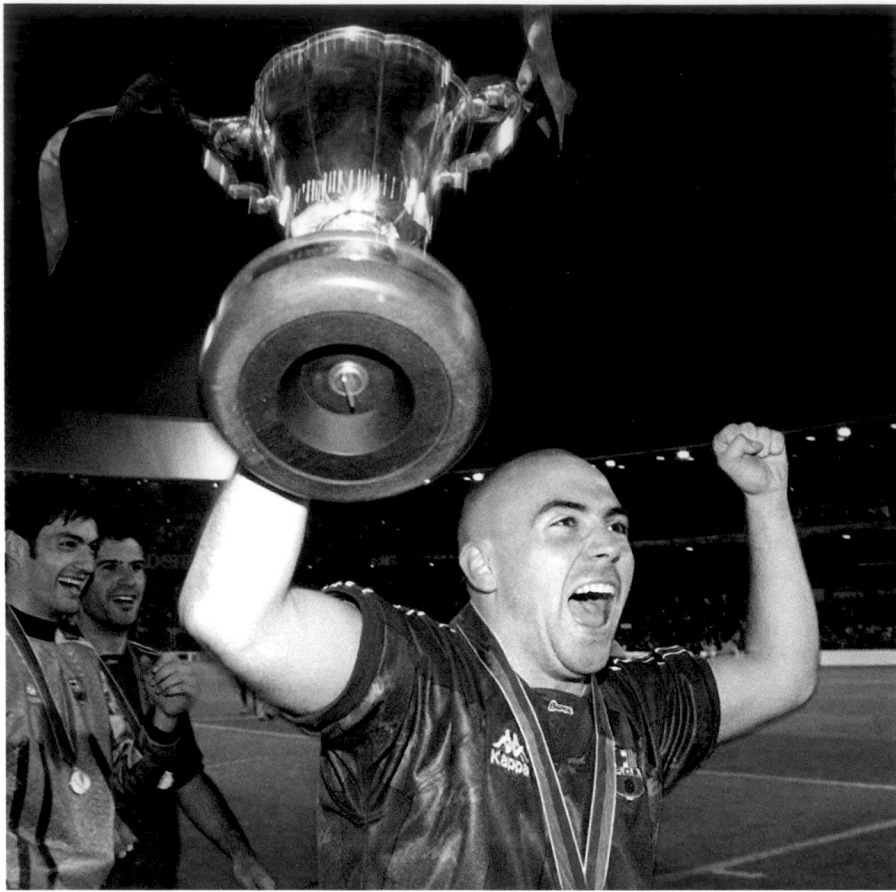

Italian's Sampdoria in 1989 at the Wankdorf Stadium in Switzerland saw them complete a hat-trick of victories. The string of successes was rounded off in the 1997 final when Ronaldo's 37th minute penalty was enough to defeat Paris Saint-Germain. The French side were the holders of the trophy, and with no side ever managing to retain the Cup Winners' Cup, history, as well as the referee's whistle, was clearly against them.

Throughout the history of the tournament many of the high-profile sides, such as

Barcelona, have laid claim to the trophy. However, part of the event's charm lay in the fact that some of the lesser known club sides were also able to compete against the major teams of European football – something that rarely happened in the UEFA Cup, and was even scarcer in the European Cup. In 1981, arguably the greatest ever shock of the Cup Winners' Cup came about when Welsh Cup winners Newport County somehow managed to eliminate the holders Valencia. Newport were in the English Division Four at the time.

Smaller clubs to go all the way to the final have included Slovan Bratislava, who in 1969 saw off the challenge of Barcelona in a famous 3-2 victory for the Slovak side. While in 1974 FC Magdeburg of East Germany held the trophy aloft after beating a star-studded AC Milan side 2-0 in Rotterdam. Georgia's Dinamo Tbilisi ran out winners in 1981, and Belgium's Mechelen also added their name to the roll of honour in 1988 with a win over Dutch giants Ajax.

Always the third tournament behind the European Cup and the UEFA Cup in terms of prestige in the European club calendar, nevertheless the Cup Winners' Cup packed a lot of passion, spectacle and great football into its 39 year history. Nedved's goal ensures that Lazio will be the holders of the trophy in perpetuity, but such giants of the game as Barcelona, AC Milan, Manchester United and Juventus all have fond memories of a trophy that for a period of time proudly sat in a special place in their trophy cabinet.

THE WINNERS OF THE EUROPEAN CUP WINNERS' CUP

1961: FIORENTINA
1ST LEG May 17
Rangers **0-2** Fiorentina
(Scotland)   (Italy)
2ND LEG May 27
Fiorentina **2-1** Rangers
Fiorentina won 4-1 on aggregate

1962: ATLÉTICO MADRID
HAMPDEN PARK, GLASGOW May 10
Atlético Madrid **1-1** Fiorentina
(Spain)   (Italy)
REPLAY: NECKARSTADION, STUTTGART
September 5
Atlético Madrid **3-0** Fiorentina

1963: TOTTENHAM HOTSPUR
DE KUIP, ROTTERDAM May 15
Tottenham **5-1** Atlético Madrid
Hotspur
(England)   (Spain)

1964: SPORTING LISBON
HEYSEL, BRUSSELS May 13
Sporting Lisbon **3-3** MTK Budapest
(aet)
(Portugal)   (Hungary)
REPLAY, BOSUILSTADION ANTWERP
May 15
Sporting Lisbon **1-0** MTK Budapest

1965: WEST HAM UNITED
WEMBLEY, LONDON May 19
West Ham United **2-0** 1860 Munich
(England)   (West Germany)

1966: BORUSSIA DORTMUND
HAMPDEN PARK, GLASGOW May 5
Borussia **2-1** Liverpool (aet)
Dortmund
(West Germany)   (England)

1967: BAYERN MUNICH
FRANKENSTADION, NÜREMBERG May 31
Bayern Munich **1-0** Rangers (aet)
(West Germany)   (Scotland)

1968: AC MILAN
DE KUIP, ROTTERDAM May 23
AC Milan **2-0** Hamburg
(Italy)   (West Germany)

1969: SLOVAN BRATISLAVA
ST JAKOB, BASLE May 21
Slovan Bratislava **3-2** Barcelona
(Czechoslovakia)   (Spain)

1970: MANCHESTER CITY
PRATER, VIENNA May 29
Manchester City **2-1** Górnik Zabrze
(England)   (Poland)

1971: CHELSEA
KARAISKAKIS, PIRAEUS May 19
Chelsea **1-1** Real Madrid
(England)   (Spain)
REPLAY: KARAISKAKIS, PIRAEUS May 21
Chelsea **2-1** Real Madrid

1972: RANGERS
NOU CAMP, BARCELONA May 24
Rangers **3-2** Dinamo Moscow
(Scotland)   (USSR)

1973: AC MILAN
KAFTANTZOGLIO SALONICA May 16
AC Milan **1-0** Leeds United
(Italy)   (England)

1974: FC MAGDEBURG
DE KUIP, ROTTERDAM May 8
FC Magdeburg **2-0** AC Milan
(East Germany)   (Italy)

1975: KIEV DYNAMO
ST JAKOB, BASLE May 14
Dynamo Kiev **3-0** Ferencváros
(USSR)   (Hungary)

1976: RSC ANDERLECHT
HEYSEL, BRUSSELS May 5
Anderlecht **4-2** West Ham United
(Belgium)   (England)

1977: HAMBURG
OLYMPISCH, AMSTERDAM May 11
Hamburg **2-0** RSC Anderlecht
(West Germany)   (Belgium)

1978: RSC ANDERLECHT
PARC DES PRINCES, PARIS May 3
Anderlecht **4-0** Austria Vienna
(Belgium)   (Austria)

1979: BARCELONA
ST JAKOB, BASLE May 16
Barcelona **4-3** Fortuna
Düsseldorf (aet)
(Spain)   (West Germany)

1980: VALENCIA
HEYSEL, BRUSSELS May 15
Valencia **0-0** Arsenal (aet)
(Spain)   (England)
Valencia won 5-4 on penalties

1981: DYNAMO TBILISI
RHEINSTADION, DÜSSELDORF May 13
Dynamo Tbilisi **2-1** FC Carl-Zeiss
Jena
(USSR)   (East Germany)

1982: BARCELONA
NOU CAMP, BARCELONA May 12
Barcelona **2-1** Standard Liège
(Spain)   (Belgium)

1983: ABERDEEN
NYA ULLEVI, GOTHENBURG May 11
Aberdeen **2-1** Real Madrid (aet)
(Scotland)   (Spain)

1984: JUVENTUS
ST JAKOB, BASLE May 16
Juventus **2-1** FC Porto
(Italy)   (Portugal)

1985: EVERTON
DE KUIP, ROTTERDAM May 15
Everton **3-1** Rapid Vienna
(England)   (Austria)

1986: DYNAMO KIEV
GERLAND, LYON May 2
Dynamo Kiev **3-0** Atlético Madrid
(USSR)   (Spain)

1987: AJAX
OLYMPIC STADIUM, ATHENS May 13
Ajax **1-0** Lokomotive
Leipzig
(Netherlands)   (East Germany)

1988: KV MECHELEN
MEINAU, STRASBOURG May 11
KV Mechelen **1-0** Ajax
(Belgium)   (Holland)

1989: BARCELONA
WANKDORF, BERNE May 10
Barcelona **2-0** Sampdoria
(Spain)   (Italy)

1990: SAMPDORIA
NYA ULLEVI, GOTHENBURG May 9
Sampdoria **2-0** Anderlecht (aet)
(Italy)   (Belgium)

1991: MANCHESTER UNITED
DE KUIP, ROTTERDAM May 15
Manchester **2-1** Barcelona
United
(England)   (Spain)

1992: WERDER BREMEN
ESTADIO DA LUZ, LISBON May 6
Werder Bremen **2-0** Monaco
(Germany)   (France)

1993: PARMA
WEMBLEY, LONDON May 12
Parma **3-1** Royal Antwerp
(Italy)   (Belgium)

1994: ARSENAL
PARKEN, COPENHAGEN May 4
Arsenal **1-0** Parma
(England)   (Italy)

1995: REAL ZARAGOZA
PARC DES PRINCES, PARIS May 10
Real Zaragoza **2-1** Arsenal (aet)
(Spain)   (England)

1996: PARIS SAINT-GERMAIN
KING BAUDOUIN, BRUSSELS May 8
Paris Saint- **1-0** Rapid Vienna
Germain
(France)   (Austria)

1997: BARCELONA
DE KUIP, ROTTERDAM May 14
Barcelona **1-0** Paris Saint-
Germain
(Spain)   (France)

1998: CHELSEA
RASUNDA, STOCKHOLM May 13
Chelsea **1-0** Stuttgart
(England)   (Germany)

1999: LAZIO
VILLA PARK, BIRMINGHAM May 19
Lazio **2-1** Mallorca
(Italy)   (Spain)

COPA LIBERTADORES

(THE SOUTH AMERICAN CLUB CUP)

Above from left to right: Copa Libertadores winners in recent years have included Olimpia (2002), River Plate (1996) and Vasco da Gama (1998).

Opposite clockwise from top left: Boca Juniors triumphed in 2000; victors in 1999, Palmeiras; 1997 champions Cruzeiro; Grêmio take home the title in 1995.

The Copa Libertadores is the premier club event in South America, and has been played between the continent's top sides on an annual basis since its inception in 1960. Very much the equivalent of the European Cup, the competition was sparked into life when UEFA proposed that the champions of Europe should play against the South American champions for a world title (the World Club Cup). Seven national league winners competed home and away on a knock-out basis. In the inaugural tournament it was Uruguay's Peñarol who were first to lift the trophy, beating Olimpia of Paraguay 1-0 in the first leg and drawing 0-0 in the second. Rather than winning on goal aggregate, however, they were deemed to have won on points aggregate having a win and a draw to Olimpia's one draw and one defeat. This system continued until 1988 when goal aggregate was introduced.

The competition was not without historical precedent, as in 1948 a similar tournament was held in Chile, staged by Santiago's leading club, Colo Colo. The event was won by Brazil's Vasco Da Gama, but proved to be such a financial disaster for all involved that it was not staged again. It was with such an uncertain legacy that the current Copa Libertadores was launched. However, the tournament has not only survived but flourished over the years, despite many format changes and many moments of controversy, to become the most important date in the South American football calendar – far exceeding the national Copa América in terms of popularity.

In 1962 Pele, by then a star on the global stage, gave the competition's profile a much-needed image boost as his Santos side got the better of Peñarol (still the champions after having retained their title in 1961). Sadly, the final is not remembered for the glamour of the occasion. The first leg in Montevideo had been played out without incident, resulting in a 2-1 win for Santos. But the second leg was far more unsavoury, the game being suspended shortly after half-time as the referee was knocked unconscious by a stone thrown from the crowd. After a considerable delay the game was restarted with Peñarol ahead 3-2, only for a linesman to endure the same fate, just as Peñarol were on the verge of adding to their lead. The game was suspended and awarded to the Uruguayans, forcing a play-off which saw Santos come out eventual winners 3-0. The following year they retained the trophy, beating Boca Juniors convincingly both home and away with Pele at the fore.

It was to be the last time a Brazilian side won the Copa Libertadores for 13 years. This was due, in part, to the strong Argentinian teams taking the event more seriously, but also due to a four-year Brazilian boycott of the competition from 1966 to 1970, after an amendment to the competition's format, as originally proposed by the Uruguayan football association, accommodated the entry of league runners-up. The extra fixtures not only caused disruption to the Brazilian national league, but reduced the tournament's financial rewards. The boycott opened the door for Peñarol to

claim another title, this time snatching victory from River Plate with 4-2 win after a replay – two of the goals were scored by Alberto Spencer, one of the tournament's most prolific marksmen. Sadly, the event was again spoilt by controversy, as two former Peñarol players in the River Plate side, Cubilla and Matosas, were accused of deliberately performing badly and 'throwing' the game.

In 1969, Argentinian clubs followed Brazil's example and played no part in the tournament in protest over fixture congestion. This action inevitably lead to CONMEBOL streamlining the tournament by reducing the number of group matches.

In 1970 the powerhouses of Brazil and Argentina rejoined the passionate fray. And it was the latter, in the shape of Buenos Aires club side Independiente, who dominated proceedings with a remarkable run of four consecutive titles. In 1972 The Red Devils got the better of Universitario de Deportes of Peru, while Colo Colo were their victims the following year in a close fought play-off game. Once again the 1974 final couldn't be decided over two legs, but Independiente held their nerve to claim a 1-0 victory over São Paulo.

Their fantastic run culminated with a win over Chile's Unión Española in 1975. Again the tournament was won as a result of a play-off game, with the Argentinian side coming out 2-0 winners with goals from Ruiz Moreno and Bertoni. Independiente still hold the record for the most Copa Libertadores wins with seven (followed by Peñarol with five).

Above: Boca Juniors beat Santos to win the title in 2003.

Below right: Paraguay's Olimpia celebrate victory over São Caetano in 2002.

Opposite: Action from the 2002 final between Olimpia and São Caetano.

Independiente's run of unparalleled success was finally brought to an end by Brazil's Cruzeiro, who included veteran Jairzinho in their side. However, with the notable exception of a Zico-inspired Flamengo in 1981, it was to be Argentinian and Uruguayan teams that continued to dominate the Copa Libertadores in the late Seventies and through the Eighties. Boca Juniors won the trophy in 1977 and 1978, with Argentinian sides River Plate, Argentinos Juniors and Independiente also savouring victory during a rich period for the nation. For Uruguay, both Peñarol (1982 and 1987) and Nacional (1980 and 1988) completed a brace of victories. The latter's 1988 win was to be the last time a Uruguayan side picked up the cup.

The smaller nations, however, were at last beginning to challenge the long-established Argentina/Brazil/Uruguay monopoly. The first instance of success outside this triumvirate was Olimpia of Paraguay's surprise victory in the 1979 competition – they defeated the mighty Boca Juniors 2-0 in their home leg, and managed to secure a 0-0 draw in Buenos Aires to claim the Copa Libertadores. From 1985 through to 1987, Colombian side America de Cali competed in three consecutive finals, but were unfortunate to be runners-up each time. A similar fate was undergone earlier by Cobreloa of Chile, who finished on the losing end of consecutive finals in 1981 and 1982. But the less celebrated nations were not to be denied their place in the sun: Colombia's Atletico Nacional narrowly defeated Olimpia in 1989, and the following year the Paraguayan

side made it to the final again, this time defeating Ecuador's Barcelona on aggregate. In 1991 the pattern continued and the big boys were once again frozen out, Chile claiming its first ever Copa Libertadores trophy with Colo Colo's triumph over Olimpia.

These successes coincided with the format change in 1988 of two-leg knockouts for the quarter-finals and semi-finals, and extra-time and penalties to decide the outcome of the final (replacing the play-off).

Considering the country's dominance on the international stage, the record of Brazilian club sides coming into the Nineties was a relatively poor one. This was all set to change, however. In 1992, with talented midfielder Rai pulling the strings in midfield, São Paulo beat Newell's Old Boys 3-2 on penalties. The following year, including internationals such as Cafu, Palinha and Muller among their ranks, they defeated Chile's Universidad Catolica 5-3 on aggregate. The competition, always reflecting the shift in power of South American club football, then saw Brazilian sides win a further four of the next six titles, with separate wins for Grêmio, Cruzeiro, Vasco da Gama and Palmeiras.

Trends never last forever in the South American Club Cup though, and the new millennium saw a resurgence from Argentine giants, Boca Juniors. A talented side, under the management of Carlos Bianchi, claimed back-to-back titles in 2000 and 2001 with victories on penalties against Palmeiras and Cruz Azul (clubs from Mexico were first invited to play in 1999). Indeed, 2001 saw the Copa Libertadores relaunched with yet another new format, plus a lucrative TV deal and extended sponsorship. Where previously only five sides were eliminated at the group stages, now 16 dropped out. This has helped to discourage negative play, and the more attacking style of football has made the competition much more entertaining.

The competition has now become more popular than ever. Despite its many problems in the past, and the current dire financial plight of many of South America's high-profile club sides, the ever-improving Copa Libertadores has the strength and will to keep evolving, and is now truly established as one of the great international club competitions.

THE WINNERS OF THE COPA LIBERTADORES

1960: PEÑAROL

1ST LEG June 12
Peñarol **1-0** Olimpia
(Uruguay)   (Paraguay)

2ND LEG June 19
Olimpia **1-1** Peñarol
Peñarol won on points aggregate

1961: PEÑAROL

1ST LEG June 9
Peñarol **1-0** Palmeiras
(Uruguay)   (Brazil)

2ND LEG June 11
Palmeiras **1-1** Peñarol
Peñarol won on points aggregate

1962: SANTOS

1ST LEG July 28
Peñarol **1-2** Santos
(Uruguay)   (Brazil)

2ND LEG August 2
Santos **2-3** Peñarol

PLAY-OFF August 30
Santos **3-0** Peñarol

1963: SANTOS

1ST LEG September 3
Santos **3-2** Boca Juniors
(Brazil)   (Argentina)

2ND LEG September 11
Boca Juniors **1-2** Santos
Santos won on points aggregate

1964: INDEPENDIENTE

1ST LEG August 6
Nacional **0-0** Independiente
(Uruguay)   (Argentina)

2ND LEG August 12
Independiente **1-0** Nacional
Independiente won on points aggregate

1965: INDEPENDIENTE

1ST LEG April 9
Independiente **1-0** Peñarol
(Argentina)   (Uruguay)

2ND LEG April 12
Peñarol **3-1** Independiente

PLAY-OFF April 15
Independiente **4-1** Peñarol

1966: PEÑAROL

1ST LEG May 12
Peñarol **2-0** River Plate
(Uruguay)   (Argentina)

2ND LEG May 18
River Plate **3-2** Peñarol

PLAY-OFF May 20
Peñarol **4-2** River Plate (aet)

1967: RACING CLUB

1ST LEG August 15
Racing Club **0-0** Nacional
(Argentina)   (Uruguay)

2ND LEG August 25
Nacional **0-0** Racing Club
(aet)

PLAY-OFF August 29
Racing Club **2-1** Nacional

1968: ESTUDIANTES DE LA PLATA

1ST LEG May 2
Estudiantes **2-1** Palmeiras
de La Plata
(Argentina)   (Brazil)

2ND LEG May 7
Palmeiras **3-1** Estudiantes
de La Plata

PLAY-OFF May 15
Estudiantes **2-0** Palmeiras
de La Plata

1969: ESTUDIANTES DE LA PLATA

1ST LEG May 15
Nacional **0-1** Estudiantes
de La Plata
(Uruguay)   (Argentina)

2ND LEG May 22
Estudiantes **2-0** Nacional
de La Plata
Estudiantes de La Plata on points aggregate

1970: ESTUDIANTES DE LA PLATA

1ST LEG May 21
Estudiantes **1-0** Peñarol
de La Plata
(Argentina)   (Uruguay)

2ND LEG May 27
Peñarol **0-0** Estudiantes
de La Plata
Estudiantes de La Plata on points aggregate

1971: NACIONAL

1ST LEG May 26
Estudiantes **1-0** Nacional
de La Plata
(Argentina)   (Uruguay)

2ND LEG June 2
Nacional **1-0** Estudiantes
de La Plata

PLAY-OFF June 9
Nacional **2-0** Estudiantes
de La Plata

1972: INDEPENDIENTE

1ST LEG May 17
Universitario **0-0** Independiente
de Deportes
(Peru)   (Argentina)

2ND LEG May 24
Independiente **2-1** Universitario
de Deportes
Independiente won on points aggregate

1973: INDEPENDIENTE

1ST LEG May 22
Independiente **1-1** Colo Colo
(Argentina)   (Chile)

2ND LEG May 29
Colo Colo **0-0** Independiente

PLAY-OFF June 6
Independiente **2-1** Colo Colo (aet)

1974: INDEPENDIENTE

1ST LEG October 12
São Paulo **2-1** Independiente
(Brazil)   (Argentina)

2ND LEG October 16
Independiente **2-0** São Paulo

PLAY-OFF October 19
Independiente **1-0** São Paulo

1975: INDEPENDIENTE

1ST LEG June 18
Unión Española **1-0** Independiente
(Chile)   (Argentina)

2ND LEG June 25
Independiente **3-1** Unión Española

PLAY-OFF June 29
Independiente **2-0** Unión Española

1976: CRUZEIRO

1ST LEG July 21
Cruzeiro **4-1** River Plate
(Brazil)   (Argentina)

2ND LEG July 28
River Plate **2-1** Cruzeiro

PLAY-OFF July 30
Cruzeiro **3-2** River Plate

1977: BOCA JUNIORS

1ST LEG September 6
Boca Juniors **1-0** Cruzeiro
(Argentina)   (Brazil)

2ND LEG September 11
Cruzeiro **1-0** Boca Juniors

PLAY-OFF September 14
Boca Juniors **0-0** Cruzeiro (aet)
Boca Juniors won 5-4 on penalties

1978: BOCA JUNIORS

1ST LEG November 23
Deportivo Cali **0-0** Boca Juniors
(Colombia)   (Argentina)

2ND LEG November 28
Boca Juniors **4-0** Deportivo Cali
Boco Juniors won on points aggregate

1979: OLIMPIA

1ST LEG July 22
Olimpia **2-0** Boca Juniors
(Paraguay)   (Argentina)

2ND LEG July 27
Boca Juniors **0-0** Olimpia
Olimpia won on points aggregate

1980: NACIONAL

1ST LEG July 30
Internacional **0-0** Nacional
Porto Alegre
(Brazil)   (Uruguay)

2ND LEG August 6
Nacional **1-0** Internacional
Porto Alegre
Nacional won on points aggregate

1981: FLAMENGO

1ST LEG November 13
Flamengo **2-1** Cobreloa
(Brazil)   (Chile)

2ND LEG November 20
Cobreloa **1-0** Flamengo

PLAY-OFF November 23
Flamengo **2-0** Cobreloa

1982: PEÑAROL

1ST LEG November 26
Peñarol **0-0** Cobreloa
(Uruguay)   (Chile)

2ND LEG November 30
Cobreloa **0-1** Peñarol
Peñarol won on points aggregate

1983: GRÊMIO

1ST LEG July 22
Peñarol **1-1** Grêmio
(Uruguay)   (Brazil)

2ND LEG July 28
Grêmio **2-1** Peñarol
Grêmio won on points aggregate

1984: INDEPENDIENTE

1ST LEG July 24
Grêmio **0-1** Independiente
(Brazil)   (Argentina)

2ND LEG July 27
Independiente **0-0** Grêmio
Independiente won on points aggregate

1985: ARGENTINOS JUNIORS

1ST LEG October 17
Argentinos **1-0** América Cali
Juniors
(Argentina)   (Colombia)

2ND LEG October 22
América Cali **1-0** Argentinos
Juniors

PLAY-OFF October 24
Argentinos **1-1** América Cali (aet)
Juniors
Argentinos Juniors won 5-4 penalties

1986: RIVER PLATE

1ST LEG October 22
América Cali **1-2** River Plate
(Colombia)   (Argentina)

2ND LEG October 29
River Plate **1-0** América Cali
River Plate won on points aggregate

1987: PEÑAROL

1ST LEG October 21
América Cali **2-0** Peñarol
(Colombia)   (Uruguay)

2ND LEG October 28
Peñarol **2-1** América Cali

PLAY-OFF October 31
Peñarol **1-0** América Cali

1988: NACIONAL

1ST LEG October 19
Newell's Old Boys **1-0** Nacional
(Argentina)   (Uruguay)

2ND LEG October 26
Nacional **3-0** Newell's Old Boys
Nacional won 3-1 on aggregate

1989: ATLÉTICO NACIONAL

1ST LEG May 24
Olimpia **2-0** Atlético Nacional
(Paraguay)   (Colombia)

2ND LEG May 31
Atlético Nacional **2-0** Olimpia (aet)
Atlético Nacional won 5-4 on penalties

1990: OLIMPIA

1ST LEG Oct 3
Olimpia **2-0** Barcelona
(Paraguay)   (Ecuador)

2ND LEG October 10
Barcelona **1-1** Olimpia
Olimpia won 3-1 on aggregate

1991: COLO COLO

1ST LEG May 29
Olimpia **0-0** Colo Colo
(Paraguay)   (Chile)

2ND LEG June 5
Colo Colo **3-0** Olimpia
Colo Colo won 3-0 on aggregate

1992: SÃO PAULO

1ST LEG June 10
Newell's Old Boys **1-0** São Paulo
(Argentina)   (Brazil)

2ND LEG June 17
São Paulo **1-0** Newell's Old Boys
(aet)
São Paulo won 3-2 on penalties

1993: SÃO PAULO

1ST LEG May 19
São Paulo **5-1** Universidad
Católica
(Brazil)   (Chile)

2ND LEG May 26
Universidad **2-0** São Paulo
Católica
São Paulo won 5-3 on aggregate

1994: VÉLEZ SARSFIELD

1ST LEG August 24
Vélez Sarsfield **1-0** São Paulo
(Argentina)   (Brazil)

2ND LEG August 31
São Paulo **1-0** Vélez Sarsfield
(aet)
Vélez Sarsfield won 5-3 on penalties

1995: GRÊMIO

1ST LEG August 24
Grêmio **3-1** Atlético Nacional
(Brazil)   (Colombia)

2ND LEG August 30
Atlético Nacional **1-1** Grêmio
Grêmio won 4-2 on aggregate

1996: RIVER PLATE

1ST LEG June 19
América Cali **1-0** River Plate
(Colombia)   (Argentina)

2ND LEG June 26
River Plate **2-0** América Cali
River Plate won 2-1 on aggregate

1997: CRUZEIRO

1ST LEG August 6
Sporting Cristal **0-0** Cruzeiro
(Peru)   (Brazil)

2ND LEG August 13
Cruzeiro **1-0** Sporting Cristal
Cruzeiro won 1-0 on aggregate

1998: VASCO DA GAMA

1ST LEG August 12
Vasco da Gama **2-0** Barcelona
(Brazil)   (Ecuador)

2ND LEG August 26
Barcelona **1-2** Vasco da Gama
Vasco da Gama won 4-1 on aggregate

1999: PALMEIRAS

1ST LEG June 2
Deportivo Cali **1-0** Palmeiras
(Colombia)   (Brazil)

2ND LEG June 16
Palmeiras **2-1** Deportivo Cali
(aet)
Palmeiras won 4-3 on penalties

2000: BOCA JUNIORS

1ST LEG June 14
Boca Juniors **2-2** Palmeiras
(Argentina)   (Brazil)

2ND LEG June 21
Palmeiras **0-0** Boca Juniors (aet)
Boca Juniors won 4-2 on penalties

2001: BOCA JUNIORS

1ST LEG June 20
Cruz Azul **0-1** Boca Juniors
(Mexico)   (Argentina)

2ND LEG June 28
Boca Juniors **0-1** Cruz Azul (aet)
Boca Juniors won 3-1 on penalties

2002: OLIMPIA

1ST LEG July 27
Olimpia **0-1** São Caetano
(Paraguay)   (Brazil)

2ND LEG July 31
São Caetano **1-2** Olimpia (aet)
Olimpia won 4-2 on penalties

2003: BOCA JUNIORS

1ST LEG June 25
Boca Juniors **2-1** Santos
(Argentina)   (Brazil)

2ND LEG July 2
Santos **1-3** Boca Juniors
Boca Juniors won 5-2 on aggregate

THE WORLD CLUB CUP

Above from left to right: Real Madrid triumph against Olimpia in 2002; Ajax celebrate after defeating Grêmio on penalties in 1995; Juventus beat River Plate to take the 1996 title.

Opposite clockwise from top left: Bayern Munich defeat Boca Juniors in 2001; Real Madrid lift the cup in 1998, with a 2-1 victory over Vasco da Gama; European defeat in 1994 as Velez Sarsfield beat AC Milan; Manchester United lift the trophy in 1999.

Despite its grandiloquent title, the World Club Cup is widely regarded as an annual sideshow by all but the holders and their fans. Since the first contest – held between the winners of the European Cup and the Copa Libertadores – in 1960, it has enjoyed a chequered history, marred by violent encounters, withdrawals and tinkering. If anything, its legacy has been its magnification of the cultural divide between Europe and South America.

The Intercontinental Cup, as it was first known, was a logical progression from the European Champions Cup for UEFA general secretary Henri Delaunay, though it took several more years to organise.

Played over two legs, home and away, the inaugural trophy was won by Real Madrid who had enjoyed an unbroken run of success in the European Cup since its commencement five years earlier. Just two months after their legendary 7-3 victory over Eintracht Frankfurt Madrid travelled to Montevideo to face the Uruguayans, Peñarol. The encounter, a 0-0 draw, was played in monsoon conditions, but Real romped to a 5-1 win in the return with Puskás bagging two goals.

Peñarol were back the following year and this time they struck the first blow for South America, beating Portugal's Benfica. The contest went to its first play-off – aggregate goals did not count at the time – with Eusébio making his debut in the deciding match after he was flown in especially for the final game.

The cup was to reside in South America for three years with Pele's awesome Santos

winning it twice in succession. However, their second match against Milan began the trend towards foul play, with two players sent-off in the bad-tempered play-off game. The cup did eventually arrive in the city of Milan after the ultra defensive Inter side triumphed twice in succession, conceding only one goal in two dour encounters with Argentinian team Independiente between 1964 and 1965.

The competition's descent into bad feeling plumbed a new level as the decade came to an end. In 1966 the Spanish press had rubbished the quality of the Uruguayan pitch, but it was the introduction of British teams that led to the competition's descent into anarchy. In 1967 Celtic's 'Lisbon Lions' had become the first British side to lift the European Cup. Five months later they faced Argentinians Racing Club in a series of matches memorable only for the violence of the encounters. Anti-English feeling in Argentina was still running high after the 1966 World Cup encounter, which provoked England manager Ramsey to describe them as 'animals', and the Scots took the brunt of this sentiment.

Celtic won a bad-tempered first leg 1-0, but in the return leg, at the Avellaneda Stadium, goalkeeper Ronnie Simpson was struck by a missile before kick-off and stand-in John Fallon took up his position. The deciding game, staged in Montevideo, degenerated into war as Celtic had four players sent-off and Racing two. By the final whistle the 1-0 scoreline in the South Americans' favour was of little consequence. 'We should have stuck

to our guns and refused to play a third match,' lamented Celtic chairman Bob Kelly after the event. 'We couldn't have expected it to be anything but a disgrace.'

If at all possible the spirit of competition worsened still further the following year when Manchester United met Estudiantes. Upon landing in Buenos Aires for the first leg, the English team were greeted with a polo match in their honour, but when the Argentinian team boycotted the official reception the tone was set. The game rapidly descended into hostility with Nobby Stiles, described in the match programme as 'brutal, badly intentioned and a bad sportsman', a particular target for ill-treatment. The aggression of Estudiantes was led by Carlos Bilardo, who was later to become the manager of the Argentinian national team, lifting the World Cup in 1986.

Kicked and punched regularly, Stiles was eventually dismissed, not for retaliating, but for gesturing at a linesman over an offside call. George Best later recalled objects raining down on him every time he got the ball and deciding he was better off not calling for it. In the equally bad-tempered return leg at Old Trafford he was dismissed for thumping his tormentor while the referee was in the process of booking him. Matt Busby later declared: 'Holding the ball out there put you in danger.'

Paddy Crerand's conclusion that 'the whole thing was a total waste of time' began to take seed with many European sides. The travelling was demanding, especially mid-season, and clubs were not willing to risk injury.

Above: Celtic's John Hughes in action against Racing Club in the 1967 final.

Opposite top: Real Madrid celebrate after defeating Olimpia in 2002.

Opposite bottom: Boca Juniors' victory over Real Madrid brought them the 2000 title.

Below left to right: Juan Véron scores against Manchester United as Estudiantes de La Plata win in 1968; Luis Figo in action for Real Madrid during their 2000 final against Boca Juniors.

The Seventies were marked by a succession of withdrawals, beginning with Ajax, who declined to take part in 1971 and 1973. They were subsequently replaced by defeated finalists Panathinaikos and Juventus, both losing out to their South American opposition.

The withdrawals continued. In 1975 Bayern Munich's decision to opt out led to the competition's complete cancellation, but the Germans agreed to enter when they held on to their European crown the following season and were subsequently rewarded with the title 'world club champions' after beating Brazilians Cruzeiro. However, two years later the event was pulled again when Liverpool balked at travelling. Nottingham Forest followed suit in 1979 to be replaced by Swedes Malmö.

The competition was clearly doomed unless action was taken. The solution arrived in 1980 when Japanese vehicle manufacturers Toyota offered to sponsor the trophy if it was held in Tokyo. On February 11, 1981, 62,000 fans packed into the city's national stadium to witness the first Toyota Cup match between Nacional Montevideo and Brian Clough's Nottingham Forest. The Uruguayans won the tie 1-0 in a tight defensive encounter that saw them shut up shop after Victorino scored the only goal in the tenth minute.

With English clubs dominating Europe they contested the trophy for the next two seasons, but both Liverpool and Aston Villa lost out. In fact an English side would not lift the cup until 1999, when the all-conquering Manchester United of that year capped their unique treble when Roy Keane volleyed home the only goal against Brazilians Palmeiras.

The competition's farcical side was again demonstrated when Brazilians Cruzeiro signed several players on loan, including Bebeto, for their 1997 encounter with Borussia Dortmund. Fortunately they were defeated.

The impact of Manchester United's 1999 win was undermined by the knowledge that the trophy was to be superseded by the World Club Championship just a few months later. After ten years in which the competition had degenerated into a pleasant sideshow, FIFA decided a revamp was necessary, allowing it to flex its muscles over rivals UEFA in the process. Architect Sepp Blatter decreed the trophy was now to be decided by a mini-tournament, something not greeted with much warmth by European leagues already suffering from fixture congestion. Manchester United and Real Madrid were selected to represent Europe against sides from South America, Oceania, Africa and Central America. In England there was controversy over the withdrawal of the holders from the FA Cup to take part in the tournament, the club being put under pressure to go by a government wanting to secure the 2006 World Cup.

In the end the European sides failed to progress and the final was contested between Brazilian sides Corinthians and Vasco da Gama. The São Paulo club duly became first Club World Champions after a penalty shoot-out, pocketing a purse of $6m.

Having rejigged the template once, FIFA attempted to expand the competition to 12 teams the following year, adding Japan's Jubilo Iwata as compensation for the curtailment of the Toyota Cup. But the 2001 tournament, scheduled to be played in Spain, had to be cancelled due to the bankruptcy of ISMM-ISL, FIFA's former marketing partner. All teams and Spain's government were compensated.

The World Club Cup continued in its usual format in Tokyo in November 2000, with Boca Juniors, Bayern Munich and Real Madrid lifting the trophy one after the other. But the competition's future looks as uncertain as its past. Inevitably it will continue to be the object of political tampering and the power struggle between UEFA and FIFA, with the former determined to limit the competition to just one game, the latter intent on turning it into a showpiece. What is certain is that it will never carry the same weight as a domestic title or a Champions League victory for the cream of Europe. It is simply not that important.

THE WINNERS OF THE WORLD CLUB CUP

1980: REAL MADRID
1ST LEG July 3
Peñarol **0-0** Real Madrid
(Uruguay)   (Spain)
2ND LEG September 4
Real Madrid **5-1** Peñarol
Real Madrid won 5-1 aggregate

1961: PEÑAROL
1ST LEG September 4
Benfica **1-0** Peñarol
(Portugal)   (Uruguay)
2ND LEG September 17
Peñarol **5-0** Benfica
PLAY-OFF September 19
Peñarol **2-1** Benfica

1962: SANTOS
1ST LEG September 19
Santos **3-2** Benfica
(Brazil)   (Portugal)
2ND LEG October 11
Benfica **2-5** Santos
Santos won 8-4 on aggregate

1963: SANTOS
1ST LEG October 16
AC Milan **4-2** Santos
(Italy)   (Brazil)
2ND LEG November 14
Santos **4-2** AC Milan
PLAY-OFF November 16
Santos **1-0** AC Milan

1964: INTER MILAN
1ST LEG September 9
Independiente **1-0** Inter Milan
(Argentina)   (Italy)
2ND LEG September 23
Inter Milan **2-0** Independiente
PLAY-OFF September 26
Inter Milan **1-0** Independiente
(aet)

1965: INTER MILAN
1ST LEG September 8
Inter Milan **3-0** Independiente
(Italy)   (Argentina)
2ND LEG September 15
Independiente **0-0** Inter Milan
Inter Milan won 3-0 on aggregate

1966: PENAROL
1ST LEG October 12
Peñarol **2-0** Real Madrid
(Uruguay)   (Spain)
2ND LEG October 26
Real Madrid **0-2** Peñarol
Peñarol won 4-0 on aggregate

1967: RACING CLUB
1ST LEG October 18
Celtic **1-0** Racing Club
(Scotland)   (Argentina)
2ND LEG November 1
Racing Club **2-1** Celtic
PLAY-OFF November 4
Racing Club **1-0** Celtic

1968: ESTUDIANTES DE LA PLATA
1ST LEG September 25
Estudiantes **1-0** Manchester
de la Plata   United
(Argentina)   (England)
2ND LEG October 16
Manchester **1-1** Estudiantes
United   de la Plata
Estudiantes de la Plata won 2-1 on aggregate

1969: AC MILAN
1ST LEG October 8
AC Milan **3-0** Estudiantes
(Italy)   de la Plata
(Argentina)
2ND LEG October 22
Estudiantes **2-1** AC Milan
de la Plata
AC Milan won 4-2 on aggregate

1970: FEYENOORD
1ST LEG August 26
Estudiantes **2-2** Feyenoord
de la Plata
(Argentina)   (Holland)
2ND LEG September 9
Feyenoord **1-0** Estudiantes
de la Plata
Feyenoord won 3-2 on aggregate

1971: NACIONAL MONTEVIDEO
1ST LEG December 15
Panathinaikos **1-1** Nacional
Montevideo
(Greece)   (Uruguay)
2ND LEG December 29
Nacional **2-1** Panathinaikos
Montevideo
Nacional Montevideo won 3-2 on aggregate

1972: AJAX
1ST LEG September 6
Independiente **1-1** Ajax
(Argentina)   (Holland)
2ND LEG September 28
Ajax **3-0** Independiente
Ajax won 4-1 on aggregate

1973: INDEPENDIENTE
OLYMPIC STADIUM, ROME November 28
Independiente **1-0** Juventus
(Argentina)   (Italy)

1974: ATLÉTICO MADRID
1ST LEG March 12
Independiente **1-0** Atlético Madrid
(Argentina)   (Spain)
2ND LEG April 10
Atlético Madrid **2-0** Independiente
Atlético Madrid won 2-1 on aggregate

1975
Bayern Munich v Independiente
(West Germany)   (Argentina)
Not contested

1976: BAYERN MUNICH
1ST LEG November 23
Bayern Munich **2-0** Cruzeiro
(West Germany)   (Brazil)
2ND LEG December 21
Cruzeiro **0-0** Bayern Munich
Bayern Munich won 2-0 on aggregate

1977
1ST LEG March 22
Boca Juniors **2-2** Borussia
Mönchengladbach
(Argentina)   (West Germany)
2ND LEG March 26
Borussia **0-3** Boca Juniors
Mönchengladbach
Boca Juniors won 5-2 on aggregate

1978
Liverpool v Boca Juniors
(England)   (Argentina)
Not contested

1979: OLIMPIA
1ST LEG November 18
Malmö **0-1** Olimpia
(Sweden)   (Paraguay)
2ND LEG March 3 2nd leg
Olimpia **2-1** Malmö
Olimpia won 3-1 on aggregate

1980: NACIONAL
NATIONAL STADIUM, TOKYO February 11
Nacional **1-0** Nottingham
Forest
(Uruguay)   (England)

1981: FLAMENGO
NATIONAL STADIUM, TOKYO December 13
Flamengo **3-0** Liverpool
(Brazil)   (England)

1982: PEÑAROL
NATIONAL STADIUM, TOKYO December 12
Peñarol **2-0** Aston Villa
(Uruguay)   (England)

1983: GRÊMIO
NATIONAL STADIUM, TOKYO December 11
Grêmio **2-1** Hamburg
(Brazil)   (West Germany)

1984: INDEPENDIENTE
NATIONAL STADIUM, TOKYO December 9
Independiente **1-0** Liverpool
(Argentina)   (England)

1985: JUVENTUS
NATIONAL STADIUM, TOKYO December 8
Juventus **2-2** Argentinos
Juniors (aet)
(Italy)   (Argentina)
Juventus won 4-2 on penalties

1986: RIVER PLATE
NATIONAL STADIUM, TOKYO December 14
River Plate **1-0** Steaua
Bucharest
(Argentina)   (Romania)

1987: FC PORTO
NATIONAL STADIUM, TOKYO December 13
FC Porto **2-1** Peñarol (aet)
(Portugal)   (Uruguay)

1988: NACIONAL
NATIONAL STADIUM, TOKYO December 11
Nacional **2-2** PSV Eindhoven
(aet)
(Uruguay)   (Holland)
Nacional won 7-6 on penalties

1989: AC MILAN
NATIONAL STADIUM, TOKYO December 17
AC Milan **1-0** Atlético Nacional
(aet)
(Italy)   (Columbia)

1990: AC MILAN
NATIONAL STADIUM, TOKYO December 9
AC Milan **3-0** Olimpia
(Italy)   (Paraguay)

1991: RED STAR BELGRADE
NATIONAL STADIUM, TOKYO December 8
Red Star Belgrade **3-0** Colo Colo
(Yugoslavia)   (Chile)

1992: SÃO PAULO
NATIONAL STADIUM, TOKYO December 13
São Paulo **2-1** Barcelona
(Brazil)   (Spain)

1993: SÃO PAULO
NATIONAL STADIUM, TOKYO December 12
São Paulo **3-2** Milan
(Brazil)   (Italy)

1994: VÉLEZ SARSFIELD
NATIONAL STADIUM, TOKYO December 1
Vélez Sarsfield **2-0** AC Milan
(Argentina)   (Italy)

1995: AJAX
NATIONAL STADIUM, TOKYO November 25
Ajax **0-0** Grêmio (aet)
(Holland)   (Brazil)
Ajax won 4-3 on penalties

1996: JUVENTUS
NATIONAL STADIUM, TOKYO November 26
Juventus **1-0** River Plate
(Italy)   (Argentina)

1997: BORUSSIA DORTMUND
NATIONAL STADIUM, TOKYO December 2
Borussia **2-0** Cruzeiro
Dortmund
(Germany)   (Brazil)

1998: REAL MADRID
NATIONAL STADIUM, TOKYO December 1
Real Madrid **2-1** Vasco da Gama
(Spain)   (Brazil)

1999: MANCHESTER UNITED
NATIONAL STADIUM, TOKYO November 30
Manchester **1-0** Palmeiras
United
(England)   (Brazil)

2000: BOCA JUNIORS
NATIONAL STADIUM, TOKYO November 28
Boca Juniors **2-1** Real Madrid
(Argentina)   (Spain)

2001: BAYERN MUNICH
NATIONAL STADIUM, TOKYO November 27
Bayern Munich **1-0** Boca Juniors (aet)
(Germany)   (Argentina)

2002: REAL MADRID
YOKOHAMA STADIUM December 3
Real Madrid **2-0** Olimpia
(Spain)   (Paraguay)

OTHER INTERNATIONAL CLUB COMPETITIONS

WORLD CLUB CHAMPIONSHIP

The first FIFA Club World Championship was hosted by Brazil in January 2000. Eight teams representing the cream of the world game took part with two teams from Europe (Real Madrid and Manchester United) and South America (Corinthians and Vasco da Gama) and one each from Asia (Al Nasr), Africa (Raja Casablanca), CONCACAF (Necaxa) and Oceania (South Melbourne). Corinthians defeated Vasco da Gama 4-3 on penalties after a goalless draw in the final. The second 12-team tournament was scheduled to be hosted by Spain in July/August 2001. However, following the collapse of ISL Worldwide, FIFA's marketing partners, the tournament was cancelled. The second tournament has been rescheduled to take place in 2005.

EUROPEAN SUPERCUP

The Supercup was originally conceived by UEFA as a celebration match between the winners of the European Cup and the Cup Winners' Cup. The latter competition is now defunct and the place is taken up by the UEFA Cup winners. It is a match played on neutral territory and squeezed into the calendar when both teams can accommodate it.

SUPERCOPA LIBERTADORES

A competition which was open only to previous winners of the Copa Libertadores or

the South American Championship (Vasco da Gama won the only one in 1948), that ran from 1988 to 1997. Six out of ten editions were won by Argentinian teams. Independiente and Brazilian side Cruzeiro were the only teams to win it twice.

COPA MERCOSUR

The Copa Mercosur effectively replaced the Supercopa in 1998. Five groups of four teams play each other home and away. The group winners and the three best runners-up qualify for the quarter-finals. It is a competition that has been dominated by Brazilian clubs.

COPA SUDAMERICANA

A knockout competition with ties played over two legs. It is sponsored by a sports marketing firm in Argentina and entry is by invitation only. Brazilian clubs are notable by their absence, citing their own domestic fixture congestion for their non-participation. San Lorenzo won the first competition in 2002.

RECOPA

From 1988 to 1997 the Recopa was contested between the winners of the Copa Libertadores and the Supercopa. Between 1998 and 2001 the Recopa was absorbed by the Copa Mercosur. However, from 2002 the winners of the Copa Libertadores and the Copa Sudamericana will battle it out in Los Angeles.

Olimpia were the first winners under the new arrangements.

AFRICAN CHAMPIONS' CUP

The African Champions' Cup was born in 1964 when an international club competition on the continent became feasible. Many nations had become independent from their former colonial rulers and formed their own leagues. With the exception of the first tournament the competition was based on the format of Europe's established club competitions. Ties were to be played home and away including the final. Zaïre's TP Englebert were a leading force early on, appearing in four successive finals between 1967 and 1970, winning the first two and losing the second pair. Guinea's Hafia Conakry were the team to beat during the 1970s as they reached the final on five occasions, winning in 1972, 1975 and 1977. Hafia's presence confirmed the early dominance of west and central Africa. This was largely because the north of the continent showed little interest until the 1980s. Then the teams of the north – Algeria, Egypt, Morocco and Tunisia – put a stranglehold on the African Champions' Cup. Egyptian clubs have won nine times, with Zamalek the most successful side, earning the title of African champions on five occasions in 1984, 1986, 1993, 1996 and 2002. It is a long drawn out competition with the preliminary round kicking off in February with the final being resolved in December each year.

Above from left to right: Lazio lift the European Supercup after their 1999 win over Manchester United; Vasco da Gama and Manchester United meet at the first World Club Championship in 2000; Vasco da Gama are crowned FIFA World Club champions after beating Corinthians in the final.

AFRICAN CUP WINNERS' CUP

The African Cup Winners' Cup began in 1975 following the established success of the Champions' Cup. The new competition was open to the main cup winners of each country. It has been dominated by northern sides, with Egypt a real force in the 1980s as its clubs held the trophy for five successive years. Al Mokaoulum won it 1982 and 1983, with Al Ahly clinching a hat-trick of wins over the next three years, beating Canon Yaounde, Leventis United and AS Sogara respectively. For their third success Al Ahly turned down a chance to compete in the Champions' Cup in 1986.

CAF CUP

The CAF Cup is Africa's equivalent of Europe's UEFA Cup and was introduced in 1992. One team from each member nation (plus the holders) are allowed to enter the competition. All ties are played over two legs and, like its two sister cups, the competition is dominated by clubs from the north. Algeria's JS Kabylie, under coach Jean-Yves Chay, completed a hat-trick of victories in the competition, winning in 2000, 2001 and 2002. Tunisia's Etoile du Sahel have also been successful, appearing in four finals and winning twice in 1995 and 1999, while losing in 1996 and 2001.

AFRICAN SUPER CUP

The African Super Cup pitches together the African Champions' Cup winners against the African Cup Winners' Cup holders in a one-off encounter. It was first played in 1992 when Cup Winners' Cup winners Africa Sports beat champions WAC Casablanca after a penalty shoot-out in Abidjan. Since then it has been the African champions have held sway on all but two occasions. Zamalek have won the trophy three times in 1993, 1996 and 2002.

ASIAN CHAMPIONS LEAGUE

The Asian Champions League has four qualifying rounds split into West Asia and East Asia, with ties played over two legs. The qualifying period leads to the Champions League section of four groups of four teams, with each group played in a different city. In 2003, for example, the cities of Bangkok, Dalian, Al Ain and Tashkent hosted the group games. The group winners then play a two-legged semi-final and final. There had been a fledgling Asian Champion Teams Cup between 1967 and 1971 which was dominated by the Israelis. Maccabi Tel Aviv won it twice 1968 and 1971 while Hapoel Tel Aviv won the inaugural competition and lost the 1970 final to Iran's defunct Taj Club. The Champions Cup was revived in the mid-Eighties with increasing success. Recent years have seen the competition dominated by South Korea. Between 1996 and 2002 Korean clubs won the event five times. In fact on two occasions, the cup climaxed with an all-Korean final, in 1997 and 2002. Suwon Samsung Bluewings won it in 2001 and 2002 and were preceded by Pohang Steelers in 1997 and 1998 and Ilhwa Chunwa in 1996. Japan's Jubilo Iwata broke the Korean stranglehold in 1999.

ASIAN CUP WINNERS' CUP

The Asian Cup Winners' Cup was introduced in 1990 and has proved a successful hunting ground for international honours for Saudi Arabian clubs. Al Hilal won it in 1997 and 2002, while Al Nasr, with a winning goal from Hristo Stoichkov, lifted the trophy in 1998 and Al Ittihad won in 1999.

ASIAN SUPER CUP

The Asian Champions take on the Asian Cup winners over two legs in this annual fixture which was inaugurated in 1995. Japan's Yokohama Flugels beat Thai Farmers Bank 4-3 on aggregate in the first final. The ties have been close encounters with away goals and penalty shoot-outs coming into play.

Above: UEFA Cup holders Liverpool celebrate their win over Champions League winners Bayern Munich in the 2001 European Supercup Final.

191

GREAT CLUBS OF THE WORLD

AJAX

AMSTERDAM, HOLLAND
Stadium: Amsterdam Arena
(50,200)

Founded: 1900 **Honours:** World Club Cup 1972, 1995; Champions Cup 1971, 1972, 1973, 1995; Cup Winners' Cup 1987; UEFA Cup 1992; European Supercup 1972, 1973, 1995; League 28; Cup 15

The name Ajax is synonymous with the term 'Total Football'. This was a concept of play that saw footballers of supreme technical ability able to interchange positions during a game in a way that had never previously been seen on the European stage. Not only was it magnificent to watch, it was also highly successful. At the height of their powers in the early Seventies, Ajax not only lifted the European Champions Cup on three successive occasions but they also enjoyed back-to-back Super Cup wins and a World Club Cup.

Already dominant in Holland, this took Ajax on to the world stage. There was talent in abundance with the likes of Johan Neeskens, Arie Haan and Rudi Krol, but the star of the side was Johan Cruyff. These names, like so many past and future players at the club, were products of the revered Ajax youth system – a system that has continued to produce talent, spawning such players as Frank Rijkaard, Marco Van Basten, Dennis Bergkamp, Marc Overmars and Patrick Kluivert.

While the relaxation of overseas signings has seen Ajax lose many of their homegrown talents, with the club in turn fielding a more international line-up, it was fitting that their last major success on the European front, a 1-0 Champions Cup victory over Milan, was sealed by Patrick Kluivert.

ANDERLECHT

BRUSSELS, BELGIUM
Stadium: Constant Vanden Stock (28,063)

Founded: 1908 **Honours:** Cup Winners' Cup 1976, 1978; UEFA Cup 1983; European Supercup 1976, 1978; League 26; Cup 8

Anderlecht are Belgium's most successful club. Formed in Brussels on May 27, 1908, it wasn't until 1947 that they won their first Belgian league title. However, a further 25 championships, a national record by some margin, illustrates the Mauves' willingness to make up for lost time, and the level of their domestic dominance.

Success on the European stage came in the late 1970s, a golden period, when the club reached three consecutive Cup Winners' Cup finals. In 1976 they got the better of West Ham United, winning 4-2 to claim their first

European title. The following campaign they lost to Hamburg, but a year later they again lifted the silverware after thrashing FK Austria 4-0. The club added the UEFA Cup to their honours list in 1983 with a 2-1 aggregate victory over Benfica. The following season saw them reach the final again, this time losing out to Tottenham after a penalty shoot-out.

The following decade saw a decline in the club's fortunes, with the occasional relegation scare and many managerial changes. However, in recent years, Anderlecht have once again risen right to the top of the Belgian ladder with Champions League football following successive league titles in 2000 and 2001.

ARSENAL

LONDON, ENGLAND
Stadium: Highbury
(38,500)

Founded: 1886 **Honours:** Cup Winners' Cup 1994; Fairs Cup 1970; League 12; Cup 9; League Cup 2

Arsenal were formed as Dial Square by workers at the Woolwich armaments factory in south London, before turning professional in 1891 as Woolwich Arsenal. The prefix was dropped as the club gained election to Division Two in 1893 and promotion followed 11 years later. Relegation in 1913 was tempered by the club's move to Highbury, a decision made by chairman Sir Henry Norris who saw great potential in the north London catchment area.

Promotion back to Division One was 'engineered' by Norris in somewhat strange circumstances when the league resumed after World War I and his appointment of manager Herbert Chapman in 1925 transformed the club into one of the greatest in world football.

Not only did Arsenal get white sleeves and their own tube station, under Chapman they

won five championships in the 1930s and two FA Cup wins. Following Chapman's death, there was something of a decline and, although championships were won in 1948, 1953 and the 'double' of 1971, it wasn't until the appointment of George Graham in 1986 that the team emerged as a consistent force.

Graham's disciplinarian style, shrewd buying and faith in the club's youth system yielded the championship within three years. As the team matured, they won the title again in 1991, the League Cup and FA Cup double in 1993 and enjoyed Cup Winners' Cup success against Parma a year later.

Arsenal's one-dimensional play won them few friends, but the appointment of Arsene Wenger in 1996 changed the club's image emphatically. The Frenchman has championed a stylish approach on the pitch and forward-thinking preparation off it. Winning the double in 1998 and 2002, and plans for the construction of a new 60,000-seater capacity stadium, are an indication of the rapid strides made.

ASTON VILLA

BIRMINGHAM, ENGLAND
Stadium: Villa Park
(39,217)

Founded: 1874 **Honours:** Champions Cup 1982; European Supercup 1982; League 7; Cup 7; League Cup 5

A founding member of the Football League, Aston Villa are one of the oldest clubs in the world. Five of their seven titles and three of six FA Cups were won by 1900. Between the turn of the century and the club's first relegation in 1936, Villa remained powerful: champions in 1910, runners-up on seven occasions, and FA

Above: Peter Withe, after scoring Aston Villa's winning goal against Bayern Munich in the 1982 European Cup Final.

Left: A familiar sight at Ajax, club legend John Cruyff on the attack in 1972

Opposite clockwise from top: the stars of Arsenal – Tony Adams lifts the FA Cup in 1998 after defeating Newcastle in the final; George Graham wheels away after scoring the equaliser against Liverpool in the 1971 Cup Final; goalscoring legend Cliff Bastin.

Above: Juninho, who played for Atlético Madrid in the mid-1990s, when they were worthy challengers to their great rivals, Real Madrid.

under Ron Atkinson. But while Villa are now seen as secure in the Premiership, they are rarely considered genuine title contenders. League Cup victories in 1994 and 1996, and an FA Cup final appearance in 2000, at least give their fans a case for arguing that Villa remain a major force in English football.

ATHLETIC BILBAO

BILBAO, SPAIN
Stadium: San Mamés
(46,223)

Founded: 1898 **Honours:** League 8; Cup 23

Among the oldest football clubs in Spain, Athletic Bilbao share the honour of having never been relegated from the Spanish top flight with Real Madrid and Barcelona. This Basque club's English name originally stems both from British influence in the region, and local suspicion of anything Spanish! Engineers from the UK brought football to the quarry-workers of this proud area of northern Spain in the late 1800s, and the club still sticks to the selection policy of 'la cantera' or 'the quarry' – only picking players of Basque origin. The most famous of these was Rafael Moreno Aranzadi, or 'Pitxitxi' (the top goalscorer in La Liga still wins a trophy named after him).

Bilbao also employed English coaches. Freddy Pentland won three championships and five cups in the 1920s and 1930s, the club's most successful era. In fact, despite their lack of impact on the European stage, at home Bilbao are second only to Barcelona as winners of the Spanish Cup.

These glory days were recaptured in the 1980s when Javier Clemente's fearsome team, including notorious defender Goikoetxea, 'The Butcher Of Bilbao', won the league in 1983 and the treble in 1984. Bilbao's magnificent stadium, nicknamed 'La Catedral', has been home to many legends: goalkeepers Iríbar and Zubizarreta, striker Zarraonandia, and modern heroes Guerrero and Etxeberría. And the club's domestic achievements – though their last good season was as runners-up in 1998, their centenary year – are incredible given their stubborn loyalty to 'la cantera'.

ATLÉTICO MADRID

MADRID, SPAIN
Stadium: Vicente Calderón
(57,500)

Founded: 1903 **Honours:** World Club Cup 1974; Cup Winners' Cup 1962; League 9; Cup 9

Formed in 1903 by three Basque students based in Madrid, the club performed poorly in its early years. Indeed, it wasn't until after the Civil War and a merger with the Spanish

air force's side, Atlético Aviacion, that success came to the football club.

Although Atlético Madrid have spent a large proportion of their history in the shadow of illustrious neighbours Real Madrid, the club has regularly won titles in Spanish domestic competitions. Nicknamed 'Los Colchoneros' (The Mattressmakers – due to the club's kit), they have also performed credibly on the European stage. In 1959 they reached the semi-finals of the European Cup, but, ironically, were beaten to a place in the final by Real. The club can boast success in the now defunct European Cup Winners' Cup with victory against Fiorentina in 1962.

In the late 1980s the club was taken over by the flamboyant Jesus Gil, and it has been his erratic and often dubious financial behaviour that has defined the club in the decades ever since. In his first ten years at the club he managed to hire and fire more than 25 coaches. However, his unique approach was vindicated in 1996 when Atlético won the Spanish league and cup double, and for a short while crept out of the shadow of Real.

ATLETICO NACIONAL

MEDELLIN, COLOMBIA
Stadium: Atanasio Girardot
(52,000)

Founded: 1936 **Honours:** Copa Libertadores 1989; Inter-American Cup 1989; Copa Merconorte 1998, 2000; League 7

Atletico Nacional's first league title in 1954 coincided with the Colombian FA rejoining FIFA after a four-year dispute over transfer payments. The club have subsequently added a further six domestic league titles to their honours list – the latest being in 1999 when they narrowly pipped America De Cali in a close-run title race.

However, it was ten years earlier in 1989 that the club experienced its most golden hour by becoming the first Colombian team to win the Copa Libertadores, the South American Club Cup. Future national team coach Francisco Maturana led Nacional to the trophy with a narrow win over Olimpia of Paraguay. This was followed by an appearance in the final of the prestigious World Club Cup, and a 1-0 reverse against AC Milan in Tokyo.

Medellin is an area at the epicentre of Colombia's drug industry and, as a result, controversy has never been far away from the club. Indeed, Pablo Escobar, the leader of the country's biggest drug cartel was a lifelong Nacional fan, and the club flag was draped over the coffin at his funeral in 1993. Recent players to wear the green and white include the flamboyant goalkeeper Jose Luis Chilavert, and Medellin-born striker Juan Pablo Angel, who went on to play for Aston Villa.

Cup winners three times. Although return to the top flight on this occasion was swift, after relegation the club were never the same force, sinking as far as the Third Division in 1970.

Controversially, Villa won the FA Cup in 1957 against Manchester United and 'the Busby Babes' (United played some of the match with ten men after their goalkeeper was injured), and they also triumphed in the League Cup in 1961. They were finalists again as a Third Division team ten years later, but winning the Division Three title under Vic Crowe in 1972 proved the impetus that the club needed. Ron Saunders continued the revival after his appointment in 1974, taking them in to the top flight the following year and winning the title in 1981. Midway through the next season Saunders resigned, leaving his assistant Tony Barton to take over the team just three months before Villa's greatest ever night – Peter Withe's single goal beating Bayern Munich in Rotterdam to win the 1982 European Champions Cup.

Relegation in the late 1980s saw Graham Taylor take charge and reverse the fortunes of the club. They finished runners-up in the title race in 1990, a feat they achieved again in 1993

BARCELONA

SPAIN
Stadium: Nou Camp
(98,600)

Founded: 1899 **Honours:** Champions Cup 1992;
Cup Winners' Cup 1979, 1982, 1989, 1997; Fairs
Cup 1958, 1960, 1966; European Supercup 1992,
1997; League 16; Cup 24

One of the biggest and best-supported clubs
in European football, FC Barcelona have only
won the ultimate prize – the Champions Cup
– on one occasion. By the standards of almost
any football club, 16 national titles, 24
domestic cups and ten European trophies
would be seen as an incredible record, but
Barcelona's achievements have always been
judged by the yardstick set by bitter rivals Real
Madrid, who dominated the Champions Cup
for much of its first ten years.

With a club history mired in the politics of
mid 20th Century Spain, Barcelona were, for
many, a symbol of Catalan defiance in
a country oppressed by Franco's centralist
government in Madrid. But ironically for a
club so synonymous with the spirit of
Catalonia, its roots were originally in the
expatriate communities of the city. In October
1899 Swiss football enthusiast Hans Gamper
placed an advert in the local sports newspaper
Los Deportes and recruited a team largely
drawn from the various English businesses
of the city, the club's famous strip inspired by
the school colours of one of the English
players, Arthur Witty. FC Barcelona played
their first game on Christmas Eve 1899,
fielding a team comprised largely of
foreigners to beat local side FC Catala 3-1, with
Arthur Witty scoring to seal the win.

Swift progress was made in the early years
of the century, with Barcelona reaching the
first final of the Spanish Cup (the Copa Del
Rey) in 1902, although by the time they finally
won the competition in 1910, Real Madrid
had already lifted the trophy four times.

When the first Spanish national league
came into being in the 1928-29 season,
Barcelona beat Real Madrid to the title by just
two points, and since then, along with Real
and Athletic Bilbao, they share the honour of
having never been relegated. But although
Barça continued to win domestic honours for
the next 20 years, it was really in the period
between 1948 and 1960 that the club built
a team of substance and a stadium to house
it, the Nou Camp, which opened in 1957.

Barcelona's greatest period of achievement
was under the management of Argentinian
Helenio Herrera, who arrived at the club in
1958, shortly after their first European
triumph in the Fairs Cup. During his two-
year spell at Barça, Herrera shook the club at

Above: Under Johan Cruyff Barcelona finally win the European Cup for the first time, beating Sampdoria at Wembley
in 1992. Playing in their orange away strip, the team changed into their famous Blaugrana shirts to collect the trophy.

its roots, placing his faith in both young
Catalan players nurtured through the youth
team and his 'tricky foreigners', Hungarians
Sandor Kocsis and Zoltan Czibor. In Herrera's
first season in charge, Barça eclipsed the Real
Madrid of Di Stéfano and Puskás to take the
league title with a record haul of points.

Victory over Birmingham City in the 1960
Fairs Cup was followed by another league title,
but no amount of success could ease the pain
caused by the end of that season's European
Cup campaign when, despite recording
significant aggregate victories over CNDA
Sofia (8-4), AC Milan (7-1) and Wolves (9-2),
semi-final humiliation by Real Madrid was
deemed disastrous. Before the clash Herrera
had fallen out with his star Ladislao Kubala
over bonus payments. Zoltan Czibor backed
his fellow Hungarian and both were dropped,
Barcelona lost both legs 3-1. Herrera took the
blame and was forced to resign.

The following season saw a 3-2 defeat to
Benfica in the Champions Cup final. Despite
having dumped Real Madrid from the
competition en route to the final, in La Liga
it was the onset of a decade of dominance by
Madrid, who won eight of the remaining nine
titles during the Sixties (Atlético Madrid
interrupting this run in 1966). Triumphs in

The Nou Camp: the greatest venue in European football?

the Copa Del Rey in 1963 and 1968 were
scant consolation, and while Barcelona again
won the Fairs Cup in 1966, they would not
retake the championship until 1974, after
securing the services of Johan Cruyff. In the
mid-Sixties the Spanish league had banned
imported players, but the ban was lifted in
1973 in time for the club to spend a world
record fee of £922,000 on Cruyff, who took
them from the relegation zone to the league
title for the first time in 14 years. Better than
that, the season also included a 5-0 away
thrashing of Real Madrid.

Although success in La Liga would evade
the club for another 11 years, when Terry
Venables secured the title, it was Cruyff who
would again prove saviour, returning as coach
to deliver Barça their one and only triumph
in the Champions Cup, a single Ronald
Koeman goal at Wembley in the 1992 final
beating Sampdoria to the prize. However, a
4-0 defeat to Milan in the final two years later
did little to endear Cruyff to the Barcelona
board, and despite having taken the club to
four league titles in a row, failure to win
a trophy in 1995 and 1996 ultimately led to
his acrimonious departure.

Dutchman Louis Van Gaal brought back-
to-back titles to the Nou Camp in 1998 and
1999, but by filling the side with so many of
his countrymen – Kluivert, Overmars, Cocu,
Zenden, Reiziger and the De Boers – he
proved unpopular and was forced to resign.
A second spell at the club for Van Gaal just
a year later was unsuccessful and he was
replaced midway through his second season.
Since then Radomir Antic has had the good
fortune to oversee the conclusion of a
Champions League record of 11 consecutive
wins. But to find a worse season than their
sixth-place finish in La Liga in 2003 you
would have to go back to 1942.

1895

1899: Barcelona play
their first game at
Bonanova Racetrack
on Christmas Eve
against FC Catala.

1900

1905

1902: Barça are
losing finalists in the
first Copa Del Rey to
Vizcaya Bilbao. They
also play
Madrid for the
first time,
winning 3-2.

1910

1905: The club play
Madrid for the first
time in Barcelona,
winning 3-2.

1915

1920

1922: Barça move
to a new stadium at
Les Corts.

1925

1930

1929: The club
wins the first
ever Spanish
league title.

1935

1937-39: The
national league is
abandoned during
Spanish Civil War.

1940

1945

1951: The club sign
Hungarian legend
Ladislao Kubala.

1950

1955

1957: The first game
is played at The Nou
Camp.

1960

1958: Barça win their
first European trophy,
the Fairs Cup.

1965

1961: Despite
beating Real Madrid
on the way, the club
loses the European
Cup final to Benfica.

1970

1974:
Johan
Cruyff is
signed
from Ajax.

1975

1979: Barça
lift the Cup
Winners' Cup
for first time.

1980

1985

1982: After four years
of chasing, the club
finally sign Maradona.

1990

1988: Johan Cruyff
returns as manager.

1995

1992: Barça
win the
European Cup
for the first
time, beating
Sampdoria 1-0
at Wembley.

2000

2005

Above: Boca Juniors coach Carlos Bianchi celebrates winning the 2001 league title with his players.

BAYERN MUNICH

  MUNICH, GERMANY
Stadium: Olympic Stadium (63,000)

Founded: 1900 **Honours:** World Club Cup 1976; Champions Cup 1974, 1975, 1976, 2001; Cup Winners' Cup 1967; UEFA Cup 1996; League 17; Cup 11

Bayern celebrated their centenary year by winning the Bundesliga and DFB Cup double for the third time, and followed it up in 2001 with their seventh appearance – and fourth victory – in the European Cup final. Yet, incredibly, Bayern weren't even their city's representative in the initial Bundesliga of 1963. That honour fell to TSV 1860 Munich.

Bayern had triumphed only once in the regional play-offs which previously decided the German championship – back in 1932. It wasn't until attack-minded Yugoslav coach Tschik Cajkovski took over in 1963 that Bayern started their climb to the top. In the 1965 Bundesliga promotion play-offs, Cajkovski included three promising youngsters in his team: Sepp Maier in goal, Franz Beckenbauer in midfield and Gerd Müller in attack. Maier holds Bayern's appearances record, including 422 consecutive games; Müller, 'Der Bomber', netted an astonishing 365 goals in 427 games; and Beckenbauer, 'Der Kaiser', is, quite simply, one of the greatest footballers ever.

This trio helped Bayern to cup wins in 1966 and 1967, and a Cup Winners' Cup victory in 1967 against Rangers. They completed their first league and cup double in 1969 under new boss Branko Zebec. With the addition of three more world-class players, Paul Breitner, Uli Hoeness and Georg Schwarzenbeck, Bayern saw the dawn of a golden era. Zebec's replacement, Udo Lattek, led them on a four-year unbeaten home run. They won three titles in a row, and notched-up their first of three consecutive European Cup wins in 1974, with a 4-0 victory over Atlético Madrid, following it up with wins over Leeds and St Etienne.

Domestically their triumphs dried up as the old guard left or retired, but the club were revitalised by the emergence of striker Karl-Heinz Rummenigge and the return of Breitner. The arrival of the influential Lothar Matthäus in 1984 prompted another trio of league wins. In the early 1990s, however, Bayern struggled and 'Der Kaiser' returned as club president in 1994 to reverse their fortunes, overseeing the team's UEFA Cup win in 1996 as coach.

A new breed of Bayern stalwarts then emerged under wünder-coach Ottmar Hitzfeld, with players such as Kahn, Effenberg and Linke. They put their heartbreaking last minute defeat by Manchester United in the 1999 Champions Cup Final behind them to win in 2001 against Valencia, while pocketing another string of German titles, including the league and cup double in 2003.

In 1974 West Germany won the World Cup on Bayern's home ground. Bayern are now moving to a new stadium which will host the 2006 World Cup Final.

BENFICA

  LISBON, PORTUGAL
Stadium: Stadium Of Light (45,000)

Founded: 1904 **Honours:** Champions Cup 1961, 1962; League 30; Cup 26

Though in terms of silverware Benfica have fallen on barren times, they remain Portugal's most famous and successful side. But while there may have been a great deal to celebrate over the years as a Benfica fan, the trophy cabinet should not have been quite so barren.

Few sides in history could compare with the Benfica side of the 1960s, yet while they swept all before them on home soil, an amazing six Champions Cup final appearances in that decade alone brought just two victories. Spanish opposition was beaten in both 1961 and 1962 in the shape of Barcelona and Real Madrid – the 1962 final ending in a remarkable 5-3 victory as the great Eusébio (a statue of whom now stands outside Benfica's ground) scored twice after Ferenc Puskás fired a first half hat-trick for Real. The Italian clubs were not quite so charitable, with both Inter Milan and AC Milan foiling Benfica in the three finals that followed. And in 1968 it was Manchester United's turn to heap further final misery on the Lisbon giants.

In 1978 the club scrapped its policy of fielding only Portuguese citizens (and those from the colonies – Eusébio was born in Mozambique) in an effort to compete with Europe's best once again. The policy seemed to work as the club returned to European final action. However, as before, the club fell at the final hurdle on each occasion, finishing runners-up in the UEFA Cup in 1983 and in the Champions Cup in 1988 and 1990. The most galling defeat of all was losing 6-5 on penalties to PSV Eindhoven in 1988.

Of greatest concern to the Benfica sporting empire (the football club itself funds numerous other sports clubs) is that you have to go back to 1994 for the club's last Portuguese league title – and there is currently little to suggest that they can wrestle the balance of power back from rivals Porto.

BOCA JUNIORS

 BUENOS AIRES, ARGENTINA
Stadium: La Bombonara (58,750)

Founded: 1905 **Honours:** World Club Cup 1977, 2000; Copa Libertadores 1977, 1978, 2000, 2001, 2003; Super Cup 1989; League 23

Boca Juniors will be forever associated with former player and fervent fan Diego Maradona, but, in truth, the great man has only played a bit part in the club's long and eventful history. They were founded in 1905 by Irishman Patrick MacCarthy, together with a group of Italian immigrants, in the poor docklands of Buenos Aires – the neighbourhood that gave birth to the tango. To this day the club's humble roots have not been forgotten, and Boca Juniors will forever represent working class Argentina.

Six titles in the national amateur league signalled the club's arrival as a domestic force, and there hasn't been a decade since that

Opposite: Two years after their heartbreaking last minute defeat against Manchester United, Bayern Munich win the Champions League in 2001, defeating Valencia in the final.

the club hasn't got its hands on silverware. In 1931 they were the first winners of the inaugural Argentine Professional League. A decade later Boca moved to the Estadio Dr Camilo Cichero, or as it is more commonly known, 'La Bombonera' (The Chocolate Box).

Despite a flurry of domestic titles it was only with the arrival of disciplinarian coach Juan Carlos Lorenzo in 1976 that Boca emerged as a force outside of Argentina. During his five-year tenure, Boca won the South American Club Cup for the first time in 1977. A year later the title was defended with victory over Colombia's Deportivo Cali. While Boca's physical style of play under Lorenzo didn't win them too many friends among the football purists, a 5-2 aggregate victory against Borussia Mönchengladbach in 1977's World Club Cup kept their fans in a satisfied state of frenzy.

In 1980 Boca paid Argentinos Juniors £1million for Diego Maradona, but he was quickly sold on to Spanish club Barcelona in a £3million world record deal two seasons later. After his departure Boca's dominance waned, and it wasn't until the club's back-to-back successes in the Copa Libertadores in 2000 and 2001, under Carlos Bianchi, that status as a genuine intercontinental superpower was reaffirmed. A 2-1 victory over Real Madrid in the final of the World Club Cup in 2000, and their 2003 Copa Libertadores win, helped cement that reputation.

BORUSSIA DORTMUND

DORTMUND, GERMANY
Stadium: Westfalenstadion (68,600)

Founded: 1909 **Honours:** World Club Cup 1997; Champions Cup 1997; Cup Winners' Cup 1966; League 6; Cup 2

Borussia Dortmund's history has seen success in two distinct eras separated by a barren period stretching more than 30 years. The first taste of silverware occurred in the 1956-57 campaign when the club gained its first West German league title, a feat that was duly repeated the following season.

This heralded the start of what was to be the first golden era for the club: another title in 1963 was followed by the German Cup in 1965 and triumph in the European Cup Winners' Cup a year later. The 2-1 extra-time victory over Liverpool at Hampden Park gave Dortmund a special place in the record books, as the first German side to win a European trophy.

With the exception of a second German Cup in 1989, nothing but dust was added to the trophy cabinet at the Westfalenstadion until 1995, when a Matthias Sammer-inspired Dortmund pipped Werder Bremen to the Bundesliga title. The following year they ran out league winners again, but better was to

come. The 1997 Champions League Final in Munich's Olympic Stadium saw Dortmund, with two goals by Karl-Heinz Riedle and one by Lars Ricken, defeat a strong Juventus side 3-1. A subsequent 2-0 victory over Brazil's Cruzeiro in the World Club Cup final that year established the club's position as a force on the global football stage.

CELTIC

GLASGOW, SCOTLAND
Stadium: Celtic Park (61,000)

Founded: 1888 **Honours:** Champions Cup 1967; League 38; Cup 31; League Cup 12

Celtic's crowning moment was the 1967 European Cup final in Lisbon, when they beat Inter Milan 2-1 to become the first British side to win the competition. The team nearly repeated the feat in 1970 when, skippered again by Billy McNeill, they lost 2-1 to Feyenoord. The achievement of 'The Lions Of Lisbon' was especially heartening because all their players came from within a 30-mile radius of Celtic Park.

Celtic were very much the team of Glasgow's Irish immigrant community. A Catholic priest founded them as a charity, but they were never charitable to opponents and

their ongoing fierce rivalry with the Protestants of Rangers started early.

Under long-serving manager Willie Maley, their superb pre-First World War team won six consecutive championships. Between the wars Maley introduced such legends as Patsy Gallagher and Jimmy McGrory, still the club's leading goalscorer. After World War II Celtic faltered until the appointment of ex-player Jock Stein in 1965. He soon moulded the European Cup-winning side from the likes of Tommy Gemmell, Bertie Auld and tricky winger 'Jinky' Jimmy Johnstone. The team won every competition they entered that season and, joined by he likes of Kenny Dalglish and Lou Macari, raced to nine titles in a row.

In the years that followed, the league was shared among Celtic, their 'Old Firm' adversaries Rangers, and new force Aberdeen. The 1990s, however, belonged to Rangers. Celtic underwent a transformation to be able to compete, and new owner Fergus McCann rebuilt the club and their stadium. Following the example set by Rangers, Celtic began importing foreign players, including goal machine Henrik Larsson. The strategy paid off as it prevented Rangers from breaking Celtic's own record of successive title wins.

Martin O'Neill arrived at the helm in 2000 and won the treble in his first season. In 2003 he took Celtic to their first European final in 33 years, but they lost the UEFA Cup to Porto.

COLO COLO

SANTIAGO, CHILE
Stadium: David Arellano
(62,500)

Founded: 1925 **Honours:** Copa Libertadores 1991; South American Recopa 1991; League 21; Cup 10

Chile's most successful club side gained their exotic name from the local slang term for a 'wildcat'. Based in the capital, Santiago, they were one of the first South American teams to tour Europe and visited both Spain and Portugal in 1927. Founder members of the Chilean league in 1933, Colo Colo have tasted championship victory on an unprecedented 21 occasions. Their record in the haphazardly scheduled Chilean Cup – established in 1958, but not played between 1962 and 1973 – is also peerless, with ten wins.

In 1973 they became the first Chilean side to reach the final of the South American Club Cup, but lost 2-1 to Independiente of Argentina in a close-fought play-off game. However, with a 3-0 aggregate win in 1991 over Olimpia of Paraguay, Colo Colo finally became the first (and only) Chilean club to lift the trophy. The triumph was made all the greater for a well-deserved victory over the might of Boca Juniors in the semi-final. Their subsequent appearance in the World Club Cup ended in a heavy 3-0 defeat against Red Star Belgrade.

In recent years, like many other South American teams, the club has experienced significant money problems, but the club have now bounced back from bankruptcy in 2002.

CORINTHIANS

SÃO PAULO, BRAZIL
Stadium: Alfredo Schurig,
Parque São Jorge (14,000)

Founded: 1910 **Honours:** World Club Championship 2000; League 3; Cup 2

In 1910 the famed Corinthians, one of English football's pioneering clubs, toured Brazil, winning all its games. Such was their influence that a group of students from the Tatuapé area of São Paulo were inspired to set up their own club, adopting the English team's name in their honour. São Paulo expanded rapidly to become one of the world's biggest cities and the club grew with it to become one of the best supported clubs in Brazil – so much so that the team regularly switches matches from its modest home ground, the Parque São Jorge, to the council-owned Pacaembu stadium with its 40,000 capacity.

Their fans, known as the 'Fiel' – the 'faithful' – are also among the country's most fervent, so much so that when the team was flirting with relegation during the mid-Nineties a group of them ambushed the Corinthians' team bus on the motorway.

Despite their mass popularity Corinthians failed to win a national title until 1990 and then had to wait until the end of the decade to repeat the feat. The team cashed in on that success by winning the inaugural World Club Championship, beating rivals Vasco De Gama on penalties in the Maracana in January, 2000.

Among the famous players to have worn the Corinthians shirt are the celebrated World Cup winning quartet of Rivelino, Socrates, Dunga and Rivaldo.

DYNAMO KIEV

KIEV, UKRAINE
Stadium: Valeri Lobanovsky
Dynamo Stadium (82,000)

Founded: 1927 **Honours:** Cup Winners' Cup 1975, 1986; European Supercup 1975; Ukrainian League 10, Soviet League 13; Ukrainian Cup 6, Soviet Cup 8

Founder members of the Soviet Union league in 1936, Dynamo Kiev had to wait until 1961 for their first championship. After this landmark was reached, the club established itself as a major force in Soviet football, and Kiev's final total of 13 Soviet League titles, beating the 12 of their rivals Spartak Moscow, will forever remain a record following the dissolution of the Soviet Union in 1991.

In 1975, under the guidance of legendary coach Valeri Lobanovsky, Kiev became the first Soviet team to win a European trophy, demolishing Ferencváros 3-0 in the final of the Cup Winners' Cup. Indeed, the history of the club cannot be separated from that of Lobanovsky, who guided them to success in the same competition in 1986. His death in May 2002 cast a great shadow over Ukrainian football, and as a mark of respect Dynamo renamed their stadium after him.

Since the formation of the post-Communist Vischcha Liga in Ukraine few clubs can boast such a stranglehold over domestic football. With the aid of former luminaries such as Andriy Shevchenko and Sergei Rebrov, Dynamo Kiev have won ten of the 11

championships contested. The exception occurred in the 2002 season when Shaktar Donetsk finally broke the monopoly, and consigned Kiev to second place. Things were put right in 2003 as Kiev won the double.

Above: Andriy Shevchenko, one of the players who helped Dynamo Kiev to nine league titles in ten years.

DYNAMO MOSCOW

MOSCOW, RUSSIA
Stadium: Dynamo
(36,800)

Founded: 1923 **Honours:** Soviet League 11; Soviet Cup 7, Russian Cup 1

Dynamo Moscow will always be known for their association with goalkeeping legend, Lev Yashin. The 'Black Panther' played 326 times for the club, winning the league title on six occasions and the Soviet Cup twice. It was during his tenure between the sticks that the club experienced its most successful era. After his departure Dynamo have for the great part lived in the shadow of their great rivals, Spartak Moscow, though they can lay claim to being the first Soviet team to reach a European final, when in 1972 they went down 3-2 to Rangers in the Cup Winners' Cup.

In 1923 Dynamo Moscow were ominously taken under the control of Felix Dzerzhinsky, the leader of the Russian secret police and future head of the KGB. The club is more famed, however, for an historic four-match tour of Britain in 1945. Helping to feed the appetite of a public starved of competitive football due to the Second World War, the Russians greatly impressed with their ball skills and progressive play, beating a strong Arsenal side, demolishing Cardiff 10-1, and gaining creditable draws against Chelsea and Rangers.

The formation of the post-Communist Vysshaya Liga in 1991 has seen a largely disappointing Dynamo, with only a Russian

Left: Lev Yashin, Russia's Black Panther, played 326 times for Dynamo Moscow.

Above: Feyenoord's Johan Elmander and Pierre Van Hooijdonk celebrate winning the 2002 UEFA Cup at their home stadium in Rotterdam, where they beat Borussia Dortmund.

Cup victory in 1995 to add to the roll of honour. To add insult to injury, in 1998 Dynamo's undersoil heating malfunctioned and managed to scorch the playing surface rendering it unplayable.

EINTRACHT FRANKFURT

FRANKFURT, GERMANY
Stadium: Waldstadion (48,000)

Founded: 1899 **Honours:** UEFA Cup 1980; League 1; Cup 4

Eintracht Frankfurt may have been formed more than 100 years ago, and were founder members of the Bundesliga in 1963, but to most people the club's reputation is based on just one game. The 90 minutes in question is the 1960 European Cup Final at Hampden, when they were on the wrong end of a 7-3 scoreline dished out by a Real Madrid side inspired by the combined genius of Ferenc Puskás and Alfredo Di Stéfano. Many football pundits still look back on the match as the finest ever played.

This is of scant consolation to Frankfurt, as the club has perpetually struggled to get out from under the shadow of that game. That's not to say there haven't been successes, with 1980's UEFA Cup triumph over fellow German side Borussia Mönchengladbach being an obvious exception. Inspired by such world-class stars as German midfielder Andy Möller and Ghanaian striker Tony Yeboah, the club underwent a brief renaissance in the early Nineties with a series of impressive tilts at the domestic league title.

In recent years, however, Frankfurt have bounced between the two top divisions in the Bundesliga, and have been beset by crippling financial problems, so much so that they were very nearly expelled to the amateur leagues in 2002, but eventually managing to retain their status after appeal.

FK AUSTRIA VIENNA

VIENNA, AUSTRIA
Stadium: Franz Horr Stadion (11,800)

Founded: 1911 **Honours:** League 22; Cup 23

Founded in the Austrian capital on March 12, 1911 by members of the Vienna Cricket and Football Club, the team were initially known as SV Amateure Vienna, and won their first league title under this name in 1924. With the onset of a professional league the name changed to FK Austria two years later.

The early 1930s were the club's most famous years and corresponded with the Austrian national team's domination of European football. It was no coincidence as the so-called Austrian 'Wunderteam' contained many players from FK Austria, including the legendary Matthias Sindelar.

Club success came not only in the form of domestic league titles, but also with victories in the Mitropa Cup, a forerunner of the Champions League. FK Austria claimed this prestigious trophy in 1933 and 1936.

In 1977 a new sponsor changed the club's name to the unwieldy FK Austria Memphis, and the modern side have failed to live up to the Violets' glorious past. An appearance in the 1978 Cup Winners' Cup Final led to a heavy 4-0 defeat at the hands of Anderlecht. There are signs, however, that the good times are returning, and with the club winning the league and cup double in 2003, the promise of Champions League football has led the club to make plans to increase the capacity of the Franz Horr Stadium.

FEYENOORD

ROTTERDAM, HOLLAND
Stadium: De Kuip Stadium (51,000)

Founded: 1908 **Honours:** World Club Cup 1970; Champions Cup 1970; UEFA Cup 1974, 2002; League 14; Cup 10

Feyenoord became the first Dutch side to land a European trophy when they won the Champions Cup in 1970. Amsterdam-based rivals Ajax had missed out in the final the previous year to Milan, but the Rotterdam side's 2-1 victory over Celtic at the San Siro stadium in Milan began a four-year monopoly of Europe's top prize for Dutch clubs. Sadly for Feyenoord, whose defence of their trophy ended in the ignominy of going out to Romanian minnows UT Arad, their 1970 victory was just the forerunner to an Ajax hat-trick of successes.

More European glory followed in 1974 with victory over Tottenham Hotspur in the UEFA Cup final, but the Eighties and Nineties saw Feyenoord eclipsed by both Ajax and PSV Eindhoven in the Dutch league. Domestic cup triumph proved to be their biggest area of success during this period, as problems off the pitch took more of the headlines, with financial difficulties for the club and a disturbing hooligan element among their support mirroring the decline in fortunes on the field.

Manager Leo Beenhakker helped Feyenoord to their most recent league title in 1999 and PSV, Inter Milan and Borussia Dortmund were among those beaten as the Rotterdam side gained more UEFA Cup success in 2002 and gave hope that better times may lie ahead.

FLAMENGO

RIO DE JANEIRO, BRAZIL
Stadium: Gavea (13,000)
Maracana (95,095)

Founded: 1911 **Honours:** World Club Cup 1981;
Copa Libertadores 1981; Copa Mercosur 1999;
Rio State League 22; Brazil Championship 5

Football in Rio still reflects the divisions of race and class in the city, and while arch rivals Fluminense are seen to represent the middle classes, Flamengo have always been the club of the people. This appeal makes them by far the most popular club in Brazil, and 'Fla's' support is garnered not just from the favellas of Rio itself, but from districts throughout the country. Ironically enough, the club was formed when disaffected members of Fluminense joined the Flamengo rowing club in 1911 to create a football team.

Despite enormous popularity within their own country it wasn't until the early 1980s that the club established itself as a force to be reckoned with on the world stage. Under the influence of Zico, one of the club's greatest players, Flamengo finally got its hands on both the South American Club Cup and the World Club Cup in 1981. With what is still regarded as one of the strongest ever Brazilian club sides, they beat Cobreloa of Chile in an ill-tempered game to lift the Copa Libertadores. To cap the achievement they produced another great performance, with Zico again to the fore, to dismiss a strong Liverpool team 3-0 in the World Club Cup final.

FLUMINENSE

RIO DE JANIERO, BRAZIL
Stadium: Laranjeiras (8,000)
Maracana (95,095)

Founded: 1902 **Honours:** Rio State League 27;
Brazil championship 4

Fluminense were founded in 1902 by the wealthy expat British community, and those privileged origins continue to define the club, as 'Flu' are still regarded as the club of Rio's elite middle classes, in direct contrast to the 'everyman' appeal of bitter rivals Flamengo. The club were founder members of the Rio de Janeiro Amateur League, and trophies came early with four successive titles spanning 1906 to 1909. Further domestic league trophies have continued to be captured, including five consecutive Rio State League titles between 1936 to 1941.

For all their success in Brazil, Fluminense have amazingly yet to win an international tournament. Flu's overall record in the South American Club Cup – not reaching a single final – is a poor one. This comes as more of

a surprise when you consider the list of great players that the club has had to call on over the years. The magical Didi played for the club in the early 1950s, pulling the strings in midfield as much as he did for Brazil's World Cup winning sides of 1958 and 1962. Carlos Alberto, Brazil's 1970 World Cup winning captain, is another former Fluminense great.

GALATASARAY

ISTANBUL, TURKEY
Stadium: Ali Sami Yen
Stadium (40,000)

Founded: 1905 **Honours:** UEFA Cup 2000; Super
Cup 2000; League 15; Turkish Cup 13

Galatasaray are Turkey's most successful club side, with a long and distinguished history that has passion written through it at every stage. Founded by Ali Sami Yen and a group of friends from the Galatasaray Lycée school, the club's stated aim was 'to play together like Englishmen, to have a colour and a name, and to beat the non-Turkish teams'.

Winners of the Istanbul league nine times between 1924 and 1958, it took the club four seasons before they won the national Turkish league after its establishment in 1959, lifting their first championship trophy in 1962, having been eclipsed in the preceding campaigns by both of their Istanbul rivals Fenerbahçe (twice) and Besiktas.

Their greatest triumph came in 2000 when they beat Arsenal on penalties to win their first UEFA Cup, having already won the domestic league. A few months later they beat Real Madrid in the Super Cup final with a golden goal from Mario Jardel. The manager at the time, Fatih Terim, was already a club legend, having played 327 times for the team, but UEFA Cup success raised him above other Galatasaray greats like Metin Oktay, Turgay Seren and Gheorghe Hagi.

The intimidating atmosphere created by their supporters led to the Ali Sami Yen Stadium being dubbed 'Hell'. Despite a planned revamp of the ground, that reputation is likely to remain for many years to come.

HAMBURG

HAMBURG, GERMANY
Stadium: Volksparkstadion
(55,000)

Founded: 1887 **Honours:** Champions Cup 1983;
Cup Winners' Cup 1977; League 6; Cup 3

On paper Hamburg are the oldest club in Germany. Having been formed in 1887 as SC Germania, in June 1919 the club merged with Hamburg FC and FC Falke to create Hamburg SV, with the red and white strip picked as a compromise that was suitable for all parties.

National champions twice in the 1920s when the title was decided in a play-off format

Left: Hamburg's Kevin
Keegan playing in the 1980
European Cup Final against
Nottingham Forest.

between the winners of the various regional leagues, Hamburg would not win the title again until they clinched the West German championship in 1960 under the leadership of legendary centre-forward Uwe Seeler.

Seeler's Hamburg side took Barcleona close in the semi-final of the 1961 Champions Cup, losing in a play-off, and seven years later finished as runners-up to Milan in the Cup Winners' Cup. But by the time of his retirement in 1972, the club had yet to taste European glory. That changed in 1977 with a Cup Winners' Cup triumph over Anderlecht, goals from Georg Volkert and Felix Magath sealing the 2-0 victory in Amsterdam.

Spearheaded in the late Seventies by Kevin Keegan – his performances for the club saw him voted European Player Of The Year for both 1978 and 1979 – Hamburg clinched their first Bundesliga title in 1979, ushering in a truly golden period for the club. The magic of Keegan couldn't help Hamburg avoid a 1-0 defeat to Nottingham Forest in the Champions Cup final of 1980, but without him they went on to win the Bundesliga in 1982 and 1983 (finishing runners-up four times in the decade too) and the German Cup in 1987.

In 1983 Felix Magath was the Hamburg hero once again as he scored the only goal of the 1983 Champions Cup Final against a Juventus team that boasted Platini, Zoff, Gentile, Tardelli and Rossi. But since the golden period of the Eighties, Hamburg fans haven't had too much to cheer about, the side too often settling for mid-table mediocrity.

INDEPENDIENTE

BUENOS AIRES, ARGENTINA
Stadium: Doble Visera De Cemente (57,901)

Founded: 1905 **Honours:** World Club Cup 1973, 1984; Copa Libertadores 1964, 1965, 1972, 1973, 1974, 1975, 1984; Inter-American Cup 1973, 1974, 1976; Super Cup 1994, 1995; League 14

Formed in the Avellaneda suburb of Buenos Aires, Independiente were founded, strangely enough, by employees of the City Of London department store. The club may not possess the global glamour of River Plate or Boca Juniors, but can boast far greater success in the prestigious South American Club Cup than either of their higher-profile city rivals. Indeed, they were the first Argentine side to claim the trophy in 1964, getting the better of Uruguay's Nacional. A record-breaking seven Copa Libertadores titles, including an unlikely-to-be-equalled run of four successive triumphs from 1972 to 1975, has earned the club the nickname of 'The King of Cups'.

The silverware spree doesn't end there, and a brace of World Club Cups have also competed for space in the crowded trophy cabinet. The first of these wins was by a single goal against Juventus in Rome in 1973, followed 11 years later by victory over Liverpool by the same scoreline in Tokyo.

Since the glory days, Independiente's fortunes have declined, with mounting debts, bad management, and declining crowds forcing the club to sell top players. The joint sale of Diego Forlan to Manchester United (£7.5million) and Vincente Vuoso (£3.5million) to Manchester City proving absolutely vital to the club's survival in 2002.

INTER MILAN

MILAN, ITALY
Stadium: Giuseppe Meazza (85,700)

Founded: 1908 **Honours:** World Club Cup 1964, 1965; Champions Cup 1964, 1965; UEFA Cup 1991, 1994, 1998; League 13; Cup 3

Giovani Paramithotti founded Football Club Internazionale Milano on March 9, 1908, after he and a group of his supporters broke away from AC Milan following a major policy disagreement with that club's owners. The name Internazionale was chosen because the club was to be open to players of all nationalities, unlike AC Milan who only allowed Italians to join them. To underline its commitment to internationalism, the club's first captain hailed from Switzerland. All things considered, it comes as no surprise that the rivalry between Milan's AC and Inter remains one of the fiercest in world football almost a century after the split.

Inter won their first Italian championship in 1910, picked up another in 1920, and were one of the founders of Serie A in 1929. They remain, along with Juventus, one of only two clubs never to have lost top-flight status. Along the way they have boasted many world-class players, including Brazilians such as Ronaldo and Jair, German trio Jürgen Klinsmann, Andreas Brehme and Lothar Matthäus, goal-scoring defender Giacinto Facchetti and Giuseppe Meazza, the prodigious striker after whom the stadium is named – a stadium, incidentally, shared with AC Milan.

When the fascists under Benito Mussolini came to power in Italy Inter were forced to take on a less cosmopolitan name: in 1929 they became Ambrosiana, after the patron saint of the city of Milan.

The name switch didn't do Inter any harm on the pitch and they won three Serie A titles – in 1930, 1938 and 1940 – as well as the Coppa Italia in 1939. They were also successful in the Mitropa Cup, a prototype of today's UEFA and European Champions cups, making the semi-finals twice (1930 and 1936) and the final once (1933).

After World War II and the defeat of fascism, Inter reverted to their original name, appointed Alfredo Foni as coach and continued adding trophies to their cabinet, winning back-to-back titles in 1953 and 1954.

It wasn't until the 1960s under another coach – Helenio Herrera – that they were able to enjoy domestic, European and international success at the same time though. Serie A winners in 1963, Inter were crowned European champions for the first time the following season, comfortably beating Real Madrid 3-1 in the final in Vienna with two goals from striker Sandro Mazzola. They then beat Independiente of Argentina in the same year's World Club Cup, before pulling off an even more impressive trophy haul in 1965.

Having already been crowned Italian title winners and eliminating Liverpool in the semi-finals, Inter retained the European Champions Cup with a 1-0 win in Milan over mighty Benfica. They then beat Independiente 3-0 over two legs to keep their world crown intact. Inter retained their league title the following season and made it to the final of the Champions Cup in 1967, only to lose to Celtic 2-1 after initially taking the lead through a Mazzola penalty.

A title win in 1971 and a European Champions Cup final appearance the following season (they lost 2-0 to Ajax) couldn't disguise the fact that without their massively influential coach Herrera, who had joined Roma, Inter's time as one of the world's biggest clubs had come to an end.

The rest of Seventies and Eighties were hardly unkind to the club – they won Serie A in 1980 and 1989, and the Coppa Italia in 1978 and 1982, but it wasn't until the Nineties that the Milan club once again made significant waves in Europe. In 1991 they won the UEFA Cup for the first time, beating AS Roma 2-1 in a two-legged all-Italian final, and repeated the feat three years later in a 2-0 aggregate victory over Austria Salzburg. Another UEFA Cup final appearance followed in 1997, but having battled out a draw over two legs with German side Schalke, Inter lost 4-1 on penalties in Milan. Inter returned to put matters right in 1998 in their fourth final appearance in eight years, beating Lazio 3-0 in the competition's first one-off final.

In a concerted attempt to re-establish Inter as a force in both the Italian league and the much-coveted Champions Cup, the club appointed Argentinian Hector Cúper as coach in 2001. Cúper had taken his previous side, Valencia of Spain, to successive Champions Cup finals, and it didn't take long for him to make an impact at Inter. The club were involved in the fight for the 2001-02 domestic title right up until the very last day of the season. Inter eventually finished third behind Juventus and Roma, with just two points separating the top three.

Opposite clockwise from top left: the stars of Inter Milan – Ivan Luis Zamorano scores against FC Schalke in the 1997 UEFA Cup Final; Dennis Bergkamp in action in 1994; Ronaldo lifts the 1998 UEFA Cup; Giuseppe Bergomi in 1998.

JUVENTUS

TURIN, ITALY
Stadium: Delle Alpi
(69,000)

Founded: 1897 **Honours:** World Club Cup 1985,
1996; Champions Cup 1985, 1996; Cup Winners'
Cup 1984; UEFA Cup 1977, 1990, 1993;
League 27; Cup 9

Famously founded on a Turin park bench by
a group of high school students in November
1897, Juventus have become the most
successful Italian club of all time. Never out
of Serie A since its formation in 1929, and
crowned champions on 27 occasions between
1905 and 2003, the club has also featured
some of the world's most celebrated players,
including Michel Platini, Zinedine Zidane,
Dino Zoff and Giampiero Boniperti, who still
holds club records for goals (177) and
appearances (444) more than 50 years after
first making his mark in the team. Originally
playing in pink, Juventus adopted their famous
black-and-white stripes in 1903 after a club
official visited England and liked Notts
County's shirts so much that he took a bundle
of them back home with him.

It wasn't until the 1930s that Juventus truly
emerged as a superpower in the Italian league.
They won five consecutive championships
between 1931 and 1935 under coach Carlo
Carcano, a feat that remains unrepeated.
Players such as goalkeeper Gianpiero Combi,
centre-half Monti, winger Raimondo Orsi and
striker Giovanni Ferrari went on to help Italy
win the World Cup in 1934 – Orsi even scored
his country's equaliser against Czechoslovakia
in the final. During this time Juventus also
reached the semi-finals of the Mitropa Cup
(the forerunner of European tournaments
such as the UEFA Cup and Champions Cup)
on four consecutive occasions. Unfortunately,
they never made it to the final and on one

occasion were actually disqualified from the
tournament altogether after a brutal semi final
tie against Slavia (who were also banned).

Intermittent success in the league and cup
continued throughout the Fifties and Sixties
(they won back-to-back cups in 1959 and 1960
and league titles in 1960 and 1961), but it
wasn't until the Seventies that the club
translated their domestic success into
European progress. They made it to the final
of the Fairs Cup in 1971, but after three drawn
games with Leeds (one a replay of the first leg),
they lost out on the away goals rule. In 1977
they won the UEFA Cup on the same rule
against Athletic Bilbao, although they came
close to throwing the tie away having led 2-0
on aggregate before being pegged back by the
determined Spaniards. Juventus added the
Cup Winners' Cup to their trophy cabinet in
1984 with a 2-1 victory over Porto.

The European Champions Cup continued
to elude them: their first final came in 1973
but they were defeated 1-0 by Ajax, and history
repeated itself in 1983 when they lost to
Hamburg by the same scoreline. Juventus
were finally crowned European champions for
the first time in the Heysel Stadium in 1985,
when a team featuring Italy's 1982 World Cup
hero Paolo Rossi defeated Liverpool 1-0. Sadly
their long awaited moment of glory was
overshadowed by the deaths of 39 Italian fans
during pre-match violence between the two
sets of supporters.

The 1990s promised much for Juventus –
massive sums of money were spent on
securing the services of Roberto Baggio from
Fiorentina and Gianluca Vialli from
Sampdoria, and the club won the UEFA Cup
twice, in 1990 and 1993. It was only when
Marcelo Lippi joined as coach from Napoli,
though, that the Juventus success story moved
up a gear. The Turin side claimed their first
league title in nine years in 1995 (also claiming

the Coppa Italia) and won back-to-back
championships in 1997 and 1998. Even more
impressively, Lippi's side beat Ajax on penalties
to lift the European Champions Cup for
a second time in 1996, following it up with a
crushing 9-2 aggregate win over Paris Saint-
Germain in the same year's European Super
Cup. Juventus also reached the final of the
European Champions Cup in 1997 and 1998,
but despite starting the games as favourites,
lost on both occasions – 3-1 to Borussia
Dortmund and then 1-0 to Real Madrid.

Lippi left for Internazionale in 1999 after
a final trophy-free season at the Delle Alpi, but
returned after only a year in Milan. He won
the Serie A title in dramatic fashion in his first
season back, pipping Lazio and Inter to the
championship on its final day. The challenge
now, however, is to make genuine progress in
the Champions League, which the club has
failed to do since the late 1990s.

Above: Alessandro Del Piero celebrates Juve's league title win in 1998. Opposite clockwise from top: the stars of Juventus
– Gianluca Vialli lifts the European Cup in 1996; 'The White Feather', Fabrizio Ravanelli; Roberto Baggio lifting the UEFA
Cup in 1993; and 2000 World Player Of The Year, Zinedine Zidane. Below: Irish export Liam Brady with Juventus in 1980.

STADIO DELLE ALPI

The Stadio Delle Alpi was built in Turin to
host the 1990 World Cup, but has never been
popular with fans, who prefer the city's old
Stadio Comunale. Delle Alpi is being rebuilt,
with the athletics track being removed and
capacity reduced to 35,000. The hope is that
the arena will become more intimate and live
down its 'stadium without a soul' tag.

Timeline

1895

1897: Students from Turin's Liceo D'Azeglio form a sports club. The team play in pink shirts.

1900

1903: Juve adopt the famous black and white shirt, inpired by the strip of Notts County.

1905

1905: Juventus beat more experienced teams from Genoa and Milan to win their first Italian title.

1910

1915

1923: Edoardo Agnelli, son of FIAT's founder, is elected club president. The club moves to a new stadium.

1920

1925

1926: Juventus win their second title.

1930

1931: Juve win the title for five years in a row, from 1931-35.

1933: Juve move home again. A stadium is built for the World University Games and the team plays here until 1990.

1935

1940

1945

1947: Giovanni Agnelli becomes president of Juventus.

1950

1955: Umberto Agnelli takes over the presidency from his older brother Giovanni.

1955

1957: John Charles is bought for £70,000 from Leeds, doubling the British transfer record.

1960

1961: Juve become the first Italian club entitled to wear the star after winning ten titles.

1965

1970

1972 to 1986: Juve win nine titles and all major European and Intercontinental tournaments.

1975

1985: Juventus defeat Liverpool to win the European Cup, but it is a game remembered for the deaths of fans in the Heysel Stadium.

1980

1985

1990: Juve win the UEFA Cup and Italian Cup. They move to the 69,041-capacity Stadio Delle Alpi.

1990

1994: Coach Marcelo Lippi guides the team to their first title in nine years.

1995

1996: Juve beat Ajax on penalties to win the Champions League.

2000

2003: Title-winners again, they lose the European Cup to Milan.

2005

KASHIMA ANTLERS

KASHIMA, JAPAN
Stadium: Kashima Soccer
Stadium (41,800)

Founded: 1991 **Honours:** League 4; League Cup 2;
Emperor's Cup 4

Formerly the factory team of Sumitomo Metals, the club transformed into the Kashima Antlers in 1991, taking its name and logo from the town's literal translation as Deer Island. Kashima began its J.League life by winning the first ever stage of the two-stage race, but the club had to wait until 1996 for its first full championship. Since then it has overtaken more traditional sides like Verdy Kawasaki to become the most dominant team in Japan, winning an unprecedented treble (league title, Nabisco Cup, Emperor's Cup) in 2000.

Kashima's footballing dominance has been built on the presence of Brazilian imports including Jorginho, Alcindo and, most importantly, the legendary Zico, who joined the club on its foundation in 1991 and eventually became its general manager. Zico retired before the club won its first title but is revered in Kashima, having not one but two statues dedicated to him there. He was appointed Japan national coach in 2002.

Although based in a modest-sized town, Kashima Antlers are one of the best supported sides in the league, averaging 17,000 fans per game, who flock to a state-of-the-art dedicated stadium which was dramatically redeveloped for the 2002 World Cup.

LAZIO

ROME, ITALY
Stadium: Olympic Stadium
(82,000)

Founded: 1900 **Honours:** Cup Winners' Cup 1999;
Super Cup 1999; League 2; Cup 3

Until the arrival of Sven Göran Eriksson as coach at the start of the 1997-98 season, it's safe to say that Lazio had been one of Italian football's great underachievers. Founded on January 9, 1900, by Luigi Bigiarelli and eight friends, the club had endured decades waiting in the wings while Juventus and AC Milan paraded centre stage. However, Lazio's threadbare trophy cabinet – containing an Italian Cup (1958) and a single league title (1974) – was soon filled to bursting as the Rome side took seven trophies in three heady seasons of achievement.

Eriksson and a team that included the likes of Chilean striker Marcelo Salas, Argentinian midfielder Juan Sebástian Verón and Italian hitman Christian Vieri, won two Italian Cups, two domestic Super Cups (played between the Italian league champions and cup winners), the UEFA Super Cup (beating Manchester United) and a European Cup Winners' Cup (2-1 over Mallorca). Most significantly of all, Eriksson steered Lazio to a second league title in 2000, before leaving the club the following season – during a run of bad results – to take up the post of England coach. Since the genial Swede's departure, Lazio, under coaches such as Dino Zoff, Alberto Zaccheroni and Roberto Mancini, have struggled to match the string of achievements during his remarkably successful period in charge, although they remain one of Italy's biggest clubs.

LEEDS UNITED

LEEDS, ENGLAND
Stadium: Elland Road
(40,204)

Founded: 1919 **Honours:** Fairs Cup 1968, 1971;
League 3; Cup 1; League Cup 1

Following allegations of illegal payments to players, Second Division Leeds City were wound-up by the FA in October 1919. Leeds United were formed the following month. With Port Vale having taken over Leeds City's remaining fixtures, the new United initially began playing in the Midland League, before entering the Second Division after turning professional in 1920.

In the 1930s, in Edwards, Hart and Copping, Leeds United boasted one of the great half-back lines in English football, while in 1957 the club made headlines by selling John Charles to Juventus for a British-record of £70,000. For much of their first 40 years, however, Leeds United merely bounced between the top two divisions. It wasn't until the mid-1960s that the team really became a major force in English football, mainly as a result of the appointment in 1959 of Don Revie as player-manager.

Although relegated in 1960, over the next five years Revie would transform the club, changing the team colours from blue and gold to their now famous all-white (inspired by the European triumphs of Real Madrid), and rebuilding the team around a talented group of young players that included the celebrated names of Jack Charlton, Billy Bremner, Peter Lorimer, Norman Hunter, Paul Reaney, Paul Madeley, Eddie Gray and Johnny Giles.

Promoted to Division One in 1964 as champions, in their first year back in the top flight they narrowly lost the title on goal average to Manchester United and the FA Cup final to Liverpool, helping to establish a reputation that would haunt the club for the next decade. Under Revie they would be known as the greatest runners-up in English football: five times they would finish second in the league, three times in the FA Cup, and once each in all three European competitions.

That's not to say that success eluded them. In 1968 they first beat Arsenal to win the League Cup, before lifting the Fairs Cup with a 1-0 aggregate win over Ferencváros. The following year they won their first league title, and in 1971 they beat Juventus to again lift the Fairs Cup. In 1972 a single Allan Clarke goal beat Arsenal to win the centenary FA Cup, and in 1974, at the end of the Revie era, they won their second league championship.

Following this success, Revie left Elland Road to take charge of the national team. Brian Clough was the nominated successor, but his tenure in the Leeds hotseat lasted days rather than months, leaving Jimmy Armfield to complete the season and take the team to the 1975 European Cup Final. The match proved pivotal in the history of Leeds United – not only did they lose 2-0 to an understrength Bayern Munich, but after a riot by their fans, the club were banned from all European competition for the next five years.

Leeds were relegated in 1982, their glory days seemingly behind them. Managed in turn by former legends Allan Clarke, Eddie Gray and Billy Bremner, Leeds turned to Howard Wilkinson – poached from nearby Sheffield Wednesday – who finally brought the good times back to Elland Road after joining the club in 1988. Achieving promotion in 1990, he took Leeds back to the very top of the English game two years later when – inspired by the mercurial Frenchman Eric Cantona – the club clinched the final Football League title before the onset of the Premier League.

Building on that revival, at the turn of the century, under David O'Leary, Leeds were once again regarded as a force to be reckoned with in European football, reaching the semi-finals of the Champions Cup in 2001. But in attempting to reach those heady Euro heights, the club financially overstretched themselves – and they are still paying the price for their ambition today.

Right: Leeds United's Allan Clarke, whose goal won the 100th FA Cup final in 1972, celebrates another strike.

LIVERPOOL

LIVERPOOL, ENGLAND
Stadium: Anfield
(46,000)

Founded: 1892 **Honours:** Champions Cup 1977, 1978, 1981, 1984; UEFA Cup 1973, 1976, 2001; Super Cup 1977; League 18; Cup 5; League Cup 7

Strangely, Liverpool have their city neighbours and great rivals, Everton, to thank for their existence. Then residents at Anfield, The Toffees became embroiled in an argument with the stadium's owner, John Houlding, over rent payments, and, unable to find a mutually acceptable solution, left to set up a new home at Goodison Park. In possession of a football ground but no team to play in it, Houlding formed Liverpool Football Club on March 15, 1892, and soon saw them rise from the local Lancashire League to the English Second Division – and then gain promotion to the top-flight in 1894.

The first of 18 league titles came in 1901, with four more championships arriving over the course of the next 40 or so years. However, Liverpool returned to the Second Division in 1954 and it wasn't until the arrival of charismatic Scotsman, Bill Shankly, as manager in late 1959 that the foundations for the huge success enjoyed by the club in the Seventies and Eighties were laid.

Shankly's approach combined great tactical acumen with infectious enthusiasm, and his ability to instill self-belief in his players was second to none. Liverpool finally returned to Division One in 1962 and claimed a sixth league title two years later. But Shankly was only just getting started: two more championships (1966 and 1973) and two FA Cups (1965 and 1974) followed, before his retirement in 1974. Most significant of all Shankly's achievements though was the club's first European trophy – they beat Borussia Mönchengladbach 3-2 over two legs to lift the UEFA Cup in 1973.

Michael Owen, bringing pace and goals to the club.

Shankly's successor was Bob Paisley, a quietly spoken Geordie, who'd been first team coach and a vital member of the legendary Anfield 'boot room'. Paisley's achievements at Liverpool have never been matched in the English game. In nine extraordinary years he took The Reds to six league championships, three League Cups, one UEFA Cup and three Champions Cups – the first of which came in 1977 with a 3-1 win against Borussia Mönchengladbach. Liverpool retained the trophy the following year with a 1-0 win over Club Brugge and lifted it again in 1981 as they beat Real Madrid 1-0.

When Paisley stepped down as manager in 1983 he was replaced by another member of the Anfield backroom staff, Joe Fagan. Any notions that the Liverpool success story was about to come to a halt were despatched in the new manager's first season in charge as Liverpool claimed an impressive trophy treble of league title, League Cup and European Cup (won on penalties against AS Roma).

Liverpool reached the Champions Cup final the following year but lost 1-0 to Italian champions Juventus in the Heysel stadium in Brussels. However, the game itself was overshadowed by the terrible events that occurred as supporters of the two sides rioted. Thirty-nine Italian fans lost their lives when a wall collapsed, leading to a ban that kept English clubs, including Liverpool, out of European competition for the next five years.

Fagan's reign at Anfield was surprisingly short and when he stepped down at the end

of the 1984-85 season he was replaced by Kenny Dalglish, the first player-manager in the club's history. The Scottish international guided The Reds to a league and FA Cup double in his first season in charge (1985-86) and further championships in 1988 and 1990. Dalglish's side also won the FA Cup in 1989, but their triumph was tinged with tragedy – on April 15 of that year 96 Liverpool fans were crushed to death at Sheffield Wednesday's Hillsborough ground before kick-off in an FA Cup semi-final tie between The Reds and Nottingham Forest.

Dalglish quit suddenly at the end of the 1991 season to be replaced with former Anfield midfield hero Graeme Souness, who had enjoyed great success in Scotland as manager of Rangers. In his three seasons in charge, Souness won the FA Cup (1992) but Liverpool's primacy in the league started to slip. He was replaced in 1994 by veteran Anfield coach, Roy Evans, an appointment that suggested Liverpool were trying to recapture the old 'boot room' philosophy of promoting from within. When Evans failed to demonstrably improve Liverpool's league standing, Gerard Houllier was brought in to work alongside him, eventually taking over the manager's role altogether.

Although Houllier has returned Liverpool to trophy-winning ways, with triumphs in the FA Cup, UEFA Cup, Super Cup and League Cup in 2001, and the League Cup again in 2003, a 19th league title and progress in the Champions League continues to elude them.

Above: Bill Shankly, the legendary Liverpool manager, who laid the foundations for success during his 15-year tenure.

1892: Liverpool FC are founded on March 15. They win their first game 7-1, a friendly against Rotherham played on September 1.

1901: Liverpool clinch their first league title.

1906: The club wins a second title and builds the Spion Kop.

1947: The club win their fifth league title, 24 years after the previous one.

1954: After finishing 22nd in the league, Liverpool are relegated to Division Two.

1959: Bill Shankly is appointed manager.

1964: A title win sparks a golden era for the club, with further titles in 1966 and 1973, and the FA Cup in 1965 and 1974.

1973: Kevin Keegan scores two goals to win the UEFA Cup.

1974: Bill Shankly retires and is replaced by coach Bob Paisley.

1977: Liverpool beat Mönchengladbach to win the European Cup.

1981: Alan Kennedy's goal is enough to defeat Real Madrid and win the European Cup.

1984: New manager Joe Fagan wins a title, a European Cup and a League Cup in his first season.

1986: Kenny Dalglish is appointed manager and guides the club to the double.

1989: During an FA Cup semi-final 96 Liverpool fans die.

1998: Gerard Houllier joins Liverpool.

2001: Liverpool win the League Cup, the FA Cup and the UEFA Cup.

THE CHAMPIONS CUP WITH FOUR WINS, LIVERPOOL HAVE THE BEST RECORD OF ANY ENGLISH CLUB IN THE EUROPEAN CUP.

1977
Liverpool 3
B. Mönchengladbach 1
Olympic Stadium, Rome

1978
Liverpool 1
Club Brugge 0
Wembley Stadium, London

1981
Liverpool 1
Real Madrid 0
Parc Des Princes, Paris

1984
Liverpool 1
Roma 1
Liverpool 4-2 on penalties
Olympic Stadium, Rome

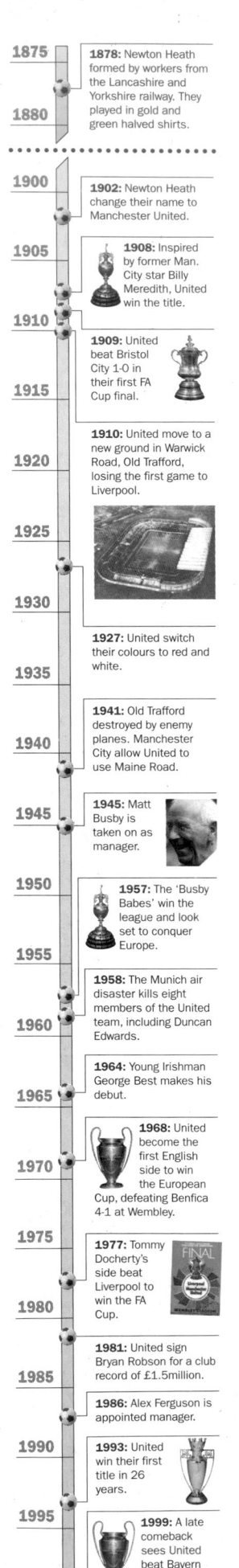

1875

1878: Newton Heath formed by workers from the Lancashire and Yorkshire railway. They played in gold and green halved shirts.

1880

1900

1902: Newton Heath change their name to Manchester United.

1905

1908: Inspired by former Man. City star Billy Meredith, United win the title.

1910

1909: United beat Bristol City 1-0 in their first FA Cup final.

1915

1910: United move to a new ground in Warwick Road, Old Trafford, losing the first game to Liverpool.

1920

1925

1927: United switch their colours to red and white.

1930

1935

1941: Old Trafford destroyed by enemy planes. Manchester City allow United to use Maine Road.

1940

1945: Matt Busby is taken on as manager.

1945

1950

1957: The 'Busby Babes' win the league and look set to conquer Europe.

1955

1958: The Munich air disaster kills eight members of the United team, including Duncan Edwards.

1960

1964: Young Irishman George Best makes his debut.

1965

1968: United become the first English side to win the European Cup, defeating Benfica 4-1 at Wembley.

1970

1975

1977: Tommy Docherty's side beat Liverpool to win the FA Cup.

1980

1981: United sign Bryan Robson for a club record of £1.5million.

1985

1986: Alex Ferguson is appointed manager.

1990

1993: United win their first title in 26 years.

1995

1999: A late comeback sees United beat Bayern Munich to win the European Cup 2-1.

2000

MANCHESTER UNITED

ENGLAND
Stadium: Old Trafford
(69,000)

Founded: 1878 **Honours:** World Club Cup 1999; Champions Cup 1968, 1999; Cup Winners' Cup 1991; European Supercup 1991; League 15; Cup 10; League Cup 1

The story of Manchester United is a real rags-to-riches tale. Now a commercial giant across the world, United have grown out of recognition from their humble beginnings. Formed as Newton Heath by employees of the Lancashire and Yorkshire Railway Company, the club had severe financial problems and were saved from bankruptcy in 1902 by a local brewery owner. The club took on the name Manchester United and almost immediately a period of success followed with a first league championship in 1908, followed 12 months later with victory in the FA Cup final.

To cope with growing attendances United left their Bank Street home, moving to Old Trafford in 1910, losing the first game at their new ground 4-3 to Liverpool. The Twenties and Thirties saw United yo-yo between Divisions One and Two, and in 1934 relegation to Division Three was only avoided on the final day of the season. Financial difficulties again struck the club as attendances fell and during the Second World War the main stand at Old Trafford was destroyed during a German bombing raid. But United's fortunes were to change forever when the club appointed Matt Busby as manager in 1945.

Claiming his first silverware with the 1948 FA Cup victory over Blackpool, Busby made the club a force in English football once again, giving youth its chance by promoting players like Jackie Blanchflower and Roger Byrne to the first team. His policy paid dividends in 1952 when the club finally won the league.

OLD TRAFFORD

Constructed in 1909, Old Trafford was rebuilt after Second World War bomb damage. In the 1970s it became the first English stadium to erect perimeter fencing. With the rebuilding of the Stretford End in 1994, it became a perfect bowl. Known as 'The Theatre Of Dreams', the stadium features a memorial clock outside, commemorating the Munich air disaster.

Above: George Best lifts the European Cup in 1968 as Manchester United become the first English champions of Europe. Opposite clockwise from top left: the stars of Old Trafford – Munich air disaster survivor Bobby Charlton; the class of 1999 lift the Champions League trophy; the enigmatic Eric Cantona; United with the 2003 Premiership trophy.

Rising star Duncan Edwards was thrown into the first team as a 16-year-old and further league success followed in 1956 and 1957. But the club were rocked by tragedy the following year when a plane carrying the team back from a European match against Red Star Belgrade crashed after refuelling in Munich, killing 22 people – including seven players. Fifteen days later Edwards also died, failing to recover from his injuries in a German hospital.

United still managed to reach the FA Cup final that year but Busby had to rebuild the club and he did so with the likes of Nobby Stiles, Denis Law and George Best, combining brilliantly with players such as Bobby Charlton, a survivor of the Munich crash.

The championship was won again in 1965 and 1967 and this time United made sure that they left their mark on Europe. Extra-time goals at Wembley from Best, Brian Kidd and Charlton gave United a 4-1 victory over Benfica to lift the 1968 Champions Cup for the first time – a remarkable achievement just ten years after the Munich air crash. Busby was knighted but he bowed at the top, retiring in 1969, and United found he was a difficult man to replace.

Briefly out of the top flight in the mid-Seventies, United fans were becoming starved of the kind of success that they had become accustomed to, despite FA Cup victories in 1977, 1983 and 1985. Alex Ferguson was appointed manager in November 1986 and soon the balance of football power in England began to shift from Merseyside to Manchester.

The Nineties began with Ferguson guiding the club to success in the FA Cup, the Cup Winners' Cup and the League Cup in three consecutive years, but the championship still eluded them. The wait, having now stretched to 25 years, looked certain to come to an end in 1992, but United somehow contrived to hand the title to Leeds.

Leeds repaid the favour as they sold Eric Cantona to Old Trafford and he provided the missing link for Ferguson's side. Inspired by the Frenchman, the Red Devils won the title in 1993 and 1994, and were to be crowned champions five times in the Nineties.

Cantona retired in 1997 at the age of 30, but by now Ferguson, like Busby, had built his side around the products of the club's youth system, with players like Ryan Giggs, David Beckham, Paul Scholes and the Neville brothers. United's crowning year came in 1999, when their all-conquering side added a Champions Cup and World Club Cup to their domestic double. Not only was the manner of the European Cup victory amazing (substitutes Sheringham and Solskjaer each scored in injury-time to beat Bayern 2-1), it enabled Ferguson to emulate the achievements of Busby.

Ferguson too was knighted as the league domination continued in 2000 and 2001, and though he reneged on his promise to retire, bringing the title back again in 2003, United fans know that when his days at Old Trafford come to an end he will prove just as difficult to replace as Busby.

MARSEILLE

MARSEILLE, FRANCE
Stadium: Vélodrome
(60,000)

Founded: 1898 **Honours:** Champions Cup 1993;
League 9 (inc. 1993 revoked); Cup 10

Olympique Marseille have cut a swathe through the history of French football to become the most famous club from France across the world. Winning their first French league title in 1937, they added a second in 1948 during the early days of professional football. Known as 'l'OM', they enjoyed huge popular support in their native south of France.

Further success was difficult to come by, but in 1971 and 1972 they enjoyed another period of glory and won back-to-back titles, Yugoslav striker Josip Skoblar setting a record of 44 goals in a season in the 1970-71 campaign.

Marseille failed to build on their triumphs but returned to prominence in glorious fashion in 1986 when businessman Bernard Tapie became chairman, triggering the club's most successful spell. He rebuilt the team, spending lavishly on star players such as Jean-Pierre Papin, Chris Waddle and Enzo Francescoli, and guided them to four consecutive French league titles from 1989 to 1992.

Tapie established Marseille as a force to be reckoned with at home and abroad. Papin, a talismanic figure, was the league's top scorer five seasons in a row, and Waddle became a cult hero in France. Others, such as Brazilian Carlos Mozer and the Ghanaian midfielder Abedi Pele added touches of class.

Marseille reached the Champions Cup semi-finals in 1990, losing to a controversial Benfica goal, and the final in 1991, when they lost on penalties to Red Star Belgrade in Bari. In 1993 they finally realised their dream by beating AC Milan thanks to a headed goal from Basile Boli in Munich.

Joy turned to agony when the club was found guilty of fixing a league match against Valenciennes. Tapie was forced out, the club was relegated and headed for financial ruin. Their time at the top was over, although a brief rally in 1999 saw them battle their way to the UEFA Cup final, before losing 3-0 to Parma.

Below: Marseille's joy at winning the European Cup in 1993 was short-lived, as they were found guilty of match-fixing in their domestic league the same season and were relegated.

AC MILAN

MILAN, ITALY
Stadium: Giuseppe Meazza
(85,700)

Founded: 1899 **Honours:** World Club Cup 1969, 1989, 1990; Champions Cup 1963, 1969, 1989, 1990, 1994, 2003; Cup Winners' Cup 1968, 1973; European Supercup 1989, 1990, 1995; League 16; Cup 5

Although Juventus can lay claim to being Italy's most successful club in terms of domestic competition, on the European stage they run a distant second to AC Milan, five time winners of the Champions Cup, a record only bettered by Spanish giants Real Madrid. The Milan Cricket And Football Club was founded on December 16, 1899 by Englishman Albert Edwards, and over the last century it has become one of the world's richest clubs: first bankrolled by tyre magnate Piero Pirelli, but in more recent times by Silvio Berlusconi, Italy's richest man and also its Prime Minister.

The club won its first Italian title in 1901, with two more added in 1906 and 1907. Milan finished third in 1929-30, Serie A's first season, and contested their first Coppa Italia final in 1942, losing to Juventus after a replay. It wasn't until the 1950s, however, that Milan really found their feet, winning four titles in nine years, with their success initially stemming from the purchase of Gunnar Gren, Nils Liedholm and Gunnar Nordahl, the stars of Sweden's Olympic gold-medal-winning team in 1948. Nordahl went on to score 210 goals in 257 games for the club, while Liedholm later became club coach in the early 1980s.

Milan's first serious foray into European competition was in 1956 when they reached the semi-finals of the Champions Cup, which was being held for the very first time that year. They lost out to Real Madrid 5-4 on aggregate and were beaten again by the Spanish giants in the 1958 final, 3-2 after extra-time. Starting the 1960s in impressive form, Milan notched their fifth Serie A title in 1962 and won their first Champions Cup the following year at Wembley against holders Benfica. The Italians won 2-1, despite falling behind to a Eusébio goal.

In 1965 they claimed another European title after beating German side Hamburg 2-0 in the final of the Cup Winners' Cup. A second Champions Cup followed in 1969, when Milan put out holders Manchester United in the semi-finals, before thumping Ajax 4-1 in the final itself – Pierino Prati scoring a hat-trick. In the same year Milan won their first World Club Cup, beating Estudiantes de la Plata of Argentina 4-2 on

aggregate, despite their opponents' inexcusably violent behaviour in the second leg.

Milan started the Seventies brightly with appearances in two consecutive Cup Winners' Cup finals. In 1973 they beat Leeds 1-0, but they lost the second 2-0 to FC Magdeburg. With that defeat European success dried-up for Milan and they had to rely on domestic honours to assuage the ambitions of their fans. The club won the Italian title in 1979 and the Coppa Italia three times between 1972 and 1977, but dark days were just around the corner. In 1980 a betting scandal broke, implicating the club's goalkeeper, Enrico Albertosi, and President, Felice Colombo. Milan were relegated to Serie B as punishment

THE SAN SIRO

The home of both AC Milan and Inter Milan, the Stadio Giuseppe Meazza is still largely known as the San Siro, the original name it took from the district in which it is located. Built in 1926, a £50 million overhaul for the 1990 World Cup included the addition of a third tier built on impressive cylindrical towers at the corners of the stadium.

and nearly went out of business altogether, before Berlusconi stepped in to save them from bankruptcy in 1986.

Much rejuvenated by Berlusconi's millions and the inspired management of Arrigo Sacchi, the club dominated European football in the late 1980s and early 1990s. They beat Steaua Bucharest 4-0 in the 1989 Champions Cup Final, with Dutch superstars Ruud Gullit and Marco Van Basten both scoring twice. Milan retained the trophy the following year, a single Frank Rijkaard goal this time giving them victory over Benfica. Defeat in the 1993 final to Marseille was a momentary blip as the Milan giants triumphed once again the following year with a solid 4-0 demolition of Barcelona. A further Champions Cup final appearance came in 1995 when Patrick Kluivert, who'd go on to play for Milan, scored a late winner for Ajax.

Milan were equally impressive domestically, winning their first league title for nine seasons in 1988 and three more consecutively between 1992 and 1994. The trio of titles coincided with an extraordinary 58-match unbeaten streak between 1991 and 1993. A fifth title in nine years came in 1996, with George Weah providing the firepower up front.

The club's last championship came in 1999 when they won their final seven games to pip Lazio to the title by just a point. The dearth of success on the European stage was addressed with a semi-final appearance in 2002's UEFA Cup, followed by a Champions Cup win in 2003, when they beat Juventus on penalties at Old Trafford.

Above clockwise from top left: AC Milan's Paolo Maldini fends off Inter's Ronaldo; Marcel Dessailly lifts the European Cup in 1994; back on top again – AC Milan beat Juventus to win the 2003 Champions Cup at Old Trafford.

MILLONARIOS

BOGOTA, COLOMBIA
Stadium: Estadio Nemesio
Camacho (56,000)

Founded: 1938 **Honours:** Copa Merconorte 2001;
League 13

Millonarios are the most successful club in Colombia in terms of domestic league titles, but they have never managed to consistently translate this dominance into silverware outside of their own country. Their overall record in the Copa Libertadores is particularly poor for a club of their stature.

The bulk of the club's major triumphs were achieved in the Fifties, an era known as 'El Dorado', when Millonarios were at the centre of a worldwide transfer controversy. Along with Independiente Santa Fe, the Bogota club refused to pay transfer fees to overseas clubs, and a rebel league was consequently formed. This coincided with a player strike in Argentina, and lured by the massive signing-on fees and wages on offer, Millonarios were able to attract their most famous player, Alfredo Di Stéfano. Along with his fellow Argentines, Nestor Rossi and Adolfo Pedernera, the team won four league titles in five years. In the process they earned the nickname the 'Blue Ballet' for their artistry on the pitch. Di Stéfano scored a remarkable 267 goals in 292 games for Millonarios before swapping Colombia for further fame and fortune with Real Madrid.

In recent years, the club has not been without its problems, and is closely associated with the Medellin drug cartel.

NACIONAL

MONTEVIDEO, URUGUAY
Stadium: Parque Central
(16,000), Centenario (73,609)

Founded: 1899 **Honours:** World Club Cup 1971,
1980, 1988; Copa Libertadores 1971, 1980,
1988; South American Recopa 1988;
Inter-American Cup 1972, 1989; League 39

Fans of Nacional proudly lay claim to being the first South American club formed by its citizens rather than the ex-patriot community. In 1903 the entire Nacional team to a man was selected to play for Uruguay in an international against Argentina – they won 3-2 and the date continues to be part of the club's annual celebrations. Along with city rivals Peñarol, they have remained a controlling force in Uruguayan football ever since – there have only been eight occasions, in a league that was formed way back in 1900, when neither of the teams have won the championship.

Triumphs have not only been confined to home soil, and a trio of victories in the Copa

Libertadores is matched by the same number of successes in the World Club Cup, the most eye-catching of which was a 1-0 victory against Brian Clough's Nottingham Forest in 1980, when the trophy was contested in the National Stadium, Tokyo.

Famous footballers to play in Nacional's colours include Hèctor Scarone, one of Uruguay's greatest ever forwards and the inspiration behind his country's World Cup triumph in 1930. After years plying his trade abroad with Barcelona and Inter Milan, he returned to Nacional and finally retired as a player at the age of 55.

NOTTINGHAM FOREST

NOTTINGHAM, ENGLAND
Stadium: City Ground
(30,602)

Founded: 1865 **Honours:** Champions Cup 1979,
1980; Supercup 1979; League 1; Cup 2;
League Cup 4

Before Brian Clough took charge of Second Division Nottingham Forest in 1975 they had never won the league and had won the FA Cup just twice – in 1898 and 1959. A mere five years later they had become Champions of Europe twice over.

Promoted to Division One in 1977, Forest clinched the title in their first season back in the top flight. To consolidate the club's bid for European glory the following season Clough signed Trevor Francis from Midlands rivals Birmingham City, making him English football's first million-pound player. In his first European game Francis's single goal brought victory against Malmö in the Champions Cup final, helping Forest to become only the third club in the competition's history to lift the trophy at the first attempt. One year later they repeated the feat, beating Hamburg – complete with their European Footballer Of The Year, Kevin Keegan – 1-0 to lift the trophy in Real Madrid's Bernabéu Stadium.

Under Clough's stewardship Forest went on to appear in six League Cup finals in 12 years, running out winners four times. Their one appearance in the FA Cup final in this period resulted in defeat to Tottenham in 1991, and two years later Forest were relegated in Clough's last game before retirement.

Bouncing between divisions with little impact, Forest's subsequent progress has been hampered by the financial problems besetting the club. Powered by the goals of striker Stan Collymore they secured promotion to the top flight under Frank Clark in 1994, and returned again as Division One champions in 1998 – but relegation the following year signalled that the once-great club's glory days may now be well and truly behind them.

PENAROL

MONTEVIDEO, URUGUAY
Stadium: Las Acacias
(12,000), Centenario (73,609)

Founded: 1893 **Honours:** World Club Cup 1961,
1966, 1982; Copa Libertadores 1960, 1961,
1966, 1982, 1987; Inter-American Cup 1969;
League 46

Peñarol were founded in 1893 by the large British expatriate community in Montevideo under the rather cumbersome name of Central Uruguayan Railways District Club, and were inaugural winners of the league in 1900. As British influence waned, the club officially changed its name to the more acceptable Peñarol on December 13, 1913 – after the poor, rural area of the city from where they emerged. To this day, the club's support is associated with the working class element of the nation's capital. Along with bitter rivals, Nacional, the two clubs have completely dominated Uruguayan football with more than 80 championship titles shared between them.

However, Peñarol have also been fantastic ambassadors for the Uruguayan game outside of its borders, and won the first ever South

Right: In 1979 Nottingham Forest celebrated the first of two consecutive European Cup victories.

American Club Cup in 1960 against Olimpia of Paraguay, and successfully defended the crown a year later against Brazil's Palmeiras. Three more Copa Libertadores titles have come their way, the last being a play-off victory against America de Cali of Colombia.

Further proof of Peñarol's durability, and a defining achievement, is that they were the first club to win the World Club Cup three times. These victories came with a win against a Eusébio-inspired Benfica in 1961, a 4-0 aggregate win over Real Madrid in 1966, and a 2-0 victory against Aston Villa in 1982.

PORTO

OPORTO, PORTUGAL
Stadium: Estadio das Antas (50,000)

Founded: 1893 **Honours:** World Club Cup 1987; Champions Cup 1987; UEFA Cup 2003; European Supercup 1987; League 18; Cup 12

There can be no doubting that 1987 will take some surpassing as the finest year of Porto's history. While it may have been a year when they enjoyed no domestic success, they did complete a memorable international treble of the Champions Cup, Supercup and World Club Cup. The Champions Cup came at the expense of Bayern Munich in Vienna with two late goals in a 2-1 victory. It made up for their disappointment three years earlier, when the club lost the final of the Cup Winners' Cup.

It was in the mid-1970s that Porto really came of age and began to threaten the Lisbon monopoly of Sporting and Benfica. That they have succeeded in shifting the balance of power owes much to the presidency at that time of Pinto da Costa and the management of Jose Maria Pedroto.

Porto assumed almost total dominance of the Portuguese league, and despite the rotation of managers and high profile players, they won nine titles in the 12 years up until the end of the Nineties. In 2003 they asserted their dominance further, adding the UEFA Cup to their domestic league and cup double.

PSV EINDHOVEN

EINDHOVEN, HOLLAND
Stadium: Philips Stadium (36,000)

Founded: 1913 **Honours:** Champions Cup 1988; UEFA Cup 1978; League 17; Cup 7

Funded by electronics giants Philips, PSV were champions just 15 years after joining the Dutch league and have overtaken Feyenoord to offer the greatest challenge to Ajax's domination of Dutch football.

PSV have housed some of the top Dutch

and international players of recent times. Ronald Koeman, Ruud Gullit and Ruud van Nistelrooy all had spells in Eindhoven, while Brazilian stars Romario and Ronaldo each preceded their Barcelona careers with spells at the Philips Stadium.

The late Eighties and early Nineties saw Eindhoven at the height of their powers, capped with a penalty shootout victory over Benfica in the 1988 Champions Cup Final. On the domestic front the club were almost unstoppable, with six league titles in seven seasons between 1986 and 1992. The final two came under the management of Sir Bobby Robson, who had joined Eindhoven for two seasons straight after leading England to the semi-finals of Italia 90.

The millennium began with PSV back in command in Holland. Former player Eric Gerets led them to consecutive league titles in 2000 and 2001, and Guus Hiddink brought the trophy back again in 2003, but with star players often lured to other European leagues, the club have been unable to make much of an impact in the Champions Cup.

RANGERS

GLASGOW, SCOTLAND
Stadium: Ibrox Park (50,500)

Founded: 1873 **Honours:** Cup Winners' Cup 1972; League 50; Cup 31; League Cup 23

Rangers are the historically Protestant half of perhaps the most passionate rivalry in all football: the 'Old Firm' battle with Catholic Celtic. The Gers have the edge in domestic triumphs, due largely to three sustained periods of dominance. The first came in the inter-war years (1918-39) under manager William Struth, when Alan 'Wee Blue Devil' Morton and Bob McPhail terrorised defences. The second great Rangers team emerged after the Second World War, built around George Young in their 'Iron Curtain' defence, and schemer Willie Waddell.

The third era of success arrived with the appointment of ex-Liverpool player Graeme Souness as player-manager in 1986. With the lavish financial backing of the club's new owner, David Murray, he brought in English players like Terry Butcher and Trevor Steven, and to the horror of the more bigoted fans, signed Mo Johnston – both a Catholic and a former Celtic player!

Walter Smith continued the modernisation through the 1990s, bringing Paul Gascoigne to the club from Italy and equalling Celtic's record of nine consecutive titles. Rangers stopped a Celtic hat-trick in 2003, retaking the league title after two years as runners-up.

Other players who have contributed to the club's success over the years include midfield

genius Jim Baxter and record goalscorer Ally McCoist, while the Rangers team of 1972 won the club their only European trophy, with skipper John Greig lifting the Cup Winners' Cup before going on to manage one of the two treble-winning sides of the Seventies.

Above: It was Rangers' turn to lift the Scottish Cup in 1969, a feat they have managed on 31 occasions.

RAPID VIENNA

VIENNA, AUSTRIA
Stadium: Hanappi (19,600)

Founded: 1899 **Honours:** League 32; Cup 14

One of Austria's oldest teams, Rapid Vienna possess a long and eventful history. The Viennese side captured the inaugural Austrian League title in 1911, and matched this achievement by reclaiming the title on eight more occasions in the following 12-year period. An overall total of 32 championships is a European record. After the 1938 annexation by Germany they competed in the German National Championship, and even managed to win the 1941 league title.

The club has also had the distinction of producing many famous players over the years, including master goal poacher Franz 'Bimbo' Binder, who scored more than 1,000 club goals in a remarkable career. Midfielder Gerhard Hanappi not only played 93 times for Austria, but also designed the club stadium (now named after him). Other legends include Karl Rappan, Walter Zeman, Ernst Happel, Franz Hasil and the prolific marksman Hans Krankl, who won the European Golden Boot in 1978 after scoring 41 goals.

Despite the overwhelming success at home, Rapid Vienna have never won a European trophy, and the closest they have come is a brace of runners-up spots in the Cup Winners' Cup in 1985 and 1996, losing out to Everton and Paris Saint-Germain respectively.

REAL MADRID

MADRID, SPAIN
Stadium: Santiágo Bernabéu
(106,000)

Founded: 1902 **Honours:** Champions Cup 1956, 1957, 1958, 1959, 1960, 1966, 1998, 2000, 2002; UEFA Cup 1985, 1986; League 29; Cup 17

In the ongoing debate to decide the greatest club of all time it's hard to make a case for anyone other than Real Madrid. In 101 years of existence the club have won the Spanish championship 29 times and the Champions Cup, the toughest of all European tests, a record nine times.

Madrid Football Club was officially born in 1902 but did not take the regal prefix 'Real' until 1920 when King Alfonso XIII granted the title in recognition of their role in founding the tournament that eventually became the Copa Del Rey, the Spanish FA Cup.

The club's first chairman Julian Palacios was aided – with some irony, given their bitter rivalry with Barcelona – by two Catalans, the Padrós brothers, Carlos and Juan. The former went on to become club president and Spain's representative at the inaugural meeting of FIFA in 1904, a gesture symbolic of the club's status at the centre of the national game.

While Madrid's founding fathers were all Spaniards its first player-manager was an Englishman, former Corinthians player Arthur Johnson, and it was he who also instigated the famous all-white strip. In its early years the club struggled to make its mark on the fledgling football scene in Spain, with Athletic Bilbao and Barcelona holding sway.

ESTADIO SANTIAGO BERNABEU

The home of Real Madrid, the Bernabéu was built in 1943 to replace their previous Charmartín ground, which was all but destroyed in the war. Initially financed by a membership scheme, at one time the ground boasted a capacity of 125,000. Overhauled for the 1982 World Cup, it was the venue for that year's World Cup Final.

Above: The fans of Real Madrid turned out in force to welcome David Beckham when he joined the Bernebéu allstars in 2003. **Opposite:** Fernando Hierro and Raúl lift the 2002 European Champions Cup at Hampden Park.

The most significant development at this time was the arrival at the club of the young Santiágo Bernabéu, the single most important individual in its history. Bernabéu joined the club as a junior in 1909, helped erect its first purpose-built ground, the O'Donnell Stadium, went on to captain the side and be associated with the fortunes of the club for nearly 70 years until his death in 1978.

By the Twenties the newly-titled Real Madrid had embarked on a strategy designed to install it as the most prestigious club in the land. It demonstrated its intention, as it has done on many occasions since, with a string of big-name signings, an act which accelerated professionalism in the Spanish league. However, when the first national league was installed in 1929 Real were runners-up to Barcelona. It took them three more years to win the first of two back-to-back titles, but by the time they won the league again in 1954, the capital had been destroyed by civil war, rebuilt, and Bernabéu was the club's president.

His presence at the helm ushered the club into an era of dominance. It was he who brokered a bold new stadium in the city's richest district in 1947, eventually named after him, and it was he who financed deals to bring in a string of impressive talents including Gento, Puskás, Kopa and, the biggest of all, Alfredo Di Stéfano, 'the Blond Arrow'.

It was Di Stéfano, more than any other player, who propelled Real to glory, scoring 228 league goals between 1953 and 1964. More importantly, his 49 goals in Europe established the club's name outside Spain as Real drove on to improbable heights by securing the newly-created Champions Cup for five years in succession, an unparalleled feat. Di Stéfano

scored in all five finals, crowning his efforts with a hat-trick in the 7-3 victory over Eintracht Frankfurt at Hampden Park in 1960, a game regarded as one of the finest ever.

League titles continued at regular intervals, but while there was one more Champions Cup triumph in 1966 over Partizan Belgrade – making an astonishing six winners medals for their outstanding winger Gento – Real could not maintain their high standards.

The next 29 years became known as 'The Wilderness Years' as the team strived in vain to rekindle the chemistry that had made it so unbeatable. Two successive UEFA Cup wins in the mid-Eighties would have satisfied most fans, but not those of Real. Significantly the club refused to even enter the competition until 1972. Nevertheless, that squad – which featured the striker Emilio Butragueño, Michel and Martin Vásquez (dubbed 'the Vulture Squadron') and the backflipping Mexican goal machine Hugo Sanchez – revived memories.

The glory days finally returned in 1998 with Predrag Mijatovic's strike against Juventus that won the Champions Cup. That victory began a fresh golden era as Real embarked on a huge spending spree financed by the sale of their training ground. Signings of superstars like Zidane and Figo smashed the transfer barrier successively and embellished a team already packed with stars like Raúl and Iker Casillas.

Real have won the Champions Cup three times since the beginning of the Champions League format, the most special win coming in their centenary year in Glasgow, 42 years on from the legendary 7-3 victory. FIFA rapidly declared Real 'The Best Club Of The 20th Century', a title they could well walk away with again in a hundred years time.

1900
1905
1902: Founded as Madrid Football Club on March 6, the team takes its all-white strip from English club, Corinthians. Their first coach is Englishman Arthur Johnson.

1910
1912: Santiago Bernabéu debuts in the first team in 1912.

1915
1920: The club's name is changed to Real Madrid in June 1920 after King Alfonso XIII gives his official blessing to the team.
1920

1925
1924: The opening of Chamartín Stadium is celebrated with a match between Madrid and Newcastle United.

1930
1932: Real win their first Spanish title.
1935
1943 Santiago Bernabéu is appointed club president.

1940

1945
1947: A new stadium is built and will be named after the club president.
1950
1953: Argentine legend Alfredo Di Stéfano is signed.

1955
1956: Real win the first European Cup with a 4-3 victory over Reims.
1960
1958: Hungarian star Ferenc Puskás signs for Madrid.

1965
1960: Real defeat Eintracht Frankfurt 7-3 to claim their fifth successive European Cup title.
1970
1971: Paco Gento winds up an 18-year career with the club in a Cup Winners' Cup final defeat.

1975

1980
1986: The UEFA Cup is won for a second consecutive year with a victory over Köln.
1985
1990: Real sweep to their fifth consecutive Spanish title, setting a goal-scoring record of 107 goals in 38 games.
1990

1995
1998: Named by FIFA as the best club in football history, they also win the Champions League, beating Juventus 1-0.
2000
2001: One year after signing Luis Figo for £37.5million, Real splash out £45.8million on Zinedine Zidane.
2005

KINGS OF EUROPE

REAL MADRID'S VICTORIES IN THE CHAMPIONS CUP FINAL

1956	Real Madrid	4	1957	Real Madrid	2	1958	Real Madrid	3	1959	Real Madrid	2
	Stade De Reims	3		Fiorentina	0		Milan	2		Stade De Reims	0
	Parc Des Princes, Paris			*Bernabéu, Madrid*			*Heysel, Brussels*			*Neckar, Stuttgart*	

1960	Real Madrid	7	1966	Real Madrid	2	1998	Real Madrid	1	2000	Real Madrid	3	2002	Real Madrid	2
	Eintracht Frankfurt	3		Partizan Belgrade	1		Juventus	0		Valencia	0		Bayer Leverkusen	1
	Hampden Park, Glasgow			*Heysel, Brussels*			*Arena, Amsterdam*			*Stade De France, Paris*			*Hampden Park, Glasgow*	

RED STAR BELGRADE

BELGRADE, SERBIA AND
MONTENEGRO
Stadium: Red Star (56,000)

Founded: 1945 **Honours:** Champions Cup 1991;
World Club Cup 1991; League 22; Cup 19

Known as Crvena Zvezda in their native Serbia and Montenegro (formerly Yugoslavia), it was students of the city's university who founded Red Star Belgrade in March 1945. The first football team to be created in Yugoslavia after liberation, they won their first league title in 1951. Since then they've dominated their country's domestic football – outstripping bitter rivals Partisan to record successes in both league and cup.

Red Star have always been associated with playing precise, technical football, and of producing a constant stream of home-grown talent. The club's reputation in European competitions is a very strong one and was established early when they reached the semi-final of the second Champions Cup in 1957, losing to Fiorentina. The Red Star Stadium was the first ground in the old Eastern bloc to host a major European final, and is known affectionately to home fans as 'the Marakana'.

The club's finest moment was achieved in 1991 when they captured the Champions Cup, winning a penalty shoot-out after a negative performance in a 0-0 draw against Marseille. There may have been many more successes in European competitions, had it not been for the fact that Red Star have always struggled to hold on to their best players. The exit door at the Marakana has seen such world-class talent as Dragan Stojkovic, Robert Prosinecki, Dejan Stankovic and Darko Pancev walk through it.

RIVER PLATE

BUENOS AIRES, ARGENTINA
Stadium: Monumental
(76,689)

Founded: 1901 **Honours:** World Club Cup 1986;
Copa Libertadores 1986, 1996; Inter-American Cup
1986; League 29

Founded in 1901, the side was originally formed in the poor Boca district of Buenos Aires, but later migrated north to the altogether more affluent Retiro area of the city. The move led to the nickname of the 'Millionaires', and established in their erstwhile neighbours, the equally-celebrated Boca Juniors, one of the fiercest rivalries in world football.

A major force in the foundation of the first Argentine professional league, River Plate have enjoyed two distinct golden eras. From 1936 to 1957 they swept all beside them, winning a total of 12 national titles, and in the late 1940s producing the much-admired forward line of Moreno, Labruna, Sivori, Muñoz and Padernera – known to the fans as 'La Maquina' (The Machine).

The 1960s was a lean decade for the club, but since winning the league title in 1975 River have re-established themselves as one of the giants of the game in Argentina, adding a seemingly endless stream of championship triumphs. In 1986, inspired by Uruguayan playmaker Enzo Francescoli and Norberto Alonso, River Plate finally won the Copa Libertadores, beating America of Colombia, and went on to get the better of Steaua Bucharest to gain the club's only World Club Cup trophy. A decade later, River once again beat America to capture a second South American Club Cup title. This time they were denied a second World Club Cup by a single Alessandro Del Piero strike in a close fought match with Juventus.

While Boca Juniors can name Diego Maradona as their most famous former player, the roll call of River Plate old boys reads like a who's who of goalscoring greats. Alfredo Di Stéfano scored 27 league goals for River during the 1946-47 season, while prolific marksmen such as Omar Sivori, Luis Artime, Mario Kempes, Marcelo Salas, Hernan Crespo and, more recently, Javier Saviola have all played for the Buenos Aires club with distinction.

ROMA

ROME, ITALY
Stadium: Olimpico
(82,000)

Founded: 1927 **Honours:** Fairs Cup 1961;
League 3; Cup 7

Founded in 1927 when four local clubs merged (Roman, Pro Patria, Alba and Fortitudo), Associazone Sportiva Roma were members of Serie A when it was inaugurated in 1929. Their record since has been one of occasional highs and rather more frequent lows.

A first Serie A title didn't arrive until 1942, although they did finish as runners-up in both 1931 and 1936. Relegated from Serie A at the start of the 1950s, Roma bounced back a decade later to become one of the first Italian teams to win a European trophy, defeating Birmingham City in the Fairs Cup final in 1961, winning 4-2 on aggregate.

Domestic cup wins in 1964 and 1969 couldn't disguise the fact that Roma spent much of the next two decades in the football wilderness, but things improved dramatically in the 1980s. They won the Coppa Italia four times in seven seasons, added a second Serie A title in 1983 and reached the Champions Cup final the following season, eventually losing to Liverpool 4-2 on penalties after a 1-1 draw in their home stadium.

Under former AC Milan coach Fabio Capello, Roma won their first Serie A title for 18 years in 2001, helped by the enormous firepower of Gabriel Batistuta, Vincenzo Montella and Francesco Totti. The following season they only missed out on the title on the season's last day in a terrific three-way tussle with Juventus and Inter, with just two points separating the three teams.

SANTOS

BRAZIL
Stadium: Vila Belmiro
(22,000)

Founded: 1912 **Honours**: World Club Cup 1962, 1963; Copa Libertadores 1962, 1963; Inter-American Cup 1998; São Paulo League 17; Brazil championship 6 (including Rio-São Paulo Tournament)

There are very few clubs in the world game whose reputation is based so solely on the exploits of one player. However, when that player affords the iconic status of Pele, the synonymous relationship becomes all the more understandable. The great man joined Santos as a 15-year-old in 1956, and made his final appearance in the famous all-white kit in 1974. During his tenure the São Paulo side won many national titles, and achieved back-to-back Copa Libertadores titles in 1962 and 1963. Along with this success also came two World Club Cups with victories over AC Milan and Benfica – the latter featuring a Pele hat-trick in the Stadium Of Light.

Of course, it would be unjust to label Santos as a one-man team during this era, and the club provided the Brazilian national side with many other players who took part in the victorious World Cup campaigns of 1958, 1962 and 1970 – including goalkeeper Gilmar, centre-back Mauro and midfielder Zito. In demand and in the glare of the global spotlight, the club took to the world stage with a stream of friendly match tours, and subsequently reaped the financial benefits.

Not unsurprisingly Pele was a difficult act to follow, and with his retirement the club saw fortunes both on and off the pitch take a severe dip. Debts mounted and the lack of silverware gradually took the club away from the elite group in Brazilian football.

Victory in the Rio-São Paulo Tournament in 1997 was the exception rather than the rule. Supporters seemed to have lost the faith and even the appointment of Pele as the club's youth academy director in 1999 was regarded more as a promotional tool rather than an effective measure. Nonetheless it proved to be something of a turning point, and against the odds Santos revived the glory days by adding the 2002 Brazilian championship to their long list of silverware success.

Opposite: an ambassador for football across the globe, Pele was a Santos player for 18 years from 1956 to 1974.

Above: Brazil's Cafu was at the centre of São Paulo's success in the 1990s.

SAO PAULO

SÃO PAULO, BRAZIL
Stadium: Morumbi
(80,000)

Founded: 1935 **Honours:** World Club Cup 1992, 1993; Copa Libertadores 1992, 1993; Super Cup 1993; Inter-American Cup 1998; São Paulo League 19; Brazil championship 4 (including Rio-São Paulo Tournament)

The youngest of the five São Paulo-based clubs that participate in the Brazilian National Championships, São Paulo FC were founded in 1935, the result of a coming together of two clubs, CA Paulistino and AA de Palmeiras. A convincing five São Paulo titles between 1943 and 1949 soon signalled the arrival of a new major force in the industrial city. As a result of this success, the massive 140,000 capacity Morumbi Stadium was built in 1960 (now reduced to 80,000 for safety reasons). However, the club spent much of this decade in the shadow of their crosstown rivals Santos.

Under the attack-minded guidance of the legendary Brazilian coach Tele Santana, São Paulo's very own glory days were to arrive in the early 1990s, when they were arguably the strongest club side in the world. Two consecutive South American Club Cups – with victories over Paraguay's Olimpia and Newell's Old Boys of Argentina – were followed up by back-to-back triumphs in the World Club Cup. The first saw São Paulo defeat Barcelona 2-1 with both goals from Brazilian international Rai, while the 1993 final witnessed them overcome the much-heralded masters of Europe, AC Milan, with full-back Cafu at the centre of everything good that the team produced. It was the first time a side had successfully defended the title in the Tokyo National Stadium.

São Paulo's position as the major power in the city from which they take their name has diminished, and Corinthians and Palmeiras are currently in the ascendancy. The club were back in the news in 1998, however, when they sold Denilson for a then world record £22m to Spanish club Real Betis.

SPARTA PRAGUE

PRAGUE, CZECH REPUBLIC
Stadium: Stadion Letná
(21,000)

Founded: 1893 **Honours:** League 29; Cup 21

Sparta are the most successful Czech club ever – and that's in spite of several periods when their fortunes have faltered. During the 1970s they even suffered the indignity of relegation. Established as Kralovske Vinohrady (King's Vineyard) in 1893, it wasn't until after the First World War that their reputation as 'Iron Sparta' really grew, when they competed under the name of AC Sparta.

In the inter-war years they vied constantly with neighbours Slavia Prague, winning numerous trophies and achieving the league and cup double in 1936. They also proved a dominant force in Europe, winning the Mitropa Cup – a prestigious forerunner of the Champions Cup – in both 1927 and 1934. Their star player, Oldrich Nejedly, finished top scorer in the 1934 World Cup, playing in a Czechoslovakia team who lost out in the final to Italy (Sparta and rivals Slavia provided all 11 Czech players for the match). Another World Cup hero, Andrej Kvasnak – who played in the 1962 final – was the playmaker of the fine Sparta team of the mid 1960s.

The club finally settled on their current moniker in 1965. After World War II they had suffered several name changes, becoming for a time Sparta Bratrstvi and Spartak Praha Sokolovo, but fans always called them Sparta.

After the relatively dark days of the Seventies, the club started to win trophies again, including the double in 1988 and 1989. Players like Skuhravy, who shone at the World Cup in 1990, and Hasek were followed by Frydek and Kouba, and the club continued to succeed despite seeing much of their talent travel abroad.

Throughout the post-Communist era – and despite some financial and managerial upheavals – Sparta have dominated Czech football, and have even ruffled the feathers of bigger clubs in European competition.

SPARTAK MOSCOW

MOSCOW, RUSSIA
Stadium: Lokomotiv
(29,300)

Founded: 1922 **Honours:** Soviet League 12; Russian League 9; Soviet Cup 10, Russian Cup 3

Spartak Moscow are without question Russia's most successful and popular club, completely dominating post-Communist football in the Vysshaya Liga since its formation in 1991. They have captured all but two of 11 league titles, achieving a hat-trick of league/cup doubles in this fruitful period.

The club was formed in 1922 and was initially linked to the Moscow food producers' co-operative. It wasn't until the Spartak name was adopted in 1935 that the club began to prosper. The first Soviet league championship was won in 1936, and the club triumphed again in 1938 and 1939. Always leading lights in the Soviet Union, a stage they shared with Dynamo Kiev, they were champions a further four times in the 1950s, and inspired the founding of the Champions Cup with their friendly matches against Wolverhampton Wanderers in 1954 and 1955.

Despite appearing in the Champions League on a regular basis and enjoying several encouraging campaigns, European silverware has remained elusive. Spartak's best ever performance came in 1995-96, when they walked their qualification group with a 100 per cent record, only to fall at the quarter-final hurdle to Nantes.

SPORTING LISBON

LISBON, PORTUGAL
Stadium: Estadio Jose de Alvalde (52,411)

Founded: 1906 **Honours:** Cup Winners' Cup 1964; League 18; Cup 17

Sporting have always been in the difficult position of competing for Lisbon domination with local rivals Benfica, and while Sporting can lay claim to being the current pride of the city after achieving league and cup double success in 2002, not even they have been able to prevent the balance of power in Portugal from switching to Porto.

Back in the Forties and Fifties Sporting could just about lay claim to having the upper hand over Benfica, with five league titles in each decade, but only six more championships were to follow between the beginning of the Sixties and the end of the millennium. There was European success in Antwerp, with a 1-0 replay victory over MTK Budapest in the Cup Winners' Cup in 1964, but the club flattered to deceive over a long period of time.

Their cause was not aided by the fact that a number of top players had to be sold due to financial problems, among them Luis Figo, who left for Barcelona after helping the club to Portuguese Cup success in 1995.

The departures on the field have been mirrored by the changes off it, with the likes of Sir Bobby Robson and Carlos Queiroz paying the ultimate price for the dearth of championship success, but league victories in 2000 and 2002 suggest the another era of success may be on the horizon.

STEAUA BUCHAREST

BUCHAREST, ROMANIA
Stadium: Ghencea
(30,000)

Founded: 1947 **Honours:** Champions Cup 1986; League 21; Cup 20

Unlike most Eastern bloc army teams since the dissolution of the Soviet Union, Steaua continue to be their nation's most powerful and successful team. Initially formed as Armata in 1947, they adopted the name CCA Bucharest two years later, and won the national league three times in a row in the early 1950s. The Steaua name – the word means 'star' – wasn't adopted until 1962, and silverware under this title wasn't long in coming, with the capture of a welter of league and cup titles in the late Sixties and early Seventies.

However, the 1980s proved to be a golden decade for the Bucharest side, and the league and cup double in 1985 was followed by Champions Cup triumph the following year. Disposing of Rangers and Anderlecht on the way to the final, Steaua pulled off the improbable to beat Terry Venables' Barcelona 2-0 in a penalty shoot-out, after a goal-less game. A remarkable achievement in itself, it was also the first time a Communist country had lifted the Champions Cup.

Buoyed by this success, the talented Gheorghe Hagi was added to the squad a year later, and the result was a hat-trick of doubles from 1987 to 1989. This era also produced another Champions Cup final appearance, but this time Steaua were caught on the wrong side of a 4-0 scoreline by a Gullit and Van Basten inspired AC Milan.

VALENCIA

VALENCIA, SPAIN
Stadium: La Mestalla
(55,000)

Founded: 1919 **Honours:** Fairs Cup 1962, 1963; Cup Winners' Cup 1980; Euopean Supercup 1; League 5; Cup 6;

Valencia's defeats in consecutive Champions Cup finals – to Real Madrid in 2000, and to Bayern Munich in 2001 – were more than just a disappointment to their fans. Neutrals everywhere admired the underdogs and their style of play. To make matters worse, they hadn't even won their league to qualify for the competition. But the team eventually got their reward when they won their first title in La Liga for more than 20 years in 2002, having been coached to their previous championship in 1971 by the great Alfredo Di Stéfano.

Nevertheless, 'Los Chés' – nicknamed after a local greeting, roughly translated as 'mate' – have always had a tradition for silky play. They won three titles in the 1940s, with goal-getting wizard Edmundo 'Mundo' Suárez twice lifting the 'Pichichi' award as the league's top-scorer. In the early Sixties another classy incarnation of the team played in the style of a junior Real, appearing in three consecutive Fairs Cup finals, winning two.

Argentinian World Cup giant Mario Kempes helped the club to their Cup Winners' Cup final triumph over Arsenal in 1980 (although he missed his spot-kick in the penalty shoot-out), and lately, under the astute guidance of Hector Cúper and then Rafael Benítez, players such as Claudio López, Gaizka Mendieta and Kily González, have kept up the club's reputation for fiesta football.

VASCO DA GAMA

RIO DE JANERIO, BRAZIL
Stadium: São Januario
(35,000)

Founded: 1915 **Honours:** Copa Libertadores 1998; Copa Mercosur 2000; Rio State League 18; Brazil championship 6 (including Rio-São Paulo Tournament)

Vasco are the club of Rio's Portuguese community, and were named after the celebrated explorer. Football in Rio had been the preserve of the elite until Vasco broke the mould by winning the 1923 championship with a team that included mixed-race and working class players. Outraged, Rio's leading teams launched a breakaway league, and were only persuaded back with the agreement that players would have to complete a registration form – a task deemed beyond most of Brazil's illiterate poor. The literacy test was eventually abolished in 1929, but the club will always be revered for paving the way for democracy in Brazilian football.

With Flamengo and Fluminense's history inexorably entwined, Vasco are regarded as the perpetual outsiders in the battle for footballing superiority in Rio. That's not to say they haven't brought home a number of trophies. The club's greatest triumph was capturing the Copa Libertadores in 1998 with a 4-1 aggregate win over Barcelona of Ecuador. Following on from this success, Vasco were invited to play in the inaugural World Club Championships in 1999, where they beat Manchester United 3-1 on the way to the final. But it wasn't to be, and after contesting a 0-0 draw with São Paulo's Corinthians, they lost out on penalties.

Below: Valencia showed consistency in reaching consecutive European Cup finals at the turn of the millennium, but lost on both occasions.

LEGENDS OF FOOTBALL

Right: Florian Albert of Hungary,
the 1967 European Footballer
Of The Year.

ADEMIR

Country: Brazil
Born: November 8, 1922
Position: Centre-forward
Clubs: Recife, Vasco da Gama, Fluminense, Vasco Da Gama

Son of the famous 1938 World Cup defender Domingos, goalscorer Ademir Marques de Menezes went a long way in establishing Brazil as a post-War footballing power. He made his international debut in 1945 and went on to score 32 goals in 37 games, placing him an impressive seventh on his country's all-time goalscorers list. His finest hour came in the 1950 World Cup when he fully deserved the Golden Boot for his total of eight goals, including four against Sweden in the final pool game. The forward line trio of Ademir, Zizinho and Jair is still considered one of Brazil's finest ever. A prolific goalscorer at club level in the Rio State League, he was a five times league winner with Vasco da Gama, and he continued his success with a further title at city neighbours Fluminense.

MOHAMED AL-DEAYEA

Country: Saudi Arabia
Born: August 2, 1972
Position: Goalkeeper
Clubs: Al Tae, Al Hilal

Mohamed Al-Deayea is the greatest goalkeeper that Asia has ever produced. He played 165 times for his country after succeeding his elder brother in the national side, who had been part of the Asian Cup winning teams of 1984 and 1988. His international career began against Bangladesh at the Asian Games in Beijing in 1990, and ended, through retirement, in June 2002 against the Republic of Ireland in Japan (at Al-Deayea's third successive World Cup). His 100th appearance had been at the 1998 World Cup against South Africa. By then he was team captain. He plans to retire from the club game at the end of the 2004 season.

Right: Ivor Allchurch of Wales,
second only to Ian Rush as his
country's highest goalscorer.

FLORIAN ALBERT

Country: Hungary
Born: September 15, 1941
Position: Centre-forward
Clubs: Ferencváros

Florian Albert was an elegant and gifted striker who enjoyed a long and successful career at club and international level. He was difficult to mark and had an ability to bring others into play. At the 1966 World Cup he shone as Hungary beat holders Brazil 3-1 at Goodison Park and was impressive during their run to the quarter-finals with his guile and skill.

Albert appeared for Hungary at the 1960 Olympic Games when they finished third, and he also turned out at the 1962 World Cup Finals in Chile. At that tournament he scored a superb solo goal against England and struck a hat-trick against Bulgaria. Tall and slender, he was different from previous Hungarian strikers but equally effective and had shown his promise while still at school, making his international debut at the age of 17.

Albert spent his career with Ferencváros, picking up four titles. He helped them become the first Hungarian club to win a continental trophy when they lifted the Fairs Cup in 1965 and he was voted European Footballer Of The Year in 1967. He played 75 times for Hungary, scoring 31 goals. He retired in 1974.

IVOR ALLCHURCH

Country: Wales
Born: October 16, 1919
Position: Inside-forward
Clubs: Swansea City, Newcastle United, Cardiff City, Swansea City

Grace and elegance were the watchwords of Ivor Allchurch, an inside-forward who still stands second in the record books in his country's goalscoring charts – just behind Ian Rush. Tall and blond, inevitably he was known as the 'Golden Boy', but he sadly failed to gain just reward for his ample talents as he spent his entire career playing for clubs at the wrong end of the table. Only at the 1958 World Cup in Sweden did a wider audience get to appreciate his sublime talents, when he was part of a talented Welsh team that narrowly went down Pele's Brazil in the quarter-finals. The 251 goals he scored in nearly 700 league appearances attest to both the quality of his finishing and his durability, while eight of his 68 Welsh caps were gained partnering his brother Len, who also played for Swansea.

JOSE ALTAFINI

Country: Brazil, Italy
Born: August 27, 1938
Position: Centre-forward
Clubs: Palmeiras, São Paulo, AC Milan, Napoli, Juventus, Chiasso

Jose Altafini's career spanned three decades, two international careers and a change of name. In the unique nickname tradition of his native Brazil he was known as 'Mazzola' for his resemblance to the Torino captain killed in the Superga air crash, and he represented his country with distinction in the 1958 World Cup. The re-adoption of his birth name came with a move to AC Milan, and four years later he represented Italy in the same tournament, making him one of only five World Cup players to have turned-out for two countries. His finest hour came in Milan's 1963 European Champions Cup campaign when he scored 14 goals, including both goals in a 2-1 win over Benfica in the final.

ANTONIO ALZAMENDI

Country: Uruguay
Born: June 7, 1956
Position: Forward
Clubs: Sud America, Independiente, River Plate, Nacional, UNAM, Peñarol, Logrones, Deportivo Mandiyú, Corrientes, Rampla Juniors

Antonio Alzamendi was the 1986 South American Player Of The Year when the continent may have thought the year belonged to Diego Maradona. Alzamendi helped River Plate to the Argentinian championship and the Copa Libertadores, and rounded off by scoring the decisive goal in the World Club Cup final in Tokyo against Steaua Bucharest. He had also featured in the 1986 World Cup finals, and later at Italia 90. He helped Uruguay win the Copa América in Argentina where he had spent ten successful years in club football as a prolific striker, scoring 105 goals in 204 games. He also played club football in Spain, Mexico and Uruguay.

AMARO AMANCIO

Country: Spain
Born: October 12, 1939
Position: Inside-right/Outside-right
Clubs: Deportivo La Coruna, Real Madrid

Amancio was one of Spain's most exciting players of the 1960s. He was groomed by the great Real Madrid, winning the European Cup in an all-Spanish side in 1966. Two years earlier, he had helped Spain to their 1964 European Championship triumph. He scored 11 goals in 42 appearances for his country. The brilliance of the player was in his ability to play, primarily, as an inside or outside right but with equal aplomb switch to the other flank. A leg injury in a Spanish Cup game looked to have ended his career but he recovered to feature in the resurgence of Real Madrid in the 1970s.

JOSE LEANDRO ANDRADE

Country: Uruguay
Born: November 20, 1898
Position: Wing-half
Clubs: Bella Vista, Nacional

Jose Leandro Andrade was one of the mainstays of the great Uruguayan side of the late 1920s and early 1930s, and helped his country to gain Olympic gold medals in Paris in 1924 and Amsterdam in 1928. His career looked as though it was to finish prematurely when injury struck in 1929, but he battled back, and his experience was a vital factor when his Uruguayan side lifted the inaugural World Cup in 1930 on home soil. Andrade is regarded as one of the greats of the golden generation of Uruguayan football, alongside defender Jose Nasazzi and influential striker Hector Scarone. An old fashioned wing-half, Andrade played 41 times for his country before hanging up his international boots in 1933.

VICTOR ANDRADE

Country: Uruguay
Born: February 14, 1927
Position: Left-half
Clubs: Wanderers, Peñarol

Victor Andrade emulated the triumph of his uncle, the great Jose Leandro Andrade, by winning the World Cup with Uruguay in 1950. The diminutive Andrade was a tenacious left-half who was an excellent ball winner, which was perfectly epitomised in the decisive 1950 World Cup match against Brazil in which he often frustrated the hosts. Four years later in an injury-hit Uruguayan side he played as an attacking centre-half and was captain in the semi-finals. He was part of the Peñarol side that never finished lower than runners-up in the national league in the 1940s and 1950s.

ROBERTO BAGGIO

Country: Italy
Born: February 18, 1967
Position: Centre-forward
Clubs: Fiorentina, Juventus, AC Milan, Bologna, Inter Milan, Brescia

One of eight children and born in the small town of Caldogno, Baggio first made his name as a 15-year-old winger in Italy's Serie C1 (or third division) with local club side Lanerossi Vicenza. When he was 18, Baggio was signed by Fiorentina, then in Italy's top-flight, and became a regular in their first team during the 1987-88 season. He stayed with the Florence side for five seasons, in that time becoming one of Italian football's hottest properties and making his international debut against Holland on November 16, 1988. His last two seasons in Florence saw Baggio score 32 league goals in 62 appearances (better than a goal every other game), and in the 1989-90 season, his final year with the club, Fiorentina made it to the final of the UEFA Cup, only to lose out 3-1 on aggregate to Juventus.

Astonishingly, just a week after going down to Juventus, Fiorentina sold Baggio to them for a then world record £8million. The news provoked such fury amongst fans in Florence that the riot police had to be called in to quell two days of violent disturbances. Aged 23 and a recent convert to Buddhism, Baggio made his World Cup debut for Italy in 1990. He started the tournament on the bench but, against Czechoslovakia, scored one of the best goals that the tournament had ever seen: a powerful run from the halfway line that left defenders for dead. Italy still only managed to finish third though.

Baggio's time at Juventus was extremely successful. The Turin club won the UEFA Cup in 1993, finished runners-up in 1995, and under coach Marcelo Lippi, claimed back-to-back league titles in 1995 and 1996. Baggio himself was named European and World Footballer Of The Year in 1993, and continued to score regularly for Juventus (78 goals in 99 league appearances spread over five seasons). However, with the precociously talented Alessandro Del Piero waiting in the wings, and a wealth of strike talent elsewhere in the squad, Baggio was finding it harder to hold down a first team place. He joined AC Milan in 1995, and played for both Bologna and Inter Milan before settling at Brescia.

By 1994, Baggio had arguably become the most famous, if not the most popular, player in Italy, and it was these talismanic qualities that made him the focus of his country's World Cup campaign the same year. Italy had barely qualified for the second round stage and, as the tournament wore on, seemed to rely more and more on 'the Divine Ponytail' (as Baggio was nicknamed). He scored a last-minute

equaliser and an extra-time penalty winner to eliminate Nigeria in the second round, before snatching the decider in the quarter-final against Spain. Another brace of goals dispatched Bulgaria in the semi-finals and when it came down to penalties against Brazil in the final, even though he'd been carrying an injury, it seemed certain that Baggio would net the deciding spot kick and keep Italy's World Cup hopes alive. Alas, it was not to be and he scooped his penalty – Italy's fifth and last – over the bar, handing Brazil victory.

With a record of 29 goals in 55 games for Italy, Baggio was recalled to the national team for the 1998 World Cup finals in France where he was able to atone for the penalty miss of four years before, converting a vital spot-kick against Chile to give Italy a 2-2 draw.

Above: Roberto Baggio scored 78 goals for Juventus in 99 league games and was voted World Player Of The Year.

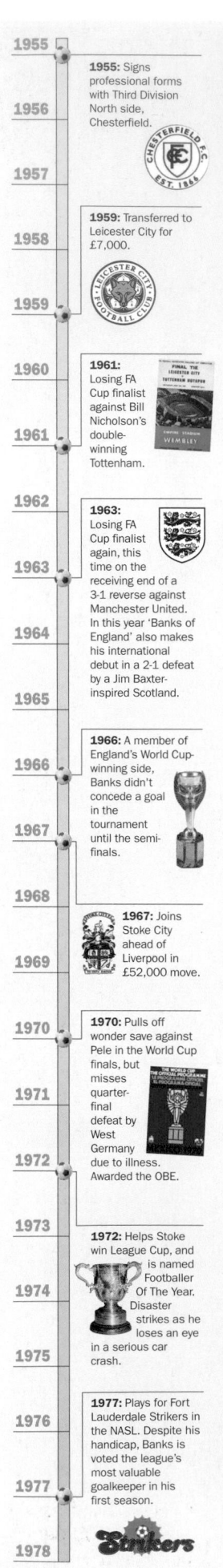

1955: Signs professional forms with Third Division North side, Chesterfield.

1959: Transferred to Leicester City for £7,000.

1961: Losing FA Cup finalist against Bill Nicholson's double-winning Tottenham.

1963: Losing FA Cup finalist again, this time on the receiving end of a 3-1 reverse against Manchester United. In this year 'Banks of England' also makes his international debut in a 2-1 defeat by a Jim Baxter-inspired Scotland.

1966: A member of England's World Cup-winning side, Banks didn't concede a goal in the tournament until the semi-finals.

1967: Joins Stoke City ahead of Liverpool in £52,000 move.

1970: Pulls off wonder save against Pele in the World Cup finals, but misses quarter-final defeat by West Germany due to illness. Awarded the OBE.

1972: Helps Stoke win League Cup, and is named Footballer Of The Year. Disaster strikes as he loses an eye in a serious car crash.

1977: Plays for Fort Lauderdale Strikers in the NASL. Despite his handicap, Banks is voted the league's most valuable goalkeeper in his first season.

GORDON BANKS

Country: England
Born: December 30, 1937
Position: Goalkeeper
Clubs: Chesterfield, Leicester City, Stoke City, Fort Lauderdale Strikers

Only one Englishman can lay claim to the title World's Greatest Goalkeeper. Gordon Banks became a legend for his composure, his agility, consistency and all-round technique, yet never played for a major club.

Banks was born the son of a foundryman in Tinsley, Sheffield, in December 1937 and developed his physical strength hauling bags of coal and hod-carrying when he left school. He took up goalkeeping as an amateur and was picked up by Third Division Chesterfield at the age of 15, making his league debut against Colchester on November 29, 1958. Leicester City spotted his potential and Banks moved to Filbert Street in July 1959 for £7,000, making his Division One debut that September in a 1-1 draw with Blackpool.

Banks is today credited with developing many of the facets of modern goalkeeping. He would stay behind for hours after training, concentrating on technique, learning angles and inventing specialised routines designed to improve his strength and agility. However, he did not adopt gloves regularly until 1970, preferring to spit sticky saliva from chewing gum on to his hands and let it dry.

In May 1961, in his second season, Banks made his first Wembley appearance, picking up a loser's medal in the FA Cup final against double-winners Tottenham Hotspur. Two years later he picked-up another against Manchester United.

Banks was called into the England squad by Walter Winterbottom for a 1962 friendly against Portugal while at Leicester, but it was Alf Ramsey who awarded him his first cap on April 6, 1963. Though the game ended in a defeat to Scotland, Banks rapidly became a fixture in the England side.

He was the rock of the 1966 World Cup-winning team, conceding just one goal before the final against West Germany, a penalty to Eusébio. But his finest performance came at Mexico 70, the day after he was awarded an OBE. Facing Pele for the first time in his career in the titanic clash between the holders and the tournament favourites, he managed to scoop the Brazilian's sharp, downward header up and over the bar. It became the most replayed save of all time. But when it came to the most crucial game of the tournament Banks was unfortunately absent through illness, felled by 'Montezuma's revenge'. Peter Bonetti took his place and conceded three goals against West Germany in the quarter-final, ending England's dream

of retaining the Jules Rimet trophy in Mexico.

A year after lifting the World Cup, Stoke City moved for Banks, and Leicester, knowing they had the promising Peter Shilton in reserve, let him go for £52,000 in April 1967. Banks won the League Cup with Stoke in 1972 but never achieved FA Cup or league honours. But he was FIFA Goalkeeper Of The Year on six occasions and Football Writers' Player Of The Year in 1972. He would undoubtedly have played at the top for much longer had a car crash that summer not cost him the sight in one eye.

He kept 35 clean sheets in 73 games for England and lost just nine games. He enjoyed a spell in the North American Soccer League playing for the Fort Lauderdale Stikers, before returning in 1979 for an unsuccessful stint as manager of Telford United. He now sits on the Pools Panel.

Above: Gordon Banks won the World Cup with England, the League Cup with Stoke City and was voted FIFA Goalkeeper Of The Year six times.

FRANCO BARESI

Country: Italy
Born: May 8, 1960
Position: Sweeper
Clubs: AC Milan

Born near Brescia, in the Lombardy region of Italy, Baresi enjoyed two decades of football with his only club, AC Milan. Making his professional debut in an away game against Verona on April 23, 1978, Baresi went on to establish himself as the finest sweeper in the world during Milan's glory years of the late Eighties and early Nineties.

The consummate modern defender, Baresi was nicknamed 'The Steel Man' – he was a formidable stopper but was also comfortable bringing the ball out of defence and joining in with attacking moves. He captained Milan to numerous league titles (the last in 1996), World Club Cups and Italian Cups, as well as to European Champions Cup glory in 1989 and 1990. Sadly, he missed his club's 4-0 demolition of Barcelona in the European Cup final of 1994 as he was suspended.

Baresi made his international debut for Italy against Romania in December 1982, although he had been a non-playing member of the squad which had won the World Cup in Spain a few months earlier. He went on to play for his country 81 times, 31 of them as captain, but suffered heartbreak in the World Cup final of 1994, Italy losing to Brazil in a game where he missed a penalty in the climactic shoot-out. When Baresi retired from the game in 1997, Milan retired his famous Number 6 shirt.

CLIFF BASTIN

Country: England
Born: March 14, 1912
Position: Left-winger
Clubs: Exeter City, Arsenal

'Boy Bastin' started his career with hometown club Exeter but joined Arsenal as a raw 16-year-old in 1929. He was not just a great left-winger, but also a talented inside-forward, the position he preferred. He helped The Gunners to their first trophy, the FA Cup, in his debut season, and four goals on the way to the final against Huddersfield set the tone for his career. An incredible turn of pace and uncanny dribbling ability made Bastin the pivotal figure in an Arsenal team that yielded five league titles and an FA Cup win in the 1930s, while he became a mainstay of the England squad from the age of 19. A cartilage operation in 1934 curtailed his career, but his tally of 178 goals in 396 games remained an Arsenal record until Ian Wright passed the barrier in 1997.

BEBETO

Country: Brazil
Born: February 16, 1964
Position: Centre-forward
Clubs: Flamengo, Vasco da Gama, Deportivo De La Coruna, Vitoria Bahia, Gremio, Botafogo, Vasco da Gama, Jubilo Cerezo

The fresh-faced striker is best known outside of Brazil for his 'cradling the baby' celebration during the 1994 World Cup, but it is his unfailing ability to find the back of the net that has established him as a player of pedigree. Admittedly he rarely won the headlines when partnering Romario, though his 38 goals in 75 internationals entitles him to stand fourth on Brazil's all-time goalscoring list. Domestic football saw Bebeto controversially transferred in 1980 from Flamengo, where he was the fans' favourite, to rivals Vasco da Gama. A move to Europe followed, but he was unable to reproduce his earlier form.

FRANZ BECKENBAUER

Country: Germany
Born: September 11, 1945
Position: Midfield/Sweeper
Clubs: Bayern Munich, New York Cosmos, Hamburg

What Franz Beckenbauer touches invariably turns to gold. Both as player and manager, at club and international level, he is a winner. Beckenbauer picked up his nickname – 'The Kaiser' – for his imperious style. As a footballer he was utterly in control, a chess player who read the game in his head, but was also blessed with an excellent touch, a good change of pace and flawless distribution.

Beckenbauer joined Bayern as a junior in 1959 playing on the left but gradually moved inside, making his debut at 18 years of age. The club were promoted to the top division of the Bundesliga in 1965, finishing third in their first season behind city rivals TSV 1860 Munich. In the following two seasons Bayern won the German Cup twice, then a European Cup Winners' Cup in 1967.

Beckenbauer's classy performances led to a rapid call-up to the West Germany squad and he made his international debut in a 2-1 victory over Sweden on September 26, 1965.

At the 1966 World Cup he established himself at the heart of the German side, scoring four goals, including the winner in the semi-final with Russia, but he was unable to stop England from lifting the trophy.

Four years later in Mexico he had a measure of revenge in the quarter-finals. When Alf Ramsey withdrew Bobby Charlton from the game while England were leading, it freed up Beckenbauer in midfield and he scored the first goal that propelled West Germany's

Left: Franco Baresi lifts the European Cup in the Nou Camp after Milan's 4-0 win over Steaua in 1989.

Above: George Best takes on Wolves in 1971.

Opposite: A legend in his own lifetime and an icon of his age, George Best was dubbed 'the fifth Beatle'.

comeback. He lost out in the semi-final with Italy and finished the game with a dislocated shoulder, playing on with his arm strapped across his chest.

A year later Beckenbauer took over as captain of the national team and led them to a European Championship win over the Soviet Union in 1972, having redefined the sweeper's role by gliding out of defence with mazy runs to set up devastating counter-attacks.

In 1974 he experienced his crowning moment as a player, captaining the national side to World Cup victory on home soil in a game where Holland threatened to overrun the West Germans. Beckenbauer remained unfazed and when the Dutch flagged he marshalled his forces and pushed his side to victory. He retired from international football in 1977 with 103 caps.

On the domestic front he helped Bayern dominate the mid-Seventies, leading them to an impressive hat-trick of European Cups between 1974 and 1976. He finished his Bayern career with three titles and four cup wins, twice being voted European Footballer Of The Year, in 1972 and 1976. He played for three years with New York Cosmos, winning the NASL Soccer Bowl three times before returning to Germany with Hamburg. After one final season with the Cosmos he retired.

His cerebral style and ability to lift others made him a natural for management and, without experience of club management, he took over his country in 1984, coaching the players to two World Cup finals. At Italia 90 he became the first person to captain and manage a World Cup-winning side when his team defeated Argentina 1-0.

After a spell with Marseille he returned to Bayern as manager in 1994, winning the Bundesliga in his first season before becoming

the club president, and then vice president of the German Football Federation. In 2001 he became president of the German World Cup 2006 Organising Committee.

IGOR BELANOV

Country: Soviet Union
Born: September 25, 1960
Position: Forward
Clubs: Chernomerets Odessa, Dynamo Kiev, Borussia Mönchengladbach

Igor Belanov was voted European Footballer Of The Year in 1986 after a sensational period when he topped the goalscoring charts in Dynamo Kiev's title-winning season, won the European Cup Winners' Cup and, just three weeks before the Mexico World Cup, found himself catapulted into the Soviet squad along with 11 other Kiev team-mates. He went on to score a hat-trick against Belgium in the second round, but the Soviets lost 4-3. After 1986 Belanov was plagued by injuries, although he did earn a move to West Germany and played in the 1988 European Championship final, missing a penalty in the 2-0 defeat by Holland.

MIODRAG BELODEDICI

Country: Romania, Yugoslavia
Born: May 20, 1964
Position: Sweeper
Clubs: Steaua Bucharest, Real Star Belgrade, Valencia, Real Valladolid, Villarreal

Miodrag Belodedici was the first player to win the Champions Cup with two different clubs, Steaua Bucharest in 1986 and Red Star Belgrade in 1991. On both occasions the final was decided on penalties, with Steaua beating Barcelona 2-0 and Red Star defeating Marseille 5-3 after goalless draws. Belodedici was born in Serbia but raised in Romania, and played for them 20 times between 1984 and 1988. In 1988 he visited Yugoslavia and successfully sought asylum there, returning to Romania in 1992 and going on to feature in the 1994 World Cup and even Euro 2000 for them.

GEORGE BEST

Country: Northern Ireland
Born: May 22, 1946
Position: Centre-forward
Clubs: Manchester United, Stockport County, Fulham, Los Angeles Aztecs, Motherwell, Hibernian, Bournemouth, Brisbane Lions

The name George Best became a byword for 'booze' and 'birds' in an era when footballers broke the superstar barrier, but the image overshadowed the talent of a man who is arguably the greatest player to have emerged from the British Isles.

Best was the complete all-round player. Blessed with quick feet and even quicker intelligence he would toy with defenders like a cat with a mouse. He could pass and finish but he never forgot to work for the team. For all his razzmatazz a Best goal was generally celebrated with a hand half raised, perhaps a finger pointing upwards. Gordon Banks cites a dazzling run which left him lying on his backside as the best goal ever scored against him. Not long after that encounter the two met again in an international. As Banks prepared to kick the ball upfield, Best flipped it out of the goalkeeper's hands and headed it in the back of the net. It was typical of Best's impudence but the referee disallowed it.

Best arrived in Manchester from Belfast in 1961 aged just 15 years and made his Old Trafford debut two years later against West Bromwich Albion. Sharp, quick-witted and stylish, he launched the club into a new era that helped it overcome the loss of the 'Busby Babes' and, teamed with Bobby Charlton and Denis Law, brought two league titles in 1965 and 1967. In six seasons he scored 190 goals in 290 games, but his crowning moment was lifting the European Champions Cup in 1968 after characteristically rounding the goalkeeper to score in the 4-1 win over Benefica.

Best was named European Player Of The Year but his taste for the game was diminishing. With the retirement of the patrician Sir Matt Busby, his behaviour became increasingly rebellious. Managers came and went in an awkward period of transition at the club and when Tommy Docherty dropped Best, the Irishman responded by walking out. FIFA became involved, issuing a ban, but it was rescinded allowing Best to join Stockport County in 1975. It was to be the first stationing post in a spiralling career.

Living the life of a popstar – he was dubbed 'the fifth Beatle' – Best joined the football revolution in the USA before returning home to join Fulham in September 1976. There he rediscovered a taste for the game, forming an entertaining partnership with another wayward genius, Rodney Marsh. Fulham's gate doubled for their first home game together and Best put them one up with barely a minute on the clock. Shortly afterwards he became the first player to receive a red card for foul language under the new system.

While Best succumbed to alcoholism, the great tragedy of his career was that despite winning 37 caps for Northern Ireland he was never able to perform on the world stage as his talent merited.

Best received a liver transplant in July 2002 and has since returned to writing and broadcasting. His legacy is still felt, not least at Manchester United, where every young prodigy is still hailed as 'the new George Best'. Not surprisingly it has been an impossible billing for anyone to live up to.

FRANZ 'BIMBO' BINDER

Country: Austria, Germany
Born: December 1, 1911
Position: Centre-forward/Inside-forward
Clubs: St Polten, Rapid Vienna

Franz 'Bimbo' Binder is credited as being the first European player to score a thousand goals in his career with clubs St Polten and Rapid Vienna, as well playing internationally for Austria (20 times) and Germany (9 times). Binder is purported to have scored 1,006 goals in 756 games before hanging up his boots in 1950, when he turned to management with Rapid Vienna. He later took charge of Austria's national team. He was certainly the greatest Austrian player of the 1930s, gaining success with Rapid both in the Austrian league and, after the Anschluss of 1938, the Greater Germany Championship.

DANNY BLANCHFLOWER

Country: Northern Ireland
Born: February 10, 1926
Position: Half-back
Clubs: Barnsley, Aston Villa, Tottenham Hotspur

Having cut his teeth with Barnsley, Danny Blanchflower's annoyance at the club's lack of ambition prompted a move to Aston Villa in 1951. But it was at Tottenham Hotspur where the Belfast-born defender emerged as one of the most astute defenders of his generation. When Arsenal pulled out of a proposed transfer in 1954, the White Hart Lane club stepped into the breach, signing Blanchflower for £30,000 – then a record fee for a half-back.

His outspoken ways did not go down well initially, but the appointment of Bill Nicholson as manager in 1958 proved to be a defining moment in the Irishman's career. He was the manager's voice on the pitch, while his cultured yet steadfast defending became the foundation on which the club's 1961 'double' success was built.

Twice voted Footballer Of The Year, he also skippered Tottenham to FA Cup success in 1962, the European Cup Winners' Cup the following year, and helped his country to the last eight of the World Cup finals in 1958.

OLEG BLOKHIN

Country: Soviet Union
Born: November 5, 1952
Position: Centre-forward
Clubs: Dynamo Kiev, Vorwärts Steyr

Oleg Blokhin was one of the quickest players ever to play the game, a claim that becomes all the more creditable when it is revealed that his personal trainer was Olympic sprint champion Valeri Borzov. But you don't become the Soviet

Union's most-capped player through pace alone, and after moving inside from the left-wing to centre-forward, Blokhin became a reliable and prolific goalscorer. His 39 goals in 101 international appearances is a record, and he was crowned European Footballer Of The Year in 1975 for leading Dynamo Kiev to their European Cup Winners' Cup triumph. As a reward for his services to Soviet football Blokhin was allowed to move to Western Europe, and played out the rest of his career with Vorwärts Steyr in Austria.

ZBIGNIEW BONIEK

Country: Poland
Born: March 3, 1956
Position: Forward
Clubs: Zawisza Bydgoszcz, Widzew Lodz, Juventus, Roma

Zbigniew Boniek made his name in Poland's magnificent team that played at the 1978 and 1982 World Cups. After the latter tournament, in which he missed the crucial semi-final through suspension against Italy, he was snapped-up by Juventus and featured in a star-studded side alongside Michel Platini and Paolo Rossi. With Juventus, Boniek won both the European Cup Winners' Cup in 1984, scoring the winner against Porto in the final, and the European Champions Cup in 1985. Boniek also won a number of Italian domestic trophies with Juventus and Roma. He scored 24 goals in 80 appearances for Poland.

JÓZSEF BOZSIK

Country: Hungary
Born: September 28, 1929
Position: Right-half
Clubs: Kispest, Honvéd

József Bozsik was a member of the 'Magical Magyars' side that inflicted a humiliating 6-3 defeat on England at Wembley in 1953. One of the goals was a stunning 30-yard effort from Bozsik. His 15-year international career began with a debut in the 9-0 thrashing of Bulgaria in August 1947 and ended with his 100th appearance in April 1962, a 1-1 draw with Uruguay in which he scored. In that period, Bozsik went to two World Cups with Hungary and made an appearance in the final against West Germany in 1954. He also won a gold medal at the Olympic Games in 1952. At club level he was a star player alongside the likes of Ferenc Puskás at Kispest (later Honvéd).

LIAM BRADY

Country: Republic Of Ireland
Born: February 13, 1956
Position: Midfield
Clubs: Arsenal, Juventus, Sampdoria, Inter Milan, Ascoli, West Ham United

In an era where cultured footballers at Arsenal had become a rarity, Brady's ball skills and sweet left foot made him shine like a beacon. Given the nickname 'Chippy', for his love of fast food rather than his football ability, he made his debut in 1973 for a team in transition. As The Gunners continually struggled in the lower reaches of Division One, the Irish international's skillful performances were worthy of a higher stage – his swirling 25-yard effort against Tottenham in 1978 remains one of Arsenal's greatest goals.

Despite their inconsistencies, the club did reach three successive FA Cup finals and it was following the 1980 defeat against West Ham that Brady decided to try his luck abroad. His emphatic performances against Juventus in the European Cup Winners' Cup that season – Arsenal lost the final to Valencia on penalties – made him a target for the Italian giants and it was no surprise when he moved to Turin for £600,000 that summer.

Brady's skills were custom-made for life in Serie A, and as a fundamental component of Giovanni Trapattoni's side he helped Juventus to successive Scudetto titles. Shockwaves were created when he was then sold to make way for Michel Platini, and following two seasons at Sampdoria and spells at Inter and Ascoli, he ended his career back in England. He played over 100 games in three seasons for West Ham before retiring in 1990.

ANDREAS BREHME

Country: West Germany
Born: November 9, 1960
Position: Left-back
Clubs: Kaiserslautern, Bayern Munich, Inter Milan, Real Zaragoza, Kaiserslautern

Brehme started and finished his career at Kaiserslautern but was most famous for winning the 1990 World Cup for West Germany – putting an end to one of the most disappointing finals of all time. Germany were making hard work of beating an ill-disciplined Argentina side when Brehme converted an 85th minute penalty to win the game 1-0. That was a richly deserved personal triumph for Brehme, who was acknowledged as one of the world's best left-backs during the Eighties and Nineties. Typically German in style – Brehme was all about determination, strength, endeavour and uncompromising tackling, though in the German tradition he was always willing to thunder forward too – the defender

also had a successful club career, notably with Inter Milan. Brehme was one of a trio of high-profile German internationals, the others being Lothar Matthäus and Jurgen Klinsmann, in the Inter Milan side which won the 1989 Serie A title and 1991 UEFA Cup.

PAUL BREITNER

Country: West Germany
Born: September 5, 1951
Position: Left-back
Clubs: Bayern Munich, Real Madrid, Eintracht Braunschweig, Bayern Munich

Nicknamed 'Der Afro' for his distinctive curly hairstyle, Paul Breitner has won everything there is to win in the game. A member of the all-conquering West Germany team of the 1970s, he enjoyed success in the 1972 European Championship, two years later adding a World Cup winners' medal to his collection. The 1974 tournament saw Breitner adding attacking flair to Germany's play from left-back, converting a penalty in the final against Holland. The same year also saw 'Der Afro' claim the Champions Cup with Bayern Munich, and seal a move to Real Madrid. A falling out with the national coaching staff saw him miss the 1978 World Cup, but he returned in 1982 and again scored in the final.

BILLY BREMNER

Country: Scotland
Born: December 9, 1942
Position: Midfield
Clubs: Leeds United, Hull City, Doncaster Rovers

Bremner was Leeds United's midfield general during the club's glory years of the 1960s and 1970s and the perfect leader for Don Revie's ruthlessly single-minded side. He signed for Leeds as a 15-year-old and broke into the first team during the 1959-60 season. They were relegated that year, but returned to Division One in 1964 with a formidable team – and Bremner was the heartbeat of it.

By the time he left Leeds in September 1976 he had won two league titles, an FA Cup, a League Cup, and narrowly missed out on so much more – Leeds were title runners-up five times, beaten FA Cup finalists three times, and European Cup runners-up once. The winner of 54 Scotland caps, Bremner's fiery temper was never far from the surface and his career was littered with flashpoints, most famously in the 1974 Charity Shield when he squared up to Liverpool's Kevin Keegan, resulting in both players being sent-off. But incidents like that didn't detract from the fact Bremner was a supremely talented footballer.

He later managed the club for a spell in the 1980s, and was hugely mourned when he died of a heart attack in 1997.

EMILIO BUTRAGUEÑO

Country: Spain
Born: July 22, 1963
Position: Centre-forward
Clubs: Real Madrid, Celaya

Throughout the Eighties and Nineties defences lived in fear of 'The Vulture'! That was Butragueño's nickname and he lived up to it well. Save for a final hurrah at Mexican club Celaya, Butragueño spent his career at Real Madrid, where his avalanche of goals brought trophies galore. Graduating from Real's youth ranks and Castilla's second team, Emilio established himself as a penalty-box poacher, inspiring Madrid to consecutive UEFA Cups in 1985 and 1986. But he's best remembered for an extraordinary four-goal display for Spain against Denmark in the 1986 World Cup. He was a Real legend by the time he left in 1995.

KALUSHA BWALYA

Country: Zambia
Born: August 16, 1963
Position: Midfield
Clubs: Mufulira Blackpool, Mufulira Wanderers, Cercle Brugge, PSV Eindhoven, América, Necaxa, Leon, Al Wahda, Irapuato, Vera Cruz, Correcaminos

Kalusha Bwalya, a player of exciting promise with enthralling dribbling skills and a powerful shot, was the star of Zambian soccer. He initially came to prominence at the African Nations Cup in 1986, but it was a sensational performance at the 1988 Olympics – his hat-trick inspiring Zambia to a shock 4-0 thrashing

Below: Liam Brady, a star at Arsenal who went on to build a career in Italy.

Right: A much loved star for both Brazil and Napoli, Careca in action for his country in 1990.

of the mighty Italy – that made his name. By then he had been transferred to Belgian club Cercle Brugge, the first Zambian player since the Sixties to do so. Not surprisingly that year he was also voted Zambia's Player Of The Year and Africa's Player Of The Year.

ERIC CANTONA

Country: France
Born: May 24, 1966
Position: Striker
Clubs: Martigues, Auxerre, Marseille, Bordeaux, Montpellier, Marseille, Nimes, Leeds United, Manchester United

Eric Cantona became a legend in English football for helping Manchester United win their first league title for 26 years. He began his career at Auxerre and became the most expensive player in France when he joined hometown club Marseille for £2.2million in 1988. A gifted but temperamental striker, he struggled to make an impact in France despite winning the French Cup at Montpellier, and came to life only when he moved to England at the age of 25.

At Leeds United he inspired the team to the league title in 1992, before controversially joining Manchester United – much to the consternation of the fans at Elland Road. His skill and leadership lifted Manchester United back to the top of the English game as he claimed four more league titles, two FA Cups and the PFA Player Of The Year award, but he was unable to inspire them to a Champions League triumph. He made just 45 appearances for his country, scoring 19 goals. He retired from the game in 1997.

Below: Eric Cantona was the catalyst for Manchester United's biggest successes in the early years of Alex Fergusson's reign at Old Trafford.

ANTONIO CARBAJAL

Country: Mexico
Born: June 7, 1929
Position: Goalkeeper
Clubs: Espana, Leon

Antonio Carbajal has been awarded FIFA's gold award for services to football, recognising his achievement as a player and coach. Carbajal carved out his legendary status by becoming the first player to appear in five World Cups, playing in each tournament between 1950 and 1966. He was only once on the winning side, against Czechoslovakia in 1962. In the same game Carbajal became the goalkeeper who conceded the then quickest ever World Cup goal after just 15 seconds. He gained his first and only clean sheet at the finals in his 11th and last appearance. He had made his international debut at the 1948 Olympics.

CARECA

Country: Brazil
Born: October 5, 1960
Position: Centre-forward
Clubs: Guarani, São Paulo, Napoli, Hitachi

Adored equally in Brazil and Naples, Careca was one of the main supporting players in the Diego Maradona years that brought such unprecedented success to the Italian club. He forged his name at unfashionable Guarani, who he helped to win the championship in Brazil. Careca's powerful shot and pace

constantly unnerved defenders, but injury denied him a place in the 1982 World Cup. He made amends, however, in both 1986 and 1990, scoring seven goals in nine games. He then teamed up with Diego Maradona and compatriot Alemao at Napoli in 1987 for his greatest years, winning the Scudetto and the UEFA Cup.

JAN CEULEMANS

Country: Belgium
Born: February 28, 1957
Position: Centre-forward/Midfield
Clubs: Lierse, Club Brugge

Arguably the greatest player that Belgium has produced, Jan Ceulemans had an impressive international career that spanned almost 14 years and saw him score 23 goals in 96 games for his country. For a nation of its size, Belgium over-achieved on the international stage throughout the 1980s, and Ceulemans was the team's driving force. Peaking in fourth place at the Mexico World Cup of 1986, Belgium lost out in the semi-finals to the eventual winners, Argentina.

Unusually, Ceulemans resisted the lure of the more wealthy leagues, and appeared happy to stay in his native country despite being courted by some of Europe's top clubs – most notably AC Milan, who were reportedly close to signing him at one point.

Ceulemans was the Belgian league's record signing when he moved from Lierse to Brugge in 1978 for £250,000.

BOBBY CHARLTON

Born: October 11, 1937
Country: England
Position: Centre-forward/Left-wing
Clubs: Manchester United, Preston North End

"There has never been a more popular footballer," remarked former Manchester United manager Sir Matt Busby of Bobby Charlton. "He was as near perfection as man and player as it is possible to be." Certainly Charlton had his fans as part of a rejuvenated Manchester United side and an England World Cup winning team in the 1960s (Jimmy Hill once claimed that at the peak of his powers, Charlton was the most famous living Englishman), but fate so nearly cut short a wonderful career at an early age.

On February 8, 1958, Charlton was caught up in the Munich air disaster that killed eight of the 'Busby Babes' – a name given to Sir Matt Busby's Manchester United side because of their youth. Charlton was thrown 40 yards from the wreckage as the British Airways plane skidded across the runway and ploughed into the airport's perimeter fence. Charlton escaped with a head wound, but it so easily could have been worse: 21 people died in the crash, including the exciting United player Duncan Edwards.

Charlton and Manchester United recovered that year to make it to the FA Cup final, and Charlton, who had already impressed the club by scoring 10 goals in his first 14 appearances, became central to Busby's plans. With his quick thinking, powerful shooting boots and dipping, fizzing crosses, Charlton was used to devastating effect by Busby, first as an inside-forward, then as a left-winger and centre-forward, and later in central midfield. He helped United sweep their way to FA Cup victory in 1962, and two championships in

Above: Bobby Charlton was a part of England's 1970 World Cup side, often regarded as the country's best ever team.
Below left: Warming up for his last World Cup. Bobby Charlton on the ball away to Wales in April 1970. Below right: in action against Austria at Wembley in 1962.

1965 and 1967, as well as a famous European Champions Cup victory in 1968 – United beating Lisbon 4-1 in the final at Wembley.

He was equally explosive for England. Geoff Hurst might have stolen the headlines after his celebrated World Cup-winning hat-trick in 1966, but it was Charlton who steered England to the final. Alf Ramsey's side had started poorly with a 0-0 draw against Uruguay, but during the next game against Mexico Charlton kick-started their campaign with a dazzling goal. Running 30 yards from midfield, he blasted a drive from outside the

penalty area that flew into the net, helping England to a 2-0 win. It was one of the more spectacular efforts from among his 49 goals scored in an England shirt, a record that still stands, but psychologically it was also vital, boosting confidence as England swept aside France, Argentina, Portugal, and West Germany. That year, Charlton was voted Footballer Of The Year, European Footballer Of The Year and Player Of The World Cup.

After a disappointing World Cup in 1970, when Charlton was controversially substituted during England's defeat to West Germany, he played out his final years at United before retiring in 1973 (on the same day as his brother, Leeds United star Jack Charlton). He signed for Preston the following season as manager and later moved to Wigan Athetic.

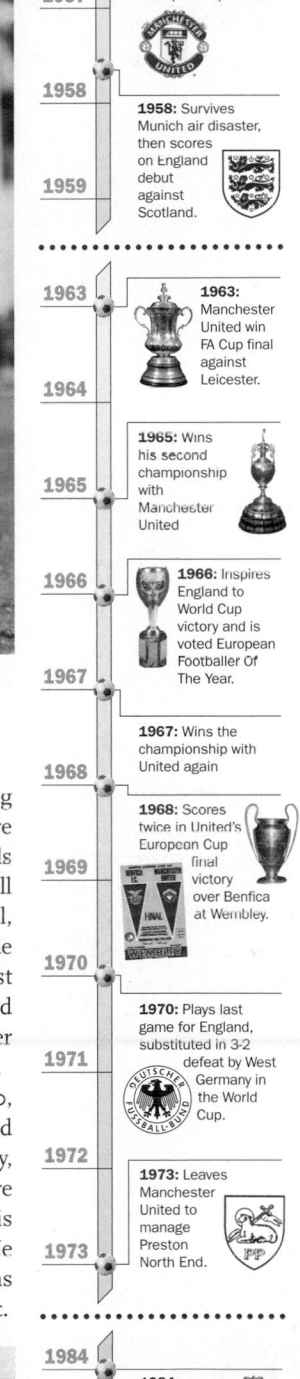

1956: Scores twice on debut for Manchester United and wins first league championship medal.

1958: Survives Munich air disaster, then scores on England debut against Scotland.

1963: Manchester United win FA Cup final against Leicester.

1965: Wins his second championship with Manchester United

1966: Inspires England to World Cup victory and is voted European Footballer Of The Year.

1967: Wins the championship with United again

1968: Scores twice in United's European Cup final victory over Benfica at Wembley.

1970: Plays last game for England, substituted in 3-2 defeat by West Germany in the World Cup.

1973: Leaves Manchester United to manage Preston North End.

1984: Returns to Manchester United to take up a place on the board.

1994: Receives a knighthood from the Queen in her Birthday Honours List.

1956
1957
1958
1959

1963
1964
1965
1966
1967
1968
1969
1970
1971
1972
1973

1984
1986
1988
1990
1992
1994

Right: Mario Coluna, who appeared in five European Cup finals for Benfica before becoming Mozambique's Minister for Sport.

HECTOR CHUMPITAZ

Country: Peru
Born: April 12, 1944
Position: Centre-back
Club: Sporting Cristal

Hector Chumpitaz was, for much of his international career, Peru's inspirational captain. The Peruvian authorities recognised him as playing for the national team on 147 occasions – of which only 110 were officially recognised by FIFA. Chumpitaz had made his international debut in 1966 and went on to appear in two World Cups, in 1970 and 1978. The latter was the most significant as the 34-year-old captain helped Peru through to the second phase. Three years earlier he was part of Peru's Copa América triumph in Colombia. He was a one club man throughout his career, representing Sporting Cristal with some success in the Peruvian championship.

CLODOALDO

Country: Brazil
Born: September 26, 1949
Position: Midfield
Clubs: Santos

Clodoaldo played in every game of Brazil's successful 1970 World Cup campaign at the age of just 20. He scored the equaliser in their 3-1 semi-final win over Uruguay, launching their comeback for victory. A defensive midfielder, he was the baby of Mario Zagalo's team and provided a platform for the likes of Jairzinho and Rivelino to launch attacks. Yet despite the rock-like security he supplied, he never played at a World Cup again.

At club level, Clodoaldo spent his entire career at Santos, making over 500 appearances and winning the Paulista championship five times, in 1967, 1968, 1969, 1972 and 1978.

MARIO ESTEVES COLUNA

Country: Portugal
Born: August 6, 1935
Position: Midfield/Centre-forward
Clubs: Deportivo Lourenço Marques, Benfica

Mario Coluna was a member of the great Benfica side of the 1950s and 1960s. He began as a lethal centre-forward then, after the arrival of the legendary Eusébio, he turned into a formidable midfielder. Born in Mozambique, Coluna was to make 73 appearances for Portugal and he captained the side that reached the 1966 World Cup semi-finals. His greatest achievements were with Benfica, winning a host of domestic trophies and scoring in the 1961 and 1962 European Champions Cup victories, as well as making three other Champions Cup final appearances in 1963,

1965 and 1968. Coluna also played in Mozambique with Marques, and later became the country's Sports Minister.

GIANPIERO COMBI

Country: Italy
Born: December 18, 1902
Position: Goalkeeper
Club: Juventus

Gianpiero Combi was the first of the truly great Italian goalkeepers. He captained Italy to triumph in the 1934 World Cup, beating Czechoslovakia 2-1 after extra-time. The final was Combi's 47th and last appearance for his country, a career which had started dauntingly ten years earlier with a 7-1 defeat by Hungary. He also retired from club football in 1934, and had gone out on a high with Juventus, winning a fourth successive Italian league championship. Combi also won a bronze medal at the 1928 Amsterdam Olympics when Italy finished third, beating Egypt 11-3 in the third place play-off game.

JOHAN CRUYFF

Country: Holland
Born: April 25, 1947
Position: Forward
Clubs: Ajax, Barcelona, Los Angeles Aztecs, Washington Diplomats, Levante, Ajax, Feyenoord

Hugely talented, wilful and unpredictable, Johan Cruyff symbolises the golden era of Dutch football and remains inextricably linked with the concept of Total Football.

Brought up just around the corner from Ajax's ground where his mother was a cleaner, Cruyff joined the club in 1959 and made his debut on November 1964, aged 17, scoring the only Ajax goal in a 3-1 defeat to Groningen. With the arrival of Rinus Michels, the architect

of Total Football, the club accelerated into the modern era with breathtaking style.

Lightweight but blessed with superb balance and huge stamina, Cruyff could cover acres of space and dictate the play. Ajax won five league titles in his first spell with the club but it was three consecutive European Champions Cups between 1971 and 1973 that helped define the legend of the 'Flying Dutchman', resulting in a hat-trick of European Footballer Of The Year awards. Scoring both his side's goals in the 2-0 win over Inter Milan in 1972 capped one of his finest performances.

Making his first international appearance on September 7, 1966, Cruyff scored on his debut in a 2-2 draw with Hungary. But he also became the first Dutchman to be dismissed in an international two months later.

By the time the World Cup came around in 1974 the Dutch team were hot favourites and Cruyff was skipper. Wearing the celebrated Number 14 shirt he orchestrated play with teasing skills and dazzling surges, unveiling the celebrated 'Cruyff turn' to the watching millions. The shift in the balance of power was vividly demonstrated when the Dutch beat a physical Brazil 2-0 in a game notable for a sublime volley from the captain. Losing the final to West Germany did nothing to diminish Cruyff's stature, even though he was shackled by Berti Vogts during its most crucial phase.

Four years later he withdrew unexpectedly from the Holland squad, a gesture typical of his rebellious personality. He had won 48 caps and scored 33 goals.

By the summer of 1974 he had moved to Barcelona for a record fee of £922,300. The Catalan side were struggling but Cruyff scored twice on his debut and led them to their first championship since 1960.

In 1978 he announced his retirement to go into business but returned to playing in the American NASL a year later. He eventually rejoined Ajax in December 1981, taking them to two more championships, but his swansong came with bitter rivals Feyenoord, whom he guided to a league and cup double in 1984. In his last season, at 37, he was voted Dutch Player Of The Year.

Cruyff inevitably went into management with Ajax in 1985, winning a European Cup Winners' Cup, but quit three years later after another dispute. In May 1988 he took over at Barcelona, guiding the club to four consecutive league titles between 1991 and 1994. His greatest achievement though was bringing them the European Cup for the first time in 1992, but four years later his influence had waned and he was sacked.

A heavy smoker with a congenital heart condition, he had a bypass operation in 1991, but his health does not stop him from being linked with Barcelona and Holland every time there is a vacancy. From his record it is not hard to fathom why.

Opposite: A majestic Johan Cruyff rounds the floored Argentinian goalkeeper to score for Holland during the 1974 World Cup.

Right: Teofilo Cubillas in action at the 1978 World Cup, where he scored five goals.

TEOFILO CUBILLAS

Country: Peru
Born: March 8, 1949
Position: Midfield
Clubs: Alianza, Basel, FC Porto, Alianza, Fort Lauderdale Strikers

Teofilo Cubillas is a name few Scottish football fans are ever likely to forget. In 1978 he shot down Scotland's World Cup hopes with two goals in a surprise 3-1 win for Peru, and then went on to score a hat-trick against Iran, taking his World Cup finals tally to ten – he also played in the 1970 competition as a 21-year-old. Easily Peru's greatest ever player, Cubillas was named South American Footballer Of The Year in 1972 and helped the country to the 1975 Copa América. In great contrast to his impressive international achievements – 117 caps and 47 goals – his club career was modest. A hero in his own country, however, he eventually became the Peruvian Minister for Sport.

ZOLTAN CZIBOR

Country: Hungary
Born: August 23, 1929
Position: Left-winger
Clubs: Ferencváros, Csepel, Honvéd, Barcelona, Espanyol

Below: Kenny Dalglish scores Liverpool's winning goal against Chelsea in 1986, a goal that secured the league title for the player-manager.

Czibor was the talented left-footer who supplied much of the ammunition for the great Hungarian forward line of Puskás and Kocsis in the 1950s. Having won the Olympic title in 1952, Czibor's talents helped Hungary to the World Cup final in Switzerland in 1954. He was outstanding in the 4-2 semi-final success over Uruguay, but the Hungarians surrendered a two goal lead to lose the final to West Germany.

At the time of the Hungarian revolution in 1956, Czibor – like Puskás and Kocsis – took advantage of a Honvéd tour to settle in Spain, where he was to win back-to-back league titles with Barcelona.

KENNY DALGLISH

Country: Scotland
Born: March 4, 1951
Position: Centre-forward
Clubs: Celtic, Liverpool

Alan Shearer tells a story about trying to mark his then manager at Newcastle in a practice game. Dalglish kept spinning off him and racing away with the ball. "How did you know where I was?" Shearer asked. "I could see your shadow," was the reply from his boss. With a football at his feet Kenny Dalglish had the instincts of a gunslinger.

Possessed of quickfire reflexes, an acute awareness of opponents and team-mates, exquisite touch, and the ability to shield the ball seemingly forever, Dalglish ranks among the finest players Scotland has ever produced.

He joined Celtic as a junior in 1967 and might have gone straight to Liverpool at 15 but for a failed trial. Instead Celtic farmed him out to Cumbernauld to toughen him up. Jock Stein's Celtic were a top European side and though he made his league debut against Raith Rovers on October 4, 1969, it took time to establish himself. However, in seven seasons there he was to make 204 appearances, score 112 goals and win four league championships and four Scottish Cups.

In August 1977 he made the move to Liverpool for a UK record fee of £440,000. Bought to replace the departing Kevin Keegan, he won the European Champions Cup in his first season. The trophies continued to come: three European Cups in Europe, a hat-trick of league titles between 1982 and 1984 at home, and two Footballer Of the Year awards.

Dalglish also played for Scotland at every level, making his debut as a substitute against Belgium on November 10, 1971. He was part of the 1974 Scotland World Cup squad, but despite not losing, and holding Brazil to a draw, they crashed out on goal difference.

In Argentina four years later Dalglish opened the scoring against Holland in the superb 3-2 win, but the team were again on a plane home after the first round. No matter how far Scotland got in the World Cup, the 'Tartan Army' idolised him just for scoring in the 1977 2-1 victory at Wembley.

He travelled to a third World Cup in 1982, and scored in the opening game against New Zealand, and would have appeared at a fourth tournament under Alex Ferguson but for injury. He made his last appearance against Luxembourg in November, 1986, retiring with 102 caps, having equalled Denis Law's scoring record of 30 goals.

In 1985 Dalglish succeeded Joe Fagan when he became player-manager of Liverpool, winning the elusive league and cup double in his first season in charge, and going on to win a total of three league titles as manager.

When the Hillsborough disaster struck the city in 1989, Dalglish conducted himself impeccably, but following on as it did from the deaths at Heysel four years earlier it was

a significant added pressure and he quit the club unexpectedly in February 1991.

Eight months later he surprised everyone by coming out of retirement to manage Blackburn Rovers, taking the dormant club into the Premier League and then to a championship in 1995. He was unable to repeat the trick when he moved to Newcastle United in February 1997 but still took the club to their first major cup final in 20 years.

Dalglish stepped back from the firing line and subsequently became part of a consortium that took over at Celtic briefly, but it is hard to believe the game has seen the last of him.

JIMMY DELANEY

Country: Scotland
Born: September 3, 1914
Position: Outside-right
Clubs: Celtic, Manchester United, Aberdeen, Falkirk, Derry City, Cork Athletic, Elgin City

Jimmy Delaney's career spanned both sides of the Second World War and he made a unique mark on the game by becoming the only player to have won the Scottish Cup, the FA Cup and the Irish Cup. He won the Scottish Cup with Celtic in 1937, beating Aberdeen 2-1 in the final. He also won two league titles with the club. He lifted the FA Cup with Manchester United in 1948 in a thrilling 4-2 win over Blackpool, and in 1954, at the age of 39 and as the Irish league's most expensive player at £1,500, he finally won the Irish Cup with Derry City after two replays with Glentoran.

DIDIER DESCHAMPS

Country: France
Born: October 15, 1968
Position: Midfield
Clubs: Nantes, Marseille, Bordeaux, Marseille, Juventus, Chelsea, Valencia

A hugely successful footballer, Deschamps started out at Nantes and captained Marseille to a European Champions Cup triumph aged just 24 in 1993. He joined Juventus and became a key figure, winning the European Cup and World Club Cup in 1996, and Italian titles in 1995, 1997 and 1998. Deschamps captained France to World Cup victory on home soil in 1998 and led the side to the European Championship in 2000 before quitting international football. A prodigious worker, he read the game well and provided a platform for more creative players. He won 103 caps, retiring in 2001.

Above: Didier Deschamps holds off Brazil's Bebeto as France win the World Cup on home soil in 1998.

KAZIMIERZ DEYNA

Country: Poland
Born: October 23, 1947
Position: Midfield
Clubs: Wlokniarz Starogard Gdanski, LKS Lodz, Legia Warsaw, Manchester City, San Diego Sockers

Kazimierz Deyna was the creative midfield driving force of Poland's greatest ever team during the 1970s. The Legia Warsaw player had shot to prominence at the 1972 Olympics, scoring both goals in the 2-1 victory over Hungary in the final. He went on to win 102 caps and was captain of Poland at two successive World Cups. In 1974, Deyna helped a free-scoring Poland to third place, and then in 1978 helped them to the second round group stage. During this period he figured in the top ten of Europe's Footballer Of The Year Award on three occasions. He also appeared in the film *Escape To Victory*.

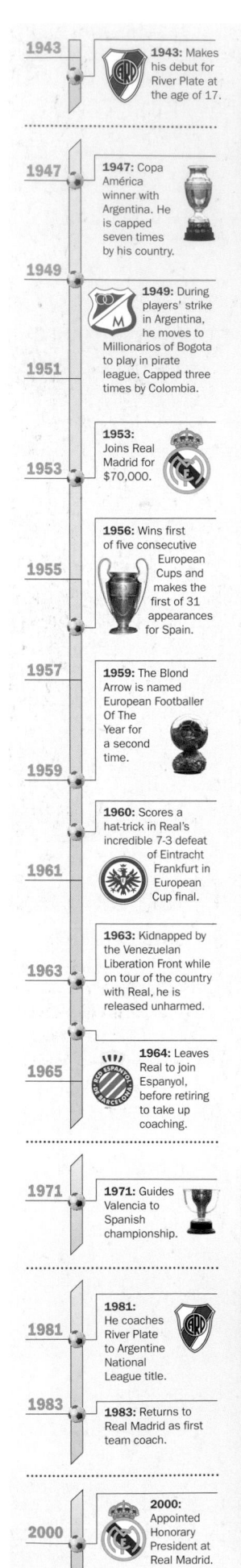

1943: Makes his debut for River Plate at the age of 17.

1947: Copa América winner with Argentina. He is capped seven times by his country.

1949: During players' strike in Argentina, he moves to Millonarios of Bogota to play in pirate league. Capped three times by Colombia.

1953: Joins Real Madrid for $70,000.

1956: Wins first of five consecutive European Cups and makes the first of 31 appearances for Spain.

1959: The Blond Arrow is named European Footballer Of The Year for a second time.

1960: Scores a hat-trick in Real's incredible 7-3 defeat of Eintracht Frankfurt in European Cup final.

1963: Kidnapped by the Venezuelan Liberation Front while on tour of the country with Real, he is released unharmed.

1964: Leaves Real to join Espanyol, before retiring to take up coaching.

1971: Guides Valencia to Spanish championship.

1981: He coaches River Plate to Argentine National League title.

1983: Returns to Real Madrid as first team coach.

2000: Appointed Honorary President at Real Madrid.

ALFREDO DI STÉFANO

Country: Argentina, Colombia, Spain
Born: July 4, 1926
Position: Centre-forward
Clubs: River Plate, Huracan, Millonarios, Real Madrid, Espanyol

Born in Argentina of Italian parentage, Alfredo was just 15 years of age when he joined the famous River Plate side of the 1940s and within a year he had made his debut in a team that included Adolfo Pedernera and Labruna, two of Argentina's greatest ever players.

Unable to make an immediate impression in an attack that lauded such players, he was loaned to Huracan to hone his skills, and some 50 goals in 66 games saw his return following Pedernera's departure to Atalanta. Now 20 years of age, his impact on the team was immediate as he led River Plate to the 1947 championship with 27 goals in 30 games. His elevation to the Argentinian national team was inevitable, and five goals helped his country retain the Copa América championship that year.

A players strike in 1949, the result of a poor wage structure, led to an exodus of players into the pirate 'Di Mayor' league in Colombia. As this league was outside of the jurisdiction of FIFA, no transfer fees were paid, therefore the clubs could afford to tempt the players with higher wages. Alongside Pedernera, Di Stéfano joined Millonarios of Bogota and became the club's second highest goalscorer of all time as they won five titles in six seasons.

With his place in the country's football history assured, Di Stéfano represented the Colombian national team, regardless of the fact that he had already played for Argentina. But with so few fixtures arranged, he made just four appearances for his adopted nation.

Di Stéfano was regarded as the best player in South America and when he was lured to join Real Madrid in 1953, the opportunity

Above: Di Stéfano in full flight for Real Madrid against Zamalek Sporting Club in Cairo in 1961. Below left: 11 days after bitter rivals Barcelona had knocked Real out of the European Cup for the first time, Di Stéfano scores the first goal in a 5-3 victory over their rivals in the league in 1960. Below right: posing for Barcelona's other team, Espanyol in 1964.

came late in his career. Santiago Bernabéu, president of the Spanish club, orchestrated the move after the 27-year-old impressed in a friendly between Real and Millonarios. For a while they were involved in a tug-of-war with Barcelona for his services, but he signed for Madrid that summer for $70,000.

The next ten seasons would see him rival Pele as the greatest player on the planet and he became the most revered player in Real's history. His first season heralded the Spanish title, and within three years his opening goal inspired the club to an inaugural European Cup victory against Stade de Reims. Di Stéfano would score in each of the next four finals as Real made the trophy their own.

The second triumph against Fiorentina was significant as it capped a tremendous season in which he not only topped the scoring in the competition, but also in the Spanish

league, where Real reigned supreme. His exploits made him a household figure across the continent and it was little surprise when he was named European Player Of The Year.

It was the fifth European Cup success that highlighted both Di Stéfano's standing in the game and Real's dominance. Having finished the previous campaign as Spain's top scorer for the fourth consecutive season, he led the club to a 7-3 drubbing of Eintracht Frankfurt in the final. His hat-trick, allied to the four goals of Ferenc Puskás, saw Di Stéfano at his peak, and although he would reach two more finals, Di Stéfano's star was on the wane.

A 3-1 Champions Cup defeat by Inter Milan in 1964 proved to be his last major game for the club, and although he scored 19 goals in two seasons for Barcelona-based Espanyol, a back injury forced him to hang up his boots at the ripe old age of 40.

DIDI

Country: Brazil
Born: October 8, 1928
Position: Midfield
Clubs: FC Rio Branco, FC Lencoes, Madureiro, Fluminense, Botafogo, Real Madrid, Valencia, Botafogo

Waldyr Pereira, more famously known as Didi, was the inspiration behind Brazil's successive World Cup triumphs of 1958 and 1962. Indeed, Brazil's free-flowing 4-2-4 system owed much to Didi's speed, thoughtful play and extraordinary technique. He was the first of the great free-kick specialists, scoring 12 of his 31 international goals from dead ball situations. He represented Brazil on 85 occasions, including at the 1954 World Cup, and made his name with Fluminense and Botofogo. A dream move to Real Madrid did not work out. He later became coach of Peru and guided them to the 1970 World Cup.

DOMINGOS

Country: Brazil
Born: November 19, 1912
Position: Centre-back
Clubs: Bangu, Vasco da Gama, Nacional, Boca Juniors, Flamengo, Corinthians

Domingos da Guia is regarded as one of the all-time great Brazilian defenders. He played at the 1938 World Cup, where they reached the semi-finals, and enjoyed a superb club career across South America. He started at Bangu and starred for Vasco da Gama and Flamengo. He also played abroad and won the Uruguayan league championship at Nacional and the Argentine title at Boca Juniors.

Nicknamed 'The Divine Master', Domingos was a highly skilled player, introducing a refined technique at the back. He often dribbled the ball out of the penalty area, something rarely seen at the time. He made 30 appearances for Brazil and died in 2000.

DRAGAN DZAJIC

Country: Yugoslavia
Born: May 30, 1946
Position: Left-winger
Club: Red Star Belgrade, SEC Bastia

Dragan Dzagic is regarded as the greatest Yugoslav player of all time. After making his international debut at the age of 17, the Red Star Belgrade winger scored 23 goals in 85 appearances for his country. He helped Yugoslavia to the European Championship final of 1968 and the semi-finals in 1976, as well the 1974 World Cup finals. A winger who truly mesmerised defenders with his speed and agility in carving out chances, his power

also made him a direct threat to any goalkeeper. With Red Star he won five Yugoslav championships and four Yugoslav Cups between 1961 and 1975, scoring 287 goals in 590 appearances.

DUNCAN EDWARDS

Country: England
Born: October 1, 1936
Position: Midfield
Clubs: Manchester United

Even today, some people still rate Duncan Edwards as the greatest player to have worn the Manchester United shirt. For someone who played only 151 matches for his club and 18 for his country before his death following the Munich air disaster at the age of 21, that appears difficult to believe – but not to those who saw him play.

Unusually strong and quick, he played his first game for Manchester United aged 16. Comfortable anywhere on the pitch, he could play in defence, midfield or attack. His all round game, speed and power meant he was the brightest of the 'Busby Babes' who won back-to-back championships before the heart

of the side was lost on an icy runway. Edwards clung to survival for 15 days before slipping away. He would have been 29 at the 1966 World Cup. Had he lived, many believe he, rather than Bobby Moore, would have been the man who lifted the World Cup.

PREBEN ELKJAER-LARSEN

Country: Denmark
Born: October 5, 1960
Position: Striker
Clubs: Köln, Lokeren, Verona

Denmark matured as a football nation in the 1980s when they boasted three players of world class: the Laudrup brothers and Elkjaer-Larsen. Explosive on and off the field, Elkjaer-Larsen was the kind of player who made things happen. First capped in 1977, he starred in the 1984 European Championship and was voted third best player of the 1986 World Cup Finals, in which he scored a hat-trick in Denmark's 6-1 rout of Uruguay. His 25 goals in 66 matches in Italy helped Verona to the Scudetto in the 1984-85 season. He had retired by the time of his country's greatest triumph, the 1992 European Championship.

Above: Manchester United's Duncan Edwards in action against Aston Villa in the 1957 FA Cup Final. The greatest football talent of his generation, he died from injuries sustained in the Munich air disaster at just 21.

ARSENIO ERICO

Country: Paraguay
Born: March 30, 1915
Position: Centre-forward
Clubs: FC Asuncion, Independiente, Huracan

In 1937 the Argentine league witnessed a goalscoring sensation when Independiente's Arsenio Erico netted a record 47 goals during the league season. It was a record that epitomised Erico as a prolific goalscorer, and on numerous occasions he managed to find the net five times in a game.

He was discovered at the age of 17 when he played in a charity match for the Paraguay Red Cross in Buenos Aires. He was immediately signed by Independiente in exchange for a donation to the Red Cross. His career was blighted by injury though, which enforced his retirement in 1944.

EUSÉBIO

Country: Portugal
Born: January 25, 1942
Position: Centre-forward
Clubs: Sporting Lourenço Marques, Benfica, Boston Minutemen, Toronto Metros, Las Vegas Quicksilver

Eusébio Da Silva Ferreira was born in the Portuguese colony of Mozambique in 1942 and although he excelled at basketball and athletics, he made his name as a footballer with local club Sporting Lourenço Marques, a feeder for Portuguese side Sporting Lisbon.

In 1960, he was deemed ready for the Portuguese league, but having successfully arrived at Lisbon airport, en-route to Sporting's headquarters he was 'kidnapped' by rival club Benfica and hidden in an Algarve fishing village until a deal was struck in the best interests of all parties.

Benfica were prompted to take such evasive action after their coach, Bela Guttmann, heard about Eusébio in a hairdresser's salon. Having flown out to Mozambique to witness his talent at first hand, Guttmann made it his mission to sign 'The Black Panther' as soon as the opportunity presented itself.

As a fresh-faced 18-year-old, it took Eusébio a little time to adapt to his new surroundings, but within two years he had managed to secure a place in Benfica folklore as a member of the triumphant European Champions Cup side that beat Spanish giants and five-times winners, Real Madrid. Eusébio scored twice in the 5-3 victory and the following year was selected to play for a Rest Of The World side against England at Wembley, as part of the Football Association's centenary celebrations.

He endeared himself to the British public and the bond was further cemented three years later when he became a star of the 1966 World Cup finals as a member of the Portuguese team. Having reached the quarter-finals, Portugal were shocked when North Korea took a 3-0 lead, but Eusébio inspired his team-mates into one of the greatest ever World Cup comebacks. He scored four goals as Portugal won the game 5-3, and although he left the tournament in tears following semi-final defeat against England, he was the competition's top-scorer with nine goals. Such was his impact, he even had a waxwork model erected in his honour at Madame Tussaud's.

Goals were certainly Eusébio's forte and from 1964 to 1968, and again in 1970 and 1973, he was Portugal's top league scorer. He was also the continent's top scorer in 1968 and 1973, with 42 and 40 goals respectively, and in his 15 years at Benfica there were just two seasons in which he didn't win a domestic or European honour.

With a European Champions Cup winners' medal already to his name, when Benfica faced Manchester United at Wembley in 1968 he again had an opportunity to go one better than the runner-up medals he'd picked up in 1963 and 1965. With the scores at 1-1, he was denied a late winner by a fine save from Alex Stepney and United went on to win in extra-time. Eusébio again left Wembley in tears but the bittersweet experience of the competition was tempered by his total tally of 46 cup goals, second only to the great Alfredo Di Stéfano.

A knee injury forced Eusébio to end his top-flight career at 32 and he saw out his playing days in the NASL with the Boston Minutemen, Toronto Metros and Las Vegas Quicksilver. He returned to Benfica as coach in 1977, but having scored 38 goals in 46 games for Portugal, and 727 goals in 715 games in total, it is undoubtedly as a scorer of goals that he will be best remembered.

GIACINTO FACCHETTI

Country: Italy
Born: July 18, 1942
Position: Defender
Clubs: Trevigliese, Inter Milan

Starting out as a striker at his first club Trevigliese, Facchetti was converted into a left-back by team coach Helenio Herrera when he joined Inter Milan. Encouraged to attack as well as taking care of his defensive duties – something unique at the time in Italian football – Facchetti netted 60 league goals in an Inter career lasting 17 years. His most celebrated goal came in 1965 in a European Cup semi-final second-leg match against Liverpool, when despite being 3-1 down from the first leg at Anfield, Inter defeated the English side 3-0 in the return match, with Facchetti netting the decider. He made 94 appearances for Italy and was team captain when his country made the World Cup final in 1970.

Above: Italy's Giacinto Facchetti shakes hands with Nazaire, the captain of Haiti, during the 1974 World Cup.

FALCAO

Country: Brazil
Born: October 16, 1953
Position: Midfield
Clubs: Internacional, Roma, São Paulo

Paulo Roberto Falcao was an elegant and graceful midfielder who sprang to prominence as part of the outstanding Brazil side at the 1982 World Cup. He played alongside Zico, Socrates and Toninho Cerezo in a wonderfully creative midfield and brought his own flair and style to the team.

At club level Falcao played in Brazil for Internacional and was their greatest-ever player. With excellent passing vision and an eye for goal – he often scored from long range – he led the side to three national titles in 1975, 1976 and 1979.

He moved to Italy in 1980, and in 1983 led Roma to their first title triumph in over 50 years. Roma reached the European Cup final the following year, where they lost to Liverpool on penalties in their own Stadio Olimpico. Falcao returned to Brazil in 1985 and played a final season at São Paulo. He won 38 caps for his country, scoring nine goals.

BERNABE FERREYRA

Country: Argentina
Born: February 12, 1909
Position: Inside-forward
Clubs: Tigre, River Plate

Ferreyra was the first legendary player of Argentine football, although he only made four appearances for his country. His name was made in the domestic game, however, firstly with Tigre and then River Plate. He joined River Plate in 1932, and during his debut season with the club he scored a record 43 goals. No-one, it seems, could stop the player. His reputation as unstoppable was such that a Buenos Aires newspaper offered a gold

Opposite: 'The Black Panther', Eusébio of Benfica.

Right: Just Fontaine, scorer of a record 13 goals in the 1958 World Cup, is chaired off after the third-place play-off.

medal to any goalkeeper who kept a clean sheet against him. Ferreyra though was not fêted with honours, winning the Argentine title just twice in 1936 and 1937.

ELIAS FIGUEROA

Country: Chile
Born: March 25, 1946
Position: Left-back
Clubs: Peñarol, Internacional, Club Palestino, Fort Lauderdale Strikers, Colo Colo

Elias Figueroa Brander is the greatest Chilean player ever, having won consecutive South American Footballer Of The Year titles in 1974, 1975 and 1976. No other player has achieved such a feat. His talent was recognised early on and he was captain of Chile's Under-17 team. The Valpariso-born Figueroa very quickly established himself as a player of elegance, earning himself the respected nickname 'Don Elias'. At the 1974 World Cup he was voted the tournament's best defender, while at club level he won the national titles in three different countries: five times in Uruguay, three times in Brazil, and twice in Chile.

TOM FINNEY

Country: England
Born: April 5, 1922
Position: Winger
Clubs: Preston North End

Finney started his love affair with Preston North End in the summer of 1940 when he signed as a part-time professional. Slight of build and with a quick turn of pace, he made an immediate impression by scoring on his debut in a 2-1 defeat at Liverpool that August.

He continued to impress his hometown club but the Second World War interrupted his progress and he was shipped off to the Middle East before he could sign on as a full professional. On his return at the start of the 1946-47 season, Finney scored in a 3-2 victory against Leeds United and his flourishing reputation was soon rewarded with an England debut against Northern Ireland. His debut goal in a 7-2 victory was the first of 30 he would score in 72 appearances for his country, and with 18 of them coming in his first 24 appearances, he was vying with Stanley Matthews for the title of the greatest England player of his generation.

A host of clubs tried to prise Finney from Preston's grasp, including Italian club Palermo, who reportedly offered him £10,000, a car, a villa and huge salary – but he stayed fiercely loyal and spent his entire career at Deepdale. Although he failed to win a major honour with the club, he was twice voted Footballer Of The Year in 1954 and 1957 and his 187 league goals remain a club record.

Opposite: Paul Gascoigne scores one of the most memorable England goals of all time against Scotland at Euro 96.

JUST FONTAINE

Country: France
Born: August 18, 1933
Position: Centre-forward
Clubs: AC Marrakesh, US Marocaine Casablanca, Nice, Reims

Just Fontaine made history when he scored 13 goals at the World Cup finals in 1958 to set a record that looks unlikely ever to be beaten. It stands as the highest number of goals scored by one player in a single tournament, yet he was not even France's first-choice centre-forward before the World Cup began. Only an injury to Rene Bliard gave him the chance to make football history.

Fontaine was born in Morocco and won his first cap for France in 1953. He was left out for nearly three years and returned to the international fold to play just four times before the World Cup in 1958.

At the finals held in Sweden he formed a wonderful partnership with Raymond Kopa. Fontaine's assets were pace and a potent left foot, and he couldn't stop scoring. He was a star in the French league with Nice and Reims, with whom he lost in the 1959 European Cup final. To prove his World Cup exploits were no fluke, he finished as the European Cup's leading scorer in the 1958-59 season with ten goals. A broken leg ended his career and he went on to briefly manage France. He won 21 caps and scored 30 goals.

ENZO FRANCESCOLI

Country: Uruguay
Born: November 12, 1961
Position: Forward/Midfield
Clubs: Wanderers, River Plate, Racing Club Paris, Marseille, Cagliari, Torino, River Plate

When a footballer of the stature of Zinedine Zidane names his first born son after his hero, you know the player receiving such a tribute is exceptionally special. Enzo Francescoli certainly was. He graced Latin and European football for two decades in a career that yielded almost 200 club goals. He was voted South American Footballer Of The Year in 1984, and again when he returned from Europe for one final season in 1995. Nicknamed 'El Principe' (The Prince), he combined silky movement with great attacking play from midfield, and he was as adept at creating chances as he was converting them. He was top scorer in the Argentine league in 1984, 1986 and 1995.

ARTHUR FRIEDENREICH

Country: Brazil
Born: July 18, 1892
Position: Striker
Clubs: Germania, Ipiranga, Americao, Paulistano, São Paulo, Flamengo

Few players can claim to be better than Pele, but in sheer volume of goals scored, Arthur Friedenreich can. In a 26-year career, 'The Tiger' scored a world record 1,329 goals – 49 more than Pele. Of German and Brazilian parentage, his significance extends far beyond the playing field. An Englishman had originally introduced football to Brazil in the late 19th century, and for the first two decades of the 20th century it remained the preserve of white people. Friedenreich helped to change that. He played for the first Brazilian national side in a friendly against Exeter City in 1914 and went on to win 17 caps, scoring eight goals, until his final international appearance in 1930.

GARRINCHA

Country: Brazil

Born: October 28, 1933

Position: Right-wing

Clubs: Pau Grande, Botafogo, Corinthians, Flamengo, Bangu, Portuguesa Santista, Olaria, Atletico Junior Barranquilla, Red Star Paris

It was a miracle that Garrincha became one of Brazil's greatest players because, despite an operation, a childhood illness had left one leg curved and the other slightly shorter. Nicknamed the 'Little Bird', he was an outstanding dribbler with the ball and he possessed a wonderful swerving 'banana' shot.

Garrincha was part of the Brazil side which lifted the 1958 World Cup but, although he might have been overshadowed by the exciting young Pele on that occasion, in the 1962 finals he was Brazil's inspiration. He scored twice in the quarter-final win over England and then twice again in the semi-finals against hosts Chile, fully deserving his second winners' medal. His last game for Brazil was against England in 1966, and in 60 matches for his country, he only lost once. Sadly, his wild off-the-field lifestyle caught up with him in 1983 when he died at the age of 49.

PAUL GASCOIGNE

Country: England

Born: May 27, 1967

Position: Midfield

Clubs: Newcastle United, Tottenham Hotspur, Lazio, Rangers, Middlesbrough, Everton, Burnley, Gansu Tianmu

The English game has produced legends like Bobby Moore, Bobby Charlton and Stanley Matthews, but none more talented than Paul Gascoigne. At his best Gascoigne could do things with a football beyond the scope of those men. He could run with it at pace, dance through tackles, see a pass no-one else could, strike the ball with power or caress it. Yet he proved incapable of handling his talent.

Born in nearby Gateshead, Gascoigne joined Newcastle United as a boy and made his senior debut at just 17 years of age, coming on as a substitute against QPR on April 13, 1985. He went on to make 106 league and cup appearances for the club, scoring 22 goals, but never truly won over the Geordie crowd.

He moved south to Spurs in July 1988 for £2million and rapidly flowered under manager Terry Venables in a stylish attacking side. England manager Bobby Robson gave him his international debut as a substitute against Denmark on September 14, 1988, and he forced his way into the World Cup squad for Italia 90. There England rode their luck to the semi-finals, losing on penalties to Germany. As the dream of World Cup glory ebbed away,

Gazza lifted his shirt to wipe away the tears, creating one of the game's most iconic images.

In May 1991 Spurs agreed an £8million move to Lazio after that season's FA Cup final against Nottingham Forest, but Gascoigne ruptured a cruciate ligament in a wild challenge on Gary Charles. Four months later he fell outside a nightclub, smashing the same kneecap, delaying his comeback by three months. In subsequent years 27 operations would take their toll on his body.

He made a belated debut appearance for Lazio in a friendly with Spurs on September 23, 1992, and two months later scored his first goal in Serie A, an 87th minute headed equaliser in the Rome derby that forever endeared him to the Lazio fans.

Gascoigne's career in Italy proceeded in stops and starts as he drifted in and out of games. Then, in April 1994, a wild training ground tackle on Alessandro Nesta shattered his shin in two places. It was a year before he managed to return to the game, but within a month of the season ending he joined Rangers, where he won the Scottish Player Of The Year award in 1996, two Scottish Cups, and two championship medals.

Terry Venables, now England coach, brought him back for Euro 96, where he demonstrated flashes of his old brilliance, not least with a delicious goal against Scotland.

A £3.5million move to Middlesbrough in March 1998 failed to convince critics he was anything but a shadow of the player he one was. He made his debut in the League Cup final but could not wrench the game from Chelsea's grasp. Glenn Hoddle subsequently omitted him from the 1998 World Cup squad, adding to his anguish.

Former Rangers boss Walter Smith took him to Everton in July 2000 and the move initially worked for Gascoigne, but he was also plagued by injury niggles exacerbated by years of heavy drinking. Following Smith's dismissal he headed for Burnley, a stint that lasted just four months. Attempts to find a suitable British club the following season foundered and he eventually moved to Gansu Tianmu in the Chinese B League, marking another bizarre downward turn in the Gazza soap opera.

FRANCISCO GENTO

Country: Spain
Born: October 22, 1933
Position: Left-wing
Clubs: Santander, Real Madrid

Supporters love to see wingers in full flight and none came more dazzling or decorated than outside-left Francisco 'Paco' Gento. Blessed with electric pace and intricate dribbling ability, he provided the ammunition to Puskás and Di Stéfano in Real's heyday. Gento joined Real from Santander in 1953 and

played 800 games for the club, scoring 256 goals and winning 11 championship medals. He was capped 43 times for Spain and featured in the 1960 European Championship winning squad, but his greatest achievement was to appear in all eight of Real Madrid's European Champions Cup finals between 1956 and 1966, picking up a winner's medal in six of them and scoring the extra-time winner in the 1958 game against AC Milan.

ERIC GERETS

Country: Belgium
Born: May 18, 1954
Position: Right-back
Clubs: Standard Liège, AC Milan, MVV Maastricht, PSV Eindhoven

The Belgian defender is one of his country's most celebrated players, picking up 86 caps in an international career that stretched between 1975 and 1991. Gerets was also part of the Belgian team which reached the final of the 1980 European Championship in Italy, where they ultimately lost out to a West Germany winner only two minutes from time. At club level, Gerets' greatest achievement came with Dutch side PSV Eindhoven, who he captained to victory in the 1988 Champions Cup final against Benfica on penalties. Now a coach, Gerets guided Lierse and Club Brugge to the Belgian title, and won back-to-back championships with PSV in 2000 and 2001.

GÉRSON

Country: Brazil
Born: January 1, 1941
Position: Midfield
Clubs: Botafogo, São Paolo

Gérson was the successor to Didi as Brazil's midfield general in the 1966 World Cup, but

his country's ageing team were eliminated early. Four years later, however, it was a very different story. Gérson had a superb World Cup in 1970 where he orchestrated most of Brazil's attacking moves. In the first round, against Romania, he provided a trademark 40-yard pass from midfield for Pele to score, and his range of distribution, together with his midfield scheming, was a consistent delight for all. In the final against Italy, Gérson was arguably the man of the match and scored Brazil's second goal in the memorable 4-1 rout. He will be forever remembered as an integral part of Mario Zagalo's Brazil 1970 side.

JOHNNY GILES

Country: Republic of Ireland
Born: January 6, 1940
Position: Midfield
Clubs: Manchester United, Leeds United, West Bromwich Albion, Vancouver Whitecaps, Shamrock Rovers

When Leeds recruited Giles in 1963 it proved a brilliant bit of business and a crucial move in manager Don Revie's team-building plans. The Irishman became one of the key players in Revie's superb side of the Sixties and Seventies, forming a lengthy partnership in central midfield with Billy Bremner. It was Bremner who supplied the fire and Giles the coolness of passing, though he wasn't shy of a strong challenge himself when it was needed.

His period at Elland Road would be filled with honours. Leeds won the championship in 1969 and 1971, and the FA Cup in 1972, but while Giles twice picked up Fairs Cup winners' medals, the closest he came to success in the European Cup was defeat to Bayern Munich in the 1975 final.

After leaving Leeds, Giles became player-manager at West Brom and later managed the Republic Of Ireland, stepping down in 1980.

GILMAR

Country: Brazil
Born: August 22, 1930
Position: Goalkeeper
Clubs: Jabaquara São Paulo, Corinthians, Santos

Gilmar is regarded as the finest goalkeeper Brazil has ever produced. He played in goal when they became world champions for the first time in 1958 and retained the title four years later. In 1958 he let in only three goals in six matches and was equally impressive at the 1962 World Cup in Chile. Agile and brave, he proved a formidable last line of defence.

Gilmar played for Corinthians, and after a decade joined Santos, where he enjoyed his greatest moments at club level, clinching the World Club Cup in 1962 and 1963. He won 94 caps and retired in 1969.

FERNANDO GOMES

Country: Portugal
Born: November 22, 1956
Position: Centre-forward
Clubs: FC Porto, Sporting Gijon, Sporting Lisbon

Fernando Mendes Soares Gomes was Portugal's legendary striker who twice won Europe's Golden Boot, in 1983 and 1985. On both occasions he was captaining Porto, his hometown club, scoring 36 and 39 league goals respectively. Both Porto, with whom he signed at the age of the 17, and Gomes were at the height of their powers. Gomes, however, missed out on the highlight of the 1987 European Cup final with a broken leg. He was the Portuguese league's top goalscorer six times in all and won five titles and three Portuguese Cups. During a 17-year career Gomes also played 46 times for Portugal.

JIMMY GREAVES

Country: England
Born: February 20, 1940
Position: Centre forward
Clubs: Chelsea, AC Milan, Tottenham Hotspur, West Ham United

Jimmy Greaves always knew how to make an impression, scoring on every debut he made. But then he had a habit of scoring goals, his guile and pace helping him to notch up 357 of them throughout his career,.

After working his way through the Chelsea youth ranks in the late 1950s, he quickly entertained management and fans alike with his quick feet and imaginative individualism. After four seasons at Stamford Bridge (including two seasons as the league's top scorer), Greaves moved to AC Milan in search

of higher wages but found it difficult to settle and returned home to Spurs only six months later for a then record £99,999. He settled at White Hart Lane quickly, helping Spurs to two FA Cups and European glory in the Cup Winner's Cup, a first for any British club.

An England favourite throughout his career, the disappointment of sitting out the World Cup final in 1966 took its toll (injured early in the tournament, he was fit enough to return to the starting line-up but Alf Ramsey perserverd with a winning team). Greaves slipped into alcoholism and by the time he signed for West Ham as part of a cash/player exchange with Martin Peters in 1969, his ability was on the slide. During the latter stages of his career, and then in his retirement years, Greaves struggled with the bottle and became a shadow of his former self. He later recovered and resurrected his career as a football pundit on the popular ITV show *Saint And Greavsie*.

GUNNAR GREN

Country: Sweden
Born: October 31, 1920
Position: Inside-right
Clubs: IFK Gothenburg, AC Milan, Fiorentina, Genoa, Orgryte, GAIS Gothenburg

Gunnar Gren was the inside-right of AC Milan's famous 'Grenoli' Swedish midfield triumvirate – alongside Nordahl and Liedholm.

Gren had been spotted by the Italian club at the 1948 London Olympics, where he had captained Sweden to the gold medal, scoring twice in the 3-1 victory over Yugoslavia in the final. The lure of a professional career – as opposed to the strictly amateur one in Sweden – took him to Milan and later Fiorentina and Genoa. When his native Sweden opened the doors to professionalism, Gren returned and was instrumental in helping hosts Sweden reach the 1958 World Cup final.

GYULA GROSICS

Country: Hungary
Born: February 4, 1926
Position: Goalkeeper
Clubs: Dorog, Honvéd, Tatabanya

A member of the 'Magical Magyars' team of the 1950s, Grosics was Hungary's greatest ever goalkeeper. Spectacular and assured in equal measure, he was a resilient last line of defence, dominating his penalty area and directing the play. He represented his country 86 times from 1947 onwards, winning a gold medal at the 1952 Helsinki Olympics, as well as playing at the World Cups of 1954, 1958 and 1962.

He was turned from hero to villain in 1954 after helping Hungary to the World Cup final; he was then found guilty of smuggling and was suspended for a year and exiled from army club Honvéd to Second Division Tatabanya.

Above: One of the true greats of the English game, Tottenham's Jimmy Greaves rounds the Arsenal goalkeeper at Highbury.

RUUD GULLIT

Country: Holland

Born: September 1, 1962

Position: Centre-forward/sweeper/midfield

Clubs: Haarlem, Feyenoord, PSV Eindhoven, AC Milan, Sampdoria, AC Milan, Sampdoria, Chelsea

Ruud Gullit (who changed his birth name from 'Rudi Dil') is one of the most versatile and intelligent players the European game has yet produced, comfortable in a number of positions and enormously successful with clubs from three different countries, as well as at international level.

He made his professional debut in 1978, aged 16, for Haarlem, who were then managed by former West Bromwich Albion player Barry Hughes. His confident appearances at sweeper for the Dutch minnows led to Gullit's debut for Holland on his 19th birthday in 1981, in a 2-1 win over Switzerland. Successful moves to Feyenoord (1982 for £300,000) and PSV Eindhoven (1985 for £400,000) followed, but when the Dutchman became unhappy at PSV he was snapped up by Italian giants AC Milan in 1987 for a world record fee of £5.5million.

The following year was truly extraordinary for Gullit, as Milan won their first league title for a decade and Holland became European Champions for the first time. Gullit captained the Dutch side that day and scored one of their goals in the 2-0 win over the Soviet Union. To cap a fantastic year, he was named European and World Player Of The Year. Gullit's success story continued the following season as AC Milan thumped Steaua Bucharest 4-0 in the European Cup final, with the Dutchman recovering from a serious knee injury in time to not only play in the match, but to also score two of the goals. Milan retained their European crown the following season but Gullit's year was again disrupted by knee problems, causing doubts to arise about the future of his career.

Frustrated by injuries and after failing to make the side for Milan's European Cup final loss to Marseille in 1993, Gullit joined Sampdoria on a free transfer. But his form there was so good that his former club quickly swooped to re-sign him. Around the same time Gullit called time on an international career that had seen him grace just one World Cup final, despite the fact that he was regarded as one of the best players on the planet.

After quitting Holland in 1992 for 'personal reasons' Gullit had a change of heart and returned to the fold. However, it was a short-lived affair and after a spat with national team coach Dick Advocaat, he walked out on the Holland camp just three weeks before the 1994 World Cup finals. It took Dutch fans a long time to forgive him.

After one last season with Sampdoria, Gullit finally left Italian football for good in 1995 to join Chelsea on a free transfer. And when the man who signed him, Glenn Hoddle, quit the club to become England coach, the Dutchman took over as player-manager.

In 1997 Chelsea beat Middlesbrough 2-0 in the FA Cup final, but Gullit's time at Stamford Bridge turned sour following disputes with both players and the club's hierarchy. He was sacked in February 1998, only to resurface as manager of Newcastle later the same year, another relationship that was to end in his dismissal.

GHEORGHE HAGI

Country: Romania

Born: February 5, 1965

Position: Midfield

Clubs: FC Constanta, Sportul Studentesc, Steaua Bucharest, Real Madrid, Brescia, Barcelona, Galatasaray

Known as the 'Maradona of the Carpathians', Gheorghe Hagi arrived on the world stage as the inspirational, goalscoring flair behind the Steaua Bucharest team of the 1980s. Upon his controversial arrival in 1986 (with government approval, he was all but kidnapped from his previous team, Sportul Studentesc), they won three consecutive national league titles and also reached the final of the European Cup.

Such performances didn't go unnoticed and a big money move to Real Madrid followed. But despite glimpses of his trademark magic he failed to fulfil his enormous potential and moved on to Italy to play for Brescia.

Hagi has never been anything less than a talismanic figure for his country, and has inspired them to great things over the course of three World Cup finals. In 1990, his Romanian side were eliminated in the second round after doing well to qualify out of a tough group. The following tournament saw them perform fantastically well, winning their group and getting the better of a strong Argentina 3-2 in the second round. At the World Cup in 1998 his ageing side played admirably, beating England in the group stage, before narrowly losing out to Croatia. He retired from international football after Euro 2000.

Towards the end of his playing career Hagi joined Galatasaray, where his famed creative qualities had a significant impact, and he led the Turkish side to their first ever piece of European silverware when they beat Arsenal in 2000 to lift the UEFA Cup.

HOSSAM HASSAN

Country: Egypt

Born: August 10, 1966

Position: Striker

Clubs: Al Ahly, PAOK Salonica, Neuchatel Xamax, El Ain, Zamalek

In 2002, Hossam Hassan, along with twin brother Ibrahim, bowed out in style by winning the African Champions League with Zamalek, some 15 years after winning the trophy with Al Ahly. It is testament to the his enduring consistency that he was able to feature in six African Nations Cups, as well as the 1990 World Cup. He made his debut in September 1985 in a friendly international against Norway in Oslo. He quickly established himself as captain of the national team, his performances earning him a move to Europe, the first of several Egyptians to do so.

Opposite: Ruud Gullit captained the Dutch side which lifted the 1988 European Championship.

Below: Gheorghe Hagi led Turkish side Galatasaray to UEFA Cup success in 2000.

Above left: The first British player to earn £100 a week, Fulham inside-forward Johnny Haynes, battles with Norman Hunter.

Above right: England's Geoff Hurst, the only player to score a hat-trick in a World Cup final.

JOHNNY HAYNES

Country: England
Born: October 17, 1934
Position: Inside-forward
Clubs: Fulham, Durban City

For two decades, Johnny Haynes was Fulham's star and even now, over 50 years since his 1952 debut, he's still considered the best player in the club's history. Renowned for his superb passing, Haynes became the first British player to earn £100 a week and repaid Fulham's faith in him by staying loyal to the club. For England, Haynes won 56 caps, scoring 18 goals, and captained the side 22 times – he also played in the 1958 and 1962 World Cups and scored twice in the 9-3 win over Scotland in 1961. He joined South African side Durban in 1970 after 594 league appearances for Fulham – still a club record.

NANDOR HIDEGKUTI

Country: Hungary
Born: March 3, 1922
Position: Centre-forward
Clubs: Herminamezo, MTK Budapest

Nandor Hidegkuti was the first foreign player to score a hat-trick against England at Wembley in Hungary's historic 6-3 win in 1953. A star of MTK Budapest, Hidegkuti scored 39 international goals in 68 appearances – but it was more than the statistics alone that made

him special, it was also the way he played. Hidegkuti was not an out-and-out striker but a deep-lying centre-forward. It was this role that contributed to Hungary's free-scoring reputation. It created space for others and opportunities for himself in equal measure. Appearances at two Worlds Cups (1954 and 1958) and an Olympic gold in 1952 underlined Hidegkuti's reputation in the 1950s.

JOSE RENE HIGUITA

Country: Colombia
Born: August 27, 1966
Position: Goalkeeper
Clubs: Millonarios, Real Cartegena, Junior Barranquilla, Deportivo Pereira

Eccentric on the pitch and troubled off it, there has never been a goalkeeper quite like Colombia's 'El Loco'. Renowned for dribbling the ball out of his area, taking on opposition players and even getting on the scoresheet, Higuita's defining moment came at Wembley in 1995 against England: to save a lob from Liverpool's Jamie Redknapp, Higuita flipped in mid air, his feet above his head, and flicked the ball away with the bottom of his boots. The move became known as the 'scorpion kick' and the fame it bought Higuita marked an upturn in his fortunes. His earlier mistake at the World Cup finals in 1990 had seen Colombia eliminated from the competition, and he had also spent six months in jail in 1993 for his involvement in a kidnapping case.

GEOFF HURST

Country: England
Born: December 8, 1941
Position: Forward
Clubs: West Ham United, Stoke City, West Bromwich Albion, Seattle Sounders, Cork Celtic

Though not England's most prolific ever goalscorer, Geoff Hurst will always be his nation's most celebrated for scoring the first hat-trick in a World Cup final – the three goals which secured England the Jules Rimet trophy for the first and only time.

The son of a pre-war centre-half, Hurst was born in Ashton-Under-Lyme but moved to Essex as a boy. He joined West Ham as a junior, making his league debut in February 1960, against Nottingham Forest. Manager Ron Greenwood fashioned The Hammers into an exciting, stylish unit and Hurst, a fierce striker of the ball and powerful in the air, became its cutting edge. He won the FA Cup in 1964 and the European Cup Winners' Cup a year later, scoring 180 goals in 410 appearances before moving to Stoke City in August 1972 and West Brom three years later.

Hurst scored 24 goals in 49 appearances for his country but was only a fringe member of the England squad in the early stages of the 1966 World Cup. He would not have played in the final but for an injury to Jimmy Greaves earlier in the tournament. Hurst seized the opportunity, and even when Greaves was declared fit before the final, Hurst held on to his place in the line-up.

He became player-manager of Telford in 1976, coached with England for five years and had an unsuccessful six-month spell as manager of Chelsea. He was knighted in 1998.

VALENTIN IVANOV

Country: Soviet Union
Born: November 19, 1934
Position: Forward
Club: Torpedo Moscow

Soviet football enjoyed a purple patch in the early 1960s: the national team won the inaugural European Championship in 1960, and two years later they reached the quarter-finals of the World Cup, thanks largely to Ivanov's lethal finishing. He had been on target once in the 1958 finals but in 1962 he scored four goals, finishing the tournament as joint top scorer. It was an accolade he shared with five other players, including the Brazilians Garrincha and Vava. Scoring in the opening match against Yugoslavia, he was on target twice in the 4-0 rout of Colombia, and again against Uruguay before the Soviets bowed out 2-1 to Chile in the quarter-final. He scored 26 international goals between 1955 and 1966 and was Russian Player Of The Year in 1957.

JAIRZINHO

Country: Brazil
Born: December 25, 1944
Position: Winger
Clubs: Botafogo, Marseille, Cruzeiro, Portuguesa

If Pele was the greatest player ever to play for Brazil, then there's a long list of legends not too far behind him battling it out to be recognized as the next best. Jairzinho would be close to the top of that list, essentially for his fantastic performances in the team's 1970 World Cup triumph. The winger had already played in the 1966 finals in England, though there was little evidence then that he would take the tournament by storm four years later. With Garrincha still in the side, Jairzinho, then just 21 years old, made do with a role on the left wing of Brazil's attack and wasn't at his best. He played in all three of his team's matches, but Brazil were poor and went home after the group stages.

Four years later it was another story. Jairzinho arrived in Mexico as a member of a very different Brazil side indeed and, with Garrincha retired, was able to play in his natural position as an attacking right-winger. Blessed with a direct style, scorching pace and a fierce shot, he was simply too much for opposing defenders to handle, and by the end of the tournament he had collected a winners' medal and made history by scoring in every round of the competition.

Jairzinho started off with a double in his first match, a 4-2 win over Czechoslovakia,

Above: Jairzinho was a star of the 1970 World Cup Final against Italy, a game Brazil won 4-1. Below: Jairzinho takes on Romania, on the way to scoring a goal in every round of the 1970 World Cup tournament.

and then scored the winning goal in the victory over England, lauded as one of the most memorable matches of all time. The outstanding incident from that encounter has always been Gordon Banks' gravity-defying save from Pele's downward header, but it's often forgotten that it was Jairzinho's run and cross which provided the chance. And that it

was the winger who settled a tight game with a close-range finish. Next up, Romania, and a goal in a 3-2 success, then another in the quarter-final win over Peru. In the semi-finals, Jairzinho scored again as Brazil beat Uruguay, and he made it a goal in every round with the third in the 4-1 win against Italy in the final – even if the did ball roll in off his chest!

Jairzinho's achievement was remarkable; one other player in World Cup history has done the same, but Uruguay's Alcide Ghiggia only had to play in four games in 1950. Jairzinho also played in the 1974 finals, scoring twice as Brazil finished fourth.

His club career was always overshadowed somewhat by his international achievements and, typically for many Brazilian players of his generation, Jairzinho rarely strayed far from his homeland. He did have a short spell with French side Marseille, but he enjoyed a highlight when he returned to more familiar surroundings with Cruzeiro, when he scored the winning goal to secure the 1976 Copa Libertadores – the South American Club Cup. He played on for Brazil's national team until the age of 38, finishing with 98 caps.

He can justifiably claim a permanent place in the World Cup Hall Of Fame.

1959: Joins Rio club Botafogo, and learns trade from his hero Garrincha.

1964: Makes international debut against Portugal.

1966: Plays in the same World Cup squad as Garrincha.

1970: The Hurricane comes back from injury after breaking his leg twice. Scores seven goals, and becomes the only player to have scored in every round of the World Cup finals.

1974: Sporting a huge afro hairstyle for the World Cup finals in Germany, Jairzinho plays as centre-forward but fails to make an impression.

1975: Leaves Botafogo after a long career and joins French giants Olympique Marseille. Returns to Brazil after an altercation with a linesman.

1976: Wins the Copa Libertadores with Belo Horizonte side Cruzeiro against River Plate, scoring the winning goal.

1978: Fails to make the Brazilian World Cup squad.

1979: Joins Venezuelan club Portuguesa.

1981: Retires from football.

1991: Working as a scout he is credited with discovering the teenage Ronaldo.

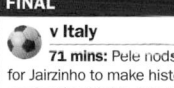

JAIRZINHO'S RECORD-BREAKING GOALS At Mexico in 1970 Jairzinho became the only player to score in every game of every round of the finals.

1ST GROUP GAME		2ND GROUP GAME	3RD GROUP GAME	QUARTER-FINAL	SEMI-FINAL	FINAL
v Czechoslovakia	**v Czechoslovakia**	**v England**	**v Romania**	**v Peru**	**v Uruguay**	**v Italy**
61 mins: Puts Brazil 3-1 ahead after receiving a pass in an offside position.	**81 mins:** Beats four men to score the final goal, making it 4-1.	**59 mins:** Pele lays off a Tostao cross for Jairzinho to fire home for a 1-0 win.	**22 mins:** The second goal in a 3-2 win, Jairzinho scores from close range.	**75 mins:** Jairzinho rounds the goalkeeper to score, completing a 4-2 win.	**76 mins:** Scores the second goal in a 3-1 win after starting move in his own half.	**71 mins:** Pele nods on for Jairzinho to make history, scoring the third in 4-1 victory.

Above: Northern Ireland goalkeeper Pat Jennings perfecting his big kick. In the 1967 Charity Shield between Tottenham and Manchester United, he scored from his own penalty area.

ALEX JAMES

Country: Scotland
Born: September 14, 1901
Position: Forward
Clubs: Raith Rovers, Preston North End, Arsenal

Lanarkshire born James was the inspiration behind the great Arsenal side of the 1930s, winning four championships and two FA Cups. The diminutive Scot was probably the most influential player of his generation and a huge favourite with the fans, being a natural showman and easily recognisable by his trademark baggy shorts.

This showmanship often infuriated his managers, and it was this, coupled with a fiery temper, which probably contributed to the fact that James only gained eight Scotland caps throughout his career, though he was one of the Wembley Wizards who crushed the mighty England 5-1 in 1928. The legendary Arsenal striker of the period Cliff Bastin, along with his contemporaries in The Gunners' attack, had much to thank him for, because James was the creator who supplied them with the ammunition they needed.

PETAR JEKOV

Country: Bulgaria
Born: October 10, 1944
Position: Centre-forward
Clubs: Bepoe, CSKA Sofia

Opposite clockwise from top: Kevin Keegan celebrates Liverpool's first European Cup with Ray Clemence; Keegan winning another cap for England; leading The Reds out.

Throughout a career that spanned from 1962 to 1975, Petar Jekov was an outstanding goalscorer. He was the first Bulgarian to win the Golden Boot (awarded each season to the leading scorer in the European leagues) after netting 36 goals for CSKA Sofia in the 1968-69 season, and his career total of 253 goals in 333 club appearances points to his lethal finishing ability. Added to that, he remains near the top of the goalscoring charts for the Bulgarian national side with 25 goals.

PAT JENNINGS

Country: Northern Ireland
Born: June 12, 1945
Position: Goalkeeper
Clubs: Newry Town, Watford, Tottenham Hotspur, Arsenal.

If you were designing the perfect goalkeeper on a computer, the finished article would end up very much like Pat Jennings. With all the attributes a great goalkeeper needs, Jennings was tall but agile, athletic but sturdy. He famously possessed huge hands, was great on crosses, superb in one-on-one confrontations with strikers, and could improvise point-blank saves. He was also a superb shot-stopper and penalty saver.

Jennings had even more than that though, because you can add to the mix the fact he was consistent, making very few errors in his career. Jennings was even-tempered too, and he had excellent powers of concentration. He was also incredibly durable, completing over 1,000 first class games in his long and distinguished career.

Jennings shot to fame after moving, via Watford, from his native Ireland to Tottenham Hotspur, where he kept goal for over 600 games over a 13-year spell before the club, mistakenly suspecting his career was on the wane at 33, sold him to bitter North London rivals Arsenal.

He continued his incredible career with The Gunners, winning more major honours until finally retiring in 1985 with 119 caps, four FA Cup finals, two Player Of The Season accolades and two World Cup campaigns under his belt.

JIMMY JOHNSTONE

Country: Scotland
Born: September 30, 1944
Position: Right-winger
Clubs: Celtic, San Jose, Sheffield United, Dundee, Shelbourne

'Jinky' Jimmy Johnstone will be remembered as one of Scotland's greatest ever players. The former ballboy at Celtic Park rose to become one of the stars of the great side of the late Sixties and early Seventies and was a key player in the team that won nine back-to-back league titles and seven Scottish Cups. Johnstone loved the big occasion and his finest season probably came in 1967, when Celtic became the first British side to lift the European Cup after beating Inter Milan in the final, crowning a season in which the club had won every competition they entered.

Johnstone, who left Celtic in 1975 to play for San Jose in the North American league, could perhaps have made even more of his career, but a typically fiery redhead, he led a less than exemplary off-the-field lifestyle.

Johnstone was a superb dribbler, an accurate crosser of the ball, and an expert finisher. But like many inspirational players, consistency was his problem and he tended to have his fair share of off games.

KEVIN KEEGAN

Country: England
Born: February 14, 1951
Position: Centre-forward
Clubs: Scunthorpe United, Liverpool, Hamburg, Southampton, Newcastle United

It seems apt that Kevin Keegan was born on Saint Valentine's Day. During his career as both player and manager, the man nicknamed 'Mighty Mouse' (because of his diminutive stature and physical power) has been one of the game's great romantics, whipping up enthusiasm amongst fans and players alike.

That wasn't how Bill Shankly viewed him in 1971, however, when he bought the Scunthorpe United striker to Anfield for £33,000. But after describing him as 'playing like a rat after a weasel', Shankly was repaid for his veiled compliment as Keegan scored a goal on his debut in a 3-1 victory against Nottingham Forest.

The striker immediately became a crowd favourite (one popular Anfield chant was 'Kevin Keegan walks on water') and was arguably Shankly's best signing for the club. Certainly he had an impact, scoring 100 goals in 321 appearances and helping Liverpool to three league titles (1973, 1976, 1977), two UEFA Cups (1973, 1976) and the European Cup (1977) before moving to the German side Hamburg in 1977 for £500,000.

His England career was successful too, and after forcing his way into Alf Ramsey's side in 1972 he soon became an international regular, later forging an exciting partnership with Trevor Brooking in the early 1980s. 'He was the first person to admit he wasn't a naturally gifted player,' says Brooking now, 'but he was fabulous with man markers and would run them into the ground with his determination by twisting and turning and he was a strong little fella as well. People would knock him down and he would just get up again.'

Sadly trophies would elude England during that period and Keegan missed out on the chance of international glory when Ron Greenwood's team were knocked out of the 1982 World Cup in the second group stage, Keegan missing most of the tournament through a recurring back injury.

Despite a lack of trophies with England, he had already made his mark on the continent with Hamburg. In 1978 he claimed the European Player Of The Year award, a feat he repeated the following year when he helped Hamburg to the Bundesliga title before returning to England in 1980 to play for Southampton in a £420,000 deal.

Despite Southampton's lowly status in the old First Division, Keegan sparkled, scoring 42 goals in 80 games for the club, helping The Saints lead the title race for two months during the 1981-82 campaign before finally finishing seventh. Keegan was to pick up the PFA Player

Of The Year Award that year, but, almost as quickly as he had arrived, he moved again, this time to Newcastle for £100,000.

Newcastle were languishing in the old Second Division at the time of Keegan's arrival, but after scoring on his debut against QPR he helped The Magpies to promotion in 1984. Bizarrely, as soon as this happened, Keegan announced his retirement from the game and in May of that year, directly after the end of his final match, a helicopter picked him up from the centre of the pitch at St James' Park. He was looking to a life away from the game on a golf course in Spain. Little did he know that

he would be returning to football, and Newcastle United, much sooner than he thought, for an explosive period as manager. His subsequent jobs – in charge of Fulham and England – have been no less eventful, and he has subsequently revived the fortunes of Manchester City after years of turmoil.

WIM KIEFT

Country: Holland
Born: November 12, 1962
Position: Centre-forward
Clubs: Ajax, Pisa, Torino, PSV Eindhoven, Bordeaux, PSV Eindhoven

Had Marco Van Basten not been around at a similar time, Wim Kieft would undoubtedly have figured on a far more regular basis than the 43 occasions he represented his country. Frequently those appearances came from the bench, but that did not stop him from scoring some important goals. As part of the squad that won the 1988 European Championship, Kieft netted the crucial winner against the Republic Of Ireland in the group stage. His goalscoring talents were equally at home in the Dutch top flight and Italy's Serie A.

SANDOR KOCSIS

Country: Hungary
Born: September 23, 1929
Position: Inside-right
Clubs: Ferencváros, Honvéd, Young Fellows, Barcelona

Sandor Kocsis was top scorer at the 1954 World Cup with 11 goals and was nicknamed 'Golden Head' for his superb ability in the air. He recorded a remarkable tally of 75 goals in 68 internationals and is regarded as one of the finest Hungarian footballers of all time.

Kocsis was born in Budapest and made his international debut in 1949. During the 1950s he was three times Hungarian league top scorer, won four titles and made his name as part of the fabulous Hungary side that beat England 6-3 at Wembley in 1953.

He played for Ferencváros and Honvéd and formed a superb partnership at club and international level with Ferenc Puskás. Having won the Olympic gold medal in 1952 Kocsis went into the 1954 World Cup as a member of the Hungary side expected to claim the trophy, but despite his outstanding personal exploits, including two goals in the semi-final against Uruguay, Hungary lost to West Germany in the final.

Kocsis moved to Barcelona in 1958 and during his eight years with the Catalan giants won an impressive two Spanish league titles, two Spanish Cups and the UEFA Cup in 1960. He retired from playing football in 1966 and died in 1979.

MARIO KEMPES

Country: Argentina
Born: July 15, 1954
Position: Forward
Clubs: Instituto Cordoba, Rosario Central, Valencia, River Plate, Hercules, First Vienna, SV Austria Salzburg

Dubbed 'El Matador' for his incisive finishing, Kempes ranks only behind Maradona in the pantheon of Argentinian footballing heroes.

Born in Cordoba, he joined local team Instituto Cordoba and then moved to Rosario, where he became top scorer in the Argentine league with 21 goals.

Kempes made his international debut aged 19, against Bolivia during the qualifying rounds of the 1974 World Cup, and was part

of the squad at the finals in West Germany. He was to appear in three successive tournaments, making 18 of his total of 43 international appearances on the biggest stage, scoring 20 goals. At the finals in 1978 he was the only European-based player in Cesar Menotti's squad and went on to win the Golden Boot with six goals, including two in the victory over Holland in the final.

By then Kempes had made his name at Valencia where he was top scorer in the Spanish league for two successive seasons. He subsequently moved on to Austria and then to the Far East before retiring at 41. Coaching took him to obscure shores. He became a manager in Albania but was forced to flee during civil unrest and then won a league title with The Strongest in Bolivia before moving to Independiente Petrolero.

Above: Mario Kempes celebrates Argentina's 3-1 defeat of Holland in the 1978 World Cup final.

JURGEN KLINSMANN

Country: Germany
Born: July 30, 1964
Position: Forward
Clubs: Stuttgart Kickers, Stuttgart, Inter Milan, Monaco, Tottenham Hotspur, Bayern Munich, Sampdoria

Klinsmann was an athletic and charismatic striker who first played for West Germany in 1987 and made an impact with his intelligent, all-round play. Club success followed when Klinsmann and fellow countrymen Lothar Matthäus and Andreas Brehme helped Inter Milan to the Serie A title. He loved testing himself in different football cultures and eventually played top-flight football in Germany, Italy, France and England.

Klinsmann is best remembered for his outstanding feats at international level, most notably in 1990 when West Germany lifted the World Cup in Italy. Klinsmann's apparent dive for the penalty that won the match added a less appealing facet to his reputation, but one that barely dimmed his popularity. Four years later, representing the newly unified Germany, he scored five more World Cup goals in the side that lost in the quarter-final.

His performances at Tottenham made him England's Player Of The Year in 1995 and the following year he inspired Germany to the European Championship. His World Cup swansong in 1998 yielded another three goals. He retired with 108 caps and 47 goals.

RONALD KOEMAN

Country: Holland
Born: March 21, 1963
Position: Central defender
Clubs: FC Groningen, Ajax, PSV Eindhoven, Barcelona, Feyenoord

Ronald Koeman's strike-rate belied his role as a defender. He netted almost 200 goals in a career spanning over 500 league games, earning himself a reputation as a set-piece specialist, both from the penalty spot and from free-kicks. His power and accuracy also meant that he was capable of delivering precision passes into the attacking third of the field for his strikers and he was comfortable on the ball in any area of the pitch.

He began his career alongside his brother Erwin at FC Groningen before joining Ajax. It was with PSV Eindhoven though, and then Barcelona, that Koeman was to enjoy his most successful spells, winning the European Champions Cup with both clubs, becoming only the second player, after Belododici the year before, to win the competition with two different sides. He also had a key role to play in both finals, netting for PSV Eindhoven in the penalty shoot-out victory over Benfica in

1988 and then scoring Barcelona's winner against Sampdoria at Wembley in 1992.

Success for Koeman wasn't consigned to club football however, as he was also a member of the Dutch side that won the European Championship in 1988.

After ending his playing days in Holland with Feyenoord, he moved into coaching, first joining the staff of the Dutch national side before moving on to Barcelona. His first managerial role was with Vitesse Arnhem, before he successfully took over at Ajax.

KALMAN KONRAD

Country: Hungary, Austria
Born: March 23, 1896
Position: Inside-forward
Clubs: MTK Budapest, FK Austria Vienna, Brooklyn Wanderers

Kalman Konrad was part of the dominant MTK Budapest side that ruled the Hungarian game from 1914 to 1925. By the mid 1920s after scoring 88 goals in 94 games for MTK, Konrad was lured to the Austrian club FK Austria for a brief spell that lasted until 1928. Konrad was an overtly skilful ball player, effectively making him the grandfather of the

'Magical Magyars' – his abilities were known to have inspired a generation of Hungarian footballers, including Alfred Schaffer and Gyorgy Orth. These players in turn inspired the players that were to become legends in their own right in the 1950s.

RAYMOND KOPA

Country: France
Born: October 13, 1931
Position: Centre-forward
Clubs: Angers, Reims, Real Madrid, Reims

Raymond Kopa became France's first winner of the European Footballer Of The Year prize in 1958 and was his country's greatest player until Michel Platini came along. He made his name as a deep-lying centre-forward at Reims and helped the side reach the first European Champions Cup final, where they lost to Real Madrid. The Spaniards snapped him up in 1956 and he played as a right-winger when Real Madrid won the European Cup in 1957, 1958 and 1959.

He was outstanding at the World Cup in Sweden in 1958, helping France reach the semi-finals. In total he scored 18 goals in 45 international appearances.

Above: Jurgen Klinsmann celebrates one of his 47 international goals for Germany.

Right: Hans Krankl, who won the European Cup Winners' Cup with Barcelona, lining up for Austria.

HANS KRANKL

Country: Austria
Born: February 14, 1953
Position: Centre-forward
Clubs: Rapid Vienna, Vienna AC, Barcelona, First Vienna, Barcelona, Rapid Vienna, Wiener Sportclub

Hans Krankl was one of Austria's most successful footballers and a prolific goalscorer, racking up a staggering 320 goals in 427 Austrian league appearances, as well as 34 goals in a 69-game international career which ran from 1973 to 1985. Included in this total for the national side was a six-goal haul in April 1977 when Austria thrashed Malta 9-0. The following season Krankl was the winner of Europe's Golden Boot with 41 goals for Rapid Vienna. It was the second of four occasions when he was the Austrian league's top scorer, and in 1979 he became the Spanish league's top scorer while at Barcelona, with whom he won the European Cup Winners' Cup in 1979 and the Spanish league.

RUDI KROL

Country: Holland
Born: March 24, 1949
Position: Defender
Clubs: Ajax, Napoli, Cannes, Vancouver Whitecaps

Below: Poland's most capped player, Grzegorz Lato, at the World Cup in 1982.

Rudolf Josef Krol epitomised Holland's Total Football philosophy. Described as an all-round defender he could play at full-back on either flank or in the centre of defence. Indeed, he was one of the first attacking full-backs. He played 83 times for the Dutch, including successive appearances in the World Cup final in 1974 and 1978 – the second time as captain. Krol was also a European Cup and European Super Cup winner in 1972 and 1973 with the great Ajax side that featured Cruyff, Neeskens and Haan and formed the backbone of the Holland's national team.

LADISLAV KUBALA

Country: Czechoslovakia, Hungary, Spain
Born: June 10, 1927
Position: Forward
Clubs: Ferencváros, Bratislava, Vasas, Barcelona, Espanyol, FC Zurich, Toronto Falcons

Ladislav Kubala is revered at Barcelona and was voted the club's greatest player above Cruyff and Maradona in a poll carried out in the club's 1999 centenary year. Born to Slavic parents in Budapest in 1927, he began his career at Ferencváros and had just moved to Vasas when he defected in 1949, a decision that saw him banned from playing by FIFA.

A powerful, hard-running striker, good in the air and a lethal finisher, he was approached by Real Madrid in 1950 but snatched by Barcelona who made him their highest paid player ever. He went on to win four titles and five cups for them between 1951 and 1957, playing 329 times and scoring 256 goals. He also has the distinction of playing for three countries, Hungary, Czechoslovakia and Spain, with whom he won 19 caps, scoring 11 goals.

Afer stints with Espanyol and Toronto Falcons, he managed Malaga, then Barcelona, before coaching the Spanish national team for 68 games between 1969 and 1980, longer than any other incumbent. There were further coaching stints with Barcelona, before he became president of the Barcelona Veterans Association in 1990. He died aged 74 on May 17, 2002 and was posthumously awarded FIFA's Order Of Merit.

ANGEL AMADEO LABRUNA

Country: Argentina
Born: September 26, 1918
Position: Inside-left
Clubs: River Plate, Platense, Green Cross, Rampla Juniors

At the age of 40, and nicknamed 'El Viejo' (the old one), Labruna represented Argentina at the 1958 World Cup Finals. His two appearances in Sweden took his tally to 36 international appearances, in which he scored 17 goals and reaped two South American Championships in 1946 and 1955. Labruna also served River Plate like no other player, turning out for them in 1,150 games and scoring 457 goals over a 29-year period, finally

retiring at the age of 41. He won the league championship nine times, earning a feared reputation as part of the club's famed 'Maquina' forward line.

GRZEGORZ LATO

Country: Poland
Born: April 8, 1950
Position: Winger
Clubs: Stal Mielec, KSC Lokeren, Atlanta de Mexico, Toronto

Grzegorz Lato is Poland's most capped player and also one of their leading goalscorers. His international career, spanning 13 years, saw him make 95 appearances for Poland, scoring 42 goals. He starred in three consecutive World Cups and was the tournament's top goalscorer in 1974, scoring seven of Poland's 14 goals in an attacking team that featured him alongside Gadocha, Deyna and Szarmach. In 1982 his international swansong brought him closest to success, Lato bowed out with a third place at the World Cup in Spain.

BRIAN LAUDRUP

Country: Denmark
Born: February 22, 1969
Position: Forward/Midfield
Clubs: Brondby, Bayer Uerdingen, Bayern Munich, Fiorentina, AC Milan, Rangers, Chelsea, FC Copenhagen, Ajax

A mazey dribbler and crowd entertainer, Brian Laudrup is the brother of Denmark's 1986 World Cup star Michael Laudrup. Starting his career at Brondby in 1986, the forward moved to Germany in 1989, first with Bayern Uerdingen and later Bayern Munich, before making the glamorous move to Italian side Fiorentina after winning the 1992 European

Championship with Denmark. A brief stint at AC Milan followed a season later but Laudrup left after only nine games to become a crowd favourite at Rangers in 1994.

After four seasons and 44 goals he left Scotland for Chelsea (on a free 'Bosman' deal), before controversially returning home to FC Copenhagen after a bout of homesickness. He retired in 2000 after a recurring Achilles heel problem hampered his performances.

MICHAEL LAUDRUP

Country: Denmark
Born: June 15, 1964
Position: Midfield/Forward
Clubs: Brondby, Lazio, Juventus, Barcelona, Real Madrid, Vissel Kobe, Ajax

Laudrup was the most elegant cog in the Danish side that electrified world football in the mid-1980s. Supremely gifted, Ajax wooed him at 13 and by the age of 18 he was scoring on his international debut. His list of super clubs is testament to a player of sublime skill. Laudrup won the European Champions Cup while with Barcelona in 1992 and league championships in three countries. Highly technical and unselfish, he shone in both midfield and attack. Laudrup played in the 1986 and 1998 World Cup finals before retiring with 37 goals in 104 games. He missed Denmark's 1992 European Championship success after falling out with the coach.

DENIS LAW

Born: February 22, 1940
Country: Scotland
Position: Forward
Clubs: Huddersfield Town, Manchester City, Torino, Manchester United, Manchester City

Nicknamed 'The King' at Old Trafford, Denis Law was arguably one of the most popular players to have worn a Manchester United shirt during his reign in the 1960s, with his trademark over-sized shirt and his one-armed goal celebrations. Starting his career at Huddersfield Town, Law made his professional debut in 1956, aged 16. By 18 he was wearing the Scotland jersey and a move to Maine Road followed in 1960 at the age of 20. He later moved to Torino in Italy in 1961, where despite a car crash, he still scored a creditable ten goals in 27 games.

In August 1962, Manchester United paid a British record fee of £115,000 for his services and Law's impact on the club was immediate. He scored two goals on his debut, notching up a total of 160 goals during his 222 matches for the club, winning a European Player Of The Year award in 1964, as well as two league titles (1965 and 1967). He was later transferred to Manchester City in 1973, where he made

headlines by famously back-heeling the goal at Old Trafford that helped to consign his former club to relegation in 1974. Distraught, he retired after the game.

TOMMY LAWTON

Country: England
Born: October 6, 1919
Position: Forward
Clubs: Burnley, Everton, Chelsea, Notts County, Brentford, Arsenal

A big, powerful, bustling centre-forward, recognisable as much by his centre parting as his physique, Lawton's best years were probably lost to the Second World War. Even so he can still claim an impressive record of 231 goals in 390 league games, and 22 goals in 23 internationals. For England his record was helped by the regular supply he received from the likes of Finney and Matthews.

Lawton famously scored on his league debut for Burnley aged just 16 before being picked up by Everton, keen to find a replacement for

the great Dixie Dean. Lawton first donned an England shirt at just 19 and his career took him to numerous clubs.

Above: Denmark's Michael Laudrup skips past the Scots during the 1986 World Cup.

LEÓNIDAS

Country: Brazil
Born: November 11, 1910
Position: Centre-forward
Clubs: Havanesa, Barroso, Sul Americano, Sirio Libanes, Bomsucesso, Nacional, Vasco da Gama, Botafogo, Flamengo, São Paulo

In World Cup history, nine players can boast of scoring four goals in a game. Leónidas da Silva was the first to do so. The Brazilian, dubbed the 'Black Diamond', enjoyed his 90 minutes of fame in the 1938 finals when the South Americans beat Poland 6-5 in the first round – Leónidas, renowned for his overhead kick, scored a hat-trick in the first-half and added a fourth in the second. He ended up as top goalscorer with eight, but the competition ended in disappointment; he was rested for the semi-final against Italy – and Brazil lost!

NILS LIEDHOLM

Country: Sweden
Born: October 8, 1922
Position: Inside-forward/Wing-half/Sweeper
Clubs: Norrköpping, AC Milan

Nils Liedholm was the longest serving member of AC Milan's famed 'Grenoli' midfield trio. After winning two championship medals with Swedish club Norrköpping, he signed for AC Milan, playing in 367 league games for the Italians, scoring 60 goals and helping them to win the title in 1951, 1955, 1957 and 1959. He also helped the club to their first European Cup final appearance in 1958.

On the international stage Liedholm captained Sweden to the World Cup final in 1958, ten years after winning the Olympic Games title as an amateur.

Because of Sweden's reluctance to select professionals for the national team, Liedholm played just 18 games for his country. In the latter part of his career AC Milan converted him into a formidable sweeper.

GARY LINEKER

Country: England
Born: November 30, 1960
Position: Forward
Clubs: Leicester City, Everton, Barcelona, Tottenham Hotspur, Nagoya Grampus Eight

Gary Lineker, the son of a market trader, enjoyed a glittering career as one of England's finest ever goalscorers. After seven seasons with his hometown club Leicester, Lineker became a target for England's bigger outfits and Everton clinched his prized signature in 1985 for £800,000.

In his first, and as it turned out only, season on Merseyside, Lineker's performances were phenomenal. He hit 30 league goals in the campaign, but The Toffees finished runners-up in the championship, beaten into second place by Liverpool. When the two teams clashed again in the 1986 FA Cup Final Lineker scored early to put Everton ahead, only for The Reds to triumph 3-1.

But the striker didn't have long to mope about the defeat, as in the summer he headed off to the World Cup finals in Mexico as England's number one goalscorer. It was a tournament which was to change the direction of his career. With Bobby Robson's team lurching towards a disastrous first round exit, Lineker hit a first-half hat-trick in the must-win game against Poland and his name made international headlines.

Two further goals against Paraguay, then another in the quarter-final defeat against Argentina, put the England striker on six goals – enough to clinch the Golden Boot and earn the attentions of Spanish giants Barcelona.

After returning from the World Cup Lineker swapped Goodison Park for the famous Nou Camp, where he spent the next three seasons.

At Barcelona, under Terry Venables, Lineker was an immediate success, far more so than Mark Hughes, another Venables recruit. Lineker scored goals freely and pleased the critical Nou Camp fans with his pace and sharp finishing. A hat-trick against Barcelona's bitter rivals Real Madrid in 1987 cemented his popularity, but when Venables was replaced by Dutchman Johan Cruyff, Lineker found that his influence was marginalized, the new coach inexplicably deploying him as a right-winger.

Despite winning the European Cup Winners' Cup with Barcelona in 1989, a parting of the ways was inevitable. Lineker returned to English football, teaming up with Venables again at Tottenham.

He quickly showed that he had lost none of his ability. At international level he remained a permanent threat, claiming four goals in the 1990 World Cup as England reached the semi-finals, including the equaliser in the epic encounter with West Germany. For Spurs, Lineker developed a fine understanding with Paul Gascoigne and in 1991 he won his only English domestic trophy when Tottenham toppled Nottingham Forest 2-1 to win the FA Cup. Lineker actually missed a penalty during the game, yet still ended up a winner.

The following year he accepted a lucrative offer to play for Grampus Eight in Japan, and although a toe injury limited his appearances, he proved a wonderful ambassador for a developing league until his retirement two years later opened up a second successful profession as a presenter on British television for the BBC.

Alongside all the goalscoring acclaim, one other major statistic stands out; throughout his career, Lineker's disciplinary record was exemplary – he wasn't booked once.

RABAH MADJER

Country: Algeria
Born: December 12, 1958
Position: Midfield/Forward
Clubs: Sempac, MA Hussein Dey, Racing Paris, Porto, Qatar

No-one will ever forget Rabah Madjer's outrageous back-heeled goal in the 1987 European Cup final. He later set-up the winner as Porto beat Bayern Munich. Later in the year he scored the winner in the World Club Cup and was a deserving winner of the 1987 African Player Of The Year Award. Not that he was an unknown – five years earlier he had been part of Algeria's 1982 World Cup victory over West Germany, scoring the first goal in a 2-1 win. He also appeared in the 1986 finals and helped Algeria to the quarter-finals of the 1980 Olympics.

Above: Sepp Maier was ever present during West Germany's golden era in the 1970s.

SEPP MAIER

Country: West Germany
Born: February 28, 1944
Position: Goalkeeper
Clubs: TSV Haar, Bayern Munich

Josef-Dieter 'Sepp' Maier spent 19 seasons at Bayern Munich, including a run of 422 consecutive games in goal (of a total of 473 appearances in all) for the German giants. Maier played in each of Bayern's three consecutive European Cup successes between 1974 and 1976, keeping clean sheets in three of the four games involved. 'Die Katze' (the Cat), as he was nicknamed, had established himself as his country's first choice goalkeeper in time for the 1970 World Cup, and although West Germany only reached the semi-finals, success was just around the corner.

Captained by Franz Beckenbauer, the Germans were crowned champions of Europe in 1972 and world champions two years later, Maier memorably stopping a formidable Johan Neeskens' volley as his side beat Holland 2-1.

Named German Player Of The Year three times in the 1970s, a car accident in 1979 ended Maier's career at the age of just 35 (still relatively young for a goalkeeper). Following his retirement, Maier returned to his first sporting love, setting up a tennis school.

Opposite: Gary Lineker gives the Republic Of Ireland defence plenty to worry about at the 1988 European Championship.

1976: Makes his debut for Argentinos Juniors as a 15-year-old and a week later plays his first full match against Newell's Old Boys.

1977: Makes his debut for Argentina as a sub in a 5-1 friendly victory against Hungary.

1978: Makes the squad of 25 players for World Cup, but Cesar Menotti elects not to take him.

1979: Member of Argentina's World Youth Cup winning side in Japan.

1982: Sent-off in World Cup against Brazil. Bought by Barcelona for £3million, a new record transfer fee.

1983: Suffers the worst injury of his career after a tackle by Goicoechea, the 'Butcher of Bilbao'.

1984: Joins Serie A's Napoli for £5million, another record transfer fee.

1986: Captains Argentina to World Cup win, and is the star of the show. Remembered for his two goals against England.

1987: Leads Napoli to their first ever Scudetto title.

1990: Cannot prevent Argentina from losing in the World Cup final against West Germany.

1991: Fails a drugs test and is banned for 15 months.

1992: After completion of the ban he refuses to rejoin Napoli, and makes a disappointing comeback for Seville.

1994: Fails another drugs test at the World Cup finals in the USA.

1997: Plays his last match for Boca Juniors, retires from football on his 37th birthday.

2000: He is named as FIFA's internet Player Of The Century following an online poll.

DIEGO MARADONA

Country: Argentina
Born: October 30, 1960
Position: Centre-forward
Clubs: Argentinos Juniors, Boca Juniors, Barcelona, Napoli, Seville, Newell's Old Boys, Boca Juniors

As well as being one of the greatest players to ever grace the world game, Maradona is also one of the most controversial. Indeed, there are times when the Argentine's career history reads more like a rap sheet than the biography of the world's greatest sportsmen. But his various bans, drug problems and occasionally perverse behaviour (he once shot at journalists with an air rifle) shouldn't distract from Diego Maradona's formidable achievements in a game he bestrode like a colossus throughout the 1980s.

Born to working class parents in a Buenos Aires suburb, Maradona and football were inseparable from an early age. After playing for a couple of local boys clubs (one of whom he inspired to go 136 matches unbeaten), he joined first division Argentinos Juniors, making his debut as a raw but undoubtedly talented 15-year-old on October 20, 1976. Barely four months later Maradona was making another debut – this time as a fully-fledged Argentine international, coming on as a substitute in a friendly against Hungary. Although he was angry at missing out on a place in the squad for the 1978 World Cup finals, Maradona was a vital part of the Argentine side that won the World Youth Championship in 1979 in Japan.

After scoring 116 goals in 166 appearances for Argentinos Juniors, Maradona was transferred to Boca Juniors (35 goals in 71 appearances) for £1million in 1981. He stayed only one season, before Barcelona snapped him up for £3million. Although again prodigious in front of goal, netting 38 times in 58 appearances, his two-year stay in Spain was undermined by injury. Far more successful was his transfer to Napoli for £5million in 1984. He led them to league titles in 1987 and 1990 (the club's first ever) and a UEFA Cup win in 1989.

Maradona's first World Cup finals in 1982 ended badly for the Argentines as they failed to make it beyond the second round, while Maradona himself was sent-off against Brazil. It was a very different story at the 1986 tournament, though, as Argentina became world champions for the second time and Maradona lived up to his reputation as the world's best but most controversial player. The Argentine's schizophrenic nature was perfectly illustrated by his performance in the quarter-final against England, where he scored both goals in a 2-1 win. The first he

pushed past goalkeeper Shilton with his hand (the infamous 'Hand Of God' goal) but the second saw Maradona weave the ball around an army of defenders from the halfway line before stroking it into the net.

The 1986 finals proved to be the high point of Maradona's career, although he inspired a below par Argentina to another World Cup final in 1990. The following year he was banned from the game for 15 months after testing positive for cocaine and then arrested in Argentina for possession of the drug.

Maradona's World Cup swansong came in 1994 and ended in ignominy when he was sent home for failing another dope test. Short spells as a coach back home with Argentine club sides came to nothing and he soon returned as a player with Newell's Old Boys. The curtain finally fell on Maradona's incredible playing career on October 29, 1997, when he turned out for Boca Juniors against rivals River Plate.

Above: Maradona celebrates more success for Argentina.
Above top: Napoli saw the best of Maradona as a player at club level – he led them to their first ever league title.

SILVIO MARZOLINI

Country: Argentina
Born: October 4, 1940
Position: Left-back
Clubs: Ferro Carril Oeste, Boca Juniors

Silvio Marzolini is a Boca Juniors legend and was part of the team that dominated the Argentine league in the mid-Sixties, winning three championships. One of the first of a new breed of full-backs to make a mark in the modern game, his dynamic, all-round style of play still gets him selected in many people's all-time XIs. He appeared in two World Cups for his country, in 1962 and 1966, and played in the infamous quarter-final against England at Wembley. After retirement he went on to manage Boca Juniors, and even took them to a league title in 1981.

JOSEF MASOPUST

Country: Czechoslovakia
Born: February 9, 1931
Position: Midfield
Clubs: SK Most, Teplice, Dukla Prague, Molenbeek

Known as the 'Czech Cavalier', Josef Masopust was named Czech Player Of The Century. Born in Most, he began his career in 1950 playing up front but was switched to midfield where his stamina and vision covered his lack of speed. He joined Dukla Prague in 1952 and went on to win eight titles and three cups with them, making 386 appearances including the 1967 European Cup semi-final against Celtic.

At international level Masopust won 63 caps, scoring ten goals, and was part of the 1958 World Cup squad before reaching the semi-final of the 1960 European Championship. The high point of his career was leading his country to the runners-up spot in the 1962 World Cup, scoring the 15th minute goal that gave them the lead in the final over Brazil. His performance and his legendary sportsmanship saw him named 1962 European Footballer Of The Year – he remains the only Czech player to win the coveted award.

Offers flooded in from Italy and West Germany, but the communist regime did not allow him to leave until 1969 when, aged 38, he moved to Molenbeek in the Belgian second division, taking them up into the top flight. He later returned to coach them, then Dukla, and became assistant manager of the national side in 1984.

LOTHAR MATTHÄUS

Country: West Germany, Germany
Born: March 21, 1961
Position: Midfielder
Clubs: Borussia Mönchengladbach, Bayern Munich, Inter Milan, Bayern Munich, New York Metro Stars

For a man who is Germany's most capped star, Lothar Matthäus' popularity appears to be inversely low. A powerful but arrogant and often outspoken midfielder, Matthäus made his debut for Mönchengladbach in 1979, before moving to Bayern Munich in 1984. He won six championships in two spells there, broken by a move to Inter Milan in 1988 where he won the Scudetto as captain and a UEFA Cup, scoring in the 2-1 win over Roma in 1991.

Matthäus made his international debut at 19 in a 3-2 European Championship win over Holland on June 14, 1980, picking up a winners' medal in the final with Belgium, and he became a fixture in the side for 20 years, winning an incredible 150 caps. He played in no less than five World Cups and holds the record for the most appearances in the tournament with 25 games.

He was runner-up in the 1986 World Cup, then lifted the trophy as captain four years later in Italy, being named European Footballer Of The Year. He extended his career to 39 years of age by moving to sweeper and finishing with New York Metro Stars, before taking over as coach of Rapid Vienna and then Partizan Belgrade. He caused a scandal by resigning his life membership of Bayern Munich and threatening to sue the club over the gate money from his testimonial game.

STANLEY MATTHEWS

Country: England
Born: February 1, 1915
Position: Winger
Clubs: Stoke City, Blackpool, Stoke City

Regarded as 'The Wizard Of The Dribble', Matthews made his league debut for hometown club Stoke City just six weeks after his 17th birthday. The son of a featherweight boxer, his appearance was slight against his more burly opponents, but it was his lightning burst of pace, balance and timing that few defenders could live with. Within two seasons Matthews had already made his England debut and, as the most exciting young player to emerge in the First Division at the time, it was reported that his presence regularly put 10,000 extra fans on the gate wherever Stoke played.

In 1938, Matthews fell out with manager Bob McGrory and asked to be put on the transfer list, but such was the furore in the local area that business managers claimed that production was being affected by the ongoing saga. Following a massive protest meeting, Stan decided to stay. But following the war, hostilities resumed with McGrory and in 1947 he was sold to Blackpool for £11,500, aged 32.

Despite his veteran status, Matthews reached new heights as he led his club to three FA Cup finals in six years. Defeats against Manchester United and Newcastle led many to believe that a Cup hoodoo had a hold and with 20 minutes to go of the 1953 final against Bolton, that appeared to ring true for the 38-year-old. With Blackpool having fallen 3-1 behind, Matthews suddenly sprang into action and, having set up Stan Mortensen for his second of the game, he took a hold of the match and ran his opposing number, Ralph Banks, ragged. Then with just three minutes

Left: Stanley Matthews attracted thousands of extra fans to stadiums around the country throughout his career.

remaining, he skipped past his marker yet again to give Mortensen his hat-trick, and deep into stoppage time he reached the by-line one last time to set up South African winger Bill Perry to snatch a dramatic winner. Despite Mortensen's heroics and Perry's goal, the game became known as 'The Matthews Final'.

In 1961, Matthews decided to end his career back at Stoke and, having paid £3,500 for his services, the club recouped their money by regularly putting an extra 26,000 on their gate at the Victoria Ground. Matthews acted as a catalyst as The Potters marched to the 1962-63 Second Division championship and incredibly, at the age of 48, he played 35 of the club's 42 league games. Two years later, he finally bowed out of top-flight football, aged 50 years and five days.

Although he won few honours in his career, Matthews was a truly unique phenomenon, and as a result of his exemplary disciplinary record on the pitch, he was also regarded as a true gentleman. He received the Footballer Of The Year trophy twice, in 1948 and 1963, and was knighted in the 1965 New Year's Honours list, five days after his 50th birthday.

He played for England between 1934 and 1957 and, although scoring on his first outing for his country, he found himself in and out of the team. In all, he played only 54 of 119 full internationals during that period, a statistic that consistently outraged fans.

SANDRO MAZZOLA

Country: Italy
Born: November 8, 1942
Position: Forward
Club: Inter Milan

Sandro followed in the footsteps of his father Valentino to become an Italian football legend. Though Torino star Valentino died in the Superga plane crash when Sandro was just seven, his passion for the game had already been instilled in Mazzola junior. Inter Milan were to be his sole club, and he made more than 400 top flight appearances for the Nerazzurri, winning consecutive European and World Club Cups with them.

Although not as effective at international level, he did still make 70 appearances for his country and was in the Italian side that won the 1968 European Championship.

VALENTINO MAZZOLA

Country: Italy
Born: January 26, 1919
Position: Forward
Clubs: Venezia, Torino

Mazzola formed one half of a formidable strike partnership with Ezio Loik, with whom he combined superbly, initially at Venezia and then, from 1942 onwards, with Torino who bought both men as a pair. The move was a shrewd one because Mazzola went on to lead the dominant Torino to five league titles between 1943 and 1949.

Tragically killed in his prime in 1949 in the Superga aircrash alongside 17 of his team mates, with only 12 caps to his name, Mazzola would surely have gone on to achieve greater international recognition in the following year's World Cup finals.

GIUSEPPE MEAZZA

Country: Italy
Born: August 23, 1910
Position: Inside-forward
Clubs: Inter Milan, AC Milan, Juventus, Varese, Atalanta, Inter Milan

The man after whom the former San Siro stadium in Milan is now named was considered the complete forward player; a perfect predator in front of goal, but skilled enough to create chances for others as well as himself. He made his debut for Inter in 1927 at the age of 17 and remained with the club for the next 12 seasons. In that time, he was Serie A's top scorer on three occasions, hitting 33 goals in the 1929-30 season alone, including six in a 10-2 win against Venezia.

Having hit 241 goals for Inter in 344 games, Meazza succumbed to a leg injury and missed the whole of the 1939-40 season, before joining Inter's arch-rivals AC Milan the following year. Further moves to Juventus and Atalanta followed, but Meazza returned to Inter for the 1946-47 season as player/coach to help them battle against relegation.

Meazza's time on the international stage proved to be equally impressive, scoring twice on his debut as a 19-year-old against Switzerland in 1930, and hitting a hat-trick against Hungary later that year, in a 5-0 win. One of only two players to have played in both Italian World Cup wins in 1934 and 1938, Meazza died in 1979 aged 68.

ROGER MILLA

Country: Cameroon
Born: May 20, 1952
Position: Forward
Clubs: Eclair de Douala, Léopard de Douala, Valenciennes, Monaco, Bastia, Saint-Etienne, Montpellier, JS Saint-Pierroise

Dancing the Makossa around a corner flag, Albert Roger Milla gave the World Cup one of its most memorable goal celebrations in 1990. A natural goalscorer, Milla won the African Golden Ball and played in France for 12 years. He scored on his international debut in 1978 and was part of the squad that returned unbeaten from the 1982 World Cup. At 38 he was playing on Reunion Island when the Cameroon president begged him to come back for Italia '90. Milla became a talisman with four goals from the bench as his team reached the quarter-finals. At 42 he was back at USA '94, with a goal against Russia making him the oldest World Cup goalscorer ever.

LUISITO MONTI

Country: Argentina, Italy
Born: May 15, 1901
Position: Central defender
Clubs: Huracan, Boca Juniors, San Lorenzo, Juventus

Monti tasted both victory and defeat in World Cup finals, but for different nations. He was on the losing side with Argentina in 1930, going down to Uruguay, but four years later he helped Italy beat Czechoslovakia. His eligibility for Italy came after he moved to Juventus. Monti was one of three Argentinian-born players in the successful Italy side as players were permitted to represent more than one nation in the World Cup. Having won league titles with both Huracan and San Lorenzo in Argentina, Monti won four consecutive Serie A titles in Turin.

BOBBY MOORE

Country: England
Born: April 12, 1941
Position: Central defender
Clubs: West Ham United, Fulham, San Antonio Thunder, Herning FC, Seattle Sounders

In the pantheon of English sporting heroes no footballer ranks above Bobby Moore, the only England captain ever to lift the World Cup. His name remains synonymous with honour, dignity and sportsmanship.

Bobby Moore was born in Barking, East London, and joined West Ham as a schoolboy, turning professional at 17. He rose rapidly to the first team, playing flawlessly in a 3-2 win over Manchester United on his debut on September 8, 1958. He did not establish himself fully until 1960, but thereafter became a fixture in the side. In 1964 he led the team an to an FA Cup final win over Preston as Footballer Of The Year. The following season he was back at Wembley to guide West Ham to victory over TSV 1860 Munich in the European Cup Winners' Cup.

Moore won his first England cap against Peru in 1962 and played in all four games in that summer's World Cup in Chile. At 22 he became the country's youngest ever captain when he led the team against Czechoslovakia on May 20, 1963. Just three years later his crowning moment arrived when he lifted the World Cup following the historic 4-2 win over West Germany. The famous fourth goal was

Opposite: England's greatest ever football hero, Bobby Moore kisses the World Cup that he won as captain in 1966.

the result of Moore measuring a long pass to striker Geoff Hurst rather than listening to the entreaties of his partner Jack Charlton to put the ball over the stand.

Yet Moore's finest performance was not Wembley 66, but Mexico 70. Before that summer's World Cup tournament had kicked-off he was falsely accused of the theft of a bracelet from a jeweller in Bogota, Columbia. Moore, held under house arrest, remained calm, destroyed the false testimony of the main witness and rejoined the squad. Three weeks later he played the game of his life against Brazil in the heat of Guadalajara, thwarting the tide of gold shirts that flooded towards him. When the final whistle blew, signifying a narrow 1-0 defeat, Pele stepped past everyone, including Alan Mullery who had marked him through the game, to swap shirts with Moore. The moment became an iconic football image.

Moore would win 108 caps for England, 90 of them as captain, but his career was virtually ended by an uncharacteristic error in a World Cup qualifier against Poland in 1973.

After 544 games for West Ham he moved across London to Fulham in March 1974 and enjoyed one more Wembley appearance in the FA Cup final, ironically against his old club, but this time he collected a loser's medal. Thereafter, his career tailed off as he joined Seattle Sounders, Herning FC in Denmark, then San Antonio Thunder in Texas.

Bizarrely he won three caps for Team America, playing alongside his old adversary Pele and finishing his international career playing against England.

Back home Moore struggled to make a mark in management. He began at lowly Oxford City in 1979, coached in Hong Kong and took over for an unsuccessful stint at Southend. By the late Eighties he had fallen out of the game and was working as a radio summariser. He was diagnosed with bowel cancer and died on February 24, 1993.

In June 2000, West Ham United purchased Bobby Moore's World Cup memorabilia for their museum, having named a stand at the Boleyn Ground after him six years earlier. Subsequently a strong campaign to name the redeveloped Wembley Stadium after him seemed the only way to honour his memory, given his legacy to English football.

JUAN MORENO

Country: Argentina
Born: August 3, 1916
Position: Forward
Clubs: River Plate, Espana, Universidad Catolica, Boca Juniors, Defensor, FC Oeste, Medellin

Moreno is one of the greatest Argentine players of all time and a winner of four league titles with River Plate, where he spent most of his playing career. The first of Moreno's league winners' medals came in 1936 when he broke into the side from the youth team as a raw but talented 20-year-old.

Moreno was part of the legendary River Plate 'Maquina' attack in the 1940s which included the likes of Munoz, Pedernera, Labruna and Loustau. Morena played for two years with the Mexican club Espana before returning to River Plate for a second spell and then spending the later years of his career representing different clubs in Chile, Uruguay and Columbia. Moreno scored an impressive 20 goals in 33 internationals for his country.

GERD MÜLLER

Country: West Germany
Born: November 3, 1945
Position: Forward
Clubs: TSV Nordingen, Bayern Munich, Fort Lauderdale Strikers

Gerd Müller holds a special place in World Cup history, as the the all-time highest scorer in the finals. His 14 goals in two World Cups were the high points of an astonishing international career which saw him average more than a goal a game. He remains his country's highest goalscorer, and he also struck the winning goal in the 1974 World Cup Final.

The early 1970s were a golden period for West German football, forged on the athleticism and unquenchable spirit that Müller typified. Besides reaching the World Cup semi-final of 1970 and winning in 1974, the West Germans also lifted the European Championship in 1972. Müller, inevitably, scored twice in the final.

Müller's international success was repeated at club level with the dominant Bayern Munich, with whom he won the European Champions Cup in 1974, 1975 and 1976. That he enjoyed such a glittering career is even more remarkable given his background. Short and stocky, he grew up in a small village with no football ground but trained hard to make the most of his ability.

Never giving less than 100 per cent, he acquired a fearsome reputation as the ultimate predator in the penalty area, earning the nickname 'Der Bomber'.

Below right: Gerd Müller in action for Bayern Munich against Borussia in 1972.

Below: A familiar sight for West Germany and Bayern fans alike, Gerd Müller finding the back of the net. This one for Bayern, against St Etienne, was disallowed.

JOSE NASAZZI

Country: Uruguay
Born: May 24, 1901
Position: Right-back
Clubs: Lito, Roland Moor, Nacional, Bella Vista

Right-back Jose Nasazzi is not only one of Uruguay's most famous players, but one of the great captains in the history of the game. His leadership qualities and organisational skills earned him the nickname 'The Marshall'. As Uruguay captain Nasazzi won Olympic gold in 1924 and 1928, as well as the Copa América in 1923, 1924 and 1926. But the best was yet to come, and Nasazzi etched himself into football history when he became the first man to lift the Jules Rimet trophy after his country's 4-2 triumph over Argentina in the inaugural 1930 World Cup final. This was no mean feat, as Nasazzi was captaining a side who competed without a team manager and whose players made all the tactical decisions. When asked to coach the national team in 1945, he did so for just one South American Championship. He didn't believe in coaches.

Müller made his international debut in 1966, shortly after West Germany had lost the World Cup final to England. When the 1970 tournament arrived he was already known as one of the great strikers in world football. But despite the pressure, Müller delivered in spectacular style, hitting ten goals in six games. He recorded hat-tricks against Bulgaria and Peru and the winner against Morocco. He also got the deciding goal in a quarter-final which saw West Germany come from 2-0 down to beat defending champions England. In the semi-final Müller scored twice more but West Germany bowed out of the competition 4-3 against Italy. He was, however, the tournament's top scorer.

Four years later Müller was less prolific, but was to prove equally lethal when it mattered most. Determined to make amends for their recent near misses, West Germany ground their way to a final on home soil against the more fluent and outrageously talented team from Holland.

Despite going a goal down, the hosts weren't going to let it slip this time and after equalising it was Müller who scored the winning goal just before half-time. The moment couldn't have been sweeter: not only had he achieved the greatest dream in football but he had done so in the Olympic Stadium, where he had scored so many of his 365 goals in 427 games for Bayern.

Müller retired from the international game and considered quitting altogether, but instead he decided to continue playing club football with Bayern, with whom he had won the European Cup Winners' Cup in 1967. It was

JOHAN NEESKENS

Country: Holland
Born: September 15, 1951
Position: Midfield
Clubs: Ajax, Barcelona, New York Cosmos, Fort Lauderdale Strikers, FC Groningen, FC Baar

Although he often lived in the shadows of Johan Cruyff, Johan Neeskens was regarded as one of the greatest midfielders of the 1970s and was an integral part of the talented Dutch side that reached the final at both the 1974 and 1978 World Cups.

In the 1974 match against West Germany he scored the fastest goal in a World Cup final – converting a penalty kick in the second minute – and his terrific pace, skill and control was also an integral feature of the Ajax side that swept all before them, both domestically and in the European Cup.

He followed his Ajax team-mate Johan Cruyff to Barcelona after the 1974 final before moving to the NASL five years later. Having returned home to Groningen, he saw out his career as a player-coach in Switzerland.

an inspired decision. In a fruitful autumn to his career, he achieved three European Cup triumphs before leaving Bayern in 1979 to wind down his career in the United States with Fort Lauderdale.

Named European Footballer Of The Year in 1970, Müller was a two-time winner of the European Golden Boot, and scored a total of 628 first class goals.

IGOR NETTO

Country: Soviet Union
Born: September 4, 1930
Position: Left-back
Club: Spartak Moscow

Netto will be remembered by his countrymen as the man who led the Soviet Union to Olympic Games success in 1956 in Australia, and then four years later, to the European Championship in France. All this during an international career that saw him gain 57 caps and score four goals. Sadly for Netto, injury kept him out of the 1958 World Cup but he was an ever present member of the team in 1962, when the Soviets got as far as the quarter-finals before losing to Chile. A strong tackler, Netto moved into central defence when he'd lost a little of his pace later in his career. A one-club man, he made more than 350 appearances for Spartak Moscow in his career, winning five league titles in that time.

GUNTER NETZER

Country: West Germany
Born: September 14, 1944
Position: Midfield
Clubs: Borussia Mönchengladbach, Real Madrid, Grasshoppers

A flamboyant, long-haired playmaker who was the star of West Germany's European Championship winning side of 1972. Netzer played a crucial hand in his country's advance to the final with a match-winning performance against England in the quarter-finals at Wembley, and he was equally inspirational in the 3-0 defeat of the Soviet Union in the final. Known for his long, accurate passing and ability to inspire others, Netzer usually operated just behind the strikers. He made 38 international appearnaces before losing his place in the national team in 1974. After hanging up his boots, he went on to become a leading commentator and businessman.

THOMAS NKONO

Country: Cameroon
Born: July 19, 1955
Position: Goalkeeper
Clubs: Douala, Canon Yaoundé, Espanyol

Thomas Nkono was twice voted African Footballer Of The Year, in 1979 and 1982. On the second occasion it was for his magnificent performance at the 1982 World Cup. Dubbed the 'Black Spider' he conceded just one goal in three unbeaten games. He had become a goalkeeper by accident. Initially a winger with Douala he went between the posts when the regular goalkeeper failed to turn up. His performances at the 1982 World Cup led to a move to Europe with, most notably, Espanyol, with whom he reached the 1988 UEFA Cup final. During 2002's African Championship in Mali, while working as goalkeeping coach to Cameroon, he was arrested for witchcraft!

GUNNAR NORDAHL

Country: Sweden
Born: October 19, 1921
Position: Forward
Clubs: Degerfors, Norrköpping, AC Milan, Roma, Karlstad

Former fireman Gunnar Nordahl set a blazing goal trail wherever he went. In Sweden, he scored 77 goals in 58 games for Degerfors, followed up with a sensational 93 goals in 92 appearances for Norrköpping, before leading the charge for Sweden's gold medal success at the 1948 London Olympics. A chance to turn professional with AC Milan saw no change in his abilities as a goalscorer, netting 225 goals in 257 Serie A matches, playing alongside fellow Swedes Gren and Liedholm. For Sweden he racked up some 44 goals in 33 internationals, including the 1958 World Cup where Sweden finished as runners-up.

ERNST OCWIRK

Country: Austria
Born: March 10, 1926
Position: Centre-half/Midfield
Clubs: Floridsdorfer, FK Austria, Sampdoria

Ernst Ocwirk was the last of a dying breed of attacking centre-halves – and he was excellent at the role. While the rest of Europe went for a stopper, FK Austria Vienna and the Austrian national side exploited Ocwirk's skill and intuition. FK won the Austrian championship three times, in 1949, 1950 and 1953.

Ocwirk, nicknamed 'Clockwork' by the English for his ability to create and dictate matches, helped make Austria one of the strongest teams in Europe, playing 62 times for his country. Later in his career he had a five-year spell with Italian club Sampdoria where he was re-modelled as a midfielder.

MORTEN OLSEN

Country: Denmark
Born: August 14, 1949
Position: Defender/Forward/Midfield
Clubs: Vodingborg, B1901 Nykobing, Cercle Brugge, Racing White Bruxelles, Anderlecht, Köln

Morten Olsen's 18-year playing career saw him play in every outfield position, but he will be remembered as a gifted libero in the thrilling Denmark side of the 1980s. The role had come to him care of his Anderlecht coach, Tomislav Ivic, after Olsen had recovered from injury. To extend his playing career Ivic cast him as libero and this was embraced by Danish national coach Sepp Piontek. Olsen was instrumental in Denmark's exciting performances at the 1984 European Championship and 1986 World Cup. In later years he became a coach and in his first season won the Danish championship with Brondby.

WOLFGANG OVERATH

Country: West Germany
Born: September 29, 1943
Position: Midfield
Clubs: SV Siegburg 04, Köln

When Wolfgang Overath helped the West Germans to World Cup success on home soil in 1974, not only did he bring his international career to a fitting end, but he also completed a remarkable treble. Having been a beaten finalist in the 1966 final, he scored the winner in the third placed play-off in 1970, so like Beckenbauer, he can claim to have finished first, second and third in the World Cup.

Overath won the Bundesliga in his first season with Köln and, almost 800 games for the club later, he bowed out of football after helping them to German Cup success in 1977.

JEAN-PIERRE PAPIN

Country: France
Born: November 5, 1963
Position: Forward
Clubs: INF Vichy, Valenciennes, Club Brugge, Marseille, AC Milan, Bayern Munich, Bordeaux, Guingamp

Jean-Pierre Papin won the European Footballer Of The Year award in 1991 and was one of the most prolific strikers of his era. A stocky goalscorer with a powerful shot on either foot, he starred at the 1986 World Cup for France and finished top scorer in the French league for Marseille for five consecutive seasons. Papin found the net from every angle and became synonymous with Marseille's success across Europe. He flourished at international level too, helping France qualify for the 1992 European Championship with nine goals in eight matches, and was also a regular scorer in European club competitions.

He struggled to make an impact after moving to AC Milan and injuries marred his spell at Bayern Munich. Yet he won four French titles, two Italian titles, one UEFA Cup with Bayern and scored an impressive 30 goals in 54 appearances for France, a total that puts him joint-second on their all-time scorers list.

DANIEL PASSARELLA

Country: Argentina
Born: May 25, 1953
Position: Defender
Clubs: Sarmiento, River Plate, Fiorentina, Inter Milan

Passarella, who captained Argentina to World Cup glory in 1978 aged only 25, was an instinctive sweeper who exuded calm. His leadership in the face of overwhelming expectations earned him the nickname 'El Gran Capitan'. Passarella was an unusually skilful defender who contributed enormously in attack, scoring 22 goals in 70 internationals. He was particularly dangerous at set pieces. Three goals were notched in 12 World Cup appearances in 1978 and 1982. Passarella was also selected for the 1986 finals but withdrew through injury. He achieved notoriety as a coach, banning players with long hair, or who wore earrings, for being homosexual.

ADOLFO PEDERNERA

Country: Argentina
Born: November 15, 1918
Position: Forward
Clubs: River Plate, Atlanta, Huracan, Millonarios

Adolfo Pedernera provided the cutting edge of the famous River Plate 'Maquina' attack. Pedernera won five league titles with River Plate in 11 years and was capped 21 times for his country. In 1948, during the Argentine players strike, he moved to Colombia where he signed for Millonarios of Bogota, attracting huge crowds when he was presented to the fans for the first time, tripling their normal gate receipts of $18,000. And on his actual debut, that figure doubled again.

Pedernera's move began an exodus of top South American talent to Colombia, beginning a golden age for the league called 'El Dorado'. Pedernera himself recruited the top talent to Columbia, including his replacement at River Plate, Alfredo Di Stéfano.

Below: Fans lift Argentina captain Daniel Passarella as he holds aloft the World Cup in 1978.

PELE

Country: Brazil
Born: October 23, 1940
Position: Forward
Clubs: Santos, New York Cosmos

Edson Arantes do Nascimento, or Pele as he is more commonly known, began kicking a ball around the yard of his Três Corações home at the age of two and had the perfect role model in his father, Dondinho, who was a striker for leading Brazilian side Fluminese.

After playing for a few amateur teams, including Baquinho and Sete Setembro, Pele was discovered by the former Brazilian World Cup player Waldemar de Brito, who recognized the 11-year-old's potential and invited him to join his Clube Atlético Bauru team. Within four years, de Brito had seen enough and took his protégé to top São Paulo outfit Santos FC for a trial, telling the club at the time: "This boy will be the greatest soccer player in the world."

Pele went on to score on his debut that September and, although appearances were extremely limited in that opening campaign, he netted 32 times the following season, leading the São Paulo league goal charts in the process.

Brazil's national coach Sylvio Pirilo gave Pele his international debut on July 7, 1957, and the 16-year-old scored in a 2-1 defeat against Argentina. His appearances in a gold shirt made Pele a worldwide phenomenon and the early signs of his greatness were seen at the 1958 World Cup finals in Sweden.

Already guaranteed their place in the quarter-finals, Pele made his bow in Brazil's final group game against the Soviet Union.

Above: Pele trots out for Santos, the club for whom he averaged more than a goal a game, for over a thousand games.
Below left: Pele celebrates another World Cup highlight. Below right: Pele ended his career with New York Cosmos.

He then went on to score the only goal against Wales in the quarter-finals. His pace, trickery and eye for goal ensured he remained in the side and a semi-final hat-trick in a 5-2 defeat of France, and a further two goals in the final against Sweden, made sure he was not out of the headlines.

Although Brazil successfully defended their title four years later in Chile, a pulled muscle prematurely ended Pele's tournament, and the 1966 campaign would also end in tears and frustration. The greatest player in the world became a marked man in England and was brutally fouled against Bulgaria and Portugal as Brazil crashed out at the first stage. "I don't want to end my life as an invalid," moaned Pele, as he threatened to boycott the next World Cup in Mexico.

Pele's frustrations eased though, and his performances in 1970 proved to be the pinnacle of an illustrious career. He was again the focal point in a Brazil team that is still regarded as the greatest ever. A free flowing brand of football swept all challengers aside and the team's 4-1 final victory against Italy emphasised the dominance. Pele scored in that game, taking his tally to four and his overall World Cup tally to 12 in 14 matches. He would eventually end his international career with 96 goals in 111 appearances.

In 1974, Pele left Santos, having made 1,036 appearances and scoring an alleged 1,216 goals. He helped the team to win eight league championships in 11 years before bringing down the curtain on his career with the New York Cosmos. He scored a further 65 goals for the club before playing his final game, a friendly match against Santos, on October 1, 1977.

1950 **1950:** Begins playing for local team Bauru Athletic Club, where his father was a coach.

1956 **1956:** Joins Santos, scores as a 15-year-old on his debut against Corinthians; finishes the season as top scorer with 32 goals.

1957

1958 **1957:** Scores on his international debut for Brazil against Argentina.

1959

1960 **1958:** At 17 he becomes the youngest ever World Cup winner in Sweden. Scores twice in the final in a 5-2 victory over the hosts.

1961

1962

1963

1964 **1962:** Misses the World Cup through injury but helps Santos to World Club Cup crown.

1965 **1966:** Brutal opposition tactics see the world's best player fouled out of the World Cup.

1966

1967 **1969:** Scores his 1,000th first-class goal, a penalty against Vasco Da Gama.

1968

1969 **1970:** Star of the World Cup finals, he inspires Brazil to win the Jules Rimet trophy for the third time in Mexico.

1970

1971 **1971:** Makes his 111th and final appearance for Brazil, against Yugoslavia.

1972

1973 **1974:** Plays his final game for Santos against Ponte Preta.

1974

1975 **1975:** Comes out of retirement to appear for New York Cosmos in NASL.

1976

1977 **1977:** Retires after helping Cosmos win a third successive NASL championship.

1994 **1994:** Appointed as Brazil's Minister for Sport.

Above: The 1991 African Player Of The Year, Abedi Pele, in action for German club TSV 1860 Munich.

ABEDI PELE

Country: Ghana
Born: January 5, 1962
Position: Winger/Midfield
Clubs: Real Tamale United, Al Satar, Dragons de Louéme, FC Zurich, Niort, Marseille, Mulhouse, Lille, Torino, TSV 1860 Munich

At the age of 17 Abedi Ayew Pele won the 1982 African Nations Cup with Ghana. The precocious teenager, although not yet an automatic choice, was a sensation. A European club career beckoned, with his greatest success achieved with the French club Olympique Marseille, where he won the 1993 European Champions Cup, beating the mighty AC Milan 1-0 just two years after losing the final on penalties to Red Star Belgrade. He was given an influential free role in that talented team that included Barthez, Desailly, Deschamps, Boksic and Völler and he excelled. In 1991 he was voted African Player Of The Year for his performances in Europe.

SILVIO PIOLA

Country: Italy
Born: September 29, 1913
Position: Forward
Clubs: Pro Vercelli, Lazio, Torino, Juventus, Novara

Right: Pirri was the ultimate one club man, serving Real Madrid in a variety of on and off the field roles over three decades.

Silvio Piola was an early Italian football hero and one of the great pre-war strikers. He scored five goals at the 1938 World Cup in France,

including two in the final as Italy triumphed with a 4-2 win over Hungary. At times he was impossible to play against, his strength and skill showing he was ahead of his peers.

At club level Piola started at Pro Vercelli, earning his international debut in 1935. He continued after the war but he will always be remembered for 1938, when he was a pivotal figure and, alongside Léonidas of Brazil, arguably the greatest striker of his era.

PIRRI

Country: Spain
Born: March 11, 1945
Position: Striker/Midfield/Defender
Clubs: Real Madrid

Few players have ever served one club as loyally as Pirri did Real Madrid. For three decades he was at the heart of the Spanish giants, firstly as a player, then in a variety of positions, including sports director. He made his debut for the club as a striker in 1964 but over the years moved back first into midfield and then defence, playing until 1979, after which he became the club doctor and later a scout. A long career with a great club inevitably yields honours but Pirri's with Madrid were particularly numerous, totalling eight Spanish championships, three domestic cups and the European Cup. He also played 44 times for Spain between 1966 and 1978.

FRANTISEK PLÁNICKA

Country: Czechoslovakia
Born: June 2, 1904
Position: Goalkeeper
Club: Slovan Prague, Bubenec, Slavia Prague

Frantisek Plánicka was one of Czechoslovakia's most successful players as part of Slavia Prague's unstoppable side of the 1920s and 1930s. Plánicka won nine league titles, six Czech Cups and the 1938 Mitropa Cup. He was an automatic choice for the national team between 1925 and 1938, captaining them in two World Cups in 1934 and 1938.

In the 1934 competition his magnificent, agile performances helped the Czechs to the runners-up spot, while in the 1938 quarter-final clash with Brazil, Plánicka played much of the game with a broken arm. All in all Plánicka made 73 appearances for his country in a 13-year international career.

MICHEL PLATINI

Country: France
Born: June 21, 1955
Position: Midfield
Clubs: Nancy, St Etienne, Juventus

Michel Platini is firmly established as one of the greatest players of all time. With his remarkable technique, superb passing and

sublime free-kicks, he was the world's best player during the first half of the 1980s. His astonishing goalscoring record from midfield made him a match-winner at the highest level and his ability to peak on the biggest occasions set him apart from his peers.

Platini excelled for France throughout an 11-year international career and he won a string of club honours at Juventus, wowing football followers across the world.

He started at Nancy, who took a chance on him after others famously turned him down because of his frail physique. He showed elegant natural skills and worked hard on his technique on the training field. At the relatively small club he was able to develop after making his league debut at 17 and emerged as a bright French talent, making his international debut against Czechoslovakia on March 27, 1976.

He took part impressively in the 1978 World Cup finals, hinting at things to come, and moved to St Etienne after the tournament. But

the club's golden era was over and despite brilliant individual performances, Platini returned to the international spotlight only in 1982. That year he helped France to the semi-finals of the World Cup, where they lost on penalties to West Germany following a thrilling 3-3 draw. Platini was the leader of their gifted generation, showing the vision and goalscoring ability that was his trademark.

At 27 he was coming to the peak of his powers and he moved to Juventus. It was in Serie A that he truly developed into the world's greatest player, helping the squad win the Italian title in 1984 and 1986, the Italian Cup in 1983, the European Cup Winners' Cup and the European Super Cup in 1984, and the European Cup and the World Club Cup in 1985. Platini was the master, his range of skill unrivalled in the toughest league in the world and his achievements at the highest level overshadowing those of any other player. More remarkable still was his goals record. Three

times he finished as the highest goalscorer in the Italian league, thanks largely to his ability with free-kicks and penalties.

In the midst of club success Platini also tasted victory with France, inspiring them to win the European Championship in 1984 with a series of astonishing displays in the finals. He struck nine goals in five matches, including two hat-tricks and the winner in the semi-final. The opener in the 2-0 final win over Spain completed a remarkable run.

He was voted European Footballer Of The Year in 1983, 1984 and 1985, becoming only the second player to win the award three times after Johan Cruyff. He appeared at the 1986 World Cup as France again reached the semi-final, but he retired aged 31 in May 1987. He won 72 caps for France and scored 41 goals, becoming their all-time highest goalscorer. Alongside his haul of trophies, he averaged more than one goal in every two games throughout his career.

Above: Michel Platini was the greatest player in world football in the first half of the 1980s.

Above: After leaving Aston Villa, David Platt forged a career in Italy's top flight with Bari, Juventus and Sampdoria.

Opposite: Hardly the classic build for a footballer Ferenc Puskás, seen here turning out for his native Hungary, was a true legend with Honvéd and Real Madrid.

DAVID PLATT

Country: England
Born: June 10, 1966
Position: Midfield
Clubs: Manchester United, Crewe Alexandra, Aston Villa, Bari, Juventus, Sampdoria, Arsenal

After a modest start to his professional career – released by Manchester United then moving to Crewe and Aston Villa – Platt made his name in the 1990 World Cup, where one goal effectively changed his life. His fantastic volley against Belgium gave England victory in the final minute of extra-time and sent his team into the quarter-finals. The midfielder returned from the tournament as a player in demand and after one more season with Villa he established a fine career in Italian football, first with Bari, who bought him for a British record transfer fee of £5.5 million, then with Juventus, where he won the UEFA Cup in 1993 despite not holding down a regular first team place, and finally with Sampdoria.

At the same time his international career boomed. He was one of England's key players during the Nineties, playing in the 1992 and 1996 European Championship, eventually winning a total of 62 caps and scoring 27 goals. He was also captain on several occasions. Platt's Italian adventure ended in 1995 when he signed for Arsenal, and although he was troubled by knee problems, he won the league and FA Cup double in 1998 with The Gunners before moving into coaching.

TONI POLSTER

Country: Austria
Born: March 10, 1964
Position: Forward
Clubs: Austria Vienna, Torino, Seville, Logrones, Rayo Vallecano, Köln, Borussia Mönchengladbach, SV Salzburg

Toni Polster remains the biggest name in Austrian football. Such was his importance to the national side he was still considered one of their key-players at the age of 34 during France 98. He made his final appearance for Austria against Iran, by which time he was 36, bringing down the curtain on a career spanning 95 internationals and making him Austria's most-capped player of all time.

In a side that was only able to qualify for the 1990 and 1998 World Cups during Polster's career, his haul of 44 international goals made him a feared opponent all over the world.

FERENC PUSKÁS

Country: Hungary, Spain
Born: April 2, 1927
Position: Forward
Clubs: Honvéd, Real Madrid

Football can have few more unlikely stars than Ferenc Puskás, the short, barrel-chested Hungarian goal machine who became known as the 'Galloping Major'. Puskás possessed one of the most powerful and accurate left feet in the history of the game and his goalscoring record is phenomenal: 83 goals in 84 matches for Hungary and 35 goals in 39 European matches for Real Madrid from 1961 to 1965.

As a small child Puskás was entranced by the roar of the Kispest crowd, audible from his kitchen window in Budapest. The smallest kid on the block, he became inseparable from the five-year-old next door, József Bozsik. Their fathers worked together in a slaughterhouse and when Bozsik was picked up by Kispest (renamed Honvéd after 1949 and turned into the army side, hence Puskás's nickname) his friend went with him. Together they forged one of the most dynamic strike partnerships in the history of the game.

Puskás scored on his international debut against Austria on August 20, 1945, and in the epochal 6-3 victory at Wembley in 1963 he underlined the gulf between the Magyars and England with a memorable drag back and shot past the home side's goalkeeper Gil Merrick.

In the 1954 World Cup he captained the side and came back from an injury in the first match to play in the final. Though clearly unfit he opened the scoring after six minutes and had a late equaliser disallowed.

In a time of hardship he became chief smuggler among the Hungarian players, returning from away fixtures loaded with razor blades or machine parts, twice having to talk himself out of trouble with the secret police.

Puskás won four Hungarian league titles with Honvéd but his life took a dramatic turn in 1956 when the Soviet Union invaded his country to quell the nationalist uprising. Honvéd were touring Europe at the time, and Puskás, along with Kocsis and several others, refused to return and was banned by UEFA.

Real Madrid arranged for the ban to be rescinded and he made his debut for them in 1958 aged 30, rapidly forging a devastating partnership with Argentine Alfredo di Stéfano that yielded six league championships and a staggering 240 goals in 260 appearances, explaining his Spanish nickname 'Cañoncito Pum' (the Little Canon).

Puskás became the first player to score a hat-trick in the European Cup final against Eintracht Frankfurt in 1960 (Di Stéfano became the second in the same game, while Puskás finished with four). He was the Cup's top scorer on three occasions, scoring another hat-trick in losing to Benfica in 1962 at 35.

Puskás even picked up four caps as a naturalised Spaniard in the 1962 World Cup finals before retiring at 40. He moved to Athens to coach Panathinaikos whom he took to their only European Cup final in 1971, and finally resettled in Budapest. In 1993 he became caretaker manager of the national side but failed to guide Hungary to the 1994 World Cup. This did not deter the Hungarian government from marking his 75th birthday in 2002 by naming the Népstadion (which he had helped build as a youth) the Ferenc Puskás Stadium. A fitting tribute to a genuine legend.

HELMUT RAHN

Country: West Germany
Born: August 16, 1929
Position: Forward
Clubs: Altenessen 12, Oelde 09, Sportfreunde Katernberg, Rot-Weiss Essen, Köln, Enschede, Duisburg

Rahn will be best remembered for the part he played in an unfancied West German side's World Cup success in 1954. Rahn scored twice in the final against the red-hot favourites Hungary, netting the equaliser and then the late winner. Yet Rahn nearly didn't get to Switzerland as he was on the verge of signing for Nacional of Uruguay while on a tour with club side Rot-Weiss Essen, before his coach

Above: Roberto Rivelino became an international star after his performances in the 1970 World Cup Finals.

summoned him home. Rahn was well known for having a thunderous shot and figured strongly in the 1958 finals when he scored six goals, to take his total World Cup tally to ten.

THOMAS RAVELLI

Country: Sweden
Born: August 13, 1959
Position: Goalkeeper
Clubs: Osters Vaxjo, IFK Gothenburg, Tampa Bay Mutiny

The adage that you have to be a bit mad to be a goalkeeper was never more appropriate than when applied to Ravelli. Known as the clown prince of Swedish football for his humourous approach to the game, he was a magnificent, agile keeper who led his country to the semi-finals of the 1994 World Cup in America.

Ravelli made an incredible 143 appearances for his country between 1981 and 1997, a period in which Swedish football grew in stature. The commanding six-footer was the international game's most capped player until Lothar Matthäus surpassed his total.

ROBBIE RENSENBRINK

Country: Holland
Born: July 3, 1947
Position: Left-winger
Clubs: OVVO, OSV, DWS Amsterdam, Club Brugge, Anderlecht, Portland Timbers, Toulouse

The outstanding Dutch winger spent much of his career in Belgium with Anderlecht, helping them to two European Cup Winners' Cup victories, while on the international scene he was a leading figure in the exciting Dutch team of the Seventies.

He played in two successive World Cup finals in 1974 and 1978, taking runners-up medals in each, but he does hold the honour of scoring the 1,000th goal in World Cup history – that came with a penalty against Scotland in the 1978 tournament. He ended his playing career with brief spells in both America and France.

FRANK RIJKAARD

Country: Holland
Born: September 30, 1962
Position: Midfield/Central defender
Clubs: Ajax, Sporting Lisbon, Real Zaragoza, AC Milan, Ajax

Enormously versatile, Frank Rijkaard made his Ajax debut in 1979 under Johan Cruyff, but left the club for brief spells in Portugal and Spain after the two men fell out. He ended up in Italy where he was an integral part of the all-conquering AC Milan team of the late Eighties and early Nineties, along with fellow Dutchmen Ruud Gullit and Marco van Basten.

Milan won two European Champions Cups, two league titles and two World Club Cups with Rijkaard in the side and his return to Ajax resulted in another European Cup triumph 1995. Having made his international debut at just 19 years of age, he also went on to play an important role in the exciting Holland side that won the European Championship in 1988. Following his retirement from playing Rijkaard became national team coach in 1998. He resigned, however, immediately after his promising Dutch tournament favourites were eliminated from Euro 2000 by Italy on penalties at the semi-final stage.

GIGI RIVA

Country: Italy
Born: November 7, 1944
Position: Forward
Clubs: Legnano, Cagliari

Originally a left-winger, Riva's pace saw him develop into a prolific and popular striker both for Italy and Cagliari. He helped the Sardinian side into Serie A and then on to win the Scudetto. He was also Italy's top scorer in the 1970 World Cup in Mexico, scoring in extra-time during the semi-final victory over West Germany. At that time it was his 22nd goal in 21 internationals. Riva then suffered the second broken leg of his career in a European Championship qualifier before turning down the opportunity of a big money move to Juventus. The 1974 tournament was not such a success for Riva and he subsequently lost his place in the Italian side.

ROBERTO RIVELINO

Country: Brazil
Born: January 1, 1946
Position: Midfield
Clubs: Corinthians, Fluminese, El Hilal

The arrival of Mario Zagalo as Brazil manager in the lead up to the 1970 World Cup finals proved to be a watershed in the career of Roberto Rivelino. Under former coach Joao Saldanha, the Corinthians midfielder had to be content with fleeting appearances, but as the tournament got underway in Mexico, it became evident that the first exponent of the 'banana shot' free-kick was ready to unleash his talents on a worldwide audience.

Rivelino joined in perfect harmony with Pele, Gérson, Jairzinho and Tostão to form the most potent attacking force Brazil has ever had. The highlight of his career came against Czechoslovakia, where a swerving long-range shot inspired his teammates to victory.

Brazil were victorious in the final, beating Italy 4-1, and with three tournament goals to his name, Rivelino had played his part. He would play in two further World Cups, representing his country a total of 96 times, scoring 44 goals.

GIANNI RIVERA

Country: Italy
Born: August 18, 1943
Position: Inside-forward
Clubs: US Alessandria, AC Milan

Gianni Rivera was an Italian hero who made his Serie A debut for his local team aged just 15, transferring to AC Milan just a year later. Staying at the San Siro throughout his long and successful career, he starred in four consecutive World Cups and helped the Milan side become Italian champions in 1962 and European Cup winners in 1963. His superb passes twice put José Altafini through the Benfica defence to score the goals that made Milan champions of Europe. Slender and graceful, he was a technically superb player with tremendous passing skills and a powerful shot, particularly from distance.

He was the dominating figure when Milan became Italian champions again in 1968 and followed this triumph by winning the European Champions Cup and the World Club Cup the following year. He landed the European Footballer Of The Year award in 1969 for his outstanding exploits.

Rivera featured at the 1968 European Championship, which Italy won, but had to battle for his place in the national team with great rival Sandro Mazzola. Indeed, he was left on the bench for the 1970 World Cup Final against Brazil, getting on for just the last eight minutes. He won 60 caps, scoring 14 goals.

BRYAN ROBSON

Country: England
Born: January 11, 1957
Position: Midfield
Clubs: West Bromwich Albion, Manchester United, Middlesbrough

Robson earned the nickname 'Captain Marvel' for his unflinching and inspiring midfield performances in what was an undistinguished era for club and country. For a decade he was consistently the most outstanding player to wear England and Manchester United's colours. Signed by United for a then British record fee of £1.5million, Robson's battling, defensive qualities, combined with regular

goals, made him a natural leader. He managed 26 strikes for England, including a 27-second effort against France in the 1982 World Cup, and a total of 97 for Manchester United.

He led Manchester United to three FA Cup triumphs, but at the time of Liverpool's great dominance he looked destined to become one of the greatest players never to lift the championship. However, Manchester United finally achieved back-to-back Premiership titles in 1993 and 1994, in the autumn of Robson's career. He then joined Middlesbrough as player-manager. Capped 90 times by England, 65 as captain, Robson paid the price for his fearlessness by suffering regular injuries, most significantly in the 1986 World Cup Finals.

ROMARIO

Country: Brazil
Born: January 29, 1966
Position: Forward
Clubs: Olario, Vasco da Gama, PSV Eindhoven, Barcelona, Flamengo, Valencia, Fluminese, Al Sadd

Frustrating to coaches, adored by fans and feared by defenders, Romario was one of the most exciting and colourful players in the world in his heyday. At his peak in the early

1990s, Romario was arguably the greatest striker on earth and a worthy heir to the tradition of great Brazilian attackers. In 1994, the year in which Brazil won the World Cup, he was at his deadliest. He was named FIFA World Footballer Of The Year after scoring five goals in the finals, although he failed to get on the scoresheet in the final itself, a drab 0-0 draw with Italy. He was, however, among the successful penalty takers.

A year before the World Cup, Romario had joined Barcelona for £3million. It was a move that brought the Spanish championship but by now he was attracting as much coverage for his playboy lifestyle as for his feats on the pitch. In 1996, he returned to Brazil to join Flamengo, only to be sacked three years later. By then injury had denied him a place alongside Ronaldo at the 1998 World Cup. Unsettled and with his international career in decline, he remained in demand at club level, hopping between clubs according to whichever coach most tolerated his indulgences.

JULIO CESAR ROMERO

Country: Paraguay
Born: 1961
Position: Forward
Clubs: Fluminese, Barcelona, Necaxa, New York Cosmos

The 1985 South American Footballer Of The Year, Romero was the star of the Paraguay side that reached the second phase of the 1986 World Cup. Romero, alongside strike partner Cabanas, spearheaded his team to a win over Iraq and gain creditable draws with hosts Mexico and tournament dark horses Belgium, finishing second in their group before losing out in the second phase to England. 'Romerito', as he was nicknamed, lit up the Brazilian league as one of the leading lights of the Fluminese team of the mid-1980s.

Above: Romario's off the field antics often overshadowed the fact that at his peak he was one of the world's best strikers.

Left: Captain Marvel Bryan Robson led Manchester United to FA Cup and eventually league championship success in his time as Old Trafford captain.

Above: Ian Rush strikes against
Everton in Liverpool's 3-1 1989
FA Cup Final win.

PAOLO ROSSI

Country: Italy
Born: September 23, 1956
Position: Centre-forward
Clubs: Prato, Juventus, Como, Lanerossi
Vicenza, Perugia, Juventus, AC Milan

Although Rossi retired young, at the age of 29, he packed a great deal of incident into a short, controversial career. A problematic knee injury saw Juventus release him in 1975 but he recovered, prospered and eventually joined Perugia for £3.5million. Despite being banned

Right: Paolo Rossi made
a dramatic return to the
international fold as top scorer
in the 1982 World Cup in Spain.

for two years in the early 1980s, following his alleged involvement in a match-fixing scandal, Rossi was nevertheless part of the Italian squad for the 1982 World Cup Finals in Spain. It was there that his ailing reputation enjoyed an extraordinary resurrection. Rossi ended up as the tournament's top scorer with six goals (including a hat-trick against Brazil) as Italy went on to win their third world title – he was also named European Player Of The Year in the same year.

KARL-HEINZ RUMMENIGGE

Country: West Germany
Born: September 25, 1955
Position: Forward
Clubs: Bayern Munich, Inter Milan, Servette

For several years, Rummenigge was the leading player and personality in West German football. A prolific goalscorer, he starred for Bayern Munich in the 1976 European Champions Cup victory over St Etienne and hit a World Cup brace in 1978 before reaching his peak two years later, helping West Germany to win the European Championship. Twice named European Footballer Of The Year, Rummenigge scored 45 goals in 95 games for his country but didn't have the best of luck; he was captain when the Germans lost the 1982 World Cup to Italy, and again four years later in defeat to Argentina.

IAN RUSH

Country: Wales
Born: October 20, 1961
Position: Striker
Clubs: Chester City, Liverpool, Juventus,
Liverpool, Leeds United, Newcastle United,
Sheffield United, Wrexham

Ian Rush was one of the greatest goalscorers of his, or any other era. Rush was signed by Bob Paisley from Chester City for £300,000 and became a Liverpool stalwart for 16 years, barring a short spell in Italy with Juventus, where he failed to settle. As a result Rush now stands as Liverpool's second highest goalscorer of all time (just behind Roger Hunt) with an impressive 229 league goals to his name.

Rush can also claim to be one of the most highly-decorated players in English football as his career peaked in conjunction with the greatest period in Liverpool's history, when league titles, FA Cups and European Cups flowed. Aside from his Italian sojourn, which was not quite as disastrous as has been made out, Rush's other great career disappointment was failing to grace the finals of any major international championship, but he was still capped 73 times by Wales, scoring 28 goals.

After setting up his own soccer school, Rush was recruited by Liverpool into becoming one of the coaching staff to work specifically with the current crop of Anfield strikers.

HUGO SANCHEZ

Country: Mexico
Born: June 11, 1958
Position: Forward
Clubs: UNAM, Atlético Madrid, Real Madrid, América, Rayo Vallecano

Human jack-in-the-box Hugo Sanchez is probably the greatest-ever player to emerge from Central America. The livewire Mexican, whose trademark was an acrobatic somersault celebration after each goal (taught to him by his Olympic gymnast sister), was the top goalscorer in Spanish league football for an incredible five consecutive seasons. He totted up 234 goals, mainly for Madrid's senior clubs, and his partnership with Emilio Butragueño at the Bernabéu remains the stuff of legend – as does his propensity for the bicycle kick. His international career spanned from 1977 to 1998, and he captained his country during several World Cup tournaments, scoring for Mexico 29 times in 58 appearances.

LEONEL SANCHEZ

Country: Chile
Born: April 25, 1936
Position: Left-winger
Club: Universidad de Chile

Leonel Sanchez was the star player of the Chilean team that finished third as hosts in the 1962 World Cup. Raiding from the left-wing in typically direct fashion, Sanchez ended the tournament as the Golden Boot winner with four goals, a distinction he shared with five other players (Florian Albert, Valentin Ivanov, Vava, Garrincha and Drazan Jerkovic).

Sanchez is also remembered for his part in the infamous 'Battle of Santiago' at the 1962 World Cup in Chile. Initially he was the unfortunate victim on the end of a disgraceful neck-high challenge from Italian Mario David, but his punch that flattened Humberto Maschio was inexcusable, even if it did show impressive timing.

JOSE SANTAMARIA

Country: Uruguay, Spain
Born: July 31, 1929
Position: Centre-half
Clubs: Nacional, Real Madrid

The hard-as-nails Uruguayan centre-back was the defensive lynchpin of the all-conquering Real Madrid team of the mid-1950s. Playing behind the attacking talents of Puskás, Di Stéfano and Gento, he won a hat-trick of European Cups for his trouble. Santamaria is also one of five players to have represented two countries at the finals of the World Cup. In 1954 he was one of the stars of the tournament playing in the centre of defence for Uruguay. In 1962, however, he was to be found in Spanish colours, and collected 17 caps in total for his adopted country. He later went on to become manager of a disappointing Spain side during the 1982 World Cup Finals.

DJALMA SANTOS

Country: Brazil
Born: February 27, 1929
Position: Right-back
Clubs: Portuguesa, Palmeiras, Atletico Curitiba

Santos was aged 37 when he played in his fourth World Cup in the 1966 tournament in England. However, it was not to be a happy competition for the outstanding full-back and he lost his place after the defeat to Hungary. Four years previously, though, he was at the height of his powers as he formed a terrific understanding with Garrincha. He set up the third goal as Brazil retained their World crown with victory over Czechoslovakia, while in Sweden in 1958 his sole appearance was in Brazil's final defeat of the hosts.

NILTON DOS SANTOS

Country: Brazil
Born: May 16, 1925
Position: Left-back
Clubs: Botafogo

Referred to as a left-back Dos Santos loved to push forward, more like a modern wing-back. He represented his country over a 14-year spell, which included two victorious World Cup campaigns in 1958 and 1962 and saw him make 82 international appearances before he retired in 1963 at the age of 37.

He made his debut for Brazil in 1949 and the following year embarked upon an ill-fated World Cup campaign and failed to take to the field. In 1954 Brazil fared slightly better, making the quarter-finals, but its was four years later in Sweden when he tasted glory as part of the Brazil side who became the first nation to lift the trophy outside of their own continent. Dos Santos earned the respect of his team-mates and his opponents wherever he played. At club level he represented Rio de Janeiro side Botafogo throughout his career.

GYORGY SAROSI

Country: Hungary
Born: September 12, 1912
Position: Centre-forward/Centre-half
Club: Ferencváros

Gyorgy Sarosi was an educated man with a law degree and was duly nicknamed 'The Doctor' because of it. Between the wars he truly was one of the best footballers around, enhancing the reputation of both his club Ferencváros – eight times Hungarian league champions and Mitropa Cup winners in 1937 – and his country. Sarosi captained Hungary to the 1938 World Cup Final. The previous year he scored seven goals against Czechoslovakia in an 8-3 win, the haul contributing to his overall tally of 42 goals. Later, he carved out an impressive coaching career in Italy and Switzerland.

JUAN SCHIAFFINO

Country: Uruguay, Italy
Born: July 28, 1925
Position: Inside-forward
Clubs: Peñarol, AC Milan, Roma

Small but lethal, Schiaffino was the key striker in the Uruguay team which won the 1950 World Cup in Brazil, scoring the first goal in a 2-1 win against the hosts in the final. He played again in the 1954 finals and was his country's most dynamic performer as they fell at the semi-final stage to the might of Hungary. This prompted AC Milan to shell out a then world record fee of £72,000 for his services, and once there he crafted a reputation as one of the greatest imports ever to play in Serie A. Schiaffino could have represented Italy at the World Cup in 1958 due to his mixed ancestry, but couldn't stop them from losing out to Northern Ireland in qualification.

Below: Hugo Sanchez got to perform his somersault goal celebration 29 times for Mexico.

SALVATORE SCHILLACI

Country: Italy
Born: December 1, 1964
Position: Centre-forward
Clubs: Messina, Juventus, Inter Milan, Jubilo Iwata

Lasting less than a year and a half after his debut against Switzerland in March 1990, 'Toto' Schillaci's international career was nothing if it wasn't short. His place in history is assured, however, thanks to the six goals he netted for Italy in the 1990 World Cup Finals, which made him the tournament's top scorer. The Juventus hitman claimed crucial strikes against Austria (a game in which he came on as a substitute to score after four minutes) and the Republic Of Ireland. He also put Italy ahead in their semi-final clash with Argentina

only to see Diego Maradona's team come back to win on penalties. Despite his heroics, Schillaci played just eight more games for his country after the finals ended and scored just one more goal.

PETER SCHMEICHEL

Country: Denmark
Born: November 18, 1963
Position: Goalkeeper
Clubs: Gladsaxe, Hvidovre, Brondby, Manchester United, Sporting Lisbon, Aston Villa, Manchester City

For ten years, the Danish giant was regarded as perhaps the best goalkeeper in the world. He collected numerous domestic trophies and made over 100 international appearances (even scoring once for his country), as well as forming the impregnable barrier behind Denmark's surprise European Championship-winning side in 1992. But his greatest period was at Manchester United. While Eric Cantona was the charismatic and enigmatic talisman up front, Schmeichel was the brick wall at the back, equally important to the club winning their first domestic title for more than a quarter of a century – and the many that followed.

Athletic and domineering, he was always shouting at – and organising – his defenders, never letting them lose their concentration. Schmeichel pulled off many memorable saves through his agility and speed of thought, and his long throws and accurate kicks set up many successful attacking moves from the back.

Keen not to be exposed by the advancing years, he left United after their Champions League triumph in 1999, spending two years in Portugal before returning to the English Premiership with Aston Villa.

A year later he was on the move again, this time to the other half of Manchester, playing a vital role in stabilising Kevin Keegan's Manchester City on their return to the top

flight. He finally announced his retirement at the end of his first season with the club, making his farewell appearance at City's last ever game at their Maine Road ground.

UWE SEELER

Country: West Germany
Born: November 5, 1936
Position: Centre-forward
Club: Hamburg

Seeler spent his entire 18-year career with Hamburg, scoring more than 550 goals for them. But while his individual achievements are many, the sides in which he featured regularly fell at the last hurdle.

His career took him to four World Cups, reaching one final, two semi-finals and one quarter-final. He scored in each tournament, an achievement matched only by Pele, and his 21 appearances in the finals was a record that was only broken by Lothar Matthäus.

Having skippered the German side to defeat in the World Cup final at Wembley in 1966, Seeler had dropped back into a deeper role by the 1970 tournament as he turned creator for Gerd Müller, who was to succeed him as Germany's most prolific striker.

PETER SHILTON

Country: England
Born: September 18, 1949
Position: Goalkeeper
Clubs: Leicester City, Stoke City, Nottingham Forest, Southampton, Derby County, Plymouth Argyle, Wimbledon, Bolton Wanderers, Coventry City, West Ham United, Leyton Orient

Shilton is England's most capped player with 125 international appearances, yet his final tally could have been higher. For years he vied with Ray Clemence for the goalkeeper's jersey and it wasn't until his early 30s that Shilton clearly emerged as England's regular shot stopper.

Shilton enjoyed an extraordinarily long career: he played for England until the age of 40 and club football up to 48. He succeeded Gordon Banks, another England legend, at Leicester City when he was just 16 years of age but, although towards the end of his career he became increasingly nomadic, at club level his name is forever associated with Nottingham Forest, who enjoyed a fairytale story of success in the late 1970s. Under Brian Clough they won the league championship in 1978 at the first attempt after promotion to the top flight and went on to win back-to-back European Cups in 1979 and 1980.

When Ron Greenwood selected Shilton as his first choice goalkeeper for the 1982 World Cup it signalled the end of the Shilton-Clemence rivalry. For the next eight years and three eventful World Cups, Shilton would be

a regular fixture in the England goal. He kept ten clean sheets in 17 World Cup matches but is most remembered for the two goals he conceded to Diego Maradona in 1986: the first to a handball, the second to one of the greatest goals ever. He quit the international game after helping England to fourth place in the World Cup in Italy in 1990.

ALLAN SIMONSEN

Country: Denmark
Born: December 15, 1952
Position: Forward
Clubs: Vejle, Borussia Mönchengladbach, Barcelona, Charlton Athletic, Vejle

Simonsen was the man for the big occasion, scoring in the finals of all three major European club competitions. He was on target twice for Borussia Mönchengladbach in the 1975 UEFA Cup Final and once in the 2-1 aggregate defeat of Red Star Belgrade in the 1979 UEFA Cup Final, a season which saw him finish as the competition's top scorer with nine goals. He also netted in the 1977 European Cup Final defeat against Liverpool and for Barcelona in the 1982 European Cup Winners' Cup Final with Standard Liege, which the Spanish giants won 2-1. In 1977 he celebrated his third consecutive Bundesliga title along with the accolade of being named European Footballer Of The Year.

Opposite top: Peter Schmeichel at his best for Manchester United against Liverpool.

Opposite bottom: Toto Schillaci shoots for goal. The Italian's 15 minutes of fame came as he top-scored at the 1990 World Cup.

Below: Peter Shilton was 40 when he kept goal for England at the 1990 World Cup.

MATTHIAS SINDELAR

Country: Austria
Born: February 10, 1903
Position: Forward
Clubs: Hertha Vienna, FK Austria Vienna

A certain amount of mystery still surrounds the death of Matthias Sindelar, a slight man who was known on the football field as 'The Man of Paper'. Some sources have claimed that he was murdered for his anti-fascist beliefs at the time of the Anschluss, others that he committed suicide rather than live in Nazi-run Austria – but that he died of carbon monoxide poisoning remains the only certainty.

Sindelar was the star of Austria's talented 'Wunderteam' of the Thirties, falling to the hosts in the semi-finals of the 1934 World Cup in Italy. A knee injury almost ended his career before it began, and following surgery he was always easy to spot due to what became a trademark bandage on his right knee.

OMAR ENRIQUE SIVORI

Country: Argentina, Italy
Born: October 2, 1935
Position: Inside-left
Clubs: River Plate, Juventus, Napoli

Below: Socrates led talented, but ultimately unsuccessful, Brazil sides in their 1982 and 1986 World Cup campaigns.

Omar Enrique Sivori had a remarkable career, playing international football for Argentina, the country of his birth, and Italy. Sivori started at Argentinian club River Plate and established himself as an extremely gifted inside-left, playing for Argentina before Italian side Juventus paid a world record £91,000 for him

in 1957. Defecting to Turin cost Sivori his international place with Argentina, but his club career took off spectacularly.

With Juventus he struck up a fabulous understanding with Welshman John Charles, and inspired the Bianconeri to a trio of league championships in 1958, 1960 and 1961. His personal contribution to these triumphs was significant. In the 1960 championship, he was the league's leading scorer with 27 goals from 31 games, and in 1961 he was named as the European Footballer Of The Year. In the following year he represented his adopted country in the 1962 World Cup, playing three times in the finals in Chile.

Sivori's glorious reign at Juve ended in 1965, but to this day he is fondly remembered as one of club's legends. He joined Napoli and played until a knee injury forced retirement in 1968.

JOSIP SKOBLAR

Country: Yugoslavia
Born: March 12, 1941
Position: Forward
Clubs: NK Nadar, OFK Belgrade, Marseille, Hannover 96, Marseille

Josip Skoblar became a legend at Marseille for his goalscoring exploits. He struck 44 times in the 1970-71 season to win the European Golden Boot and help the club win the league. He topped the scoring charts the next year as they won the double and was league top scorer in 1972-73 for a third successive season.

He turned out for Yugoslavia at the 1962 World Cup when they reached the semi-finals, but in total he made only 35 appearances for his country because of a rule that prevented players based abroad playing for the national team. He will always be best remembered for his exploits at club level.

SOCRATES

Country: Brazil
Born: February 19, 1954
Position: Midfield
Clubs: Botafogo, Corinthians, Fiorentina, Flamengo, Santos

An unlikely footballer, Socrates emanated from an educated middle-class background, and played as an amateur for Botafogo while studying for a medical degree. After qualifying as a doctor he put his stethoscope in storage and signed pro forms for São Paulo side Corinthians in 1977. A tall, lean and elegant midfielder, he captained his country with great distinction but limited success in the 1982 and 1986 World Cup finals.

At the 1982 finals he scored a wondergoal against the Soviet Union, yet was unable to prevent his side being eliminated by eventual winners Italy. A similar pattern occurred four

GUILLERMO STÁBILE

Country: Argentina, France
Born: January 17, 1906
Position: Forward
Clubs: Huracán, Genoa, Napoli, Red Star Paris

Stábile wrote his name in World Cup history when he became the first player to score a hat-trick in the final stages of the competition. He achieved the feat in the inaugural tournament in 1930 when he helped Argentina to a 6-3 defeat of Mexico. Stábile had begun the tournament as a reserve but his three goals earned him a regular place in the starting line-up. He proved he was no one-hit wonder by finishing the competition as leading scorer with eight goals. He scored and hit the woodwork in the final but ended up on the losing side. Stábile, whose game was based on blistering pace, also played for France after moving to Europe to play club football.

FRANK STAPLETON

Country: Republic Of Ireland
Born: July 10, 1956
Position: Forward
Clubs: Arsenal, Manchester United, Ajax, Derby County, Le Havre, Blackburn Rovers, Anderlecht, Huddersfield Town, Bradford City

Frank Stapleton is the Republic Of Ireland's all-time leading scorer, with 20 goals in 71 internationals. He also registered 149 goals at club level, leading the line admirably in a 17-year career for many outstanding sides. Strong and powerful in the air, he was a model professional who worked hard on his game after joining Arsenal as an apprentice in 1973. Signed by Manchester United for £900,000 in 1981, Stapleton became the first player to score for different teams in the FA Cup final. After leaving United in 1987 he failed to make an impact at Ajax and returned to England to finish a career that included appearances in five FA Cup finals.

HRISTO STOICHKOV

Country: Bulgaria
Born: August 2, 1966
Position: Midfield
Clubs: Plovdiv, CSKA Sofia, Barcelona, Parma, Al Nasr, Kashiwa Reysol, Chicago Fire

Stoichkov came to prominence as an integral figure of the CSKA side that reached the semi-finals of the European Cup Winners' Cup in 1989 against Barcelona. He also won the European Golden Boot award the following

years later, where his mercurial performances were eclipsed by the pain of defeat in the quarter-finals against France.

year, prompting Barcelona coach Johan Cruyff to splash out £3million for his services.

It proved to be an inspirational signing as Barcelona went on to win the European Champions Cup for the only time in their history. Not to mention the fact that he fired the club to five Spanish championships between 1991 and 1997. In the mid-Nineties Stoichkov was arguably the greatest footballer on the planet and at the 1994 World Cup Finals he inspired Bulgaria to third place, winning the Golden Boot in the process.

A temperamental player, his clash of personality with Johan Cruyff led to a brief spell with Parma in 1995, but he returned to inspire the Barça side under Louis van Gaal before his career petered out with spells in the Middle East, Japan and the United States, where he now lives.

LUIS SUAREZ

Country: Spain
Born: May 2, 1935
Position: Inside-forward
Clubs: Barcelona, Inter Milan, Sampdoria

Luis Suarez was one of the most gifted inside-forwards of his generation. Despite a fiery nature, he was voted European Footballer Of The Year in 1960, which led to Inter Milan to pay a staggering £210,000 to sign him the following year. He became Inter's midfield general and was influential in the European Cup-winning teams of 1964 and 1965. He was already a fully established international by the late 1950s but his moment of glory came when Spain won the 1964 European Championship. His Inter career came to an abrupt end when the club sold him to Sampdoria while he was on holiday in Spain. Aged 37 he was recalled to the injury-ravaged national team in 1972.

JEAN TIGANA

Country: France
Born: June 23, 1955
Position: Midfield
Clubs: Toulon, Lyon, Bordeaux, Marseille

Jean Tigana became a midfield star in the 1980s when a glorious France side ruled Europe and shone as one of the greatest teams on earth – despite never managing to win the ultimate international trophy, the World Cup. His tireless performances for Les Bleus, notably at the World Cup finals in 1982 and again in 1986, and also at the European Championship that France won on home soil in 1984, made him hugely admired by football fans the world over.

Born in Mali, Tigana moved to France aged just three years old, making his name at Lyon before joining Bordeaux in 1980. He played

JAN TOMASZEWSKI

Country: Poland
Born: January 9, 1948
Position: Goalkeeper
Clubs: Legia Warsaw, LKS Lodz, Beerschot, Hercules

Brian Clough dubbed him 'a clown' in 1973, but after the Polish goalkeeper's memorable performance that kept England from the World Cup finals, no-one in England was laughing. Tomaszewski made his international debut in 1971 but his fifth game was a home victory over England in a World Cup qualifier. Poland were not expected to survive the return leg at Wembley, but held out for a crucial 1-1 draw with Tomaszewski pulling off a string of improbable saves.

At the finals in West Germany, Poland demonstrated the result was no fluke as Tomaszewski conceded just five goals and saved two penalties on the way to third place. Two years later he won a silver medal at the 1976 Olympics and returned for the 1978 World Cup. His 65 appearances for Poland in total make him his country's most capped goalkeeper. The communist regime finally let him move abroad to Belgium in 1978, before subsequently moving to Spain. He retired in 1982 and entered sports journalism.

TOSTÃO

Country: Brazil
Born: January 25, 1947
Position: Forward
Clubs: Cruzeiro, Vasco da Gama

Tostão played in two successive World Cup tournaments for Brazil – in 1966 and 1970 – but in between faced the biggest challenge of

Above: England could only beat Tomaszewski once in their famous 1971 World Cup qualifier with Poland, and missed the World Cup finals as a result.

his career when he battled against a serious eye injury. The striker needed surgery to repair a detached retina and, though the problem eventually took its toll, he recovered to win the 1970 World Cup. As a member of the Brazilian team regarded as the greatest of all time, Tostão played in all six matches, where he was joined in a fearsome forward line by Pele, Jairzinho and Rivelino. Although he didn't score in the final, he will be remembered for the cross which led to Brazil's winner against England, and his two goals against Peru in the quarter-finals. His eye injury eventually forced him into early retirement.

successfully there under the coaching of Aime Jacquet, winning the French championship in 1984, 1985 and 1987, and the French Cup in 1986 and 1987.

Tigana made his international debut in 1980 and became a fixture in the line-up alongside fellow midfielders Michel Platini, Alain Giresse and Luis Fernandez. Slight and wiry, he was a prodigious worker and a great reader of the game. His most famous moment came during the 1984 European Championship when he ran half the length of the pitch deep in extra-time and crossed for Platini to score the winning goal in the 3-2 semi-final victory over Portugal.

Tigana finished his career at Marseille, adding league titles in 1990 and 1991, before moving into coaching. He won 52 caps for France, scoring one goal.

Since moving into coaching he has enjoyed spells with Marseille and Fulham.

Left: Jean Tigana shone for France in the Eighties.

Above: Carlos Valderrama, though Colombia's distinctive talisman, often underperformed on the big stage.

CARLOS VALDERRAMA

Country: Colombia
Born: September 2, 1961
Position: Midfield
Clubs: Santa Marta, Millonarios, Atlético Nacional, Montpellier, Real Valladolid, Medellin, Atletico Junior Barranquilla, Tampa Bay Mutiny, Miami Fusion

Carlos Valderrama's crazy hair overshadowed a special football talent. An elegant player, during the Nineties Valderrama orchestrated Colombia's play from midfield with an unhurried air and he is rightly recognized as the country's best-ever player. Twice South American Footballer Of The Year, he became the first Colombian to pass the 100-cap mark, eventually finishing with 110 international appearances and ten goals.

Valderrama perhaps didn't deliver as often as he should have done through his career. He didn't shine outside his native country at club level, and in 1994, when great things were expected of Colombia at the World Cup, the team didn't get past the first round.

MARCO VAN BASTEN

Country: Holland
Born: October 31, 1964
Position: Centre-forward
Clubs: Ajax, AC Milan

Opposite clockwise from top: Gianluca Vialli ended his glittering career playing for Chelsea; Marco Van Basten, the complete centre-forward; Paul Van Himst, perhaps Belgium's finest ever player.

Some goals are so stunning they will never be forgotten. Marco van Basten was the scorer of such a goal. During the 1988 European Championship final against the Soviet Union, Arnold Mühren hoisted a high ball towards the penalty area, Van Basten met the ball as it

dropped, and from a tight angle sent a volley screaming into the net. It clinched the trophy for the Dutch and set the seal on a tournament of great personal success for the striker. Van Basten had earlier destroyed England with a hat-trick in the group stage and beaten Germany with a semi-final winner.

After astounding performances for Ajax – he once scored 37 goals in a season – he joined Italian giants AC Milan in 1987. Even in Serie A, the goals didn't dry up and the Dutchman helped Milan to league glory in 1988, 1992 and 1993, and European Cup wins in 1989 (when he scored twice) and 1990. But against Marseille in the 1993 final, Van Basten sustained an ankle injury that forced his retirement before the age of 30. Had it not been for that, he may just have helped Holland to World Cup victory in 1994.

PAUL VAN HIMST

Country: Belgium
Born: October 2, 1943
Position: Forward
Clubs: Anderlecht, RWD Molenbeek, Eendracht Aalst

Paul Van Himst is arguably the most decorated player in Belgian history. Four times he was named the Belgian Player Of The Year and he made 81 appearances for the national side, scoring 31 goals.

A product of the Anderlecht youth team, Van Himst made his club debut at the age of 16 and just a year later he was drafted into the national side. A technically outstanding and elegant player, he was so highly regarded that he was once dubbed 'the White Pele'.

He won the Belgian title eight times with Anderlecht and later led them as coach to UEFA Cup success in 1983.

OBDULIO VARELA

Country: Uruguay
Born: September 20, 1917
Position: Centre-half
Clubs: Wanderers, Peñarol

Obdulio Varela, a gifted attacking centre-half, was the inspiration behind Uruguay's 1950 World Cup triumph. In the decisive match against hosts Brazil, team captain Varela magnificently held his defence firm against relentless Brazilian attacks. After the break he drove his team forward and helped them turn a single goal deficit into a shock 2-1 win. Varela was in charge again for his swansong four years later when Uruguay finished third.

At the age of 24 he had won his first international honour in Uruguay's triumphant Copa América team. He was subsequently signed by Peñarol with whom he won six Uruguayan league titles.

VAVA

Country: Brazil
Born: November 12, 1934
Position: Forward
Clubs: Recife, Vasco da Gama, Atlético Madrid, Palmeiras, Botafogo

Real name Edvaldo Izidio Neto, Vava originally played as a winger but converted to centre-forward to accommodate Pele in the 1958 Brazilian starting line-up. Curiously under-used by his country, he only played 20 full internationals spread over a decade – scoring 15 goals – but he was the ultimate big stage player. He scored two of Brazil's five goals in the 1958 World Cup Final victory against Sweden, and another in the 3-1 win over the Czechs in 1962. At club level his spell at Atlético Madrid was successful in terms of goals, but it was cut short due to homesickness and a desire to represent his country.

GIANLUCA VIALLI

Country: Italy
Born: July 9, 1964
Position: Forward
Clubs: Cremonese, Sampdoria, Juventus, Chelsea

Vialli started his career with hometown club Cremonese, before joining Sampdoria in 1984. His eight seasons with the Genoa-based side coincided with the most successful period in their history. Sampdoria won three Italian Cups, the European Cup Winners' Cup in 1990 and enjoyed a first league title success in 1991, with Vialli scoring 19 goals in 26 games. Vialli left Sampdoria for Juventus for £12million in 1992 and his personal success story continued, captaining the Turin side to European Champions Cup glory against Ajax in 1996. A somewhat lacklustre international career with Italy now over, he joined Chelsea later the same year, going on to become the most successful coach in the club's history.

IVO VIKTOR

Country: Czechoslovakia
Born: May 21, 1942
Position: Goalkeeper
Club: Dukla Prague

Ivo Viktor will always be remembered for his magnificent performances for Czechoslovakia on their way to winning the 1976 European Championship. The goalkeeper, who was never booked in his career, was outstanding in the two-legged quarter-final clash with the Soviet Union, equally superb in both the semi-final against Holland and in the final against West Germany, where he made the decisive save in a 5-4 penalty shoot-out win. In that year

he was voted the Czech Player Of The Year for the fifth time. The first two of his 63 international appearances were won at the Maracana Stadium against Brazil and at Wembley against England in the 1960s.

RUDI VÖLLER

Country: West Germany, Germany
Born: March 13, 1960
Position: Forward
Clubs: Stuttgart Kickers, Munich 1860, Werder Bremen, Roma, Marseille, Bayer Leverkusen

A classic goal poacher, Rudi Völler is remembered as much for his bubble perm and the spittle Frank Rijkaard deposited in it in 1990. He began his career in 1978 with Stuttgart Kickers but established his reputation as a top predator with Werder Bremen, being named German Footballer Of The Year in 1982. He joined Roma in 1987 where he scored 69 goals in 197 appearances and reached a UEFA Cup final. He left for Marseille in 1992, winning the European Cup before finishing at Bayer Leverkusen.

Playing 90 times for his country, and with 47 goals, Völler ranks only behind Gerd Müller as his nation's top scorer. Having made his debut in 1982, he came on to score the equaliser that took the 1986 World Cup Final with Argentina to extra-time. Four years later he was a winner when West Germany had their revenge in a scrappy final.

Despite his lack of managerial experience he was appointed national manager in 2000 and surprised doubters by taking the team to the final of the 2002 World Cup.

FRITZ WALTER

Country: West Germany
Born: October 31, 1920
Position: Midfield/Forward
Clubs: Kaiserslautern

Only Franz Beckenbauer outranks Fritz Walter in the list of German football legends. Making his debut for home town club Kaiserslautern in 1937, Walter remained there for his entire career, playing 379 games and scoring an impressive 306 goals. He won two league titles in 1951 and 1953 with the club, top-scoring in the latter campaign with 38 goals. In 1985 Kaiserslautern recognised his achievements by renaming their stadium after him.

Walter made his international debut in 1940, scoring a hat-trick against Romania, but World War II interrupted his career. In 1948 he returned to football, now alongside his brother. At the age of 33, national team coach Sepp Herberger made him captain of the West German team for the 1954 World Cup in Switzerland. Walter scored three goals in the tournament, and his brother two, as the West Germans came back from a disastrous start against Hungary to win the final in the 'Miracle of Berne', making them the first siblings to win a World Cup.

Walter led his team again at the 1958 World Cup in Sweden, this time losing at the semi-final stage to the hosts. He retired the following year after 61 matches and 33 goals, but could have gone to Chile in 1962 had he listened to Herberger's entreaties. As Germany closed in on another World Cup final in June 2002, Walter died aged 81.

GEORGE WEAH

Country: Liberia
Born: October 1, 1966
Position: Centre-forward
Clubs: Young Survivors, Bongrang, Mighty Barolle, Tonnerre de Yaoundé, Monaco, Paris Saint-Germain, AC Milan, Chelsea, Manchester City, Marseille

Although born in Liberia, Weah holds French citizenship and has played for many different clubs in five different countries. He helped

Monaco win the French league title in 1991 and repeated the trick with Paris Saint-Germain in 1995. The striker's most successful period came in Italy with AC Milan, who he joined for £3.5million in 1995, his goals firing the club to the Serie A title in both 1996 and 1999. The former African, European and World Footballer Of The Year, Weah was also part of the Chelsea team which won the FA Cup in 2000 – the last one ever to be staged at the old Wembley Stadium.

In addition to his football skills, Weah is also known for the amount of charity work he does. He is as a chairman of UNICEF and has provided substantial financial support to the Liberian national team.

BILLY WRIGHT

Country: England
Born: February 6, 1924
Position: Centre-half
Club: Wolverhampton Wanderers

One of the most celebrated footballers of his day, Billy Wright joined Wolverhampton Wanderers as a ground staff boy in 1938 and stayed at Molineux in a one-club career that spanned 13 seasons and 490 appearances. During his tenure at the club he led them to FA Cup success in 1949, and three league titles in the 1950s. He was hardly the tallest centre-half in the world, but still managed to command the game both in the air and on the ground. Wright's popularity wasn't confined to the Black Country either, and as an automatic pick for the national team, he was captain of his country for 90 of the 105 games in which he played. He died of cancer in North London on September 3, 1994.

Above: Bobby Smith sees his effort stopped by Yashin in an England v Rest Of The World XI match. Below: Soviet hero Yashin playing England again, this time for his country in 1958.

LEV YASHIN

Country: Soviet Union
Born: October 22, 1929
Position: Goalkeeper
Club: Dynamo Moscow

Goalkeeping legends don't come much larger or imposing than Lev Yashin. Dressed in black, possessed of huge hands and, according to Gordon Banks, 'fingers the size of bananas', his nickname, the 'Black Spider', (also the 'Black Panther') was not hard to fathom.

Lev Ivanovich Yashin went to work in the same Moscow tool factory as his father at the age of 13 and played in goal for their football team. He was spotted by Dynamo Moscow but was on the verge of taking up a career as 'keeper for the club's ice hockey team when an injury to first choice football goalkeeper Aleksei 'Tiger' Khomich opened the door for him. He made his league debut in 1949 and went on to play 326 matches for the club, staying for a total of 22 years and winning five league championships and three cups.

Yashin is seen as the greatest goalkeeper in the history of the game and the first of the modern era. Extremely vocal, he kept his defence constantly on its toes and was one of the first goalkeepers to venture out of his area to kick the ball away. His huge throws helped launch rapid counter-attacks and he was also a penalty specialist, saving 150 in his career.

In 1963 he was named European Footballer Of The Year after letting in a miserly 14 goals in 38 league games, the only time the award has ever gone to a goalkeeper.

Yashin made his debut for the Soviet Union on September 8, 1954, in a 6-0 win over Sweden. In 1956 he won a gold medal with the Soviet team at the Melbourne Olympics, marking the beginning of a golden era for Soviet football. Yashin proved instrumental in securing the USSR its only major trophy of the modern era, making a string of crucial saves in the inaugural European Nations Cup in 1960 to deny Yugoslavia. Four years later he was still between the posts when the Soviet Union were runners-up.

Yashin was also instrumental in taking the Soviet Union to the quarter-finals of the World Cups of 1958 and 1962, where they were eliminated by the hosts on both occasions. However, he was blamed for both goals against Chile in 1962 and he subsequently went into premature retirement.

Four years later he was back at the World Cup in England as the side recorded its best performance in the tournament, reaching the semi-finals and losing narrowly to Germany with ten men. Named in the squad for the 1970 World Cup in Mexico, he would have set new records had he appeared in a match. In total he won 78 caps.

By the time of his retirement Yashin was regarded as a Soviet national hero to rank alongside cosmonaut Yuri Gagarin. He received the Order Of Lenin and Honoured Master Of Soviet Sport, and in 1971 some 120,000 spectators turned up for his final testimonial game between Dynamo Moscow and a Rest Of The World XI.

Sadly he suffered pain from a knee injury in his later years and had a leg amputated in 1986. He died on March 20, 1990, following complications from surgery. To celebrate his achievements FIFA introduced the Lev Yashin Award for the best goalkeeper at the World Cup in 1994. Its recipients so far have been Michel Preud'Homme of Belgium, France's Fabian Barthez and Germany's Oliver Kahn.

1946: Joins Dynamo Moscow ice hockey team as a goaltender.

1953: Opting for football, establishes himself as Dynamo Moscow's first-choice goalkeeper.

1954: Wins first of 78 caps for the Soviets in a 3-2 victory against Sweden.

1956: Forms part of the Soviet Union's Olympic gold medal winning team in Melbourne.

1959: Wins Soviet championship with Dynamo Moscow.

1960: Wins his first European Championship with the Soviet Union, with a 2-1 victory against Yugoslavia in the final.

1963: The 'Black Panther' is named European Footballer Of The Year.

1964: Soviet Union are beaten by Spain in the European Championship final.

1966: Stars in World Cup, as Soviet Union reach semi-finals.

1968: Receives the Order Of Lenin awarded by the Soviet government.

1970: Retires from the game with a testimonial match watched by 120,000 at the Lenin Stadium in Moscow.

1986: Has leg amputated after complications with a knee injury.

1990: Lev Yashin passes away on March 20 at the age of 60.

MARIO ZAGALO

Country: Brazil
Born: August 9, 1931
Position: Left-winger
Club: Botafogo

Mario Zagalo's name is synonymous with the World Cup, and he is the most successful individual in the history of the tournament having won it on four occasions with Brazil in various roles. In 1958 he played in his country's World Cup team as a left-winger. An intelligent player, Zagalo had a great match against Sweden in the final, scoring the fourth and creating Pele's second goal of the match as Brazil ran out 5-2 winners. He struck gold again in 1962, having dropped back to midfield and assuming a harder working role (he was known as 'the Little Ant' for his industry on the pitch). Ultimately it was his versatility that converted Brazil from the 4-2-4 formation to their trademark 4-3-3 playing style. In 1970, Zagalo coached one of the greatest attacking teams in World Cup history to success, and in 1994 he repeated the trick as technical adviser to coach Carlos Alberto.

RICARDO ZAMORA

Country: Spain
Born: January 21, 1901
Position: Goalkeeper
Clubs: Espanyol, Barcelona, Espanyol, Real Madrid, OGC Nizza

Ricardo Zamora was the first real hero of Spanish football, making just short of 50 appearances for Spain. He also became the first goalkeeper to save a World Cup penalty, against Brazil in the 1934 finals in Italy.

His first club was Espanyol, the city of Barcelona's 'other team', and after a short stint with Barça he returned to Espanyol and then completed a record-breaking transfer to Real Madrid. He won two titles and two Spanish cups at Real, having already won the cup twice with Barça and once with Espanyol.

He moved into management with Atlético Madrid, and later took over at Espanyol. He also had a stint in charge of the Spanish national side. Fittingly it was in his home city of Barcelona that Zamora died at the age of 77.

ZICO

Country: Brazil
Born: March 3, 1953
Position: Forward/Midfield
Clubs: Flamengo, Udinese, Flamengo, Kashima Antlers

The great Zico represented Brazil in three consecutive World Cups from 1978, and was seen at his best in Spain in 1982 where he was the outstanding player of the tournament. One of the game's greatest ever dead-ball strikers, he scored with one of his speciality free-kicks on his debut against Uruguay in 1977. He went on to add a further 51 goals to this total in his 73 internationals for his country, to leave himself second only behind Pele in Brazil's all-time goalscoring list. A wiry, dynamic yet tricky forward, he was just as adept at setting up his centre-forward as he was finding the goal for himself.

At club level he inspired Flamengo to victory in the Copa Liberatores in 1981, and was almost single-handedly responsible for the subsequent undoing of Liverpool in the World Club Cup in the same year. After the 1982 World Cup Finals he moved to Italy's Udinese, and was voted World Footballer Of The Year in 1983 – such accolades came easy to the great man, and he added this title to the three South American Player Of The Year awards he already possessed.

After a spell as Brazil's Minister of Sport, he joined Kashima Antlers to play his part in the setting up of the J-League in 1993. He took over as the coach of the Japanese national team after the 2002 World Cup.

DINO ZOFF

Country: Italy
Born: February 28, 1942
Position: Goalkeeper
Clubs: Udinese, Mantova, Napoli, Juventus

One of the finest goalkeepers of all-time, Zoff's career is packed with honours. He captained Italy to World Cup glory in Spain in 1982, held the Italian record for international appearances (112, with 59 as captain) and between 1973 and 1974 went 1,142 minutes without conceding a goal (an international record).

Initially rejected as a 14-year-old by Inter Milan and Juventus for being too small, he first signed professional forms with Udinese in 1961. But on his debut he was beaten five times by Fiorentina and the club were soon relegated. A more successful spell at Mantova followed, but it was at Napoli that Zoff's career truly took off, leading to an international call-up.

He made his debut for Italy in a European Championship quarter-final match against Bulgaria in April 1968, and he retained his place as the Italians went on to win the tournament. Zoff then joined Juventus in 1972, and went on to win six titles, two Italian cups and a UEFA Cup in 11 years at the club. His only major career disappointment was that he never won the European Cup, despite reaching the final twice.

Zoff retired from playing as a 40-year-old in 1982, going on to coach Italy's Olympic team, Juventus and Lazio, before taking the Italian senior team all the way to the final of the European Championship in 2000, where

after leading until the last minute of the game, they were beaten by France in extra-time, provoking his immediate resignation.

Above: Andoni Zubizarreta ended his international career at the France 98 World Cup.

ANDONI ZUBIZARRETA

Country: Spain
Born: October 23, 1961
Position: Goalkeeper
Clubs: Athletic Bilbao, Barcelona, Valencia

In January 1985 Andoni Zubizarreta made his international debut for Spain against Finland. Some 13 years later he played his 126th game for his country, capping an incredible career which included appearances in four separate World Cup tournaments – in 1986, 1990, 1994 and 1998.

He started out with Athletic Bilbao, winning two Spanish titles, before switching to Barcelona and enjoying the most successful spell of his club career. As well as further domestic honours, Zubizarreta triumphed in Europe, with Barça winning the European Cup Winners' Cup in 1989 and the European Cup in 1992; both against Sampdoria – and the 'keeper didn't concede a goal in either.

Zubizarreta left the Nou Camp in 1994 to join Valencia but continued to defy the years with top-level performances. He bowed out of international football after captaining Spain in the 1998 World Cup at the age of 37.

Opposite: Zico runs at the Argentina defence during the 1982 World Cup in Spain, a tournament at which he was the outstanding player.

GREAT PLAYERS OF TODAY

Above: Pablo Aimar, Argentina's Player Of The Year in 2000, challenges Liverpool's Dietmar Hamann in a Champions League tie at Anfield.

PABLO AIMAR

Country: Argentina
Born: November 3, 1979
Position: Midfield
Clubs: River Plate, Valencia

Pablo Cesar Aimar, son of Ricardo Aimar of Newell's Old Boys, made his name at River Plate as an excellent playmaker. 'The Little Clown' was part of Argentina's 1997 World Youth Cup winning team and at 18 he inherited the great Enzo Francescoli's number 10 shirt. Three years later Valencia coach Hector Cuper signed the 21-year-old for a staggering £13million. He played his first game for Valencia against Manchester United in the European Champions League. By then he was already an established Argentine international, having made his debut against Bolivia in June 2000. He was voted Argentina's Player Of The Year in 2000 at the age of 21.

SAMI AL-JABER

Country: Saudi Arabia
Born: December 11, 1972
Position: Forward
Clubs: Al Hilal, Wolverhampton Wanderers, Al Hilal

Right: Michael Ballack, a great German talent and a goalscoring threat from midfield.

Discovered as a 15-year-old by Al Hilal, Sami Al-Jaber has been Saudi Arabia's golden boy. Winning the Saudi championship in 1996, he was voted Most Valuable Player in the club's 1996 Asian Cup Winners' Cup triumph. The following year he was the match winner with both goals in the Asian Super Cup. For Saudi Arabia his direct style of running at defenders made him one of the most feared strikers in Asia. He won the 1994 Gulf Cup, the 1996 Asian Cup, and played at three successive World Cup finals up until 2002. He had a four-month period on loan at Wolves in 2000.

KARIM BAGHERI

Country: Iran
Born: February 20, 1974
Position: Midfield
Clubs: Teraktor, Keshavarz, Pirouzi, Arminia Bielefeld, Charlton Athletic, Al Nasr, Persopolis, Pirouzi

Along with Ali Daei, Karim Bagheri Koroygh became the first Iranian to play professional football in Europe when he signed for Germany's Arminia Bielefeld. Although he had to endure relegation and was a stop-gap for every outfield position, Bagheri did reasonably well. However, on the international stage he has demonstrated his natural ability as a goalscorer with six goals in Iran's 19-0 thrashing of Guam and a World Cup qualifying record seven goals in the 17-0 defeat of the Maldives on their way to the 2002 World Cup Finals. He is regarded as the heart of the national team, where his ball-winning skills are responsible for making things happen.

MICHAEL BALLACK

Country: Germany
Born: September 29, 1976
Position: Midfield
Clubs: BSG Motor Karl-Marx-Stadt, Chemnitzer FC, Kaiserslautern, Bayer Leverkusen, Bayern Munich

Ballack is the biggest talent in German football and the main goal threat from midfield in both the current Bayern Munich team and the German national sides. He is often likened to the great German legend of the 1970s, Franz Beckenbauer. Ballack was booked early in the 2002 World Cup semi-final, which meant he was suspended for the final, yet showed tremendous character to score the goal against South Korea that took an otherwise average German team to the final where, without him, they were comprehensively beaten by Brazil.

Ballack has played at the highest level of German football from a young age, having won the 1998 league title with Kaiserslautern, steered Bayer Leverkusen to a Champions Cup final in 2002, and spearheaded a successful season with Bayern Munich in 2003. Like many great German players over the years, Ballack is not afraid to air his views in public, sometimes to the annoyance of his bosses.

FABIEN BARTHEZ

Country: France
Born: June 28, 1971
Position: Goalkeeper
Clubs: Toulouse, Marseille, Monaco, Manchester United

Ever the extrovert, Barthez has won all the major honours in the game, with domestic titles in both France and England and success in the Champions Cup with Marseille. He played a leading role in helping France to the magnificent double of the World Cup on home turf in 1998 and the European Championship in 2000. Superbly athletic and excellent at distributing the ball from the hand or with his feet, he is one of the most entertaining goalkeepers in the game. His father had been a top-class rugby player.

YILDIRAY BASTURK

Country: Turkey
Born: December 24, 1978
Position: Midfield
Clubs: Spfr Wanne-Eickel, Wattenschied 09, VfL Bochum, Bayer Leverkusen

Born and raised in Germany to Turkish parents, Basturk has developed into one of the most exciting players in the Bundesliga and the Turkish national team. In 2000, at the age of 21, he became the youngest captain in the Bundesliga when he led out Bochum. Relegation after 104 appearances led to a £4million move to Bayer Leverkusen. Basturk is a natural playmaker who was spotted by Turkey very early – he was selected at Under-16 level and his full debut followed in January 1998 in Albania. He was instrumental in Turkey's third place at the 2002 World Cup.

GABRIEL BATISTUTA

Country: Argentina
Born: February 1, 1969
Position: Forward
Clubs: Newell's Old Boys, River Plate, Boca Juniors, Fiorentina, Roma, Inter Milan, Al Arabi

Born in Avellaneda north of Buenos Aires, Gabriel Batistuta idolised Mario Kempes but outstripped his hero to become Argentina's all-time top scorer with 56 goals in 78 appearances, earning the nickname 'Bati-Gol' for his exploits. He starred in three World Cups in 1994, 1998 and 2002, but made his league debut for Newell's Old Boys in 1988. He built his reputation with Boca Juniors, becoming the league's top scorer in their championship-winning season, before moving to Fiorentina. There he became a club legend, top scoring in 1994-95 before switching to Roma and finally winning the Scudetto in 2001. He joined Inter, and then Al Arabi, in the twilight of his career.

DAVID BECKHAM

Country: England
Born: May 2, 1975
Position: Right midfield
Clubs: Manchester United, Real Madrid

On the opening day of the 1996-97 season David Beckham chipped the opposition goalkeeper from the halfway line, and in scoring the type of goal that had eluded even Pele, he began his inexorable rise to football superstardom. The London-born Manchester United trainee's subsequent marriage to Spice Girl, Victoria Adams, did little to take the media spotlight off him. His assured performances and long-range goals helped United to the Premier League title that season, and earned him a place in Glenn Hoddle's England team.

Despite rattling in a trademark free-kick against Colombia in the World Cup group stages, France 98 was a personal disaster for Beckham, who was sent-off against Argentina for a petulant kick at Diego Simeone in his country's narrow quarter-final defeat. As a result, the United Number 7 was made into a national pariah, and brainlessly booed by opposing fans whenever he played for his club the following season.

A testament to his strength of character, the barracking failed to have a detrimental effect on his football, Beckham playing a vital role in United's treble-winning team (Premier League, FA Cup and Champions League), his efforts also earning him second place behind Rivaldo in the voting for both World and European Player Of The Year awards. His main attributes are his fantastic range of passing and crossing, coupled with a world-class ability at free-kicks. However, his game is also based on tireless running, a steely determination, and a ferocious will to win.

Caretaker England manager Peter Taylor rewarded his accomplishments with the England captaincy for a friendly against Italy in November 2000, and 'Becks' was to retain the armband with the appointment of Sven Goran Eriksson. The winning goal in the 2002 World Cup qualifier against Finland at Anfield signalled the start of David Beckham's rehabilitation from scapegoat to national hero, the culmination of which was a remarkable individual performance against Greece at Old Trafford, where he scored the last-ditch free-kick equaliser that took England to the World Cup in Japan. It also landed him the BBC's coveted Sports Personality Of The Year Award.

A broken metatarsal received in a game against Deportivo La Coruña threatened Beckham's participation in the tournament, and his lack of fitness hampered much of his play. However, he was still able to gain a degree of revenge when he slotted home the winning penalty against Argentina. Much speculation about a move to Spanish giants Real Madrid surrounded Beckham at the end of the 2003 season, but he still managed to pick up a sixth league winner's medal with United before moving to the Spanish giants.

Above: The most famous living Englishman. David Beckham's pinpoint long-range free-kicks and tireless energy have saved his country from embarrassment on several occasions.

Opposite clockwise from top left: Alen Boksic, who scored the winner for Hadjuk Split in the last ever Yugoslav Cup; Laurent Blanc enjoyed a long international career with France, but missed the 1998 World Cup Final through suspension; central defender Sol Campbell, who made a controversial move from Tottenham to Arsenal; and Cafu captained 2002 World Cup winners Brazil.

DENNIS BERGKAMP

Country: Holland
Born: May 10, 1969
Position: Centre-forward
Clubs: Ajax, Inter Milan, Arsenal

Dennis Bergkamp is one of the most famous products of the famed Ajax youth system, and having made his debut against Roda JC in December 1986, he went on to become the pivotal figure in a side that won the Dutch championship, the UEFA Cup and the Cup Winners' Cup in his time at the club. He was the Dutch league's top goalscorer between 1991 and 1993, and his total of 103 goals in 185 games made him a most wanted striker.

He joined Inter Milan in a £12million deal in 1993 but his 11 goals in two seasons – despite another UEFA Cup success – was regarded as a failure. A £7.5million transfer to Arsenal in the summer of 1995 shocked the football world, but it proved to be a shrewd move by the north London club. Bergkamp soon began to weave his magic as both provider and scorer following Arsene Wenger's arrival at the club.

Under Wenger Bergkamp played an instrumental part in Arsenal's league and cup double of 1998, and he capped the season by winning the PFA and Footballer Writers' Player Of The Year awards. He also played a prominent role in the Dutch side that reached the semi-finals of the World Cup.

Although many argue he failed to recapture his form in the ensuing seasons, Bergkamp was back to his best as Arsenal secured their second double in 2002.

Below: Dennis Bergkamp's magic touches made him the Dutch league's top goalscorer between 1991 and 1993.

OLIVER BIERHOFF

Country: Germany
Born: May 1, 1968
Position: Forward
Clubs: Bayer Uerdingen, Hamburg, Borussia Mönchengladbach, Casino Salzburg, Ascoli, Udinese, AC Milan, Monaco, Chievo

German striker Oliver Bierhoff has often confounded his critics. A brilliant header of the ball, he has consistently added to his game, reaching the heights of Serie A. Born in Karlsruhe, he made his reputation at Borussia Mönchengladbach before moving to Austria and then to Italy, signing for Inter Milan but being loaned to Ascoli. He moved on to Udinese in 1995 and became top scorer in Serie A with 27 goals, earning a transfer to AC Milan. He won 70 caps for Germany, scoring 37 goals, and is best remembered for his 'Golden Goal' in the final of the 1996 European Championship and a six-minute hat-trick against Northern Ireland.

LAURENT BLANC

Country: France
Born: November 19, 1965
Position: Defender
Clubs: Montpellier, Napoli, Nimes, Saint-Etienne, Auxerre, Barcelona, Marseille, Inter Milan, Manchester United

A graceful defender, Laurent Blanc began as an attacking midfielder but converted to defence early in his career. He switched regularly from one club and league to another, winning few trophies, but made his name at international level playing for France for more than a decade. He impressed at three European Championships, particularly in 2000 when France emerged as winners, and he starred at the 1998 World Cup, but missed the final through suspension. Superbly confident on the ball and a calming influence in the team, he won 97 caps and scored 16 goals in becoming one of France's greatest players. He retired in the summer of 2003.

CUAUHTEMOC BLANCO

Country: Mexico
Born: January 17, 1973
Position: Forward
Clubs: América, Necaxa, América, Real Valladolid, América

One moment from the 1998 World Cup that will be forever recalled is Cuauhtemoc Blanco's two-footed trickery that so mesmerised his South Korean opponents. That moment epitomises Blanco as a player too. He is a quick-thinking and nimble footballer who is unpredictable and exciting to watch, one of the most thrilling players and prolific goalscorers to grace the international stage currently. However, with the exception of two seasons in Spain with Real Valladolid, his club career has been restricted to the Mexican league, with América (three spells) and Necaxa.

ALEN BOKSIC

Country: Yugoslavia, Croatia
Born: January 31, 1970
Position: Forward
Clubs: Hajduk Split, Cannes, Marseille, Lazio, Juventus, Lazio, Middlesbrough

Alen Boksic was one of the most technically gifted strikers to emerge from the former Yugoslav league. He earned the reputation of not only being a goalscorer but a creator of goals too, securing a place in Yugoslavia's 1990 World Cup squad. He also scored the winner in the last politically-charged Yugoslav Cup for Hajduk Split against Red Star Belgrade. He moved to France to join Marseille, where he partnered Rudi Völler to French league and Champions Cup success. Boksic was sold to Lazio for £8million and he stayed in Italy for six years before moving to Middlesbrough. He retired in the summer of 2003.

CAFU

Country: Brazil
Born: June 19, 1970
Position: Right-back
Clubs: São Paulo, Real Zaragoza, Palmeiras, Roma, AC Milan

Marcos Evangelista de Moraes Cafu has played in a record three successive World Cup finals for Brazil and ended up a winner twice, in 1994 and 2002. The latter was extra special as he was captain of the side that defeated Germany 2-0 to lift the trophy. Cafu is regarded as Brazil's greatest right-back, succeeding Jorginho in the role. He made his international debut in September 1990 against Spain. He gained success with São Paulo in the Copa Libertadores in 1992 and 1993, and went on to win the UEFA Cup with Real Zaragoza in 1995 and the Italian Serie A title with Roma in 2001, before signing for AC Milan in 2003.

SOL CAMPBELL

Country: England
Born: September 18, 1974
Position: Defender
Clubs: Tottenham Hotspur, Arsenal

Sol Campbell stunned British football when he quit Tottenham for arch-rivals Arsenal in the summer of 2001. As a free agent, it was expected Campbell would join either Barcelona or Bayern Munich, but when he was paraded

Right: Hernan Crespo became one of the most expensive players ever when he made his £36million move from Parma to Lazio in 2000.

at a press conference in an Arsenal shirt, his actions outraged Spurs fans who felt a real sense of betrayal. Their disgusted reactions were understandable as Campbell had been with the club since a schoolboy and had enjoyed nine seasons as a first-team player and captain, and had become an England regular.

Fine displays at the 1998 World Cup saw Campbell's status elevated, and as a fiercely ambitious individual, a lack of investment and silverware at White Hart Lane prompted him to take such decisive action. The move was controversial, but justified as he won the league and cup double in his first season.

ROBERTO CARLOS

Country: Brazil
Born: April 10, 1973
Position: Left-back
Clubs: União São João, Palmeiras, Inter Milan, Real Madrid

As a regular starter for both Brazil and Real Madrid, Roberto Carlos is one of the most admired players in world football, and his dynamic, rampaging style of play from left-back has won him many of the game's major honours, including the World Cup in 2002. After failing to settle at Inter Milan following his move from Brazil in 1995, he found himself part of a very talented Real Madrid side. Legendary for his ability with a dead ball, Carlos scored one of the most memorable free-kicks the game has ever seen in the pre-World Cup Tournoi in France in 1997.

Below: In spite of being an excellent left-back for club and country, Roberto Carlos will always be remembered for his remarkable swinging free kick for Brazil during a World Cup warm-up tournament in France.

IKER CASILLAS

Country: Spain
Born: May 20, 1981
Position: Goalkeeper
Club: Real Madrid

Born in Madrid, Iker Casillas' potential came to fruition when he helped Spain to both World Youth Championship and Meridian Cup success in 1999. His progress continued when he replaced the injured Bodo Illgner to perform heroics as Real defeated Valencia in the 2000 Champions Cup Final but, at the tender age of 19, he failed to live up to his newly-found fame and was replaced in the Real goal by Cesar Sanchez. A little older and wiser, he reclaimed the jersey for the 2002 final against Bayer Leverkusen and, having helped preserve a slender 2-1 lead with a number of fine saves, he has remained in goal for club and country ever since.

ANDY COLE

Country: England
Born: October 15, 1971
Position: Forward
Clubs: Arsenal, Fulham, Bristol City, Newcastle United, Manchester United, Blackburn Rovers

Much-maligned and under-rated, Cole has proven to be one of the best forwards of his generation in club football, yet has never been able to prove himself on the international stage. Unable to break through at Arsenal, Cole dropped down the leagues to become an immediate hit at Bristol City. Kevin Keegan provided the headline writers with a dream by taking Cole to Newcastle, where he grabbed 55 goals in 70 games, before Manchester United paid a British record £6.25million for

him. In seven years at Old Trafford he proved his game was more than just scoring, helping United land the Champions League, before moving on to Blackburn in December 2001.

HERNAN CRESPO

Country: Argentina
Born: July 5, 1975
Position: Forward
Clubs: River Plate, Parma, Lazio, Inter Milan, Chelsea

In 2000 Hernan Crespo moved from Parma to Lazio in a staggering £36million deal. Lazio parted with Maitias Almeyda, Sergio Conceicao and £12million in cash. Crespo had been instrumental in Parma's success in winning the UEFA Cup, the Italian Cup and Super Cup in 1999. Parma themselves had parted with £10million for Argentina's 1994 Young Player Of The Year. He made his international debut in February 1995 against Bulgaria. River Plate coach Daniel Passarella groomed Crespo to become a prolific goalscorer for both club and country and in 1996 he scored twice for River Plate in their Libertadores Cup final victory.

ALI DAEI

Country: Iran
Born: March 21, 1969
Position: Forward
Clubs: Javanan Ardabil, Esteghlal Ardabil, Tahirani Tehran, Tejarat Tehran, Pirouzi Tehran, Alasad, Arminia Bielefeld, Bayern Munich, Hertha Berlin, Al Shabab, Pirouzi Tehran

Ali Daei is one of Iran's most popular and famous players. He was the first Iranian (along with Karim Bagheri) to play professional football in Europe. In 1998, after he was dropped from the national team for criticising tactics, fans organised a poll calling for (and getting) his reinstatement. Daei made his international debut in June 1993 against Oman and went on to become one of Asia's most dangerous strikers, forming an excellent partnership with Khodadad Azizi. In 1996 he scored 22 international goals including eight at the Asian Cup tournament. He was voted the 1999 Asian Player Of The Year.

FRANK DE BOER

Country: Holland
Born: May 15, 1970
Position: Defender
Clubs: Ajax, Barcelona, Galatasaray

Frank De Boer started his Ajax career at 14 and developed as an attack-minded left-back. Having made his debut as an 18-year-old, he quickly established himself to feature in the Ajax sides that won the 1992 UEFA Cup against Torino and the 1995 Champions Cup Final against Milan. In just over ten seasons, he had won five league titles and two Dutch Cups, while becoming a prominent figure in the Dutch side. His versatility promted Louis Van Gaal to take him to Barcelona in 1999 for £8million, but his career at the Nou Camp has been chequered, including a failed drugs test in March 2001 that was later quashed. He transferred to Galatasaray in July 2003.

ALESSANDRO DEL PIERO

Country: Italy
Born: November 9, 1974
Position: Centre-forward/midfielder
Clubs: Padova, Juventus

Signed from Serie B side Padova in 1993 as a 19-year-old, it wasn't long before the mercurial Alessandro Del Piero had forced himself into the Juventus first team, where he has since become an inspirational figure. Although mostly known for his passing and creative play, it isn't unusual for Del Piero to get among the goals: he scored an impressive 21 times in 32 league appearances during the 1997-98 season as Juventus went on to win the title.

Del Piero has never really hit the same heights for the Italian national team, his slow recovery from a knee ligament injury that had kept him sidelined for nine months limited his effectiveness at the 1998 World Cup Finals. He started Euro 2000 in fine form, netting an exquisite goal against Sweden, but having come on as a second-half substitute in the final, missed two gilt-edged opportunities to score. Coach Giovanni Trapattoni used Del Piero only sparingly in the 2002 World Cup, but he still came off the bench against Mexico to score the equaliser five minutes from time that helped Italy qualify for the second round phase.

MARCEL DESAILLY

County: France
Born: September 7, 1968
Position: Defender
Clubs: Nantes, Marseille, AC Milan, Chelsea

A colossal player at club and international level, Marcel Desailly is one of the greatest defenders of all time. He started his career alongside Didier Deschamps at Nantes, moved to Marseille, winning the Champions Cup in 1993, and scored in the final when AC Milan clinched the trophy the following year. Immensely strong and powerful, he was a midfielder during five years at Milan but always played in defence for France and was a key figure as they won the World Cup in 1998 and the European Championship in 2000. He became France's most capped player of all time in April 2003.

EL HADJI DIOUF

Country: Senegal
Born: January 15, 1981
Position: Forward
Clubs: Linguere, Sochaux, Rennes, Lens, Liverpool

El Hadji Diouf is one of the brightest talents to emerge from Africa. This gifted footballer, like many of his fellow Senegalese players, was quickly snapped up by the French league as a teenager. Initially he earned a reputation as a wild player but he has matured into one of the most dangerous strikers in European football. In April 2000 Diouf made his international debut against Benin. His nine-goal haul in eight appearances, including successive hat-tricks against Algeria and Namibia, helped Senegal to their first World Cup in 2002 and led to a £10million move to the English Premiership with Liverpool.

Above: Marcel Desailly, France's most capped player of all time.

LANDON DONOVAN

Country: United States
Born: March 4, 1982
Position: Forward
Clubs: Bayer Leverkusen, San Jose Earthquakes

Donovan is the golden boy of American football. He has progressed through the ranks, representing his country at every level, becoming Player Of The Tournament at the 1999 Under-17 World Championship. A brief spell with Bayer Leverkusen followed but Donovan was unable to establish himself. As a teenager, he was instrumental in San Jose's 2001 MLS Championship winning team. He scored on his full international debut, being voted Player of the Game in the 2-0 win over Mexico in October 2000. He became an automatic choice in the national team, helping the USA to the 2002 World Cup quarter-finals.

EDMILSON

Country: Brazil
Born: July 10, 1976
Position: Centre-back
Clubs: São Paulo, Lyon

Edmilson Jose Gomes de Moraes, the son of an orange picker and amateur footballer, was Brazil's attack-minded centre-back in a three-man defence in the 2002 World Cup winning team. He magnificently dealt with Germany's aerial attack in the final, while his desire to cross the halfway line at every opportunity led to a spectacular first international goal with an overhead kick against Costa Rica. He made his name with São Paulo as a midfielder and was captain of the Paulista championship-winning team in 2000 before joining French club Lyon, with whom he won the 2002 French title.

Left: El Hadji Diouf, whose performances in the 2002 World Cup earned him a £10million move to Liverpool.

Above: Luis Enrique, one of the few players to represent both Barcelona and Real Madrid.

STEFAN EFFENBERG

Country: Germany
Born: August 2, 1968
Position: Midfield
Clubs: Borussia Mönchengladbach, Bayern Munich, Fiorentina, Borussia Mönchengladbach, Bayern Munich, Wolfsburg, Al-Arabi

Stefan Effenberg has graced some of Europe's top teams and at his peak was one of Europe's top players, but he will probably be best remembered for being sent home from the 1994 World Cup for making obscene gestures at the German fans. It was a rash act that more or less ended his international career as he only added two more German caps to his collection afterwards, bringing his overall tally up to 35. A German championship winner with Mönchengladbach aged just 22, he had two spells at the club, as he did with Bayern Munich, with whom he won two further championship medals. Effenberg also had a spell with Fiorentina in the early 1990s, but is now nearing the end of his career, accepting a lucrative contract with Qatari side Al-Arabi.

EMERSON

Country: Brazil
Born: April 4, 1976
Position: Midfield
Clubs: Gremio, Botafogo, Bayer Leverkusen, Roma, Boavista, Spartak Moscow

Emerson Ferreira da Rosa is that rare breed: a tenacious Brazilian who has the reputation as a hard man. His propensity to commit fouls is offset by his versatility – he can play just about anywhere in any formation. He made his international debut against Ecuador in September 1997, won the 1999 Copa América and was named captain of Brazil's 1999 Confederations Cup squad. However, he missed out on Brazil's 2002 World Cup

campaign by dislocating his shoulder after going in goal in training for the benefit of photographers before the tournament. He has proved equally adept in the German and Italian leagues, enjoying spells with Bayer Leverkusen and Roma respectively.

LUIS ENRIQUE

Country: Spain
Born: May 8, 1970
Position: Midfield
Clubs: Sporting Gijon, Real Madrid, Barcelona

One of a very few players ever to represent both Barcelona and Real Madrid at senior level, Luis Enrique has been one of the most consistent performers in La Liga over the past decade and has more than 100 goals to his name in Spain's top flight. The hardworking but temperamental Enrique began his career at Gijon as a striker before reverting to midfield while at Real Madrid. He picked up a Spanish league title in 1995 with Real, and has added two more and a Cup Winners' Cup with Barcelona. Enrique made his international debut in 1996 and has been a permanent fixture in the national side ever since, featuring in the last two Spanish World Cup campaigns.

RIO FERDINAND

Country: England
Born: November 8, 1978
Position: Defender
Clubs: West Ham, Leeds United, Manchester United

Rio Ferdinand is the YTS kid from Peckham who became the world's most expensive defender. Signed to West Ham United in 1995 he soon earned comparisons to local legend Bobby Moore for his composure on the ball.

He made his league debut on May 5, 1996 and his international debut against Cameroon in November 1998, demonstrating the class that would later make him such a success at the 2002 World Cup. He joined Leeds United in November 2000 for a record fee of £18million and helped them to the semi-final of the Champions Cup. Manchester United moved in with another record fee of £30million and he won a championship medal in his first season with the club.

LUIS FIGO

Position: Midfield
Country: Portugal
Born: November 4, 1972
Clubs: Sporting Lisbon, Barcelona, Real Madrid

A strong, tricky winger, Luis Felipe Madeira Figo has enthralled fans across Europe – particularly in Spain, where he has worn the shirts of both Barcelona and Real Madrid. His career began in the humble surroundings of the alleyways of Lisbon where he played for the street team Os Pastilhas, and it was here that he attracted the attentions of Sporting Lisbon, signing schoolboy forms at 11.

Even as a teenage player Figo received international acclaim, helping Portugal to third place in the FIFA Under-16s tournament in 1989 before winning the FIFA World Junior Championship two years later with the Under-20s team. After making his full debut for Sporting Lisbon at the age of 17, and helping them to second place in the league and a Portuguese Cup win in 1995, he attracted the attention of Europe's big guns and signed for Barcelona for £1.5million.

Under managers Johan Cruyff, Bobby Robson and Louis Van Gaal, Figo developed into a world-class player, mesmerising fans and defenders with his quick feet and acute football brain. Figo helped the team too, driving them to success in the Cup Winners' Cup and Super Cup in 1997, two Spanish league titles in 1998 and 1999, and two Spanish Cups in 1997 and 1998.

After a three-year love affair with the Nou Camp and a hugely successful Euro 2000 (Figo helped Portugal to the semi-finals and was viewed by many as the best player of the tournament), he made a controversial big-money move to arch rivals Real Madrid. His impact was immediate, both on an off the pitch. Alongside team-mates Roberto Carlos and Raúl, and later Zinedine Zidane and Ronaldo, Figo steered the best club side in the world to the league championship in 2001 and 2003, plus the Champions Cup in 2002.

Away from the field he had caused an outrage that would never be forgiven in Barcelona, but the anger that greeted his departure (a pig's head was thrown at him

Opposite: Luis Figo was regarded as the best player of the tournament at Euro 2000.

Right: Rio Ferdinand became the world's most expensive defender with his £30million move from Leeds to Manchester United.

Right: Thierry Henry's conversion from winger to striker at Arsenal has seen him become one of the most deadly goalscorers in Europe.

during a clash between the two teams) was as much to do with his exceptional talent as it was to do with traditional rivalry, as testified by Real Madrid's technical director, Jorge Valdano. 'We are so used to Figo playing brilliantly,' he said, 'that we think he's playing badly when he just plays normally.'

STEVEN GERRARD

Country: England
Born: June 16, 1976
Position: Midfield
Clubs: Liverpool

A product of the Liverpool youth academy, Steven Gerrard is one of the brightest prospects in English football. Making his debut in a European tie during the 1998-99 season against Celta Vigo at Anfield, his robust, all-action style from the centre of midfield has seen him establish a regular place in the first team at club level, and he was an integral part of the Liverpool side that won a trio of cup competitions in 2001 (UEFA Cup, League Cup and FA Cup). He is also a valuable member of the national team, and scored England's second goal from long range in the historic 5-1 demolition of Germany in the 2002 World Cup qualifier. He missed the subsequent finals through injury, but looks to have a long international career ahead of him.

RYAN GIGGS

Country: Wales
Born: November 29, 1973
Position: Winger
Club: Manchester United

As one of the original members of Sir Alex Ferguson's 'Fledglings', Ryan Giggs has become the most decorated player in Manchester United's history. He made his debut as a 17-year-old substitute against Everton in March 1991 and immediately caught the eye with his unmatchable pace and dribbling skills. The comparisons with United legend George Best were plentiful and although he became a regular the following season, making his debut for Wales and winning the PFA Young Player Of The Year in the process, the campaign would end in disappointment as Leeds United pipped their rivals to the championship.

The title finally arrived at Old Trafford in 1993 for the first time in 26 years, signalling the start of the most illustrious period in the club's history. Giggs has played a prominent role every season and, despite constant links with a move to Serie A, has remained loyal to the club, winning eight Premiership titles, three FA Cups and, most famously, the Champions Cup in 1999.

JOSEP 'PEP' GUARDIOLA

Country: Spain
Born: January 18, 1971
Position: Midfield
Clubs: Barcelona, Brescia, Roma, Brescia

Josep Guardiola, or 'Pep', is the man who made Barcelona tick throughout the 1990s. After being handed his debut as a 19-year-old, he was at the heart of the team that won the Champions Cup two years later, and went on to win six titles. Very comfortable on the ball, he was the one who supplied ammunition for the likes of Michael Laudrup, Hristo Stoichkov, Romario and Ronaldo. He has won more than 40 caps for his country, but injury forced him out of the 1998 World Cup. He left Spain in 2001 for Brescia, moved to Roma, and was then loaned back to Brescia before quitting Italy to return to Spain.

THIERRY HENRY

Country: France
Born: August 17, 1977
Position: Forward
Clubs: Monaco, Juventus, Arsenal

A wonderfully fast and powerful striker, Henry is among the finest in the world. Currently scoring goals at Arsenal, he started as a winger

at Monaco and was France's top scorer with three goals when they won the World Cup in 1998. Signing for Juventus in 1999, he quickly moved on and found success at Arsenal, where he converted to a centre-forward. He was outstanding at Euro 2000 and helped Arsenal clinch the double in 2002. Capable of scoring goals from every range, he is one of the best all-round strikers of the current era and a terrific sight in full flight.

Right: Ryan Giggs, Manchester United's most decorated player, made his first team debut at the age of 17 in 1991.

FERNANDO HIERRO

Country: Spain
Born: March 23, 1968
Position: Centre-back/Midfield
Clubs: Real Valladolid, Real Madrid, Al Rayyan

Fernando Hierro, Spain's most-capped outfield player, was justifiably described by coach Fabio Capello as 'the Spanish Baresi'. Malaga-born Hierro is a tough-tackling ball-winner who holds the record for the most bookings and sendings-off in the history of the Spanish league. However, he is also a skilful player, comfortable as a centre-back with Real Madrid or in a midfield holding role with Spain. He has featured in four successive World Cup squads, evolving from non-playing member in 1990 to captain in 2002. He has won the Champions Cup three times, the Spanish title five times, as well as the Spanish Cup and World Club Cup. He moved to Qatar in 2003.

JUNICHI INAMOTO

Country: Japan
Born: September 18, 1979
Position: Midfield
Clubs: Gamba Osaka, Arsenal, Fulham

Junichi Inamoto wrote his name in the record books when he scored against Russia to record Japan's first ever World Cup win in 2002. Inamoto is a defensive midfielder with a holding role for the national team. He made his debut at schoolboy level at just 14 years of age, went on to win the Asian Under-16 Championship in 1994 and played in the World Under-17 Championship a year later. In 1997, at the age of 17, he made his debut in J.League with Gamba Osaka after winning the Youth Cup. By August 2000 he had 100 J.League appearances to his name. His move to Arsenal wasn't a success, as he made just a handful of cup appearances, but after catching the eye at the 2002 World Cup, he found a more appreciative home in Fulham.

FILIPPO INZAGHI

Country: Italy
Born: August 9, 1973
Position: Centre-forward
Clubs: Piacenza, Leffe, Piacenza, Parma, Atalanta, Juventus, AC Milan

A lethal opportunist in the penalty area, Filippo Inzaghi's best season to date as a striker came with Atalanta in 1996-97, when he netted 24 times in 33 league games. He was immediately snapped up by Juventus and stayed in Turin for four seasons, winning a league title in 1998 and losing 1-0 to Real Madrid in the final of the 1998 Champions Cup. Inzaghi played three matches for Italy at the 1998 World Cup

Finals, and scored twice for his country at the European Championship two years later. He also scored seven times in six games for Italy during their qualification campaign for the 2002 World Cup Finals. More recently, he was part of the AC Milan side which won the 2003 Champions Cup.

JOAO PINTO

Country: Portugal
Born: August 19, 1971
Position: Forward
Clubs: Boavista, Atlético Madrid, Boavista, Benfica, Sporting Lisbon

Joao Pinto is a fast and skilful striker who emerged as part of Portugal's 'Golden Generation' who won the World Youth Cup in 1989 and 1991. He made his international debut in 1991 and enjoyed a successful club career in Portugal. He had to wait until 1996 to make an impact on the international stage at the European Championship. He starred at Euro 2000, but suffered an ill-fated World Cup in 2002, getting sent-off and receiving a lengthy ban after clashing with a referee. He is third on Portugal's all-time appearances list and only Eusebio and Luis Figo have scored more goals for the national team.

OLIVER KAHN

Country: Germany
Born: June 15, 1969
Position: Goalkeeper
Clubs: Karlsrühe, Bayern Munich

Highly motivated and imposing, Oliver Kahn is one of the contemporary game's great 'keepers. He started at Karlsrühe but was snapped up by Bayern Munich in 1994 for £1.6million, a record fee for a goalkeeper in the Bundesliga. There he has won six league titles, a UEFA Cup and the 2001 Champions Cup, crucially saving three times in the penalty shoot out. It was a performance that saw him voted German Player Of The Year. Khan made his international debut in 1995 and was a non-playing squad member in two World Cups until he captained the side at Japan and Korea. He was instrumental in guiding the team to the final and was subsequently named Player Of The Tournament, the first time a goalkeeper has received the award.

NWANKWO KANU

Country: Nigeria
Born: August 1, 1976
Position: Forward
Clubs: Ajax, Inter Milan, Arsenal

Kanu signed for Ajax aged 16 and was a member of the side that won the 1995

Champions Cup against AC Milan. He won further silverware the following season as Nigeria won Olympic gold in Atlanta, where his unpredictability and breathtaking skill secured his move to Inter Milan. A life-threatening heart problem, which required surgery, brought an end to his Serie A career before it had really begun, but he was given a lifeline by Arsenal boss Arsene Wenger, who signed him for £4million in January 1999. Kanu has since failed to establish himself as a regular for The Gunners, but has made a number of breathtaking contributions, the highlight being a late 15-minute hat-trick against Chelsea in 1999.

Above: Filippo Inzaghi's nose for a goal around the penalty area has made him popular with a succession of Italian clubs.

ROBBIE KEANE

Country: Republic Of Ireland
Born: July 8, 1980
Position: Forward
Clubs: Wolves, Coventry, Inter Milan, Leeds United, Tottenham Hotspur

Robbie Keane made the breakthrough with both Wolves and the Republic Of Ireland at the age of 17, his creative skills not only forging goalscoring opportunities for himself, but for his strike partners too. While few expected the Midlands club to be able to hold on to such

a hot talent for long, not many would have predicted that within six years he would have moved club four times and commanded combined transfer fees of almost £40million. His spell in Italy was short and unsuccessful but he has shown with both Leeds and Tottenham that he is one of the most expressive players in the Premiership. On the international stage he is one of Ireland's greatest talents with plenty still to come.

ROY KEANE

Country: Republic Of Ireland
Born: August 10, 1971
Position: Midfield
Clubs: Cobh Ramblers, Nottingham Forest, Manchester United

A strong, fiery, ball-winning midfielder, Roy Keane has been one of the Premier League's most outstanding and consistent performers since its inception in 1992. He began his footballing career with Cobh Ramblers in his native Cork before Brian Clough took him to Nottingham Forest as an 18-year-old. Clough gave him his debut away at Liverpool and the combative youngster instantly won many admirers with his tireless box-to-box running and ability to score vital goals. At the end of his first full season at Forest Keane made an appearance in the 1991 FA Cup Final, collecting a runners-up medal after the defeat by Tottenham. A Republic Of Ireland debut against Switzerland was to follow under the guidance of Jack Charlton.

Seen as the natural successor to Bryan Robson at Manchester United, Alex Ferguson got his man for what is now seen as a bargain £3.75million in 1993 (at the time it was a record fee between English clubs). His presence and fearless tackling in the centre of midfield, coupled with his intelligent, accurate passing, has contributed much to United's success, and he was made club captain after Eric Cantona's retirement. However, months later a serious knee injury saw him miss much of the 1997-98 campaign, but his return coincided with his club's historic treble-winning season. After an inspired performance in the semi-final against Juventus, where he scored a goal and bossed the game majestically, Keane was unfortunate to miss the 1999 Champions Cup Final victory due to suspension.

Highly regarded by his peers and critics alike, he was voted Player Of The Year for the 1999-2000 season by the Football Writers Association and the PFA. A passionate and brutally honest man, Keane has courted notoriety throughout his time as a player. His biting 'prawn sandwich' outburst against United's executive fans was followed by a series of stinging comments about his fellow players. However, these remarks were nothing compared to his fall-out with Republic Of

Ireland team manager Mick McCarthy. Keane had gone to the 2002 World Cup in Japan and Korea as the Republic Of Ireland captain, but the personality clash with McCarthy saw him return without kicking a ball.

HARRY KEWELL

Country: Australia
Born: September 22, 1978
Position: Left-winger
Clubs: Leeds United, Liverpool

The young Australian was brought to the UK at the age of 16, having been recruited from the New South Wales Soccer Academy. Howard Wilkinson threw the youngster, who was already a full Australian international, into the first team at the age of 17, but under George Graham he was forced to bide his time on the sidelines. Kewell really blossomed when David O'Leary gave him, and several other Leeds youngsters, a chance in the first team and the 1999-2000 campaign saw him pick up the PFA Young Footballer Of The Year Award. Since then, Kewell has risen to become a genuine world star, signing for Liverpool in July 2003 for £5million. His performance in Australia's 3-1 win over England in February 2003 was hailed by many as the greatest individual performance by an Australian football international for his country.

KLEBERSON

Country: Brazil
Born: June 19, 1979
Position: Midfield
Clubs: Atletico Paranaense, Manchester United

Just five months after making his international debut, Kleberson became a World Cup winner at the age of 23. Although he had made an immediate impact, scoring on his Brazilian debut against Bolivia, he began the World Cup on the bench. When Luis Felipe Scolari opted to strengthen the heart of his midfield he turned to the man from Atletico Paranaense and he proved to be well up to the task. Not surprisingly his performances in Japan and Korea earned Kleberson many new admirers among the major clubs in Europe. He signed for Manchester United in August 2003.

MIROSLAV KLOSE

Country: Germany
Born: June 9, 1978
Position: Forward
Clubs: SG Blaubach-Diedelkopf, FC Homburg, Kaiserslautern

Miroslav Klose's meteoric rise from regional football to the 2002 World Cup Final took less two years. Signed by Kaiserslautern in 2000,

within seven months he had made a dramatic match-winning international debut as a substitute for Germany against Albania. He did likewise in his next appearance against Greece. The striker's blistering pace and sharp reactions in the box were a godsend for a national team crying out for a lethal striker. A World Cup hat-trick against Saudi Arabia followed on the way to the final and he finished the tournament as second-highest scorer behind Ronaldo. Polish-born Klose is a natural athlete with a sporting family history – his father was a professional footballer and his mother was a Poland handball international.

PATRICK KLUIVERT

Country: Holland
Born: July 1, 1976
Position: Forward
Clubs: Ajax, AC Milan, Barcelona

Following in the footsteps of his father Kenneth, who was a professional footballer in Surinam, Patrick was given his Ajax debut by Louis Van Gaal in 1994. The following season he scored the only goal against AC Milan in the Champions League final, which became a defining moment in the 18-year-old's life.

As the most talked about young striker in Europe, his 39 league goals in 70 games for Ajax prompted a move to AC Milan the following year, although it proved to be a somewhat unhappy spell at the San Siro. In a star-studded side, which included international team-mates Edgar Davids and Michael Reiziger, Kluivert failed to command a regular place in a team that itself struggled to make an impression in the title race.

He was made scapegoat by the fans but managed to rediscover his form as Holland reached the semi-finals of the 1998 World Cup. When Van Gaal invited him to join Barcelona that September, he needed little persuading. In his first season he helped Barça to the

Opposite clockwise from top left: Roy Keane's tenure as captain of Manchester United coincided with the club's success in the 1990s; Kleberson broke into the Brazil side five months before the team won the World Cup; Miroslav Klose has provided Germany with much-needed firepower up front; and Harry Kewell's impact at club and national level have made him Australia's most celebrated player of the current era.

Below: Dutch star Patrick Kluivert has grown from an exciting young prospect at Ajax to become Barcelona's leading front man.

championship and continued his form at Euro 2000, where he was joint leading scorer with five goals. Now approaching 100 goals for Barça he is once again the centre of intense transfer speculation.

HENRIK LARSSON

Country: Sweden
Born: September 20, 1971
Position: Forward
Clubs: Hogaborg, Helsingborg, Feyenoord, Celtic

Celtic have had an amazing return for the £650,000 they paid Feyenoord for Henrik Larsson in 1997. Despite serious injuries the Swedish striker has never been far from the top of the Scottish goalscoring charts. With an incredible strike rate he has become the darling of the Celtic fans, and not only the most feared striker in Scottish football but one with a reputation that spreads worldwide.

He has risen from humble beginnings, starting out as a teenager with Third Division Swedish side Hogaborg. Making the journey from Hogaborg to the UEFA Cup final with Celtic, as well as European Championships and the World Cup with Sweden, owes much to both his ambition and attitude.

Tricky, fast and good in the air, Larsson has the full repertoire required of a striker. It is not just at club level that he has been a prolific goalscorer, as he has averaged almost a goal in every three games he has played for his country. He scored eight of their 20 goals in qualifying for the 2002 World Cup, and there are plenty of Swedish fans who will point to the fact that without Larsson the team would not have reached the finals.

PAOLO MALDINI

Country: Italy
Born: June 26, 1968
Position: Left-back/Sweeper
Clubs: AC Milan

Paolo Maldini is one of the finest defenders ever to grace the world stage. An unflappable, cultured and resilient presence at left-back for AC Milan, he is equally proficient when deployed at sweeper or centre-half. His ability to bring the ball out of defence and help out in attack is merely the icing on the cake of a truly prodigious reputation.

He began his long and exclusive association with his local club Milan when only a boy. Making his debut for the first team as a 16-year-old substitute against Udinese in January 1985, Maldini was following in the footsteps of his father, Cesare, who'd starred for Milan and Italy in the Sixties and later coached the national team. To say Paolo's time at Milan has been successful is a great understatement; in 15 years in the first team he has helped them accrue a vast collection of silverware, including six Italian league titles, two World Club Cups, three Super Cups, and three Champions Cups. The 1994 final saw Milan thrash Barcelona 4-0 and Maldini deputise at sweeper for the suspended Franco Baresi. Maldini was also part of the Milan sides that lost Champions Cup finals in 1993 and 1995, to Marseille and Ajax respectively.

Maldini made his debut for Italy as a 19-year-old on March 31, 1988, against Yugoslavia, but his career with the national team hasn't been quite as successful as his father's (Cesare Maldini was captain of Italy when they lifted the European Championship trophy in 1963). Italy came third in the World Cup in 1990 and reached the final in 1994, before losing to Brazil on penalties. The Italian captain was unlucky again at Euro 2000. Despite missing a penalty in the semi-final shoot-out against Holland, Maldini found himself in the final and seconds away from emulating his father by lifting the Henri Delauney trophy. But Italy's slender 1-0 lead over France was obliterated in the game's final minute and the French went on to grab a heartbreaking extra-time winner.

Maldini announced his retirement from international football after Italy's exit from the 2002 World Cup Finals with a record-breaking

126 caps for his country. He's expected to bring down the curtain on his club career with Milan at the end of the 2003-04 season as he nears his 36th birthday.

PATRICK MBOMA

Country: Cameroon
Born: November 15, 1970
Position: Forward
Clubs: Stade de L'Est, Chateauroux, Paris Saint-Germain, Metz, Gamba Osaka, Cagliari, Parma, Sunderland, Al-Ittihad, Tokyo Verdy

Patrick Mboma turned down the chance to play for Cameroon at the 1994 World Cup because, although born in Douala, he had been raised in France. Two years later he succumbed to Cameroon's call and went on to win the African Nations Cup in 2000 and 2002, the Olympic Games in 2000, and play in two World Cups. He was also voted African Player Of The Year for 2000. He was initially overlooked for France 98 but was drafted into the squad as a replacement for the injured Marc-Vivien Foe. He has graced the French League, Japan's J.League, Italy's Serie A and England's Premiership.

STEVE McMANAMAN

Country: England
Born: February 11, 1972
Position: Midfield
Clubs: Liverpool, Real Madrid, Manchester City

One of the first high-profile Bosman transfers, McManaman – a gangly, clever winger – made his name at Liverpool before signing for Real Madrid in 1999. Things started well as Madrid picked up a Champions League title in 2000 (McManaman scored in the final) but his first-team opportunities were rare, due to the club's embarrassment of riches in midfield. He remained a regular substitute and a crowd favourite, but inconsistency and little first-team football hindered his international career. He signed for Manchester City at the beginning of the 2003-04 season.

GAIZKA MENDIETA

Country: Spain
Born: March 27, 1974
Position: Midfield
Clubs: Castellón, Valencia, Lazio, Barcelona, Middlesbrough

Basque-born Mendieta became one of the hottest properties in football for his part in Valencia's run to two successive Champions League finals. Signed from second division Castellón at 19 years of age, he blossomed under Claudio Ranieri, drifting out wide and helping launch rapid counter-attacks. He made his international debut in 1999 and figured at both Euro 2000 and the World Cup of 2002. However, a £30million move to Lazio turned sour as he struggled to make an impact in Serie A. Barcelona brought him back on loan, where he attempted to rebuild his career before signing for Middlesbrough in 2003.

PREDRAG MIJATOVIC

Country: Yugoslavia, Serbia & Montenegro
Born: January 19, 1969
Position: Forward
Clubs: Buducnost Titograd, Partizan Belgrade, Valencia, Real Madrid, Fiorentina, Levante

Predrag Mijatovic came to prominence in the early 1990s with his goalscoring prowess in the Yugoslav league with Buducnost Titograd, and then Partizan Belgrade, with whom he scored 45 goals in 104 games, culminating in Partizan's 1993 championship win. Spanish

club Valencia signed him for £4.8million and he was a hit, netting 28 goals as Valencia finished runners-up. Mijatovic being voted Spain's Player Of The Year. Real Madrid signed him for £6.3million with his goals contributing to the 1997 championship and the 1998 Champions League title. He also topped Europe's World Cup qualifying goal charts with 14 goals, including seven in Yugoslavia's play-off win over Hungary in 1997.

FERNANDO MORIENTES

Country: Spain
Born: April 5, 1976
Position: Forward
Clubs: Albacete, Real Zaragoza, Real Madrid

Fernando Morientes is a talented forward who has lacked as much first-team action as he would have liked in recent times because of Real Madrid's abundance of riches up front. He is a full Spanish international, who would have been the golden boy of Spanish football had his career not coincided with that of his club team-mate Raúl. Like Raúl, Morientes is tremendously experienced for his age and boasts two Spanish titles and three Champions League medals to his name. Morientes has also proved to be a success at international level, reaching 20 goals in just 26 games, though his appearances on the greatest stage of all, the World Cup finals, have been

disappointing. In 1998 Spain crashed out of the World Cup in the opening phase despite beating Bulgaria 6-1 in their final game, with Morientes scoring twice. And then in 2002 Spain were surprisingly beaten by hosts South Korea on penalties. Morientes remains a favourite at the Bernabéu, but if Real continue with their policy of adding star players to the team, his future may now lie elsewhere.

HONG MYUNG-BO

Country: South Korea
Born: February 12, 1969
Position: Sweeper
Clubs: Posco Atoms, Pohang Steelers, Bellmare Hiratsuka, Kashiwa Reysol, Pohang Steelers, Los Angeles Galaxy

Hong Myung-bo is regarded as Asia's best sweeper. His experience and leadership has been gained through playing in four successive World Cups with South Korea. His influence was apparent in South Korea's run to the semi-finals in 2002. It was Hong, the captain, who converted the decisive penalty that knocked out Spain and inspired the win over Italy. He has been equally successful in club football, being voted Most Valuable Player in the Korean League in 1992 and the Japanese League in 1999. In 2000 he became the first Korean to captain a Japanese club, Kashiwa Reysol, and in 2002 he signed for Los Angeles Galaxy.

Above: Gaizka Mendieta's time at Valencia coincided with the club's successive Champions League finals.

Left: Predrag Mijatovic enjoyed a successful period in Spain, where he was voted Player Of The Year in 1996.

Opposite: Michael Owen exploded onto the world stage with his wonder goal against Argentina during France 98.

HIDETOSHI NAKATA

Country: Japan
Born: January 22, 1977
Position: Midfield
Clubs: Bellmare Hiratsuka, Perugia, Roma, Parma

Quite simply the greatest player Japan has produced so far, Nakata managed to show that players from the fledgling J.League could hold their own in Europe. Individualistic, skilful and with an iron will, playmaker Nakata carries the weight of his country on his shoulders, and does it well, with massive media and public interest in his every move. He impressed at the 2002 World Cup, where Japan proved a surprise package, but has been frustrated at club level, despite helping Roma to their first title in 18 years. A big money move to Parma in the summer of 2001 could have provided him with the platform his skills deserve.

PAVEL NEDVED

Country: Czech Republic
Born: August 30, 1972
Position: Midfield
Clubs: Dukla Prague, Sparta Prague, Lazio, Juventus

Dubbed the 'Czech Cannon' for his powerful but cultured left-foot, Pavel Nedved is the most talented and charismatic Czech footballer since Josef Masopust, a tireless runner capable of leading the line or acting as playmaker. He played for two of Prague's major sides, winning three championships with Sparta, and became an automatic choice for the national side, starring in the final of the 1996 European Championship. He joined Lazio, becoming the club's top scorer in 1998 and clinching the winning goal in the last ever Cup Winners' Cup final. He won the Scudetto in 2000 and was nominated Best Foreign Player In Serie A before Juventus secured him for £26million as a replacement for Zidane.

Below: Pavel Nedved was nominated Best Foreign Player in Serie A in 2000.

ALESSANDRO NESTA

Country: Italy
Born: March 19, 1976
Position: Central defender
Clubs: Lazio, AC Milan

A product of the Lazio youth system, Nesta made his senior debut for the Rome side when he was 17. After a marathon 18-year association with the club, which included winning the Cup Winners' Cup in 1999, the Italian league title in 2000, and a long spell as captain, he transferred to Italian rivals AC Milan in August 2002 for £19million. On the international stage, Nesta was part of the Italy squad at the 1996 European Championship, but didn't get a game, finally making his debut in October of the same year. A defensive rock with sublime ball control, Nesta has gone on to become a regular fixture in the national side under a succession of coaches and effectively marked Patrick Kluivert out of the game in Italy's win over Holland in the semi-final at the 2000 European Championship.

EMMANUEL OLISADEBE

Country: Poland
Born: December 22, 1978
Position: Forward
Clubs: Jasper United, Polonia Warsaw, Panathiniakos

Nigerian-born Emmanuel Olisadebe was discovered by Jerzy Engel, and although Olisadebe had failed trials at Wisla Krakow and Ruch Chorzow, Engel signed him for Polonia Warsaw. His goals helped Polonia to the Polish league and cup double in 2000. When Engel became Poland's national team coach he was desperately searching for a striker. It was former Polish legend Zbigniew Boniek who suggested Polish citizenship for Olisadebe and in July 2000 it was granted. Olisadebe's impact was immediate – he scored on his debut against Romania and his goals fired Poland to the 2002 World Cup. In January 2001 he joined Greek giants Panathinaikos.

SUNDAY OLISEH

Country: Nigeria
Born: September 14, 1974
Position: Midfield
Clubs: Julius Berger, FC Liege, Reggiana, Köln, Ajax, Juventus, Borussia Dortmund, Bochum

Sunday Oliseh retired from international football in 2002 after a nine-year career in which he won the 1994 African Nations Cup, 1995 Afro-Asian Nations Cup and the 1996 Olympic Games, where they beat both Brazil and Argentina on the way to a gold medal. Since his debut as an 18-year-old in April 1993 against Ethiopia, he has played in three successive World Cups, the highlight being his stunning strike that defeated Spain in 1998. Oliseh's club career has seen him play in the leagues of Nigeria, Belgium, Germany, Holland and Italy, making him one of the most experienced players in the African and European game.

MARC OVERMARS

Country: Holland
Born: March 29, 1973
Position: Winger
Clubs: Go Ahead Eagles, Willem II, Ajax, Arsenal, Barcelona

After brief spells at Go Ahead Eagles and Willem II, the career of Marc Overmars really took off when he joined Ajax in 1992 and became a member of the side that won three titles and then the Champions Cup final in 1995. The following season he was already eyeing a move abroad when he suffered a cruciate knee ligament injury and was sidelined for 12 months. Once recovered, he joined Arsenal and in his first season proved an influential team member as the club won the league and FA Cup double. He moved to Barcelona for £25million a year later and has been a regular at the Nou Camp ever since.

MICHAEL OWEN

Country: England
Born: December 14, 1979
Position: Forward
Club: Liverpool

A prolific scorer for club and country, Michael Owen made his Liverpool debut against Wimbledon in May 1997, and as a regular in the side the following season, he showed his predatory instincts by netting 18 league goals. He was rewarded with an England debut against Chile in February 1998, making him the youngest player of the last century to represent his country, and he went on to make a real international impact at the World Cup that year, scoring one of the tournament's most outstanding goals against Argentina.

In each of his six full seasons at Anfield, Owen has been Liverpool's leading scorer, and even a serious hamstring injury, sustained against Leeds at the tail end of the 1998-99 season, has not dented a goalscoring ratio of more than one goal in every two league games. Although he has already enjoyed many highs in a red shirt, 2001 proved to be the highlight of a flourishing career when, after helping Liverpool to success in three cup competitions, including the UEFA Cup, he was voted European Footballer Of The Year. Owen has also scored more goals for England than any other Liverpool player.

Above: Raúl, so much a part of his club that they have been dubbed Raúl Madrid.

Below right: Ronaldinho's name is etched on the hearts of England fans after his freak goal for Brazil in the 2002 World Cup.

ROBERT PIRES

Country: France
Born: January 29, 1973
Position: Forward
Clubs: Metz, Marseille, Arsenal

Robert Pires came to life at Arsenal following a £6million move from Marseille in 2000 and was voted England's Footballer Of The Year in 2002 after helping the club win the league and FA Cup double. A gifted attacker, he can play in a variety of positions and is capable of both creating and scoring goals. Earlier in his career, he won the French Young Player Of The Year award while at Metz in 1996 and was a squad member at both the World Cup in 1998 and the European Championship in 2000. He endured two disappointing seasons as he struggled at Marseille before returning to prominence in England.

RAÚL

Country: Spain
Born: June 27, 1977
Position: Forward
Clubs: Real Madrid

So closely is Raúl Gonzalez identified with the Spanish giants, they have been dubbed Raúl Madrid. A predator to rank alongside club legends like Di Stéfano and Butragueno, local-born Raúl was a first-team regular at just 17 years old and continues to rewrite the record books. Sharp, two-footed and agile, Raúl is the complete striker, becoming an international fixture at 19, and a frequent topscorer in the Spanish league. He already stands as the all-time top scorer in the Champions League with 43 goals, nine of them during the 2002-03 campaign. His exploits have resulted in four championship medals (1995, 1997, 2001 and 2003) and two Champions Cup medals, scoring in the victory over Valencia in 2000.

ALVARO RECOBA

Country: Uruguay
Born: March 17, 1976
Position: Forward
Clubs: Danubio, Nacional, Venezia, Inter Milan

Alvaro Recoba is reputedly among the highest-paid players in Serie A, but the Inter staff must be happy with what they are getting for their money as he has been at the club since 1997. He made an immediate impact, scoring twice on his debut in a 2-1 victory over Brescia, with one strike from more than 30 yards out. The Uruguayan is a technically-gifted player with a fantastic left foot, dangerous with his pace and is a set-piece specialist. He is also equally adept at playing as a central striker or in a free role behind the front men.

FERNANDO REDONDO

Country: Argentina
Born: June 6, 1969
Position: Midfield
Clubs: Argentina Juniors, Tenerife, Real Madrid, AC Milan

Perhaps the most effective midfield player in the world, Redondo was voted Champions League Player Of The Year when he guided Real Madrid to the Champions Cup in 2000, yet was shown the door as the Spaniards looked to finance the purchase of Luis Figo. He dominates the middle of the park, and his performances in the 2000 campaign versus Bayern Munich, Valencia and Manchester United were dazzling. He suffered a terrible knee injury in his first week at AC Milan and fought a long battle for fitness – even renouncing his salary until fit to play. He is now looking to return to the heights of the past and end his career at Milan.

RIVALDO

Country: Brazil
Born: April 19, 1972
Position: Forward/Midfield
Clubs: Paulista, Santa Cruz, Corinthians, Palmeiras, Deportivo La Coruña, Barcelona, AC Milan

Reinaldo Vitor Borba Ferreira, or Rivaldo as he is more commonly known, began his road to fame and fortune with local club Paulista at the age of 17. Following spells at Santa Cruz and Corinthians, he joined Palmeiras in 1994, helping the club to two championships. His goalscoring potential was spotted by Spanish side Deportivo La Coruna in 1996, and in one season at the Riazor, he scored an incredible 30 goals in 30 games. Now a regular for Brazil, he moved to Barcelona for £18million as a replacement for Ronaldo and his impact was

immediate, as he inspired Barça to league and cup success in his first season.

Rivaldo's outstanding form at the Nou Camp was rewarded with the FIFA World Player Of The Year award in 1999 and his worth to the side was never more evident than on the final day of the 2000-01 season when his hat-trick secured Barça a place in the following season's Champions League tournament. It is widely regarded as one of the best hat-tricks ever scored, but with the club's continued lack of success both in Europe and domestically, Rivaldo was offloaded to AC Milan in the summer of 2002. He had played a prominent role in his country's World Cup success in Korea and Japan, where he finished the tournament as joint second-highest scorer.

RONALDINHO

Country: Brazil
Born: March 21, 1980
Position: Forward
Clubs: Gremio, Paris Saint-Germain, Barcelona

One of the best players at the 2002 World Cup, he helped Brazil to victory by forming a spectacular attacking trio with Ronaldo and Rivaldo. He was shortlisted for FIFA Player Of The Tournament and made headlines with his free-kick goal from great distance against England in the quarter-finals. He first came to prominence at the Copa America in 1999, where his ball skills were clear for all to see. A sublimely gifted player, he took time to settle after a protracted move to PSG, but he is one of the most exciting players in the world and will be a star for years to come.

RONALDO

Country: Brazil
Born: September 22, 1976
Position: Forward
Clubs: Cruzeiro, PSV Eindhoven, Barcelona, Inter Milan, Real Madrid

Once dubbed 'The Phenomenon', Ronaldo is the closest thing to a modern day Pele that Brazil has produced. At his peak he demonstrated searing pace, skill and finishing ability, whether breaking from his own half to score alone or tapping in from a few feet.

Ronaldo Luiz Nazario de Lima was born in Bento Ribeiro, in the suburbs of Rio De Janeiro. He made his debut for Cruzeiro aged 16 and earned a place in the squad for the World Cup in 1994, having made his debut that year against Argentina. He left Brazil to join Bobby Robson's PSV Eindhoven, following in the footsteps of another great Brazilian predator, Romario. In two seasons in Holland he scored 42 goals, despite playing only 13 matches in the 1995-96 season. When Robson took over at Barcelona in 1996 he promptly spent £20million on Ronaldo, who scored 47 goals in his one season with the Catalans, winning the Cup Winners' Cup in the process.

At the 1998 World Cup in France, Ronaldo's world began to unravel. The team leant heavily on him but he managed only four goals on the way to the final. On the eve of the big match Ronaldo suffered a fit, which led to his name being struck-off the team sheet in the hour leading up to the kick-off. However, when the Brazilians took to the pitch he was there, though patently unfit. Brazil lost the game amid much acrimony, but worse was to come.

He joined Inter Milan for £19million and scored 25 goals in his first season, but wear and tear after years of playing top-level football from a young age resulted in a serious knee injury in November 1999. Five months later he made his return in the final of the Italian Cup, but collapsed in agony after just seven minutes without being touched.

Many wrote off his chances of returning to football but he fought back after extensive rehabilitation to prove his fitness in time for the 2002 World Cup Finals. The tournament proved his redemption as he scored eight goals on the way to lifting the trophy, winning the Golden Boot and being named FIFA Player Of The Year for the third time. There was bitterness at Inter, however, for after spending significant periods of his contract injured, as soon as he was fit he jumped ship to join the elite of Real Madrid for £23million in September 2002.

Carrying extra weight he struggled to convince Real fans that he merited a place above favourite Morientes, but eventually proved his worth in the Champions League.

Above: Ronaldo's rehabilitation was capped with the Golden Boot at the 2002 World Cup Finals.

WAYNE ROONEY

Country: England
Born: October 24, 1985
Position: Forward
Club: Everton

Already England's youngest ever international, having made his debut as a substitute against Australia aged just 17 years and 111 days, Rooney has the natural talent to become a major star. England boss Sven Goran Eriksson certainly thinks so. He selected Rooney for the crucial European Championship qualifier against Turkey and the youngster impressed with a confident display. In September 2003 he confirmed his arrival on the international scene when a strike against Macedonia made him England's youngest goalscorer ever.

RUI COSTA

Country: Portugal
Born: March 29, 1972
Position: Midfield
Clubs: Fafe, Benfica, Fiorentina, AC Milan

On his day a brilliant playmaker, the man around whom his national and club sides tick, Rui Costa was a member of Portugal's 'Golden Generation' which won the World Under 17 title in 1989 and the World Youth Cup in 1991. His passing and creativity have seen him lured to some of Europe's top clubs, AC Milan paying £28million for him in 2001. In his homeland many believe him more vital to the side than Luis Figo. Able to score spectacular goals, injury has hampered his career. He was a disappointment in the last World Cup when not fully fit, but he had an outstanding Euro 2000. Inconsistency is his only real weakness.

MARCELO SALAS

Country: Chile
Born: December 24, 1974
Position: Forward
Clubs: Universidad de Chile, River Plate, Lazio, Juventus, River Plate

Dubbed 'The Matador' for his finishing, Salas is a quicksilver forward with a dynamic left foot. Born of Indian blood in Temuco, he joined Universidad de Chile in 1990 but moved to River Plate in 1996, winning three league titles. He made his name at the World Cup in 1998, outdoing the record of Chilean legend Zamorano with four goals, a tally which helped him secure a move to Lazio, scoring 12 goals in their 2000 double-winning season. He left for Juventus in 2001 but was sidelined by injury and returned to River Plate in 2003.

HASAN SAS

Country: Turkey
Born: August 1, 1976
Position: Forward
Clubs: Ankaragucu, Galatasaray

An exciting talent who has been attracting some of the top clubs in Europe, his shaven head marking him out as a star of the Turkish squad that reached the semi-finals of the 2002 World Cup. Able to play up front or on the left flank, injuries and indiscipline – including a suspension for substance misuse – have cost him appearances, but he rose to the fore during Galatasaray's UEFA Cup triumph of 2000. He is equally at home as provider or goalscorer, as Champions League strikes versus Real Madrid and AC Milan have proved.

JAVIER SAVIOLA

Country: Argentina
Born: December 11, 1981
Position: Forward
Clubs: River Plate, Barcelona

The world's most expensive teenager at nearly £18million, Saviola is a goalscoring sensation for Barcelona and, like any talent from his nation, is often touted as 'the next Maradona'.

Like his famous predecessor, he is short and explosive, strong enough to worry the biggest defenders, blessed with superb skills, and has a great knack of finding the back of the net. He has often seemed weighed down by the pressure of expectation, but his country is guiding him gently, including him in the pre-World Cup squad in 2002, but not taking him along for the final stages.

PAUL SCHOLES

Country: England
Born: November 16, 1974
Position: Midfield
Club: Manchester United

Paul Scholes may not get the same media attention as some of his team-mates, but there are few players who can be as assured of a starting role at Old Trafford. His fantastic runs into the box, and his shooting and heading ability, have meant that his goalscoring record from midfield for club and country is impressive. But there is a discipline to his game that is rarely found in attacking midfielders. Never one to neglect his defensive duties, Scholes is a terrifically hard-working and tough-tackling player.

DAVID SEAMAN

Country: England
Born: September 19, 1963
Position: Goalkeeper
Clubs: Peterborough United, Birmingham City, QPR, Arsenal, Manchester City

Shown the door by Leeds United as an apprentice, David Seaman was Arsenal's first-choice goalkeeper for 13 years, winning every domestic honour at Highbury, including the league and FA Cup double in both 1998 and 2002. He signed from QPR for £1million and

helped the team secure the 1991 league title in his debut season, conceding just 18 league goals. Within three years Seaman went on to win FA Cup, League Cup and Cup Winners' Cup honours.

As an integral member of the club's fabled 'back five', Seaman's consistent performances won him international recognition, and although he missed England's 1990 World Cup campaign through injury, he was firmly established as first choice by the time of the 1996 European Championship. He was, arguably, the finest goalkeeper in the world at the time, and he kept Scotland and Spain at bay with a number of top-class saves as England progressed to the semi-finals.

At 38 years of age David Seaman remained England's first choice at the 2002 World Cup, and although his tournament was tainted by conceding Ronaldinho's long-range free-kick, his performances against Sweden and Argentina justified Sven Goran Eriksson's faith in the veteran 'keeper. His desire to continue playing was demonstrated by his decision to move to Manchester City in 2003, rather than remain at Arsenal in a coaching position.

ALAN SHEARER

Born: August 13, 1970
Country: England
Position: Forward
Clubs: Southampton, Blackburn Rovers, Newcastle United

It's a shame Newcastle United didn't recognise the talents of a young schoolboy by the name of Alan Shearer when he failed his trial at the club. It certainly would have saved them the world record fee of £15million that they paid to Blackburn Rovers for the highly sought-after England captain. Nevertheless, in his seven years leading the line at St James' Park, Shearer has become a Geordie hero.

After failing his Newcastle trials, Shearer was snapped up on schoolboy forms by Southampton, progressing through the ranks. After two substitute appearances, he made an impressive full debut in 1988, scoring a hat-trick against Arsenal to become the youngest player ever to do so in the English Football League. It was just an injury that prevented Shearer making the journey to Sweden for the 1992 European Championship, and during that summer Blackburn Rovers paid a record £3.6million for his services.

The sizeable transfer fee was repaid almost immediately. After scoring more than 30 goals in each of his first three seasons at the club, in 1995 Shearer helped Blackburn pip Manchester United to their first league title in 81 years under Kenny Dalglish's stewardship.

In 1996, Shearer had his most successful spell in an England shirt, helping Terry Venables' team win through to the European

Championship semi-finals and forming a devastating partnership with Spurs striker, Teddy Sheringham. Shearer notched up an impressive five goals, including a brace in the 4-1 demolition of Holland, and became the tournament's top scorer.

The disappointment of losing to Germany on penalties in the semi-final was soon washed away as Shearer announced he would be returning to St James' Park on August 6. Manager Kevin Keegan was aware that the cost of Shearer's services would cause a strain on the club's finances, but that was quickly forgotten as the England hitman forged a devastating partnership with Les Ferdinand in attack, complementing the guile and vision of Ginola and Beardsley in midfield.

Sadly, trophies eluded Kevin Keegan's side and the team later struggled under the leadership of Kenny Dalglish and Ruud Gullit. But with Bobby Robson installed as manager, Newcastle have begun to challenge for honours again, with Shearer, having retired from international football after Euro 2000, enjoying one of the best spells of his career.

ANDRIY SHEVCHENKO

Country: Ukraine
Born: August 29, 1976
Position: Forward
Clubs: Dynamo Kiev, AC Milan

A hero in his homeland and one of Europe's most prolific strikers, Andriy Shevchenko has everything a great striker needs – vision, pace, strength, and an uncanny eye for goal. Brought up through the ranks at Kiev, his first trophy was presented to him at age 13 by Ian Rush at a tournament in Wales. He formed a lethal partnership with Sergei Rebrov in Dynamo Kiev's 1997 Champions League campaign, scoring a hat-trick at Barcelona. The following year he was the competition's top scorer with 11 goals. He was lured to AC Milan in the summer of 1999, where his goalscoring has continued in Serie A against some of the world's toughest defences.

DIEGO SIMEONE

Country: Argentina
Born: April 28, 1970
Position: Midfield
Clubs: Velez Sarsfield, Pisa, Sevilla, Atlético Madrid, Inter Milan, Lazio, Atlético Madrid

Diego Simeone is best remembered for his role in the sending-off of England's David Beckham at the 1998 World Cup Finals, but there is more to the tough-tackling midfielder than that one moment of controversy. Making his international debut against Australia in 1988, Simeone became the first Argentine player to win 100 caps for his country, a feat not even achieved by Diego Maradona. He was also a part of his country's silver medal winning team at the 1996 Olympics.

In club football, he was a part of the Atlético Madrid side that won the Spanish title in 1996 and he scored the winner for Lazio in the 2000 Italian Cup Final, helping them to a first league and cup double. He returned to Atlético in August 2003.

JAAP STAM

Country: Holland
Born: July 17, 1972
Position: Centre-back
Clubs: Zwolle, Cambuur, Willem II, PSV Eindhoven, Manchester United, Lazio

Jaap Stam became the world's most expensive defender when he joined Manchester United in 1998, and he enjoyed a dream first season.

Sir Alex Ferguson's team won the treble, including the Champions League, but things were to turn sour. After spending just three of his five contracted years with United, Stam was bound for Lazio. The move seemed to shock the imposing defender as much as the rest of the football world, though many reports at the time blamed Stam's autobiography for his departure. Life at Lazio did not get off to the best of starts with a five-month ban imposed after testing positive for nandrolone.

HAKAN SÜKÜR

Country: Turkey
Born: September 1, 1971
Position: Forward
Clubs: Galatasaray, Torino, Inter Milan, Parma, Blackburn Rovers, Galatasaray

Known as the 'Bull of the Bosphorus', Hakan Sükür is Turkey's greatest striker ever and

a legend with Galatasaray fans, having scored 173 goals during his eight seasons with them, winning six championships, plus the 2000 UEFA Cup. However, Sükür struggled to make an impact abroad. He could not settle at Torino, moved to Inter Milan for £4.9million in 2000, and then to Parma in January 2002. He signed for Blackburn Rovers but broke his leg before he could make his debut. Though Turkey's top scorer, he laboured at the 2002 World Cup, scoring only once – in the the place play-off. Timed at 10.8 seconds, it was the fastest ever goal in World Cup history.

LILIAN THURAM

Country: France
Born: January 1, 1972
Position: Defender
Clubs: Monaco, Parma, Juventus

Lilian Thuram came to prominence at the 1998 World Cup as arguably the player of the tournament and produced an unforgettable performance by scoring both goals in the 2-1 semi-final win over Croatia. He started his career at Monaco and joined Parma in 1996, quickly becoming one of the outstanding defenders in Serie A.

Capable at centre-back or right-back, his strengths are power and man-marking. He added another honour when France won Euro 2000 and became the world's most expensive defender when he joined Juventus for £22million in 2001, helping them win the Italian title the following year.

FRANCESCO TOLDO

Country: Italy
Born: February 12, 1971
Position: Goalkeeper
Clubs: AC Milan, Verona, Trento, Ravenna, Fiorentina, Inter Milan

Part of Italy's Under-21 side which won the European Championship in 1994, Francesco Toldo had begun his club career with AC Milan's youth team. As a 19-year-old he joined Trento of Italy's Serie C2, but two years later was playing in Serie A with Fiorentina, where he stayed for eight seasons.

When Italy's first choice goalkeeper, Gianluigi Buffon, broke his hand a week before the start of the European Championship in 2000, Toldo stepped in to deputise. His penalty saves in the semi-final against Holland – first from Frank De Boer in normal time, and then from De Boer (again) and Paul Bosvelt in the shoot-out that followed – took Italy to the final and had many proclaiming him as the tournament's best goalkeeper. Although part of the Italian squad for the 2002 World Cup Finals, he was left on the bench for all four of his country's matches.

JON DAHL TOMASSON

Country: Denmark
Born: August 29, 1976
Position: Forward
Clubs: Heerenveen, Newcastle United, Feyenoord, AC Milan

It would have been easy for Jon Dahl Tomasson to disappear after a disappointing time at Newcastle, but Kenny Dalglish's £2million 'flop' has since proved himself a hit. That lean spell followed a fine goal-scoring record in Holland for Heerenveen, and a return to Holland allowed his prodigious talent to shine once again. Tomasson is fast and elusive, a good target man as well as hard-working, and his return to form at Feyenoord was capped by a starring role in the 2002 UEFA Cup Final. He followed that with a great World Cup and earned a move to AC Milan, where his goals have already proved vital.

FRANCESCO TOTTI

Country: Italy
Born: September 27, 1976
Position: Midfield/Forward
Club: Roma

Francesco Totti made his debut for AS Roma in March 1993, aged just 16, but didn't become a first-team regular until two years later. In 2001 he captained the club to their first Italian title for 18 years and scored 13 goals in 30 league appearances. Preferring to play as an attacking midfielder or deep-lying forward, Totti made his first appearance for the Italian national side against Switzerland on October 10, 1998. He went on to impress at Euro 2000, scoring a superb goal against Romania, converting a crucial penalty in the semi-final shoot-out with Holland. He was Italy's best player in the final defeat to France, however, his red card against South Korea in Italy's disastrous 2002 World Cup campaign means Totti still has much to prove on the world stage.

EDWIN VAN DER SAR

Country: Holland
Born: October 29, 1970
Position: Goalkeeper
Clubs: Ajax, Juventus, Fulham

It was a shock to many when Edwin Van Der Sar arrived at unfashionable Fulham for the start of their English Premiership adventure, but it was an excellent signing for Jean Tigana. The giant goalkeeper has proved his class in winning four Dutch titles and the Champions Cup with Ajax, whom he joined as a teenager, before another league championship at Juventus. His quality is well known by the Dutch, for whom he is their undisputed

number one. He proved an instant crowd favourite in West London, helping Fulham to an FA Cup semi-final and top-flight survival with some inspirational performances, but he struggled with injury in 2003.

RUUD VAN NISTELROOY

Position: Forward
Born: July 1, 1976
Country: Holland
Clubs: Den Bosch, Heerenveen, PSV Eindhoven, Manchester United

Strong, fast and with a killer instinct for goal, Dutch striker Ruud Van Nistelrooy plied his trade for a while in the Dutch league before making his name with PSV Eindhoven. It was here that Van Nistelrooy first attracted the attentions of Manchester United boss, Sir Alex Ferguson, but a proposed deal fell through after a medical revealed a weak right knee in 2000. The knee was to rupture two days later, but after a lengthy spell on the sidelines, Van Nistelrooy signed for United for £19million in April 2001 and has scored more than 100 goals in two years at the club, bringing the title back to Old Trafford in his second full season.

Above: Ruud Van Nistelrooy scored 100 goals for Manchester United in his first two years at the club.

Opposite clockwise from top left: French defender Lilian Thuram in action for Juventus; goalkeeper Francesco Toldo salutes another Inter Milan goal; Italian striker Francesco Totti celebrates with Roma; and Denmark's Jon Dahl Tomasson playing for AC Milan.

Above: Frenchman Patrick Vieira contributed his midfield dominance to Arsenal's recent league and cup doubles.

Right: Christian Vieri is as famous for his numerous transfers as he is for his goalscoring ability.

JUAN SEBASTIÁN VERÓN

Country: Argentina
Born: March 9, 1975
Position: Midfield
Clubs: Estudiantes de la Plata, Boca Juniors, Sampdoria, Lazio, Manchester United, Chelsea

The son of striker Juan Ramon Verón, 'Seba' was born in Buenos Aires and joined his father's team, Estudiantes de la Plata, before moving to Boca Juniors in 1996. He made his international debut against Poland that year and has starred in two World Cups. He moved to Sven Goran Eriksson's Sampdoria in August 1996 before a £15million move to Parma. He rejoined Eriksson at Lazio for £18million in 1999 and was instrumental in the team's championship run. He then moved on to Manchester United for £28million in July 2001. Despite question marks over his impact, in his second season at the club he became the first Argentinian to win the league in England, before moving to Chelsea for £15million.

PATRICK VIEIRA

Country: France
Born: June 23, 1976
Position: Midfield
Clubs: Cannes, AC Milan, Arsenal

Patrick Vieira began his career with French side Cannes, and even captained the club as a 17-year-old before moving to AC Milan in 1995. He made just two appearances for the Serie A giants before switching to Highbury a year later in a £3.5million deal. His impact was immediate and in his second season he linked up with compatriot Emmanuel Petit to help the club win the league and FA Cup double. He was again instrumental, this time as captain, as the club repeated the feat in 2002. He was also a member of the French side that won the 1998 World Cup on home turf and the European Championship in 2000.

CHRISTIAN VIERI

Country: Italy
Born: July 12, 1973
Position: Centre-forward
Clubs: Prato, Torino, Pisa, Ravenna, Venezia, Atalanta, Juventus, Atlético Madrid, Lazio, Inter Milan

As famous for the number of clubs he's joined as for his goalscoring exploits, Christian Vieri first rose to prominence while at Juventus. Originally acquired from Atalanta as a squad player, Vieri stepped into the first team after injuries to Alessandro Del Piero and Alen Boksic. He joined Spanish side Atlético Madrid in July 1997 and scored 24 goals in 24 games before a move to Lazio, with whom he won the Cup Winners' Cup. In July 1999 he was transferred to Inter Milan for a world record fee of £31million.

Vieri shone at the 1998 World Cup Finals, scoring five goals in five games, including a superb chip over the goalkeeper in a 3-0 win

against Cameroon. The tournament proved less fruitful in 2002, however. Vieri had put Italy ahead in the second round game against South Korea but they ultimately crashed out 2-1 in one of the tournament's biggest shocks.

SYLVAIN WILTORD

Country: France
Born: May 10, 1974
Position: Forward
Clubs: Rennes, Bordeaux, Arsenal

Wiltord became Arsenal's record signing when he joined the club for £13million in the summer of 2000, but the transfer was drawn out as Deportivo La Coruna, the club he was on loan to, demanded a share of the fee. Once he took his place, Wiltord was shunted on to the wing as Thierry Henry and Dennis Bergkamp limited his chances in attack. He still netted 15 goals in his first season, and followed up with a further 17 as the club won the league and FA Cup double. Wiltord also earned a place in his country's footballing history by scoring a late equaliser against Italy in the Euro 2000 final, paving the way for David Trezeguet's winner.

DWIGHT YORKE

Country: Trinidad & Tobago
Born: November 3, 1971
Position: Forward
Clubs: Signal Hill, Aston Villa, Manchester United, Blackburn Rovers

Yorke has put a smile on the faces of fans at all of the clubs he has played for and he regularly reciprocates that cheerful outlook on the pitch. A natural athlete, the Trinidad & Tobago international found himself frozen out of the first team at Manchester United after winning three league titles and the Champions League. His 'playboy' lifestyle off the pitch undoubtedly did not go down well with United

and his ability to devote his full attentions to his career at Blackburn will go a long way to determining how he will be remembered.

IVAN ZAMORANO

Country: Chile
Born: January 18, 1967
Position: Forward
Clubs: Cobresal, Cobre Andino, St Gallen, Seville, Real Madrid, Inter Milan, América, Colo Colo

Perhaps Chile's most influential footballer ever, he has played with some of the great forwards of his time, including Ronaldo at Inter and Salas for his country. Born in the suburbs of Santiago, he quickly made a name for himself in Chile before a move to Switzerland in 1988. He kept on banging the goals in, living up to the nickname 'Bam Bam'. He earned a move to Real Madrid, where he scored 80 goals in four years. A switch to Inter in 1996 was hampered by injury, but after a spell in Mexico with América he returned to Chile in 2003. Intending to play out his career with Colo Colo, he then received an 11-month ban for pushing a referee in a Chilean league game.

ZINEDINE ZIDANE

Country: France
Born: June 23, 1972
Position: Midfield
Clubs: Cannes, Bordeaux, Juventus, Real Madrid

It's impossible to overstate how great a player Zinedine Zidane is. The Marseille-born midfielder can rightly be mentioned in the same breath as Puskás, Pele, Cruyff and Maradona, and in the modern game he is just untouchable. His awareness on the ball, sublime skill, peerless touch, and unmatched big-game mentality have marked him out as a genuine superstar.

The world first took note of Zidane in 1996 when, as the master of Bordeaux's midfield, his incisive passing and instinctive skill inspired the French First Division side to the UEFA Cup final. Bayern Munich scuppered their hopes of glory, but for Zidane, it marked the entrance to football's hall of fame.

The same summer he was bought by Italian giants Juventus, and helped them to the Serie A title. Appearances in consecutive Champions League finals underlined what every football fan knew about his exceptional talent, but at France 98 he bettered that, inspiring his country to the World Cup triumph. Despite blotting his copy book early on in the tournament with an ugly stamping incident, 'Zizou' – his French nickname – ran rings around the world's best players and scored the two goals that killed off Brazil in the final.

It was no surprise, after his superlative performance on the world's biggest stage, that the game's top honour soon came the Frenchman's way – in 1998 FIFA announced Zidane as their World Player Of The Year. The honour was repeated in 2000, when his mastery of the beautiful game was still beguiling football fans around the world.

But, as is fitting for such a talent, an even greater compliment was soon to be bestowed upon him. In the summer of 2001, Zidane, quite deservedly, became the world's most expensive player. It was Real Madrid who lured him away from Juventus, and they did it with the kind of deal that the game will probably never see again. The exact figure paid is still unclear, as the arrangement of payment was typically complicated, but the most accurate estimates put it at around £45million.

To this day, the unassuming playmaker continues to demonstrate his utter genius – anyone who saw the volley he scored to win the 2002 Champions League will know that – and it's doubtful whether the world will ever see a talent like his again.

GIANFRANCO ZOLA

Country: Italy
Born: July 5, 1966
Position: Inside-forward
Clubs: Nuorese, Torres, Napoli, Parma, Chelsea, Cagliari

Learning his trade as Diego Maradona's understudy at Napoli in the early Nineties, Sardinian-born Gianfranco Zola soon became known as a creative but hard-working attacker with a speciality in long-range free-kicks. He joined Parma in 1993, and helped them lift the Super Cup in 1994 and beat Juventus over two legs to win the UEFA Cup in 1995. Following his countrymen Gianluca Vialli and Roberto Di Matteo to Chelsea in December 1996 for £4.5million proved to be a great move for Zola. He came off the bench to score the London side's winner in the final of the Cup Winners' Cup against Stuttgart in 1998, and in 2003 fans voted him the club's best ever player.

His international career has been one of few highlights. He is probably best remembered for missing a penalty at Euro 96 that effectively eliminated Italy from the tournament. He was also sent-off in a World Cup game against Nigeria in 1994. But neither incident should overshadow his superb winner in a World Cup qualifier against England in 1997.

In July 2003, Zola opted not to extend his contract at Chelsea for a further year and decided to honour a longstanding promise and return home to Sardinia to play out his career at Serie B side Cagliari.

Left: Twice World Player Of The Year, Zinedine Zidane in action for Real Madrid.

Below: Gianfranco Zola's exceptional form in his twilight years earned him the honour of being crowned Chelsea's best ever player.

GREAT MANAGERS

Right: Sir Matt Busby, a legend of both Manchester United and the craft of football management itself.

RADOMIR 'RADDY' ANTIC

Born: November 22, 1948

Management Career: Partizan Belgrade, Real Zaragoza, Real Madrid, Real Oviedo, Atlético Madrid, Real Oviedo, Barcelona

A Yugoslavia international, Antic carved out a successful career as a player at home and abroad, with Fenerbahce, Real Zaragoza and Luton Town and has followed suit as a manager. His greatest success came in guiding Atlético to the 1996 double, sweet revenge after he was sacked by rivals Real Madrid in January 1991 despite his team sitting eight points clear at the top of the table. A later spell at Atlético saw them relegated, a trick he repeated the following season with Oviedo. In early 2003 he replaced Louis Van Gaal at Barcelona, but despite leading them to the Champions League semi-finals, they failed to re-qualify for the Champions League and he himself was replaced by Frank Rijkaard.

ENZO BEARZOT

Born: September 26, 1927

Management Career: Prato, Italy

Major honours: World Cup 1982

Enzo Bearzot masterminded Italy's only World Cup triumph since 1938. After qualifying as a coach he joined the national set-up in 1969, becoming sole manager in 1977. Little was expected of his team in the 1978 World Cup,

Below: Enzo Bearzot led Italy to the World Cup in 1982.

but Bearzot's commitment to teamwork, loyalty and a more adventurous approach, meant they finished fourth. The 1982 World Cup campaign began badly, but again his loyalty was rewarded when he stuck by out-of-form striker Paolo Rossi. 'Pablito' went on to bag the goals that won the trophy. Bearzot's ageing side failed at the World Cup in 1986, but that should not devalue his reputation as a canny tactician and superb man-manager.

FULVIO BERNARDINI

Born: December 28, 1905

Management Career: Lazio, Fiorentina, Bologna, Italy

Fulvio Bernardini was an educated and elegant centre-half who earned the nickname 'Il Dottore' (the Doctor). However, he really made his name as one of the best coaches in the Italian game, taking modest clubs and making them successful. In 1956 he guided Fiorentina to their first ever championship success and followed it up by taking them to the 1957 European Cup Final. In 1964 he took Bologna to their first title in 23 years. In the mid-Seventies he took charge of the national team, helping Italy through the World Cup qualifiers before handing the reins to Enzo Bearzot.

VICENTE DEL BOSQUE

Born: December 23, 1950

Management career: Real Madrid

Major honours: Champions Cup 2000, 2002; World Club Cup 2002; European Supercup 2002

Opinion is divided on Vicente del Bosque. Some class him as the luckiest coach ever, a man for whom Luis Figo, Zinedine Zidane and Ronaldo were bought in successive seasons to add to a Real Madrid squad already packed with talent. With such a team, they argue, how could he fail?

Others think the Spaniard was terribly unlucky to be sacked in June 2003 after delivering two Champions League triumphs and two Spanish league titles in four years. When he desperately needed to bolster a failing defence, he was instead given more of the world's finest attacking stars and did magnificently to smooth over the super-egos of the dressing room and fashion a style of play that fitted his attack-heavy team – a team often referred to as the Harlem Globetrotters of the footballing world.

Whatever the truth and whatever else he may do in his coaching career, Del Bosque will forever be associated with Madrid. As a player, he turned out for Cordoba and Castellon, but it was at the Bernabéu that he enjoyed his greatest success, collecting five league titles, four cups and 18 caps. So enamoured was Del

Bosque with the club that when his playing days came to an end, he stayed there, filling a variety of roles, initially as manager of Madrid's B-team, Castilla.

Having stepped in as first-team boss for an 11-game spell in the 1993-94 season, and for one game during the 1995-96 campaign, he did so for a third time during 1999-2000, a season that was to culminate in a glorious Champions League final victory over Valencia at the Stade de France in Paris.

Asked to stay on, he delivered another Champions League, two league titles, the European Supercup and the World Club Cup, but when Madrid lost to Juventus in the Champions League semi-finals in 2003, the writing was on the wall. Offered a role as technical director, Del Bosque instead decided to finally sever his ties with the club.

MATT BUSBY

Born: May 26, 1909

Management career: Manchester United

Major honours: Champions Cup 1968

Revered at Old Trafford, Sir Matt Busby remains one of the great post-war British managers, a man who built a succession of great teams and forged a dynasty. Like Jock Stein and Bill Shankly, Busby hailed from Scottish mining stock. Born in Orbiston, Lanarkshire, he escaped a life at the coal-face through football. He played at half-back, winning one international cap for Scotland in 1933 and an FA Cup winner's medal for Manchester City the following year before finishing his career with Liverpool.

Manchester United was his first managerial appointment and, although just 36 years old, he became quick to assert his authority, demonstrating a tough disciplinary approach and a ruthless streak, belied by his amiable exterior. When he took over in 1945 the club was in disarray. Old Trafford was being rebuilt following severe bomb damage, money was short and the team was struggling.

Busby began his own rebuilding process, setting up a coherent youth policy and reorganising the scouting system. The first sign of progress was the 1948 FA Cup win

which was followed, after a couple of close calls, by the 1952 league championship – United's first since 1911. His team scored prolifically that season but Busby was not content and began rebuilding immediately, bringing in talented youth squad players. The era of the Busby Babes was born, with Bobby Charlton, Duncan Edwards, Dennis Viollet, Tommy Taylor and Jackie Blanchflower.

Two successive league titles followed in 1956 and 1957 before Busby defied the Football League to enter United for the European Cup, making them the first English club to compete. Famously, his decision rebounded with tragic consequences when the team plane crashed on a Munich airfield in 1958 en route home from an encounter with Red Star Belgrade. Eight of the team were killed and Busby himself was severely injured.

He recovered and began rebuilding the team with iron determination, unearthing major international talents like Denis Law and George Best. Two more league championships followed before Manchester United finally triumphed in Europe, beating Benfica 4-1 in 1968 to become the first English team in history to win the coveted trophy.

Busby's retirement in 1969 did not sever his influence on the team and a succession of managers, including Wilf McGuinness, Frank O'Farrell and Tommy Docherty, struggled to fill the vacuum he left and deal with the influence he continued to wield in the boardroom. It took another Scotsman to restore the club to its former glory. Busby lived to see the his club dominate the league again before dying, aged 84, on January 20, 1994.

FABIO CAPELLO

Born: June 18, 1946
Management career: AC Milan, Real Madrid, Roma
Major honours: Champions Cup 1994

One of the most decorated coaches in Italy, Fabio Capello commands a massive salary, and usually delivers the silverware in return, winning league titles with AC Milan, Roma and Real Madrid. A no-nonsense and fiery character, he has often had run-ins with opposition players and coaches, as well as top officials at his own clubs – controversially quitting Milan in 1996 after winning the Serie A title four times in five seasons. But his record speaks for itself and his hard-working

teams often play in his own image. He rarely hides his emotions, but he is always linked with every big job that comes up, including vacancies with the England national team and Manchester United. He was an excellent player in his own right, winning 32 Italian caps between 1972 and 1976 while playing for Juventus and AC Milan.

HERBERT CHAPMAN

Born: January 19, 1878
Management career: Northampton Town, Leeds City, Huddersfield Town, Arsenal

One of English football's great managers, Herbert Chapman was a visionary who, in his career, advocated numbered shirts, European football, white balls, floodlit matches and attempted to keep pace with the best of foreign tactical developments.

Chapman enjoyed an undistinguished playing career, spending time with, among others, Northampton Town and Tottenham reserves. He returned to Northampton as player-manager in 1907 and began to demonstrate his ability, leading them to the Southern League championship in his second

Above: Brian Clough, one of the English game's most charismatic football managers.

season. He moved on to Leeds City, finishing fourth in Division Two in 1914. However, he was suspended over illegal payments to guest players and quit the game, only returning in 1920 when his appeal was upheld. He took over at Huddersfield Town and began a golden era for the club, winning consecutive titles in 1924 and 1925 with limited resources.

He moved to Arsenal and sparked a revival in the club's fortunes, toying with their formation in the wake of changes to the offside rule. The reversal of north-south power was demonstrated when Arsenal won the 1930 FA Cup, beating Huddersfield 2-0. With some bold transfer coups, including Alex James and David Jack, Arsenal embarked on an era of total dominance that included five league titles. Sadly Chapman did not live to see them all. He died in January 1934 after contracting pneumonia watching his third team play.

JAVIER CLEMENTE

Born: March 12, 1950
Management Career: Athletic Bilbao, Espanyol, Spain, Real Betis, Real Sociedad, Marseille

Injury put an end to Javier Clemente's promising playing career at the age of 23, and he went straight into coaching. His first job was at the club he played for – Athletic Bilbao – where he joined the coaching staff. He quickly rose through the ranks, eventually leading them to the Spanish title in 1983. His next job saw him move to Espanyol, where

despite winning no trophies, he reached the 1988 UEFA Cup Final. That success won him the Spain job, and he coached the national team to three successive tournaments, before taking on successful relegation battles at Real Betis, Real Sociedad and Marseille.

BRIAN CLOUGH

Born: March 21, 1935
Management career: Hartlepool United, Derby County, Brighton & Hove Albion, Leeds United, Nottingham Forest
Major honours: Champions Cup 1979, 1980

Brian Clough was a free-scoring centre-forward before injury ended his playing days. Aged 30, he embarked on one of the greatest, and most colourful, managerial careers in history. At Fourth Division Hartlepool he forged an enduring partnership with Peter Taylor. The pair moved to Derby, and in five seasons rebuilt the club, taking them from 18th in Division Two to their first league title. The duo left The Rams after interference from the board – a perennial bugbear with Clough. Brief and eccentric sojourns at Brighton and Leeds United followed (Clough lasted 44 days at Elland Road before player-power had him removed), but Nottingham Forest were similar to Derby – a club he could mould.

This time it took four seasons to go from Division Two to the league championship. He cemented his reputation as England's foremost club boss by winning the European Cup in consecutive seasons, against Malmö and Hamburg. League Cup victories followed in the Eighties, but in 1993 his final season was marred by relegation from the newly-established Premiership. Always outspoken, he knew how to motivate ordinary players, but wasn't afraid to buy big either, signing the first million-pound player, Trevor Francis. He believed football was a simple game, but his teams always played it skilfully and wholeheartedly.

JOHAN CRUYFF

Born: April 25, 1947
Management career: Ajax, Barcelona
Major honours: Champions Cup 1992; European Cup Winners' Cup 1987, 1989; European Supercup 1992

One of the game's greatest playing talents, the three-time European Footballer Of The Year proved himself to be almost as gifted in the manager's office at Ajax and Barcelona, the clubs with which he had spent his prime as a player. Without any coaching qualifications, Cruyff guided the Amsterdam giants to the league title, two Dutch Cups and the 1987 European Cup Winners' Cup before being tempted back to the Nou Camp.

Two years later, his Barcelona side defeated Sampdoria to lift the Cup Winners' Cup at the start of what was to be a golden era for the Catalan giants. Playing sumptuous attacking football, Barça won two Spanish Cups, four consecutive league titles and, finally, in 1992, the trophy the club had been so desperately waiting for: the European Champions Cup. Again Sampdoria were the victims as Ronald Koeman's stunning extra-time free-kick gave Barça the one trophy they most desired.

Two years later Barça again reached the European Cup final, only to find themselves on the receiving end of a 4-0 thumping from AC Milan. With his side's success waning at home and abroad, Cruyff was forced out in 1996 and though he remains enormously popular with Barcelona fans, serious heart problems make a permanent return to football management unlikely.

SVEN GORAN ERIKSSON

Born: February 5, 1948
Management Career: Degerfors, IFK Gothenburg, Benfica, Roma, Fiorentina, Benfica, Sampdoria, Lazio, England
Major honours: UEFA Cup 1982; European Cup Winners' Cup 1999; European Supercup 1999

Sven Goran Eriksson's achievements are too numerous to mention individually; suffice it to say that he is a natural winner. His ice cool, intellectual approach rubs off on his players, making his teams play with confidence and intelligence, and although he is yet to win anything with his present charges, the England team, it is surely only a matter of time before he does. Working with his life-long coach Tord Grip he has won the league and cup in every country he has coached – Sweden, Portugal and Italy. Europe has also been a happy hunting ground, as he has won the UEFA Cup, Cup Winners' Cup and Supercup, and been a Champions League runner-up.

Right: England manager Sven Goran Eriksson enjoyed continental club success with Lazio, lifting the European Cup Winners' Cup in 1999.

ALEX FERGUSON

Born: December 31, 1941

Management career: East Stirlingshire, St Mirren, Aberdeen, Scotland, Manchester United

Major honours: Champions Cup 1999; European Cup Winners' Cup 1983, 1991; World Club Cup 1999; European Supercup 1991

A handy but limited player with a string of Scottish clubs, most notably Rangers, Alex Ferguson got his chance in management with Scottish minnows East Stirling. There he began to develop the motivational skills that would make him one of the world's most successful coaches, before moving to St Mirren and recording his first success, the First Division title.

Offered the manager's job at Aberdeen, Ferguson seized his opportunity to shake up Scottish football and break the 'Old Firm' duopoly. Rangers and Celtic had shared 14 successive league titles, but driven on by their workaholic manager's extraordinary hunger, Aberdeen snatched the 1980 championship. Two further league titles followed, along with four Scottish Cups and a memorable victory over Spanish giants Real Madrid in the 1983 European Cup Winners' Cup Final.

In 1986, Ferguson led Scotland at the World Cup finals after the sudden death of Jock Stein, and three months later Manchester United asked him to be their manager. After decades of underachievement, England's biggest club were desperate for success. But for four years Ferguson struggled as he sought to revolutionise United, cutting out the dead wood and shaping the club in his image.

As results dipped, and the pressure on Ferguson's job intensified, the Glaswegian finally delivered his first trophy, the 1990 FA Cup, to kick-start a golden era for United. The European Cup Winners' Cup and League Cup

Above left: Alex Ferguson in his Aberdeen days. Above: Lifting the 1999 Premier League trophy with Manchester United.

were added before, in 1993, after 26 years of trying, the league championship finally returned to Old Trafford.

The following year, United won their first league and FA Cup double, adding a second two years later as the team racked up eight league championships and four FA Cup victories in an 11-year spell. But it was 1999's historic and seemingly impossible treble that really established Ferguson in the pantheon of great managers.

Faced with mounting challenges in the league, FA Cup and Champions League, Ferguson brilliantly juggled his resources, tweaking and tinkering, resting players where

he could, and all the while exhorting his team to play thrilling attacking football.

It made for memorable games, none more so than the Champions League final against Bayern Munich, where two injury-time goals saw United crowned European Champions for the first time since 1968.

Knighted for his achievements, Ferguson announced his intention to retire at the end of the 2001-02 season. But as United faltered, he could not resist one last challenge, extending his contract and leading his team to their seventh successive Champions League quarter-final and another league championship in 2003.

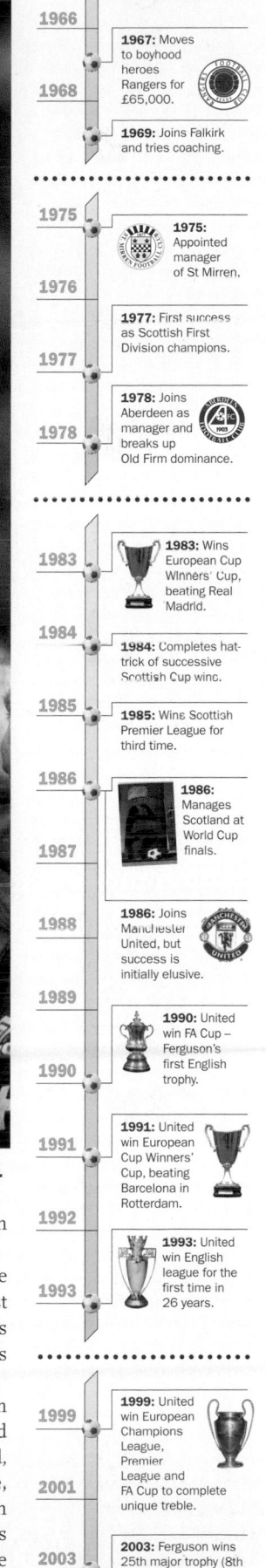

1964

1964: Signs on as a professional at Dunfermline.

1966

1967: Moves to boyhood heroes Rangers for £65,000.

1968

1969: Joins Falkirk and tries coaching.

1975

1975: Appointed manager of St Mirren.

1976

1977: First success as Scottish First Division champions.

1977

1978: Joins Aberdeen as manager and breaks up Old Firm dominance.

1978

1983

1983: Wins European Cup Winners' Cup, beating Real Madrid.

1984

1984: Completes hat-trick of successive Scottish Cup wins.

1985

1985: Wins Scottish Premier League for third time.

1986

1986: Manages Scotland at World Cup finals.

1987

1988

1986: Joins Manchester United, but success is initially elusive.

1989

1990

1990: United win FA Cup – Ferguson's first English trophy.

1991

1991: United win European Cup Winners' Cup, beating Barcelona in Rotterdam.

1992

1993: United win English league for the first time in 26 years.

1993

1999

1999: United win European Champions League, Premier League and FA Cup to complete unique treble.

2001

2003

2003: Ferguson wins 25th major trophy (8th Premier League title).

Right: Helenio Herrera, whose defensive tactics brought him success with Inter Milan.

BELA GUTTMAN

Born: March 13, 1900
Managerial career: AC Milan, Peñarol, Benfica
Major honours: Champions Cup 1961

A hugely respected coach, Hungarian Bela Guttman retired as a player in 1935 and embarked on a 40-year management career. He coached several teams in Eastern Europe, took the reins of AC Milan in Italy, and was one of the first from Europe to work in South America when he led Peñarol. The highlights of his career came at Benfica, whom he led to European Champions Cup triumph in 1961. He was feted for taking the trophy away from Real Madrid for the first time and retained it the following year. Guttman won a total of seven national titles during his trek around the globe. He died in 1981.

ERNST HAPPEL

Born: June 25, 1929
Management Career: Wacker Innsbruck, Feyenoord, Den Haag, Club Brugge, Holland, Hamburg, FC Swarovski Tirol, Austria
Major honours: Champions Cup 1970, 1983; World Club Cup 1970

Ernst Happel was one of the world's most successful and disciplined coaches, winning a staggering 17 trophies, including the national league titles of Austria, Belgium, Holland and West Germany. He was the first manager to have won the European Champions Cup with two different clubs: Feyenoord in 1970 and Hamburg in 1983. In addition Club Brugge were losing finalists in the 1978 final. In that same year he almost won the World Cup with Holland, but Ronnie Rensenbrink's shot late in the game hit the post and the Dutch went on to lose 3-1 in extra-time to Argentina.

JOSEF 'SEPP' HERBERGER

Born: March 28, 1897
Management Career: Germany, West Germany
Major honours: World Cup 1954

Josef 'Sepp' Herberger was coach of Germany from 1938 to 1963 without ever managing a club side. He proved to be tactically shrewd, a great motivator, pragmatic yet adaptable. He built the foundation that was to make West Germany one of the strongest teams in the world. In 1954 Herberger's strategies earned West Germany the World Cup. The late call-up of Rot Weiss Essen winger Helmut Rahn was a stroke of genius, as was the bold gamble of fielding a second-string side against the mighty Hungary early on in the competition – the result earned them the easier route to the final, where a full strength Germany beat Hungary 3-2 with two goals from Rahn.

Opposite: Guus Hiddink's club successes have been somewhat overshadowed by his achievement with South Korea, whom he took to the World Cup semi-finals in 2002.

HELENIO HERRERA

Born: April 17, 1917
Management career: Puteaux, Red Star 93, Stade Francais, Atlético Madrid, Malaga, Valladolid, Sevilla, Barcelona, Italy, Spain, Inter Milan, Roma
Major honours: Champions Cup 1964, 1965; World Club Cup 1964, 1965

In terms of trophies, Helenio Herrera's record is impressive enough, but the impact of the man they called 'Il Mago' (the Magician) cannot be measured in silverware alone. Herrera was a revolutionary manager, a well-paid control freak who dominated his club and whose use of man-management techniques was way ahead of its time. His tactical innovations can still be felt in the game today, most notably his role in creating the highly-defensive system of 'catenaccio' with which Inter Milan enjoyed such success in the mid-1960s.

Using tough man-for-man markers supported by a sweeper, Herrera asked his team to focus primarily on defending, pressing their opponents hard and then hitting them on the counter-attack at pace.

So successful was this approach that Inter won three league titles and successive European and World Club Cups in 1964 and 1965. However, it would be wrong to remember Herrera merely as the godfather of defensive Italian football.

Born in Argentina, but raised in Morocco, Herrera played his club football in France and it was there that he began his managerial career with little Puteaux. On moving to Spain, he guided Atlético Madrid to back-to-back league titles before embarking on a tour of the country that ended with Barcelona and another league title. Far from being defensive, at Barcelona Herrera earned a reputation for coaching a wildly attacking team, often playing forwards in defensive positions and encouraging them to go forward in search of goals.

He coached the Italian national team during qualification for the 1962 World Cup Finals, but by the time the tournament came round, he was at the helm of the Spanish team (though he could do nothing to stop them finishing bottom of their group). After the glorious successes of 'Il Grande Inter', Herrera was snapped up by Roma, but could only add an Italian Cup.

GUUS HIDDINK

Born: November 8, 1946
Management Career: De Graafschap, PSV Eindhoven, Fenerbahce, Valencia, Holland, Real Madrid, Real Betis, South Korea, PSV
Major honours: Champions Cup 1988

Guus Hiddink rose to prominence during his time at PSV Eindhoven, where he won the league and cup three times each, and topped his reign by claiming the Champions Cup in 1988. His attractive, free-flowing football won him many admirers, and after spells at Fenerbahce and Valencia he took charge of the Dutch national team, where only a penalty shoot-out prevented an appearance in the final of the 1998 World Cup. A move back to Spain followed, to take charge of Real Madrid and then Real Betis. Now back at PSV, he may well be best remembered for taking South Korea to the semi-finals of the 2002 World Cup.

OTTMAR HITZFELD

Born: January 12, 1949.
Management career: Zug, Aarau, Grasshoppers Zurich, Borussia Dortmund, Bayern Munich
Major honours: Champions Cup 2001

Composed, determined, steely – all could apply to the man who became the first to win the new format of the Champions League with two different clubs following its inception in the early 1990s. There wasn't much of a stir when he took over at Ruhr Valley side Dortmund in 1991, but within four years they were dominating the Bundesliga and then Europe. Poached by Bayern Munich, perceived as the 'glamorous' team of Germany, his authoritarian style was just what was needed. He transformed them in his own image, winning three titles in succession as well as the Champions League in 2001 – beating Valencia on penalties. A disciplinarian, he regards himself as a teacher of football, and Munich have learned the lesson.

ROY HODGSON

Born: August 9, 1947
Management Career: Halmstad, Bristol City, Orebro SK, Malmo, Xamax Neuchatel, Switzerland, Inter Milan, Blackburn Rovers, Grasshoppers, FC Copenhagen, Udinese, United Arab Emirates

Roy Hodgson has been one of the most successful English coaches abroad. He made his name in Sweden with the championship-winning sides of Halmstad and Malmo. With the latter he reached the 1979 European Cup Final before losing out to Brian Clough's Nottingham Forest. He went on to manage

clubs in Switzerland, Italy, Denmark and England. He succeeded the German Uli Stielike as Switzerland's national team boss and got the Swiss to the 1996 European Championship – their first major tournament appearance since 1966. In 2002 he became national coach of the United Arab Emirates.

JIMMY HOGAN

Born: October 16, 1882
Management Career: Holland, Austria, MTK Hungaria, Fulham, Aston Villa

Moderately successful as an inside-forward for Burnley and Fulham, Jimmy Hogan was enticed to coach in Vienna in 1912 by Hugo Miesl. He failed to get his message across to the educated university students, but the unwavering support of Miesl encouraged Hogan to persist with the principles of ball control and intelligent passing that was to be the hallmark of football in Austria, Germany and Hungary. The Vienna School's emphasis on skill led to the 'Wunderteam' of Austria, the rise of West Germany as a football force after the war and the 'Magical Magyars' of Hungary. By way of an acknowledgement of his influence on Hungarian football, Hogan was the team's guest of honour when Hungary memorably defeated England 6-3 at Wembley. He died in January 1974.

AIME JACQUET

Born: November 27, 1941
Management career: Lyon, Bordeaux, Montpellier, Nancy, France
Major honours: World Cup 1998

Aime Jacquet led France to their greatest-ever sporting triumph, victory on home soil at the 1998 World Cup. A decent player in his time, he picked up five league titles and three French Cups at St Etienne in the 1960s and 1970s. He had a brief international spell, playing twice for France, before turning to management at Lyon, where his talent was quickly spotted.

He took over at Bordeaux in 1980 and led the club through the most successful period in their history. Under Jacquet, Bordeaux won three titles, two French Cups and starred impressively in Europe, reaching the semi-finals of the European Cup and the European Cup Winners' Cup, confirming his reputation as France's foremost club manager.

Jacquet was a meticulous planner who prided himself on knowing his players well and paid rigorous attention to detail – qualities that would later serve him well during international tournaments.

After leaving Bordeaux in 1989 he took a Montpellier side including Eric Cantona to an unexpected French Cup triumph. However, a downturn in fortunes followed when he left

for Nancy. He was sacked and moved into the French Football Federation set-up, working as assistant to Gerard Houllier before taking over the national team in 1993 and leading a side built around a solid defence to the semi-finals of the European Championship in 1996.

Despite press criticism he held on to his job to deliver the ultimate prize in 1998. He quit immediately after the finals, becoming the FFF's technical director and elder statesman.

MARCELLO LIPPI

Born: April 12, 1948
Management Career: Sampdoria, Pontedera, Siena, Pistoiese, Carrarese, Cesena, Lucchese, Atalanta, Napoli, Juventus, Inter Milan, Juventus
Major honours: Champions League 1996; World Club Cup 1996; European Supercup 1996

Just one glance at Marcello Lippi's Serie A titles confirms his managerial greatness, but he has worked hard to get where he is. After being in charge of an endless succession of minor Italian clubs, it wasn't until he finished seventh and sixth with Atalanta and Napoli respectively – on shoestring budgets – that his reputation was sealed. His achievements earned him a chance to take over at the helm of Juventus, where he delivered the Champions League – beating Ajax on penalties – the Italian Cup, and a series of three Serie A titles in four seasons between 1995 and 1998. He spent a brief period away from the club, managing Inter Milan, before returning to pick up the league title in both 2002 and 2003. During his time in Turin, he has continued to dominate the Italian game.

VALERY LOBANOVSKY

Born: January 6, 1939
Management career: Dnepr Dnepropetrovsk, Dynamo Kiev, Soviet Union, United Arab Emirates, Kuwait, Ukraine
Major honours: European Cup Winners' Cup 1975, 1986

Notorious for his solemn expression and ruling teams with an iron fist, the late Valery Lobanovsky was the man responsible for making Dynamo Kiev a force in European football. As coach he took the club to victory in the European Cup Winners' Cup in 1975 and 1986, and to the semi-finals of the Champions League in 1999. A left-winger, as a player he won the league and cup with Dynamo before moving to Chernomorets Odessa. But he made his name as a coach, starting in the late 1960s. Teamwork was the cornerstone of his teams, but he also brought through outstanding individuals such as Oleg Blokhin, and latterly Sergei Rebrov and Andriy Shevchenko. He died on May 13, 2002.

Left: Cesar Luis Menotti won two World Cups as manager of Argentina.

CESARE MALDINI

Born: February 5, 1932
Management Career: Foggia, Ternana, Parma, Italy, Paraguay

Cesare Maldini believes in the traditional Italian values of a solid defence, with teams that win games by the odd goal. It has worked for him though. He was second in command to Enzo Bearzot when Italy won the 1982 World Cup, and his highly successful spell in charge of the Italy Under-21s was enough to earn him the stewardship of the national team, but a quarter-final exit from the 1998 World Cup cost him the Italy job. He went on to manage Paraguay at the 2002 World Cup, although the appointment was controversial as coaches in Paraguay were furious that an old-fashioned foreigner was preferred to them. He retired after the World Cup campaign.

CESAR LUIS MENOTTI

Born: November 5, 1938.
Management career: Independiente, Argentina, Barcelona, Peñarol, Boca Juniors, River Plate, Mexico, Atlético Madrid, Sampdoria, Valencia, Rosario Central
Major honours: World Cup 1978

A decent player in North and South America, it was not until chain-smoking Cesar Luis Menotti went into management that he became a football legend for reviving the national team of Argentina. 'El Flaco' (The Thin One) was a highly-strung coach who had already enjoyed a spell as the manager of Independiente when he took over the national team before the 1978 World Cup. He broke the mould by going for all-out attack, with stars such as Mario Kempes, Osvaldo Ardiles and later Diego Maradona at the heart of his teams. He has variously enjoyed and endured short spells at many clubs, including some in Europe, and most recently the side he first played for, Rosario Central.

Opposite: Aime Jacquet lifts the 1998 World Cup, after France beat Brazil in the final.

1940

1940s/50s: Enjoys a career as a centre forward with Ajax during which time he wins five caps with Holland.

1950

1965

1965: Becomes head coach of Ajax, where he develops the Total Football concept.

1967

1967: Success arrives with a Dutch league and cup double.

1968: Ajax win third successive Dutch championship.

1968

1971: Ajax win European Cup for the first time, beating Panathinaikos at Wembley.

1971

1971: Moves to Spain to take over as manager at Barcelona.

1972

1973: Signs Cruyff, who epitomised Total Football.

1973

1974: Wins Spanish league title.

1974

1974: Takes Holland to World Cup final, but loses to West Germany.

1975

1975: Returns to Ajax as coach.

1980

1980: Tackles the German Bundesliga by joining Köln.

1984

1984: Returns to international coaching with Holland.

1986

1988: Holland win European Championship with a team which includes the talents of Gullit, Rijkaard and Marco Van Basten.

1988

1988: Takes over at Bayer Levekusen.

1990

1990: Becomes Dutch coach for third time, only to retire in 1992.

2002

2002: Recognised with UEFA Lifetime Achievement Award.

MARINUS 'RINUS' MICHELS

Born: February 9, 1928

Management career: Ajax, Barcelona, Holland, Ajax (technical director), Barcelona, Los Angeles Aztecs, Köln, Holland (technical director), Holland, Bayer Leverkusen, Holland

Major honours: Champions Cup 1971; European Championship 1988

An Ajax centre-forward who won five caps for Holland, it is as the coach who invented Total Football that Michels will always be remembered. With Johan Cruyff as its heartbeat, Total Football – a philosophy dependent on versatility, adaptability and all-round ball skills – was first developed with Ajax in the late 1960s, and then with the brilliant Dutch team of the Seventies.

But 'Iron Rinus' was no soft touch. For him, playing beautiful football was a serious business and he demanded a high level of professionalism from his players. That combination of silk and steel took Ajax to their first European Cup final in 1969, and although they lost to Milan, the foundations for future success had been firmly laid. Ajax went on to win three successive European Cups and, while Michels left for Barcelona after the first victory, he could still claim much of the credit for the legacy he left behind.

At Barça he at first found progress hard but, having taken Cruyff to the Nou Camp, he celebrated league success in 1974 and lifted the Spanish Cup in 1978 during a second spell in charge. He also found time to lead an outstanding Holland team to the 1974 World Cup Final, captivating fans across the world, only to see them throw away a 1-0 lead against West Germany and finish as runners-up.

In 1978 Michels joined the Los Angeles Aztecs in the NASL before going back to Germany and a successful spell with Köln. He returned as coach of Holland in time to mould individuals like Ruud Gullit and Marco Van Basten into a disciplined Dutch unit good enough to win their first international trophy, the 1988 European Championship.

After a spell with Bayer Leverkusen, Michels led Holland to the 1992 European Championship, but when they slipped up on penalties to surprise winners Denmark, he called time on a glorious career.

Above: Rinus Michels capped his return to managing the Dutch national side by taking them to the 1988 European Championship, but retired after defeat to Denmark in the same competition four years later.

HUGO MIESL

Born: November 16, 1881

Management Career: Amateure, Austria

Hugo Miesl developed the famed Vienna School alongside Englishman Jimmy Hogan. Miesl was a highly educated man and a believer in 'pure' football. He was an admirer of the English game and his recruiting and encouragement of Hogan not only had a profound effect on football in Austria – notably with 'Wunderteams' of the 1930s and 1950s – but also on football in Hungary and Germany. Austria finished fourth at the 1934 World Cup but the country was annexed by the Nazis' Greater Germany by the time of the 1938 tournament. He founded Amateure (later FK Austria) and was an advocate of FIFA and the international game.

BORA MILUTINOVIC

Born: September 7, 1944

Management Career: Pumas UNAM, Mexico, San Lorenzo, Almagro, Costa Rica, Udinese, USA, Mexico, Nigeria, MetroStars, Peru, China

Major honours: CONCACAF Championship 1989; Gold Cup 1991, 1996

Bora Milutinovic is a true coaching legend, having taken charge of five different countries at five successive World Cups: Mexico (1986), Costa Rica (1990), USA (1994), Nigeria (1998) and China (2002). The Yugoslav-born coach has the ability to get teams to exceed expectation and Milutinovic's sides have been responsible for a number of World Cup shocks over the years, including Costa Rica's defeat of Scotland in 1986 and Nigeria's win over Spain in 1998. His best World Cup finals performance was taking hosts Mexico to the quarter-finals of the competition in 1986. His management career had begun in Mexico with Pumas UNAM in 1977 and, between international appointments, he has managed clubs in Argentina, Italy and the USA.

MIGUEL MUNOZ

Born: September 15, 1924

Management Career: Plus Ultra, Real Madrid, Hercules, Sevilla, Las Palmas, Spain

Major honours: Champions Cup 1960, 1966

Miguel Munoz was, arguably, the greatest manager Real Madrid ever had. During his 14-year reign in charge Real won the Spanish championship nine times and the Spanish Cup twice. Of greater significance were the European Cup wins of 1960 and 1966. The 1960 victory was the classic 7-3 triumph over Eintracht Frankfurt at Hampden Park in Glasgow, regarded as one of the best matches of all time. It was Real's fifth successive

Champions Cup triumph. As a player, Munoz had won the trophy twice with Real in 1956 and 1957. Inevitably, Munoz became coach of the Spanish national team, taking them to the 1984 European Championship Final and the 1986 World Cup quarter-finals.

BILL NICHOLSON

Born: January 26, 1919
Management Career: Tottenham Hotspur
Major honours: UEFA Cup 1972; European Cup Winners' Cup 1963

Bill Nicholson guided Tottenham Hotspur to a host of domestic and European trophies between 1958 and 1974. However, his most famous and enduring achievement was winning the 1961 league championship and FA Cup double. In their 42 league games that season Tottenham scored 115 goals, playing outstanding and attractive football. Nicholson achieved the double after spending more money than any other British manager in history. His Tottenham side, featuring Danny Blanchflower and the skilful John White, began the season with 11 straight wins and ended up winning 31 games (including 16 away). The double was successfully completed by defeating Leicester City 2-0 in the FA Cup final at Wembley Stadium.

BOB PAISLEY

Born: January 23, 1919
Management career: Liverpool
Major honours: Champions Cup 1977, 1978, 1981; UEFA Cup 1976;

Bob Paisley began his playing career with the famous amateur side Bishop Auckland in his native North-East, but from just before the war in 1939 until his retirement from the board in 1992, he was Liverpool through and through. Few, if any, other football professionals can have been a player, a coach, a physiotherapist, a manager and a director of the same club. Paisley fulfilled all these roles at Anfield. He forged his 'odd couple' partnership with Bill Shankly in 1959, and for 15 years was happy to play second fiddle to the extrovert Scotsman.

Shankly relied heavily on Bob Paisley's shrewd judgment of a player's strengths and weaknesses, and when Shankly suddenly resigned in 1974, the unassuming Paisley was reluctant to take on the mantle. With the support of his senior players, he agreed to take on the challenge and was able to help Liverpool continue to develop the footballing philosophy that he had helped formulate. His teams, like Shankly's before him, played a simple, fast passing game, the players working tirelessly for each other. Soon Paisley's Liverpool were surpassing the achievements of the Shankly era. After a worryingly trophyless first season,

his side went on to win Division One the following year, and a 4-3 aggregate victory over Club Brugge gave them the UEFA Cup too.

In 1977 Liverpool won the league by a point from Manchester City and, four days after an FA Cup final defeat to Manchester United, they outplayed Borussia Mönchengladbach to win the European Champions Cup in Rome. As a member of the British Army in World War II, Paisley was able to joke that the last time he had visited the city he had helped liberate it! That was Kevin Keegan's last game for the club, but in keeping with his reputation as a good judge of a footballer, Paisley replaced Keegan with Kenny Dalglish. The Scotsman went on to score the winner against Club Brugge the following year as Liverpool retained the European Cup. Other useful investments included Alan Hansen, Graeme Souness and Mark Lawrenson, as he strove to motivate and renew his incredibly successful side.

The Reds continued to dominate in the league, winning four of the five titles between 1979 and 1983. In that year off, 1981, they added a third European Cup, beating Real Madrid 1-0. Paisley also managed three League Cup triumphs in his final three years, before he called it a day in 1983, staying on as an advisor to Joe Fagan and then Kenny Dalglish. He died on February 14, 1996.

Above: Liverpool manager Bob Paisley and friend head back on the train after the side's 1-0 European Cup final win over Club Brugge at Wembley in 1978.

CARLOS ALBERTO PARREIRA

Born: February 27, 1943
Management career: Fluminense, Kuwait, United Arab Emerates, Metrostars, Saudi Arabia, Corinthians, Brazil
Major honours: World Cup 1994

Now back in charge of Brazil for the third time following the success of Luiz Felipe Scolari's 2002 World Cup side, to many people the man known as 'The Professor', Carlos Parreira, is modern Brazilian football. He is famous for combining modern coaching techniques with the exciting tradition of his national team.

Parreira was not a distinguished player himself, arriving instead from a background of physical preparation, having been on the coaching staff when Brazil won the 1970 World Cup in Mexico. He then married the attacking and exciting play forever demanded by the public following that success to a more pragmatic, match-winning approach. But for his 1994 side he was also blessed with stars such as Bebeto and Romario, enabling the team to claim Brazil's first World Cup win for 24 years. He is one of only two men to lead four different nations to World Cup finals (Kuwait, UAE, Saudi Arabia and Brazil), Bora Multinovic being the other.

VITTORIO POZZO

Born: March 2, 1886
Management Career: Torino, Italy
Major honours: World Cup 1934, 1938;
Olympics 1936

Many believe Pozzo only won the World Cup because the all-powerful Mussolini 'arranged' it – others see him as a managerial genius. He is certainly the only manager to win the World Cup twice, and he was the first man to lead Italy in a competitive game. The war broke up his career, and 'Il Vecchio Maestro' (the Old Master) never really rediscovered his touch, despite remaining manager of the national team. Part of the problem was that Italy had been largely ignored by the footballing world after its involvement in the war, but Pozzo had already done enough to earn his reputation.

JOSEF 'SEPP' PIONTEK

Born: March 5, 1940
Management Career: Fortuna Düsseldorf, Haiti, Denmark, Turkey, Silkeborg, Greenland

Despite a CV exempt of any major honours, Piontek is a huge talent, and one highly regarded in the game. After learning his trade as boss of Haiti, he moulded a Denmark national team of no-hopers into a major force, guiding them to the semi-finals of the 1984 European Championship and the second round of the 1986 World Cup. His team earned the nickname 'Danish Dynamite' as they constantly over-achieved, and when he finally left the role in 1990, the opportunity to take over the burgeoning Turkey side arose. He spent three years there before returning to Denmark to win the league with Silkeborg, and is now the manager of Greenland.

ALF RAMSEY

Born: January 21, 1920
Management Career: Ipswich Town, England, Birmingham City
Major honours: World Cup 1966

Though he never coached a major club, Alf Ramsey is one of the game's top managers for his success at both ends of the spectrum – in piloting a relatively minor club to the First Division championship and in guiding the national team to World Cup triumph.

Ramsey was a high grade full-back who played for Southampton and Tottenham. A natural leader and an instinctive reader of the game, he won 32 caps, captaining both club and country. Retiring at the age of 35 in 1955, he immediately took up management with Ipswich Town, then in the Third Division South. Playing with a deep-lying striker and his wide players tucked, the club embarked on

an extraordinary seven-year run of success, moving swiftly through the divisions until they secured the First Division title in 1962.

Ramsey was an enigmatic character: unflappable, pragmatic and iron-willed. His clipped vowels concealed a working-class upbringing in Dagenham, but while he was never close to his players, he commanded their utmost respect. It was these characteristics that led to his appointment as England manager in 1962, following the retirement of Walter Winterbottom. On taking the job he promptly announced that England would win the World Cup, but in his first match in charge they exited the European Nations Cup with a 2-5 defeat to France.

Ramsey set about building a team with the ability to take on the world, shoring up the defence with the addition of goalkeeper Gordon Banks and refining his 'wingless wonders' system. Captain Bobby Moore became the heartbeat of his side.

England's World Cup victory was a triumph for Ramsey's preparation and planning. He drafted Geoff Hurst into the squad late, but when injury ruled Jimmy Greaves out of the notorious confrontation with Argentina, Ramsey put Hurst in and then played him in

the final, with match-winning consequences.

A knighthood did not go to Ramsey's head and his preparation for the World Cup in 1970 was even more meticulous. Bad luck played its part in undermining an even better squad, but the quarter-final defeat to West Germany raised questions about his cautious tactics.

Two disastrous results against Poland home and away in 1973 led to failure to qualify for the 1974 tournament and Ramsey's eventual dismissal. He had a brief spell at Birmingham as caretaker-manager in 1977, and was later technical director with Panathinaikos in 1979, before retiring from the game completely. He died on April 28, 1999, but will always be remembered for his role in England's greatest sporting achievement.

GEORGE RAYNOR

Born: January 13, 1907
Management Career: Sweden, AIK Stockholm, Atvidaberg, Juventus, Lazio, Skegness Town, Djurgardens, Skegness Town, Doncaster
Major honours: Olympics 1948

Englishman George Raynor took Sweden to Olympic Games gold in 1948 and the 1958 World Cup Final as hosts. Stanley Rous, chairman of the FA, noticed Raynor when he was coaching in Iraq during the Second World War. After the war Raynor moved from reserve trainer at Aldershot to national team coach of Sweden. In his first game in charge he made his mark by devising a strategy that outwitted Switzerland's revolutionary 'Swiss bolt' system. A series of training camps were then set up aimed at improving promising young players. The scheme was certainly a roaring success and by 1948 Raynor had helped Sweden to gold at the Olympics with a team that included Gren, Nordahl and Liedholm.

DON REVIE

Born: July 10, 1927
Management Career: Leeds United, England, UAE, Al Nasr, Al-Al FC
Major honours: Fairs Cup 1968, 1971

Between the mid-Sixties and mid-Seventies, Don Revie turned Leeds United into the fiercest contenders in British football, winning six trophies, and finishing as runners-up to a further 11. Revie had been a decent centre-forward for Leicester, Hull, Manchester City and Sunderland before joining a broke and demoralised Leeds in the Second Division as player-manager in 1958.

By 1964 he had taken the club from the relegation zone of the Second Division to the brink of the Division One title and to the FA Cup final, where they lost to Liverpool. The following ten seasons saw Revie construct a team renowned for a win-at-all-costs attitude. And win they did: the league in 1969 and 1974; the FA Cup in 1972; the Fairs Cup in 1968 and 1971; and the League Cup in 1968.

In 1974 Revie left Leeds to replace Sir Alf Ramsey as manager of the England team. But he couldn't recreate the same magic on the international stage and, after failing to take the team to the 1978 World Cup Finals, he caused consternation when he resigned to take up a £240,000 four-year contract to manage the United Arab Emirates.

Revie subsequently coached Saudi side Al Nasr and had a short spell in Cairo with Al-Al FC, before returning home in 1984. After his resignation from the England job, the FA had banned him from the English game for ten years. The ban was overturned but, despite brief negotiations with QPR, Revie never returned to club management. He died in May 1989.

BOBBY ROBSON

Born: February 18, 1933
Management career: Vancouver Royals, Fulham, Ipswich Town, England, PSV Eindhoven, Sporting Lisbon, Porto, Barcelona, PSV Eindhoven, Newcastle United
Major honours: UEFA Cup 1981; European Cup Winners' Cup 1997

Sir Bobby Robson is now the grand old man of football management. He started his coaching career more than 35 years ago, with a brief spell in Canada, before returning to Fulham, where he had spent much of his distinguished playing career. He was, however, sacked in short order, and began his long and successful stint at Ipswich. He turned this small-town club into one of the country's best and most attractive sides, winning the FA Cup in 1978 and the UEFA Cup against AZ 67 Alkmaar in 1981, though never won the league.

Robson was rewarded for his sterling achievements in 1982 when he was offered the role of England manager. His side lost unluckily to Argentina, and Maradona's dextrous subterfuge, in the quarter-finals of the 1986 World Cup; performed badly in the 1988 European Championship; and nearly made it to the World Cup final of 1990. Robson then began his decade-long journey around the continent, winning trophies galore in Holland, Portugal and Spain. Finally it was back to his Geordie homeland, where his decency, enthusiasm and football nous have helped breathe new life into Newcastle.

ARRIGO SACCHI

Born: April 1, 1946
Management career: Rimini, Parma, AC Milan, Italy, AC Milan, Atlético Madrid, Parma
Major honours: Champions Cup 1989, 1990; World Club Cup 1989, 1990

Having never played the game professionally, Arrigo Sacchi's big break came after his up-and-coming Parma team knocked AC Milan out of the 1986-87 Italian Cup. The following summer Milan president Silvio Berlusconi moved to bring Sacchi to the San Siro and within a year he had created a brilliant attacking team. The Serie A league title in his first season in charge was followed by two successive European Cup triumphs in 1989 and 1990, before he was tempted away to coach the Italian national side.

He guided the Azzurri to the 1994 World Cup Final in the USA, where they were beaten on penalties by Brazil, but resigned after the 1996 European Championship and returned to Milan for a brief, unsuccessful spell. He then had a short stint at Atlético Madrid, an even shorter one (just 28 days) back at Parma, who he left for health reasons before resurfacing at the club as Parma's general manager in December 2001.

HELMUT SCHÖN

Born: September 15, 1915
Management Career: Saarland, West Germany
Major honours: World Cup 1974; European Championship 1972

Helmut Schön scored 17 goals in 16 internationals before the war forced him to flee his native Dresden. His first 'national' coaching job was with the postwar limbo state, Saarland. Then from 1955 he was West Germany's assistant manager, taking over the reins from Sepp Herberger in 1964.

Schön's fine, undervalued team nearly upset England in the 1966 World Cup Final, eventually losing in extra-time. In the 1970 quarter-final the Germans exacted revenge, beating England, and eventually finishing third. Schön's natural inclination, as an inside-forward, was to produce ball-playing teams. His truly great 1972 European Championship-winning side, boasting Franz Beckenbauer, Gerd Müller and Gunter Netzer, epitomised that Dutch ideal of Total Football.

Despite arguments over money – which depressed the benign, erudite Schön deeply – his flexible, powerful 1974 team pulled through to beat Holland and win the ultimate prize. West Germany then lost in the final of the 1976 European Championship, before failing again at the 1978 World Cup. That final performance, however, cannot devalue Schön's many achievements in a long career.

LUIZ FELIPE SCOLARI

Born: November 9, 1948.
Management career: Gremio, Criciuma, Palmeiras, Cruzeiro, Brazil, Portugal
Major honours: World Cup 2002; Copa Libertadores 1995, 1999

'Big Phil' led Brazil from the doldrums to a record fifth World Cup, but his style is different to many in that country. With a reputation for making tough decisions and sticking by them – especially over selection – Scolari preferred home-based stars to some playing in Europe. He placed an emphasis on a workmanlike midfield and strong defence, and he put the team before all individuals.

His playing career was hardly sparkling, being a defender for modest Brazilian teams, but when called upon by his nation as a manager, he transformed their fortunes from Copa América strugglers to world champions in just over a year. Under-achieving Portugal now hope for the same result.

BILL SHANKLY

Born: September 2, 1919
Management Career: Carlisle United, Grimsby Town, Workington, Huddersfield Town, Liverpool
Major honours: UEFA Cup 1973

Bill Shankly was the founding father of the great Liverpool dynasty of the Sixties, Seventies and Eighties. After a good playing career, which included several caps for Scotland, he spent a decade as manager at various lowly clubs who lacked his drive and vision. In 1959, he finally alighted at Liverpool, then languishing in Division Two. He dispensed with the services of 24 players, but was canny enough to retain two members of the coaching staff, Joe Fagan and Bob Paisley. Together they would go on to form the legendary Anfield 'Boot Room'. With their help, and through his own willpower, charisma and native intelligence, he transformed the club, taking them to promotion to Division One in 1962, and to the championship in 1964. He emphasised neat passing, constant movement and indefatigable teamwork, hallmarks which stayed with Liverpool teams through the decades.

The FA Cup was collected in 1965 after beating Leeds United 2-1, and the league title was won again in 1966, though they failed at the final hurdle in the European Cup Winners' Cup against Borussia Dortmund the same year. As the team built around Ron Yeats, Ian St John and Roger Hunt began to fade, Shankly set about rebuilding. His enthusiasm was embodied on the pitch in the shape of new signing, Kevin Keegan. The pocket-sized powerhouse helped The Reds to another Division One title in 1973. That year they also achieved one of Shankly's much-coveted

ambitions: a European honour, in the shape of a UEFA Cup final victory over Borussia Mönchengladbach. After the 3-0 FA Cup final trouncing of Newcastle in 1974, Shankly unexpectedly announced his retirement. He left behind a powerful legacy, and will be eternally venerated by the club's fans for his passion for the game, his commitment to good football, and his witticisms ('This city has two great teams: Liverpool and Liverpool reserves,' he once famously quipped). He died on September 29, 1981.

JOCK STEIN

Born: October 1, 1922
Management Career: Dunfermline Athletic, Hibernian, Celtic, Leeds United, Scotland
Major honours: Champions Cup 1967

Jock Stein, 'The Big Man', announced his arrival as a manager by guiding unfancied Dunfermline Athletic to the Scottish Cup of 1961, beating Celtic – the team Stein had captained to the double of 1954. Stein moved to Hibs for a spell, but by 1965 he was in charge at Celtic Park. With a determination born of his background as miner, he quickly built one of the best British club sides ever. In 1966 he won the first of an unprecedented nine titles in succession. Their exuberant, skilful victory over dour Inter Milan in the European Cup final of 1967 was also a victory for football. They nearly repeated the feat in 1970, losing narrowly to Feyenoord.

Celtic tried to move Stein into a more senior role after his final championship in 1977, but he decided instead on a new challenge at Leeds United. This engagement lasted mere weeks before he returned north to manage the Scottish national team. He steered them to the 1982 World Cup Finals, but they failed to progress beyond the first round. Tragically he died of a heart-attack immediately after the game which ensured Scotland a place at the 1986 finals in Mexico. His balance of honesty, intelligence, steel and likeability mark him as one of the very greatest managers.

GUY THYS

Born: December 6, 1922
Management Career: Racing Lokeren, Wezel Sport, Herentals, SK Beveren, Union St Gilloise, Antwerp, Belgium

When Guy Thys, a club manager with no real success, was appointed national team coach of Belgium in 1976 he inherited an old team from his predecessor Raymond Goethals. Thys embarked on a policy of developing young players and went on to build one of the best national sides in the history of Belgian football. Thys's team proved to be the surprise package of the 1980 European Championship, only

losing the final with West Germany to a goal two minutes from time. Belgium played exciting open football and also reached the World Cup semi-finals under Thys.

GIOVANNI TRAPATTONI

Born: March 17, 1939
Management Career: AC Milan, Juventus, Inter Milan, Bayern Munich, Cagliari, Bayern Munich, Fiorentina, Italy
Major honours: Champions Cup 1985; UEFA Cup 1977, 1991; European Cup Winners' Cup 1984; World Club Cup 1985; European Supercup 1984

Italy's most successful coach actually won two European Cups as a player with AC Milan, but it was during a glorious spell as coach of Juventus that he really made his name, winning all three major European trophies, the European Supercup, the World Club Cup, six Italian league titles and two Italian Cups. He added another league title and UEFA Cup with Inter Milan before succeeding Franz Beckenbauer at Bayern Munich. He struggled with the language in Germany, but after a spell at Cagliari he returned to become the first foreign manager to win the German league. He graduated from club football to become coach of the Italian national side in July 2000.

Below: 'Big Phil' Scolari led Brazil to their latest World Cup triumph in 2002.

PHILIPPE TROUSSIER

Born: March 21, 1955

Management career: Alencon, Red Star, ASEC Abidjan, Ivory Coast, Kaizer Chiefs, CA Rabat, FUS Rabat, Nigeria, Burkino Faso, South Africa, Japan, Qatar

Major honours: Asian Nations Cup 2000

Paris-born Philippe Troussier started coaching in his native France but only really found success after moving to Africa, where he led ASEC Abidjan to three consecutive league titles. He gained a huge reputation with spells in charge of Ivory Coast, Nigeria and Burkina Faso, who he led to fourth place in the African Nations Cup on home soil in 1998.

Nicknamed 'The White Sorcerer', Troussier took South Africa into the 1998 World Cup Finals, held in his homeland, but switched to Japan afterwards, revolutionising the team and winning the Asian title in 2000. The country reached the last 16 of the 2002 World Cup and he quit after the finals.

LOUIS VAN GAAL

Born: August 8, 1951

Management career: Ajax, Barcelona, Holland, Barcelona

Major honours: Champions Cup 1995; UEFA Cup 1992; World Club Cup 1995; European Supercup 1995

A fine creative midfielder in the 1970s, Louis Van Gaal became head coach of his former club Ajax in 1991. Putting his faith in youth, he created a fast, accomplished, ball-playing side who peaked with their 1995 Champions League triumph over AC Milan. Having lost the 1996 final, and seen his best players leave, Van Gaal headed for Barcelona in 1997, winning back-to-back Spanish league titles but proving unpopular with the fans who resented his preference for Dutch players. He resigned in 2000, becoming Holland coach, but failure to qualify for the 2002 World Cup forced him out and he returned to Barcelona for a short, unsuccessful spell.

TERRY VENABLES

Born: January 6, 1943

Management career: Crystal Palace, Queens Park Rangers, Barcelona, Tottenham Hotspur, England, Australia, Crystal Palace, Middlesbrough, Leeds United

Terry Venables represented England at every level as a player, but after a bright start with Chelsea and Spurs his career was fading by the time Malcolm Allison offered him a coaching post at Crystal Palace. As manager from 1976, Venables guided The Eagles to two promotions with a young side dubbed 'The Team of the Eighties', but then left in 1980 for QPR, who he lead to the FA Cup final.

In 1984 he took over at Barcelona, earning the nickname 'El Tel' as he brought the club their first league title in 11 years and took them to the 1986 European Cup Final.

Back in England Venables collected his only major English trophy in 1991, winning the FA Cup with Tottenham, before falling out with chairman Alan Sugar. In 1994 he took charge of England, leading them to the semi-finals of the 1996 European Championship on home turf, but left the job amid controversy. He then dabbled in ownership at Portsmouth, coached Australia and returned to Palace.

In December 2000, he was summoned to join Bryan Robson at Middlesbrough and saved them from relegation, but decided not to stay on. So it was a surprise when he accepted the manager's job at Leeds United in 2002. But after the club's severe financial troubles saw their best players sold, Venables was sacked in March 2003.

ARSENE WENGER

Born: September 22, 1949

Management career: Nancy, Monaco, Nagoya Grampus Eight, Arsenal

An average player with Strasbourg, Arsene Wenger joined the club's coaching staff in 1981, going on to become head coach at Nancy and then Monaco in 1987, where he won the league, the French Cup and reached the European Cup Winners' Cup final before departing for Japan. Having transformed Grampus Eight from also-rans to title hopefuls, Wenger took over at Arsenal, arriving in September 1996 to newspaper headlines of 'Arsene Who?' In 1998, however, he became the first foreign coach to win the English championship, throwing in the FA Cup for good measure. After a series of near misses, a second double followed in 2002.

WALTER WINTERBOTTOM

Born: January 31, 1913

Management Career: England

Between 1946 and 1962 Walter Winterbottom was England manager and Director of FA Coaching. He was in charge for 139 games, winning 78 times. He lifted the British Championship outright on seven occasions and took charge of England at four World Cups. Winterbottom considered coaching as the most important aspect of his job. For much of his tenure he did not have control over team selection – that was done by committee – and Winterbottom's job was to prepare the team for the match concerned (as well as the Under-23 and Youth teams). It is a testament to Winterbottom that England still had the reputation of being one of the world's best teams during this period.

MARIO ZAGALO

Born: August 9, 1931

Management career: Botafogo, Brazil, Fluminense, Flamengo, Brazil, Kuwait, Saudi Arabia, UAE, Brazil (technical director), Brazil, Portuguesa de Desportes, Flamengo, Brazil (technical director)

Major honours: World Cup 1970, 1994 (as technical co-ordinator); Copa América 1997

Having won the 1958 and 1962 World Cups as a player (scoring as Brazil defeated Sweden 5-2 in the 1958 final), Mario Zagalo began his coaching career as youth team boss at Botafogo. In 1967 he became manager, winning two Rio State Championships, before his big opportunity came just three months before the 1970 World Cup Finals, when he was asked to take charge of the national side. He did so, allowing his team to play with such freedom and panache that many regard their performances as the greatest ever seen.

Continuing as Brazil coach, he also lead Rio rivals Fluminense and Flamengo to State Championships before a fourth-place finish with Brazil at the 1974 World Cup.

After a seven-year stint in the Middle East with Kuwait, Saudi Arabia and the UAE (who he led to the 1990 World Cup Finals), Zagalo became Brazil's technical co-ordinator in 1991, teaming up with coach Carlos Alberto Parreira to win the 1994 World Cup in the United States, and becoming the first man ever to be involved in four World Cup victories.

It would have been five, had Zagalo's team not stalled in the 1998 final against France. But after winning another State Championship with Flamengo, in autumn 2002 he returned for one last crack with the national team, again in partnership with Carlos Alberto Parreira.

Opposite clockwise from top left: Arsene Wenger with the FA Cup; 'El Tel' at Barcelona; Louis Van Gaal enjoys Ajax's European Cup win; Philippe Troussier, Japan coach for the 2002 World Cup.

Below: Mario Zagalo hoists aloft his fourth World Cup as Brazil's technical co-ordinator in 1994.

WOMEN'S FOOTBALL

THE HISTORY OF WOMEN'S FOOTBALL

Above from left to right: Kelly Smith, England; Sun Wen, China; and Julie Foudy, USA.

Below: Hanna Ljungberg of Sweden celebrates.

Women's football may not have come to the public's attention until the last decade of the 20th Century, but its history began in Europe 100 years earlier. The first recorded women's football match in the world was staged in England in 1895, held between a northern team and southern XI on March 23 – the North winning 7-1. The popularity of women's football in England continued to grow and, in the early 1900s, crowds of up to 50,000 watched teams such as Dick, Kerr Ladies from Preston play matches to raise money for charity. However, the Football Association banned women from playing on league grounds in 1921 and this effectively destroyed the game in England for more than 40 years. The Dutch and German federations followed suit in the 1950s, although they were to adopt the women's game 20 years later.

The game continued to develop in other countries in Europe, most notably in Scandinavia and Italy. By the early 1970s the Italian women's league, run by the amateur women's football association, was attracting players from across Europe, offering to pay living expenses while some of the better home-grown players were earning weekly wages.

A key step forward in the development of the game came from UEFA in 1971. Dismayed that its member nations had participated in two 'unofficial' World Cups in Italy and Mexico between 1970 and 1971, UEFA held a vote of its states where an overwhelming majority voted in favour of national associations taking over the governance of women's football in their countries. Most European nations did this, although Italy (1986) and England (1993) left it until much later. Germany, Sweden and Norway, whose associations did take control of the women's game in the 1970s, are three of the top five teams in the world today, while Italy and England struggle to compete regularly at the highest level, both having failed to qualify for the 2003 World Cup.

This change allowed for official international competition to begin, albeit limited to just friendlies at first. A UEFA women's committee established in 1971 (and composed entirely of men) folded seven years later, having failed to establish successfully an official championship tournament for nations.

Across the Atlantic, another political decision was being taken that would help to shape the future development of women's football. The US government introduced an equity funding programme, Title IX, which ensured the same investment would be put into women's collegiate sport as men's. The whole North American sports structure relies upon competitive college sport, from which the country's top leagues draft their talent annually. While the men's scholarships were centred around basketball, baseball and American football, the minority sport of soccer soon began to emerge as the preferred women's scholarship sport.

Today there are more than 300 colleges in America providing football scholarships, drawing on the best young players from across the world to supplement their own talented players. This programme has helped drive the participation rates to more than eight million by giving the players an exit route. It also enables the national team to hen-pick their world-beating squad. It wasn't until 1985 that the USA team first played an international, but by playing numerous competitive fixtures each year – with funding most national women's teams across the world could only dream of – the side became the world's first official champions just six years later.

With the growing number of national teams and competitions, FIFA followed UEFA's call to member associations in 1983, and then

announced three years later that a Women's World Cup would be established, the first to be staged in China in 1991. An official world tournament would not only give more credibility to the women's game, but it would have an impact on the development of the game through elite competition. It was to be an occasion where the USA team – for whom striker Michelle Akers starred – would stamp their mark on football. The potential of women's football as a serious spectator sport – with 65,000 attending the final to see USA beat Norway – became apparent at this stage.

At the 1995 World Cup FIFA president Sepp Blatter made the now famous statement that 'the future of football is feminine'. The sentiment turned out to be more than just lip service because the next two major women's tournaments, following the 1995 World Cup in Sweden, ensured that the game could live up to those expectations. Women's football was launched at the 1996 Atlanta Olympics, with the host nation sweeping all before them to take the gold medal from China in front of 76,000 cheering fans.

But while a section of the American audience was being won over, it was the 1999 World Cup that launched women's football across the world as a sport in its own right –

a sport that could complement the men's game, rather than be forever regarded as its poor relation. Over half a million fans packed into stadia to watch the games, while 40 million tuned in across the world to watch the tournament on television.

It is a valid question whether the cup would have left such a legacy had the USA not triumphed on home soil. But triumph they did, giving rise to a wave of enthusiasm that enabled the launch of world's first fully professional women's league – Women's United Soccer Association (WUSA) – that launched 18 months later to a modest, yet encouraging audience.

Several seasons later and the Americans still lead the development of the women's game as the only arena where women can make a career from their sport. The Chinese FA, in preparation for hosting the 2003 World Cup, established a semi-professional league, while the superior youth development structures of the European nations could see a turnaround in the powerbase in the game. England boast 42 girls' centres of excellence, while France has a national girls' academy alongside the established boys' programme at Clarefontaine.

It's not true to say that the women's game is now at an advanced stage of development

across the world, in many places the sport is in the early stages of its infancy. Women's football in Asia, Africa and the South Americas still remains a major area for improvement. Many countries do not operate a national league or a national team and the opportunity for girls to play organised, structured football is limited. FIFA's plans to take its second Under-19 World Championship to Thailand in 2004 could help encourage associations in Asia to appreciate the value of developing the women's game, while the AFC president, Mohamed bin Hammam, has set the target of having as many as 20 nations (from 44 member states) competing at the 15th Asia women's championships in 2005.

Despite a survey in 2001 showing that there are now 22 million girls and women playing affiliated football across the world, most of these are concentrated in the North Americas, Europe, Oceania and China. Of the 207 FIFA member states, there are 120 countries now actively competing on the international stage in women's football, all of which were grouped into the first world rankings launched on July 16, 2003. Unsurprisingly, this list ranked the USA as the leading nation, followed by Olympic gold medallists Norway and European champions Germany.

Above left: Sissi of Brazil is regarded as one of the most entertaining players in the women's game.

Above right: One of the most famous images in women's football – USA's Brandi Chastain celebrating her World Cup goal in 1999.

GREAT PLAYERS OF WOMEN'S FOOTBALL

LIU AILING

Country: China
Born: February 5, 1967
Position: Midfield
Clubs: Beijing, Philadelphia Charge

Rated as highly as her team-mate Sun Wen in their homeland China, Ailing is a midfield dynamo whose fearless style of play puts fear into opposing teams. She has great vision and brings her team-mates into the game through slick passes with both feet. She played for China in the 1995 and 1999 World Cups, losing on penalties to the USA in the final of the latter. After making her name with Beijing, in 2001 she jumped at the opportunity to play professionally in the USA with Philadelphia Charge. She was the top scorer in the opening season, before returning to China.

Opposite: The golden girl of women's football, Mia Hamm.

Right: Mexico captain Maribel Dominguez.

Below: China's Liu Ailing, who played in both the 1995 and 1999 World Cups.

BRANDI CHASTAIN

Country: USA
Born: July 21, 1978
Position: Defender
Club: San Jose CyberRays

Brandi Chastain has the glory of being the most recognisable player in women's football. However, most would only recognise the endearing image of her celebrating victory at the 1999 World Cup rather than know her name or where she plays.

After scoring the winning penalty against China at the Pasadena Rose Bowl in front of a television audience of 40 million, Chastain sunk to her knees and whipped off her shirt to reveal her sports bra – 'momentary insanity' she claimed in the subsequent press conference. She started off her early career as a striker, before a two-year injury-enforced break, and when she made her comeback she was playing in defence. She has represented her country on more than 160 occasions, and the majority of these appearances have been as a defender.

MARIBEL DOMINGUEZ

Country: Mexico
Born: November 18, 1978
Position: Centre-forward
Clubs: Kansas City Mystics, Atlanta Beat

The captain of the Mexican national team, Maribel Dominguez had been a closely-guarded secret in the American amateur W-League for Kansas City Mystics. But her consistent good form in 2002, when she was named as the league's Player Of The Year, caught the eye of several WUSA teams and she was signed by Atlanta Beat for 2003.

Small and fast, Dominguez is a forward who regularly hits the back of the net. Having made an immediate impact on the American professional league, she is fast becoming a popular player with the fans. Despite her best efforts, Mexico often find it hard to make any significant mark on the world stage, and are often in the shadow of the stronger teams of the USA and Canada.

JULIE FLEETING

Country: Scotland
Born: December 18, 1980
Position: Centre-forward
Clubs: Ayr United, San Diego Spirit

Born into a footballing family, Julie Fleeting's father Jim played for Norwich City. Like many British girls, Fleeting's early footballing years were served playing for a boys team and she followed in her father's footsteps by playing for Ayr United, where she won several honours. She caught the eye of US scouts in 2002 and, after the culmination of the Scottish season, Fleeting made the switch to San Diego Spirit. A tall striker, who is comfortable running at defenders and obviously good in the air, her typical British-style of play has helped her flourish in WUSA. Undoubtedly the star of the Scotland team, by the beginning of the 2003-04 international season, Fleeting has amassed 60 goals in 62 starts and hit goals aplenty to try to shoot the Scots to Euro 2005.

JULIE FOUDY

Country: USA
Born: January 23, 1971
Position: Central midfield
Club: San Diego Spirit

The current captain of the USA national team, Julie Foudy is one of their most experienced players, having made her debut in 1988 as a 17-year-old. She plays the role of an attacking midfielder, showing the typical all-American desire to win every ball, let alone every game. Foudy is now a veteran of more than 220 internationals, which makes her the third most capped player in the world. Aged 20, she played every minute of every game when the Americans lifted the inaugural World Cup in 1991, and she helped them win the gold medal in the first women's football event at the 1996 Olympics in Atlanta. Also captain for her club side, Foudy had the responsibility of leading USA's campaign to become the first women's team to retain the World Cup in 2003.

KELLY GOLEBIOWSKI

Country: Australia
Born: July 26, 1981
Position: Midfield
Clubs: Hampton Road Piranhas, Washington Freedom

Kelly Golebiowski became the youngest player to ever represent The Matildas in a warm-up to the 1996 Olympics against hosts America – she was just 14 years old. Her promise as one of the best players in the world was clear, but a serious injury early in her career curtailed her progress. She played in the 1999 World Cup, and was a part of the disappointing Australia side at the 2000 Olympics (they failed to reach the semi-finals on home soil, despite training together as a team for a year). She signed her first professional club contract for Mia Hamm's Washington Freedom in early 2003 and helped Australia qualify for that year's World Cup with ease.

MIA HAMM

Country: USA
Born: March 17, 1972
Position: Centre-forward
Club: Washington Freedom

Hamm is the golden girl of women's football. After helping to shoot the USA team to World Cup victory in 1999 in front of more than 90,000 home fans, she became the most-requested world footballer – male or female – on internet search engines. Her profile is such that she has fronted a campaign to promote milk across America, signed a multi-million dollar sponsorship deal with Nike, written

a best-selling autobiography, and she is undoubtedly the star of WUSA, America's professional women's league (games featuring her team, Washington Freedom, regularly attract the biggest attendances whenever she plays). Being an out-and-out striker, Hamm has scored more international goals than any footballer in history, and this has certainly helped endear her to the glory-thirsty American public.

At 15 years of age, in a game against China, she became the youngest player to debut for USA in what would be the first of many important matches in her career. Four years later she was the youngest member of the squad that travelled to China to lift the inaugural World Cup, playing five of the six matches. She was also a part of the World Cup squad in 1995, where she stepped in as goalkeeper after a sending-off, but the team was unsuccessful. She played with a sprained ankle but helped the USA win the 1996 Olympic gold medal, and she then netted the opening goal of the 1999 World Cup.

Now in her early thirties, and after a string of injuries, Hamm's presence in front of goal is as threatening as ever and the 2003 World Cup – in front of those home fans – may well be her swansong to end an unbelievable career.

CHARMAINE HOOPER

Country: Canada
Born: January 15, 1968
Position: Centre-forward
Clubs: Atlanta Beat, Chicago Cobras

Charmaine Hooper isn't a particularly fast or skilful striker, her main attribute being her consistency – she hits the net in virtually every game she plays. She holds the record number of caps for a Canadian, and is her country's top scorer. She was also Player Of The Year for Atlanta Beat in the first two seasons of America's pro league. Hooper has a wealth of experience, having played on a professional contract in Italy, Norway and Japan, and has regularly topped goalscoring charts along the way. Although set to play in the 2003 World Cup, she has stated that she may retire to start a family following the 2004 Olympics.

KARA LANG

Country: Canada
Born: December 22, 1986
Position: Centre-forward
Club: Vancouver Whitecaps

Kara Lang was the undoubted star of the FIFA Under-19 World Championship, staged for the first time in August 2002 in her homeland Canada. Her height, combined with deadly pace when running on to long balls and the ability to shoot from seemingly anywhere in the opposition's half, was enough to see Canada through to the final – losing only on penalties to the Americans. She made the transition to senior national team with ease, notching a brace against Wales in her second international while still a student. By her 24th game she had scored 14 goals. The signing of a professional contract in February 2003 has added further to her potential.

KRISTINE LILLY

Country: USA
Born: July 22, 1971
Position: Winger
Club: Boston Breakers

Kristine Lilly's finest moment in a 16-year international career was undoubtedly the 1999 World Cup Final: a speedy winger and an occasional forward, she jumped to clear a goal-bound header from China's Fan Yunjie in the last minute of extra-time to force penalties. Lilly then netted the USA's third spot kick to put them ahead after China had missed, leading them to a 5-4 win. Like Foudy and Hamm, it was her second World Cup win after the inaugural victory in China in 1991.

A year after that famous second World Cup victory, Lilly was making history again: this time becoming the first player in footballing history – male or female – to reach the 200-cap mark. A more illuminating fact, and testimony to the influence this midfielder has had on the success of the USA, is that she has played in more than 85 per cent of all internationals played by the US team.

At club level, Lilly has captained Boston Breakers since the launch of WUSA in 2001. One of the fittest players in the game, she can dictate the pace of play and creates many of the Breakers' attacking moves. Off the pitch, like Hamm and Chastain, she is one of the most famous faces in US women's football. She runs her own soccer school, her former school named a football pitch after her, and her home town had a parade in her honour when she was part of the USA team that won Olympic gold in 1996.

HANNA LJUNGBERG

Country: Sweden
Born: January 8, 1979
Position: Centre-forward
Club: Umea IK

Hanna Ljungberg made a name for herself as one of the best emerging players in world football when she burst on to the scene at the 2001 European Championship. A fast and tricky striker, she starred up front as Sweden reached the final, losing to hosts Germany. Ljungberg has since been in startling form for both club and country, scoring regularly as Sweden qualified for the fourth FIFA World Cup with ease. She virtually put on a one-player show as Umea IK won the 2003 UEFA Women's Cup, netting two goals (with two assists) in the first leg win over Fortuna Hjorring, and adding another in the return match. She has scored more than a goal every game at international level.

MARIEN MEINERT

Country: Germany
Born: August 5, 1973
Position: Centre-forward
Club: Boston Breakers

The biggest compliment that can be paid to Marien Meinert is that teams regularly change their defensive tactics when playing against the German striker, often employing a man-marker in the hope that she won't find the back of the net. Meinert was the sixth overseas player selected to play for WUSA in 2000, a month after Germany had won bronze at the Sydney Olympics. A season later she shot her country to the 2001 European Championship title, but surprised the women's football world by retiring from the international scene. She showed in the 2003 WUSA All Star game that she is still one of the hardest players to defend against in the world.

Opposite clockwise from top left: Canada's top scorer Charmaine Hooper; Kristine Lilly, who played a major part in the USA's 1999 World Cup win; Canada's emerging star, Kara Lang; Hanna Ljungberg of Sweden, who has scored more than a goal a game at international level.

Below: Marien Meinert retired from international football after winning the 2001 European Championship with Germany.

Opposite: China's Sun Wen, voted FIFA World Player Of The Century in 2000.

DAGNY MELLGREN

Country: Norway
Born: June 19, 1978
Position: Centre-forward
Clubs: Klepp, Bjornar, Boston Breakers

Dagny Mellgren is a short but tricky forward who has an aptitude for beating the offside trap to get into the space behind defenders. The best moment of her career was scoring the golden goal that helped Norway beat world champions USA to the gold medal at the 2000 Olympics in Sydney. She was in good form a year later at the European Championship, but she couldn't help Norway beyond the semi-finals. She was one of the first foreign players to be selected for WUSA, where she has been a key player for Boston Breakers, scoring more than 30 goals since signing in 2000.

MARINETTE PICHON

Country: France
Born: November 26, 1975
Position: Centre-forward
Clubs: Saint Memmie, Philadelphia Charge

Above right: Dagny Mellgren, scorer of Norway's golden goal in the 2000 Olympics.

Below: England's Kelly Smith, now playing club football in WUSA with Philadelphia Charge.

In her first season in professional football in 2001, Marinette Pichon stepped into the boots of the fans' favourite, the injured Kelly Smith, and shot Philadelphia Charge to the semi-finals of the Founders Cup. She finished the second top scorer in the league, was voted the Player Of The Year and also Striker Of The Year. In October 2002 she notched an important winner away against England in the UEFA play-off first leg to help France through to the 2003 World Cup – their first ever foray on to the world stage. Pichon is a tall, strong forward whose pace helps her pick up on loose balls in the area.

BIRGIT PRINZ

Country: Germany
Born: October 25, 1977
Position: Centre-forward
Clubs: FFC Frankfurt, Carolina Courage

A tall, strong, athletic figure, Birgit Prinz could be regarded as physically the nearest thing to a male player: she dominates a game from her centre-forward role, often tracking back and winning the ball in midfield before creating as many opportunities for her team-mates as herself. A European champion for both club and country (Euro 2001 with Germany and the inaugural UEFA Women's Cup with Frankfurt in 2002), she came to the attention of America's professional league in summer 2002 when she signed for Carolina Courage, immediately making her mark by scoring the winning goal in the final of the Founders Cup against Washington Freedom to secure the 2002 WUSA title.

HEGE RIISE

Country: Norway
Born: July 18, 1969
Position: Midfield
Clubs: Nikko Securities, Asker, Carolina Courage

Hege Riise has the two biggest attributes required to rank her among the top players in the world – strength and technical ability. While the Americans dominate the world of women's football through their strength, fitness and sheer desire to win, US players admittedly don't have the same understanding that their European peers nurture in countries where football is the national sport.

The Norwegians are technically gifted at football and their record at world level is testimony to that: they were beaten finalists at both the 1991 World Cup and 1993 European Championship, before winning the 1995 World Cup and beating the USA to take the gold medal at the 2000 Olympics in Sydney.

After a spell as a professional with Nikko Securities in Japan between 1995 and 1997, with whom she won the league and cup double, she was voted the Player Of The Year in Norway for club Asker in 2000. She was signed by Carolina Courage in October 2001 and continued to impress, winning the Player Of The Year award for the first two seasons.

SISSI

Country: Brazil
Born: June 2, 1967
Position: Midfield
Club: San Jose CyberRays

A veteran of three World Cups and two Olympics for Brazil, Sissi is regarded as one of the most entertaining players in the world. When she was a young girl, she would tear heads off her dolls to kick around and her obvious hero was Pele. Formerly a teacher, she was one of a handful of foreign stars integrated into the WUSA professional league in 2001, joining San Jose CyberRays. Although she's more likely to set up goals, free-kicks have become her trademark and she jointly won the Golden Boot at the 1999 World Cup.

KELLY SMITH

Country: England
Born: October 28, 1979
Position: Centre-forward/central midfield
Clubs: Arsenal, Philadelphia Charge

USA national coach April Heinrichs voted Kelly Smith as her World Player Of The Year after the England striker debuted in WUSA's inaugural year, but her first three seasons were blighted with injury. Though a midfielder for Philadelphia Charge, Smith plays as out-and-out striker for England and is a crowd-pleaser. She's at her best with the ball at her feet, taking players on and carving out opportunities from the tightest of angles. Scouted for a soccer scholarship while playing football in Watford, Smith went on to break college and league goalscoring records and was so highly regarded that Seton College retired her shirt number.

ALY WAGNER

Country: USA
Born: August 10, 1980
Position: Midfield
Club: San Diego Spirit

Aly Wagner has been tipped as the hottest young star in American soccer and the stage is set for a major breakthrough. Probably one of the most skilful and technical players the USA has produced, the midfielder just missed out on the final squad for the 1999 World Cup aged 18. Throughout her school and college days she helped her team win trophies and was regularly lauded as the best passer of her generation. San Diego Spirit had the pick of the top player coming out of college football in 2003 and Wagner was their obvious choice.

SUN WEN

Country: China
Born: April 6, 1973
Position: Midfield
Club: Atlanta Beat

Many fans of women's football regard Sun Wen as the best player in the world. She perhaps hasn't had the opportunity to play as many matches or score as many goals as Mia Hamm, but she has all the qualities you'd expect from a world class star – pace, vision, accuracy of passing and the ability to score – not only on a regular basis, but often spectacularly too. She is undoubtedly the star of the Chinese team who looked favourites to win the 2003 World Cup, before losing home advantage to the Americans due to the outbreak of the SARS virus. A well-known face in her homeland and star of chat shows, she was named as the FIFA World Player Of The Century alongside Michelle Akers in 2000.

THE HISTORY OF THE WOMEN'S WORLD CUP

Above from left to right: Mia Hamm kisses the World Cup after the USA's victory in 1999; the opening ceremony of the 1999 World Cup; Nigeria prepare to do battle.

Below from left to right: Liu Ailing in action against the USA; the 1999 World Cup Final at the Rose Bowl, Los Angeles, between China and the USA.

The inaugural women's World Cup in 1991 came 20 years after women had first contested an official international match. In the early 1970s the women's game had taken its first steps on the road to recognition, with numerous national federations taking the running of the female game under their governance, or at least forming links with amateur women's associations to allow national sides to be established. This move was widely encouraged by FIFA, the world governing body, which had issued directives to its member states to run the women's game alongside the men's.

As an increasing number of national sides emerged, international games became more competitive, with the Scandinavians' technique and fitness proving to be a generation ahead of their peers. Indeed, Denmark had the honour of being champions at the unofficial first world cup held in Mexico in 1971. USA exploded on to the world football stage in the early Eighties and competed twice in the 'Little World Cup' held in Italy in 1985 and 1988, both small tournaments won by England.

With an increasing number of unofficial world championships springing up, and with UEFA having already staged an official European Championship, FIFA felt under pressure to launch a women's World Cup. FIFA President Joao Havelange announced at the 1986 Congress in Mexico City, prior to the men's World Cup of that year, that a Women's World Cup would be launched – to take place every four years, in the year following the men's competition.

In November 1991, 12 nations descended on China for the first official women's world championship. The host media swarmed to see the home side thrash Norway 4-0 in the opening match. Norway, not to let the early Scandinavian domination of the women's

Above: USA captain Carla
Overback lifts the 1999 World
Cup after her team defeated
China in the final.

game down, hit back to reach the final, where they met the USA – the new kids on the block. The USA had benefited from mass investment into female football scholarships, and their forward line of Michelle Akers, April Heinrichs and Carin Jennings – labelled the 'Triple-Edged Sword' by local journalists – hit 18 of the team's 23 goals in five games to reach the final.

An unexpected crowd of 65,000 witnessed the final – even without the home nation competing, China having lost to Sweden in the quarter-finals. Akers hit a brace in the game to take the trophy to America for the first time thanks to a late 2-1 victory. The move to have an official women's competition on the world stage had been fully justified.

The first women's World Cup had been a unanimous success and the second event had a lot to live up to. Staged in Sweden, where participation rates were high and where there was a culture of acceptance of women playing football, it gave the European sides a chance to show a superior tactical awareness.

More than 14,000 packed into the national stadium for the opening match, only to see Brazil steal a surprise 1-0 victory against the home side. After that defeat Sweden had to pull off some good results to progress to the

final eight, where they were cruelly knocked out by China on penalties. In the semi-finals Norway avenged their 1991 final defeat by securing a tight 1-0 victory against USA, before Hege Riise and Marianne Pettersen netted a goal each to beat Germany 2-0 in the final in front of a 17,000 crowd.

While the 1995 World Cup had been a step forward in terms of performance, it was the 1999 tournament that would change the footballing world forever. The American media was highly sceptical that the tournament could be a success – after all, football was a minority sport and the women's team had previously attracted merely crowds. But the Americans had a potential audience of seven million female players to draw upon and tickets began selling out as early as Mia Hamm and her team-mates began their preparations.

As the tournament gained momentum, the interest spiralled. With 90,185 supporters in the stadium, and 40 million homes around America tuned in to watch, the final was a success, USA's Brandi Chastain going as far as to whip off her shirt in celebration of her winning penalty against China. Spectator figures for the entire tournament reached 660,000, around six times that of the 1995

tournament in Sweden, while images of the winning team adorned *Sports Illustrated* and even the illustrious *Time* – as well as every American schoolgirl's bedroom wall.

The World Cup has played a vital role in the development of the game: as competitiveness has increased, each tournament has raised the profile of the game and driven interest in women's football as a spectator sport. The 1999 World Cup stars became household names globally and the first ever professional league for women was launched off the back of its popularity in the USA.

The 2003 World Cup perhaps provides the best test of longevity of the women's game. However, the USA was awarded the tournament just four months before its kick-off, following the late decision to take the tournament away from China due to the SARS virus. The 2003 finals would be held in their original time slot of September rather than 1999's more favourable June, leaving the tournament vying for media space and crowds alongside top sports events. It would also no longer hold the novelty factor. Therefore women's football faced its ultimate battle: to win a share of the spectator sports market against established men's sport.

THE WOMEN'S WORLD CUP

WINNERS

1991: USA
1995: Norway
1999: USA

INDEX

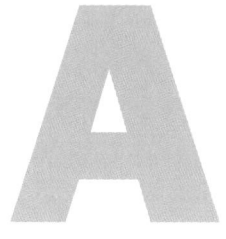

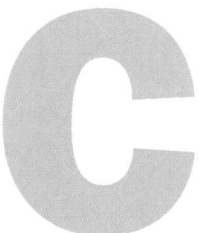

CHRIS HUNT EDITOR

Chris was the Managing Editor of *Match* for eight years, taking the weekly football title to its record-breaking circulation heights in the mid 1990s. Now a freelance editor and journalist, his travels around Japan for the World Cup in 2002 were featured in his weekly column for *Sport First* and were documented in the BBC1 television programme *Beckham For Breakfast*.

A contributor to *Four Four Two* and a football columnist in the 'lad' market for *Ice*, he was the Editor of many of the acclaimed special editions of *Q* and *Mojo*, including those on The Beatles, Punk Rock and Oasis. He was also Editor of *Supergoals – The Mag*, the 2003-04 new season preview magazine for *The Sun* newspaper. In the past he has worked as a broadcaster for BBC Radio 5, contributed to *90 Minutes*, *Sports Quarterly* and *Roy Of The Rovers*, and was the Editor of *Mega Sports* and *Sported!*

DAVID HOUGHTON ART DIRECTOR

David is an experienced designer, often specialising in football or music projects. He was the Art Director of *Match*'s *Euro 2000 Guide* and he currently oversees the creative direction of music magazine *Hip-Hop Connection*. His travels around Japan in 2002 with Editor Chris Hunt were featured in the BBC 1 television programme *Beckham For Breakfast*. He travels home and away to watch England play, and picked his latest house because it is a mere stone's throw away from the Cambridge United ground.

CONTRIBUTORS

NICK GIBBS is an international football journalist who has written for a host of publications, including *Match*, *World Soccer*, *European Football Yearbook* and preview specials of every World Cup and European Championship since 1988. He is also the author of the FA endorsed book *England – The Football Facts*.

LUKE NICOLI has worked in senior roles at both *Match* and *Shoot*, and has contributed to *The Guardian*, *Observer* and *Daily Star On Sunday*. He was co-author of *Second Time Around*, the autobiography of Kevin Phillips, he recently completed the biography *William, The People's Prince*.

GARY TIPP was formerly the Editor of *Total Football* magazine. A Pompey fan, he is a regular contributor to a number of the club's websites.

ANDREW WINTER has worked on a variety of sports magazines, including *Match* and *Sported!* He was also Editor of *Shoot!* between 1997 and 2000.

JAMES EASTHAM was editor of French football fanzine *Aux Armes!* and weekly national newspaper *Sport First*. Twice nominated for Young Journalist Of The Year, he is currently editor of weekly magazine *Soccerbet*.

KEVIN HUGHES is Assistant Editor of *Match*. He has covered World Cups, European Championships and FA Cup finals, spending many hours lurking around training grounds sharking for player interviews.

BEV WARD was a journalist on *Match* for four years and she now works to promote the women's game in England. She also established the women's football content at GiveMeFootball.com.

TIM HARTLEY was formerly Deputy Editor of *Match* and was Editor of the *Boston Standard* during a period that included their promotion to the Football League. He currently works in the sports department of the Press Association and edits Sport England's magazine *The Player*.

PAUL ROBSON has worked on both *Match* and *Total Football*, but allows himself to be distracted from his current job writing about guitars by the varying fortunes of Swindon Town.

MIKE PATTENDEN has written regular features about football for *The Times*, *Esquire*, *Goal* and *Four Four Two*. He is also the author of *Last Orders At The Liars' Bar*, the official biography of The Beautiful South.

MATT ALLEN was Assistant Editor at *Four Four Two* for two years before moving to *Q* as Features Editor. He has interviewed a number of the world's biggest players and is the author of *Jimmy Greaves: The Biography*.

RICHARD ADAMS spent three years as a writer for *Match*, and has written on football for numerous titles. He is the founding Editor of thefootyroom.co.uk.

ALISTAIR PHILLIPS was Editor of *Sports Trader* for three years before joining *Match* in 1998. He now works as a journalist on a variety of sport titles.

JOE CUSHLEY has contributed to various football fanzines, and covers the Football Conference for a digital TV station. He has also written about stadia for the *Architects' Journal*.

STEVE CRESSWELL was a staff writer with Match, before spending two seasons in the press department at Leicester City. He joined the BBC Sport website in 2000.

JOHN PLUMMER is a London-based freelance journalist who specialises in sport and fitness. He has written widely on football for newspapers and magazines, including *Match*.

ADDITIONAL CONTRIBUTIONS AND ASSISTANCE FROM: Sara Hunt, Jeff Fletcher, Alan Beeson, Darryl Tooth, Hugh Sleight, Warren Clark, Steve Rinaldi and Fiona Gilbert.

SPECIAL THANKS TO: Paul Smith, Boyd Butler, Barry Dennis, Ken Gill, Keith Nelson, Terry Pratt, Rob MacDonald, Tony Warner, Sue Peat, Phil Bagnall, Karen Munro, Dave Phillips, Lloyd Rogers, Ayumi Kita, Jonathan Wilson and Mark Rosselli at Cambridge Publishers, Chris Hull, Adrian Bevington, Ryan Giggs and David Beckham.

THE PUBLISHER WOULD LIKE TO THANK: David Jacobs, Gavin Clay and Paul Langan at Action Images.

PICTURES SUPPLIED BY: Action Images, Alfieri-Photo, Bongarts, Colorsport, GB Photo, Icon Sport Media International, Juha Tamminen, L'Equipe, Mirror Syndication International, Offside, Photo Kishimoto, Topham Picturepoint.